Lecture Notes in Computer Science 8702

Commenced Publication in 1973
Founding and Former Series Editors:
Gerhard Goos, Juris Hartmanis, and Jan van Leeuwen

Editorial Board

David Hutchison
Lancaster University, UK

Takeo Kanade
Carnegie Mellon University, Pittsburgh, PA, USA

Josef Kittler
University of Surrey, Guildford, UK

Jon M. Kleinberg
Cornell University, Ithaca, NY, USA

Alfred Kobsa
University of California, Irvine, CA, USA

Friedemann Mattern
ETH Zurich, Switzerland

John C. Mitchell
Stanford University, CA, USA

Moni Naor
Weizmann Institute of Science, Rehovot, Israel

Oscar Nierstrasz
University of Bern, Switzerland

C. Pandu Rangan
Indian Institute of Technology, Madras, India

Bernhard Steffen
TU Dortmund University, Germany

Demetri Terzopoulos
University of California, Los Angeles, CA, USA

Doug Tygar
University of California, Berkeley, CA, USA

Gerhard Weikum
Max Planck Institute for Informatics, Saarbruecken, Germany

Dimitra Giannakopoulou   Gwen Salaün (Eds.)

Software Engineering and Formal Methods

12th International Conference, SEFM 2014
Grenoble, France, September 1-5, 2014
Proceedings

 Springer

Volume Editors

Dimitra Giannakopoulou
NASA Ames Research Center
Mail Stop 269-2
Moffett Field, CA 94035, USA
E-mail: dimitra.giannakopoulou@nasa.gov

Gwen Salaün
Inria Grenoble-Rhône-Alpes
655, Avenue de l'Europe
38330 Montbonnot Saint-Martin, France
E-mail: gwen.salaun@inria.fr

ISSN 0302-9743   e-ISSN 1611-3349
ISBN 978-3-319-10430-0   e-ISBN 978-3-319-10431-7
DOI 10.1007/978-3-319-10431-7
Springer Cham Heidelberg New York Dordrecht London

Library of Congress Control Number: 2014946209

LNCS Sublibrary: SL 2 – Programming and Software Engineering

© Springer International Publishing Switzerland 2014

This work is subject to copyright. All rights are reserved by the Publisher, whether the whole or part of the material is concerned, specifically the rights of translation, reprinting, reuse of illustrations, recitation, broadcasting, reproduction on microfilms or in any other physical way, and transmission or information storage and retrieval, electronic adaptation, computer software, or by similar or dissimilar methodology now known or hereafter developed. Exempted from this legal reservation are brief excerpts in connection with reviews or scholarly analysis or material supplied specifically for the purpose of being entered and executed on a computer system, for exclusive use by the purchaser of the work. Duplication of this publication or parts thereof is permitted only under the provisions of the Copyright Law of the Publisher's location, in ist current version, and permission for use must always be obtained from Springer. Permissions for use may be obtained through RightsLink at the Copyright Clearance Center. Violations are liable to prosecution under the respective Copyright Law.
The use of general descriptive names, registered names, trademarks, service marks, etc. in this publication does not imply, even in the absence of a specific statement, that such names are exempt from the relevant protective laws and regulations and therefore free for general use.
While the advice and information in this book are believed to be true and accurate at the date of publication, neither the authors nor the editors nor the publisher can accept any legal responsibility for any errors or omissions that may be made. The publisher makes no warranty, express or implied, with respect to the material contained herein.

Typesetting: Camera-ready by author, data conversion by Scientific Publishing Services, Chennai, India

Printed on acid-free paper

Springer is part of Springer Science+Business Media (www.springer.com)

Preface

This volume contains the papers presented at SEFM 2014, the 12th International Conference on Software Engineering and Formal Methods, which was held during September 3–5, 2014, in Grenoble, France. The aim of the conference is to bring together practitioners and researchers from academia, industry, and government to advance the state of the art in formal methods, to facilitate their uptake in the software industry, and to encourage their integration with practical engineering methods. SEFM 2014 was organized by Inria and supported by Grenoble INP, University Joseph-Fourier, LIG, and CNRS.

SEFM 2014 received 138 abstracts and 106 full submissions. Papers underwent a rigorous review process, and each paper received 3 reviews. After a careful discussion phase, the international Program Committee decided to select 23 research papers and 6 tool papers. These papers cover a wide variety of topics such as program correctness, testing, static analysis, theorem proving, model checking, and automata learning. They also address a wide range of systems, including component-based, real-time, embedded, adaptive, and multi-agent.

The conference featured 3 invited talks by Patrice Godefroid (Microsoft Research, USA), Joost-Pieter Katoen (RWTH Aachen University, Germany), and Xavier Leroy (Inria, France). These talks discussed the software engineering challenges of developing *trusted* formal tools that *scale* to the size of industrial systems. Extended abstracts of the invited talks can be found in this volume.

Five international workshops were colocated with SEFM 2014: the 1st Workshop on Human-Oriented Formal Methods (HOFM 2014), the 3rd International Symposium on Modelling and Knowledge Management Applications: Systems and Domains (MoKMaSD 2014), the 8th International Workshop on Foundations and Techniques for Open Source Software Certification (OpenCert 2014), the 1st Workshop on Safety and Formal Methods (SaFoMe 2014), and the 4th Workshop on Formal Methods in the Development of Software (WS-FMDS 2014).

We thank the local Organizing Committee (Sophie Azzaro, Wassila Bouhadji, Myriam Etienne, Vanessa Peregrin) for taking care of the local arrangements, the Steering Committee chair Antonio Cerone and the Conference Chair Radu Mateescu for their guidance, the workshop chairs (Carlos Canal, Marc Frappier, and Akram Idani) for supervizing the workshops organization, Rim Abid for negotiating financial support, Lina Ye for acting as publicity chair, and Hugues Evrard for acting as Web master. We assembled an exciting technical program that would not have been possible without the excellent work of the Program Committee and external reviewers. Last, but not least, we thank the authors of all submitted papers, our invited speakers, and all the participants (speakers or not) of the conference in Grenoble. All these people contributed to the success of the 2014 edition of SEFM. Finally, EasyChair made our work as program chairs substantially easier.

June 2014
Dimitra Giannakopoulou
Gwen Salaün

Organization

Program Committee

Wolfgang Ahrendt	Chalmers University of Technology, Sweden
Bernhard K. Aichernig	TU Graz, Austria
Dalal Alrajeh	Imperial College London, UK
Farhad Arbab	CWI and Leiden University, The Netherlands
Luis Barbosa	Universidade do Minho, Portugal
Howard Barringer	The University of Manchester, UK
Domenico Bianculli	SnT Centre - University of Luxembourg, Luxembourg
Jonathan P. Bowen	Birmingham City University, UK
Mario Bravetti	University of Bologna, Italy
Tevfik Bultan	University of California at Santa Barbara, USA
Hung Dang Van	UET, Vietnam National University
Francisco Durán	University of Málaga, Spain
George Eleftherakis	The University of Sheffield International Faculty, CITY College, UK
José Luiz Fiadeiro	Royal Holloway, University of London, UK
Mamoun Filali-Amine	IRIT, France
Marc Frappier	University of Sherbrooke, Canada
Martin Fränzle	Carl von Ossietzky Universität Oldenburg, Germany
Hubert Garavel	Inria Rhone-Alpes/VASY, France
Dimitra Giannakopoulou	NASA Ames, USA
Stefania Gnesi	ISTI-CNR, France
Klaus Havelund	Jet Propulsion Laboratory, California Institute of Technology, USA
Rob Hierons	Brunel University, UK
Mike Hinchey	Lero, The Irish Software Engineering Research Centre, Ireland
Falk Howar	CMU/NASA Ames, USA
Florentin Ipate	University of Bucharest, Romania
Martin Leucker	University of Lübeck, Germany
Peter Lindsay	The University of Queensland, Australia
Antónia Lopes	University of Lisbon, Portugal
Mercedes Merayo	Universidad Complutense de Madrid, Spain
Stephan Merz	Inria Lorraine, France
Mizuhito Ogawa	Advanced Institute of Science and Technology, Japan

Fernando Orejas   UPC, Spain
Gordon Pace   University of Malta, Malta
David Parker   University of Birmingham, UK
Corina Pasareanu   CMU/NASA Ames Research Center, USA
Anna Philippou   University of Cyprus, Cyprus
Sanjiva Prasad   Indian Institute of Technology, Delhi, India
Jakob Rehof   University of Dortmund, Germany
Leila Ribeiro   Universidade Federal do Rio Grande do Sul,
                                  Brazil
Bernhard Rumpe   RWTH Aachen University, Germany
Gwen Salaün   Grenoble INP, Inria, LIG, France
Augusto Sampaio   Federal University of Pernambuco, Brazil
Gerardo Schneider   Chalmers — University of Gothenburg, Sweden
Marjan Sirjani   Reykjavik University, Iceland
Matt Staats   University of Luxembourg, Luxembourg
Martin Steffen   University of Oslo, Norway
Jing Sun   The University of Auckland, New Zealand
Jun Sun   Singapore University of Technology and Design,
                                  Singapore
Serdar Tasiran   Koc University, Turkey
Massimo Tivoli   University of L'Aquila, Italy
Dongmei Zhang   Microsoft Research, China
Jianjun Zhao   Shanghai Jiao Tong University, China

Additional Reviewers

Alkhalaf, Muath   Garnacho, Manuel
Aydin, Abdulbaki   Gerwinn, Sebastian
Bessai, Jan   Greifenberg, Timo
Bocic, Ivan   Habel, Annegret
Bodeveix, Jeanlpauk   Hojjat, Hossein
Bonenfant, Armelle   Jafari, Ali
Bove, Ana   Jaghouri, Mahdi
Colombo, Christian   Johansson, Moa
Cámara Moreno, Javier   Kaiser, Steffi
D'Souza, Deepak   Khakpour, Narges
Dang, Duc-Hanh   Khosravi, Ramtin
Decker, Normann   Kromodimoeljo, Sentot
Deharbe, David   Kuru, Ismail
Dudenhefner, Andrej   Kühn, Franziska
Duflot, Marie   Lefticaru, Raluca
Düdder, Boris   Li, Qin
Fakih, Maher   Lima, Lucas
Fantechi, Alessandro   Lin, Ziyi
Ferrari, Alessio   Lindt, Achim

Look, Markus
Lorber, Florian
Markin, Grigory
Marques, Eduardo R.B.
Martens, Moritz
Martins, Francisco
Matar, Hassan Salehe
Mateescu, Radu
Matteucci, Ilaria
Matthews, Ben
Mazzanti, Franco
Micallef, Mark
Minh Hai, Nguyen
Mostowski, Wojciech
Mousavi, Mohammadreza
Mutlu, Erdal
Mutluergil, Suha Orhun
Müller, Klaus
Müllner, Nils
Nakajima, Shin
Narayan, Chinmay
Ngo Thai, Binh
Nguyen, Tang
Nogueira, Sidney
Ogata, Kazuhiro
Ozkan, Burcu Kulahcioglu
Pelliccione, Patrizio

Pichardie, David
Pita, Isabel
Pous, Damien
Reger, Giles
Riesco, Adrian
Rodríguez Carbonell, Enric
Russo, Alejandro
Rydeheard, David
Sabouri, Hamideh
Sanchez, Alejandro
Scheffel, Torben
Schulze, Christoph
Song, Wenhao
Spadotti, Regis
Stefanescu, Alin
Stümpel, Annette
Thoma, Daniel
Tiran, Stefan
Tribastone, Mirco
Truong, Hoang
Tung, Vu
von Wenckstern, Michael
Wille, Robert
Winter, Kirsten
Yan, Dacong
Ye, Lina
Zhang, Sai

Invited Papers

Formal Proofs of Code Generation and Verification Tools

Xavier Leroy

Inria Paris-Rocquencourt, France

Abstract. Tool-assisted verification of critical software has great potential but is limited by two risks: unsoundness of the verification tools, and miscompilation when generating executable code from the sources that were verified. A radical solution to these two risks is the deductive verification of compilers and verification tools themselves. In this invited talk, I describe two ongoing projects along this line: CompCert, a verified C compiler, and Verasco, a verified static analyzer based on abstract interpretation.

500 Machine-Years of Software Model Checking and SMT Solving

Patrice Godefroid

Microsoft Research
pg@microsoft.com

Abstract. I will report on our experience running SAGE for over 500-machine years in Microsoft's security testing labs. SAGE is a whitebox fuzzing tool for security testing. It performs symbolic execution dynamically at the binary (x86) level, generates constraints on program inputs, and solves those constraints with an SMT solver in order to generate new inputs to exercise new program paths or trigger security vulnerabilities (like buffer overflows). This process is repeated using novel state-space exploration techniques that attempt to sweep through all (in practice, many) feasible execution paths of the program while checking simultaneously many properties. This approach thus combines program analysis, testing, model checking and automated theorem proving (constraint solving).

Since 2009, SAGE has been running 24/7 on average 100+ machines automatically "fuzzing" hundreds of applications. This is the largest computational usage ever for any SMT solver, with over 4 billion constraints processed to date. In the process, SAGE found many new security vulnerabilities (missed by blackbox fuzzing and static program analysis) and was credited to have found roughly one third of all the bugs discovered by file fuzzing during the development of Microsoft's Windows 7, saving millions of dollars by avoiding expensive security patches to nearly a billion PCs.

In this talk, I will present the SAGE project, highlight connections with program verification, and discuss open research challenges.

This is joint work with Michael Levin, David Molnar, Ella Bounimova, and other contributors.

Model Checking Gigantic Markov Models

Joost-Pieter Katoen

Software Modelling and Verification, RWTH Aachen University, Germany
Formal Methods and Tools, University of Twente, The Netherlands

Probabilistic model checking – the verification of models incorporating random phenomena – has enjoyed a rapid increase of interest. Thanks to the availability of mature tool support and efficient verification algorithms, probabilistic model checking has been successfully applied to case studies from various areas, such as randomized (distributed) algorithms, planning and AI, security, hardware, stochastic scheduling, reliability analysis, and systems biology [9]. In addition, model-checking techniques have been adopted by mainstream model-based performance and dependability tools as effective analysis means. Probabilistic model checking can thus be viewed as a viable alternative and extension to traditional model-based performance analysis [1].

Typical properties that are checked are quantitative reachability objectives, such as: does the probability to reach a certain set of goal states (by avoiding illegal states) exceed $\frac{1}{2}$? Extra constraints can be incorporated as well that e.g., require the goal to be reached within a certain number of transitions, within a certain budget, or within a real-time deadline. For models exhibiting both transition probabilities and non-determinism, maximal and minimal probabilities are considered. Intricate combinations of numerical (or simulation) techniques for Markov chains, optimization algorithms, and traditional CTL or LTL model-checking algorithms result in simple, yet very efficient verification procedures [2, 10]. Verifying time-bounded reachability properties on continuous-time models of tens of millions of states usually is a matter of seconds. Using symbolic representation techniques such as multi-terminal BDDs, much larger systems can be treated efficiently as well. A gentle introduction can be found in [5].

Like in the traditional setting, probabilistic model checking suffers from the curse of dimensionality: the number of states grows exponentially in the number of system components and cardinality of data domains. This hampers the analysis of real-life systems such as biological models involving thousands of molecules [12], and software models of on-board aerospace systems that incorporate probabilistic error models of various system components on top of the "nominal" system behaviour [3].

This talk considers the theory and practice of aggressive abstraction of discrete-time and continuous-time Markov models. Our abstraction technique is based on a partitioning of the concrete state space that is typically much coarser than e.g., bisimulation minimisation. We exploit three-valued abstraction [4] in which a temporal logic formula evaluates to either true, false, or indefinite. In this setting, abstraction is conservative for both positive and negative verification results; in our setting this means that the analysis yields bounds on the desired probability measures. If the verification of the abstract model yields an indefinite answer (dont know), no conclusion on the validity in the concrete model can be drawn. States in abstract Markov models are groups of concrete states and transitions are either equipped with intervals or modeled as non-deterministic choices. The resulting abstraction is shown to preserve a simulation relation: concrete states are simulated by their corresponding abstract ones.

We present the theoretical foundations of aggressive abstraction of Markov models [6] and show how this technique can be applied in a compositional way. This enables the component-wise abstraction of large models [7, 11]. We present two case studies, one from systems biology and one from queueing theory, illustrating the power of this technique. This includes strategies of which states to group, verification times of the abstract models, and the resulting accuracies of the quantitative results. We show that this abstraction technique enables the verification of models larger than 10^{250} states by abstract models of a few hundred thousands states while obtaining results with an accuracy of 10^{-6} [8].

Acknowledgement. This work is funded by the EU FP7-projects SENSATION and MEALS, the STW project ArRangeer, and the Excellence Program of the German Federal Government.

References

1. Baier, C., Haverkort, B.R., Hermanns, H., Katoen, J.-P.: Performance evaluation and model checking join forces. Commun. ACM 53(9), 76–85 (2010)
2. Baier, C., Katoen, J.-P.: Principles of Model Checking. MIT Press (2008)
3. Esteve, M.-A., Katoen, J.-P., Nguyen, V.Y., Postma, B., Yushtein, Y.: Formal correctness, safety, dependability, and performance analysis of a satellite. In: ICSE, pp. 1022–1031. IEEE (2012)
4. Huth, M., Jagadeesan, R., Schmidt, D.A.: Modal transition systems: A foundation for three-valued program analysis. In: Sands, D. (ed.) ESOP 2001. LNCS, vol. 2028, pp. 155–169. Springer, Heidelberg (2001)
5. Katoen, J.-P.: Model checking meets probability: A gentle introduction. In: Engineering Dependable Software Systems. NATO Science for Peace and Security Series - D, vol. 34, pp. 177–205. IOS Press (2013)
6. Katoen, J.-P., Klink, D., Leucker, M., Wolf, V.: Three-valued abstraction for probabilistic systems. J. Log. Algebr. Program. 81(4), 356–389 (2012)
7. Katoen, J.-P., Klink, D., Neuhäußer, M.R.: Compositional abstraction for stochastic systems. In: Ouaknine, J., Vaandrager, F.W. (eds.) FORMATS 2009. LNCS, vol. 5813, pp. 195–211. Springer, Heidelberg (2009)
8. Klink, D., Remke, A., Haverkort, B.R., Katoen, J.-P.: Time-bounded reachability in tree-structured qbds by abstraction. Perform. Eval. 68(2), 105–125 (2011)
9. Kwiatkowska, M.Z.: Model checking for probability and time: from theory to practice. In: LICS, p. 351. IEEE Computer Society (2003)

10. Kwiatkowska, M.Z., Norman, G., Parker, D.: Stochastic model checking. In: Bernardo, M., Hillston, J. (eds.) SFM 2007. LNCS, vol. 4486, pp. 220–270. Springer, Heidelberg (2007)
11. Shoham, S., Grumberg, O.: Compositional verification and 3-valued abstractions join forces. Inf. Comput. 208(2), 178–202 (2010)
12. Wolf, V., Goel, R., Mateescu, M., Henzinger, T.A.: Solving the chemical master equation using sliding windows. BMC Systems Biology 4, 42 (2010)

Table of Contents

Component-Based Systems

Real-Time and Embedded Systems

Model Checking and Automata Learning

Tool Papers

Program Correctness

Adaptive and Multi-Agent Systems

Formal Proofs of Code Generation and Verification Tools

Xavier Leroy

Inria Paris-Rocquencourt, France

Abstract. Tool-assisted verification of critical software has great potential but is limited by two risks: unsoundness of the verification tools, and miscompilation when generating executable code from the sources that were verified. A radical solution to these two risks is the deductive verification of compilers and verification tools themselves. In this invited talk, I describe two ongoing projects along this line: CompCert, a verified C compiler, and Verasco, a verified static analyzer based on abstract interpretation.

Abstract of Invited Talk

Tool-assisted formal verification of software is making inroads in the critical software industry. While full correctness proofs for whole applications can rarely be achieved [6,12], tools based on static analysis and model checking can already establish important safety and security properties (memory safety, absence of arithmetic overflow, unreachability of some failure states) for large code bases [1]. Likewise, deductive program verifiers based on Hoare logic or separation logic can verify full correctness for crucial algorithms and data structures and their implementations [11]. In the context of critical software that must be qualified against demanding regulations (such as DO-178 in avionics or Common Criteria in security), such tool-assisted verifications provide independent evidence, complementing that obtained by conventional verification based on testing and reviews.

The trust we can put in the results of verification tools is limited by two risks. The first is *unsoundness* of the tool: by design or by mistake in its implementation, the tool can fail to account for all possible executions of the software under verification, reporting no alarms while an incorrect execution can occur. The second risk is *miscompilation* of the code that was formally verified. With a few exceptions [3], most verification tools operate over source code (C, Java, ...) or models (Simulink or Scade block diagrams). A bug in the compilers or code generators used to produce the executable machine code can result in an incorrect executable being produced from correct source code [13].

Both unsoundness and miscompilation risks are known in the critical software industry and accounted for in DO-178 and other regulations [7]. It is extremely difficult, however, to verify an optimizing compiler or sophisticated static analyzer using conventional testing. Formal verification of compilers, static analyzers, and related tools provides a radical, mathematically-grounded answer to

D. Giannakopoulou and G. Salaün (Eds.): SEFM 2014, LNCS 8702, pp. 1–4, 2014.
© Springer International Publishing Switzerland 2014

these risks. By applying deductive program verification to the implementations of those tools, we can prove with mathematical certainty that they are free of miscompilation and unsoundness bugs. For compilers and code generators, the high-level correctness statement is *semantic preservation*: every execution of the generated code matches one of the executions of the source code allowed by the semantics of the source language. For static analyzers and other verification tools, the high-level statement is *soundness*: every execution of the analyzed code belongs to the set of safe executions inferred and verified by the tool. Combining the two statements, we obtain that every execution of the generated code is safe.

In this talk, I give an overview of two tool verification projects I am involved in: CompCert and Verasco. CompCert [8,9] is a realistic, industrially-usable compiler for the C language (a large subset of ISO C 1999), producing assembly code for the ARM, PowerPC, and x86 architectures. It features careful code generation algorithms and a few optimizations, delivering 85% of the performance of GCC at optimization level 1. While some parts of CompCert are not verified yet (e.g. preprocessing), the 18 code generation and optimization passes come with a mechanically-checked proof of semantics preservation. Verasco [2] is an ongoing experiment to develop and prove sound a static analyzer based on abstract interpretation for the CompCert subset of C. It follows a modular architecture inspired by that of Astrée: generic abstract interpreters for the C#minor and RTL intermediate languages of CompCert, parameterized by an abstract domain of execution states, itself built as a combination of several numerical abstract domains such as integer intervals and congruences, floating-point intervals, and integer linear inequalities (convex polyhedra).

Both CompCert and Verasco share a common methodology based on interactive theorem proving in the Coq proof assistant. Both projects use Coq not just for specification and proving, but also as a programming language, to implement all the formally-verified algorithms within Coq's Gallina specification language, in pure functional style. This way, no program logic is required to reason about these implementations: they are already part of Coq's logic. Executability is not lost: Coq's extraction mechanism produces executable OCaml code from those functional specifications.

CompCert and Verasco rely crucially on precise, mechanized operational semantics of the source, intermediate, and target languages involved, from CompCert C to assembly languages. These semantics play a crucial role in the correctness statements and proofs. In a sense, the proofs of CompCert and Verasco reduce the problem of trusting these tools to that of trusting the semantics involved in their correctness statements. An executable version of the CompCert C semantics was built to enable testing of the semantics, in particular random testing using Csmith [13].

Not all parts of CompCert and Verasco need to be proved: only those parts that affect soundness, but not those part that only affect termination, precision of the analysis, or efficiency of the generated code. Leveraging this effect, complex algorithms can often be decomposed into an untrusted implementation followed by a formally-verified validator that checks the computed results for soundness and fails otherwise. For example, CompCert's register allocation pass is composed of an untrusted implementation of the Iterated Register Coalescing algorithm, followed by a validation pass, proved correct in Coq, that infers and checks equalities between program variables and registers and stack locations that were assigned to them [10]. Likewise, Verasco's relational domain for linear inequalities delegates most computations to the Verasco Polyhedral Library, which produces Farkas-style certificates that are checked by Coq-verified validators [4]. Such judicious use of verified validation a posteriori is effective to reduce overall proof effort and enable the use of sophisticated algorithms.

In conclusion, CompCert and especially Verasco are ongoing experiments where much remains to be done, such as aggressive loop optimization in Comp-Cert and scaling to large analyzed programs for Verasco. In parallel, many other verification and code generation tools also deserve formal verification. A notable example is the verified verification condition generator of Herms et al [5]. Nonetheless, the formal verification of code generation and verification tools appears both worthwhile and feasible within the capabilities of today's interactive proof assistants.

Acknowledgments. This work is supported by Agence Nationale de la Recherche, grant ANR-11-INSE-003.

References

1. Blanchet, B., Cousot, P., Cousot, R., Feret, J., Mauborgne, L., Miné, A., Monniaux, D., Rival, X.: A static analyzer for large safety-critical software. In: Programming Language Design and Implementation 2003, pp. 196–207. ACM Press (2003)
2. Blazy, S., Laporte, V., Maroneze, A., Pichardie, D.: Formal verification of a C value analysis based on abstract interpretation. In: Logozzo, F., Fähndrich, M. (eds.) SAS 2013. LNCS, vol. 7935, pp. 324–344. Springer, Heidelberg (2013)
3. Ferdinand, C., Heckmann, R., Langenbach, M., Martin, F., Schmidt, M., Theiling, H., Thesing, S., Wilhelm, R.: Reliable and precise WCET determination for a real-life processor. In: Henzinger, T.A., Kirsch, C.M. (eds.) EMSOFT 2001. LNCS, vol. 2211, pp. 469–485. Springer, Heidelberg (2001)
4. Fouilhe, A., Monniaux, D., Périn, M.: Efficient generation of correctness certificates for the abstract domain of polyhedra. In: Logozzo, F., Fähndrich, M. (eds.) SAS 2013. LNCS, vol. 7935, pp. 345–365. Springer, Heidelberg (2013)
5. Herms, P., Marché, C., Monate, B.: A certified multi-prover verification condition generator. In: Joshi, R., Müller, P., Podelski, A. (eds.) VSTTE 2012. LNCS, vol. 7152, pp. 2–17. Springer, Heidelberg (2012)
6. Klein, G., Andronick, J., Elphinstone, K., Heiser, G., Cock, D., Derrin, P., Elkaduwe, D., Engelhardt, K., Kolanski, R., Norrish, M., Sewell, T., Tuch, H., Winwood, S.: seL4: formal verification of an operating-system kernel. Comm. ACM 53(6), 107–115 (2010)
7. Kornecki, A.J., Zalewski, J.: The qualification of software development tools from the DO-178B certification perspective. CrossTalk 19(4), 19–22 (2006)
8. Leroy, X.: Formal verification of a realistic compiler. Comm. ACM 52(7), 107–115 (2009)

9. Leroy, X.: A formally verified compiler back-end. J. Autom. Reasoning 43(4), 363–446 (2009)
10. Rideau, S., Leroy, X.: Validating register allocation and spilling. In: Gupta, R. (ed.) CC 2010. LNCS, vol. 6011, pp. 224–243. Springer, Heidelberg (2010)
11. Souyris, J., Wiels, V., Delmas, D., Delseny, H.: Formal verification of avionics software products. In: Cavalcanti, A., Dams, D.R. (eds.) FM 2009. LNCS, vol. 5850, pp. 532–546. Springer, Heidelberg (2009)
12. Yang, J., Hawblitzel, C.: Safe to the last instruction: automated verification of a type-safe operating system. In: Programming Language Design and Implementation 2010, pp. 99–110. ACM Press (2010)
13. Yang, X., Chen, Y., Eide, E., Regehr, J.: Finding and understanding bugs in C compilers. In: Proceedings of the 32nd ACM SIGPLAN Conference on Programming Language Design and Implementation, PLDI 2011, pp. 283–294. ACM Press (2011)

Lightweight Program Construction
and Verification Tools in Isabelle/HOL

Alasdair Armstrong, Victor B.F. Gomes, and Georg Struth

Department of Computer Science, University of Sheffield, UK
{a.armstrong,v.gomes,g.struth}@sheffield.ac.uk

Abstract. We present a principled approach to the development of construction and verification tools for while-programs. Our verification tool uses Kleene algebra with tests to capture the control flow of programs and its relational semantics for their data flow. It is extended to a Morgan-style program construction tool by adding one single axiom to the algebra. Our formalisation in Isabelle/HOL makes these tools themselves correct by construction. Verification condition generation and program construction steps are based on simple equational reasoning and supported by powerful Isabelle tactics. Two case studies on program construction and verification show our tools at work.

1   Introduction

Kleene algebras with tests [11] (KAT) support the analysis of while-programs by simple equational reasoning. They consist of a Kleene algebra, which models sequential compositions, nondeterministic choices and finite iteration of programs, and an embedded boolean algebra, which models assertions and test in conditionals and while-loops. KAT can verify program transformations [11], and it subsumes Hoare logic without the assignment rule [12]. The algebra has been applied, for instance, in compiler optimisation [14] and static analysis [13]. This applicability owes to its models of computational interest which include binary relations, and guarded languages and automata.

Nevertheless the role of KAT in program verification and correctness tools has so far been limited. One reason may be that these and similar algebras capture the control flow of programs elegantly and concisely, while providing limited capabilities for modelling their data flow. Only recently have KAT and similar algebraic approaches been formalised in theorem proving environments such as Coq [20] or Isabelle [3, 4] and first applications been explored.

A main contribution of this article lies in a principled approach by which program construction and verification tools can be prototyped rapidly and effectively from an algebraic layer in Isabelle/HOL [18]. It benefits from Isabelle's support for designing algebraic hierarchies with their models and its emphasis on proof automation through the integration of state-of-the-art first-order theorem proving and SMT solving technology. This technology has been optimised for equational reasoning and it interacts very efficiently with the algebraic layer.

D. Giannakopoulou and G. Salaün (Eds.): SEFM 2014, LNCS 8702, pp. 5–19, 2014.
© Springer International Publishing Switzerland 2014

The Isabelle infrastructure and our large libraries for KAT and similar algebras [4] make our approach simple and lightweight. We use variants of KAT for reasoning about the control flow of programs. The data flow, which appears in assignment statements, tests and assertions, is clearly separated from this layer. It is captured within appropriate models of KAT, in our case the standard relational semantics of imperative sequential programs. At this level we can link once more into Isabelle's extensive libraries and its extant verification infrastructure. The overall approach is illustrated through two main applications:

(i) the development of a KAT-based verification tool for while-programs which uses Hoare logic;
(ii) its extension to a program refinement tool based on Morgan's specification statement.

Relative to the formalisation of KAT in Isabelle, the main development step for the verification tool consists in refining the relational model of KAT into a detailed program semantics with program stores, in deriving assignment rules and in integrating data structures such as lists, arrays or queues.

For our program construction tool, we first show that the addition of one single algebraic axiom to KAT and its justification in the relational model suffices for deriving Morgan's basic refinement calculus.

The development in Isabelle makes both tools themselves correct by construction. It also highlights the role of algebra in program construction and verification. First of all, it allows the derivation of inference rules or refinement laws by equational reasoning which, in our case, is straightforward and fully automatic. Second, the algebraic laws can be turned into powerful tactics. In the context of verification, these support the automatic generation of verification conditions, which can be discharged by reasoning entirely at the data level. In the context of construction, they support the automated verification of refinement steps. Third, the algebraic approach is essentially open. It supports the rapid prototyping of variants and extensions, and the efficient derivation of additional inference rules or refinement laws as needed in applications.

We have applied our tools in a series of program construction and verification examples, two of which are presented in this article: the computation of sums of even Fibonacci numbers, and insertion sort. These evidence a high level of proof automation and suggest that our tools are stable enough at least for educational purposes. Optimisations to make them comparable to Isabelle's more advanced verification tools and similar tools for program construction and verification [19, 9, 7] are certainly possible, but not the purpose of this article.

The complete implementation of our tools in Isabelle and the complete program construction and verification proofs can be obtained online[1]. In particular, all mathematical statements in this article have been verified with Isabelle. Comprehensive libraries for variants of Kleene algebras, and in particular KAT, can be obtained from the Archive of Formal Proofs [5, 4].

---

[1] http://www.dcs.shef.ac.uk/~victor/refinement

2   Kleene Algebras with Tests

Kleene algebras with tests combine Kleene algebras for reasoning about the control flow of while-programs with boolean algebras that capture assertions as well as tests in conditionals or loops. Kleene algebras, in turn, are based on dioids or idempotent semirings.

A *semiring* is a structure $(S, +, \cdot, 0, 1)$ such that $(S, +, 0)$ is a commutative monoid and $(S, \cdot, 1)$ a monoid; the distributivity laws $x \cdot (y + z) = x \cdot y + x \cdot z$ and $(x + y) \cdot z = x \cdot z + y \cdot z$, and the annihilation laws $x \cdot 0 = 0$ and $0 \cdot x = 0$ hold. A semiring is *idempotent* (a *dioid*) if $x + x = x$. In that case, $(S, +, 0)$ is a semilattice with least element 0 and semilattice order defined by $x \leq y \Leftrightarrow x + y = y$.

A *Kleene algebra* is a structure $(K, ^*)$ such that K forms a dioid and the star satisfies the unfold laws and induction rules

$$1 + x^*x \leq x^*, \qquad z + yx \leq y \Rightarrow zx^* \leq y,$$
$$1 + xx^* \leq x^*, \qquad z + xy \leq y \Rightarrow x^*z \leq y.$$

Here and henceforth we drop the multiplication symbol.

Kleene algebras capture the control flow of programs. If K represents the actions of a program, then $+$ models the nondeterministic choice between actions, $\cdot$ their sequential composition, and * their finite iteration; 0 represents **abort** and 1 **skip**. The rule $sx \leq ys \Rightarrow sx^* \leq y^*s$, for instance, states that every (co)simulation s from x to y is also a (co)simulation from x^* to y^*. It is proved by equational reasoning with the first induction rule above.

For modelling concrete control structures such as conditionals or while-loops and for expressing assertions, however, additional structure is needed.

A *Kleene algebra with tests* [11] is a pair (K, B) consisting of a Kleene algebra K and a boolean algebra B of tests which is embedded into K. By this embedding, the least and greatest element of B are respectively 0 and 1; addition $+$ corresponds to join and multiplication $\cdot$ to meet. Complementation $^-$ is defined only within B. Multiplication of tests is therefore commutative: $pq = qp$. We write x, y, z for general Kleene algebra elements and p, q, r for tests; we write KAT for the class of Kleene algebras with tests and the set of its axioms.

KAT yields a simple algebraic semantics for conditionals and while-loops:

$$\textbf{if } p \textbf{ then } x \textbf{ else } y \textbf{ fi} = px + \bar{p}y, \qquad \textbf{while } p \textbf{ do } x \textbf{ od} = (px)^*\bar{p}.$$

More precisely, it is well known that KAT is sound with respect to the standard partial correctness semantics of while-programs in terms of binary relations.

Proposition 2.1 ([3]). *Let A be a set. Then $(2^{A \times A}, B, \cup, \circ, ^*, \neg, \emptyset, id_A)$ is a KAT, where $B = \{P \in A \times A \mid P \subseteq id_A\}$ is the set of all subidentities in $2^{A \times A}$.*

In this definition, $\circ$ denotes relational composition, * the reflexive transitive closure operation, $\neg P = \{(a, a) \mid (a, a) \notin P\}$, and $id_A = \{(a, a) \mid a \in A\}$ is the identity relation. The structure $(2^{A \times A}, B, \cup, \circ, ^*, \neg, \emptyset, id_A)$ is called the *full relational* KAT over A; each of its subalgebras forms again a KAT—a *relational*

KAT. The reflexive transitive closure of every element of a relational KAT exists and is equal to $\bigcup_{i \geq 0} R^i$ by standard fixpoint theory.

It can be checked in relational KAT that px models an input restriction of program x to those states where test p holds. Thus, in the above KAT-expression for the conditional, x is executed when p holds while y is executed when p fails. In the KAT-expression for the loop, x is executed zero or finitely many times after p holds, and afterwards p fails, or else the loop aborts.

3   Hoare Logic with KAT

Tests can also model assertions. Validity of Hoare triples is encoded in KAT as

$$\vdash \{p\}x\{q\} \Leftrightarrow px\overline{q} = 0.$$

The right-hand side states that there are no successful terminating executions of program x from states where assertion p holds into states where assertion q fails. In other words, if x is executed from precondition p and if it terminates, then postcondition q must hold after its execution.

KAT is expressive enough for deriving the inference rules of *propositional Hoare logic* (PHL), that is, Hoare logic without the assignment rule [12].

Proposition 3.1 ([12]). *The inference rules of* PHL *are theorems of* KAT:

$$\vdash \{p\}\mathbf{skip}\{p\},$$
$$p \leq p' \wedge q' \leq q \wedge \vdash \{p'\}x\{q'\} \Rightarrow \vdash \{p\}x\{q\},$$
$$\vdash \{p\}x\{r\} \wedge \vdash \{r\}y\{q\} \Rightarrow \vdash \{p\}x; y\{q\},$$
$$\vdash \{pb\}x\{q\} \wedge \vdash \{p\overline{b}\}y\{q\} \Rightarrow \vdash \{p\}\mathbf{if}\ b\ \mathbf{then}\ x\ \mathbf{else}\ y\ \mathbf{fi}\{q\},$$
$$\vdash \{pb\}x\{p\} \Rightarrow \vdash \{p\}\mathbf{while}\ b\ \mathbf{do}\ x\ \mathbf{od}\{\overline{b}p\}.$$

The proof is calculational. The while rule, e.g., expands to the KAT-formula

$$pbx\overline{p} = 0 \Rightarrow p(bx)^*\overline{b}(\overline{\overline{b}p}) = 0.$$

Since $px\overline{q} = 0$ is equivalent to $px \leq xq$ in KAT, we calculate

$$pbx \leq bxp \Rightarrow p(bx)^* \leq (bx)^*p \Rightarrow p(bx)^*\overline{b} \leq (bx)^*p\overline{b},$$

using the above (co)simulation rule in the first step. This illustrates the simplicity and concision of reasoning about programs in KAT. Proving the other PHL rules is even simpler. Hoare logic supplies one inference rule per programming construct. Its inference rules can therefore be applied deterministically, which simplifies the generation of verification conditions.

PHL rules for total correctness can be derived in a variant of Kleene algebra in which an operation x^∞ for the possibly infinite iteration of x is used instead of x^* [16]. This extension is, however, not considered in this paper.

4 Refinement with KAT

KAT can be extended to a Morgan-style refinement calculus by adding one single axiom. We keep the partial correctness setting, which suffices for practical program construction tasks. Extending it to a total correctness setting with termination variants seems straightforward.

Our approach follows Morgan's classical book on *Programming from Specifications* [17]. We think of specifications as programs that need not be executable. Morgan starts from the largest program which relates a given precondition p to a given postcondition q—the *specification statement*—and uses refinement laws to transform it incrementally and compositionally into an executable program which is correct by construction. In KAT, the axiomatisation of Morgan's specification statement is very simple.

A *refinement Kleene algebra with tests* (rKAT) is a KAT expanded by an operation $[\_,\_] : B \times B \to K$ which satisfies

$$\vdash \{\!|p|\!\}x\{\!|q|\!\} \Leftrightarrow x \le [p,q]. \tag{1}$$

It is easy to show that (1) implies the characteristic properties $\vdash \{\!|p|\!\}[p,q]\{\!|q|\!\}$ and $\vdash \{\!|p|\!\}x\{\!|q|\!\} \Rightarrow x \le [p,q]$ of the specification statement. First of all, program $[p,q]$ relates precondition p with postcondition q whenever it terminates. Second, it is the largest program with that property.

Morgan's basic refinement calculus provides one refinement law per program construct. Once more we ignore assignments at this stage. Deriving these laws in rKAT is strikingly easy. We use the refinement order $\sqsubseteq$, which is the converse of $\le$. One may also identify $p \le q$ on tests with the implication $p \to q$.

Proposition 4.1. *The following refinement laws are theorems of* rKAT:

$$p \le q \Rightarrow [p,q] \sqsubseteq \mathbf{skip}, \tag{2}$$
$$p' \le p \wedge q \le q' \Rightarrow [p,q] \sqsubseteq [p',q'], \tag{3}$$
$$[0,1] \sqsubseteq x, \tag{4}$$
$$x \sqsubseteq [1,0], \tag{5}$$
$$[p,q] \sqsubseteq [p,r];[r,q], \tag{6}$$
$$[p,q] \sqsubseteq \mathbf{if}\ b\ \mathbf{then}\ [bp,q]\ \mathbf{else}\ [\bar{b}p,q]\ \mathbf{fi}, \tag{7}$$
$$[p,\bar{b}p] \sqsubseteq \mathbf{while}\ b\ \mathbf{do}\ [bp,p]\ \mathbf{od}. \tag{8}$$

The laws are usually derived from Hoare logic in set theory. Two typical examples show the simplicity of deriving them with rKAT instead. For (2), we calculate

$$p \le q \Rightarrow p\bar{q} \le q\bar{q} = 0 \Rightarrow p1\bar{q} = 0 \Rightarrow \vdash \{\!|p|\!\}1\{\!|q|\!\} \Rightarrow 1 \le [p,\bar{q}] \Rightarrow [p,\bar{q}] \sqsubseteq \mathbf{skip}.$$

For (8), we calculate with the while-rule of PHL and (1), $\sqsubseteq$,

$$\vdash \{\!|pb|\!\}[pb,p]\{\!|p|\!\} \to \vdash \{\!|p|\!\}\mathbf{while}\ b\ \mathbf{do}\ [bp,p]\ \mathbf{od}\{\!|\bar{b}p|\!\}$$
$$\Rightarrow [p,\bar{b}p] \sqsubseteq \mathbf{while}\ b\ \mathbf{do}\ [bp,p]\ \mathbf{od}.$$

In (2), **skip** refines any specification statement provided its precondition implies its postcondition. $[0, 1]$ is usually called the **abort** statement, $[1, 0]$ the **magic** statement. For further discussion of these laws we refer to the literature. Finally, we verify soundness of rKAT in the relational model.

Proposition 4.2. *Let A be a set and let, for all $P, Q \subseteq \mathrm{id}_A$,*

$$[P, Q] = \bigcup \{R \subseteq A \times A \mid \ \vdash \{P\} R \{Q\}\}.$$

The structure $(2^{A \times A}, B, \cup, \circ, [\_, \_], {}^{*}, \neg, \emptyset, \mathrm{id}_A)$ then forms a rKAT.

This structure is called the *full relational* rKAT over A. Again, every subalgebra forms a rKAT; a *relational* rKAT over A.

5   Program Correctness Tools in Isabelle

We develop our tools within the Isabelle/HOL theorem proving environment [18]. Variants of Kleene algebras have already been formalised in Isabelle together with their most important models, in particular the binary relation model [5]. More recently, a comprehensive Isabelle library for KAT and a related algebra for total program correctness have been implemented [4, 3]. This includes the soundness proof for KAT with respect to the relational model (Proposition 2.1) and the derivation of the PHL rules (Proposition 3.1).

Formalising theory hierarchies is supported by Isabelle's type classes, which allow theory expansions. The class of dioids, for instance, can be specified by listing its signature and axioms. Kleene algebras are obtained by expanding dioids; fixing the star and listing its axioms. Algebras declared that way are polymorphic; their elements can have various types. This allows linking algebras formally with their model by instantiation or interpretation statements, for instance KAT and rKAT with the relational model.

By designing hierarchies like this, theorems are automatically propagated across classes and models. Those proved for Kleene algebras, for instance, become available for KAT and the relational model. Algebraic reasoning benefits from powerful proof automation supported by Isabelle's integrated automated theorem provers and SMT-solvers, whose proof output is internally verified to increase trustworthiness. Since these tools are highly optimised for equational reasoning, they interact very efficiently with the algebraic layer. Reasoning within models may require higher-order logic. This is supported by Isabelle's capabilities for modelling and reasoning with sets, polymorphic data types, inductive definitions and recursive functions as well as its tactics and simplifiers.

With this infrastructure, the implementation of verification tools for while-programs is very simple. Since the relational model of KAT is polymorphic in the underlying set, we can model the assignment rule of Hoare logic at the level of relations between generic program stores. Together with the rules of PHL at the algebraic level it can then be used for generating verification conditions.

Verifying these conditions depends on the underlying data domain, for which Isabelle, in many cases, offers excellent library support.

Implementing the refinement tool requires, as a first step, the formalisation of the material on rKAT from Section 4. This is straightforward and most proofs are fully automatic. Parts of the verification tool can then be reused for reasoning about the store and implementing Morgan's refinement rules for assignments.

We first describe the derivation of Hoare's assignment rule in the relational model. We define the store as a record of program variables. For each variable we provide a *retrieve* and an *update* function, which support variables of any Isabelle type. Isabelle's built-in list data type and its built-in list libraries can thus be used, e.g., for reasoning about list-based programs. We follow Isabelle's existing Hoare logic closely and use many of its predefined functions.

Let $\mathbf{S}$ be the set of all possible states of the store. We implement assignment statements as relations

$$(`x := e) = \{(\sigma,\ x\_update\ \sigma\ e) \mid \sigma \in \mathbf{S}\},$$

where $`x$ is a program variable, $x\_update$ the update function for $`x$ provided by Isabelle; σ is a state and e an evaluated expression of the same type as $`x$.

As usual we identify assertions with their extensions, which are sets of states. For the relational model we need to inject assertions into relational subidentities:

$$\lfloor P \rfloor = \{(\sigma,\sigma) \mid \sigma \in P\}.$$

This allows us to complete our implementation of Hoare logic in Isabelle.

Lemma 5.1. *Hoare's assignment rule is derivable in relational* KAT.

$$P \subseteq Q[e/`x] \Rightarrow\ \vdash \{\!| \lfloor P \rfloor |\!\}(`x := e)\{\!| \lfloor Q \rfloor |\!\},$$

where $Q[e/`x]$ denotes substitution of variable $`x$ by evaluated expression e in Q.

This yields the following soundness theorem of Hoare logic.

Theorem 5.2. *The rules of Hoare logic are theorems of relational* KAT.

We use the rules of Hoare logic to implement the Isabelle proof tactic *hoare* which generates verification conditions automatically and tries to blast away the entire control structure. As an enhancement of verification condition generation we have verified an additional rule for while-loops with invariants.

$$p \leq i\ \wedge\ \overline{p}i \leq q \wedge \vdash \{\!|ib|\!\}x\{\!|i|\!\} \Rightarrow\ \vdash \{\!|p|\!\}\mathbf{while}\ b\ \mathbf{inv}\ i\ \mathbf{do}\ x\ \mathbf{od}\{\!|q|\!\}.$$

In addition, our definition of assignment allows us to derive refinement laws.

Proposition 5.3. *The following refinement laws are derivable in relational* rKAT.

$$P \subseteq Q[e/`x] \Rightarrow [\lfloor P \rfloor, \lfloor Q \rfloor] \sqsubseteq (`x := e), \tag{9}$$

$$Q' \subseteq Q[e/`x] \Rightarrow [\lfloor P \rfloor, \lfloor Q \rfloor] \sqsubseteq [\lfloor P \rfloor, \lfloor Q' \rfloor];\ (`x := e), \tag{10}$$

$$P' \subseteq P[e/`x] \Rightarrow [\lfloor P \rfloor, \lfloor Q \rfloor] \sqsubseteq (`x := e);\ [\lfloor P' \rfloor, \lfloor Q \rfloor]. \tag{11}$$

(10) and (11) are called the *following* and *leading* refinement law for assignments [17]. They are particularly useful for program construction. As in the case of verification, we have programmed a *refinement* tactic which automatically tries to apply the rules of the basic refinement calculus.

6   Sum of Even Fibonacci Numbers

We now present the first example which shows our tools at work. We construct a program which computes the sum of even Fibonacci numbers below a given threshold[2]. Its input is threshold $m \in \mathbb{N}$; its return value is stored in variable 'sum. Because of typing there is no specific precondition. The postcondition is-sum-efib 'sum m, which is equivalent to $\exists n.$ 'sum = sum-efib m n $\wedge$ fib n $\leq$ m, is specified using the standard functional program fib, which can be programmed in Isabelle, and the recursive function

$$sum\text{-}efib\ m\ 0 = 0,$$

$$sum\text{-}efib\ m\ (n+1) = \begin{cases} sum\text{-}efib\ m\ n & \text{for } fib\ n\ \text{odd or } fib\ n \geq m, \\ sum\text{-}efib\ m\ n + fib\ n & \text{otherwise.} \end{cases}$$

The specification statement for our program is therefore, in Isabelle syntax,

$$[\![True,\ is\text{-}sum\text{-}efib\ \text{'}sum\ m]\!].$$

To keep track of all even Fibonacci numbers up to m, we use the function

$$efib\ 0 = 2, \qquad efib\ 1 = 8, \qquad efib\ (n+2) = 4 * efib\ (n+1) + efib\ n.$$

We have verified by induction that all numbers computed by efib are even and that efib n = fib (3n + 1) holds for all $n \geq 0$. The following classical fact about Fibonacci numbers then implies that efib computes indeed all even terms:

$$(fib\ n)\ mod\ 2 = 0 \Leftrightarrow n\ mod\ 3 = 1.$$

After this groundwork, which is an indispensable part of program construction and verification, we can start with the program construction itself. It is shown in Figure 1. Since Fibonacci numbers are defined recursively from their two predecessors, we add the variables 'x and 'y to keep track of them. In (1) we initialise 'x to 2—the first even Fibonacci number—applying the leading refinement law for assignments derived in Proposition 5.3. Our *refinement* tactic automatically applies the assignment law. In (2) we then initialise 'y to 8—the second even Fibonacci number. The *refinement* tactic now dictates the proof obligation fib 4 = 8, which is discharged by an integrated SMT solver. In (3) we initialise 'sum to 0 and state that 'sum = sum-efib m 1 by definition.

The main idea behind this program is to add the next even Fibonacci number to 'sum as long as it is below m, while storing the previous numbers in 'x and 'y. In the actual state of development, we also want to keep track of the indices of these numbers in the fib and efib series. Hence in (4) we add the variables 'n and 'k. The facts proved about Fibonacci numbers imply that the numbers stored in 'x and 'y have distance 3 in the series of Fibonacci numbers. The precondition

---

[2] The algorithm is taken from `http://toccata.lri.fr/gallery/euler002.en.html`. Fibonacci numbers start as $1, 2, 3, 5, 8, ...$, which is perhaps nonstandard.

⟦ *True*, *is-sum-efib* '*sum m*⟧

⊑   (1)

'x := 2;

⟦ 'x=*efib 0* ∧ 'x=*fib 1*, *is-sum-efib* '*sum m*⟧
  by *refinement*

⊑   (2)

'x := 2; 'y := 8;

⟦ 'x=*efib 0* ∧ 'x=*fib 1* ∧ 'y=*efib 1* ∧ 'y=*fib 4*, *is-sum-efib* '*sum m*⟧
  by *refinement* (*smt even-fib.simps(2) even-fib-correct*)

⊑   (3)

'x := 2; 'y := 8; '*sum* := 0;

⟦ 'x=*efib 0* ∧ 'x=*fib 1* ∧ 'y=*efib 1* ∧ 'y=*fib 4* ∧ '*sum*=*sum-efib m 1*,
is-sum-efib '*sum m*⟧
  by *refinement*

⊑   (4)

'x := 2; 'y := 8; '*sum* := 0; 'n := 0; 'k := 1;

⟦ 'x=*efib* 'n ∧ 'x=*fib* 'k ∧ 'y=*efib* ('n+1) ∧ 'y=*fib* ('k+3)
∧ 'n ≥ 0 ∧ 'k ≥ 1 ∧ '*sum*=*sum-efib m* 'k, *is-sum-efib* '*sum m*⟧
  by *refinement*

⊑   (5)

'x := 2; 'y := 8; '*sum* := 0; 'n := 0; 'k := 1;
while ⦃ 'x ≤ m ⦄ **do**
  ⟦ 'x=*efib* 'n ∧ 'x=*fib* 'k ∧ 'y=*efib* ('n+1) ∧ 'y=*fib* ('k+3)
    ∧ 'n ≥ 0 ∧ 'k ≥ 1 ∧ '*sum*=*sum-efib m* 'k ∧ 'x ≤ m,
    'x=*efib* 'n ∧ 'x=*fib* 'k ∧ 'y=*efib* ('n+1) ∧ 'y=*fib* ('k+3)
    ∧ 'n ≥ 0 ∧ 'k ≥ 1 ∧ '*sum*=*sum-efib m* 'k ⟧
od
  by *refinement* (*smt is-sum-efib-def*)

⊑   (6)

'x := 2; 'y := 8; '*sum* := 0; 'n := 0; 'k := 1;
while ⦃ 'x ≤ m ⦄ **do**
  ⟦ 'x=*efib* 'n ∧ 'x=*fib* 'k ∧ 'y=*efib* ('n+1) ∧ 'y=*fib* ('k+3)
    ∧ 'n ≥ 0 ∧ 'k ≥ 1 ∧ '*sum*=*sum-efib m* 'k ∧ 'x ≤ m,
    'x=*efib* 'n ∧ 'x=*fib* ('k+3) ∧ 'y=*efib* ('n+1)
    ∧ 'y=*fib* (6+'k) ∧ 'n ≥ 0 ∧ '*sum*=*sum-efib m* ('k+3) ⟧;
  'k := 'k+3
od
  by *refinement*

⊑   (7)

'x := 2; 'y := 8; '*sum* := 0; 'n := 0; 'k := 1;
while ⦃ 'x ≤ m ⦄ **do**
  ⟦ 'x=*efib* 'n ∧ 'x=*fib* 'k ∧ 'y=*efib* ('n+1) ∧ 'y=*fib* ('k+3)
    ∧ 'n ≥ 0 ∧ 'k ≥ 1 ∧ '*sum*=*sum-efib m* 'k ∧ 'x ≤ m,
    'y=*efib* ('n+1) ∧ 'y=*fib* ('k+3) ∧ (4∗'y+'x)=*efib* ('n+2)
    ∧ (4∗'y+'x)=*fib* (6+'k) ∧ ('*sum*+'x)=*sum-efib m* ('k+3) ⟧;
  '*tmp* := 'x; 'x := 'y;
  'y := 4∗'y + '*tmp*;
  '*sum* := '*sum* + '*tmp*;
  'n := 'n+1; 'k := 'k+3
od
  by *refinement*

Fig. 1. Construction of the sum of even Fibonacci numbers program

now stores the tentative loop invariant; so we can introduce the while-loop in (5). This requires that the precondition implies the postcondition, which follows from the definition of the predicate *is-sum-efib* by setting n to 'k.

Deriving the body of the loop in (6) and (7) is quite straightforward; we just need to specify the variable updates. In (6), k is updated; then, in (7), '*sum* is updated to '*sum* + 'x, 'x to 'y, 'y to the next even Fibonacci number, and so on. This can be achieved by applying the following or leading refinement law. This time we choose to apply the following law from Proposition 5.3, which forces a substitution in the postcondition. In (7) we also add a new variable '*tmp* to save the value of 'x and proceed as before until all variables have been updated.

It now remains to eliminate the surviving specification statement. Refining it to **skip** with refinement law (2) requires that its precondition implies its postcondition. Accordingly, our *refinement* tactic generates the proof obligations

$$fib\ (k+6) = 4 * fib\ (k+3) + fib\ k,$$
$$even\ (fib\ k) \wedge fib\ k \leq m \Rightarrow sum\text{-}efib\ m\ (k+3) = sum\text{-}efib\ m\ k + fib\ k,$$

which are discharged by automatic theorem proving, using induction on Fibonacci numbers. This finally gives us the program in Figure 2, which is partially correct by construction. For total correctness it remains to prove termination, for which Isabelle provides support as well [21].

We conclude this development with three remarks. First, with good libraries for Fibonacci numbers in place, the algebra and particular Isabelle technology used for constructing this algorithm remain hidden behind an interface. Developers interact with Isabelle mainly by writing mathematical expressions and pseudocode in a specification language similar to to Morgan's, and by calling the *refinement* tactic and Isabelle's theorem provers. Alternatively, they could invoke individual refinement rules. This is nicely supported by Isabelle's structured proof specification language Isar.

Second, proof automation was very high. Most refinement steps were verified by *refinement* alone, the others by automated theorem proving. Isabelle thus supported a seamless refinement process at the level of textbook proofs.

Finally, it should be pointed out that we used ghost variables such as 'n and 'k to prove correctness, which are not displayed in the final program, but have not been eliminated formally.

The Fibonacci algorithm can as well be verified with Hoare logic as shown in Figure 3. Our *hoare* tactic generates the standard proof obligations, which

```
'x := 2; 'y := 8; 'sum := 0;
while {| 'x ≤ m |} do
  'tmp := 'x; 'x := 'y;
  'y := 4*'y + 'tmp;
  'sum := 'sum + 'tmp;
od
```

Fig. 2. Sum of even Fibonacci numbers

lemma ⊢ ⦃ *True* ⦄
 '*x* := *2*; '*y* := *8*; '*sum* := *0*; '*n* := *0*; '*k* := *1*;
 while ⦃ '*x* ≤ *m* ⦄
 inv ⦃
   ('*k* ≥ *1*) ∧ ('*x*=*efib* '*n*) ∧ ('*x*=*fib* '*k*) ∧ ('*y*=*efib* ('*n*+*1*))
   ∧ ('*y*=*fib* ('*k*+*3*)) ∧ ('*sum*=*sum-efib m* '*k*)
 ⦄
 do
   '*tmp* := '*x*; '*x* := '*y*;
   '*y* := *4*∗'*y* + '*tmp*;
   '*sum* := '*sum* + '*tmp*;
   '*n* := '*n*+*1*; '*k* := '*k*+*3*
 od
⦃ *is-sum-efib* '*sum m* ⦄
apply (*hoare, auto*)
apply (*smt is-sum-efib-def*)
apply (*metis fib-6-n*)
apply (*metis efib-mod-2-eq-0 sum-efib-fib*)
by (*smt efib.simps(2) efib-correct*)

Fig. 3. Verification of the sum of even Fibonacci numbers program

can be inspected when executing our Isabelle theories, and *auto* discharges the trivial ones. The survivors are then proved by Isabelle's SMT solvers and external theorem provers, using the built-in theorem prover *metis* to verify external outputs. In this case, user interaction is restricted to calling tactics and theorem provers. Beyond that the verification is fully automatic.

7   Insertion Sort

Our next example stems from Morgan's book: the construction and verification of insertion sort. It shows that our tool can handle arrays and nested loops.

We model an array A by using Isabelle's functional lists, and therefore benefit from its excellent libraries developed for this data type. This includes the operation $A \, ! \, i$ for retrieving the i-th element of A, the function *take n A* which extracts the first n elements of A, the function *list-update A i e* which updates the i-th value of A to e, and a *sorted* predicate. Using this, array assignments are defined merely as syntactic sugar:

$$'A \, ! \, i := e \Leftrightarrow 'A := list\text{-}update \; 'A \; i \; e.$$

Our insertion sort algorithm takes an array A_0 of polymorphic data that can be linearly ordered. It returns a variable 'A which holds the sorted array; that is, the values in A_0 have been permuted so that '$A \, ! \, i \leq 'A \, ! \, j$ whenever $i \leq j$. We write '$A \sim_\pi A_0$ if 'A stores a permutation of the values of A_0. We also require that A_0 has positive length. This suggests the specification statement

$$[\![\, |A_0| > 0 \wedge {}^{\backprime}A{=}A_0, \; sorted \; {}^{\backprime}A \wedge {}^{\backprime}A \sim_\pi A_0 \,]\!].$$

The idea behind insertion sort is well known and need not be repeated. To express that we successively sort larger prefixes, we introduce a variable ${}^{\backprime}i$ such that $1 \leq {}^{\backprime}i \leq |{}^{\backprime}A|$. For ${}^{\backprime}i = 1$, we have $sorted \; (take \; {}^{\backprime}i \; {}^{\backprime}A)$.

Our refinement steps are similar to Morgan's. We show only the most important ones in Figure 4. In (1) we initialise ${}^{\backprime}i := 1$ and introduce a while-loop. The resulting proof obligation is discharged by the *refinement* tactic. In the body of the loop we now wish to take the ${}^{\backprime}i$-th element of the array and insert it in position ${}^{\backprime}j \leq {}^{\backprime}i$ such that $sorted \; (take \; ({}^{\backprime}i{+}1) \; {}^{\backprime}A)$. To express this succinctly we define the predicate $sorted\text{-}but \; A \; k$, which states that A is sorted after removing its

$$[\![\, |A_0| > 0 \wedge {}^{\backprime}A{=}A_0, \; sorted \; {}^{\backprime}A \wedge {}^{\backprime}A \sim_\pi A_0 \,]\!] \sqsubseteq \qquad\qquad (1)$$
${}^{\backprime}i := 1;$
while $\{\!|\, {}^{\backprime}i < |{}^{\backprime}A| \,|\!\}$ **do**
$\quad [\![\, sorted \; (take \; {}^{\backprime}i \; {}^{\backprime}A) \wedge {}^{\backprime}i < |{}^{\backprime}A| \wedge {}^{\backprime}A \sim_\pi A_0,$
$\quad\;\; sorted \; (take \; ({}^{\backprime}i{+}1) \; {}^{\backprime}A) \wedge ({}^{\backprime}i{+}1) \leq |{}^{\backprime}A| \wedge {}^{\backprime}A \sim_\pi A_0]\!];$
$\quad {}^{\backprime}i := {}^{\backprime}i{+}1$
od

$$\qquad\quad \sqsubseteq \qquad\qquad\qquad\qquad\qquad\qquad\qquad\qquad (2)$$
${}^{\backprime}i := 1;$
while $\{\!|\, {}^{\backprime}i < |{}^{\backprime}A| \,|\!\}$ **do**
$\quad [\![\, sorted\text{-}but \; (take \; ({}^{\backprime}i{+}1) \; {}^{\backprime}A) \; {}^{\backprime}i \wedge {}^{\backprime}i < |{}^{\backprime}A| \wedge {}^{\backprime}A \sim_\pi A_0,$
$\quad\;\; {}^{\backprime}j \leq {}^{\backprime}i \wedge sorted\text{-}but \; (take \; ({}^{\backprime}i{+}1) \; {}^{\backprime}A) \; {}^{\backprime}j \wedge ({}^{\backprime}j{\neq}{}^{\backprime}i \longrightarrow {}^{\backprime}A \, ! \, {}^{\backprime}j \leq {}^{\backprime}A \, ! \, ({}^{\backprime}j{+}1))$
$\quad\;\; \wedge \; ({}^{\backprime}i{+}1) \leq |{}^{\backprime}A| \; \wedge \; ({}^{\backprime}j{=}0 \vee {}^{\backprime}A \, ! \, ({}^{\backprime}j{-}1) \leq {}^{\backprime}A \, ! \, {}^{\backprime}j) \wedge {}^{\backprime}A \sim_\pi A_0]\!];$
$\quad {}^{\backprime}i := {}^{\backprime}i{+}1$
od

$$\qquad\quad \sqsubseteq \qquad\qquad\qquad\qquad\qquad\qquad\qquad\qquad (3)$$
${}^{\backprime}i := 1;$
while $\{\!|\, {}^{\backprime}i < |{}^{\backprime}A| \,|\!\}$ **do**
$\quad {}^{\backprime}i := {}^{\backprime}j;$
$\quad$ **while** $\{\!|\, {}^{\backprime}j{\neq}0 \wedge {}^{\backprime}A \, ! \, {}^{\backprime}j < {}^{\backprime}A \, ! \, ({}^{\backprime}j{-}1) \,|\!\}$ **do**
$\quad\quad [\![\, {}^{\backprime}j \leq {}^{\backprime}i \wedge sorted\text{-}but \; (take \; ({}^{\backprime}i{+}1) \; {}^{\backprime}A) \; {}^{\backprime}j \wedge ({}^{\backprime}j{\neq}{}^{\backprime}i \longrightarrow {}^{\backprime}A \, ! \, {}^{\backprime}j \leq {}^{\backprime}A \, ! \, ({}^{\backprime}j{+}1))$
$\quad\quad\;\; \wedge \; ({}^{\backprime}i{+}1) \leq |{}^{\backprime}A| \wedge {}^{\backprime}j{\neq}0 \wedge {}^{\backprime}A \, ! \, {}^{\backprime}j < {}^{\backprime}A \, ! \, ({}^{\backprime}j{-}1) \wedge {}^{\backprime}A \sim_\pi A_0,$
$\quad\quad\;\; {}^{\backprime}j{-}1 \leq {}^{\backprime}i \wedge sorted\text{-}but \; (take \; ({}^{\backprime}i{+}1) \; {}^{\backprime}A) \; ({}^{\backprime}j{-}1) \wedge ({}^{\backprime}i{+}1) \leq |{}^{\backprime}A|$
$\quad\quad\;\; \wedge \; ({}^{\backprime}j{-}1{\neq}{}^{\backprime}i \longrightarrow {}^{\backprime}A \, ! \, ({}^{\backprime}j{-}1) \leq {}^{\backprime}A \, ! \, {}^{\backprime}j) \wedge {}^{\backprime}j{\neq}0 \wedge {}^{\backprime}A \sim_\pi A_0]\!];$
$\quad\quad {}^{\backprime}j := {}^{\backprime}j{-}1$
$\quad$ **od**;
$\quad {}^{\backprime}i := {}^{\backprime}i{+}1$
od
$\quad \ldots$

$[\![\, \ldots previous \; specification \; statement \ldots]\!]$
$$\qquad\quad \sqsubseteq \qquad\qquad\qquad\qquad\qquad\qquad\qquad\qquad (4)$$
${}^{\backprime}k := {}^{\backprime}A \, ! \, {}^{\backprime}j;$
${}^{\backprime}A \, ! \, {}^{\backprime}j := {}^{\backprime}A \, ! \, ({}^{\backprime}j{-}1);$
${}^{\backprime}A \, ! \, ({}^{\backprime}j{-}1) := {}^{\backprime}k$

Fig. 4. Construction of insertion sort algorithm (excerpts)

```
'i := 1;
while {| 'i < |'A| |} do
  'i := 'j;
  while {| 'j≠0 ∧ 'A ! 'j < 'A ! ('j−1) |} do
    'k := 'A ! 'j;
    'A ! 'j := 'A ! ('j−1);
    'A ! ('j−1) := 'k;
    'j := 'j−1
  od;
  'i := 'i+1
od
```

Fig. 5. Insertion sort algorithm

k-th element. We then rewrite the specification statement in (2). The *refinement* tactic generates four proof obligations which are discharged automatically.

Next we wish to set 'j to 'i and iteratively swap 'A ! 'j to 'A ! ('$j − 1$) until 'A ! ('$j − 1$) $\leq$ 'A ! 'j or '$j = 0$. This requires introducing a new while-loop in (3) which is justified by calling *refinement*.

Finally, in (4) we need to prove that the remaining specification statement is refined by swapping 'A ! 'j to 'A ! ('$j − 1$). The *refinement* tactic generates six proof obligations. Discharging them automatically requires proving some general properties of sorted list and permutations absent in Isabelle's library, e.g., that swapping array elements yields a permutation. Construction of the insertion sort algorithm is then complete. The result is shown in Figure 5. Again, it is partially correct by construction; its termination can be proved by other means. Apart from adding some general-purpose lemmas about permutations and sorted lists to Isabelle's libraries, the development was fully automatic.

Decorating the algorithm with the pre- and postcondition from the above specification statement, one can also verify this algorithm with Hoare logic. After calling the *hoare* tactic and *auto* we are left with seven proof obligations, the proof of which is shown in Figure 6. It is mainly by automated theorem proving. Only the *unfold* step does not directly call a theorem prover. It unfolds two facts and then calls Isabelle's *auto* tool.

```
apply (hoare, auto)
apply (metis One-nat-def take-sorted-butE-0)
apply (metis take-sorted-butE-n One-nat-def less-eq-Suc-le not-less-eq-eq)
apply (metis One-nat-def Suc-eq-plus1 le-less-linear less-Suc-eq-le take-sorted-butE)
apply (unfold sorted-equals-nth-mono sorted-but-def, auto)
apply (smt nth-list-update)
apply (metis (hide-lams, no-types) One-nat-def perm.trans perm-swap-array)
apply (smt nth-list-update)
by (smt perm.trans perm-swap-array)
```

Fig. 6. Verification of insertion sort algorithm (proof steps)

8   Conclusion

We have used Kleene algebra with tests for developing a simple program verification tool based on Hoare logic in Isabelle. Adding one single axiom to this
algebra yielded a tool for program construction with a basic Morgan-style refinement calculus. Using the algebra in combination with Isabelle's integrated
automated theorem provers and SMT solvers made this development simple and
effective. Two extended case studies show our tools at work.

Our tools form a lightweight flexible middle layer for formal methods which
can easily be adapted and extended. Programs are analysed directly on their relational semantics, but most relational manipulations are captured algebraically.
Therefore our tools can be integrated directly into any formal method which uses
a relational semantics. Alternatively, imperative code can be verified by mapping a programming language syntax to its relational semantics. In the context
of program construction, code for a given imperative language could be generated automatically from our "relational" programs, transforming the abstract
data structures in these programs by data refinement [10].

Or approach can be enhanced and adapted flexibly to other analysis tasks.
First, equations in KAT can be decided in PSPACE. The general Horn and
first-order theories are undecidable, but universal Horn formulas of the form
$r_1 = 0 \land \cdots \land r_n = 0 \Rightarrow s = t$ are still decidable via a technique called *hypothesis
elimination*. Inference rules with Hoare triples fall into this fragment. Formally
verified decision and hypothesis elimination procedures are currently available
only in Coq [20]; they would further enhance the performance of our tools.

Second, in contrast to our semantic approach, KAT can be expanded to capture assignments at the algebraic level [1]. A flowchart equivalence proof from [1]
has already been formalised in Coq [20] and Isabelle [6] with this approach. It requires, however, more work to integrate it into tools and increase its automation.
Comparing both approaches in practice is certainly interesting.

Third, while KAT captures the deductive aspect of Hoare logic, modal Kleene
algebras [8] encompass also its partial correctness semantics [15]. The integration
of our tools into these more expressive algebras will be our next step. This
supports program analysis directly via the wlp-semantics. It may also yield more
powerful inference rules and refinement laws, and support static analysis.

Finally, KAT could be replaced by algebras for total correctness reasoning, for
which Isabelle support has already been provided [3], and by rely-guarantee style
algebras for shared variable concurrency. A simple verification tool for this, which
includes a semantics of finite transition traces, has already been developed [2].

Acknowledgements. This work has been supported by the CNPq and the
EPSRC through a DTA scholarship and grant EP/J003727/1.

References

[1] Angus, A., Kozen, D.: Kleene algebra with tests and program schematology. Technical Report TR2001-1844, Cornell University (2001)

[2] Armstrong, A., Gomes, V.B.F., Struth, G.: Algebraic principles for rely-guarantee style concurrency verification tools. In: Jones, C., Pihlajasaari, P., Sun, J. (eds.) FM 2014. LNCS, vol. 8442, pp. 78–93. Springer, Heidelberg (2014)

[3] Armstrong, A., Gomes, V.B.F., Struth, G.: Algebras for program correctness in Isabelle/HOL. In: Höfner, P., Jipsen, P., Kahl, W., Müller, M.E. (eds.) RAMiCS 2014. LNCS, vol. 8428, pp. 49–64. Springer, Heidelberg (2014)

[4] Armstrong, A., Gomes, V.B.F., Struth, G.: Kleene algebras with tests and demonic refinement algebras. Archive of Formal Proofs (2014)

[5] Armstrong, A., Struth, G., Weber, T.: Kleene algebra. Archive of Formal Proofs (2013)

[6] Armstrong, A., Struth, G., Weber, T.: Program analysis and verification based on Kleene algebra in Isabelle/HOL. In: Blazy, S., Paulin-Mohring, C., Pichardie, D. (eds.) ITP 2013. LNCS, vol. 7998, pp. 197–212. Springer, Heidelberg (2013)

[7] Cavalcanti, A., Sampaio, A., Woodcock, J.: A refinement strategy for circus. Formal Aspects of Computing 15(2-3), 146–181 (2003)

[8] Desharnais, J., Struth, G.: Internal axioms for domain semirings. Science of Computer Programming 76(3), 181–203 (2011)

[9] Filliâtre, J.-C., Marché, C.: The Why/Krakatoa/Caduceus platform for deductive program verification. In: Damm, W., Hermanns, H. (eds.) CAV 2007. LNCS, vol. 4590, pp. 173–177. Springer, Heidelberg (2007)

[10] Haftmann, F., Krauss, A., Kunčar, O., Nipkow, T.: Data refinement in Isabelle/HOL. In: Blazy, S., Paulin-Mohring, C., Pichardie, D. (eds.) ITP 2013. LNCS, vol. 7998, pp. 100–115. Springer, Heidelberg (2013)

[11] Kozen, D.: Kleene algebra with tests. ACM TOPLAS 19(3), 427–443 (1997)

[12] Kozen, D.: On Hoare logic and Kleene algebra with tests. ACM TOCL 1(1), 60–76 (2000)

[13] Kozen, D.: Kleene algebras with tests and the static analysis of programs. Technical Report TR2003-1915, Cornell University (2003)

[14] Kozen, D., Patron, M.-C.: Certification of compiler optimizations using Kleene algebra with tests. In: Lloyd, J., et al. (eds.) CL 2000. LNCS (LNAI), vol. 1861, pp. 568–582. Springer, Heidelberg (2000)

[15] Möller, B., Struth, G.: Algebras of modal operators and partial correctness. Theoretical Computer Science 351(2), 221–239 (2006)

[16] Möller, B., Struth, G.: wp is wlp. In: MacCaull, W., Winter, M., Düntsch, I. (eds.) RelMiCS 2005. LNCS, vol. 3929, pp. 200–211. Springer, Heidelberg (2006)

[17] Morgan, C.: Programming from specifications, 2nd edn. Prentice Hall (1994)

[18] Nipkow, T., Paulson, L.C., Wenzel, M.: Isabelle/HOL. LNCS, vol. 2283. Springer, Heidelberg (2002)

[19] Nipkow, T.: Winskel is (almost) right: Towards a mechanized semantics. Formal Aspects of Computing 10(2), 171–186 (1998)

[20] Pous, D.: Kleene algebra with tests and Coq tools for while programs. In: Blazy, S., Paulin-Mohring, C., Pichardie, D. (eds.) ITP 2013. LNCS, vol. 7998, pp. 180–196. Springer, Heidelberg (2013)

[21] Sternagel, C., Thiemann, R.: Certification of nontermination proofs. In: Beringer, L., Felty, A. (eds.) ITP 2012. LNCS, vol. 7406, pp. 266–282. Springer, Heidelberg (2012)

Completeness of Separation Logic with Inductive Definitions for Program Verification

Makoto Tatsuta[1] and Wei-Ngan Chin[2]

[1] National Institute of Informatics,
2-1-2 Hitotsubashi, 101-8430 Tokyo, Japan
tatsuta@nii.ac.jp
[2] Department of Computer Science,
National University of Singapore,
13 Computing Drive, Singapore 117417, Singapore
chinwn@comp.nus.edu.sg

Abstract. This paper extends Reynolds' separation logical system for pointer-based while program verification by adding inductive definitions. Inductive definitions give us a great advantage for verification, since they enable us for example, to formalize linked lists and to support the lemma reasoning mechanism. This paper proves its completeness theorem that states that every true asserted program is provable in the logical system. In order to prove its completeness, this paper shows an expressiveness theorem that states the weakest precondition of every program and every assertion can be expressed by some assertion.

1 Introduction

Reynolds proposed a new logical system based on separation logic for pointer program verification [17]. It enables us to have a concise specification of program properties and a manageable proof system. Separation logic is successful in a theoretical sense as well as a practical sense. By using separation logic, some pointer program verification systems have been implemented [13,2].

Inductive definitions in logical systems to formalize properties of programs have been studied widely, for example, in [7,15,18,11]. Inductive definitions play an important role in formalizing properties of programs in logical systems. Many important data structures such as lists and trees are naturally represented in logical systems by using inductive definitions, since they are recursively defined by nature. Specifications and properties of programs can be formally represented in a natural way in a logical system with the help of inductive definitions.

Combining with separation logic, inductive definitions give a verification system a general mechanism to formalize recursive data structures such as linked lists and circular doubly-linked lists. Instead of manually adding these data structures one by one in an ad hoc way, the system uniformly formalizes all these recursive data structures once we have inductive definitions in the system. Some properties called lemmas in [14] are important for program verification. In our system, every lemma statement corresponding to each recursive data structure is

D. Giannakopoulou and G. Salaün (Eds.): SEFM 2014, LNCS 8702, pp. 20–34, 2014.
© Springer International Publishing Switzerland 2014

also generated automatically from the description of the recursive data structure, and the consistency of the system is automatically preserved.

One of the most important theoretical questions for a verification system is its completeness [1,5,9,12]. The soundness of a system guarantees that if the correctness of a program is proved in the system, then the program will indeed run correctly. The soundness of those existing practical systems has been proved. However, it does not mean the system can prove all correct programs are correct, that is, there is a possibility that some programs are not proved to be correct by the system even though they are indeed correct. The completeness is the converse of the soundness. The completeness of the system guarantees that if a program runs correctly, then the system surely proves the program is correct. The completeness of a system shows how powerful the system is.

Our contributions are: (1) an extension of separation logic for pointer while program verification by adding inductive definitions, (2) the completeness theorem of separation logic with inductive definitions for pointer while programs, and (3) the expressiveness theorem of the separation logic with inductive definitions for pointer while programs.

We will prove the completeness by extending the completeness results of separation logic for pointer while programs given in [19] to assertions with inductive definitions. The main challenge is proving the expressiveness theorem.

We say that a logical system with the standard model is expressive for programs, if the weakest precondition of every program is definable in the logical system. At first sight, the expressiveness may look trivial, but it is indeed a subtle problem and some pathological counterexamples are known [3].

The expressiveness theorem for Peano arithmetic and separation logic was proved in [19] based on the following idea. We code the heap information as well as the store information by natural numbers, and simulating program executions as well as the truth of assertions by using Peano arithmetic. The idea uses natural numbers to encode the current store s and heap h, respectively. The store s is coded by a list of values in distinguished variables. We can construct a heapcode translation $\mathrm{HEval}_A(m)$ of an assertion A. $\mathrm{HEval}_A(m)$ is a pure formula such that A is true at (s, h) if and only if $\mathrm{HEval}_A(m)$ is true at s when the number m represents the heap h.

We will extend the expressiveness proof in [19] to inductive definitions. Since our system is proof-theoretically strictly stronger than the system in [19] because of inductive definitions [16], we did not know a possibility of this extension. The key in our proof of the expressiveness theorem for inductive definitions is to observe that if A is an inductively defined predicate, we can define $\mathrm{HEval}_A(m)$ by using another inductively defined predicate. This idea is a similar direction to the solutions used in an extension of type theory to inductive definitions [7,15], and an extension of realizability interpretations to inductive definitions [18].

An extension of bunched implications with inductive definitions was studied in [4]. Our assertion language is included in it, but ours is more specific for the aim of pointer program verification. They discussed only an assertion language and did not discuss asserted programs.

Recently the completeness of separation logic was actively studied [5,9,12]. However, the case of a predicate logic with inductive definitions has not been investigated yet, since [5] and [9] discussed only propositional logic, and [12] studied only a system without inductions.

Our long-term aim is proving completeness of the core of existing practical verification systems for pointer programs. This paper will give a step for this purpose. In order to analyze a verification system with built-in recursive data structures and their properties such as the lemma reasoning mechanism in [14], the separation logic with inductive definitions is indispensable. Since our system in this paper is simple and general, our completeness theorem can be applied to those systems in order to show the completeness of their core systems. This paper will also provide a starting point for completeness theorems in extensions with richer programming languages and assertion languages such as recursive procedure calls.

Section 2 defines our programming language and our assertion language, and gives examples of inductive definitions. Their semantics is given in Section 3. Section 4 gives a logical system for proving asserted programs, and Section 5 shows our completeness theorem as well as our soundness theorem. Section 6 gives a proof sketch of the expressiveness theorem. Section 7 is the conclusion.

2   Languages

This section defines our programming language and our assertion language. Our language is obtained from Reynolds' paper [17] by adding inductive definitions to the assertion language.

Our programming language is an extension of while programs to pointers. It is the same as that of Reynolds [17].

We have variables $x, y, z, w, \ldots$, and constants $0, 1, \text{null}$. Its expressions are defined as follows.

Expressions $e ::= x \mid 0 \mid 1 \mid \text{null} \mid e + e \mid e \times e$.

Expressions mean natural numbers or pointers. null means the null pointer.

Its boolean expressions are propositional formulas defined as follows.

Boolean expressions $b ::= e = e \mid e < e \mid \neg b \mid b \wedge b \mid b \vee b \mid b \rightarrow b$.

Boolean expressions are used as conditions in a program.

Programs are defined by:

Programs $P ::= x := e \mid \text{if } (b) \text{ then } (P) \text{ else } (P) \mid \text{while } (b) \text{ do } (P) \mid P; P \mid$
$\quad x := \text{cons}(e, e) \mid x := [e] \mid [e] := e \mid \text{dispose}(e)$.

The statement $x := \text{cons}(e_1, e_2)$ allocates two new consecutive memory cells, puts e_1 and e_2 in the cells, and puts the address into x. The statement $x := [e]$ looks up the content of the memory cell at the address e and puts it into x. The statement $[e_1] := e_2$ changes the content of the memory cell at the address e_1 by e_2. The statement $\text{dispose}(e)$ deallocates the memory cell at the address e. We will sometimes write the number n to denote the term $1 + (1 + (1 + \ldots (1 + 0)))$ (n times of $1+$). We will use i, j, k, l, m, n for natural numbers.

Our assertion language is a first-order language extended with inductive definitions and the separating conjunction $*$ and the separating implication $-\!\!*$. It is an extension of assertions in [17,19] with inductive definitions. Our assertion language is defined as follows: Terms are the same as the expressions of our programming language and denoted by t. We have predicate symbols $=, <, \mapsto$, a predicate constant emp, and predicate variables $X, Y, \ldots$. We assume that when we have a predicate variable X we also have a predicate variable $\tilde{X}$.

Open formulas $A ::= \text{emp} \mid e = e \mid e < e \mid e \mapsto e \mid X(t, \ldots, t) \mid \neg A \mid A \wedge A \mid$

$$A \vee A \mid A \rightarrow A \mid \forall x A \mid \exists x A \mid (\mu X.\lambda x \ldots x.A)(t, \ldots, t) \mid A * A \mid A -\!\!* A.$$

We assume that X occurs in A only positively for $(\mu X.\lambda x_1 \ldots x_n.A)(t_1, \ldots, t_n)$. The positivity is defined in a standard manner as follows. We define the set $\text{FPV}_+(A)$ of positive predicate variables and the set $\text{FPV}_-(A)$ of negative predicate variables for A in a standard way. We say that X occurs only positively in A when $X \notin \text{FPV}_-(A)$.

We define $\text{FPV}(A)$ as $\text{FPV}_+(A) \cup \text{FPV}_-(A)$. We call an open formula A a formula if $\text{FPV}(A) = \emptyset$. We will sometimes call a formula an assertion. We call an open formula pure when the open formula does not contain emp, $e_1 \mapsto e_2$, $A * B$, or $A -\!\!* B$.

The open formula $(\mu X.\lambda x_1 \ldots x_n.A)(t_1, \ldots, t_n)$ means the inductively defined predicate $\mu X.\lambda x_1 \ldots x_n.A$ holds for $t_1, \ldots, t_n$. The predicate $\mu X.\lambda x_1 \ldots x_n.A$ denotes the least predicate X such that $A \leftrightarrow X(x_1, \ldots, x_n)$. An open formula may contain some predicate variables. The meaning of an open formula depends on the meaning of its predicate variables. A formula does not contain any predicate variables, and its meaning is determined in an ordinary way. For an assertion, we will use only a formula, since it does not contain any free predicate variables.

emp means the current heap is empty. $e_1 \mapsto e_2$ means the current heap has only one cell at the address e_1 and its content is e_2. $A * B$ means the current heap can be split into some two disjoint heaps such that A holds at one heap and B holds at the other heap. $A -\!\!* B$ means that for any heap disjoint from the current heap such that A holds at the heap, B holds at the new heap obtained by combining the current heap and the heap. Note that $X(t_1, \ldots, t_n)$ may depend on the current heap since X could take emp or $e_1 \mapsto e_2$. The other formula constructions mean ordinary logical connectives.

$\text{FV}(A)$ is defined as the set of free variables in A. $\text{FV}(e)$ and $\text{FV}(P)$ are similarly defined. $\text{FV}(O_1, \ldots, O_n)$ is defined as $\text{FV}(O_1) \cup \ldots \cup \text{FV}(O_n)$ when O_i is an open formula, an expression, or a program. $A \leftrightarrow B$ is defined as $(A \rightarrow B) \wedge (B \rightarrow A)$. We use $A[x := t]$ for a standard substitution without variable capture.

We use vector notation to denote a sequence. For example, $\vec{e}$ denotes the sequence $e_1, \ldots, e_n$ of expressions.

Example 1 (linked lists). The predicate that characterizes singly linked lists is formalized by using inductive definitions as follows.

$$\text{Node}(x, y, z) = x \mapsto y * x + 1 \mapsto z,$$
$$\text{LL} - \mu X.\lambda x y.(x = \text{null} \wedge y = 0 \vee \exists z w(\text{Node}(x, z, w) * X(w, y - 1))).$$

$LL(p, n)$ means that there is a singly linked list pointed by p such that its length is n.

LL is the least predicate that satisfies

$$LL(p, n) \leftrightarrow p = \text{null} \wedge n = 0 \vee \exists xq(\text{Node}(p, x, q) * LL(q, n - 1)).$$

$LL(p, n)$ formalizes the predicate `p::ll<n>` given in [14]. They added their lemma properties in an ad hoc way for proof search. In our system, those properties are derived by the above general principle.

Example 2 (circular doubly-linked lists). Let

$$\text{Node2}(x, y, z, w) = x \mapsto y * x + 1 \mapsto z * x + 2 \mapsto w,$$
$$\text{DSN} = \mu X.\lambda xyzwv.(x = w \wedge z = v \wedge y = 0$$
$$\vee \exists y'w'(\text{Node2}(x, y', z, w') * X(w', y - 1, x, w, v))),$$
$$\text{DCL}(x, y) = (x = \text{null} \wedge y = 0 \vee$$
$$\exists zw(\exists u \text{Node2}(x, u, z, w) * \text{DSN}(w, y - 1, x, x, z))).$$

$\text{DSN}(q, s, p, n, t)$ means that there is a doubly linked list pointed by q such that its length is s, the previous pointer in the first element is p, the next pointer in the last element is n, and t points the last element. $\text{DCL}(p, s)$ means that there is a circular doubly-linked list of length s pointed by p.

DSN is the least predicate that satisfies

$$\text{DSN}(q, s, p, n, t) \leftrightarrow$$
$$q = n \wedge p = t \wedge s = 0 \vee \exists rs'(\text{Node2}(q, s', p, r) * \text{DSN}(r, s - 1, q, n, t)).$$

Since it is the least, we can also show that one of their lemma properties

$$\text{DSN}(q, s, p, n, t) \wedge s > 0 \leftrightarrow \exists r(\text{DSN}(q, s - 1, p, t, r) * \exists x \text{Node2}(t, x, r, n))$$

is true.

$\text{DCL}(p, s)$ formalizes the predicate `p::dcl(s)`, $\text{DSN}(r, s, p, n, t)$ formalizes `r::dseqN<s,p,n,t>`, and the last equivalence formula formalizes their lemma given in [14].

Example 3 (linked list segments). The predicate that characterizes linked list segments is formalized by using inductive definitions as follows.

$$\text{LS} = \mu X.\lambda xy.(x = y \wedge \text{emp} \vee \exists v(\exists u \text{Node}(x, u, v) * X(v, y)) \wedge x \neq y).$$

$\text{LS}(x, p)$ means that the heap is a linked list segment such that x points the first cell and p is the next pointer in the last cell.

LS is the least predicate that satisfies

$$\text{LS}(x, p) \leftrightarrow x = p \wedge \text{emp} \vee \exists v(\exists u \text{Node}(x, u, v) * \text{LS}(v, p)) \wedge x \neq p.$$

By this general principle we can show that

$$\text{LS}(x, p) * \text{Node}(p, a, b) \leftrightarrow \exists q(\text{LS}(x, q) * \text{LS}(q, p) * \text{Node}(p, a, b))$$

is true.

LS(E, F) formalizes the following predicate ls(E, F) given in [2], where we represent $E \mapsto [f_1 : x, f_2 : y]$ by Node(E, x, y). These formulas are also true in our system.

$$\text{ls}(E, F) \leftrightarrow (E = F \wedge \text{emp}) \vee (E \neq F \wedge \exists y. E \mapsto [n : y] * \text{ls}(y, F)),$$
$$\text{ls}(E_1, E_2) * \text{ls}(E_2, E_3) * E_3 \mapsto [\rho] \rightarrow \text{ls}(E_1, E_3) * E_3 \mapsto [\rho].$$

3 Semantics

The semantics of our programming language and our assertion language is defined in this section. Our semantics is obtained by combining a standard semantics for natural numbers and inductive definitions and a semantics for programs and assertions given in Reynolds' paper [17] except the following simplification: (1) values are natural numbers, (2) addresses are non-zero natural numbers, and (3) null is 0. We call our model the standard model.

The set N is defined as the set of natural numbers. The set Vars is defined as the set of variables in the language. The set Locs is defined as the set $\{n \in N | n > 0\}$.

For sets $S_1, S_2, f : S_1 \rightarrow S_2$ means that f is a function from S_1 to S_2. $f : S_1 \rightarrow_{fin} S_2$ means that f is a finite function from S_1 to S_2, that is, there is a finite subset S_1' of S_1 and $f : S_1' \rightarrow S_2$. Dom(f) denotes the domain of the function f. We use $\emptyset$ and $p(S)$ to denote the empty set and the powerset of the set S respectively. For a function $f : A \rightarrow B$ and a subset $C \subseteq A$, the function $f|_C : C \rightarrow B$ is defined by $f|_C(x) = f(x)$ for $x \in C$.

A function $f : p(S) \rightarrow p(S)$ is called monotone if $f(X) \subseteq f(Y)$ for all $X \subseteq Y$. It is well-known that a monotone function has its least fixed point. The least fixed point of f is denoted by lfp(f).

A store is defined as a function from Vars $\rightarrow N$, and denoted by s. A heap is defined as a finite function from Locs $\rightarrow_{fin} N$, and denoted by h. We will write Heaps for the set of heaps. A value is a natural number. An address is a positive natural number. The null pointer is 0. A store assigns a value to each variable. A heap assigns a value to an address in its finite domain.

The store $s[x_1 := n_1, \ldots, x_k := n_k]$ is defined by s' such that $s'(x_i) = n_i$ and $s'(y) = s(y)$ for $y \notin \{x_1, \ldots, x_k\}$. The heap $h[m_1 := n_1, \ldots, m_k := n_k]$ is defined by h' such that $h'(m_i) = n_i$ and $h'(y) = h(y)$ for $y \in \text{Dom}(h) - \{m_1, \ldots, m_k\}$. The store $s[x_1 := n_1, \ldots, x_k := n_k]$ is the same as s except values for the variables $x_1, \ldots, x_n$. The heap $h[m_1 := n_1, \ldots, m_k := n_k]$ is the same as h except the contents of the memory cells at the addresses $m_1, \ldots, m_k$. We will sometimes write $\emptyset$ for the empty heap whose domain is empty.

We will write $h = h_1 + h_2$ when Dom$(h) = \text{Dom}(h_1) \cup \text{Dom}(h_2)$, Dom$(h_1) \cap \text{Dom}(h_2) = \emptyset$, $h(x) = h_1(x)$ for $x \in \text{Dom}(h_1)$, and $h(x) = h_2(x)$ for $x \in \text{Dom}(h_2)$. The heap h is divided into the two disjoint heaps h_1 and h_2 when $h = h_1 + h_2$.

A state is defined as (s, h). The set States is defined as the set of states. The state for pointer program is specified by the store and the heap, since pointer programs manipulate memory heaps as well as variable assignments.

Definition 3.1. We define the semantics of our programming language.

We define the semantics $[\![e]\!]_s$ of our expressions e and the semantics $[\![A]\!]_s$ of our boolean expressions A under the variable assignment s by the standard model of natural numbers and $[\![\text{null}]\!] = 0$. For example, $[\![e]\!]_s$ is defined by induction on e by $[\![x]\!]_s = s(x)$, $[\![0]\!]_s = 0$, $[\![1]\!]_s = 1$, $[\![\text{null}]\!]_s = 0$, $[\![e_1 + e_2]\!]_s = [\![e_1]\!]_s + [\![e_2]\!]_s$, and so on. $[\![A]\!]_s$ is defined in a similar way.

For a program P, its meaning $[\![P]\!]$ is defined as a function from States$\cup\{$abort$\}$ to $p(\text{States} \cup \{\text{abort}\})$. We will define $[\![P]\!](r_1)$ as the set of all the possible resulting states after the execution of P with the initial state r_1 terminates. In particular, if the execution of P with the initial state r_1 does not terminate, we will define $[\![P]\!](r_1)$ as the empty set, since there are no possible resulting states in this case. Our semantics is nondeterministic since the cons statement may choose a fresh cell address and we do not allow renaming of memory addresses. $[\![P]\!]$ is defined by induction on P as follows:

$$[\![P]\!](\text{abort}) = \{\text{abort}\},$$
$$[\![x := e]\!]((s, h)) = \{(s[x := [\![e]\!]_s], h)\},$$
$$[\![\text{if } (b) \text{ then } (P_1) \text{ else } (P_2)]\!]((s, h)) = [\![P_1]\!]((s, h)) \text{ if } [\![b]\!]_s = \text{true},$$
$$[\![P_2]\!]((s, h)) \text{ otherwise},$$
$$[\![\text{while } (b) \text{ do } (P)]\!]((s, h)) = \{(s, h)\} \text{ if } [\![b]\!]_s = \text{false},$$
$$\bigcup\{[\![\text{while } (b) \text{ do } (P)]\!](r) \mid r \in [\![P]\!]((s, h))\} \text{ otherwise},$$
$$[\![P_1; P_2]\!]((s, h)) = \bigcup\{[\![P_2]\!](r) \mid r \in [\![P_1]\!]((s, h))\},$$
$$[\![x := \text{cons}(e_1, e_2)]\!]((s, h)) = \{(s[x := n], h[n := [\![e_1]\!]_s, n + 1 := [\![e_2]\!]_s])\mid$$
$$n > 0, n, n + 1 \notin \text{Dom}(h)\},$$
$$[\![x := [e]]\!]((s, h)) = \{(s[x := h([\![e]\!]_s)], h)\} \text{ if } [\![e]\!]_s \in \text{Dom}(h),$$
$$\{\text{abort}\} \text{ otherwise},$$
$$[\![[e_1] := e_2]\!]((s, h)) = \{(s, h[[\![e_1]\!]_s := [\![e_2]\!]_s])\} \text{ if } [\![e_1]\!]_s \in \text{Dom}(h),$$
$$\{\text{abort}\} \text{ otherwise},$$
$$[\![\text{dispose}(e)]\!]((s, h)) = \{(s, h|_{\text{Dom}(h) - \{[\![e]\!]_s\}})\} \text{ if } [\![e]\!]_s \in \text{Dom}(h),$$
$$\{\text{abort}\} \text{ otherwise}.$$

Definition 3.2. We define the semantics of the assertion language. For an assertion A and a state (s, h), the meaning $[\![A]\!]_{(s,h)}$ is defined as true or false. $[\![A]\!]_{(s,h)}$ is the truth value of A at the state (s, h).

A predicate variable assignment σ is a function that maps a predicate variable X with arity n to a subset of $N^n \times$ Heaps. Since an open formula A may contain free predicate variables, in order to give the meaning of A, we will use a predicate variable assignment for the meaning of free predicate variables in A. The predicate variable assignment $\sigma[X_1 := S_1, \ldots, X_n := S_n]$ is defined by σ' such that $\sigma'(X_i) = S_i$ and $\sigma'(Y) = \sigma(Y)$ for $Y \notin \{X_1, \ldots, X_n\}$. We will sometimes write $\emptyset$ for the constant predicate variable assignment such that $\emptyset(X)$ is the empty set for all X.

In order to define $[\![A]\!]_{(s,h)}$ for a formula, we first define $[\![A]\!]^{\sigma}_{(s,h)}$ for an open formula by induction on A as follows:

$[\![\text{emp}]\!]^{\sigma}_{(s,h)} = \text{true if } \text{Dom}(h) = \emptyset,$

$[\![e_1 = e_2]\!]^{\sigma}_{(s,h)} = ([\![e_1]\!]_s = [\![e_2]\!]_s),$

$[\![e_1 < e_2]\!]^{\sigma}_{(s,h)} = ([\![e_1]\!]_s < [\![e_2]\!]_s),$

$[\![e_1 \mapsto e_2]\!]^{\sigma}_{(s,h)} = \text{true if } \text{Dom}(h) = \{[\![e_1]\!]_s\}, h([\![e_1]\!]_s) = [\![e_2]\!]_s,$

$[\![X(\overrightarrow{t})]\!]^{\sigma}_{(s,h)} = \text{true if } ([\![\overrightarrow{t}]\!]_s, h) \in \sigma(X),$

$[\![\neg A]\!]^{\sigma}_{(s,h)} = (\text{not } [\![A]\!]^{\sigma}_{(s,h)}),$

$[\![A \wedge B]\!]^{\sigma}_{(s,h)} = ([\![A]\!]^{\sigma}_{(s,h)} \text{ and } [\![B]\!]^{\sigma}_{(s,h)}),$

$[\![A \vee B]\!]_{(s,h)^{\sigma}} = ([\![A]\!]^{\sigma}_{(s,h)} \text{ or } [\![B]\!]^{\sigma}_{(s,h)}),$

$[\![A \rightarrow B]\!]^{\sigma}_{(s,h)} = ([\![A]\!]^{\sigma}_{(s,h)} \text{ implies } [\![B]\!]^{\sigma}_{(s,h)}),$

$[\![\forall x A]\!]^{\sigma}_{(s,h)} = \text{true if } [\![A]\!]^{\sigma}_{(s[x:=n],h)} = \text{true for all } n \in N,$

$[\![\exists x A]\!]^{\sigma}_{(s,h)} = \text{true if } [\![A]\!]^{\sigma}_{(s[x:=n],h)} = \text{true for some } n \in N,$

$[\![A * B]\!]^{\sigma}_{(s,h)} = \text{true if } h = h_1 + h_2,$

$\quad\quad [\![A]\!]^{\sigma}_{(s,h_1)} = [\![B]\!]^{\sigma}_{(s,h_2)} = \text{true for some } h_1, h_2,$

$[\![A \mathbin{-\!\!*} B]\!]^{\sigma}_{(s,h)} = \text{true if } h_2 = h_1 + h \text{ and}$

$\quad\quad [\![A]\!]^{\sigma}_{(s,h_1)} = \text{true imply } [\![B]\!]^{\sigma}_{(s,h_2)} = \text{true for all } h_1, h_2,$

$[\![(\mu X.\lambda \overrightarrow{x}.A)(\overrightarrow{t})]\!]^{\sigma}_{(s,h)} = \text{true if } ([\![\overrightarrow{t}]\!]_s, h) \in \text{lfp}(F) \text{ where}$

$\quad n \text{ is the length of } \overrightarrow{x},$

$\quad F : p(N^n \times \text{Heaps}) \rightarrow p(N^n \times \text{Heaps}),$

$\quad F(S) = \{(\overrightarrow{l}, h) \mid [\![A]\!]^{\sigma[X:=S]}_{(s[\overrightarrow{x} := \overrightarrow{l}],h)} = \text{true}\}.$

We define $[\![A]\!]_{(s,h)}$ for a formula A as $[\![A]\!]^{\emptyset}_{(s,h)}$. We say A is true when $[\![A]\!]_{(s,h)} = \text{true for all } (s,h)$.

Note that in the definition of $[\![(\mu X.\lambda \overrightarrow{x}.A)(\overrightarrow{t})]\!]^{\sigma}_{(s,h)}$, since X appears only positively in A, F is a monotone function and there is the least fixed point of F.

Since the inductively defined predicates are interpreted by the least fixed points, we have the following lemma. We use $A[X := \lambda \overrightarrow{x}.C]$ to denote the formula obtained from A by replacing $X(\overrightarrow{t})$ by $C[\overrightarrow{x} := \overrightarrow{t}]$.

Lemma 3.3. Let μ be $\mu X.\lambda \overrightarrow{x}.A$.
(1) $A[X := \mu] \leftrightarrow \mu(\overrightarrow{x})$ is true.
(2) $\forall \overrightarrow{x}(A[X := \lambda \overrightarrow{x}.C] \rightarrow C) \rightarrow \forall \overrightarrow{x}(\mu(\overrightarrow{x}) \rightarrow C)$ is true for any formula C.

They are proved by using the definition of semantics.

The claim (1) means the folding and the unfolding of inductive definitions. The claim (2) means the inductively defined predicate is the least among C satisfying $\forall \overrightarrow{x}(A[X := \lambda \overrightarrow{x}.C] \rightarrow C)$.

Definition 3.4. For an asserted program $\{A\}P\{B\}$ with assertions A and B, its meaning is defined as true or false. $\{A\}P\{B\}$ is defined to be true if the following hold.
(1) for all (s,h), if $[\![A]\!]_{(s,h)} = \text{true}$, then $[\![P]\!]((s,h)) \not\ni \text{abort}$.
(2) for all (s,h) and (s',h'), if $[\![A]\!]_{(s,h)} = \text{true and } [\![P]\!]((s,h)) \ni (s',h')$, then $[\![B]\!]((s',h')) = \text{true}$.

$\{A\}P\{B\}$ means abort-free partial correctness. It implies partial correctness in the standard sense. It also implies that the execution of the program P with the initial state that satisfies A never aborts, that is, P does not access to any unallocated addresses during the execution.

Examples. (1) $\{0 = 1\}\text{dispose}(1); [1] := 0\{0 = 1\}$ is true. Because there is no initial state that satisfies $0 = 1$.

(2) $\{\text{emp}\}[1] := 0\{0 = 0\}$ is false. Because the abort occurs at $[1] := 0$.

(3) $\{\text{emp}\}\text{while } (0 = 0) \text{ do } (x := 0); [1] := 0\{0 = 1\}$ is true. Because we do not reach $[1] := 0$ because of the infinite loop, and the abort does not occur.

4   Logical System

This section defines our logical system. It is an extension of Reynolds' system presented in [17] so that our assertion language is extended with inductive definitions.

We will write the formula $e \mapsto e_1, e_2$ to denote $(e \mapsto e_1) * (e + 1 \mapsto e_2)$.

Definition 4.1. Our logical system is defined by the following inference rules.

$$\frac{}{\{A[x := e]\}x := e\{A\}} \ (assignment)$$

$$\frac{\{A \wedge b\}P_1\{B\} \quad \{A \wedge \neg b\}P_2\{B\}}{\{A\}\text{if } (b) \text{ then } (P_1) \text{ else } (P_2)\{B\}} \ (if)$$

$$\frac{\{A \wedge b\}P\{A\}}{\{A\}\text{while } (b) \text{ do } (P)\{A \wedge \neg b\}} \ (while)$$

$$\frac{\{A\}P_1\{C\} \quad \{C\}P_2\{B\}}{\{A\}P_1; P_2\{B\}} \ (comp)$$

$$\frac{\{A_1\}P\{B_1\}}{\{A\}P\{B\}} \ (conseq) \qquad (A \to A_1 \text{ true}, B_1 \to B \text{ true})$$

$$\frac{}{\{\forall x'((x' \mapsto e_1, e_2) \twoheadrightarrow A[x := x'])\}x := \text{cons}(e_1, e_2)\{A\}} \ (cons) \ (x' \notin \text{FV}(e_1, e_2, A))$$

$$\frac{}{\{\exists x'(e \mapsto x' * (e \mapsto x' \twoheadrightarrow A[x := x']))\}x := [e]\{A\}} \ (lookup) \ (x' \notin \text{FV}(e, A))$$

$$\frac{}{\{(\exists x(e_1 \mapsto x)) * (e_1 \mapsto e_2 \twoheadrightarrow A)\}[e_1] := e_2\{A\}} \ (mutation) \ (x \notin \text{FV}(e_1))$$

$$\frac{}{\{(\exists x(e \mapsto x)) * A\}\text{dispose}(e)\{A\}} \ (dispose) \qquad (x \notin \text{FV}(e))$$

We say $\{A\}P\{B\}$ is provable and we write $\vdash \{A\}P\{B\}$, when $\{A\}P\{B\}$ can be derived by these inference rules.

Note that in the side condition $(A \to A_1 \text{ true}, B_1 \to B \text{ true})$ of the rule $(conseq)$, the truth means one in the standard model of natural numbers and inductive definitions. Theoretically there are several interesting choices for the truth of this side condition [1]. Since we are interested in whether a given implementation of this logical system is indeed powerful enough in a real world, we choose the truth of the standard model. Hence the completeness of our system means completeness relative to all true formulas in the standard model of natural numbers and inductive definitions.

5 Soundness and Completeness Theorems

Our main results are the completeness theorem and the expressiveness theorem stated in this section. We will also show the soundness theorem. The soundness theorem is proved in a similar way to [17] and [19]. The completeness theorem is proved in a similar way to [19] if we have the expressiveness theorem. A proof of the completeness theorem requires the expressiveness theorem. Since our assertion language is extended with inductive definitions, the expressiveness theorem for our assertion language is really new. For this reason, the completeness result is also new. We will give only proof sketches of the soundness theorem and the completeness theorem.

Theorem 5.1 (Soundness). If $\{A\}P\{B\}$ is provable, then $\{A\}P\{B\}$ is true.

The soundness theorem is proved by induction on the given proof of $\{A\}P\{B\}$. Intuitively, we will show each inference rule preserves the truth.

Definition 5.2. For a program P and an assertion A, the weakest precondition for P and A under the standard model is defined as the set $\{(s,h)|\forall r([\![P]\!]((s,h)) \ni r \to r \neq \text{abort} \wedge [\![A]\!]_r = \text{true})\}$.

Our proof of the completeness theorem will use the next expressiveness theorem, which will be proved in the next section.

Theorem 5.3 (Expressiveness). For every program P and assertion A, there is a formula W such that $[\![W]\!]_{(s,h)} = \text{true}$ if and only if (s,h) is in the weakest precondition defined in Definition 5.2 for P and A under the standard model.

Theorem 5.4 (Completeness). If $\{A\}P\{B\}$ is true, then $\{A\}P\{B\}$ is provable.

This theorem says that a given asserted program $\{A\}P\{B\}$ is true (defined in Section 3), then this is provable (defined in Section 4). Note that it is relative completeness in the sense that our logical system assumes all true formulas in the standard model of natural numbers and inductive definitions. This is the best possible completeness for pointer program verification for a similar reason to that for while program verification discussed in [6].

We sketch the proof. The completeness theorem is proved by induction on the program P. The goal is showing a given true asserted program is provable. Intuitively, we will reduce this goal to subgoals for smaller pieces of the given program that state true asserted subprograms of the given program are provable. If we show that for each program construction a true asserted program is provable by using the assumption that all the asserted subprograms are provable, we can say any given true asserted program is provable.

We discuss the rule $(comp)$. Suppose $\{A\}P_1; P_2\{B\}$ is true. We have to construct a proof of $\{A\}P_1; P_2\{B\}$. In order to do that, we have to find some assertion C such that $\{A\}P_1\{C\}$ is true and $\{C\}P_2\{B\}$ is true. If we find the assertion C, since P_1 and P_2 are smaller pieces of the given program $P_1; P_2$, we can suppose $\{A\}P_1\{C\}$ and $\{C\}P_2\{B\}$ are both provable, and by the rule $(comp)$, we have a proof of $\{A\}P_1; P_2\{B\}$. In order to find the assertion C, we will use the expressiveness given by Theorem 5.3, to take the weakest precondition for P_2 and B as the assertion C.

6   Proof Sketch of Expressiveness Theorem

This section gives a sketch of proofs of the expressiveness theorem (Theorem 5.3). We extend the expressiveness proof given in [19] to inductive definitions. We assume the readers of this section have knowledge of [19] and [20].

In order to show the expressiveness theorem, we have to construct a formula that expresses the weakest precondition for given a program P and a formula A. We will follow the technique used in [19] and [20]. The main technique is to translate separation logic into ordinary first-order logic by coding a heap by a natural number and simulating a separation-logic formula by a pure formula produced by its translation. First we translate a separation-logic formula A into a pure formula $\mathrm{HEval}_A(m)$ such that A is true at the current heap h if and only if $\mathrm{HEval}_A(m)$ is true where m is a natural number that represents the current heap h. We say m is a code of h. Secondly we give a pointer program P a semantics $\mathrm{Exec}_P((n_1, m_1), (n_2, m_2))$ that manipulates the code of the current heap instead of the current heap itself. We will define the pure formula $\mathrm{Exec}_P((n_1, m_1), (n_2, m_2))$ such that when the current heap is represented by m_1, if we execute P, then the current heap is changed into some heap represented by m_2. Finally the weakest precondition for P and A is described by a formula $\mathrm{W}_{P,A}$ that transforms the current heap into its heap code m_1, requires $\mathrm{Exec}_P((n_1, m_1), (n_2, m_2))$ for executing P, and requires $\mathrm{HEval}_A(m_2)$ for enforcing A at the resulting heap m_2. This formula $\mathrm{W}_{P,A}$ proves our expressiveness theorem.

Since our assertions include inductive definitions, it is non-trivial to make this technique work for our system. In particular, the main challenge is to define a translation scheme HEval_A for assertions of form A that contain inductive definitions. This section shows it is actually possible. Similar problems occurred in type theory and realizability interpretations. An extension of type theory to inductive definitions was solved in [7] and [15], and an extension of realizability interpretations to inductive definitions was solved in [18]. Their ideas were to use another inductive definition for translating a given inductive definition. Our solution will be similar to these ideas.

We will define a heapcode translation $\text{HEval}_A(m)$ of an assertion A such that $\text{HEval}_A(m)$ is a pure formula for expressing the meaning of A at the heap coded by m. The main question is how to define $\text{HEval}_A(m)$ for inductively defined predicates. To answer this question, we will show that we can define $\text{HEval}_{(\mu X.\lambda \overrightarrow{x}.A)(\overrightarrow{t})}(m)$ as $(\mu \tilde{X}.\lambda \overrightarrow{x} y.\text{HEval}_A(y) \wedge \text{IsHeap}(y))(\overrightarrow{t}, m)$ by using another inductively defined predicate $\mu \tilde{X}.\lambda \overrightarrow{x} y.\text{HEval}_A(y) \wedge \text{IsHeap}(y)$, and we will also show that this satisfies a desired property (Lemma 6.8).

Semantics for Pure Formulas

When we simulate an inductively defined separation-logic formula by some inductively defined pure formula, in order to avoid complications, we introduce the semantics of pure formulas, which does not depend on a heap. This semantics has the same meaning as our semantics defined in Section 3, and is a standard semantics for pure formulas with inductive definitions, for example, given in [18,16].

Definition 6.1. For a store s, and a pure formula A, according to the standard interpretation of a first-order language with inductive definitions, the meaning $[\![A]\!]_s$ is defined as true or false. $[\![A]\!]_s$ is the truth value of A under the store s.

A pure predicate variable assignment σ is a function that maps a predicate variable of arity n to a subset of N^n. The pure predicate variable assignment $\sigma[X_1 := S_1, \ldots, X_n := S_n]$ and the pure constant predicate variable assignment $\emptyset$ are defined in a similar way to Section 3.

In order to define $[\![A]\!]_s$ for a pure formula A, we first define $[\![A]\!]_s^\sigma$ for a pure open formula A as follows. We give only interesting cases.

$$[\![X(\overrightarrow{t})]\!]_s^\sigma = \text{true if } [\![\overrightarrow{t}]\!]_s \in \sigma(X),$$
$$[\![(\mu X.\lambda \overrightarrow{x}.A)(\overrightarrow{t})]\!]_s^\sigma = \text{true if } [\![\overrightarrow{t}]\!]_s \in \text{lfp}(F) \text{ where } n \text{ is the length of } \overrightarrow{x},$$
$$F : p(N^n) \to p(N^n),$$
$$F(S) = \{\overrightarrow{l} \mid [\![A]\!]_{s[\overrightarrow{x} := \overrightarrow{l}]}^{\sigma[X := S]} = \text{true}\}.$$

We define $[\![A]\!]_s$ for a pure formula A as $[\![A]\!]_s^\emptyset$.

In order to show $[\![A]\!]_s = [\![A]\!]_{(s,h)}$ for a pure formula A, we need some preparation.

For a pure predicate variable assignment σ, we define a predicate variable assignment $\sigma \times \text{Heaps}$ by $(\sigma \times \text{Heaps})(X) = \sigma(X) \times \text{Heaps}$. For a subset S of $N^n \times \text{Heaps}$, we call the subset S H-independent when $S = S' \times \text{Heaps}$ for some subset S' of N^n. For a predicate variable assignment σ, we call the predicate variable assignment σ H-independent when $\sigma(X)$ is H-independent for all X.

Lemma 6.2. Suppose A is pure.

(1) $\{(s,h) \mid [\![A]\!]_{(s,h)}^\sigma = \text{true}\}$ is H-independent if σ is H-independent.

(2) $[\![A]\!]_s^\sigma = [\![A]\!]_{(s,h)}^{\sigma \times \text{Heaps}}$ for all heaps h.

Lemma 6.3. For a pure formula A, we have $[\![A]\!]_s = [\![A]\!]_{(s,h)}$ for any h.

Proof. By letting $\sigma = \emptyset$ in Lemma 6.2 (2). $\qquad\square$

Heapcode Translation

We define a heapcode translation of an assertion A that is a pure formula and describes the meaning of A in terms of the heap code. This is based on the same idea in [19]. Our key idea is to find that it is possible to define $\text{HEval}_A(x)$ for an inductively defined predicate A by using another inductively defined predicate.

Definition 6.4. We define the pure open formula $\text{HEval}_A(x)$ for the open formula A by induction on A. We give only interesting cases.

$$\text{HEval}_{X(\overrightarrow{t})}(m) = \tilde{X}(\overrightarrow{t}, m),$$

$$\text{HEval}_{(\mu X.\lambda\overrightarrow{x}.A)(\overrightarrow{t})}(m) = (\mu\tilde{X}.\lambda\overrightarrow{x}y.\text{HEval}_A(y) \wedge \text{IsHeap}(y))(\overrightarrow{t}, m).$$

For a formula A, $\text{HEval}_A(m)$ means $[\![A]\!]_{(s,h)} = \text{true}$ where s is the current store and m represents the heap h. That is, we have $[\![\text{HEval}_A(m)]\!]_s = [\![A]\!]_{(s,h)}$ if m represents the heap h. This will be formally stated in Lemma 6.8.

Note that in the definition of $\text{HEval}_{(\mu X.\lambda\overrightarrow{x}.A)(\overrightarrow{t})}(m)$, since X appears only positively in A, $\tilde{X}$ appears only positively in $\text{HEval}_A(y)$. We have $\text{FPV}(\text{HEval}_A(m)) = \{\tilde{X} | X \in \text{FPV}(A)\}$. In particular, when $(\mu X.\lambda\overrightarrow{x}.A)(\overrightarrow{t})$ is a formula, $(\mu\tilde{X}.\lambda\overrightarrow{x}y.\text{HEval}_A(y) \wedge \text{IsHeap}(y))(\overrightarrow{t}, m)$ is also a formula.

Definition 6.5. We define the pure formula $\text{Eval}_{A,\overrightarrow{x}}(n, m)$ for the assertion A. We suppose $\overrightarrow{x}$ includes $\text{FV}(A)$.

$$\text{Eval}_{A,\overrightarrow{x}}(n, m) = \text{IsHeap}(m) \wedge \exists\overrightarrow{x}(\text{Store}_{\overrightarrow{x}}(n) \wedge \text{HEval}_A(m)).$$

For a formula A, $\text{Eval}_{A,\overrightarrow{x}}(n, m)$ means $[\![A]\!]_{(s,h)} = \text{true}$ where n represents the store s and m represents the heap h.

Key Lemma

To utilize the heapcode translation defined just above, we need the key lemma that states that the semantics of a separation-logic formula equals the semantics of the corresponding pure formula obtained by the translation even if our system includes inductive definitions.

We define $(\_)^*$ for transforming semantics for heaps between that for heap codes.

Definition 6.6. We use $\text{Heapcode}(m, h)$ to mean the number m is the code that represents the heap h. For $S \subseteq N^n \times \text{Heaps}$, we define

$$S^* = \{(\overrightarrow{l}, m) \mid (\overrightarrow{l}, h) \in S, \text{Heapcode}(m, h)\},$$

For a predicate assignment σ, we define σ^* by $\sigma^*(\tilde{X}) = \sigma(X)^*$.

The role of S^* is to give the semantics of the corresponding pure formula when S gives the semantics of a separation-logic formula.

In order to prove Lemma 6.8, we need the following key lemma, which is a generalization of Lemma 6.8 for open formulas.

Lemma 6.7 (Key Lemma). Suppose A is an open formula and $y \notin \mathrm{FV}(A)$. We have $\forall mh(\mathrm{Heapcode}(m, h) \rightarrow [\![\mathrm{HEval}_A(y)]\!]^{\sigma^*}_{s[y:=m]} = [\![A]\!]^\sigma_{(s,h)})$.

The next lemma shows that the pure formula $\mathrm{HEval}_A(m)$ actually has the meaning we explained above.

Lemma 6.8. Suppose A is a formula. We have $\mathrm{Heapcode}(m, h) \rightarrow [\![\mathrm{HEval}_A(m)]\!]_s = [\![A]\!]_{(s,h)}$.

Proof. By letting $\sigma = \emptyset$ in Lemma 6.7. $\qquad\qquad\qquad\qquad\qquad\qquad\square$

Once HEval_A is defined and Lemma 6.8 is shown, we can construct the formula required in the expressiveness theorem in a similar way to [19]. Note that $\mathrm{Eval}_{A,\overrightarrow{x}}$ below is extended to inductive definitions. We will use $\mathrm{Pair2}(k, n, m)$ to mean that k represents the state (s, h) when n represents s and m represents h.

Definition 6.9. We define the formula $\mathrm{W}_{P,A}(\overrightarrow{x})$ for the program P and the assertion A. We fix some sequence $\overrightarrow{x}$ of the variables in $\mathrm{FV}(P, A)$.

$$\mathrm{W}_{P,A}(\overrightarrow{x}) = \forall xyzw(\mathrm{Store}_{\overrightarrow{x}}(x) \wedge \mathrm{Heap}(y) \wedge \mathrm{Pair2}(z, x, y) \wedge \mathrm{Exec}_{P,\overrightarrow{x}}(z, w)$$
$$\rightarrow w > 0 \wedge \exists y_1 z_1(\mathrm{Pair2}(w, y_1, z_1) \wedge \mathrm{Eval}_{A,\overrightarrow{x}}(y_1, z_1))).$$

$\mathrm{W}_{P,A}(\overrightarrow{x})$ means the weakest precondition for P and A. That is, $\mathrm{W}_{P,A}(\overrightarrow{x})$ gives the weakest assertion W such that $\{W\}P\{A\}$ is true. Note that all the free variables in $\mathrm{W}_{P,A}(\overrightarrow{x})$ are $\overrightarrow{x}$ and they appear only in $\mathrm{Store}_{\overrightarrow{x}}(x)$. This formula is the formula that describes the weakest precondition, and by this formula we can prove the expressiveness theorem (Theorem 5.3).

7   Conclusion

We have shown the completeness theorem of the pointer while program verification system which is an extension of Reynolds' separation logic with inductive definitions. For this purpose, we have also proved the expressiveness theorem of Peano arithmetic, the separation logic, and inductive definitions for pointer while programs under the standard model.

Future work would be to find a assertion language with inductive definitions that would be more suitable for automated deduction. For example, it would be interesting to find what syntactical condition guarantees that the claim (1) derives the claim (2) in Lemma 3.3. It would be also interesting to find a decidable fragment of a logical system with inductive definitions.

Another future work would be proving completeness results of various extensions of our system such as recursive procedure calls with call-by-name parameters and global variables, which have been intensively analyzed for while programs by several papers [1,8,10].

References

1. Apt, K.R.: Ten Years of Hoare's Logic: A Survey — Part I. ACM Transactions on Programming Languages and Systems 3(4), 431–483 (1981)
2. Berdine, J., Calcagno, C., O'Hearn, P.W.: Symbolic Execution with Separation Logic. In: Yi, K. (ed.) APLAS 2005. LNCS, vol. 3780, pp. 52–68. Springer, Heidelberg (2005)
3. Bergstra, J.A., Tucker, J.V.: Expressiveness and the Completeness of Hoare's Logic. Journal Computer and System Sciences 25(3), 267–284 (1982)
4. Brotherston, J.: Formalised Inductive Reasoning in the Logic of Bunched Implications. In: Riis Nielson, H., Filé, G. (eds.) SAS 2007. LNCS, vol. 4634, pp. 87–103. Springer, Heidelberg (2007)
5. Brotherston, J., Villard, J.: Parametric Completeness for Separation Theories. In: Proceedings of POPL 2014, pp. 453–464 (2014)
6. Cook, S.A.: Soundness and completeness of an axiom system for program verification. SIAM Journal on Computing 7(1), 70–90 (1978)
7. Coquand, T., Paulin, C.: Inductively Defined Types. In: Martin-Löf, P., Mints, G. (eds.) COLOG 1988. LNCS, vol. 417, pp. 50–66. Springer, Heidelberg (1990)
8. Halpern, J.Y.: A good Hoare axiom system for an ALGOL-like language. In: Proceedings of POPL 1984, pp. 262–271 (1984)
9. Hou, Z., Clouston, R., Gore, R., Tiu, A.: Proof search for propositional abstract separation logics via labelled sequents. In: Proceedings of POPL 2014, pp. 465–476 (2014)
10. Josko, B.: On expressive interpretations of a Hoare-logic for Clarke's language L4. In: Fontet, M., Mehlhorn, K. (eds.) STACS 1984. LNCS, vol. 166, pp. 73–84. Springer, Heidelberg (1984)
11. Kimura, D., Tatsuta, M.: Call-by-Value and Call-by-Name Dual Calculi with Inductive and Coinductive Types. Logical Methods in Computer Science 9(1), Article 14 (2013)
12. Lee, W., Park, S.: A Proof System for Separation Logic with Magic Wand. In: Proceedings of POPL 2014, pp. 477–490 (2014)
13. Nguyen, H.H., David, C., Qin, S.C., Chin, W.N.: Automated Verification of Shape and Size Properties Via Separation Logic. In: Cook, B., Podelski, A. (eds.) VMCAI 2007. LNCS, vol. 4349, pp. 251–266. Springer, Heidelberg (2007)
14. Nguyen, H.H., Chin, W.N.: Enhancing Program Verification with Lemmas. In: Gupta, A., Malik, S. (eds.) CAV 2008. LNCS, vol. 5123, pp. 355–369. Springer, Heidelberg (2008)
15. Paulin-Mohring, C.: Extracting F_ω's programs from proofs in the Calculus of Constructions. In: Proceedings of POPL 1989, pp. 89–104 (1989)
16. Pohlers, W.: Proof Theory. Springer (2009)
17. Reynolds, J.C.: Separation Logic: A Logic for Shared Mutable Data Structures. In: Proceedings of LICS 2002, pp. 55–74 (2002)
18. Tatsuta, M.: Program synthesis using realizability. Theoretical Computer Science 90, 309–353 (1991)
19. Tatsuta, M., Chin, W.N., Al Ameen, M.F.: Completeness of Pointer Program Verification by Separation Logic. In: Proceeding of SEFM 2009, pp. 179–188 (2009)
20. Tatsuta, M., Chin, W.N., Al Ameen, M.F.: Completeness of Pointer Program Verification by Separation Logic. NII Technical Report, NII-2009-013E (2009)

A Thread-Safe Library
for Binary Decision Diagrams*

Alberto Lovato[1,2], Damiano Macedonio[1], and Fausto Spoto[1,2]

[1] Julia Srl, Verona, Italy
[2] Dipartimento di Informatica, Università di Verona, Verona, Italy

Abstract. We describe the motivations, technical problems and solutions behind the implementation of BeeDeeDee, a new thread-safe Java library for Binary Decision Diagrams (BDDs) manipulation. BeeDeeDee allows clients to share a single factory of BDDs, in real parallelism, and reduce the memory footprint of their overall execution, at a very low synchronization cost. We prove through experiments on multi-core computers that BeeDeeDee is an effective thread-safe library for BDD manipulation. As test cases, we consider multiple instances of the n-queens problem, the construction of circuits and the parallel execution of information flow static analyses of Java programs, for distinct properties of variables. For sequential-only executions, BeeDeeDee is faster than other non-thread-safe Java libraries and as fast as non-thread-safe C libraries.

Keywords: Manipulation of Boolean functions, Binary Decision Diagrams, Java multithreading.

1 Introduction

Binary Decision Diagrams [14] (from now on BDDs) are a well-known data structure for the efficient representation of Boolean functions. Their first success story is their application for symbolic model checking [16]. They have been subsequently applied to static analysis: groundness analysis of logic programs [11], aliasing analysis of Java [18], cyclicity analysis of Java [20] and information flow analysis of Java bytecode [17]. This is because variables in Boolean functions can be very naturally seen as properties of program states or program variables, while implications between them can be seen as constraints between those properties. For instance, a Boolean function might express the fact that groundness of a variable might imply groundness of another; or that aliasing between a pair of variables might entail aliasing between other pairs; or that whenever a piece of information flows into a variable it might flow into other variables as well.

BDDs are one of many possible representations for Boolean functions. Their success is related to their compactness and efficiency. The key idea underlying their definition is to represent a Boolean function as a directed acyclic graph,

---

* Julia Srl has been partially supported by US Air Force contract n. FA8750-12-C-0174 as subcontractor of the University of Washington.

D. Giannakopoulou and G. Salaün (Eds.): SEFM 2014, LNCS 8702, pp. 35–49, 2014.
© Springer International Publishing Switzerland 2014

where each non-terminal node corresponds to the evaluation of a variable and has two outgoing edges, leading to graphs which represent the function with the variable value fixed to 1 (true) or 0 (false), respectively; terminal nodes are labeled 0 or 1 and correspond to the evaluation of the function once all variables has been assigned a value [14,15]. The order of variable evaluation can be fixed, and redundant nodes can be removed, leading to a *canonical* BDD, that is, a minimal representation for a class of equivalent functions. So, equivalence of functions can be tested by checking the structural identity of their BDD representations. Moreover, this accounts for a significant reduction in the memory space needed to hold a BDD. Furthermore, a clever implementation might allow distinct BDDs to share identical subgraphs.

There exist special purpose BDDs. For instance, *Algebraic Decision Diagrams (ADDs)* [12] can have other terminal nodes than 0 and 1. They can efficiently represent matrices and weighted directed graphs, by encoding their *characteristic functions. Zero-suppressed Binary Decision Diagrams (ZDDs)* [19] consider as redundant and remove the nodes whose positive edge points to terminal node 0. They are overall larger than BDDs in size, but they become very compact when dealing with functions that are almost everywhere 0.

C libraries, such as BuDDy [2], CUDD [4] and CAL [3], that represent and manipulate BDDs, may be used in Java via the Java Native Interface. They merely feature an API that is poorly adapted to an object-oriented language and they are not cross-platform since they must be recompiled on each platform. Java libraries, such as JavaBDD [7], JDD [8] and SableJBDD [10], are built around a common architecture, where BDDs are compactly stored in an array of integers: each integer stands for a logically distinct BDD. This array is manipulated through a centralized controller, called *factory*, that uses a *unique table* of nodes. Furthermore, caching is typically used to avoid re-computations

JavaBDD seems to be the current choice of the Java world and it offers interfaces to the native libraries BuDDy, CAL and CUDD, as well as to JDD. It includes a unique table implementation directly translated in Java from BuDDy. JDD performs well with problems that only involve simple Boolean operations, such as the *n*-queens problem, but performs rather badly in case of variable replacement or quantification. Moreover, for `replace`, `exist` and `forall` operations, it exhibits unusual behaviors, such as exiting the JVM instead of throwing exceptions. Consequently, it may not be suitable to production environments. SableJBDD is in a very early stage of development and currently exhibits low performance and very high memory consumption.

Among C libraries, CUDD can manipulate both ADDs and ZDDs. Among Java libraries, only JDD can manipulate ZDDs.

2   Our Motivation: Parallel Information Flow Analyses

The present work was sparked from a concrete problem. We were implementing many flavors of information flow analysis for Java bytecode inside our Julia static analyzer [9], by using a common framework derived from [17] and based on a translation of the program into Boolean functions.[1] Each flavor was targeted at determining where and how some specific kind of information might flow inside a Java program. These *kinds of information* were inspired from the *Top 25 Most Dangerous Software Errors* [1]: among them, one finds well-known issues such as user-provided servlet parameters flowing into SQL commands (*SQL-injection*) or into OS commands (*command-injection*); hard-coded credentials flowing into user-visible output; internal data flowing into implementation revealing output.

These distinct analyses do share a lot: namely, most program statements just transfer information from variables to variables and their abstraction into Boolean functions is identical for all flavors of information flow analysis; only a few statements have different abstraction for distinct information flow flavors. Our first implementation was based on JavaBDD. Each information flow analysis was independent from the others, that is, it was run in isolation and did not share any data structure with the others. The result was perfectly working and we could also run more analyses in parallel, in distinct threads, as long as each thread allocated its own unique table of BDDs and caches. But we immediately hit the limit of this approach as soon as we tried to analyze, in parallel, the full codebase of Hadoop Common [5], a Java implementation of a big data engine. While the computational cost in time was still acceptable, the memory footprint of the parallel analyses exploded and we had to rely on their sequential rather than parallel execution, which however takes many hours rather than minutes.

In order to reduce the memory footprint of the parallel analyses, we tried to use a single BDD unique table, shared among all threads. But this turned up to be impossible with JavaBDD. In fact, JavaBDD is not a *thread-safe* library, in the sense that by sharing the unique table among threads one just gets a runtime exception. This problem was present also with native C libraries. We realized that we needed a new library for BDD manipulation, with a thread-safe implementation. Our first version of that library was however deceiving: we built it so that all operations on the unique table were mutually exclusive, which made it thread-safe; however, any parallel execution was in reality completely sequential, since one thread at most could access the unique table, at a time. We understood that we had to allow more threads to use the unique table at the same time and synchronize them as rarely as possible. How this could be achieved was far from obvious and is the topic of this article.

3   The Features of Our Library

We assume the Java memory model: the runtime may introduce execution optimizations as long as the result of a thread in isolation is guaranteed to be exactly the same as it would have been if all the statements been executed in program order. This semantics does not prevent different threads from having different views of the data, but actions that imply communication between threads, such

---

[1] These information flow analyses are not the topic of this article and we describe them as far as it is needed for understanding our work on BDDs.

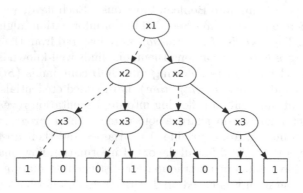

Fig. 1. An ordered read-once branching program with order $x_1 < x_2 < x_3$ for the Boolean formula $\neg(x_1 \wedge x_2 \wedge x_3) \vee (x_1 \wedge x_2) \vee (x_2 \wedge x_3)$

as the acquisition or release of a lock, ensure that actions that happen prior to them are seen by other threads.

Let us clearly state the features of our efficient thread-safe library for BDD manipulation in Java. By *thread-safe* we mean that clients can run in parallel and safely share a BDD unique table and all the needed caches. By *efficient* we mean that clients do not pay a high synchronization cost for that and are consequently blocked for a low percentage of their overall execution time.

Our library is *not* multithreaded, in the sense that it does not use multi-threading itself: BDDs are manipulated exclusively via sequential algorithms. It does use multithreading just for parallel resizing and garbage-collection, but this is a secondary aspect that does not account very much for its efficiency.

As a matter of fact, ideal parallelism is rarely achievable, since there is generally some synchronization cost to pay for. As a consequence, the parallel execution of many instances of the same task will cost, in general, slightly more than the execution of a single instance, also when enough execution cores are available. A concrete example is shown at the end of this article (see Figure 6).

4   Boolean Formulas and BDDs

Boolean formulas are generated by the grammar $f ::= x \mid 0 \mid 1 \mid \neg f \mid f \wedge f \mid f \vee f \mid f \Rightarrow f \mid f \Leftrightarrow f$, where x ranges over a given set of Boolean variables, 0 means false and 1 means true. The set of truth values is denoted as $\mathbb{B} = \{0, 1\}$. An *assignment* π binds each Boolean variable x to a truth value $\pi(x)$ and allows one to evaluate a Boolean formula f into a truth value $\pi(f)$, computed by replacing each Boolean variable in f with its value as provided by π and by applying the usual truth tables for the logical operators. If we fix an *ordering* on the Boolean variables, we can view f as defining a *Boolean function* from $\mathbb{B}^n$ to $\mathbb{B}$ where n is the number of variables in f. Two Boolean functions are *equal* if they yield the same truth value for all assignments.

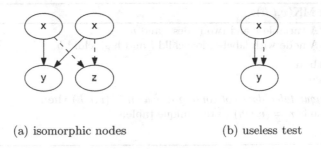

(a) isomorphic nodes   (b) useless test

Fig. 2. Types of redundancy in an ordered read-once branching program

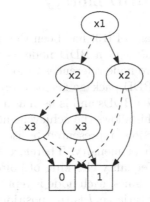

Fig. 3. BDD for $\neg(x_1 \wedge x_2 \wedge x_3) \vee (x_1 \wedge x_2) \vee (x_2 \wedge x_3)$ with $x_1 < x_2 < x_3$

We can represent a Boolean function f as a rooted, directed, acyclic graph, consisting of *decision nodes* and *terminal nodes*. Each decision node v is labeled with a Boolean variable x and has two children called *low(v)* and *high(v)*. The edge from v to *low(v)* (or *high(v)*) represents an assignment of x to 0 (respectively, 1). Terminal nodes can be either a *0-terminal* or a *1-terminal*. Each truth assignment π stands for a path from the root to a terminal node, the latter being $\pi(f)$-terminal. Each variable can be evaluated *at most once* in a path. Such a graph is called a *read-once branching program*. Moreover, it is called *ordered* if the variables on a path from the root to a terminal node are ordered according to a fixed total order, as in Figure 1. These graphs can be simplified by applying the following rules (see Figure 2): merge any isomorphic subgraphs *(merging rule)* and remove any node whose children are isomorphic *(elimination rule)*. This leads to *reduced* ordered read-once branching programs, also known as *Binary Decision Diagrams* or *BDDs* (Figure 3).

Any Boolean function has a unique BDD representation [14], up to isomorphism; *i.e.*, BDDs are a *canonical representation* of Boolean functions, where the equivalence test of functions becomes an isomorphism check on acyclic graphs.

Function MK(v,l,h)

input : A variable v and two nodes l and h
output: A node with label v, low child l and high child h

1   **if** $l = h$ **then**
2   ⌊ **return** l;

3   **if** *the unique table does not contain a node* $n = (v,l,h)$ **then**
4   ⌊ add node $n = (v,l,h)$ to the unique table;

5   **return** n.

---

5   Architecture of a BDD Library

The first efficient BDD package of [13] has been the inspiration for subsequent packages. The idea is to implement a BDD node as a data structure with, at least, a variable index and two node references to low and high children.

As we anticipated, every BDD package keeps a *unique table* of nodes, which contains all the already created BDDs and is used as a cache, so that isomorphic BDDs are never recreated. This allows the achievement of *strong canonicity*: not only are two equivalent functions represented by isomorphic graphs, but they are actually the *same* graph in memory. Therefore BDD equivalence testing boils down to constant-time equality checking of pointers. The unique table is typically an array of integral values: each node is represented as a triple (v, l, h), where v is the corresponding variable, l is the position of the low child and h is the position of the high child inside the same array.

To retrieve already created nodes from the unique table, it is convenient to organize it as a hash table, so that the array also contains, for each node, the position of the next node inside the same bucket, if any.

In order to represent strongly canonical BDDs, a package defines two constants and two functions. Constants *ZERO* and *ONE* stand for 0 and 1. Function *MK* yields a node with a given variable as a label and with two given nodes as children. Function *APPLY* implements a logical operation over BDDs and typically uses a cache for efficiency, which is implemented as a hash table.

Lines 1–2 of *MK* implement elimination rule, while lines 3–4 implement merging rule. Thanks to the use of the unique table inside *MK*, function *APPLY* keeps strong-canonicity, as it can be proved by induction. Since BDDs must be ordered, variables are put in order in the result of *APPLY*. Time complexity is $O(|n1||n2|)$. In fact, if $|n|$ denotes the number of nodes of a BDD rooted at n, then the recursive calls in *APPLY(op, n_1, n_2)* are $|n1||n2|$ at most (see [14]).

Caching is also used for non-propositional operations on BDDs such as restriction (fixing the value of a variable) and variable replacement. In fact, variables must be kept ordered subsequently to every variable replacement and reordering requires a complete and expensive rearrangement of BDDs: this is why a cache is used. Universal and existential quantification are reduced to restriction and propositional operations.

Function APPLY(op, n_1, n_2)

> **input** : A logical operator op and two nodes n_1 and n_2
> **output**: The result of the operation n_1 op n_2

1   **if** *the result of (n_1 op n_2) is already cached* **then**
2 | return that result;

3   **if** n_1, n_2 *are constants* **then**
4 | return *op* applied to n_1 and n_2;

5   **if** *var(n_1) = var(n_2)* **then**
6 | *result = MK(var(n_1),*
7 | *APPLY(op, low(n_1), low(n_2)), APPLY(op, high(n_1), high(n_2)));*

8   **else if** *var(n_1) < var(n_2)* **then**
9 | *result = MK(var(n_1),*
10 | *APPLY(op, low(n_1), n_2), APPLY(op, high(n_1), n_2));*

11   **else**
12 | *result = MK(var(n_2),*
13 | *APPLY(op, n_1, low(n_2))), APPLY(op, n_1, high(n_2)));*

14   cache *result*;
15   **return** *result*;

BDDs might be used for temporary operations and then become *garbage*, alike all dynamically allocated data structures. However, the normal garbage collector of Java is not in charge here: nodes are elements of an array of integers (the unique table) and Java garbage collector deals with the array as a whole, not with its single elements. It is hence necessary to implement a brand new garbage collector for elements of the unique table array. This garbage collector must run when that table is almost full, mark unreachable nodes and sweep them away, by compacting and rehashing the surviving nodes. Any traditional garbage collection technique may be used here. Garbage collection might be expensive or might even invalidate the caches, hence it introduces a significant overhead. When garbage collection fails to free a sufficient number of nodes, a BDD package can only resize the unique table.

6   Our Thread-Safe Library **BeeDeeDee**

The fact that a BDD library must be highly optimized, thus requiring a unique node table and caches, becomes a problem with multithreading: the unique table and all caches are shared among clients and are hence the perfect candidates for race conditions. This section shows how we overcome that problem. Avoiding race conditions was not the only requirement: we also needed to synchronize clients as little as possible, since otherwise performance would have been badly affected. We mainly applied two techniques to prevent performance degradation:

Optimistic behaviors: some operations can be performed as if a client were the only thread using the library, hence without synchronization. If this strategy fails, we synchronize and perform the access again. Statistically, most accesses won't require synchronization.

Split locks: distinct locks can be used for accessing distinct portions of a data structure, in parallel. Hence, when two clients access different parts of the unique table, or even different caches, one cannot block the other as it would happen with a single lock on the whole data structure.

Below, we show the concrete application of these techniques.

6.1   Thread-Safe Unique Table

We organize the unique table as a hash table with the following hashing function:

$$hash(v, l, h, size) = (l + h \cdot 2^{\lceil \log_2(l) \rceil}) \bmod size$$

where (v, l, h) represents the node, as described in Section 5, and $size$ is the table size (*i.e.*, the length of the array that holds the table). This hash function well distributes nodes over the hash table, as we have verified through profiling.

Once a client needs a node $n = (v, l, h)$ from the unique table, it must look for n in the table. When n is missing in the table, the client must allocate it. This, in turn, might trigger a table resize operation. Here is our code for node look-up with a possible node allocation:

```
1  int get(int v, int l, int h) {
2    do {
3      Object myLock;
4      int size = this.size;
5      int i = hash(v, l, h, size);
6      int result = getOptimistic(v, l, h, i);
7      if (result >= 0)
8        return result;
9
10     synchronized (myLock = getLocks[i % getLocks.length]) {
11       if (size == this.size || i == hash(v, l, h, this.size))
12         return expandTable(v, l, h, myLock, i);
13     }
14   } while (true);
15 }
```

Method `getOptimistic` scans the i-th bucket of the hash table for the node. It can be run in real parallelism, without synchronization, with a resize operation and with other `get` operations which just read from the table. In particular, a resize operation just extends the table and modifies only the value of `this.size`, not node positions. Thus, the hash code corresponding to n may have been changed after the assignment at line 5 and the search performed by `getOptimistic` could have scanned the wrong bucket without finding n, even though the node appears in the table. This is harmless since, in that case, the value of `result` would be -1 and the occurrence of resizing would be verified inside a `synchronized` block at line 11.

Function `get` returns the position of the node as soon as `getOptimistic` finds it (lines 7–8). Otherwise, `get` synchronizes on the i-th bucket of the hash table and expands it with a brand new node (lines 10–12). This task is accomplished by `expandTable` which first scans the i-bucket of the table to ensure that n was not concurrently added by another client and then adds the node *only* if n does not appear in the table. The code for `expandTable` is omitted for simplicity.

Split locks are used for synchronization on an element of the array `getLocks` instead of on the whole hash table. Distinct threads are still allowed to proceed in real parallelism to the update of the hash table as long as they operate on distinct buckets, modulo `getLocks.length`. The bigger `getLocks`, the smaller becomes the risk of collision, but the bigger are memory requirements. Method `expandTable` might trigger a resize operation if the unique table is full. When multiple threads want to resize inside `expandTable`, only one manages to get a resize lock, and the others wait on their `myLock`. The winning thread locks all elements of `getLocks`, resizes the table and notifies all elements of `getLocks`. Afterwards, all waiting threads can resume.

A tricky detail is the check at line 11. As we said, that check is essential since a resize might have occurred between the first computation of i (line 5) and the call to `expandTable`. Since the hash code depends on the size of the table, the bucket to be modified might have been changed. If the hash code does not match, the whole procedure starts again. In fact, the check at line 11 is equivalent to i == hash(v, 1, h, this.size), but the short-circuit operator || improves efficiency, since the hash function is expensive in elaboration time.

6.2   Thread-Safe Caches

Caches are used for *APPLY* and other expensive operations such as variable renaming. They can be made thread-safe by synchronizing their accesses. Split locks reduce the number of blocked threads and grant threads to access and modify distinct portions of the cache, in real parallelism. For instance, function *APPLY* uses a computation cache with a method `get` that allows a thread to look up for the index, inside the unique table, of the node that holds the result of the required operation in the case it has been already computed before and never overwritten later. Cache is implemented as the array `cache` of integers, which contains tuples (n_1, op, n_2, r), where n_1 and n_2 are operands, op is a logical operator and r the result. The method `get` runs the following code:

```
1  int i = hash(n1, op, n2); // not the same of the unique table
2  if (cache[i] == n1 && cache[i + 1] == op && cache[i + 2] == n2)
3    synchronized (locks[i % locks.length]) {
4      return (cache[i] == n1
5             && cache[i + 1] == op
6             && cache[i + 2] == n2) ? cache[1 + 3] : -1;
7  }
```

Namely, it first hashes the triple that must be looked up in the cache and finds at which index i of the cache it should be, if it ever exists there. Rather than the whole array, it locks only a portion of the array that includes the i-th element, by using the same split locks that are used when putting a value in the cache (for simplicity, this code is not shown). Synchronization is mandatory since the elements of the array might be modified by other threads while get tries to read them. Finally, it accesses the triple starting at i and checks again whether the result is stored there or not, this time inside the critical section marked by the synchronized at line 3. The check at line 2 is semantically useless but essential for efficiency: it allows us to abort when a (non-thread-safe) access to the cache tells that the result is not in the cache. Since the check is outside the synchronization, a race condition might induce us to think that the result is not in the cache while it was actually there. In other terms, that check avoids almost all useless synchronizations but might account for some extra cache miss. Our experiments showed that avoiding useless synchronization is definitely the direction to go since synchronization costs much more than a very unlikely cache miss.

6.3   Synchronization with the Garbage Collector

It might well be possible to let the get method of Section 6.1 allocate as many nodes as needed, inside expandTable. However, BDDs are used by clients and eventually not needed anymore. When this is the case, clients can call the free method of BDDs to request deallocation from memory.[2] This means that, in the unique table, the positions of the nodes reachable only from the root of the freed BDDs become useless *holes* and can be eventually compacted away in order to keep the size of the table small. To do that, we use a garbage collector.

Since it modifies the unique table, garbage collection cannot run while clients are using the BDD library. That is, all operations on BDDs must be synchronized with the garbage collector, as for instance the logical conjunction might be implemented as:

```
1  public BDD and(BDD other) {
2    synchronized (uniqueTable.getGCLock()) {
3      return new BDD(APPLY(AND, this.root, other.root));
4    }
5  }
```

The getGCLock method, called at line 2, yields a lock used as a barrier to enter the library; that object is acquired by the garbage collector as well, when it starts running. That way, we achieve mutual exclusion between clients and garbage collection. However, if we always returned the same object inside getGCLock,

---

[2] The free method might be called automatically inside the finalize method of the BDDs, to integrate our garbage collector of nodes with the standard garbage collector of Java. This works but we have found that redefining the finalize method currently interferes with the Just-in-Time Java compiler and makes the code much slower.

we would obtain mutual exclusion with the garbage collection but two clients would never be allowed to use the library in real parallelism, since only one of them would pass the barrier (*i.e.*, lock that object). To achieve real parallelism among clients, we use split locks also inside getGCLock:

```
1  protected Object getGCLock() {
2    return gcLocks[nextGCLocks = (nextGCLocks + 1) % gcLocks.length];
3  }
```

Here, gcLocks is an array of objects used as locks and nextGCLocks is a circular cursor over that array. Hence this method returns, in general, distinct objects for distinct calls and, consequently, clients synchronize on different objects and are allowed to access the library in real parallelism. The garbage collector must now acquire a lock on *all* the elements of gcLocks in order to block all clients. Note that the increment of nextGCLocks might give rise to a race condition since it is not synchronized, but this is not relevant since it would only introduce a small degradation (two clients synchronizing on the same barrier and hence obliged to run sequentially). This is much better than synchronizing the accesses to nextGCLock, since introducing a synchronized statement at line 2 would have a high cost and might block some client.

6.4 Parallel Resize and Garbage Collection

Resize and garbage collection of the unique node table might be expensive operations when the table is large. Resize rehashes the nodes and the hashing function depends on the size of the table (Section 6.1); garbage collection scans the not yet freed BDDs in order to collect all the nodes reachable from their root, which must be kept in the table. Both are expensive operations. We have exploited the parallelism allowed by modern multicore hardware by distributing those operations on distinct threads when the size of the table exceeds a given threshold.[3] Parallel rehashing distributes the positions at different worker threads, so that each worker rehashes a different portion of the table. Parallel garbage collection does the same distribution for the not yet freed BDDs; each worker has in this case its own bag of positions deemed reachable from the BDDs that it has already processed. That bag gets merged in a global bag only at the end of the computation of the worker: this avoids synchronization among workers.

7   Experiments and Comparisons

We first consider some sequential experiments. The *n*-queens problem consists in placing *n* queens over a checkerboard so that no one attacks another. It translates naturally into the construction of a logical function whose solutions are all possible placements of queens. Figure 4 shows the execution time for constructing this function with BeeDeeDee, compared to the time needed by using

---

[3] For small tables, the overhead of starting a multithreaded computation is proportionally too large.

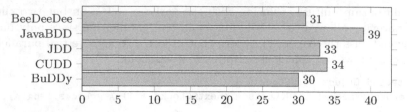

Fig. 4. Time (in seconds) for the solution of the 12-queens problem

the Java libraries JavaBDD and JDD, and the C libraries CUDD and BuDDy. BeeDeeDee is here the fastest Java library and is comparable to BuDDy, the best C library. Also the construction of the *transition relation*, as a BDD, for a circuit is a problem that applies many Boolean operations, sequentially. Figure 5 shows the time needed for three circuits from the ITC99 benchmark set [6]. Also in this case, BeeDeeDee outperforms the other Java libraries. These experiments show that BeeDeeDee can be used instead of already existing, non-thread-safe libraries, also for sequential computations.

Let us come to multithreaded examples now. Figure 6 shows the time for the construction from 1 to 4 BDDs representing the function associated to the same 12-queens problem. Such a construction was performed in parallel on a quad-core processor, by sharing unique table and caches with BeeDeeDee. We see here that we manage to achieve a high degree of real parallelism, since four BDDs are built in 33.6 seconds while a single BDD is built in 22.4 seconds. Some degradation exists, due to synchronization, but the parallel cost is much lower than the theoretical sequential cost of $4 \times 22.4 = 89.6$ seconds. This example shows that the overhead of synchronization is well acceptable for parallel computations through BeeDeeDee.

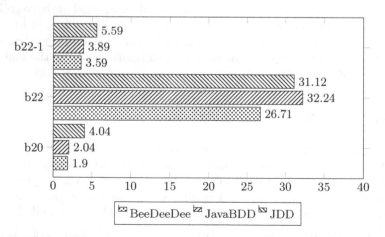

Fig. 5. Time (in seconds) for the construction of three circuits from ITC99

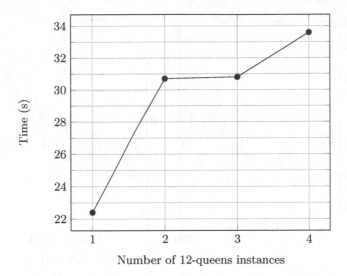

Fig. 6. Parallel 12-queens BDDs construction

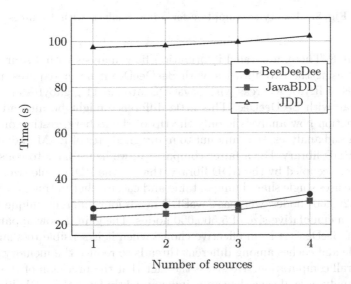

Fig. 7. Parallel information flow analysis for different sources

Figure 7 shows the time needed to perform from 1 to 4 information flow analyses of Hadoop with Julia Static Analyzer [9], in parallel on a quad-core processor, with the three libraries BeeDeeDee, JavaBDD and JDD. When we use BeeDeeDee, the BDD unique table and caches are shared, while this is not possible for the other, non-thread-safe libraries. JDD's poor performance is due to the fact that flow analysis heavily uses quantification and replacement operations, for which JDD is not optimized. JavaBDD is slightly faster in this case (it pays no synchronization overhead), but it consumes more memory, as we show next

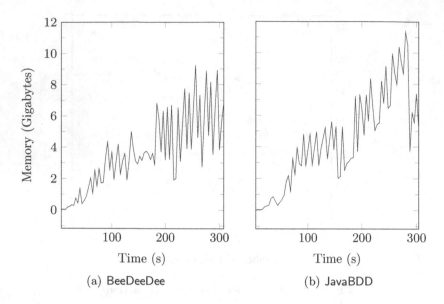

Fig. 8. Memory consumption for a flow analysis with 4 sources

with Figure 8. There, a parallel information flow analysis with 4 sources is performed by using the two libraries; with BeeDeeDee it never requires more than 9 gigabytes of RAM, whereas with JavaBDD around 11 gigabytes are required, 2 more than with BeeDeeDee. This little difference might be misleading, since the information flow analysis is only the tip of the iceberg, resting on previous processing and analyses, that amount to many gigabytes of RAM, independently from the BDD library. For a fairer comparison, we hence have to consider only the memory occupied by the BDD library, that is, the BDD table size. For that, BeeDeeDee uses single shared unique table and caches, that in this example reach a size of 2,200,000 nodes; whereas JavaBDD needs four different unique table and caches, for a cumulative size of 5,500,000 nodes. The gain is now apparent. This shows that BeeDeeDee is an effective choice when it is sensible to share unique nodes table and caches among different threads to reduce the memory footprint of the overall computation. We stress the fact that the precision of the information flow analyses is always the same, independently from the BDD library that we use, since it depends on the definition of the abstraction and of the abstract operations, not on the BDD library used for their implementation.

8   Conclusion

We have developed and evaluated a new BDD library. To the best of our knowledge, it is the first thread-safe library of that kind. This allows one to share the same unique table of nodes among clients, reduce the memory footprint and share the caches, hence avoiding repeated computations in distinct threads. It is actually faster than the already existing and non-thread-safe Java BDD libraries. Our library is consequently ready for the foreseeable development of new analysis, verification and artificial intelligence tools that exploit multithreading for real parallelism on multicore hardware. One such tool is already Julia [9], but more will be developed soon. Our library is free for non-commercial applications. It is available in source and binary formats at http://www.juliasoft.com/beedeedee.

References

1. 2011 CWE/SANS Top 25 Most Dangerous Software Errors, http://cwe.mitre.org/top25
2. BuDDy, http://buddy.sourceforge.net
3. CAL, http://embedded.eecs.berkeley.edu/Research/cal_bdd
4. CUDD, http://vlsi.colorado.edu/~fabio/CUDD
5. The Hadoop Big Data Engine, http://hadoop.apache.org
6. ITC99 Benchmark Circuits, http://www.cerc.utexas.edu/itc99-benchmarks/bench.html
7. The JavaBDD Library, http://javabdd.sourceforge.net
8. JDD, http://javaddlib.sourceforge.net/jdd
9. The Julia Static Analyzer, http://www.juliasoft.com
10. SableJBDD, http://www.sable.mcgill.ca/~fqian/SableJBDD
11. Armstrong, T., Marriott, K., Schachte, P., Søndergaard, H.: Two Classes of Boolean Functions for Dependency Analysis. Science of Computer Programming 31(1), 3–45 (1998)
12. Bahar, R.I., Frohm, E.A., Gaona, C.M., Hachtel, G.D., Macii, E., Pardo, A., Somenzi, F.: Algebraic Decision Diagrams and Their Applications. Formal Methods in System Design 10(2/3), 171–206 (1997)
13. Brace, K.S., Rudell, R.L., Bryant, R.E.: Efficient implementation of a BDD Package. In: DAC, pp. 40–45 (1990)
14. Bryant, R.E.: Graph-Based Algorithms for Boolean Function Manipulation. IEEE Transactions on Computers 35(8), 677–691 (1986)
15. Bryant, R.E.: Symbolic Boolean Manipulation with Ordered Binary Decision Diagrams. ACM Computing Surveys 24(3), 293–318 (1992)
16. Burch, J.R., Clarke, E.M., McMillan, K.L., Dill, D.L., Hwang, L.J.: Symbolic Model Checking: 10^{20} States and Beyond. Information and Computation 98(2), 142–170 (1992)
17. Genaim, S., Spoto, F.: Information Flow Analysis for Java Bytecode. In: Cousot, R. (ed.) VMCAI 2005. LNCS, vol. 3385, pp. 346–362. Springer, Heidelberg (2005)
18. Lhoták, O., Curial, S., Amaral, J.N.: Using XBDDs and ZBDDs in Points-to Analysis. Software: Practive and Experience 39(2), 163–188 (2009)
19. Minato, S.: Zero-Suppressed BDDs for Set Manipulation in Combinatorial Problems. In: Proc. of Design Automation Conference, pp. 272–277 (1993)
20. Rossignoli, S., Spoto, F.: Detecting Non-Cyclicity by Abstract Compilation into Boolean Functions. In: Emerson, E.A., Namjoshi, K.S. (eds.) VMCAI 2006. LNCS, vol. 3855, pp. 95–110. Springer, Heidelberg (2006)

Effect-Polymorphic Behaviour Inference
for Deadlock Checking*

Ka I Pun, Martin Steffen, and Volker Stolz

University of Oslo, Department of Informatics, Norway

Abstract. We present a constraint-based effect inference algorithm for deadlock checking. The static analysis is developed for a concurrent calculus with higher-order functions and dynamic lock creation. The analysis is context-sensitive and locks are summarised based on their creation-site. The resulting effects can be checked for deadlocks using state space exploration. We use a specific deadlock-sensitive simulation relation to show that the effects soundly over-approximate the behaviour of a program, in particular that deadlocks in the program are preserved in the effects.

1 Introduction

Deadlocks are a common problem for concurrent programs with shared resources. According to [4], a deadlocked state is marked by a number of processes, which forms a cycle where each process is unwilling to release its own resource, and is waiting on the resource held by its neighbour. The inherent non-determinism makes deadlocks hard to detect and to reproduce. We present a static analysis using behavioural effects to detect deadlocks in a higher-order concurrent calculus. Deadlock freedom, an important safety property for concurrent programs, is a thread-global property, i.e., two or more processes form a deadlock. The presented approach works in two stages: in a first stage, an effect-type system uses a static behavioural abstraction of the codes' behaviour, concentrating on the lock interactions. To detect potential deadlocks on the global level, the combined individual abstract thread behaviours are explored in the second stage.

Two challenges need to be tackled to make the approach applicable in practice. For the first stage on the thread local level, the static analysis must be able to *derive* the abstract behaviour, not just check compliance of the code with a user-provided description. This is the problem of type and effect *inference* or reconstruction. As usual, the abstract behaviour needs to over-approximate the concrete one, i.e., concrete and abstract descriptions are connected by some *simulation* relation: everything the concrete system does, the abstract one can do as well. For the second stage, exploring the (abstract) state space on the global level, obtaining *finite* abstractions is crucial. In our setting, there are four principal sources of infinity: the calculus allows 1) recursion, supports 2) dynamic thread creation, as well as 3) dynamic lock creation, and 4) unbounded lock counters for re-entrant locks. Our approach offers sound abstractions for the mentioned sources of unboundedness, except for dynamic thread creation. We first shortly present in a non-technical manner the ideas behind the abstractions before giving the formal theory.

---

* Partly funded by the EU projects FP7-610582 (ENVISAGE) and FP7-612985 (UPSCALE).

D. Giannakopoulou and G. Salaün (Eds.): SEFM 2014, LNCS 8702, pp. 50–64, 2014.
© Springer International Publishing Switzerland 2014

1.1 Effect Inference on the Thread Local Level

In the first stage of the analysis, a behavioural type and effect system is used to over-approximate the lock-interactions of a single thread. To force the user to annotate the program with the expected behaviour in the form of effects is impractical, so the type and especially the behaviour should be inferred automatically. Effect inference, including inferring behavioural effects, has been studied earlier and applied to various settings, including obtaining static over-approximations of behaviour for concurrent languages by Amtoft et al. [2]. We apply effect inference to deadlock detection and as is standard (cf. e.g., [11,16,2]), the inference system is constraint-based, where the constraints in particular express an approximate order between behaviours. Besides being able to infer the behaviour, it is important that the static approximation is as precise as possible. For that it is important that the analysis may distinguish different instances of a function body depending on their calling context, i.e., the analysis should be *polymorphic* or *context-sensitive*. This can be seen as an extension of let-polymorphism to effects and using constraints. The effect reconstruction resembles the known type-inference algorithm for let-polymorphism by Damas and Milner [6,5] and this has been used for effect-inference in various settings, e.g., in the works mentioned above.

Deadlock checking in our earlier work [13] was not polymorphic (and we did not address effect inference). The extension in this paper leads to an increase in precision wrt. checking for deadlocks, as illustrated by the small example below, where the two lock creation statements are labeled by π_1 and π_2:

```
let x₁ = newπ₁ L in let x₂ = newπ₂ L in
let f = fn x:L . ( x.lock; x.lock )
in spawn(f(x₂)); f(x₁)
```

The main thread, after creating two locks and defining function f, spawns a thread, and afterward, the main thread and the child thread run in parallel, each one executing an instance of f with different actual lock parameters. In a setting with re-entrant locks, the program is obviously deadlock-free. Part of the type system of [13] determines the potential origin of locks by data-flow analysis. The analysis cannot distinguish the two instances of f (the analysis is context-*insensitive*), and therefore forces that the type of the formal parameter is, at best, $L^{\{\pi_1,\pi_2\}}$. Based on that approximate information, a deadlock looks possible through a "deadly embrace" [7] where one thread takes first lock π_1 and then π_2, and the other thread takes them in reverse order, i.e., the analysis would report a (spurious) deadlock. The context-sensitive analysis presented here correctly analyzes the example as deadlock-free.

1.2 Deadlock Preserving Abstractions on the Global Level

Lock Abstraction. For dynamic data allocation, a standard abstraction is to *summarize* all data allocated at a given program point into one abstract representation. In the presence of loops or recursion, the abstracting function mapping concrete locks to their abstract representation is necessarily non-injective. For concrete, ordinary programs it is clear that identifying locks may change the behaviour of the program. Identification of locks is in general tricky (and here in particular in connection with deadlocks): on the one hand it leads to *less* steps, in that lock-protected critical sections may become larger. On the other hand it may lead to *more* steps at the same time, and deadlocks may disappear when identifying locks. This form of summarizing lock abstraction is problematic when analyzing properties of concurrent programs, and has been observed elsewhere as well, cf. e.g., Kidd et al. in [9].

To obtain a sound abstraction for deadlock detection when identifying locks in the described way, one faces thus the following dilemma: a) the abstract level, using the abstract locks, needs to show at least the behaviour of the concrete level, i.e., we expect that they are related by a form of simulation. On the other hand, to preserve not only the possibility of doing steps, but also *deadlocks,* the opposite must hold sometimes: b) a concrete program waiting on a lock and unable to make a step thereby, must imply an analogous situation on the abstract level, lest we should miss deadlocks. Let's write $l, l_1, l_2, \ldots$ for concrete lock references and $\pi, \pi', \ldots$ for program points of lock creation, i.e., abstract locks. To satisfy a): when a concrete program takes a lock, the abstract one must be able to "take" the corresponding abstract lock, say π. A consequence of a) is that taking an abstract lock is always enabled. That is consistent with the abstraction as described where the abstract lock π confuses an arbitrary number of concrete locks including, e.g., those freshly created, which may be taken.

Thus, abstract locks lose their "mutual exclusion" capacity: whereas a concrete heap is a mapping which associates to each lock reference the number of times that *at most one* process is holding it, an abstract heap $\hat{\sigma}$ records how many times an abstract lock π is held by the various processes, e.g., thrice by one process and twice by another. The corresponding natural number abstractly represents the *sum* of the lock values of all concrete locks (per process). Without ever blocking, the abstraction leads to more possible steps, but to cater for b), the abstraction still needs to appropriately define, given an abstract heap and an abstract lock π, when a process waits on the abstract lock, as this may indicate a deadlock. The definition has to capture all possibilities of waiting on one of the corresponding concrete locks (see Definition 6 later). The sketched intuitions to obtain a sound abstract summary representation for locks and correspondingly for heaps lead also to a corresponding refinement of "over-approximation" in terms of simulation: not only must the a) positive behaviour be preserved as in standard simulation, but also the b) possibility of waiting on a lock and ultimately the possibility of deadlock needs to be preserved. For this we introduce the notion of *deadlock sensitive* simulation (see Definition 9). The definition is analogous to the one from [13]. However, it takes into account now that the analysis is polymorphic and the definition is no longer based on a direct operational interpretation of the behaviour of the effects. Instead it is based on the behavioural constraints used in the inference systems.

The points discussed are illustrated in Fig. 1, where the left diagram Fig. 1a depicts two threads running in parallel and trying to take two concrete locks, l_1 and l_2 while Fig. 1b illustrates an abstraction of the left one where the two concrete locks are summarized by the abstract lock π (typically because being created at the same program point). The concrete program obviously may run into a deadlock by reaching commonly the states q_{01} and q_{11}, where the first process is waiting on l_2 and the second process on l_1. With the abstraction sketched above, the abstract behaviour, having reached the corresponding states $\hat{q}_{01}$ and $\hat{q}_{11}$, can proceed (in two steps) to the common states $\hat{q}_{02}$ and $\hat{q}_{12}$,

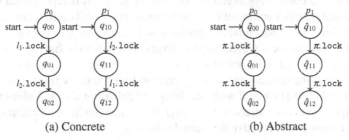

Fig. 1. Lock abstraction

reaching an abstract heap where the abstract lock π is "held" twice by each process. In the state $\hat{q}_{01}$ and $\hat{q}_{11}$, however, the analysis will correctly detect that, with the given lock abstraction, the first process *may* actually wait on π, resp. on one of its concretizations, and dually for the second process, thereby detecting the deadly embrace. Allowing this form of abstraction, summarizing concrete locks into an abstract one, improves our earlier analysis [13], which could therefore deal only with a static number of locks.

Counter Abstraction and Further Behaviour Abstraction. Two remaining causes of an infinite state space are the values of lock counters, which may grow unboundedly, and the fact that for each thread, the effect behaviour abstractly represents the *stack* of function calls for that thread. Sequential composition as construct for abstract behavioural effects allows to represent non-tail-recursive behaviour (corresponding to the context-free call-and-return behaviour of the underlying program). To curb that source of infinity, we allow for replacing the behaviour by a tail-recursive over-approximation. The precision of the approximation can be adapted in choosing the depth of calls after which the call-structure collapses into an arbitrary, chaotic behaviour. A finite abstraction for the lock-counters is achieved similarly by imposing an upper bound on the considered lock counter, beyond which the locks behave non-deterministically. Again, for both abstractions it is crucial, that the abstraction preserves also deadlocks, which we capture again using the notion of deadlock-sensitive simulation. These two abstractions have been formulated and proven in the non-context-sensitive setting of [13].

To summarize, compared to [13], the paper makes the following contributions: 1) the effect analysis is generalized to a context-sensitive formulation, using constraints, for which we provide 2) an inference algorithm. Finally, 3) we allow summarizing multiple concrete locks into abstract ones, while still preserving deadlocks.

The rest of the paper is organized as follows. After presenting syntax and semantics of the concurrent calculus in Section 2, the behavioural type system is presented in Section 3, which also includes the soundness result in the form of subject reduction. The conclusion in Section 4 discusses related and future work.

2   Calculus

This section presents the syntax and semantics for our calculus. The abstract syntax is given in Table 1 (the types T will be covered in more detail in Section 3). A program P consists of processes $p\langle t \rangle$ running in parallel, where p is a process identifier and t

is a thread, i.e., the code being executed. The empty program is represented by $\emptyset$. We assume, as usual, parallel composition $\parallel$ to be associative and commutative. A thread t is either a value v or a sequential composition written as $\texttt{let } x{:}T = e \texttt{ in } t$, where the let-construct binds the local variable x in t. Expressions include function applications and conditionals. Threads are created with the expression $\texttt{spawn } t$. For lock manipulation, $\texttt{new } L$ yields the reference to a newly created lock (initially free), and the operations $v.\,\texttt{lock}$ and $v.\,\texttt{unlock}$ deal with acquiring and releasing a lock. Values which are evaluated expressions are variables, lock references, and function abstractions, where $\texttt{fun } f{:}T.x{:}T.t$ represents recursive function definitions.

Table 1. Abstract syntax

$$
\begin{array}{llll}
P & ::= & \emptyset \mid p\langle t\rangle \mid P \parallel P & \text{program} \\
t & ::= & v \mid \texttt{let } x{:}T = e \texttt{ in } t & \text{thread} \\
e & ::= & t \mid v\,v \mid \texttt{if } v \texttt{ then } e \texttt{ else } e \mid \texttt{spawn } t \mid \texttt{new } L & \\
  &   & \mid v.\,\texttt{lock} \mid v.\,\texttt{unlock} & \text{expr.} \\
v & ::= & x \mid l \mid \texttt{true} \mid \texttt{false} \mid \texttt{fn } x{:}T.t \mid \texttt{fun } f{:}T.x{:}T.t & \text{values}
\end{array}
$$

Semantics

The small-step operational semantics, presented next, distinguishes between local and global steps (cf. Table 2). The local steps are straightforward and therefore left out here.   Global configurations are of the form $\sigma \vdash P$ where P is a program and the heap σ is a finite mapping from lock identifiers to the status of each lock, which can be either free or a tuple indicating the number of times a lock has been taken by a thread. For the analysis later, we allow ourselves also to write $\sigma(l, p) = n + 1$ if $\sigma(l) = p(n+1)$ (indicating the pair of process identifier p and lock count n) and $\sigma(l, p) = 0$ otherwise. The global steps are given as transitions between global configurations. It will be handy later to assume the transitions appropriately labeled (cf. Table 2). Thread-local transition steps are lifted to the global level by rule R-LIFT. A global step is a thread-local step made by one of the individual threads sharing the same σ (cf. rule R-PAR). R-SPAWN creates a new thread with a fresh identity running in parallel with the parent thread. All the identities are unique at the global level. Creating a new lock, which is initially free, allocates a fresh lock reference l in the heap (cf. rule R-NEWL). The locking step (cf. rule R-LOCK) takes a lock when it is either free or already being held by the requesting process. To update the heap, we define: If $\sigma(l) = \textit{free}$, then $\sigma +_p l = \sigma[l \mapsto p(1)]$ and if $\sigma(l) = p(n)$, then $\sigma +_p l = \sigma[l \mapsto p(n+1)]$. Dually $\sigma -_p l$ is defined as follows: if $\sigma(l) = p(n+1)$, then $\sigma -_p l = \sigma[l \mapsto p(n)]$, and if $\sigma(l) = p(1)$, then $\sigma -_p l = \sigma[l \mapsto \textit{free}]$. Unlocking works correspondingly, i.e., it sets the lock as being free resp. decreases the lock count by one (cf. rule R-UNLOCK).

To later relate the operational behaviour to its behavioural abstraction, we *label* the transition of the operational semantics appropriately. In particular, steps for lock manipulations are labelled to indicate which *process* has taken or released which *lock*. For instance, the labelled transition step $\xrightarrow{p\langle l\text{lock}\rangle}$ means that a process p takes a lock labelled l. We discuss further details about the labels in the next section.

Before defining the notion of deadlock, we first characterize the situation in which one thread in a program attempts to acquire a lock which is not available as follows:

Table 2. Global steps

$$\frac{t_1 \to t_2}{\sigma \vdash p\langle t_1\rangle \to \sigma \vdash p\langle t_2\rangle} \text{ R-Lift} \qquad \sigma \vdash p_1\langle \text{let } x{:}T = \text{spawn } t_2 \text{ in } t_1\rangle \to \sigma \vdash p_1\langle \text{let } x{:}T = () \text{ in } t_1\rangle \parallel p_2\langle t_2\rangle \quad \text{R-Spawn}$$

$$\frac{\sigma \vdash P_1 \to \sigma' \vdash P_1'}{\sigma \vdash P_1 \parallel P_2 \to \sigma' \vdash P_1' \parallel P_2} \text{ R-Par} \qquad \frac{\sigma' = \sigma[l \mapsto \mathit{free}] \qquad l \text{ is fresh}}{\sigma \vdash p\langle \text{let } x{:}T = \text{new L in } t\rangle \to \sigma' \vdash p\langle \text{let } x{:}T = l \text{ in } t\rangle} \text{ R-NewL}$$

$$\frac{\sigma(l) = \mathit{free} \vee \sigma(l) = p(n) \qquad \sigma' = \sigma +_p l}{\sigma \vdash p\langle \text{let } x{:}T = l. \text{ lock in } t\rangle \to \sigma' \vdash p\langle \text{let } x{:}T = l \text{ in } t\rangle} \text{ R-Lock}$$

$$\frac{\sigma(l) = p(n) \qquad \sigma' = \sigma -_p l}{\sigma \vdash p\langle \text{let } x{:}T = l. \text{ unlock in } t\rangle \to \sigma' \vdash p\langle \text{let } x{:}T = l \text{ in } t\rangle} \text{ R-Unlock}$$

Definition 1 (Waiting for a lock). *Given a configuration* $\sigma \vdash P$, *a process* p *waits for a lock* l *in* $\sigma \vdash P$, *written as* $\mathit{waits}(\sigma \vdash P, p, l)$, *if it is not the case that* $\sigma \vdash P \xrightarrow{p\langle l.\text{lock}\rangle}$, *and if furthermore there exists a* σ' *s.t.* $\sigma' \vdash P \xrightarrow{p\langle l.\text{lock}\rangle} \sigma'' \vdash P'$.

The notion of (resource) deadlock used is rather standard, where a number of processes waiting for each other's locks in a cyclic manner constitute a deadlock (see also [13]). In our setting with re-entrant locks, a process cannot deadlock "on itself".

Definition 2 (Deadlock). *A configuration* $\sigma \vdash P$ *is deadlocked if* $\sigma(l_i) = p_i(n_i)$ *and furthermore* $\mathit{waits}(\sigma \vdash P, p_i, l_{i+_k 1})$ *(for all* $0 \le i \le k-1$ *and where* $k \ge 2$*). The* $+_k$ *represents addition modulo* k. *A configuration* $\sigma \vdash P$ *contains a deadlock, if, starting from* $\sigma \vdash P$, *a deadlocked configuration is reachable; otherwise, it is deadlock free.*

3 Type System

Next we present an effect type system to derive behavioural information which is used, in a second step, to detect potential deadlocks. The type system derives flow information about which locks may be used at various points in the program. Additionally, it derives an abstract, i.e., approximate representation of the code's behaviour. The representation extends our earlier system [13] by making the analysis *context-sensitive* and furthermore by supporting type and effect *inference*, both important from a practical point of view. Being context-sensitive, making the effect system polymorphic, increases the precision of the analysis. Furthermore, inference removes the burden from the programmer to annotate the program appropriately to allow checking for potential deadlock. These extensions follow standard techniques for behaviour inference, see for instance Amtoft et al. [2] and type-based flow analysis, see e.g., Mossin [11]. The system here makes use of explicit *constraints*. Type systems are, most commonly, formulated in a syntax-directed manner, i.e., analyzing the program code in a divide-and-conquer manner. That obviously results in an efficient analysis of the code. However, a syntax-directed formulation of the deduction rules of the type system, which forces to analyze the code following the syntactic structure of the program, may have disadvantages as well. Using constraints in a type system *decouples* the syntax-directed phase of the analysis, which collects the constraints, from the task of actually *solving* the constraints. Formulations of type systems without relying on constraints can be seen as solving the underlying constraints "on-the-fly", while recurring through the structure of the code.

3.1 Types, Effects, and Constraints

The analysis performs a data flow analysis to track the usage of locks. For that purpose, the lock creation statements are equipped with labels, writing new^π L, where π is taken from a countably infinite set of labels. As usual, the labels π are assumed unique in a given program. The grammar for annotations, types, and effects is given in Tables 3 and 4. We use r to denote sets of πs with ρ representing corresponding variables. Types include basic types, represented by B, such as the unit type Unit, booleans, integers, etc., functional types with latent *effect* φ, and lock types L^r where the annotation r captures the flow information about the potential places where the lock is created. This information will be reconstructed, and the user writes types without annotations (the "underlying" types) in the program. We write T (and its syntactic variants) as meta-variables for the underlying types, and $\hat{T}$ (and its syntactic variants) for the annotated types, as given in the grammar. The universally quantified types, represented by $\hat{S}$, capture functions which are polymorphic in locations and effects.

Table 3. Types and type schemes

$$
\begin{array}{lll}
Y & ::= \rho \mid X & \text{type-level variables} \\
r & ::= \rho \mid \{\pi\} \mid r \sqcup r & \text{lock/label sets} \\
\hat{T} & ::= B \mid L^r \mid \hat{T} \xrightarrow{\varphi} \hat{T} & \text{types} \\
\hat{S} & ::= \forall \vec{Y}{:}C.\, \hat{T} \xrightarrow{\varphi} \hat{T} \mid \hat{T} & \text{type schemes} \\
C & ::= \emptyset \mid \rho \sqsupseteq r,C \mid X \sqsupseteq \varphi,C & \text{constraints}
\end{array}
$$

Whereas the type of an expression captures the results of the computations of the expression if it terminates, the effect captures the *behaviour* during the computations. For the deadlock analysis, we capture the lock interactions as effects, i.e., which locks are accessed during execution and in which order. The effects (cf. Table 4) are split between a (thread-) local level φ and a global level Φ. The empty effect is denoted by ε, representing behaviour without lock operations. Sequential composition is represented by $\varphi_1;\varphi_2$. The choice between two effects $\varphi_1 + \varphi_2$, as well as recursive effects $recX.\varphi$, is actually not generated by the algorithm; they would show up when solving the constraints generated by the algorithm. We included their syntax for completeness. Note also that recursion is not polymorphic. Labels a capture the three basic effects: spawning a new process with behaviour φ is represented by spawn φ, while r.lock and r.unlock respectively capture lock manipulations, acquiring and releasing a lock, where r refers to the possible points of creation. Silent transitions are represented by τ. Lock-creation has no corresponding effect, as newly created locks are initially free, i.e., with a lock-count of 0. On the abstract level, locks are summarized by the *sum* of all locks created at given point. Hence lock creation will be represented by a τ-transition.

Constraints C finally are finite sets of in-equations of the form $\rho \sqsupseteq r$ or of $X \sqsupseteq \varphi$,

Table 4. Effects

$$\begin{aligned}
\Phi &::= \mathbf{0} \mid p\langle\varphi\rangle \mid \Phi \parallel \Phi && \text{effects (global)} \\
\varphi &::= \varepsilon \mid \varphi;\varphi \mid \varphi+\varphi \mid \alpha \mid X \mid recX.\varphi && \text{effects (local)} \\
a &::= \text{spawn } \varphi \mid r.\text{lock} \mid r.\text{unlock} && \text{labels/basic effects} \\
\alpha &::= a \mid \tau && \text{transition labels}
\end{aligned}$$

where ρ is, as mentioned, a flow variable and X an effect or behaviour variable. To allow polymorphism we use type schemes $\hat{S}$, i.e., prefix-quantified types of the form $\forall \vec{Y}{:}C.\ \hat{T}$, where Y are variables ρ or X. The qualifying constraints C in the type scheme impose restrictions on the bound variables. The formal system presented in this paper uses a constraint-based flow analysis as proposed by Mossin [11] for lock information. Likewise, the effects captured as a sequence of behaviour are formulated using constraints.

3.2 Type Inference

Next we present a type inference algorithm which derives types and effects and generates corresponding constraints (see Table 6 below). It is formulated in a rule-based manner, with judgments of the form: $\Gamma \vdash e : \hat{T} :: \varphi; C$. The system is syntax-directed, i.e., algorithmic, where Γ and e are considered as "input", and the annotated type $\hat{T}$, the effect φ, and the set of constraints C as "output". Concentrating on the flow information and the effect part, expressions e are type-annotated with the *underlying* types, as given in Table 3. In contrast, e contains no flow or effect annotations; those are derived by the algorithmic type system. It would be straightforward to have the underlying types reconstructed as well, using standard type inference à la Hindley/Milner/Damas [6,5,8]. For simplicity, we focus on the type annotations and the effect part. For locks, the flow annotation over-approximates the point of lock creation, and finally, φ over-approximates the lock-interactions while evaluating e. As usual, the behavioural over-approximation is a form of simulation. For our purpose, we will define a particular, deadlock-sensitive form of simulation. These intended over-approximations are understood relative to the generated constraints C, i.e., *all* solutions of C give rise to a sound over-approximation in the mentioned sense. Solutions to a constraint set C are ground substitutions θ, assigning label sets to flow variables ρ and effect variables X. We write $\theta \models C$ if θ is a solution to C.

Ultimately, one is interested in the minimal solution of the constraints, as it provides the most precise information. Solving the constraints is done after the algorithmic type system, but to allow for the most precise solution afterward, each rule should generate the most general constraint set, i.e., the one which allows the maximal set of solutions. This is achieved using *fresh* variables for each additional constraint. In the system below, new constraints are generated from requesting that types are in a "subtype" relationship. In our setting, "subtyping" concerns the flow annotations on the lock types and the latent effects on function types. For instance in rule TA-APP in Table 6, the argument of a function of type $\hat{T}_2 \xrightarrow{\varphi} \hat{T}_1$ is of a subtype $\hat{T}_2'$ of $\hat{T}_2$, i.e., instead of requiring $\hat{T}_2' \leq \hat{T}_2$ in that situation, the corresponding rule will generate new constraints in requiring the subtype relationship to hold (see Definition 3). As an invariant, the type system makes sure that lock types are always of the form L^ρ, i.e., using flow *variables* and similarly that only variables X are used for the latent effects for function types.

Definition 3 (Constraint generation). *The judgment $\hat{T}_1 \leq \hat{T}_2 \vdash C$ (read as "requiring $\hat{T}_1 \leq \hat{T}_2$ generates the constraints C") is inductively given as follows:*

$$B \leq B \vdash \emptyset \quad \text{C-Basic} \qquad L^{\rho_1} \leq L^{\rho_2} \vdash \{\rho_1 \sqsubseteq \rho_2\} \quad \text{C-Lock} \qquad \frac{\hat{T}_1' \leq \hat{T}_1 \vdash C_1 \quad \hat{T}_2 \leq \hat{T}_2' \vdash C_2 \quad C_3 = \{X \sqsubseteq X'\}}{\hat{T}_1 \xrightarrow{X} \hat{T}_2 \leq \hat{T}_1' \xrightarrow{X'} \hat{T}_2' \vdash C_1, C_2, C_3} \quad \text{C-Arrow}$$

In the presence of subtyping/sub-effecting, the overall type of a conditional needs to be an upper bound on the types/effects of the two branches (resp. the least upper bound in case of a minimal solution). To generate the most general constraints, fresh variables are used for the result type. This is captured in the following definition. Note that given $\hat{T}$ by $\hat{T}_1 \vee \hat{T}_2 \vdash \hat{T}; C$, type $\hat{T}$ in itself does not represent the least upper bound of $\hat{T}_1$ and $\hat{T}_2$. The use of fresh variables assures, however, that the minimal solution of the generated constraints makes $\hat{T}$ into the least upper bound.

Definition 4 (Least upper bound). *The partial operation $\vee$ on annotated types (and in abuse of notation, on effects), giving back a set of constraints plus a type (resp. an effect) is inductively given by the rules of Table 5. The operation $\wedge$ is defined dually.*

Table 5. Least upper bound

$$\frac{B_1 = B_2}{B_1 \vee B_2 = B_1; \emptyset} \quad \text{LT-Basic} \qquad \frac{\hat{T}_1' \wedge \hat{T}_1'' = \hat{T}_1; C_1 \quad \hat{T}_2' \vee \hat{T}_2'' = \hat{T}_2; C_2 \quad X_1 \sqcup X_2 = X; C_3}{\hat{T}_1' \xrightarrow{X_1} \hat{T}_2' \vee \hat{T}_1'' \xrightarrow{X_2} \hat{T}_2'' = \hat{T}_1 \xrightarrow{X} \hat{T}_2; C_1, C_2, C_3} \quad \text{LT-Arrow}$$

$$\frac{\rho \; \text{fresh} \quad L^{\rho_1} \leq L^\rho \vdash C_1 \quad L^{\rho_2} \leq L^\rho \vdash C_2}{L^{\rho_1} \vee L^{\rho_2} = L^\rho; C_1, C_2} \quad \text{LT-Lock} \qquad \frac{X \; \text{fresh} \quad C = \{\varphi_1 \sqsubseteq X, \varphi_2 \sqsubseteq X\}}{\varphi_1 \sqcup \varphi_2 = X; C} \quad \text{LE-Eff}$$

The rules for the type and effect system then are given in Table 6. A variable has no effect and its type (scheme) is looked up from the context Γ. The constraints C that may occur in the type scheme, are given back as constraints of the variable x, replacing the $\forall$-bound variables $\vec{Y}$ in C by fresh ones. Lock creation at point π (cf. TA-NewL) is of the type L^ρ, has an empty effect and the generated constraint requires $\rho \sqsupseteq \{\pi\}$, using a fresh ρ. As values, abstractions have no effect (cf. TA-Abs rules) and again, fresh variables are appropriately used. In rule TA-Abs$_1$, the latent effect of the result type is represented by X under the generated constraint $X \sqsupseteq \varphi$, where φ is the effect of the function body checked in the premise. The context in the premise is extended by $x:\lceil T \rceil_A$, where the operation $\lceil T \rceil_A$ annotates all occurrences of lock types L with fresh variables and introduces fresh effect variables for the latent effects. Rule TA-Abs$_2$ for recursive functions works analogously. For applications (cf. TA-App), both the function and the arguments are evaluated and therefore have no effect. As usual, the type of the argument needs to be a subtype of the input type of the function, and corresponding constraints C_3 are generated by $\hat{T}_2' \leq \hat{T}_2 \vdash C_3$. For the overall effect, again a fresh effect variable is used which is connected with the latent effect of the function by the additional constraint $X \sqsupseteq \varphi$. For conditionals, rule TA-COND ensures both the resulting type and the effect are upper bounds of the types resp. effects of the two branches by generating two additional constraints (cf. Table 5). The let-construct (cf. TA-LET) for the sequential composition has an effect $\varphi_1 ; \varphi_2$. To support context-sensitivity (corresponding to let-polymorphism), the let-rule is where the generalization over the type-level variables happens. In the first approximation, given e_1 is of $\hat{T}_1$, variables which do not occur free in Γ can be generalized over to obtain $\hat{S}_1$, which quantifies over the maximal number of variables for which such generalization is sound. In the setting here, the quantification affects only flow variables ρ and effect variables X. The close-operation $close(\Gamma, \varphi, C, \hat{T})$ first computes the set of all "relevant" free variables in a type $\hat{T}$ and the constraint C by the operation $close_{\uparrow\downarrow}(fv(\hat{T}_1), C_1)$ which finds the upward and downward closure of the free variables in $\hat{T}_1$ wrt. C_1. Among the set of free variables, those that are free in the context or in the effect, as well as the corresponding downward closure, are non-generalizable and are excluded. (See also Amtoft et al. [2]). The spawn expression is of unit type (cf. TA-SPAWN) and again a fresh variable is used in the generated constraint. Finally, rules TA-LOCK and TA-UNLOCK deal with locking and unlocking an existing lock created at the potential program points indicated by ρ. Both expressions have the same type L^ρ, while the effects are $\rho.\mathtt{lock}$ and $\rho.\mathtt{unlock}$.

The type and effect system works on the thread local level. The definition for the global level is straightforward. If all the processes are well-typed, so is the corresponding global program. A process p is well-typed, denoted as $\vdash p\langle t\rangle :: p\langle\varphi;C\rangle$, if $\vdash t : \hat{T} :: \varphi;C$. In abuse of notation, we use Φ to abbreviate $p_1\langle\varphi_1;C_1\rangle \parallel \ldots \parallel p_n\langle\varphi_n;C_n\rangle$.

Table 6. Algorithmic effect inference

$$\frac{\Gamma(x) = \forall \vec{Y}{:}C.\hat{T} \quad \vec{Y}' \text{ fresh} \quad \theta = [\vec{Y}'/\vec{Y}]}{\Gamma \vdash x : \theta\hat{T} :: \varepsilon; \theta C} \text{ TA-VAR}$$

$$\frac{\hat{T}_1 = \lceil T_1\rceil_A \quad \Gamma, x{:}\hat{T}_1 \vdash e : \hat{T}_2 :: \varphi; C \quad X \text{ fresh}}{\Gamma \vdash \mathtt{fn}\, x{:}T_1.e : \hat{T}_1 \xrightarrow{X} \hat{T}_2 :: \varepsilon; C, X \sqsupseteq \varphi} \text{ TA-ABS}_1$$

$$\frac{\hat{T}_1 \xrightarrow{X} \hat{T}_2 = \lceil T_1 \to T_2\rceil_A \quad \Gamma, f{:}\hat{T}_1 \xrightarrow{X} \hat{T}_2, x{:}\hat{T}_1 \vdash e : \hat{T}_2' :: \varphi; C_1 \quad \hat{T}_2' \leq \hat{T}_2 \vdash C_2}{\Gamma \vdash \mathtt{fun}\, f{:}T_1 \to T_2, x{:}T_1.e : \hat{T}_1 \xrightarrow{X} \hat{T}_2 :: \varepsilon; C_1, C_2, X \sqsupseteq \varphi} \text{ TA-ABS}_2$$

$$\frac{\Gamma \vdash v_1 : \hat{T}_2 \xrightarrow{\varphi} \hat{T}_1 :: \varepsilon; C_1 \quad \Gamma \vdash v_2 : \hat{T}_2' :: \varepsilon; C_2 \quad \hat{T}_2' \leq \hat{T}_2 \vdash C_3 \quad X \text{ fresh}}{\Gamma \vdash v_1\, v_2 : \hat{T}_1 :: X; C_1, C_2, C_3, X \sqsupseteq \varphi} \text{ TA-APP}$$

$$\frac{\lfloor \hat{T}\rfloor = \lfloor \hat{T}_1\rfloor = \lfloor \hat{T}_2\rfloor \quad \hat{T}; C = \hat{T}_1 \vee \hat{T}_2 \quad X; C' = \varphi_1 \sqcup \varphi_2}{\Gamma \vdash v : \mathtt{Bool} :: \varepsilon; C_0 \quad \Gamma \vdash e_1 : \hat{T}_1 :: \varphi_1; C_1 \quad \Gamma \vdash e_2 : \hat{T}_2 :: \varphi_2; C_2}{\Gamma \vdash \mathtt{if}\, v\, \mathtt{then}\, e_1\, \mathtt{else}\, e_2 : \hat{T} :: X; C_0, C_1, C_2, C, C'} \text{ TA-COND}$$

$$\frac{\rho \text{ fresh}}{\Gamma \vdash \mathtt{new}^\pi\, L : L^\rho :: \varepsilon; \rho \sqsupseteq \{\pi\}} \text{ TA-NEWL}$$

$$\frac{\Gamma \vdash e_1 : \hat{T}_1 :: \varphi_1; C_1 \quad \lfloor \hat{T}_1\rfloor = T_1}{\hat{S}_1 = close(\Gamma, \varphi_1, C_1, \hat{T}_1) \quad \Gamma, x{:}\hat{S}_1 \vdash e_2 : \hat{T}_2 :: \varphi_2; C_2}{\Gamma \vdash \mathtt{let}\, x{:}T_1 = e_1\, \mathtt{in}\, e_2 : \hat{T}_2 :: \varphi_1; \varphi_2; C_1, C_2} \text{ TA-LET}$$

$$\frac{\Gamma \vdash t : \hat{T} :: \varphi; C \quad X \text{ fresh}}{\Gamma \vdash \mathtt{spawn}\, t : \mathtt{Unit} :: X; C, X \sqsupseteq \mathtt{spawn}\, \varphi} \text{ TA-SPAWN}$$

$$\frac{\Gamma \vdash v : L^\rho :: \varepsilon; C \quad X \text{ fresh}}{\Gamma \vdash v.\mathtt{lock} : L^\rho :: X; C, X \sqsupseteq \rho.\mathtt{lock}} \text{ TA-LOCK}$$

$$\frac{\Gamma \vdash v : L^\rho :: \varepsilon; C \quad X \text{ fresh}}{\Gamma \vdash v.\mathtt{unlock} : L^\rho :: X; C, X \sqsupseteq \rho.\mathtt{unlock}} \text{ TA-UNLOCK}$$

3.3   Semantics of the Behaviour

Next we are going to define the transition relation on the abstract behaviour with the effect-constraints. Given a constraint set C, we interpret $C \vdash a; \varphi_2 \sqsubseteq \varphi_1$ as φ_1 may first perform an a-step before executing φ_2, where a is one of the labels from Table 4 which do not include the τ-label. See also [2]. The relation $C \vdash \varphi_1 \sqsubseteq \varphi_2$ is defined in Table 7.

Definition 5. *The transition relation between configurations of the form* $C; \hat{\sigma} \vdash \Phi$ *is given inductively by the rules of Table 8, where we write* $C \vdash \varphi_1 \overset{a}{\Rightarrow}_{\sqsubseteq} \varphi_2$ *for* $C \vdash a; \varphi_2 \sqsubseteq \varphi_1$. *The* $\hat{\sigma}$ *represents an* abstract *heap, which is a finite mapping from a flow variable* ρ *and a process identity* p *to a natural number.*

Each transition correspondingly captures the three possible steps we describe in the behaviour, namely creating a new process with a given behaviour, locking and unlocking. Analogous to the corresponding case in the concrete semantics, rule RE-SPAWN covers the creation of a new (abstract) thread and leaves the abstract heap unchanged. Taking a lock increases the corresponding lock count by one (cf. RE-LOCK). Unlocking works similarly by decreasing the lock count by one (cf. RE-UNLOCK), where the second premise makes sure the lock count stays non-negative. The transitions of a global effect Φ consist of the transitions of the individual thread (cf. RE-PAR). As stipulated by rule RE-LOCK, the step to take an abstract lock is always enabled, which is in obvious contrast to the behaviour of concrete locks. To ensure that the abstraction preserves deadlocks requires to adapt the definition of what it means that an abstract behaviour waits on a lock (cf. also Definition 1 for concrete programs and heaps).

Definition 6 (Waiting for a lock ($\Rightarrow_{\sqsubseteq}$)). *Given a configuration* $C; \hat{\sigma} \vdash \Phi$ *where* $\Phi = \Phi' \parallel p\langle \varphi \rangle$, *a process* p waits *for a lock* ρ *in* $\hat{\sigma} \vdash \Phi$, *written as* $waits_{\sqsubseteq}(C; \hat{\sigma} \vdash \Phi, p, \rho)$, *if* $C \vdash \varphi \overset{\rho.\text{lock}}{=\!=\!=\!\Rightarrow}_{\sqsubseteq} \varphi'$ *but* $\hat{\sigma}(\rho, q) \geq 1$ *for some* $q \neq p$.

Definition 7 (Deadlock). *A configuration* $C; \hat{\sigma} \vdash \Phi$ *is deadlocked if* $\hat{\sigma}(\rho_i, p_i) \geq 1$ *and furthermore* $waits(C; \hat{\sigma} \vdash \Phi, p_i, \rho_{i+_k 1})$ *(where* $k \geq 2$ *and for all* $0 \leq i \leq k - 1$*). The* $+_k$ *is meant as addition modulo* k. *A configuration* $C; \hat{\sigma} \vdash \Phi$ *contains a deadlock, if, starting from* $C; \hat{\sigma} \vdash \Phi$, *a deadlocked configuration is reachable; otherwise it is* deadlock free.

Table 7. Orders on behaviours

$$\varepsilon; \varphi \equiv \varphi \quad \text{EE-UNIT} \qquad \varphi_1; (\varphi_2; \varphi_3) \equiv (\varphi_1; \varphi_2); \varphi_3 \quad \text{EE-ASSOC} \qquad \frac{C \vdash \varphi_1 \sqsubseteq \varphi_1' \quad C \vdash \varphi_2 \sqsubseteq \varphi_2'}{C \vdash \varphi_1; \varphi_2 \sqsubseteq \varphi_1'; \varphi_2'} \text{S-SEQ}$$

$$C, r \subseteq \rho \vdash r \subseteq \rho \quad \text{S-AX}_L \qquad C, \varphi \sqsubseteq X \vdash \varphi \sqsubseteq X \quad \text{S-AX}_E \qquad C \vdash r \subseteq r \quad \text{S-REFL}_L \qquad \frac{\varphi_1 \equiv \varphi_2}{C \vdash \varphi_1 \sqsubseteq \varphi_2} \text{S-REFL}_E$$

$$\frac{C \vdash r_1 \subseteq r_2 \quad C \vdash r_2 \subseteq r_3}{C \vdash r_1 \subseteq r_3} \text{S-TRANS}_L \qquad \frac{C \vdash \varphi_1 \sqsubseteq \varphi_2 \quad C \vdash \varphi_2 \sqsubseteq \varphi_3}{C \vdash \varphi_1 \sqsubseteq \varphi_3} \text{S-TRANS}_E$$

$$\frac{C \vdash \varphi_1 \sqsubseteq \varphi_2}{C \vdash \text{spawn } \varphi_1 \sqsubseteq \text{spawn } \varphi_2} \text{S-SPAWN} \qquad \frac{C \vdash r_1 \subseteq r_2}{C \vdash r_1.\text{lock} \sqsubseteq r_2.\text{lock}} \text{S-LOCK} \qquad \frac{C \vdash r_1 \subseteq r_2}{C \vdash r_1.\text{unlock} \sqsubseteq r_2.\text{unlock}} \text{S-UNLOCK}$$

Table 8. Global transitions

$$\frac{C \vdash \varphi \xrightarrow{p.\text{lock}}_{\sqsubseteq} \varphi' \quad \hat{\sigma}'(\rho,p) = \hat{\sigma}(\rho,p)+1}{C;\hat{\sigma} \vdash p\langle\varphi\rangle \xrightarrow{p\langle p.\text{lock}\rangle}_{\sqsubseteq} C;\hat{\sigma}' \vdash p\langle\varphi'\rangle} \text{ RE-LOCK} \qquad \frac{C \vdash \varphi \xrightarrow{\text{spawn}(\varphi'')}_{\sqsubseteq} \varphi'}{C;\hat{\sigma} \vdash p_1\langle\varphi\rangle \xrightarrow{p_1\langle\text{spawn}(\varphi'')\rangle}_{\sqsubseteq} C;\hat{\sigma} \vdash p_1\langle\varphi'\rangle \parallel p_2\langle\varphi''\rangle} \text{ RE-SPAWN}$$

$$\frac{C \vdash \varphi \xrightarrow{p.\text{unlock}}_{\sqsubseteq} \varphi' \quad \hat{\sigma}(\rho,p) \geq 1 \quad \hat{\sigma}'(\rho,p) = \hat{\sigma}(\rho,p)-1}{C;\hat{\sigma} \vdash p\langle\varphi\rangle \xrightarrow{p\langle p.\text{unlock}\rangle}_{\sqsubseteq} C;\hat{\sigma}' \vdash p\langle\varphi'\rangle} \text{ RE-UNLOCK} \qquad \frac{C;\hat{\sigma} \vdash \Phi_1 \xrightarrow{a}_{\sqsubseteq} C;\hat{\sigma}' \vdash \Phi_1'}{C;\hat{\sigma} \vdash \Phi_1 \parallel \Phi_2 \xrightarrow{a}_{\sqsubseteq} C;\hat{\sigma}' \vdash \Phi_1' \parallel \Phi_2} \text{ RE-PAR}$$

3.4 Soundness

A crucial part for soundness of the algorithm wrt. the semantics is preservation of well-typedness under reduction. This includes to check that the operational semantics of the program is over-approximated by the effect given by the type system captured by a simulation relation; in our setting, this relation has to be sensitive to deadlocks. Defining the simulation relation requires to relate concrete heaps with abstract ones where concrete locks are summarized by their point of creation.

Definition 8 (Wait-sensitive heap abstraction). *Given a concrete and an abstract heap σ_1 and $\hat{\sigma}_2$, and a mapping θ from the lock references of σ_1 to the abstract locks of $\hat{\sigma}_2$, $\hat{\sigma}_2$ is a wait-sensitive heap abstraction of σ_1 wrt. θ, written $\sigma_1 \leq_\theta \hat{\sigma}_2$, if $\sum_{l \in \{l' \mid \theta l' = \rho\}} \sigma_1(l,p) \leq \hat{\sigma}_2(\rho,p)$, for all p and ρ. The definition is used analogously for comparing two abstract heaps. In the special case of mapping between the concrete and an abstract heap, we write $\equiv_\theta$ if the sum of the counters of the concrete locks coincides with the count of the abstract lock.*

Definition 9 (Deadlock sensitive simulation $\lesssim_{\sqsubseteq}^D$). *Assume a heap-mapping θ and a corresponding wait-sensitive abstraction $\leq_\theta$. A binary relation R between configurations is a deadlock sensitive simulation relation (or just simulation for short) if the following holds. Assume $C_1;\hat{\sigma}_1 \vdash \Phi_1 R C_2;\hat{\sigma}_2 \vdash \Phi_2$ with $\hat{\sigma}_1 \leq_\theta \hat{\sigma}_2$. Then:*

1. *If $C_1;\hat{\sigma}_1 \vdash \Phi_1 \xrightarrow{p\langle a\rangle}_{\sqsubseteq} C_1;\hat{\sigma}_1' \vdash \Phi_1'$, then $C_2;\hat{\sigma}_2 \vdash \Phi_2 \xrightarrow{p\langle a\rangle}_{\sqsubseteq} C_2;\hat{\sigma}_2' \vdash \Phi_2'$ for some $C_2;\hat{\sigma}_2' \vdash \Phi_2'$ with $\hat{\sigma}_1' \leq_\theta \hat{\sigma}_2'$ and $C_1;\hat{\sigma}_1' \vdash \Phi_1' R C_2;\hat{\sigma}_2' \vdash \Phi_2'$.*
2. *If $\text{waits}_{\sqsubseteq}((C_1;\hat{\sigma}_1 \vdash \Phi_1),p,\rho)$, then $\text{waits}_{\sqsubseteq}((C_2;\hat{\sigma}_2 \vdash \Phi_2),p,\theta(\rho))$.*

Configuration $C_1;\hat{\sigma}_1 \vdash \Phi_1$ is simulated by $C_2;\hat{\sigma}_2 \vdash \Phi_2$ (written $C_1;\hat{\sigma}_1 \vdash \Phi_1 \lesssim_{\sqsubseteq}^D C_2;\hat{\sigma}_2 \vdash \Phi_2$), if there exists a deadlock sensitive simulation s.t. $C_1;\hat{\sigma}_1 \vdash \Phi_1 R C_2;\hat{\sigma}_2 \vdash \Phi_2$.

The definition is used analogously for simulations between program and effect configurations, i.e., for $\sigma_1 \vdash P \lesssim_{\sqsubseteq}^D C;\hat{\sigma}_2 \vdash \Phi$. In that case, the transition relation $\xrightarrow{p\langle a\rangle}_{\sqsubseteq}$ is replaced by $\xrightarrow{p\langle a\rangle}$ for the program configurations.

The notation $\xRightarrow{p\langle a\rangle}$ is used for weak transitions, defined as $\xrightarrow{p\langle \tau\rangle}{}^* \xrightarrow{p\langle a\rangle}$. This relation captures the internal steps which are ignored when relating two transition systems by simulation. It is obvious that the binary relation $\lesssim_{\sqsubseteq}^D$ is itself a deadlock simulation. The relation is transitive and reflexive. Thus, if $C_1;\hat{\sigma}_1 \vdash \Phi_1 \lesssim_{\sqsubseteq}^D C_2;\hat{\sigma}_2 \vdash \Phi_2$, the property of

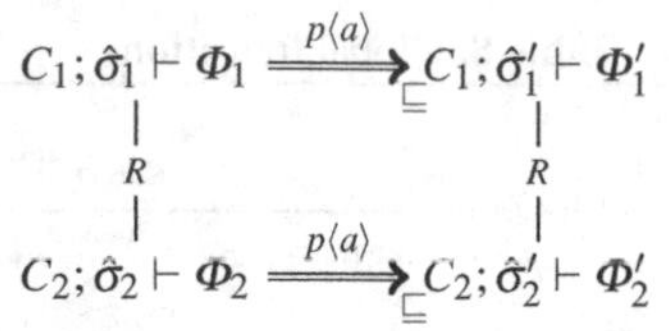

$$C_1; \hat{\sigma}_1 \vdash \Phi_1 \xrightarrow{\ p\langle a\rangle\ }_{\sqsubseteq} C_1; \hat{\sigma}'_1 \vdash \Phi'_1$$

$$\begin{array}{ccc} | & & | \\ R & & R \\ | & & | \end{array}$$

$$C_2; \hat{\sigma}_2 \vdash \Phi_2 \xrightarrow{\ p\langle a\rangle\ }_{\sqsubseteq} C_2; \hat{\sigma}'_2 \vdash \Phi'_2$$

Fig. 2. Deadlock sensitive simulation $\lesssim^D_\sqsubseteq$

deadlock freedom is straightforwardly carried over from the more abstract behaviour to the concrete one (cf. Lemma 1).

Lemma 1 (Preservation of deadlock freedom). *Assume* $C_1; \hat{\sigma}_1 \vdash \Phi_1 \lesssim^D_\sqsubseteq C_2; \hat{\sigma}_2 \vdash \Phi_2$. *If* $C_2; \hat{\sigma}_2 \vdash \Phi_2$ *is deadlock free, then so is* $C_1; \hat{\sigma}_1 \vdash \Phi_1$.

The next lemma shows compositionality of $\lesssim^D_\sqsubseteq$ wrt. parallel composition.

Lemma 2 (Compositionality). *Assume* $C; \hat{\sigma}_1 \vdash p\langle \varphi_1\rangle \lesssim^D_\sqsubseteq C; \hat{\sigma}_2 \vdash p\langle \varphi_2\rangle$, *then* $C; \hat{\sigma}_1 \vdash \Phi \parallel p\langle \varphi_1\rangle \lesssim^D_\sqsubseteq C; \hat{\sigma}_2 \vdash \Phi \parallel p\langle \varphi_2\rangle$.

The soundness proof for the algorithmic type and effect inference is formulated as a *subject reduction* result such that it captures the deadlock-sensitive simulation. The part for the preservation of typing under substitution is fairly standard and therefore omitted here. For the effects, the system derives the formal behavioural description for a program's future behaviour; one hence cannot expect the effect being preserved by reduction. Thus, we relate the behaviour of the program and the behaviour of the effects via a deadlock-sensitive simulation relation.

Lemma 3 (Subject reduction). *Let* $\Gamma \vdash p\langle t\rangle :: p\langle \varphi; C\rangle$, $\sigma_1 \equiv_{\hat{\theta}} \hat{\sigma}_2$, *and* $\theta \models C$.

1. $\sigma_1 \vdash p\langle t\rangle \xrightarrow{p\langle \tau\rangle} \sigma'_1 \vdash p\langle t'\rangle$, *then* $\Gamma \vdash p\langle t'\rangle :: p\langle \varphi'; C'\rangle$ *with* $C \vdash \theta'C'$ *for some* θ', *and furthermore* $C \vdash \varphi \sqsupseteq \theta'\varphi'$, *and* $\sigma'_1 \equiv_{\hat{\theta}} \hat{\sigma}_2$.

2. (a) $\sigma_1 \vdash p\langle t\rangle \xrightarrow{p\langle a\rangle} \sigma'_1 \vdash p\langle t'\rangle$ *where* $a \neq$ spawn φ'', *then* $C; \hat{\sigma}_2 \vdash p\langle \varphi\rangle \xrightarrow{p\langle a\rangle}_{\sqsubseteq} C; \hat{\sigma}'_2 \vdash p\langle \varphi'\rangle$, $\Gamma \vdash p\langle t'\rangle :: p\langle \varphi''; C'\rangle$ *with* $C \vdash \theta'C'$, *furthermore* $C \vdash \varphi' \sqsupseteq \theta'\varphi''$ *and* $\sigma'_1 \equiv_{\hat{\theta}} \hat{\sigma}'_2$.

   (b) $\sigma_1 \vdash p\langle t\rangle \xrightarrow{p\langle a\rangle} \sigma_1 \vdash p\langle t''\rangle \parallel p'\langle t'\rangle$ *where* $a =$ spawn φ', *then* $C; \hat{\sigma}_2 \vdash p\langle \varphi\rangle \xrightarrow{p\langle a\rangle}_{\sqsubseteq} C; \hat{\sigma}_2 \vdash p\langle \varphi''\rangle \parallel p'\langle \varphi'\rangle$ *and such that* $\Gamma \vdash p\langle t''\rangle :: p\langle \varphi'''; C''\rangle$ *with* $C \vdash \theta''C''$ *and* $C \vdash \varphi'' \sqsupseteq \theta''\varphi'''$, *and furthermore* $\Gamma \vdash p'\langle t'\rangle :: p'\langle \varphi''''; C'\rangle$ *with* $C \vdash \theta'C'$ *and* $C \vdash \varphi' \sqsupseteq \theta'\varphi''''$.

3. *If* $waits(\sigma_1 \vdash p\langle t\rangle, p, l)$, *then* $waits_\sqsubseteq(C; \hat{\sigma}_2 \vdash p\langle \varphi\rangle, p, \hat{\theta}l)$.

The well-typedness relation between a program and its effect straightforwardly implies a deadlock-preserving simulation:

Corollary 1. *Given* $\sigma_1 \equiv_\theta \hat{\sigma}_2$ *and* $\Gamma \vdash p\langle t\rangle :: p\langle \varphi; C\rangle$, *then* $\sigma_1 \vdash p\langle t\rangle \lesssim^D_\sqsubseteq C; \hat{\sigma}_2 \vdash p\langle \varphi\rangle$.

4 Conclusion

We have presented a constraint-based type and effect inference algorithm for deadlock checking. It infers a behavioural description of a thread's behaviour concerning its lock interactions which then is used to explore the abstract state space to detect potential deadlocks. The static analysis is developed for a concurrent calculus with higher-order functions and dynamic lock creation. Covering lock creation by an appropriate abstraction extends our earlier work [13] for deadlock detection using behaviour abstraction. Another important extension of that work is to enhance the precision by making the analysis context-sensitive and furthermore to support effect inference ([13] in contrast required the programmer to provide the behaviour annotations manually). The analysis is shown sound, i.e., the abstraction preserves deadlocks of the program. Formally that is captured by an appropriate notion of simulation ("deadlock-sensitive simulation").

Related work. Deadlocks are a well-known problem in concurrent programming and a vast number of techniques for statically and dynamically detecting deadlocks have been investigated. One common way to prevent deadlocks is to arrange locks in a certain partial order such that no cyclic wait on locks/resources, which is one of the four necessary conditions for deadlocks [4], can occur. For instance, Boyapati et al. [3] prevent deadlocks by introducing deadlock types and imposing an order among these. The paper also covers type inference and polymorphism wrt. the lock levels. Likewise, the type inference algorithms by Suenaga [15] and Vasconcelos et al. [17] assure deadlock freedom in a well-typed program with a strict partial order on lock acquisition. In contrast, our approach will certify two processes as safe if they take locks in orders 1-2-3 and 1-3-2, even though no fixed global order exists. Agarwal et al. [1] use above deadlock types to improve the efficiency for run-time checking with a static type system, by introducing runtime checks only for those locks where the inferred deadlock type indicates potential for deadlocks. Similar to our approach, Naik et al. [12] detect potential deadlocks with a model-checking approach by abstracting threads and locks by their allocation sites. The approach is neither sound nor complete. Kobayashi [10] presents a constraint-based type inference algorithm for detecting communication deadlocks in the π-calculus. In contrast to our system, he attaches abstract usage information onto channels, not processes. Cyclic dependencies there indicate potential deadlocks. Further differences are that channel-based communication does not have to consider reentrance, and the lack of functions avoids having to consider polymorphism and higher order. Instead of checking for deadlocks, the approach by Kidd et al. [9] generates an abstraction of a program to check for data races in concurrent Java programs, by abstracting unlimited number of Java objects into a finite set of abstract ones whose locks are binary.

Future work. As mentioned, there are four principal sources of infinity in the state-space obtained by the effect inference system. For the unboundedness of dynamic lock creation, we presented an appropriate sound abstraction. We expect that the techniques for dealing with the unboundedness of lock counters and of the call stack can be straightforwardly carried over from the non-context-sensitive setting of [13], as sketched in Section 1.2. All mentioned abstractions are compatible with our notion of deadlock-sensitive simulation in that being more abstract —identifying more locks, choosing a smaller bound on the lock counters or on the allowed stack depth— leads to a larger behaviour wrt. our notion of simulation. This allows an incremental approach, starting from a coarse-grained abstraction, which may be refined in case of spurious deadlocks. To find sound abstractions for process creation as the last source of infinity seems more challenging and a naive approach by simply summarizing processes by their point of creation is certainly not enough. We have developed a prototype implementation of the state-exploration part in the monomorphic setting of [13]. We plan to adapt the implementation to the more general setting and to extend it with implementing type inference.

For lack of space, all proofs have been omitted here. Further details can found in an extended version of this work (cf. the technical report [14]).

References

1. Agarwal, R., Wang, L., Stoller, S.D.: Detecting potential deadlocks with static analysis and run-time monitoring. In: Ur, S., Bin, E., Wolfsthal, Y. (eds.) Haifa Verification Conf. 2005. LNCS, vol. 3875, pp. 191–207. Springer, Heidelberg (2006)
2. Amtoft, T., Nielson, H.R., Nielson, F.: Type and Effect Systems: Behaviours for Concurrency. Imperial College Press (1999)
3. Boyapati, C., Lee, R., Rinard, M.: Ownership types for safe programming: Preventing data races and deadlocks. In: OOPSLA 2002, Seattle, USA. ACM (2002); SIGPLAN Notices
4. Coffman Jr., E.G., Elphick, M., Shoshani, A.: System deadlocks. Computing Surveys 3(2) (1971)
5. Damas, L.: Type Assignment in Programming Languages. PhD thesis, Laboratory for Foundations of Computer Science, University of Edinburgh, CST-33-85 (1985)
6. Damas, L., Milner, R.: Principal type-schemes for functional programming languages. In: Ninth POPL, Albuquerque, NM. ACM (1982)
7. Dijkstra, E.W.: Cooperating sequential processes. Technical Report EWD-123, TU Eindhoven (1965)
8. Hindley, J.R.: The principal type-scheme of an object in combinatory logic. Transactions of the AMS 146 (1969)
9. Kidd, N., Reps, T.W., Dolby, J., Vaziri, M.: Finding concurrency-related bugs using random isolation. STTT 13(6) (2011)
10. Kobayashi, N.: A new type system for deadlock-free processes. In: Baier, C., Hermanns, H. (eds.) CONCUR 2006. LNCS, vol. 4137, pp. 233–247. Springer, Heidelberg (2006)
11. Mossin, C.: Flow Analysis of Typed Higher-Order Programs. PhD thesis, DIKU, University of Copenhagen, Denmark. Technical Report DIKU-TR-97/1 (1997)
12. Naik, M., Park, C.-S., Sen, K., Gay, D.: Effective static deadlock detection. In: 31st International Conference on Software Engineering (ICSE 2009). IEEE (2009)
13. Pun, K.I., Steffen, M., Stolz, V.: Deadlock checking by a behavioral effect system for lock handling. J. of Logic and Algebraic Programming 81(3) (2012)
14. Pun, K.I., Steffen, M., Stolz, V.: Lock-polymorphic behaviour inference for deadlock checking. Tech. report 436, UiO, IFI (2013) (submitted for Journal Publication)
15. Suenaga, K.: Type-based deadlock-freedom verification for non-block-structured lock primitives and mutable references. In: Ramalingam, G. (ed.) APLAS 2008. LNCS, vol. 5356, pp. 155–170. Springer, Heidelberg (2008)
16. Talpin, J.-P., Jouvelot, P.: Polymorphic Type, Region and Effect Inference. J. of Functional Programming 2(3) (1992)
17. Vasconcelos, V., Martins, F., Cogumbreiro, T.: Type inference for deadlock detection in a multithreaded polymorphic typed assembly language. In: PLACES 2009. EPTCS, vol. 17 (2009)

Synthesizing Parameterized Unit Tests
to Detect Object Invariant Violations

Maria Christakis, Peter Müller, and Valentin Wüstholz

Department of Computer Science,
ETH Zurich, Switzerland
{maria.christakis,peter.mueller,valentin.wuestholz}@inf.ethz.ch

Abstract. Automatic test case generation techniques rely on a description of the input data that the unit under test is intended to handle. For heap data structures, such a description is typically expressed as some form of object invariant. If a program may create structures that violate the invariant, the test data generated using the invariant systematically ignores possible inputs and, thus, potentially misses bugs. In this paper, we present a technique that detects violations of object invariants. We describe three scenarios in which traditional invariant checking may miss such violations. Based on templates that capture these scenarios, we synthesize parameterized unit tests that are likely to violate invariants, and use dynamic symbolic execution to generate inputs to the synthesized tests. We have implemented our technique as an extension to Pex and detected a significant number of invariant violations in real applications.

1 Introduction

Automatic test case generation techniques, such as random testing or symbolic execution, rely on a description of the input data that the unit under test (UUT) is intended to handle. Such a description acts as a filter for undesirable input data. It is usually expressed as code in the test driver or as a method precondition that specifies the valid arguments for the method under test. When the inputs are heap data structures, some test case generators use predicates that express which instances of a data structure are considered valid. In an object-oriented setting, these predicates are often called *class* or *object invariants*.

Invariants may be provided by the programmer in the form of contracts, such as in the random testing tool AutoTest [11] for Eiffel and in the dynamic symbolic execution tool Pex [19] for .NET, or by the tester, like in the Korat [1] tool for Java, which exhaustively enumerates data structures that satisfy a given predicate up to a bound. Invariants may also be inferred by tools like the Daikon invariant detector [4], which is used by the symbolic execution tool Symbolic Java PathFinder [15] for obtaining input constraints on a UUT.

Using object invariants to generate test data requires the invariants to accurately describe the data structures a program may create. When an invariant is too weak, i.e., admits more data structures than the program may create, the test case generator may *produce undesirable* inputs, which are however easily detected when inspecting failing tests. A more severe problem occurs when an invariant is too strong,

D. Giannakopoulou and G. Salaün (Eds.): SEFM 2014, LNCS 8702, pp. 65–80, 2014.
© Springer International Publishing Switzerland 2014

i.e., admits only a subset of the data structures the program might actually create. The test case generator may then *not produce desirable* inputs since they are filtered out due to the overly strong invariant. Consequently, the UUT is executed with a restricted set of inputs, which potentially fail to exercise certain execution paths and may miss bugs. Too strong invariants occur, for instance, when programmers specify invariants they intend to maintain but fail to do so due to a bug, when they fail to capture all intended program behaviors in the invariant, or when invariants are inferred from program runs that do not exercise all relevant paths. Therefore, it is essential that invariants are not only used to filter test inputs but are also *checked* as part of test oracles. However, checking object invariants is very difficult as shown by work on program verification [3,12]. In particular, it is generally not sufficient to check at the end of each method that the invariant of its receiver is maintained. This traditional approach [10], which is for instance implemented in Pex and AutoTest, may miss invariant violations when programs use common idioms such as direct field updates, inheritance, or aggregate structures (see Sect. 2).

To address this issue, we propose a technique for detecting previously missed invariant violations by synthesizing parameterized unit tests (PUTs) [20] that are likely to create *broken objects*, i.e., class instances that do not satisfy their invariants. The synthesis is based on templates that capture the situations in which traditional invariant checking is insufficient. We use dynamic symbolic execution (DSE) [7], also called concolic testing [16], to find inputs to the synthesized PUTs that actually violate an invariant.

Whenever our approach detects an invariant violation, the programmer has to inspect the situation to decide which of the following three cases applies: (1) The object invariant is stronger than intended. In this case, one should weaken the invariant. (2) The invariant expresses the intended properties, but the program does not maintain it. This case constitutes a bug that should be fixed. (3) The invariant expresses the intended properties and can, in principle, be violated by clients of the class, but the entire program does not exhibit such violations. For instance, the class might provide a setter that violates an invariant when called with a negative argument, but the program does not contain such a call. In such cases, one should nevertheless adapt the implementation of the class to make the invariant robust against violations for future program changes during maintenance and for other clients of the class during code reuse.

The contributions of this paper are as follows:

- It identifies an important limitation of current test case generation approaches in the treatment of object invariants. In particular, existing approaches that use invariants as filters on input data do not sufficiently check them, if at all.
- It presents a technique that detects invariant violations by synthesizing PUTs based on templates and exploring them via DSE.
- It demonstrates the effectiveness of this technique by implementing it as an extension to Pex and using it on a suite of open source C# applications.

Outline. Sect. 2 illustrates the situations in which the traditional checks for object invariants are insufficient. Sect. 3 gives an overview of our approach.

Sect. 4 explains how we select the operations to be applied in a synthesized test, and Sect. 5 describes the templates used for the synthesis. We discuss our implementation in Sect. 6 and present the experimental evaluation in Sect. 7. We review related work in Sect. 8 and conclude in Sect. 9.

2   Violating Object Invariants

We present three scenarios in which the traditional approach of checking at the end of each method whether it maintains the invariant of its receiver is insufficient. These scenarios have been identified by work on formal verification and together with a fourth scenario—callbacks, which are not relevant here as explained in Sect. 8—have been shown to cover *all* cases in which traditional invariant checking does not suffice [3]. We assume that invariants are specified explicitly in the code as contracts. However, our technique applies equally to predicates that are provided as separate input to the test case generator or invariants that have been inferred from program runs.

```
1 public class Person {
2     Account account;
3     public int salary;
4
5     inv 0 < account.balance + salary;
6
7     public void Spend1(int amount) {
8         account.Withdraw(amount);
9     }
10
11     public void Spend2(int amount) {
12         account.balance -= amount;
13     }
14 }
15
16 public class Account {
17     public int balance;
18
19     public void Withdraw(int amount) {
20         balance -= amount;
21     }
22 }
23
24 public class SavingsAccount : Account {
25     inv 0 <= balance;
26 }
```

Fig. 1. A C# example on invariant violations. We declare invariants using a special **inv** keyword and assume that fields hold non-null values.

We illustrate the scenarios using the C# example in Fig. 1. For simplicity, we assume that all fields hold non-null values. A **Person** holds an **Account** and has a **salary**. An **Account** has a **balance**. **Person**'s invariant (line 5) requires that the sum of the **account**'s **balance** and the person's **salary** is positive. A **SavingsAccount** is a special **Account** whose **balance** is non-negative (line 25). In each of the following scenarios, we consider an object p of class **Person** that holds an **Account** a.

Direct field updates: In most object-oriented languages, such as C++, C#, and Java, a method may update not only fields of its receiver but of any object as long as the fields are accessible. For instance, method **Spend2** (which is an alternative implementation of **Spend1**) subtracts **amount** from the **account**'s **balance** through a direct field update instead of calling method **Withdraw**. Such direct field updates are common among objects of the same class (say, nodes of a list) or of closely connected classes (say, a collection and its iterator). If a is a **SavingsAccount**, method **Spend2** might violate a's invariant by setting **balance** to a negative value. A check of the receiver's invariant at the end of method **Spend2** (here, **Person** object p) does not reveal this violation. In order to detect violations through direct field updates, one would have to check the invariants of all objects whose fields are assigned to directly. However, these objects are not statically known (for instance, when the direct field update occurs within a loop), which makes it difficult to impose such checks.

Subclassing: Subclasses may restrict the possible values of a field inherited from a superclass, i.e., they strengthen the invariant for this field, as shown by class `SavingsAccount`. Methods declared in the superclass are typically designed for and tested with instances of the superclass as their receiver, and thus the tests check only the weaker superclass invariant. When such methods are inherited by the subclass and called on subclass instances, they may violate the stronger subclass invariant. In our example, in case a is a `SavingsAccount`, calling the inherited method `Withdraw` on a might set `balance` to a negative value and violate the invariant of the subclass. To detect such violations, one would have to re-test every inherited method whenever a new subclass is declared. Moreover, subclassing makes the invariant checks for direct field updates even more difficult because one would have to consider all subclasses for the objects whose fields are updated. For instance, when introducing `SavingsAccount`, testing `Withdraw` on a subclass instance is not sufficient; one has to also re-test method `Spend2` to detect the invariant violation described in the previous scenario.

Multi-object invariants: Most data structures are implemented as aggregations of several objects. For such aggregate structures, it is common that an object invariant constrains and relates the states of several objects. In our example, the invariant of class `Person` relates the state of a `Person` object to the state of its `Account`. For such *multi-object invariants*, modifying the state of one object might break the invariant of another. For instance, when `Account` a executes method `Withdraw`, it might reduce the `balance` by an amount such that it violates the invariant of `Person` p. To detect such violations, one would have to check the invariants of all objects that potentially reference a, e.g., the invariants of `Person` objects sharing the account, of collections storing the account, etc. These objects are not statically known and cannot even be approximated without inspecting the entire program, which defeats the purpose of unit testing.

These scenarios demonstrate that the traditional way of checking object invariants may miss violations in common situations and that the checks cannot be strengthened in any practical way. Therefore, simply including all necessary invariant checks in the test oracle is not feasible; other techniques are required to detect invariant violations.

3   Approach

For a given UUT we synthesize client code in the form of PUTs to detect invariant violations. The synthesis is based on a set of four fixed templates that capture the three scenarios of Sect. 2. Each template consists of a sequence of *candidate operations*, i.e., updates of public fields and calls to public methods. These operations are applied to the object whose invariant is under test or, in the case of aggregate structures, its sub-objects. (Note that since our approach synthesizes client code, it uses public candidate operations. To also synthesize code of possible subclasses, one would analogously include protected fields and methods.) The candidate operations are selected conservatively from the UUT based on whether they potentially lead to a violation of the object invariant. Depending on the template, additional restrictions are imposed on the candidate operations, e.g., that they are inherited from a superclass. By instantiating the templates with candidate operations, the synthesized PUTs become snippets of client code that potentially violate the object invariant.

Alg. 1 shows the general strategy for the PUT synthesis. Function SYNTHESIZE takes the class of the object to which candidate operations should be applied (*class*), the object

---

Alg. 1. Synthesis of parameterized unit tests.

```
1  function SYNTHESIZE(class, inv, len)
2      candOps ← COMPUTECANDOPS(class, inv)
3      puts ← GENFIELDCOMBS(candOps, len)
4      puts ← puts + GENMULTICOMBS(candOps, len, inv)
5      puts ← puts + GENSUBCOMBS(candOps, len)
6      puts ← puts + GENALLCOMBS(candOps, len)
7      return ADDSPECS(puts)
```

---

invariant under test (*inv*), and the desired length of the PUTs to be synthesized (*len*). The last argument prevents a combinatorial explosion by bounding the number of operations in each synthesized PUT. SYNTHESIZE returns a list of PUTs. Each PUT consists of a sequence of candidate operations and additional specifications, such as invariant checks, which are inserted by ADDSPECS and explained in Sect. 4. The algorithm first determines the set of candidate operations (*candOps*) of *class* that could potentially violate the object invariant *inv*. It then synthesizes the PUTs for each of the three scenarios using the corresponding templates. We discuss the selection of candidate operations as well as these templates in detail in the next sections.

We complement the templates, which cover specific scenarios for violating invariants, by an *exhaustive enumeration* of combinations (of length *len*) of candidate operations. In the algorithm, these combinations are computed by function GENALLCOMBS. As we will see in Sect. 5, this exhaustive exploration is useful for multi-object invariants where the actual violation may happen by calling a method on a sub-object of an aggregate structure.

For a given UUT, we apply function SYNTHESIZE for each class in the unit and the invariant it declares or inherits. We perform this application repeatedly for increasing values of *len*. All operations in the resulting PUTs have arguments that are either parameters of the enclosing PUT or results of preceding operations; all such combinations are tried exhaustively, which, in particular, includes aliasing among the arguments. This makes the PUTs sufficiently general to capture the scenarios of the previous section, i.e., to detect invariant violations caused by these scenarios. We employ dynamic symbolic execution (DSE) [7,16] to supply the arguments to the PUTs.

4   Candidate Operations

To synthesize client code that violates object invariants, we select candidate operations from the public fields and methods of the UUT. To reduce the number of synthesized PUTs, we restrict the operations to those that might violate a given invariant. Such operations are determined by intersecting the read effect of the invariant with the write effect of the operation. The *read effect* of an invariant is the set of fields read in the invariant. If the invariant contains calls to side-effect free methods, the fields (transitively) read by these methods are also in its read effect. The *write effect* of a method is the set of fields updated during an execution of the method including updates performed through method calls. The write effect of a field update is the field itself. Note that the effects are sets of (fully-qualified) field names, not concrete instance fields of objects. This allows us to use a simple, whole-program static analysis that conservatively approximates read and write effects without requiring alias information (see Sect. 6).

To illustrate these concepts, consider the example on the right. The read effect of the invariant is {C.x} indicating that only the value of C's field x determines whether the invariant holds. The write effect of an update to the public field x

```
public class C {
  public int x;
  int y;

  inv x == 42;

  public void SetX() { x = y; }

  public void SetY(int v) { y = v; }
}
```

and of method SetX is {C.x}, while method SetY has write effect {C.y}. By intersecting these read and write effects, we determine that field updates of x and calls to SetX must be included in the candidate operations.

With these operations, the exhaustive enumeration of sequences of length 1 (function GENALLCOMBS in Alg. 1) produces the two PUTs on the right (PUT_0, PUT_1). As shown here, each synthesized test expects as argument a non-null ob-

```
void PUT_0(C o, int v) {
  assume o != null && o.Invariant();
  o.x = v;
  assert o.Invariant();
}
void PUT_1(C o) {
  assume o != null && o.Invariant();
  o.SetX();
  assert o.Invariant();
}
```

ject o whose invariant holds, applies the synthesized sequence of candidate operations to o, and then asserts that o's invariant still holds. We encode the invariant via a side-effect free boolean method Invariant and use assume statements to introduce constraints for the symbolic execution. The assume and assert statements are inserted into the PUTs by function ADDSPECS of Alg. 1. The input object o is constructed using operations from the UUT, for instance, a suitable constructor. As explained above, the arguments of candidate operations (like the value v for the assignment to o.x in the first test) are either parameters of the PUT and supplied later via DSE, or results of preceding operations.

Whether a method call violates an invariant may not only depend on its arguments but also on the state in which it is called. For instance, a call to SetX violates the invariant only if y has a value different from 42. Therefore, tests that apply more than one candidate operation must take into account the possible interactions between operations. Consequently, for each candidate operation op_d that might directly violate a given object invariant, we compute its read effect and include in the set of candidate operations each operation op_i whose write effect overlaps with this read effect and might, therefore, indirectly violate the invariant. To prune the search space, we record that op_i should be executed before op_d. This process iterates until a fixed point is reached.

In our example, method `SetX` has read effect {C.y}. As a result, method `SetY` is used in the PUTs as a candidate operation that should be called before `SetX`. Therefore, the exhaustive enumeration of

```
void PUT_2(C o, int v) {
  assume o != null && o.Invariant();
  o.SetY(v);
  assume o.Invariant();
  o.SetX();
  assert o.Invariant();
}
```

sequences of length 2 includes the PUT above (PUT_2). Note that, by assuming o's invariant before the call to `SetX`, we suppress execution paths that have already been tested in a shorter PUT, i.e., paths that violate o's invariant before reaching the final operation.

5   Synthesis Templates

We now present the templates that capture the three scenarios of Sect. 2. Besides other arguments, each template expects an object r to which candidate operations are applied, and an object o whose invariant is under test. When the templates are used to synthesize an entire test, these two objects coincide and we include only one of them in the PUT. The templates are also used to synthesize portions of larger PUTs, and then r and o may refer to different objects.

5.1   Direct Field Updates

The direct-field-update template tries to violate the invariant of an object o by assigning to a field of r (or to an element of r when r is an array). The template has the form shown on the right. It ap-

```
void DFU(r, o, a0..aN) {
  assume r != null;
  assume o != null && o.Invariant();
  Op0(r, ...); ... OpM(r, ...);
  assume o.Invariant();
  r.f = v;
  assert o.Invariant();
}
```

plies a sequence of operations (Op0 to OpM) to r to create a state in which the subsequent update of r.f may violate o's invariant. For instance, if the invariant relates f to private fields of the same object, these operations may be method calls that update these private fields. The operations Op0 to OpM are selected from the set of candidate operations and may include a method call or field update more than once. Their arguments as well as the right-hand side v of the last field update are either parameters of the template (a0 to aN) or results of preceding operations; all such combinations are tried exhaustively.

The synthesis of PUTs from this template is performed by function GENFIELDCOMBS in Alg. 2, which is invoked from Alg. 1. Line 3 generates all possible sequences of length *len* − 1 from the set of candidate operations. Line 4 selects the set *fieldOps* of all field updates from

Alg. 2. Synthesis of parameterized unit tests from the direct-field-update template.

```
1  function GENFIELDCOMBS(candOps, len)
2    puts ← []
3    combs ← GENALLCOMBS(candOps, len − 1)
4    fieldOps ← FIELDOPS(candOps)
5    foreach comb in combs
6      foreach fieldOp in fieldOps
7        puts ← puts + [comb + [fieldOp]]
8    return puts
```

the set of candidate operations, *candOps*. Lines 5–7 append each field update *fieldOp* to each of the sequences of operations computed earlier.

Consider an invocation of the synthesis with this template, where the object to which operations are applied and the object whose invariant is being tested are the same instance of class

```
void PUT_DFU(Person o, int a, int s) {
  assume o != null && o.Invariant();
  o.Spend1(a);
  assume o.Invariant();
  o.salary = s;
  assert o.Invariant();
}
```

Person from Fig. 1. The synthesized PUTs of length 2 include the test above (PUT_DFU). Symbolically executing this PUT produces input data that causes the assertion of the invariant to fail; for instance, a Person object with salary 100 and whose Account has balance 100 for o, the value 150 for a, and any value less than or equal to 50 for s.

5.2 Subclassing

The template for the subclassing scenario (on the right) aims at breaking the invariant of an object by invoking inherited operations. It exhaustively applies a number of operations to an object of the

```
void S(r, o, a0..aN) {
  assume r != null;
  assume o != null && o.Invariant();
  Op0(r, ...); ... OpM(r, ...);
  assume o.Invariant();
  Op_super(r, ...);
  assert o.Invariant();
}
```

subclass, including any operations inherited from a superclass, and requires that the last operation is an inherited one (i.e., an update of an inherited field or a call to an inherited method) to reflect the subclassing scenario described in Sect. 2. Like in the template for direct field updates, the first $M + 1$ operations (Op0 to OpM) construct a state in which the final inherited operation may violate o's invariant as this operation was designed to maintain the weaker invariant of a superclass. This template is useful only when a subclass strengthens the invariant of a superclass with respect to any inherited fields. We identify such subclasses using a simple syntactic check: if the read effect of the invariant declared in the subclass includes inherited fields, we conservatively assume that the invariant is strengthened with respect to those.

The synthesis of PUTs based on this template is performed by function GENSUBCOMBS, which is invoked from Alg. 1. GENSUBCOMBS is analogous to

```
void PUT_S(SavingsAccount o, int a) {
  assume o != null && o.Invariant();
  o.Withdraw(a);
  assert o.Invariant();
}
```

GENFIELDCOMBS (Alg. 2) except that on line 4 it selects the candidate operations that are inherited from a superclass. Consider an invocation of the synthesis with this template, where the object to which operations are applied and the object whose invariant is being tested are the same instance of class SavingsAccount from Fig. 1. This class strengthens the invariant of its superclass Account for the inherited field balance. The synthesized PUTs of length 1 include the test above (PUT_S). The symbolic execution of this PUT produces input data that causes the assertion of the invariant to fail; for instance, a SavingsAccount object with a balance of 0 for o and any positive value for a.

5.3 Multi-object Invariants

Multi-object invariants describe properties of aggregate structures. The invariant of such a structure may be violated by modifying its sub-objects. For instance, one might be able to violate a **Person**'s invariant by reducing the balance of its account. Such violations are possible when sub-objects of the aggregate structure are not properly encapsulated [12] such that clients are able to obtain references to them: when a client obtains a direct reference to the **Account** sub-object, it can by-pass the **Person** object and modify the account in ways that violate the Person's invariant. To reflect this observation, we use two templates that allow clients to obtain references to sub-objects of aggregate structures. One template uses *leaking*, i.e., it passes a sub-object from the aggregate structure to its client. The other one uses *capturing*, i.e., it passes an object from the client to the aggregate structure and stores it there as a sub-object. Leaking and capturing are the only ways in which clients may obtain a reference to a sub-object of an aggregate structure.

Leaking. A method is said to *leak* an object l if the following three conditions hold: (1) the method takes as an argument (or receiver) an object o that (directly or transitively) references l, (2) the method returns the reference to l or assigns it to shared state, and (3) a field of l is dereferenced in o's invariant. We use a static analysis to approximate the operations that might leak a sub-object (see Sect. 6). These operations include reading public fields with reference types.

For example, assume that class **Person** from Fig. 1 provides a public getter **GetAccount** for field **account**. This method leaks the **account** sub-object of its receiver since (1) its receiver directly references the account, (2) it returns the account, and (3) **account** is dereferenced in the invariant of **Person**. Consequently, this getter enables clients to obtain a reference to the **account** sub-object and violate **Person**'s invariant, for instance by invoking **Withdraw** on the account.

In the template for leaking (on the right), we first apply a number of operations to create a state in which a sub-object l may be leaked via the operation **Op_leaking**. Once the object has been

```
void L(r, o, a0..aN) {
  assume r != null;
  assume o != null && o.Invariant();
  OpO(r, ...); ... OpM(r, ...);
  var l = Op_leaking(r, ...);
  ... // operations on leaked 'l'
  assert o.Invariant();
}
```

leaked, we try to violate o's invariant by applying operations to the leaked object l (indicated by the ellipsis with the corresponding comment in the above template). To obtain a suitable sequence of operations on l, we apply function SYNTHESIZE (Alg. 1) recursively with the class of the leaked object l and the invariant of o. This recursive call selects candidate operations on l that may break o's invariant, for instance by updating a public field of l or via complex combinations of scenarios such as repeated leaking. Note that this template attempts to violate o's invariant; whether l's invariant holds is an orthogonal issue.

Based on this template, we obtain the PUT on the right (PUT_L) for objects of class **Person** from Fig. 1. In this test, method **GetAccount** leaks the **Person**'s account object. The recursive applica-

```
void PUT_L(Person o, int a) {
  assume o != null && o.Invariant();
  var l = o.GetAccount();
  // exhaustive enumeration
  assume l != null && o.Invariant();
  l.Withdraw(a);
  assert o.Invariant();
}
```

tion of function SYNTHESIZE determines method **Withdraw** as a candidate operation because its write effect includes balance, which is also in the read effect of **Person**'s invariant. **Withdraw** is selected by the exhaustive enumeration (function GENALLCOMBS of Alg. 1) and would not be selected by any of the other templates. Symbolically executing this PUT produces input data that causes the assertion of the invariant to fail; for instance, a **Person** object with **salary** 100 and whose **Account** has **balance** 100 for o, and a value of at least 200 for a.

Capturing. A method is said to *capture* an object c if: (1) the method takes as arguments two objects o and c (o or c could also be the receiver), (2) the method stores a reference to c in a location reachable from o, and (3) the field in which c is stored is dereferenced in o's invariant. Updating a field f that has a reference type is also considered capturing if f is dereferenced in o's invariant.

The template for capturing (on the right) is analogous to leaking. In particular, it also uses a recursive application of function SYNTHESIZE to determine the operations to be applied to the captured object. In the common case that the capturing operation is a constructor of object o, the template is adjusted as shown on the right (**Cctor**). This adjustment ensures that o is actually created with a constructor that captures c instead of a

```
void C(r, o, c, a0..aN) {
  assume r != null;
  assume o != null && o.Invariant();
  OpO(r, ...); ... OpM(r, ...);
  Op_capturing(r, c, ...);
  ... // operations on captured 'c'
  assert o.Invariant();
}
void Cctor(c, a0..aN) {
  assume c != null;
  OpO(c, ...); ... OpM(c, ...);
  var o = new ctor(c, ...);
  ... // operations on captured 'c'
  assert o.Invariant();
}
```

constructor selected by the symbolic execution. Note that before the capturing operation we could also allow a number of operations on c with the goal of bringing it to a state such that, for instance, the precondition of **Op_capturing** is satisfied or the capturing execution path is taken. We omit such operations to simplify the presentation.

Synthesis. The synthesis of PUTs based on these templates is performed by the GEN-MULTICOMBS function in Alg. 3. On line 3, a new set of candidate operations, *multiOps*, is created by selecting from *candOps* the operations that leak or capture objects according to the above criteria. Since the

Alg. 3. Synthesis of parameterized unit tests from the leaking and capturing templates.

```
1  function GENMULTICOMBS(candOps, len, inv)
2    puts ← []
3    multiOps ← MULTIOPS(candOps)
4    for i = 0 to len − 2 do
5      prefixes ← GENALLCOMBS(candOps, i)
6      foreach multiOp in multiOps
7        class ← GETCLASS(multiOp)
8        suffixes ← SYNTHESIZE(class, inv, len − 1 − i)
9        foreach prefix in prefixes
10         foreach suffix in suffixes
11           put ← prefix + [multiOp] + suffix
12           puts ← puts + [put]
13   return puts
```

synthesis for these templates includes a recursive application of SYNTHESIZE, we must split the overall length of the PUT between the operations occurring before the leaking or capturing operation and the operations on the leaked or captured object occurring after. To explore all possible splits, we generate all combinations of candidate operations of length up to *len* − 2 to be applied before the leaking or capturing operation (lines 4–5). These operations create a state in which the next operation can leak or capture an object. After invoking any such operation, we recursively apply function SYNTHESIZE of Alg. 1 by taking into account the class of the leaked or captured object (*class*) and the original object invariant under test, *inv* (lines 6 8). Therefore, *suffixes* is a list of sequences of operations to be applied to the leaked or captured object. On lines 9–12, we combine the synthesized sub-sequences of lengths i, 1, and $len - 1 - i$.

6   Implementation

We have implemented our technique as an extension to Pex. Our implementation builds a static call-graph for the entire UUT that includes information about dynamically-bound calls. The call-graph is used to compute the read and write effects of all methods in the UUT with a conservative, inter-procedural, control-flow insensitive static analysis on the .NET bytecode. The effects determine the candidate operations that might, directly or indirectly, lead to an invariant violation (see Sect. 4). Our effect analysis is extended to also approximate the sets of leaking and capturing operations using their read and write effects, respectively, in addition to the read effect of the invariant under test. For simplicity, we only consider leaking operations that return the leaked object or store it in a public field of their receiver.

To detect invariant violations more efficiently, we carefully chose the order in which the synthesis (Alg. 1) applies the templates of Sect. 5 and exhaustive enumeration. The templates for direct field updates and multi-object invariants have proven to most effectively detect invariant violations and are therefore explored first. The exhaustive enumeration comes last as it produces the largest number of PUTs and requires the most effort in the symbolic execution.

7   Experimental Evaluation

We have evaluated the effectiveness of our technique using ten C# applications, which were selected from applications on Bitbucket, CodePlex, and GitHub containing invariants specified with Code Contracts [5]. This section focuses on our experiments with the nine applications for which invariant violations were detected.

Tab. 1 summarizes the results of our experiments. The third and fourth columns show the total number of classes and the number of classes with invariants for each application, respectively. We have tested the robustness of all invariants in these applications. Note that the total number of classes refers only to the classes that were included in the evaluation and not to all classes of each application. We have left out only classes that were defined in dynamic-link libraries (DLLs) containing no object invariants. The two rightmost columns of Tab. 1 show the unique and total numbers of invariant violations detected with our technique. The unique number of violations refers to the number of invariants that were violated at least once. The total number of violations refers to

Table 1. Summary of results. The third and fourth columns show the total number of classes and the number of classes with invariants for each application. The two rightmost columns show the unique and total numbers of invariant violations detected with our technique.

Application	Description	Classes	Classes w/ invariants	Invariant violations unique	total
Boogie	Intermediate verification engine[1]	355	144	21	64
ClueBuddy	GUI application for board game[2]	44	4	1	2
Dafny	Programming language/verifier[3]	310	113	15	53
Draugen	Web application for fishermen[4]	36	5	3	3
GoalsTracker	Various web applications[5]	63	5	1	1
Griffin	.NET and jQuery libraries[6]	31	3	1	1
LoveStudio	IDE for the LÖVE framework[7]	66	7	2	2
Encore	'World of Warcraft' emulator[8]	186	30	1	4
YAML	YAML library[9]	76	6	1	2

the number of distinct PUTs that led to invariant violations and may include violations of the same object invariant multiple times.

When running Pex with our technique, we imposed an upper bound of 3 on the number of operations per PUT, and an upper bound of 300 on the number of synthesized PUTs per object invariant. It turned out that all unique invariant violations were detected already with 2 operations per PUT; increasing the bound to 4 for some projects did not uncover previously undetected invariant violations. On average, 14.7 PUTs were synthesized per second. We then applied Pex to generate input data for the synthesized PUTs forcing Pex to use only public operations of the UUT (to guarantee that all inputs are constructible in practice). We counted the number of unique invariant violations and of distinct PUTs that led to invariant violations. We imposed a timeout of 3 minutes for the DSE in Pex to generate inputs for and run the synthesized PUTs. Here, we report the number of invariant violations that were detected within this time limit. Within this time limit, the first invariant violation was detected within 4–47 seconds (12.8 seconds on average) for all object invariants in all applications.

---

[1] http://boogie.codeplex.com, rev: **f2ffe18efee7**
[2] https://github.com/AArnott/ClueBuddy,
    rev: **c1b64ae97c01fec249b2212018f589c2d8119b59**
[3] http://dafny.codeplex.com, rev: **f2ffe18efee7**
[4] https://github.com/eriksen/Draugen,
    rev: **dfc84bd4dcf232d3cfa6550d737e8382ce7641cb**
[5] https://code.google.com/p/goalstracker, rev: 556
[6] https://github.com/jgauffin/griffin,
    rev: **54ab75d200b516b2a8bd0a1b7cfe1b66f45da6ea**
[7] https://bitbucket.org/kevinclancy/love-studio, rev: **7da77fa**
[8] https://github.com/Trinity-Encore/Encore,
    rev: **0538bd611dc1bc81da15c4b10a65ac9d608dafc2**
[9] http://yaml.codeplex.com, rev: 96133

The total violations found by our technique may be classified into the following categories based on the template that was instantiated: 60 due to direct field updates, 41 due to leaking, and 25 due to capturing. The remaining 6 violations were detected by the exhaustive enumeration. Out of these 6 invariant violations, 5 are also detected by the version of Pex without our technique, i.e., with the traditional approach of checking the invariant of the receiver at the end of a method. The last violation requires a sequence of two method calls and was detected only by our technique. This is because Pex could not generate appropriate input data to the second method such that the invariant check at the end of the method failed. In this case, the exhaustive enumeration served as a technique for generating more complex input data. The object invariants that were violated at least once can be classified into the following categories: 27 invariants were violated at least once due to direct field updates, 24 due to leaking, 17 due to capturing, and 5 due to the exhaustive enumeration. Note that in these applications we found no subclasses that strengthen the invariant of their superclass with respect to any inherited fields. This is why no invariant violations were detected with the subclassing template.

An example of an invariant violation detected by our technique in LoveStudio is shown on the right. A StackPanel object has a LuaStackFrame array, and its invariant holds if all array elements are non-null. In the PUT, method SetFrames captures a0 depending on the value of a1. The last operation of the test assigns a LuaStackFrame object to the array at a valid index a2. In case a3 is null, o's invariant is violated.

We have manually inspected all detected invariant violations. Violations detected with the direct-field-update template reveal design flaws and can be fixed by making fields private and providing setters that maintain the invari-

```
void PUT(StackPanel o,
        LuaStackFrame[] a0, bool a1,
        int a2, LuaStackFrame a3) {
  assume o != null && o.Invariant();
  o.SetFrames(a0, a1);
  assume a0 != null && o.Invariant();
  assume 0 <= a2 && a2 < a0.Length;
  a0[a2] = a3;
  assert o.Invariant();
}
```

ants. Violations due to leaking or capturing could be fixed either by cloning the leaked or captured objects, or by using immutable types in the interfaces of the classes whose invariants are under test. The largest number of invariant violations found with the leaking and capturing templates was detected in the Boogie and Dafny applications, which declare several multi-object invariants in their code.

The detected invariant violations indicate overly strong invariants in the sense that they may be violated by possible clients of a UUT. These clients are not necessarily present in a given application and, thus, the violations do not necessarily reveal bugs. This behavior is to be expected for unit testing, where each unit is tested independently of the rest of the application. Nevertheless, the detected violations do indicate robustness issues that might lead to bugs during maintenance or when classes are reused as libraries. We discussed the detected invariant violations in Boogie and Dafny with the lead developer, Rustan Leino. All of them seem to indicate robustness issues, which will be addressed by either weakening the invariants or changing the design of the code.

8   Related Work

Our approach to testing object invariants is inspired by static verification techniques. Poetzsch-Heffter [14] pointed out that the traditional way of checking the invariant of the receiver at the end of each method is insufficient. The checks he proposed are sufficient for sound verification, but not suitable as unit test oracles since they make heavy use of universal quantification. Some modular verification techniques for object invariants [9,12] handle the challenges mentioned in Sect. 2, but require annotation overhead that does not seem acceptable for testing.

We distilled our templates for test synthesis from a formal framework for verification techniques for object invariants [3]. This framework identifies an additional scenario (not presented in Sect. 2) involving a *call-back*. In this scenario, a method L violates the invariant of its receiver r and then calls another method M. If M performs a call-back r.N, method N finds the invariant of r broken, which may lead to an error in the body of N or a violation of the invariant check at the end of N. We omitted this scenario because Pex already detects such problems while testing L. It attempts to generate inputs for L that violate the assertions in method L and all methods it calls, in particular, the check of r's invariant at the end of N.

There are several test case generators for object-oriented programs that rely on invariants, but miss the violations presented here. AutoTest [11], a random testing tool for Eiffel, follows the traditional approach of checking the invariant of the receiver at the end of each method. Pex [19] follows the same approach, but asserts the invariant of the receiver only at the end of public methods. Korat [1] and Symbolic Java PathFinder [15] do not check object invariants of the UUT at all; they use invariants only to filter test inputs. All such tools may miss bugs when object invariants are violated and would thus benefit from our technique.

Work on synthesizing method call sequences to generate complex input data is complementary to ours. In fact, such approaches could be applied in place of the object construction mechanism in Pex to generate input objects for our PUTs. In certain cases, this might reduce the length of the synthesized tests since fewer candidate operations may be required to generate the same objects. These approaches include a combination of bounded exhaustive search and symbolic execution [22], feedback-directed random testing [13], a combination of feedback-directed random testing with concolic testing [6,2], evolutionary testing [21], an integration of evolutionary and concolic testing [8], and source code mining [17]. Moreover, Palus [23] combines dynamic inference, static analysis, and guided random test generation to automatically create legal and behaviorally-diverse method call sequences. In contrast to existing work, our technique synthesizes code that specifically targets violations of object invariants. This allows for a significantly smaller search space restricted to three known scenarios in which invariant violations may occur.

The work on method call synthesis most closely related to ours is Seeker [18], an extension to Pex that combines static and dynamic analyses to construct input objects for a UUT. More specifically, Seeker attempts to cover branches that are missed by Pex. Even though this approach does not rely on object invariants, the negation of an invariant could be regarded as a branch to be covered. However, some of the scenarios of Sect. 2 are not captured by Seeker's static analysis. For example, a multi-object invariant violation involves leaking or capturing parts of an object's representation, and might not necessarily involve a sequence of missed branches. The same holds for subclassing.

9 Conclusion

We have presented a technique for detecting object invariant violations by synthesizing PUTs. Given one or more classes under test, our technique uses a set of templates to synthesize snippets of client code. We then symbolically execute the synthesized code to generate inputs that might lead to invariant violations. As a result, our technique may reveal critical defects in the UUT, which go undetected by existing testing tools. We have demonstrated the effectiveness of our implementation on a number of C# applications with object invariants.

Acknowledgments. We thank Nikolai Tillman and Jonathan "Peli" de Halleux for sharing the Pex source code with us. We also thank Timon Gehr for implementing and evaluating parts of this technique for his Bachelor's thesis, and the reviewers for their constructive feedback.

References

1. Boyapati, C., Khurshid, S., Marinov, D.: Korat: Automated testing based on Java predicates. In: ISSTA, pp. 123–133. ACM (2002)
2. Dimjašević, M., Rakamarić, Z.: JPF-Doop: Combining concolic and random testing for Java. In: Java Pathfinder Workshop. Extended abstract (2013)
3. Drossopoulou, S., Francalanza, A., Müller, P., Summers, A.J.: A unified framework for verification techniques for object invariants. In: Vitek, J. (ed.) ECOOP 2008. LNCS, vol. 5142, pp. 412–437. Springer, Heidelberg (2008)
4. Ernst, M.D., Perkins, J.H., Guo, P.J., McCamant, S., Pacheco, C., Tschantz, M.S., Xiao, C.: The Daikon system for dynamic detection of likely invariants. Sci. Comput. Program. 69, 35–45 (2007)
5. Fähndrich, M., Barnett, M., Logozzo, F.: Embedded contract languages. In: SAC, pp. 2103–2110. ACM (2010)
6. Garg, P., Ivančić, F., Balakrishnan, G., Maeda, N., Gupta, A.: Feedback-directed unit test generation for C/C++ using concolic execution. In: ICSE, pp. 132–141. ACM (2013)
7. Godefroid, P., Klarlund, N., Sen, K.: DART: Directed automated random testing. In: PLDI, pp. 213–223. ACM (2005)
8. Inkumsah, K., Xie, T.: Evacon: A framework for integrating evolutionary and concolic testing for object-oriented programs. In: ASE, pp. 425–428. ACM (2007)
9. Leino, K.R.M., Müller, P.: Object invariants in dynamic contexts. In: Odersky, M. (ed.) ECOOP 2004. LNCS, vol. 3086, pp. 491–515. Springer, Heidelberg (2004)
10. Meyer, B.: Object-Oriented Software Construction, 2nd edn. Prentice-Hall (1997)
11. Meyer, B., Fiva, A., Ciupa, I., Leitner, A., Wei, Y., Stapf, E.: Programs that test themselves. IEEE Computer 42(9), 46–55 (2009)

12. Müller, P., Poetzsch-Heffter, A., Leavens, G.T.: Modular invariants for layered object structures. Sci. Comput. Program. 62, 253–286 (2006)
13. Pacheco, C., Lahiri, S.K., Ernst, M.D., Ball, T.: Feedback-directed random test generation. In: ICSE, pp. 75–84. IEEE Computer Society (2007)
14. Poetzsch-Heffter, A.: Specification and verification of object-oriented programs. Habilitation thesis. Technical University of Munich (1997)
15. Păsăreanu, C.S., Mehlitz, P.C., Bushnell, D.H., Gundy-Burlet, K., Lowry, M., Person, S., Pape, M.: Combining unit-level symbolic execution and system-level concrete execution for testing NASA software. In: ISSTA, pp. 15–26. ACM (2008)
16. Sen, K., Marinov, D., Agha, G.: CUTE: A concolic unit testing engine for C. In: ESEC, pp. 263–272. ACM (2005)
17. Thummalapenta, S., Xie, T., Tillmann, N., de Halleux, J., Schulte, W.: MSeqGen: Object-oriented unit-test generation via mining source code. In: ESEC/SIGSOFT FSE, pp. 193–202. ACM (2009)
18. Thummalapenta, S., Xie, T., Tillmann, N., de Halleux, J., Su, Z.: Synthesizing method sequences for high-coverage testing. In: OOPSLA, pp. 189–206. ACM (2011)
19. Tillmann, N., de Halleux, J.: Pex—White box test generation for .NET. In: Beckert, B., Hähnle, R. (eds.) TAP 2008. LNCS, vol. 4966, pp. 134–153. Springer, Heidelberg (2008)
20. Tillmann, N., Schulte, W.: Parameterized unit tests. In: ESEC/SIGSOFT FSE, pp. 119–128. ACM (2005)
21. Tonella, P.: Evolutionary testing of classes. In: ISSTA, pp. 119–128. ACM (2004)
22. Xie, T., Marinov, D., Schulte, W., Notkin, D.: Symstra: A framework for generating object-oriented unit tests using symbolic execution. In: Halbwachs, N., Zuck, L.D. (eds.) TACAS 2005. LNCS, vol. 3440, pp. 365–381. Springer, Heidelberg (2005)
23. Zhang, S., Saff, D., Bu, Y., Ernst, M.D.: Combined static and dynamic automated test generation. In: ISSTA, pp. 353–363. ACM (2011)

Formalizing DSL Semantics
for Reasoning and Conformance Testing[*]

Sarmen Keshishzadeh[1] and Arjan J. Mooij[2]

[1] Eindhoven University of Technology, Eindhoven, The Netherlands
[2] Embedded Systems Innovation by TNO, Eindhoven, The Netherlands
s.keshishzadeh@tue.nl, arjan.mooij@tno.nl

Abstract. A Domain Specific Language (DSL) focuses on the essential
concepts in a certain problem domain, thus abstracting from low-level
implementation details. In combination with code generators, DSLs bring
software development closer to domain requirements. The development
of DSLs usually centers around the grammar and a code generator; there
is little attention for the semantics of the DSL. However, a formal semantics is essential for reasoning about specifications in terms of the DSL
(i.e., DSL instances). We argue that the semantics should be expressed
independent of a code generator. Thus semantic issues can be revealed
that could otherwise remain undetected. We also use the semantics to
define the conformance of an implementation to a DSL instance, and to
automatically test conformance of the (generated) implementation code
to a DSL instance. We illustrate our approach using an industrial prototype DSL for collision prevention.

Keywords: Domain Specific Language (DSL), Semantics, Code Generation, Model-based Testing, Conformance Testing.

1 Introduction

A Domain Specific Language (DSL, [19,20]) focuses on the essential concepts
in a certain problem domain, thus abstracting from implementation details. By
trading generality for expressiveness in a limited domain, DSLs offer substantial
gains in ease of use compared with general-purpose programming and specification languages in their domain of application [10]. In combination with code
generators, DSLs bring software development closer to domain requirements.

Modern implementation technologies like the Eclipse Modeling Framework
(EMF, [16]) seem to boost the applicability of DSLs, by providing support for
the development of the language, an editor, validation and code generation.
However, the development of a DSL usually centers around the syntax of the
language and a code generator; there is little attention for the semantics of the
DSL especially for language users. The overlooking of semantics gives rise to two
important questions that we address in this paper:

---

[*] This research was supported by the Dutch national COMMIT program under the
Allegio project, and by the European ARTEMIS program under the Crystal project.

D. Giannakopoulou and G. Salaün (Eds.): SEFM 2014, LNCS 8702, pp. 81–95, 2014.
© Springer International Publishing Switzerland 2014

1. what is the precise meaning of the language elements?
2. how to validate the generated implementation code?

The first question is about semantics: it is great that DSLs focus on domain concepts, but what do we model exactly? In the literature, many approaches can be found for giving semantics to a language [2,15]. In practice, the semantics of a DSL is usually defined implicitly by implementing a transformation from the DSL to a general purpose implementation language, e.g., C++. As one would anyhow implement such a code generator, an implicit semantics comes for free. However, such a semantics is entangled with the complexities of the target language and requires that users of the DSL also understand its low-level implementation details, which contradicts the purpose of using DSLs. Thus, we aim to describe the semantics independent of transformations to other languages.

The second question is about correctness: it is great that code is generated automatically, but how do we know it is any good? This consists of two parts. First of all, whether syntactically correct code is generated. Secondly, whether the code conforms to the semantics of the DSL. We focus on the second part, and assume that the code is syntactically correct. Various authors [3,5] have argued that the correctness should be proved. However in practice code generators are improved regularly and it is important to gain confidence in the generated code in a lightweight manner. To this end we propose a testing approach.

Writing down a semantics in addition to writing a code generator requires extra effort, and hence it needs to offer added value. The first advantage is a better understanding of the language. As an extra benefit, many authors use the constructed semantics to build simulators [14]. Instead of this, we define the conformance of an implementation to a specification in terms of a DSL (i.e., a DSL instance) and derive test cases to test the compliance of an (generated) implementation with a DSL instance which describes its required behavior.

In addition to testing the generated code for a single DSL instance, the code generator itself can be tested by providing several DSL instances. The latter would be relevant as a regression test when the code generator is optimized or extended, but we focus on testing the generated code for a single DSL instance.

To illustrate our approach, we consider a prototype DSL that we have developed in collaboration [12] with Philips Healthcare in the context of interventional X-ray scanners (Fig. 1(a)). This DSL enables the description of various sets of collision prevention rules, early validation (such as verification of safety properties [9] and performance analysis [18]), and the generation and run-time monitoring of implementation code [11].

By giving several demonstrations of this DSL, we have observed that most of its features are understood quickly. Some advanced features, however, always need quite a bit of explanation. Moreover, detailed discussions about the DSL have revealed that some features can be interpreted in subtly different ways. These observations motivate again the need for a precise description of the DSL semantics. Moreover, as collision prevention is a safety-critical component, it is important to gain confidence in the generated code.

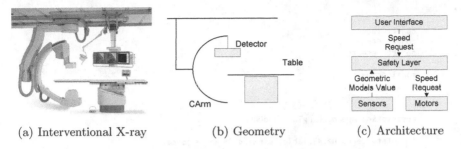

(a) Interventional X-ray   (b) Geometry   (c) Architecture

Fig. 1. Industrial Study Case

Overview. In Section 2 we introduce the collision prevention DSL and describe its structure. Its semantics is split into two modules and formalized in Section 3, which forms the basis of the conformance testing as described in Section 4. Section 5 reports some practical results from the formalization and testing. In Section 6 we argue that studying formal semantics in a modular way can improve reusability between languages. In Section 7 we discuss related work. Section 8 contains some concluding remarks and suggestions for future research.

2   Structural DSL Specification

We illustrate our approach using the interventional X-ray scanners (Fig. 1(a)) of Philips Healthcare. These systems consist of several moving objects as sketched in Fig. 1(b). For example, the Table can be moved horizontally, the Detector can be moved vertically, and the CArm can be rotated around its center.

The software architecture of these systems includes a dedicated safety layer to prevent collisions between these heavy objects; see Fig. 1(c). User speed requests for object movements should pass the safety layer. The safety layer uses certain internal resources called 'geometric models' to store data from the sensors. Geometric models store the shortest distance between each pair of objects. This data is used for making decisions about user requests and determining the speed requests that should be applied to the motors.

To describe the collision prevention logic of the safety layer from Fig. 1(c) we use the DSL from [11]. Fig. 2 depicts an instance of this collision prevention DSL[1]. The general structure of an instance of this DSL is as follows:

DSL Instance. An instance of the DSL is a tuple $DI = \langle Obj, Mod, R \rangle$ where:

- *Obj* is a finite set of objects;
- *Mod* is a finite set of geometric models;
- $R \in \mathcal{P}(Restr)$ is a finite set of restrictions (depending on *Obj* and *Mod*).

Each DSL instance declares a set of objects *Obj* and a set of geometric models *Mod*. We assume these sets as context and do not mention them as subscripts in the rest of the formalization. In Fig. 2, the object declarations correspond to the

---

[1] For confidentiality reasons, numbers and details have been changed in this example.

```
// --- Context Declarations -------
object Table
object CArm
object Detector

model Actuals
model LookAhead

// --- Restrictions -------
restriction ApproachingTableAndCArm
  activation
    Distance[Actuals](Table, CArm) < 35 mm + 15 cm
  effects
    absolute limit CArm[Rotation]
      at ((Distance[Actuals](Table, CArm) - 35 mm) / 15 cm) * 10 dgps
    absolute limit Table[Translation]
      at Distance[Actuals](Table, CArm) ^ 0.75

restriction ApproachingTableAndDetector
  activation
    Distance[LookAhead](Table, Detector) < 35 mm + 15 cm
 && Distance[LookAhead](Table, Detector) <
                                    Distance[Actuals](Table, Detector)
  deactivation
    Distance[LookAhead](Table, Detector) > 35 mm + 20 cm
  effects
    relative limit Detector[Translation]
      at ((Distance[LookAhead](Table, Detector) - 35 mm) / 15 cm)
```

Fig. 2. Example Instance of the DSL

system depicted in Fig. 1(b) and the geometric model declarations imply that the sensor data is stored in two geometric models, viz., Actuals and LookAhead.

In what follows we first relate the context declarations to the external interfaces of the safety layer. Afterwards we discuss the restrictions that form the internal logic. The goal is to understand precisely the domain notions.

2.1   External Interfaces

The external interfaces of the safety layer in the architecture of Fig. 1(c) use two concepts: speed request and geometric models value.

Speed Request. For each object, there are two kinds of movements, viz., rotation and translation. We use the data type *MovType* to describe them:

$$MovType == \{Rotation,\ Translation\}$$

Each speed request contains for each object and movement a 3D vector. We use the data type *SpReq* to describe them:

$$SpReq == Obj \times MovType \ \rightarrow \ \mathbb{R}^3$$

It should be noted that there is no language construct for speed requests.

Geometric Models Value. Each geometric model consists of the distances between each pair of objects. We describe each geometric model as a distance function $d : Obj \times Obj \ \rightarrow \ \mathbb{R}_0^+$ such that (for all $o_1, o_2 \in Obj$):

- $d(o_1, o_1) = 0$;
- $d(o_1, o_2) = d(o_2, o_1)$.

We use *Dist* to denote the set of distance functions for *Obj*. As depicted in Fig. 1(b), the objects have shapes. Each distance value refers to the shortest distance between a pair of objects, i.e., the distance between the closest pair of points from these objects. The triangle inequality does not apply in terms of the objects. We use the data type *GeoVal* to describe the geometric models value for the set of models and objects:

$$GeoVal == Mod \rightarrow Dist$$

In the DSL syntax `Distance[m](o1,o2)` denotes the distance between objects o1 and o2 in geometric model m.

2.2 Internal Logic

Finally, the collision prevention logic is specified in terms of restrictions. From Fig. 2 one can see that each restriction consists of three parts.

Restriction. A restriction is a tuple $(act, deact, eff) \in Restr$ where:

- $act \in Cond$ is an activation condition;
- $deact \in Cond$ is a deactivation condition;
- $eff \in \mathcal{P}(Eff)$ is a finite set of effects.

Condition, Expression. A condition is a function from geometric models value to booleans, and an expression is a function from geometric models value to real numbers. We use the data types *Cond* and *Expr* to describe them:

$$Cond == GeoVal \rightarrow Bool \qquad Expr == GeoVal \rightarrow \mathbb{R}$$

As a syntactic shorthand, the activation or deactivation conditions can be omitted from a restriction; in such cases the omitted condition is assumed to be true. The constants in the conditions and expressions can be annotated by measurement units (e.g., cm, dgps); we assume that all constants are transformed to a default unit and do not consider this as part of the semantics.

Effect. There are two types of effects, viz., absolute and relative. We use the data type *LimType* to describe them:

$$LimType == \{Abs, Rel\}$$

An effect is a tuple $(lt, om, e) \in Eff$ where:

- $lt \in LimType$ is a limit type;
- $om \in \mathcal{P}(Obj \times MovType)$ is a finite set of object movements;
- $e \in Expr$ is an expression.

3   DSL Semantics

Given a speed request from the user and a geometric models value from the sensors, the speed request to the motors is determined by the DSL instance. The DSL semantics consists of two modules. The first module is a symbolic transition system that determines the active restrictions (Section 3.1). The second module is a set of functions that compute the output speed request (Section 3.2).

3.1   Determining Active Restrictions

The active restrictions are determined by the first module which considers only one of the inputs to the safety layer, viz., the geometric models value. We first focus on a single restriction $r = (act_r, deact_r, eff_r)$. Each restriction can be in two states: active or passive. Initially each restriction r is passive. Given the previous state ($b \in Bool$) and the current geometric models value ($g \in GeoVal$), the current state of r is active if:

– the activation condition evaluates to true (i.e., $act_r(g)$),   or
– it was active in the previous state and the deactivation condition evaluates to false (i.e., $b \wedge \neg deact_r(g)$)

It follows from the discussion above that if both the activation and the deactivation conditions evaluate to true, the current state is active. Fig. 3 illustrates these rules as a symbolic transition system. The transition relation can be formalized by the function $CurrAct_r : Bool \times GeoVal \rightarrow Bool$ as follows:

$$CurrAct_r(b, g) = act_r(g) \vee (b \wedge \neg deact_r(g))$$

For the set of restrictions R in $DI = \langle Obj, Mod, R \rangle$, this induces an augmented symbolic transition system $ASTS_R = \langle Q, L, q, T \rangle$ such that:

– Q is a set of states;
– $L : Q \rightarrow (R \rightarrow Bool)$ is a total and one-to-one labeling function;
– $q \in Q$ is the initial state and $L(q)(r) = False$ for all $r \in R$;
– $T \subseteq Q \times Cond \times Q$ is a transition relation where the following properties hold (for all $p, q_1, q_2 \in Q, cond : Cond, f : R \rightarrow Bool, g \in GeoVal$):

$$(q_1, cond, q_2) \in T \quad \Rightarrow \quad cond(g) = \bigwedge_{r \in R} (L(q_2)(r) \Leftrightarrow CurrAct_r(L(q_1)(r), g))$$

$$\wedge \ (\exists gv \in GeoVal . cond(gv)) \qquad (1)$$

$$f \in ran(L) \Leftrightarrow f = L(q) \vee (\exists (p_1, cond_1, p_2), \dots, (p_{n-1}, cond_{n-1}, p_n) \in T.$$

$$p_1 = q \wedge p_n = p \wedge f = L(p)) \qquad (2)$$

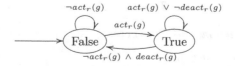

Fig. 3. A Symbolic Transition System for $R = \{r\}$

The labeling function indicates which restrictions are active; initially all restrictions are passive. Each transition symbolically represents the geometric models values that enable the move from the source state to the target state. Unreachable states (Eqn. (2)) and unsatisfiable transitions (Eqn. (1)) are not considered. The notation $ran(L)$ denotes the range of L.

This transition system is deterministic, i.e., the outgoing transitions of each state are labeled with disjoint conditions. Moreover, in each state and for every geometric models value there is an outgoing satisfiable transition. Fig. 3 depicts the $ASTS_R$ for $R = \{r\}$; the transition labels are assumed to be satisfiable.

3.2 Computing Output Speed Requests

Output speed request computation is the second module of the semantics which considers both inputs of the safety layer. In this section we first introduce the semantics of a single restriction. Then the semantics of a set of restrictions is discussed and applied for output speed request computation.

The effects of a restriction $r = (act_r, deact_r, eff_r)$ are described in the context of $b \in Bool$ which denotes the current state of r. The function $[\![Eff_r]\!]_b : Obj \times MovType \times LimType \times GeoVal \to \mathcal{P}(\mathbb{R})$ specifies the active limits of r for each object movement, limit type, and geometric models value:

$$[\![Eff_r]\!]_b(obj, m, \ell, g) = \{v \mid b \wedge \exists om \in \mathcal{P}(Obj \times MovType), e \in Expr.$$
$$(\ell, om, e) \in eff_r \; \wedge \; (obj, m) \in om \wedge e(g) = v\}$$

When r is active, for each object movement the most restrictive relative and absolute limits are considered as the effects of r. Formally, we interpret r as a partial function $[\![r]\!]_b : Obj \times MovType \times LimType \times GeoVal \nrightarrow \mathbb{R}$ such that:

$$[\![r]\!]_b(obj, m, \ell, g) = min([\![Eff_r]\!]_b(obj, m, \ell, g)) \quad \text{if } [\![Eff_r]\!]_b(obj, m, \ell, g) \neq \emptyset$$

The set of restrictions R is interpreted in the context of $B : R \to Bool$, which denotes the current state of the restrictions. The set R is interpreted as $[\![R]\!]_B : Obj \times MovType \times LimType \times GeoVal \to \overline{\mathbb{R}}$. The notation $\overline{\mathbb{R}}$ denotes the two point compactification of real numbers: $\overline{\mathbb{R}} = \mathbb{R} \cup \{-\infty, +\infty\}$.

$$[\![R]\!]_B(obj, m, \ell, g) =$$
$$\begin{cases} min\{[\![r]\!]_{B(r)}(obj, m, \ell, g) \mid r \in R\} & \text{if } (\exists r \in R. \, (obj, m, \ell, g) \in dom([\![r]\!]_b)) \\ DefLim(\ell) & \text{if } \neg(\exists r \in R. \, (obj, m, \ell, g) \in dom([\![r]\!]_b)) \end{cases}$$

where $dom([\![r]\!]_b)$ extracts the domain of r. For each geometric model value the most restrictive limits specified by R are considered for each object movement. If R does not specify a limit, an appropriate default value specified by $DefLim : LimType \to \overline{\mathbb{R}}$ is returned, i.e., $DefLim(Rel) = 1$ and $DefLim(Abs) = +\infty$.

It should be noted that the effects of R are real numbers while (user/output) speed requests are 3D vectors. The length of the requests to the motors is computed by $[\![outSpeed_R]\!]_B : Obj \times MovType \times GeoVal \times SpReq \to \mathbb{R}$ for the set of restrictions R in the context of B as follows:

$$\llbracket outSpeed_R \rrbracket_B(obj, m, g, ur) =$$
$$min\{\llbracket R \rrbracket_B(obj, m, Abs, g), \llbracket R \rrbracket_B(obj, m, Rel, g) \times norm(ur(obj, m))\}$$

where $ur \in SpReq$ is the current speed request from the user and $norm$ is defined as $norm((x, y, z)) = \sqrt{x^2 + y^2 + z^2}$. In the above definition min refers to the definition of the minimum function for $\overline{\mathbb{R}}$. Since the relative limits and norm of vectors are real numbers the computed speed is a real number (not $-\infty$ or $+\infty$).

Finally, the speed requests vectors computed by R that is applied to the motors is specified by $\llbracket output_R \rrbracket_B : GeoVal \times SpReq \to SpReq$ as follows:

$$\llbracket output_R \rrbracket_B(g, ur)(obj, m) =$$
$$\begin{cases} \frac{ur(obj,m)}{norm(ur(obj,m))} \times \llbracket outSpeed_R \rrbracket_B(obj, m, g, ur) & \text{if } ur(obj, m) \neq (0, 0, 0) \\ (0, 0, 0) & \text{otherwise} \end{cases}$$

It follows from the definition that the direction of the output is determined by computing a unit vector from the user request. The norm of the output is determined by the value computed by the DSL instance, i.e., $outSpeed_R$.

3.3   Semantics of a DSL Instance

Finally, the semantics of a DSL instance combines the two modules that determine the active restrictions and that compute the output:

Definition 1 (Semantics of an Instance). *Let* $DI = \langle Obj, Mod, R \rangle$ *be a DSL instance. The semantics of DI is the pair* $(ASTS_R, output_R)$.

In the following definition, we formalize the notion of execution for a DSL instance and show how the two modules of the semantics are linked. These definitions are guided by the manner in which the safety layer communicates with its interfacing components (Fig. 1(c)). The safety layer reads the geometric models value and the speed request from the user simultaneously at fixed intervals of time, and then produces a speed request to the motors.

Definition 2 (Run, Trace). *Let* $DI = \langle Obj, Mod, R \rangle$ *be a DSL instance:*

- *A run of DI is a sequence* $q_0(g_1, ur_1, or_1) \ldots (g_n, ur_n, or_n)q_n$ *of states* $(q_i \in Q)$ *and tuples of geometric models value, user speed requests, and outgoing speed requests* $(g_i \in GeoVal, ur_i, or_i \in SpReq)$ *such that:*

$$(q_0 = q) \wedge \forall i \in \{1, \ldots, n\} \, . \, (or_i = \llbracket output_R \rrbracket_{L(q_i)}(g_i, ur_i)) \wedge$$
$$(\exists cond \in Cond.(q_{i-1}, cond, q_i) \in T \wedge cond(g_i))$$

The notation $Runs(DI)$ *denotes the set of all runs for DI.*
- *The set of traces for DI is defined as follows where* ϵ *is the empty trace:*

$$Traces(DI) = \{\epsilon\} \cup \{(g_1, ur_1, or_1) \ldots (g_n, ur_n, or_n)|$$
$$q_0(g_1, ur_1, or_1) \ldots (g_n, ur_n, or_n)q_n \in Runs(DI)\}$$

Since $ASTS_R$ *is deterministic, the mapping from* $Runs(DI)$ *to* $Traces(DI)$ *is one-to-one.*

4 Conformance Testing

In this section we first specify for a DSL instance DI the set of test cases that can determine whether a given implementation correctly implements DI (Section 4.1). Inspired by model-based testing approaches we introduce a formalism for describing the behavior of implementations and define the conformance of an implementation to a DSL instance. Finally, we define the notions of test case and test case execution. Afterwards we address the test selection problem in our testing approach (Section 4.2). Then we discuss the procedure that we use in practice for generating test cases based on the test selection criteria (Section 4.3).

In what follows we refer to sequences over a given set A by $seq(A)$ such that:

$$seq(A) = \{f : \mathbb{N} \nrightarrow A \mid \exists n \in \mathbb{N} \, . \, dom(f) = \{1, \ldots, n\}\}$$

We write $[a, b, c]$ to denote the sequence $\{1 \mapsto a, 2 \mapsto b, 3 \mapsto c\}$.

4.1 Conformance of an Implementation to a DSL Instance

Several testing theories assume that the behavior of implementations can be described using a particular formalism [7,17]. Thus an implementation is treated as a black-box and its internal structure does not play a role in testing. This assumption is called testing hypothesis. The model of an implementation does not need to be known a-priori.

Definition 3 (Implementation). *Any implementation controlling the movements of Obj based on the values in Mod can be modeled as $imp = (STS, output)$. In this model $STS = \langle Q, q, T \rangle$ is a symbolic transition system where:*

- *Q is a set of states;*
- *$q \in Q$ is the initial state;*
- *$T \subseteq Q \times Cond \times Q$ is a transition relation.*

The function $[\![output]\!]_{STS,h} : GeoVal \times SpReq \to SpReq$ computes the output speed request based on the execution history $h \in seq(GeoVal)$ and the path navigated so far in STS. The notation Imp denotes the set of all implementations for Obj and Mod.

We use a structure similar to Def. 1 for our testing hypothesis. In Def. 3 the only assumption is that output computation is affected by the history of execution. There is no reference to DSL concepts. On the other hand, Def. 1 explicitly refers to the current state of restrictions for output computation.

A run of imp is a sequence $q_0(g_1, ur_1, or_1) \ldots (g_n, ur_n, or_n)q_n$ such that:

$$(q_0 = q) \wedge \forall i \in \{1, \ldots, n\} \, . \, (or_i = [\![output]\!]_{STS,[g_1,\ldots,g_i]}(g_i, ur_i)) \wedge$$
$$(\exists cond \in Cond.(q_{i-1}, cond, q_i) \in T \wedge cond(g_i))$$

The set of traces for imp, i.e., $Traces(imp)$, is defined similar to Def. 2. We assume that implementations are deterministic, i.e., exactly one output request is possible for each state, geometric models value, and user speed request.

In order to determine the correctness of an implementation, we define the conformance of an implementation to a DSL instance.

Definition 4 (Conformance). *An implementation* $imp \in Imp$ *conforms to* $DI = \langle Obj, Mod, R \rangle$ *if and only if* $Traces(DI) = Traces(imp)$.

From Section 3 one can see that a DSL instance specifies exactly one output request for any (reachable) state, geometric models value, and user request. In this setting trace equivalence is a natural way of describing conformance.

From Def. 4 it follows that to establish the conformance of imp to DI the set $Traces(DI)$ should be tested on imp. To investigate the conformance of an implementation to a DSL instance we perform test cases on it. A test case is an experiment where in each step we supply a geometric models value and a user speed request to the implementation and observe its output. Therefore, a test case for $imp \in Imp$ is an element of $seq(GeoVal \times SpReq \times SpReq)$.

Let $t = [(g_1, ur_1, or_1), \ldots, (g_n, ur_n, or_n)] \in seq(GeoVal \times SpReq \times SpReq)$ be a test case. Formally, execution of t on $(STS, output)$ can be described by $Exec : Imp \times seq(GeoVal \times SpReq \times SpReq) \to \{\mathbf{pass}, \mathbf{fail}\}$ such that:

$$Exec((STS, [\![output]\!]_{STS,h}), t) =$$
$$\begin{cases} \mathbf{pass} & \text{if } \forall k.1 \leq k \leq n.[\![output]\!]_{STS,[g_1,\ldots g_k]}(g_k, ur_k) = or_k \\ \mathbf{fail} & \text{otherwise} \end{cases}$$

4.2   Coverage Criteria

Conformance of an implementation to an instance DI can be tested by executing the set $Traces(DI)$. This set is complete but requires executing an infinite number of test cases. We define some coverage criteria for selecting a finite number of test cases, namely in two ways:

– reformulate existing criteria that are relevant to the semantic modules;
– define criteria that test certain language-specific aspects.

In what follows we use the function $Context_{DI} : Traces(DI) \to (R \to Bool)$ to compute the state of DI after executing a trace $t \in Traces(DI)$:

$$Context_{DI}(t) = \begin{cases} L(q_m) & \text{if } t = (g_1, ur_1, or_1) \ldots (g_m, ur_m, or_m) \wedge \\ & \quad q_0(g_1, ur_1, or_1) \ldots (g_m, ur_m, or_m)q_m \in Runs(DI) \\ L(q) & \text{if } t = \epsilon \end{cases}$$

In [1] the authors discuss an exhaustive list of coverage criteria for different artifacts (e.g., source code, specification). The node coverage criterion for graphs can be formulated for the collision prevention DSL. In our context the only test requirement will be to test the output speed request in each state. In each state arbitrary user requests are considered for each object movement. This criterion is specified in terms of the $ASTS$ module of the semantics.

Definition 5 (Coverage Criterion 1 (CC1)). *Let* $DI = \langle Obj, Mod, R \rangle$ *be a DSL instance. A test suite* $T \subseteq Traces(DI)$ *satisfies the criterion CC1 for DI if:*

$$\forall p \in Q \; \exists [(g_1, ur_1, or_1), \ldots, (g_n, ur_n, or_n)] \in T, 1 \leq i \leq n.$$
$$Context_{DI}((g_1, ur_1, or_1), \ldots, (g_i, ur_i, or_i)) = L(p)$$

In addition to reformulating existing criteria for the DSL, it is possible to formulate criteria that focus on language-specific features. We define a criterion to test the definition of $outSpeed_R$ for each object $(obj \in Obj)$ and movement $(m \in MovType)$ by enforcing two test requirements in each state:

- the output request should be determined by the relative limit for m of obj;
- the output request should be determined by the absolute limit for m of obj.

Hence the specification of this criterion refers to both semantic modules.

Definition 6 (Coverage Criterion 2 (CC2)). *Let $DI = \langle Obj, Mod, R \rangle$ be a DSL instance. A test suite $T \subseteq Traces(DI)$ satisfies the criterion CC2 for DI if:*

$$\forall p \in Q, obj \in Obj, m \in MovType$$
$$\exists[(g_1, ur_1, or_1), \ldots, (g_n, ur_n, or_n)], [(g'_1, ur'_1, or'_1), \ldots, (g'_m, ur'_m, or'_m)] \in T$$
$$\exists 1 \le k \le n, 1 \le \ell \le m \ . \ norm(or_k(obj, m)) = [\![R]\!]_{L(p)}(obj, m, Abs, g_k) \wedge$$
$$norm(or'_\ell(obj, m)) = [\![R]\!]_{L(p)}(obj, m, Rel, g'_\ell) \times norm(ur'_\ell(obj, m)) \wedge$$
$$L(p) = Context_{DI}((g_1, ur_1, or_1), \ldots, (g_k, ur_k, or_k)) \wedge$$
$$L(p) = Context_{DI}((g'_1, ur'_1, or'_1), \ldots, (g'_\ell, ur'_\ell, or'_\ell))$$

4.3   Test Case Generation

Let $DI = \langle Obj, Mod, R \rangle$ be an instance with the semantics $(ASTS_R, output_R)$. In order to generate test cases satisfying a coverage criterion CC we extract $output_R$ (i.e., the function module) automatically from a DSL instance. For actual instances of the DSL, $ASTS_R$ contains a large number of transitions. Therefore, for any criterion we try to explore $ASTS_R$ in an on-the-fly manner.

The semantics of DI implies that output computation is influenced by values from the infinite domains $SpReq$ and $Dist$. Our test case generation procedures treat data items from these domains symbolically. For a given coverage criteria CC we start exploring $ASTS_R$ from the initial state. In each state we symbolically build a condition in terms of geometric model values and user speed requests that refer to the requirements of CC. We use a solver to find a satisfiable assignment for the constructed condition. If the condition is satisfiable we compute the next state and the expected output. Otherwise, the requirement is not satisfiable. We repeat the same procedure until all requirements for CC are satisfied or known to be infeasible. It should be noted that generating minimal sets of test cases for each criterion is outside the scope of this paper.

Using a state-of-the-art SMT solver, e.g., Z3 [4], as the back-end solver is an option. However most SMT solvers provide limited support for solving non-linear expressions. In our realistic instances exponentiation is used to specify smooth brake patterns. Thus, we have decided to use Mathematica [8].

5   Formalization and Testing Results

By formalizing the semantics and testing the implementations generated by the code generator from [11] we have encountered three main issues.

5.1 Mathematically Undefined Operations

The syntax of the collision prevention DSL allows arithmetic operations inside conditions and effects. Some operations may not be mathematically defined, for example, because of a division by zero, or a square root of a negative number. Thus we should provide a semantics for interpreting undefined operations. For the collision prevention DSL, we have encountered this issue in particular with respect to effect expressions. We see two interpretations in this case:

- "ignore the effect": this is a general solution. It requires *Expr* in Section 2 to be a partial function. In turn, the semantics in Section 3.2 should be extended in order to take the partiality into account;
- "assume the effect to have value 0 for undefined cases": this is a specific solution for the collision prevention DSL which conservatively attempts to stop the objects affected by the undefined effect. It only requires a change in the way that elements of *Expr* are interpreted.

We have defined the semantics for both interpretations. The code generator from [11] uses the second interpretation. In our experiments the test cases based on the first interpretation fail, whereas the test cases based on the second interpretation pass. This was discovered by test cases satisfying criterion *CC1*; perhaps random testing could also identify this difference.

5.2 Semantics of Restrictions

The semantics from Section 3.2 resolves unspecified limits in the context of the set of restrictions R by returning values specified by *DefLim*. However, the code generator from [11] resolves unspecified limits in the context of a single restriction r; hence restrictions are interpreted as total functions. Moreover, the code generator from [11] conservatively truncates any relative limit that exceeds the value 1 into the value 1.

This makes a difference for DSL instances with individual effects above 1 for relative limits. This is related to restriction masking as discussed in [9]. Actual instances of the DSL did not include effects above 1 for relative limits. However, we discovered this mismatch by formalizing the semantics. One can also formulate a criterion to detect this mismatch by testing.

5.3 Computation Accuracies

Some test cases fail because of very small differences in the computed speed request to the motors. This is due to differences in computation accuracies between the test case generator and the generated code. To address this issue in a practical way, we have used an acceptance threshold for comparing expected and actual outputs. We consider the expected and actual speed requests $(e_x, e_y, e_z), (a_x, a_y, a_z) \in \mathbb{R}^3$ for an object to be equal if $|e_x - a_x| \leq 1 \wedge |e_y - a_y| \leq 1 \wedge |e_z - a_z| \leq 1$. This solution may not apply when individual rounding errors lead to large propagation errors.

6 Towards a Modular Semantics for DSLs

The formal semantics of a DSL can also be used by language developers as a means to characterize the main features of the language and their expressiveness. During the formalization of the semantics of the collision prevention DSL, we have observed that its semantics can naturally be split in two modules, focusing on the state-based and function-based aspects respectively. We formalized the connection of these two aspects in the definition of run (see Def. 2) where the label of the current state affects the output computation. This modularity helped us to consider variants of the language by changing the way the history of execution affects output computation. In particular, the simpler version of this DSL as discussed in [9] is stateless, and hence could be described using only a (modified) function-based module.

By their nature, DSLs usually focus on a narrow domain, and hence it may seem hard to expect any reuse among DSLs beyond frameworks like EMF for developing parsers and editors. However, many DSLs share some general semantic concepts. Ideally, this would enable the reuse of semantic modules (not necessarily their syntax). A similar direction is sketched in [13]. The authors consider a set of primary modules with well-defined semantics shared among different DSLs as analysis DSLs (e.g., expressions language module). Formalizing the semantics of DSLs can facilitate the reusability of more complex semantic models.

The separation in semantic modules can help us by selecting appropriate analysis tools for DSLs with known semantics. Since the function-based aspect is dominant in the collision prevention DSL, the use of solvers is very effective. For example, in [9] we have used solvers for verifying properties such as deadlock freedom. Similarly, in Section 4.3 we have used solvers for generating test cases. This has the potential to further reduce the required effort of developing DSLs and their tool infrastructure such as code generators and analysis techniques. In [13] the authors use analysis tools to perform certain checks on the identified primary modules (e.g., completeness of a set of boolean conditions).

7 Related Work

Various authors have formalized the semantics of DSLs to facilitate formal verification or visualization of the underlying state spaces:

- A method for prototyping visual interpreters and debugging facilities for DSLs is proposed in [14]. It is illustrated by a DSL for Petri net models. They extend the meta model of the language with the concept of configuration and use QVT (Query/View/Transformation) relations to describe the semantics.
- In [15] the authors formalize the semantics of an industrial DSL. First the concrete syntax of the language is projected onto an abstract and compositional language consisting of process terms. Then structural operational semantics (SOS) is used to assign semantics to the obtained process terms. The SOS rules are used for state space generation and model validation.
- A translational approach for prototyping the semantics of a DSL named SLCO is studied in [2]. SLCO is used in a setting with a number of transformations, e.g., to implementation code, or to restricted SLCO models with

equivalent observable behavior. The semantics of the DSL is captured by a transformation to an intermediate language called CS. They also introduce a straightforward transformation from CS to labeled transition systems and analyze them by existing tools. The correctness of the transformations is assessed by comparing the underlying labeled transition systems of the source and target models.

The DSLs studied in the mentioned works provide domain-specific abstractions for transition systems. In contrast, the dominating aspect of the collision prevention DSL is the function module. Moreover, we have used the semantics to test the generated implementation code.

For establishing the correctness of generated code, also [20] focuses on testing. However, he focuses on manually writing unit tests, either at the level of the implementation language, or at the level of the DSL.

In [6], for a model transformation it is tested whether, given source models satisfying the precondition, the transformation produces target models satisfying the postcondition. It is assumed that the meta-models of the source and target languages, precondition, and postcondition of the transformation are encoded in a constructive logic. A set of predefined criteria is used to generate source models as test data. Instead of testing the code generator, we test the generated code for a particular instance.

8   Conclusions and Further Work

The development of a DSL typically centers around the syntax of the language, whereas the semantics is defined implicitly in terms of a code generator. By formalizing the semantics independently of a code generator, we have identified semantic issues that are hard to detect due to the complexity of code generators. The formal semantics can also be used to derive test cases that check the compliance of an implementation with a DSL instance. Moreover, studying the semantics of a DSL in a modular way can improve reusability between languages.

DSLs like the collision prevention DSL are not only used to generate code, but also to generate analysis models [18,9]. It is future work to get confidence in:

- the semantic correctness of all generated artifacts and
- the consistency of artifacts with respect to a set of desired properties

in a practically feasible way. This imposes additional problems. Some aspects of the semantics may be ignored in some analysis models, because they are not relevant for a certain type of analysis. The generated code may also have properties in addition to the semantics that are important for the analysis models.

As an example of the latter, the code generator from [11] ensures that no duplicate distance computations are performed in a single computation cycle. Such properties are not part of the semantics of the DSL, but the performance models of [18] are based on this property.

References

1. Ammann, P., Offutt, J.: Introduction to software testing. Cambridge University Press (2008)

2. Andova, S., van den Brand, M.G.J., Engelen, L.: Prototyping the semantics of a DSL using ASF+SDF: Link to formal verification of DSL models. In: Proceedings of AMMSE 2011. EPTCS, vol. 56, pp. 65–79 (2011)
3. Andova, S., van den Brand, M.G.J., Engelen, L.: Reusable and correct endogenous model transformations. In: Hu, Z., de Lara, J. (eds.) ICMT 2012. LNCS, vol. 7307, pp. 72–88. Springer, Heidelberg (2012)
4. de Moura, L., Bjørner, N.: Z3: An efficient SMT solver. In: Ramakrishnan, C.R., Rehof, J. (eds.) TACAS 2008. LNCS, vol. 4963, pp. 337–340. Springer, Heidelberg (2008)
5. Ehrig, H., Ermel, C.: Semantical correctness and completeness of model transformations using graph and rule transformation. In: Ehrig, H., Heckel, R., Rozenberg, G., Taentzer, G. (eds.) ICGT 2008. LNCS, vol. 5214, pp. 194–210. Springer, Heidelberg (2008)
6. Fiorentini, C., Momigliano, A., Ornaghi, M., Poernomo, I.: A constructive approach to testing model transformations. In: Tratt, L., Gogolla, M. (eds.) ICMT 2010. LNCS, vol. 6142, pp. 77–92. Springer, Heidelberg (2010)
7. Gaudel, M.-C.: Testing can be formal, too. In: Mosses, P.D., Nielsen, M., Schwartzbach, M.I. (eds.) TAPSOFT 1995. LNCS, vol. 915, pp. 82–96. Springer, Heidelberg (1995)
8. Wolfram Research Inc. Mathematica 8.0.0.0
9. Keshishzadeh, S., Mooij, A.J., Mousavi, M.R.: Early fault detection in DSLs using SMT solving and automated debugging. In: Hierons, R.M., Merayo, M.G., Bravetti, M. (eds.) SEFM 2013. LNCS, vol. 8137, pp. 182–196. Springer, Heidelberg (2013)
10. Mernik, M., Heering, J., Sloane, A.M.: When and how to develop Domain-Specific Languages. ACM Computing Surveys 37(4), 316–344 (2005)
11. Mooij, A.J., Hooman, J., Albers, R.: Gaining industrial confidence for the introduction of Domain-Specific Languages. In: Proceedings of IEESD 2013, pp. 662–667. IEEE (2013)
12. Mooij, A.J., Hooman, J., Albers, R.: Early fault detection using design models for collision prevention in medical equipment. In: Gibbons, J., MacCaull, W. (eds.) FHIES 2013. LNCS, vol. 8315, pp. 170–187. Springer, Heidelberg (2014)
13. Ratiu, D., Voelter, M., Molotnikov, Z., Schaetz, B.: Implementing modular domain specific languages and analyses. In: Proceedings of Workshop on MoDeVVa 2012 (2012)
14. Sadilek, D.A., Wachsmuth, G.: Prototyping visual interpreters and debuggers for domain-specific modelling languages. In: Schieferdecker, I., Hartman, A. (eds.) ECMDA-FA 2008. LNCS, vol. 5095, pp. 63–78. Springer, Heidelberg (2008)
15. Stappers, F.P.M., Weber, S., Reniers, M.A., Andova, S., Nagy, I.: Formalizing a Domain Specific Language using SOS: an industrial case study. In: Sloane, A., Aßmann, U. (eds.) SLE 2011. LNCS, vol. 6940, pp. 223–242. Springer, Heidelberg (2012)
16. Steinberg, D., Budinsky, F., Paternostro, M., Merks, E.: Eclipse Modeling Framework. Pearson Education (2008)
17. Tretmans, J.: Model based testing with Labelled Transition Systems. In: Hierons, R.M., Bowen, J.P., Harman, M. (eds.) Formal Methods and Testing. LNCS, vol. 4949, pp. 1–38. Springer, Heidelberg (2008)
18. van den Berg, F., Remke, A., Mooij, A., Haverkort, B.: Performance evaluation for collision prevention based on a Domain Specific Language. In: Balsamo, M.S., Knottenbelt, W.J., Marin, A. (eds.) EPEW 2013. LNCS, vol. 8168, pp. 276–287. Springer, Heidelberg (2013)
19. van Deursen, A., Klint, P., Visser, J.: Domain-Specific Languages: an annotated bibliography. SIGPLAN Notices 35(6), 26–36 (2000)
20. Voelter, M.: DSL Engineering (2013), Version 1.0, http://dslbook.org

Test Suite Completeness and Partial Models

Adilson Luiz Bonifacio[1,*] and Arnaldo Vieira Moura[2]

[1] Computing Department, University of Londrina, Londrina, Brazil
bonifacio@uel.br
[2] Computing Institute, University of Campinas, Campinas, Brazil
arnaldo@ic.unicamp.br

Abstract. Test suite generation and coverage analysis have been widely studied for FSM-based models. Several studies focused on specific conditions for verifying completeness of test suites. Some have found necessary conditions for test suite completeness, whereas other approaches obtained sufficient, but not necessary, conditions for this problem. Most of these works restricted the specification or the implementation FSM models in several ways. Some works show how to generate specific complete test suites, but they do not deal with the general problem of checking completeness for any given test suite. In this work we describe necessary and sufficient conditions that guarantee test suite completeness even in the presence of partial FSM models, and when test cases are blocking.

Keywords: test suite completeness, partial FSMs, blocking sequences, perfectness.

1   Introduction

Many studies have investigated the automatic generation of test suites based on Finite State Machine (FSM) models. Several of them focused on the automatic generation of test suites with full fault detection. In other words, they provide test suites with complete fault coverage [3–6, 10–12, 15, 20]. Several of these methods have shown sufficient conditions that guarantee the completeness of the test suites. Some other works proved necessary conditions [13, 21] for the completeness of test suites. However, in most of them, specifications are required to be reduced machines with n states, while the corresponding implementation FSMs must have $m \geq n$ states [5]. Other works are more restrictive, either requiring $m = n$ [14, 18, 20] or completely specified specifications [8, 9, 11, 12, 20].

In a recent approach [1, 2], necessary and sufficient conditions have been proposed for test suite completeness, where the authors assume more relaxed constraints on the models, and still guarantee test completeness. On the other hand, these works still require that implementations be completely specified. Moreover, the approach also relies on the classical notion of completeness, where test cases are assumed to run in both the specification and in the implementation models, even when implementations are considered as black-boxes.

---

* Supported by FAPESP, process 2012/23500-6.

D. Giannakopoulou and G. Salaün (Eds.): SEFM 2014, LNCS 8702, pp. 96–110, 2014.
© Springer International Publishing Switzerland 2014

Here, we treat more general FSMs, allowing for partial models both as specifications and as implementations. We prove that our method succeeds in determining the completeness of test suites, even in situations where other approaches fail. Further, we relax the classical notion of completeness in order to deal with a more realistic situation in practice. More specifically, we allow for blocking test cases, that is, test cases which may not run to completion in neither the specification nor in the implementation machines. We also provide necessary and sufficient conditions for checking completeness of test suites in this new scenario.

Section 2 summarizes some recent works that are more closely related to our approach. Section 3 contains basic definitions and notations. Section 4 discusses necessary and sufficient conditions for test suite completeness with partial FSM models. We present a simple example to illustrate the application of our method in Section 5. In Section 6 we describe necessary and sufficient conditions for test suite completeness in the presence of blocking test cases. We conclude in Section 7.

2 Related Works

In this section we describe some works that address issues more closely related to our approach. Petrenko and Yevtushenko [15] propose a complete test suite generation method based on partial FSMs. They treat unreduced machines where separating sequences do not exist. However, their focus is on test suite generation only, together with sufficient conditions for the generated test suites to be complete. In our work, we give not only sufficient, but also necessary conditions under which *any given test suite* can be ascertained to be complete. Moreover, we also state necessary and sufficient conditions for checking test suite completeness even in the presence of blocking test cases.

In a recent work, Simão et al. [17] use the notion of test convergence in order to reduce the length of tests. Two tests are said to be convergent for a set of FSMs if they lead from the initial state to the same state in each FSM in the set. Their test suite generation method relies on sufficient conditions for completeness based on previous knowledge about the implementations, which are no longer complete black boxes, and other specific requirements, such as reducibility and completeness of both the specification and implementation models. In an early version [16] the authors show necessary and sufficient conditions for test suite completeness, but only when some strong constraints apply to both the specification and implementation models, such as minimality of the implementations and also reducibility and completeness of both the specification and implementation models. Further, both approaches do not deal with blocking test cases where sequences do not run to completion in one, or both, of the FSM models.

A number of other works proposed methods for checking test suite completeness. However, these approaches show only sufficient conditions for the problem, which can lead to inconclusive verdicts. Simão and Petrenko [18] uses the notion of confirmed sets. A set of input sequences is said to be confirmed when its sequences are such that when a pair of them lead to a same state in the specification, then the pair also lead to a common state in the implementation, and vice-versa. Moreover, their approach also requires complete implementations as well as reduced specification and implementation machines. They also restrict implementations to having at most as many states as the specification, giving rise to the notion of n-complete test suites, where n is the number of states in the specification. Again, they do not deal with the more general case, when blocking sequences may be present in the test suites.

More recent studies [1, 2] treat not only sufficient but also necessary conditions that can be used to guarantee m-completeness of test suites. The authors use simulation relations to characterize m-completeness of *any given test suites*. But they also require implementation candidates to be complete FSM models and, besides, blocking test cases are not considered.

In this work we provide necessary and sufficient conditions for checking test suite completeness for partial models, both in the specification side and also in the implementation side. We show that our method always succeeds in determining the completeness of any given test suite, avoiding inconclusive verdicts. Moreover, we relax the classical notion of completeness in order to treat blocking test cases, that is, test cases which may not run to completion in neither the specification nor in the implementation machines. We also provide necessary and sufficient conditions for checking completeness of test suites in this more realistic scenario.

3   Definitions and Notation

In this section we present some definitions and notation that will be useful later. Let $\mathcal{I}$ be an alphabet. The length of any finite sequence of symbols α over $\mathcal{I}$ is indicated by $|\alpha|$. The empty sequence will be indicated by ε, with $|\varepsilon| = 0$. The set of all sequences of length k over $\mathcal{I}$ is denoted by $\mathcal{I}^k$, while $\mathcal{I}^\star$ names the set of all finite sequences from $\mathcal{I}$. When we write $\sigma = x_1 x_2 \cdots x_n \in \mathcal{I}^\star$ $(n \geq 0)$ we mean $x_i \in \mathcal{I}$ $(1 \leq i \leq n)$, unless noted otherwise. Given any two sets of sequences $A, B \subseteq \mathcal{I}^\star$, their symmetric difference will be indicated by $A \ominus B$, that is $A \ominus B = (\overline{A} \cap B) \cup (A \cap \overline{B})$, where $\overline{A}$ indicates the complement of A with respect to $\mathcal{I}^\star$. By $A \setminus B$ we mean set difference.

Remark 1. $A \ominus B = \emptyset$ iff[1] $A = B$.

Next, we write the definition of a Finite State Machine [2, 7].

Definition 1. *A FSM is a system* $M = (S, s_0, \mathcal{I}, \mathcal{O}, D, \delta, \lambda)$ *where*

- S *is a finite set of* states
- $s_0 \in S$ *is the initial state*
- $\mathcal{I}$ *is a finite set of* input actions *or* input events
- $\mathcal{O}$ *is a finite set of* output actions *or* output events
- $D \subseteq S \times \mathcal{I}$ *is a* specification domain
- $\delta : D \to S$ *is the* transition function
- $\lambda : D \to \mathcal{O}$ *is the* output function. $\qquad\qquad\Box$

---

[1]   Here, 'iff' is short for 'if and only if'.

In what follows M and N will always denote the FSMs $(S, s_0, \mathcal{I}, \mathcal{O}, D, \delta, \lambda)$ and $(Q, q_0, \mathcal{I}, \mathcal{O}', D', \mu, \tau)$, respectively. Let $\sigma = x_1 x_2 \cdots x_n \in \mathcal{I}^\star$, $\omega = a_1 a_2 \cdots a_n \in \mathcal{O}^\star$ $(n \geq 0)$. If there are states $r_i \in S$ $(0 \leq i \leq n)$ such that $\delta(r_{i-1}, x_i) = r_i$ and $\lambda(r_{i-1}, x_i) = a_i$ $(1 \leq i \leq n)$, then we may write $r_0 \overset{\sigma/\omega}{\to} r_n$. When the input sequence σ, or the output sequence ω, is not important, then we may write $r_0 \overset{\sigma/}{\to} r_n$, or $r_0 \overset{/\omega}{\to} r_n$, respectively, and, if both sequences are not important we may write $r_0 \to r_n$. We can also drop the target state, when it is not important, e.g. $r_0 \overset{\sigma/\omega}{\to}$ or $r_0 \to$. It will be useful to extend the functions δ and λ to pairs $(s, \sigma) \in S \times \mathcal{I}^\star$. Let $\widehat{D} = \left\{ (s, \sigma) \mid s \overset{\sigma/}{\to} \right\}$. Now define the extensions $\widehat{\delta} : \widehat{D} \to S$ and $\widehat{\lambda} : \widehat{D} \to \mathcal{O}^\star$ by letting $\widehat{\delta}(s, \sigma) = r$ and $\widehat{\lambda}(s, \sigma) = \omega$ whenever $s \overset{\sigma/\omega}{\to} r$. When there is no reason for confusion, we may write D, δ and λ instead of $\widehat{D}$, $\widehat{\delta}$ and $\widehat{\lambda}$, respectively. Also, the function $U : S \to \mathcal{I}^\star$ will be useful, where $U(s) = \{ \sigma \mid (s, \sigma) \in \widehat{D} \}$.

Now we are in a position to define test cases and test suites.

Definition 2. *Let M be a FSM. A* test suite *for M is any finite subset of $\mathcal{I}^\star$. Any element of a test suite is a* test case. □

Since test cases must be applied from initial states, an implementation under test must be brought to its initial state before the application of a test case. This can be achieved using a homing sequence [9, 20]. If there exist more than one test case to be applied, it is assumed that the implementation under test has a reset operation. The reset operation brings the machine back to its initial state [4, 5].

The notion of simulation is given as follows.

Definition 3. *Let M and N be FSMs. We say that a relation $R \subseteq S \times Q$ is a* simulation *(of M by N) iff $(s_0, q_0) \in R$, and whenever we have $(s, q) \in R$ and $s \overset{x/a}{\to} r$ in M, then there is a state $p \in Q$ such that $q \overset{x/a}{\to} p$ in N and with $(r, p) \in R$. We say that M and N are* bi-similar *iff there are simulation relations $R_1 \subseteq S \times Q$ and $R_2 \subseteq Q \times S$.* □

4   Test Suite Completeness for Partial FSMs

In this section we give necessary and sufficient conditions for verifying test suite completeness for FSM models. Such conditions will allow for partiality in both the specification and implementation machines.

We start by writing the classical notion of distinguishability and equivalence.

Definition 4. *Let M and N be FSMs and let $s \in S$, $q \in Q$. Let $C \subseteq \mathcal{I}^\star$. We say that s and q are* C-distinguishable *iff $\lambda(s, \sigma) \neq \tau(q, \sigma)$ for some $\sigma \in U(s) \cap U(q) \cap C$, denoted $s \not\approx_C q$. Otherwise, s and q are* C-equivalent, *denoted $s \approx_C q$. We say that M and N are* C-distinguishable *iff $s_0 \not\approx_C q_0$, and they are* C-equivalent *iff $s_0 \approx_C q_0$.* □

When C is not important, or when it is clear from the context, we might drop the index. When there is no mention to C, we understand that we are taking $C = \mathcal{I}^*$. In this case, the condition $U(s_0) \cap U(q_0) \cap C$ reduces to $U(s_0) \cap U(q_0)$.

Next we introduce the concept of n-complete test suites.

Definition 5. *Let M be a FSM, let T a test suite for M and take $n \geq 1$. Then T is n-complete for M iff for any FSM N, with $U(s_0) \subseteq U(q_0)$ and $|Q| \leq n$, if $M \not\approx N$ then $M \not\approx_T N$.* □

The following result will help to show the existence of simulation relations.

Lemma 1. *Let M and N be FSMs. Let $n \geq 1$, $s_i \in S$, $p_i \in Q$ $(1 \leq i \leq n)$ and $x_i \in \mathcal{I}$, $a_i \in \mathcal{O}$, $b_i \in \mathcal{O}'$ $(1 \leq i < n)$ be such that $s_i \overset{x_i/a_i}{\to} s_{i+1}$ and $p_i \overset{x_i/b_i}{\to} p_{i+1}$ $(1 \leq i < n)$. Assume further that $s_1 \approx p_1$. Then $s_i \approx p_i$ $(1 \leq i \leq n)$ and $a_1 a_2 \cdots a_{n-1} = b_1 b_2 \cdots b_{n-1}$.*

Proof. An easy induction on $n \geq 1$ [1]. □

The next lemma states half of our desired result. We note that specifications and candidate implementations can be partial machines.

Lemma 2. *Let T be a n-complete test suite for a FSM M. Let N be a FSM such that $U(s_0) \subseteq U(q_0)$ and $|Q| \leq n$. If $M \approx_T N$ then there exists a simulation of M by N.*

Proof. Define a relation $R \subseteq S \times Q$ by letting $(s, q) \in R$ iff $\delta(s_0, \alpha) = s$ and $\mu(q_0, \alpha) = q$ for some $\alpha \in \mathcal{I}^*$. Since $\delta(s_0, \varepsilon) = s_0$ and $\mu(q_0, \varepsilon) = q_0$ we get $(s_0, q_0) \in R$.

Now assume $(s, q) \in R$ and let $s \overset{x/a}{\to} r$ in M, for some $r \in S$, $x \in \mathcal{I}$ and $a \in \mathcal{O}$. Since T is n-complete for M, $U(s_0) \subseteq U(q_0)$, $|Q| \leq n$ and $M \approx_T N$, Definition 5 gives $M \approx N$. Hence, $s_0 \approx q_0$. Since $(s, q) \in R$, the construction of R gives some $\alpha \in \mathcal{I}^*$ such that $\delta(s_0, \alpha) = s$ and $\mu(q_0, \alpha) = q$. Composing, we get $\delta(s_0, \alpha x) = \delta(s, x) = r$ and so $\alpha x \in U(s_0)$. Since $U(s_0) \subseteq U(q_0)$, we obtain $\alpha x \in U(q_0)$. Then $\mu(q_0, \alpha x) = \mu(q, x) = p$, for some $p \in Q$.

Collecting, we get $\delta(s_0, \alpha) = s$, $\mu(q_0, \alpha) = q$ and $s_0 \approx q_0$. Using Lemma 1 we conclude that $s \approx q$, and then we must have $\lambda(s, x) = a = \tau(q, x)$. So, from $(s, q) \in R$, $s \overset{x/a}{\to} r$ we obtained $p \in Q$ such that $q \overset{x/a}{\to} p$. Finally, we note that we also have $\mu(q_0, \alpha x) = p$ and $\delta(s_0, \alpha x) = r$. The definition of R now gives $(r, p) \in R$. This shows that R is a simulation relation, concluding the proof. □

We now show the converse. That is, if there is a simulation of M by any T-equivalent FSM with $U(s_0) \subseteq U(q_0)$ and with at most n states, then n-completeness of the test suite follows.

Lemma 3. *Let M be a FSM, let T a test suite for M and take $n \geq 1$. Assume that M can be simulated by any T-equivalent FSM N, with $U(s_0) \subseteq U(q_0)$ and $|Q| \leq n$. Then T is n-complete for M.*

Proof. We proceed by contradiction. Assume that T is not n-complete for M. Then, by Definition 5, there exists a T-equivalent FSM N with $U(s_0) \subseteq U(q_0)$, $|Q| \leq n$, and such that $M \not\approx N$. Using Definition 4, we get an input sequence $\sigma = x_1 \ldots x_n \in \mathcal{I}^\star$ $(n \geq 0)$ and an input symbol $y \in \mathcal{I}$ such that $\lambda(s_0, \alpha) = \tau(q_0, \alpha)$ and $\lambda(s_0, \alpha y) \neq \tau(q_0, \alpha y)$. Let $s_i \in S$, $q_i \in Q$ $(1 \leq i < n)$ be such that $\delta(s_{i-1}, x_i) = s_i$ and $\mu(q_{i-1}, x_i) = q_i$ $(1 \leq i \leq n)$. So, $\delta(s_0, \sigma) = s_n$ and $\mu(q_0, \sigma) = q_n$. Further, we get $s \in S$ and $q \in Q$ such that $\delta(s_n, y) = s$, $\mu(q_n, y) = q$ and $\lambda(s_n, y) \neq \tau(q_n, y)$.

Since N is T-equivalent to M, $U(s_0) \subseteq U(q_0)$ and $|Q| \leq n$, the hypothesis gives a simulation relation $R \subseteq S \times Q$.

CLAIM: $(s_i, q_i) \in R$ $(0 \leq i \leq n)$.

PROOF OF THE CLAIM. We go by induction on $i \geq 0$.

BASIS: we get $(s_0, q_0) \in R$ directly from Definition 3.

INDUCTION STEP: assume that $(s_i, q_i) \in R$ for some $i < n$. Since $\delta(s_i, x_{i+1}) = s_{i+1}$, Definition 3 gives a $q \in Q$ such that $\mu(q_i, x_{i+1}) = q$, $\lambda(s_i, x_{i+1}) = \tau(q_i, x_{i+1})$ and $(s_{i+1}, q) \in R$. But we already have $\mu(q_i, x_{i+1}) = q_{i+1}$ and, since μ is a function, we get $q = q_{i+1}$. Thus $(s_{i+1}, q_{i+1}) \in R$ extending the induction and establishing the Claim. $\triangle$

Using the Claim, we get $(s_n, q_n) \in R$. Since $\delta(s_n, y) = s$, Definition 3 gives a $p \in Q$ such that $(s, p) \in R$, $\mu(q_n, y) = p$, and $\lambda(s_n, y) = \tau(q_n, y)$, which is a contradiction. $\square$

Putting together the previous results we obtain necessary and sufficient conditions for n-completeness of test suites, even if we allow for partial implementation candidates.

Theorem 1. *Let M be a FSM, let T be a test suite for M and let $n \geq 1$. Then, T is n-complete for M iff M can be simulated by any T-equivalent FSM N that satisfies $U(s_0) \subseteq U(q_0)$ and $|Q| \leq n$.*

Proof. Assume that T is n-complete for M. Then, Lemma 2 guarantees that N can simulate M when N is T-equivalent to M, $U(s_0) \subseteq U(q_0)$ and $|Q| \leq n$. Now assume that M can be simulated by any T-equivalent FSM N such that $U(s_0) \subseteq U(q_0)$ and $|Q| \leq n$. Then, Lemma 3 guarantees that T is n-complete for M. $\square$

Remark 2. Note that Theorem 1 is valid even in the absence of the condition $|Q| \leq n$, if Definition 5 is also changed accordingly. But removing the condition would result in a vacuous statement, as no test suite would then be complete.

5   An Example

An algorithm for checking completeness of test suites has been investigated [1, 2]. We modify that algorithm in order to adapt it to treat partial implementations. Basically, we add a new step to check if the condition $U(s_0) \subseteq U(q_0)$ holds, given an specification M and any candidate FSM N. So, now, the algorithm proceeds in three steps, given a specification M and a test suite T: construct a T-tree; check language containment; and check for a simulation relation.

At the end of the first step, the algorithm constructs all possible FSMs, with n states and of which all T-equivalent FSMs are extensions, where n is an upper bound on the number of states for FSM implementations, as given in Definition 5. We illustrate the tree growing process by the following example depicted in Figure 2.

In the second step, we check if the condition $U(s_0) \subseteq U(q_0)$ holds, given the specification M and any candidate FSM N obtained at the end of first step. If it does hold, then N should be passed on to the final step that checks for a simulation relationship, otherwise it should be discarded. This step can be efficiently done by noting that from any FSM $M = (S, s_0, \mathcal{I}, \mathcal{O}, D, \delta, \lambda)$ we can readily extract a finite automaton $M_A = (S, s_0, \mathcal{I}, \delta, F)$ [19] where the set of final states is taken to be $F = S$. Let $L(M_A)$ be the language accepted by such an automaton. Then, clearly, $U(s_0) \subseteq U(q_0)$ if and only if $L(M_A) \subseteq L(N_A)$. And this test can be performed efficiently [19].

The final step then checks if all remaining FSMs can effectively simulate M. If the answer is positive, we declare T to be complete for M. If, on the other hand, the algorithm proves that any of the remaining FSMs was unable to simulate M, then T is declared not complete for M.

Next, as an illustration we apply the whole procedure, which is based on the main result given in Theorem 1. Let M be the FSM depicted in Figure 1, and let $T = \{01000, 000, 10\}$ be a test suite for M. Assume that we are treating implementation machines with up to $m = 3$ states. A T-tree [1, 2] for M is partially illustrated in Figure 2.

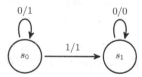

Fig. 1. Specification FSM M

The procedure starts with a root labeled (s_0, q_0), at level zero, representing a trivial machine Z_0 with empty transition and output functions. Let $\sigma = 01000$ be the first test case chosen from T. It is now the current test case. The first input symbol of σ is a 0 and so we get the two descendant nodes at level one. The leftmost corresponds to extending Z_0 according to $q_0 \xrightarrow{0/1} q_0$, and the second corresponds to adding a new state q_1 and extending Z_0 with $q_0 \xrightarrow{0/1} q_1$. The current test case is now reduced to $\sigma = 1000$, and we proceed to nodes at level 1. The leftmost node at level 1, say node u, represents a machine Z_1, as indicated in Figure 2. Since we do not have $q_0 \xrightarrow{1/}$ in Z_1, we generate new descendants for

u by extending Z_1 according to $q_0 \xrightarrow{1/1} q_0$, and also by adding a new state q_1 and letting $q_0 \xrightarrow{1/1} q_1$. Next, we examine the second node at level 1, say node w, representing a machine Z_2 in the figure. Since we do not have $q_1 \xrightarrow{1/}$ in Z_2, we generate new descendants for w by extending Z_2 according to $q_1 \xrightarrow{1/1} q$ for all states $q \in \{q_0, q_1\}$ that are already in Z_2. These are the leftmost two descendants of w. Since Z_2 has two states and we are treating implementation FSMs with at most $m = 3$ states, node w gets another descendant by adding a new state q_2 to Z_2 and extending it as required by $q_1 \xrightarrow{1/1} q_2$. This is the rightmost descendant of w.

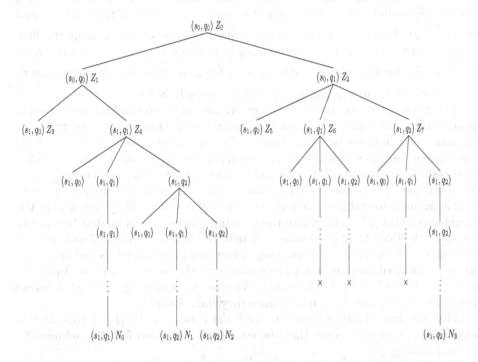

Fig. 2. T-tree for FSM depicted in Figure 1

The current test case is now reduced to $\sigma = 000$, and we proceed with nodes at level 2. When we consider the leftmost node at level 2, labeled (s_1, q_0), representing machine Z_3, we notice that we have $s_1 \xrightarrow{0/0} s_1$ in M but $q_0 \xrightarrow{0/1} q_0$ in Z_3. This indicates an incompatibility and we terminate the process for this node, leaving it behind. Next, we examine the second node at level 2, say node v, representing machine Z_4. Since we do not have $q_1 \xrightarrow{0/}$ in Z_4, we generate new descendants for v by extending Z_4 according to $q_1 \xrightarrow{0/0} q$ for all states $q \in \{q_0, q_1\}$ that are already in Z_4. These are the leftmost two descendants of v. Again, since Z_4 has two states and we are treating implementation FSMs with at most $m = 3$ states, node v gets another descendant by adding a new state q_2 to Z_4 and extending it by requiring $q_1 \overset{0/0}{\to} q_2$. This is the rightmost descendant of v.

In the third node at level 2, representing a machine Z_5, we notice that we have $s_1 \overset{0/0}{\to} s_1$ in M but $q_0 \overset{0/1}{\to} q_1$ in Z_5. This indicates an incompatibility and we terminate the process for this node, leaving it behind. We then pick the fourth node at level 2, say node r, representing a machine Z_6, as indicated in the figure. Since we do not have $q_1 \overset{0/}{\to}$ in Z_6, we generate new descendants for r by extending Z_6 according to $q_1 \overset{0/0}{\to} q$ for all states $q \in \{q_0, q_1\}$ that are already in Z_6. These are the leftmost two descendants of r. Since Z_6 has two states and we are treating implementation FSMs with at most $m = 3$ states, node r gets another descendant by adding a new state q_2 to Z_6 and extending it as required by $q_1 \overset{0/0}{\to} q_2$. This is the rightmost descendant of r. Next, we examine the fifth node at level 2, say node z, representing a machine Z_7. Since we do not have $q_2 \overset{0/}{\to}$ in Z_7, we generate new descendants for z by extending Z_7 according to $q_1 \overset{0/0}{\to} q$ for all states $q \in \{q_0, q_1, q_2\}$ that are already in Z_7.

At this point we have reduced the current test to $\sigma = 00$ and the tree growing process continues until we exhaust it. When the current test is reduced to $\sigma = \varepsilon$, we must take another test case from T. In the example, we take $\sigma = 000$ as the current test case. Because we are restarting the tree growing process with a new test case, we must relabel all nodes at level 5 with the root label, (s_0, q_0). We note that this is not explicitly indicated in Figure 2. The growing process continues until we exhaust the current test case $\sigma = 000$. The symbol $\times$ in the figure represents a branch where the growing process is terminated because of incompatibilities. After processing $\sigma = 000$, the last test case in T not already used is $\sigma = 10$. After the tree growing process terminates for this last test case, we have obtained four machines T-equivalent to M, namely, machines N_0 to N_3, indicated in the last level in Figure 2. Machine N_0 is isomorphic to M, whereas machines N_1, N_2 and N_3 are not, since they have 3 states.

After the first phase, we need to check the condition $U(s_0) \subseteq U(q_0)$. In this example, it is easily checked that the condition is satisfied for all machines N_i, $i = 0, 1, 2, 3$.

The third phase starts with a set of pairs of machines N_i and candidate simulation relations R_i, that is we have the set $\mathcal{M} = \{(N_i, R_i) \mid 0 \le i \le 3\}$. Initially, R_i contains only the pair of initial states for M and N_i. We first extract the pair (N_0, R_0) from $\mathcal{M}$, where machine N_0 can be read directly from the T-tree. Since N_0 is isomorphic to M, the third phase routinely verifies that N_0 can simulate M. We illustrate a pass of this third phase when it returns to $\mathcal{M}$ and extracts the next pair, namely, (N_1, R_1).

Machine N_1 can be read from the T-tree, and is depicted in Figure 3. Initially, R_1 contains (s_0, q_0), unmarked. We mark it as visited and proceed. For the input symbol 0 we get $s_0 \overset{0/1}{\to} s_0$ in M and $q_0 \overset{0/1}{\to} q_0$ in N_1, but the pair (s_0, q_0) is already in R_1. With input symbol 1 we get $s_0 \overset{1/1}{\to} s_1$ and $q_0 \overset{1/1}{\to} q_1$, and we add (s_1, q_1) to R_1, unmarked. Now, $R_1 = \{(s_0, q_0)^{\ddagger}, (s_1, q_1)\}$, with visited pairs indicated by

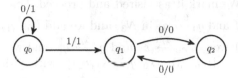

Fig. 3. FSM N_1

a ‡. We mark (s_1, q_1) as visited and, with input symbol 0, we get $s_1 \overset{0/0}{\to} s_1$ and $q_1 \overset{0/0}{\to} q_2$, and we add (s_1, q_2) to R_1, unmarked. Since $(s_1, 1) \notin D$ we are done with (s_1, q_1). Now, $R_1 = \{(s_0, q_0)^{\ddagger}, (s_1, q_1)^{\ddagger}, (s_1, q_2)\}$. We mark (s_1, q_2) as visited and need only consider the input symbol 0, since $(s_1, 1) \notin D$. We get $s_1 \overset{0/0}{\to} s_1$ and $q_2 \overset{0/0}{\to} q_1$, and so R_1 does not change. Now, $R_1 = \{(s_0, q_0)^{\ddagger}, (s_1, q_1)^{\ddagger}, (s_1, q_2)^{\ddagger}\}$. We have no more unmarked pairs in R_1 and the examination of the pair (N_1, R_1) terminates without reaching a conflict.

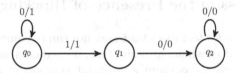

Fig. 4. FSM N_2

The procedure returns to $\mathcal{M}$ and picks the pair (N_2, R_2). Machine N_2 can also be read from the T-tree, and is depicted in Figure 4. It proceeds as it did with te pair (N_1, R_1) and reaches the point when $R_2 = \{(s_0, q_0)^{\ddagger}, (s_1, q_1)^{\ddagger}, (s_1, q_2)\}$. Then we mark (s_1, q_2) as visited and need only consider the input symbol 0, since $(s_1, 1) \notin D$. We get $s_1 \overset{0/0}{\to} s_1$ and $q_2 \overset{0/0}{\to} q_2$, and so R does not change. Now, $R_2 = \{(s_0, q_0)^{\ddagger}, (s_1, q_1)^{\ddagger}, (s_1, q_2)^{\ddagger}\}$. Again, we have no more unmarked pairs in R_2 and the examination of the pair (N_2, R_2) also terminates without reaching a conflict.

Finally, the procedure extracts the last pair, (N_3, R_3) from $\mathcal{M}$. Again, machine N_3 is read from the T-tree that is depicted in Figure 5. Initially, R_3 contains

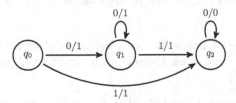

Fig. 5. FSM N_3

(s_0, q_0), unmarked. We mark it as visited and proceed. For the input symbol 0 we get $s_0 \overset{0/1}{\to} s_0$ in M and $q_0 \overset{0/1}{\to} q_1$ in N_3, and we add (s_0, q_1) to R_3, unmarked. With input symbol 1 we get $s_0 \overset{1/1}{\to} s_1$ and $q_0 \overset{1/1}{\to} q_2$, and we add (s_1, q_2) to R_3, unmarked. Now, $R_3 = \{(s_0, q_0)^\ddagger, (s_0, q_1), (s_1, q_2)\}$, with visited pairs indicated by a $\ddagger$. We mark (s_0, q_1) as visited and, with input symbol 0, we get $s_0 \overset{0/1}{\to} s_0$ and $q_1 \overset{0/1}{\to} q_1$, but the pair (s_0, q_1) is already in R_3. With input symbol 1 we get $s_0 \overset{1/1}{\to} s_1$ and $q_1 \overset{1/1}{\to} q_2$, but the pair (s_1, q_2) is already in R_3. Now, $R_3 = \{(s_0, q_0)^\ddagger, (s_0, q_1)^\ddagger, (s_1, q_2)\}$. We mark (s_1, q_2) as visited and need only consider the input symbol 0, since $(s_1, 1) \notin D$. We get $s_1 \overset{0/0}{\to} s_1$ and $q_2 \overset{0/0}{\to} q_2$, and so R_3 does not change. Now, $R_3 = \{(s_0, q_0)^\ddagger, (s_0, q_1)^\ddagger, (s_1, q_2)^\ddagger\}$. We have no more unmarked pairs in R_3 and the examination of the pair (N_3, R_3) terminates without reaching a conflict.

We would return to $\mathcal{M}$ for another pair, but now we have $\mathcal{M} = \emptyset$. So, the procedure would terminate successfully, declaring T to be 3-complete for M.

6   Completeness in the Presence of Blocking Test Cases

In this section we allow for test cases that may not run to completion in candidate implementations. That is, when put under test, implementations may not output the same number of events as there were input symbols in the test case. This kind of fault can be readily identified by observing the external behavior of the model. We show necessary and sufficient conditions for test suite completeness in the presence of blocking test cases.

Given a FSM model M, a *blocking* test case for M is one that does not run to completion in M. Given a test suite T, two FSM models M and N are considered T-equivalent in the presence of blocking test cases, if all blocking test cases for M in T are also blocking for N, and vice-versa. Furthermore, any test case that is non-blocking for both M and N must output identical behaviors when run through both models. We then investigate necessary and sufficient conditions for T to be a complete test suite, when considering this more general scenario.

We start by making precise the new notion of equivalent models.

Definition 6. *Let M and N be FSMs and let $s \in S$, $q \in Q$. Let $C \subseteq \mathcal{I}^\star$. We say that s and q are C-alike, denoted $s \sim_C q$, iff $(U(s) \ominus U(q)) \cap C = \emptyset$ and $\lambda(s, \sigma) = \tau(q, \sigma)$ for all $\sigma \in U(s) \cap U(q) \cap C$. Otherwise, s and q are C-unlike, denoted $s \nsim_C q$. We say that M and N are C-alike iff $s_0 \sim_C q_0$, otherwise they are C-unlike.* ☐

Again, when C is not important, or when it is clear from the context, we might drop the index, and when there is no mention to C, we understand that we are taking $C = \mathcal{I}^\star$.

Remark 3. Using Remark 1, we note that $s \sim q$ is equivalent to $U(s) = U(q)$ and $\lambda(s, \sigma) = \tau(q, \sigma)$ for all $\sigma \in U(s)$.

The new notion of test suite completeness now reflects the fact that we may be in the presence of blocking test cases. In order to avoid ambiguities we rename completeness to perfectness.

Definition 7. *Let M be a FSM and T be a test suite for M. Then T is perfect for M iff for any FSM N, if $M \not\sim N$ then $M \not\sim_T N$.*   □

That is when T is a perfect test suite for a specification M, then for any implementation under test N, if M and N are unlike, then they are also T-unlike.

The following result will be useful when we consider certain bi-similarities.

Lemma 4. *Let M and N be FSMs. Let $n \geq 1$, $s_i \in S$, $p_i \in Q$ $(1 \leq i \leq n)$ and $x_i \in \mathcal{I}$, $a_i \in \mathcal{O}$, $b_i \in \mathcal{O}'$ $(1 \leq i < n)$ be such that $s_i \overset{x_i/a_i}{\to} s_{i+1}$ and $p_i \overset{x_i/b_i}{\to} p_{i+1}$ $(1 \leq i < n)$. Assume further that $s_1 \sim p_1$. Then $s_i \sim p_i$ $(1 \leq i \leq n)$ and $a_1 a_2 \cdots a_{n-1} = b_1 b_2 \cdots b_{n-1}$.*

Proof. Let $\sigma = x_1 x_2 \cdots x_{n-1}$, $\omega_1 = a_1 a_2 \cdots a_{n-1}$ and $\omega_2 = b_1 b_2 \cdots b_{n-1}$. We clearly have $s_1 \overset{\sigma/\omega_1}{\to} s_n$ and $p_1 \overset{\sigma/\omega_2}{\to} p_n$. Definition 6 immediately gives $\omega_1 = \omega_2$, because $s_1 \sim p_1$ and $\sigma \in U(s_1) \cap U(q_1)$.

To see that $s_i \sim p_i$ $(1 \leq i \leq n)$ we go by induction on n. The basis is trivial and we proceed with the induction step. Let $1 \leq k < n$ and assume $s_k \sim p_k$. Let $\alpha = x_1 \cdots x_k$. Clearly $\delta(s_1, \alpha) = s_{k+1}$, $\mu(p_1, \alpha) = p_{k+1}$ and so $\alpha \in U(s_1) \cap U(p_1)$. For te sake of contradiction, assume that $s_{k+1} \not\sim p_{k+1}$. By Definition 6 we have two cases.

CASE 1: $U(s_{k+1}) \ominus U(p_{k+1}) \neq \emptyset$.
    Let $\beta \in U(s_{k+1})$ and $\beta \notin U(p_{k+1})$. This gives $\alpha\beta \in U(s_1)$ and $\alpha\beta \notin U(p_1)$. Hence $U(s_1) \ominus U(p_1) \neq \emptyset$, contradicting $s_1 \sim p_1$. The situation when $\beta \notin U(s_{k+1})$ and $\beta \in U(p_{k+1})$ is entirely analogous.
CASE 2: $\beta \in U(s_{k+1}) \cap U(p_{k+1})$ and $\lambda(s_{k+1}, \beta) \neq \tau(p_{k+1}, \beta)$, for some $\beta \in \mathcal{I}^\star$.
    This gives $\alpha\beta \in U(s_1) \cap U(p_1)$. Moreover,

$$\lambda(s_1, \alpha\beta) = \lambda(s_1, \alpha)\lambda(\delta(s_1, \alpha), \beta)) = \lambda(s_1, \alpha)\lambda(s_{k+1}, \beta), \text{ and}$$
$$\tau(p_1, \alpha\beta) = \tau(p_1, \alpha)\tau(\mu(p_1, \alpha), \beta)) = \tau(p_1, \alpha)\tau(p_{k+1}, \beta).$$

Because $|\lambda(s_1, \alpha)| = |\tau(p_1, \alpha)|$ and $\lambda(s_{k+1}, \beta) \neq \tau(p_{k+1}, \beta)$, we get $\lambda(s_1, \alpha\beta) \neq \tau(p_1, \alpha\beta)$. Since $\alpha\beta \in U(s_1) \cap U(p_1)$, this contradicts $s_1 \sim p_1$.

The proof is complete.   □

The next result guarantees the existence of bi-simulations in the presence of blocking test cases.

Lemma 5. *Let T be a perfect test suite for a FSM M. Let N be a FSM such that $M \sim_T N$. Then M and N are bi-similar.*

Proof. Define a relation $R_1 \subseteq S \times Q$ by letting $(s, q) \in R_1$ if and only if $\delta(s_0, \alpha) = s$ and $\mu(q_0, \alpha) = q$ for some $\alpha \in \mathcal{I}^\star$, $s \in S$ and $q \in Q$. Since $\delta(s_0, \varepsilon) = s_0$ and $\mu(q_0, \varepsilon) = q_0$ we get $(s_0, q_0) \in R_1$.

Now assume $(s, q) \in R_1$ and let $s \xrightarrow{x/a} r$ for some $r \in S$, $x \in \mathcal{I}$ and $a \in \mathcal{O}$. Since $(s, q) \in R_1$, the definition of R gives some $\alpha \in \mathcal{I}^*$ such that $\delta(s_0, \alpha) = s$ and $\mu(q_0, \alpha) = q$. Composing, we get $\delta(s_0, \alpha x) = \delta(s, x) = r$ and so $\alpha x \in U(s_0)$. Since T is perfect for M and $M \sim_T N$, Definition 6 gives $M \sim N$, that is $s_0 \sim q_0$. Further, Definition 6 and Remark 3 imply $U(s_0) = U(q_0)$, and so $\alpha x \in U(q_0)$. Then $\mu(q, x) = p$, for some $p \in Q$. Since $s_0 \sim q_0$, $\delta(s_0, \alpha) = s$ and $\mu(q_0, \alpha) = q$, Lemma 4 gives $s \sim q$. But $x \in U(s) \cap U(q)$, and so we must have $a = \lambda(s, x) = \tau(q, x)$. Thus, we have found $p \in Q$ with $q \xrightarrow{x/a} p$. Since $\delta(s_0, \alpha x) = r$ and $\mu(q_0, \alpha x) = p$, we also have $(r, p) \in R_1$. This shows that R_1 is a simulation relation.

A similar argument will show that $R_2 \subseteq Q \times S$, where $R_2 = R_1^{-1}$, is also a simulation relation. Thus M and N are bi-similar, as desired. $\square$

We now show the converse, that is, if M is bi-similar to any FSM N that is T-alike to it, then T is a perfect test suite for M.

Lemma 6. *Let M be a FSM and T a test suite for M. Assume that any FSM that is T-alike to M is bi-similar to it. Then T is perfect for M.*

Proof. We proceed by contradiction. Assume that T is not perfect for M. Then, by Definition 7, there exists a FSM N such that $M \sim_T N$ and $M \not\sim N$. Hence, since $M \sim_T N$, we get that N is bi-similar to M, and so there are simulation relations $R_1 \subseteq S \times Q$ and $R_2 \subseteq Q \times S$.

CLAIM: Let $s = \delta(s_0, \alpha)$ and $q = \mu(q_0, \alpha)$ for some $\alpha \in \mathcal{I}^*$. Then $(s, q) \in R_1$ and $(q, s) \in R_2$.

PROOF OF THE CLAIM. The argument is an easy induction on $|\alpha| \geq 0$ and is omitted.

Since $M \not\sim N$, by Definition 6 we have two cases:

CASE 1: $\alpha \in U(s_0) \ominus U(q_0)$, for some $\alpha \in T$.

We may assume that $|\alpha|$ is minimum.

If $\alpha \in U(q_0)$ and $\alpha \notin U(s_0)$, then we may write $\alpha = \beta x$, where $\beta \in \mathcal{I}^*$, $x \in \mathcal{I}$ are such that $\beta \in U(q_0) \cap U(s_0)$. Thus, $\delta(s_0, \beta) = s$, $\mu(q_0, \beta) = q$ and $\mu(q, x) = p$, for some $s \in S$ and some $q, p \in Q$. Since $(q_0, s_0) \in R_2$, we can use Lemma 4 and write $(q, s) \in R_2$. Because R_2 is a simulation and $\mu(q, x) = p$ we get some $r \in S$ such that $\delta(s, x) = r$. But this gives $\delta(s_0, \alpha) = \delta(s_0, \beta x) = \delta(s, x) = r$, that is $\alpha \in U(s_0)$, a contradiction.

When $\alpha \notin U(q_0)$ and $\alpha \in U(s_0)$, the argument is analogous.

CASE 2: There is some $\alpha \in U(s_0) \cap U(q_0)$ with $\lambda(s_0, \alpha) \neq \tau(q_0, \alpha)$.

Again, assume that $|\alpha|$ is minimum. Then, there are $\beta \in \mathcal{I}^*$, $x \in \mathcal{I}$, $s \in S$ and $q \in Q$ such that $\alpha = \beta x$ and $\delta(s_0, \beta) = s$, $\mu(q_0, \beta) = q$. Further, we get some $r \in S$, $p \in Q$ such that $\delta(s, x) = r$, $\mu(q, x) = p$, $a = \lambda(s, x) \neq \tau(q, x) = b$.

Using the Lemma 4, we may write $(s, q) \in R_1$. Because we have $s \xrightarrow{x/a} r$ in M and R_1 is a simulation, we know that there is some $t \in Q$ such that $q \xrightarrow{x/a} t$ in N, with $(r, t) \in R_1$. But we already had $q \xrightarrow{x/b} p$ in N. Hence, since τ is a function, we conclude that $a = b$, which is a contradiction.

The proof is now complete.   □

Combining the previous results we obtain necessary and sufficient conditions for the perfectness of test suites.

Theorem 2. *Let M be a FSM and T be a test suite for M. Then T is perfect for M iff any T-alike FSM is bi-similar to M.*

Proof. Assume that T is perfect for M. Lemma 5 guarantees that N and M are bi-similar when N is T-alike to M. Now assume that any T-alike FSM is bi-similar to M. In this case, Lemma 6 guarantees that T is perfect for M.   □

7   Conclusions

In this work we showed necessary and sufficient conditions for checking completeness of test suites for more relaxed FSM models. Our approach is general in the sense that specifications and implementations models are required to be only deterministic. So partial FSM machines are treated in the specification side and also in the implementation side. We have also presented an example in order to illustrate the application of our approach.

Further we described a new approach for checking completeness of test suites taking into account FSM models that allow for blocking test cases. For that, we introduced the new notion of test suite perfectness, a relaxation of the classical notion of test suite completeness. We have also provided necessary and sufficient conditions for checking test suite perfectness in a more realistic sceneries.

All claims herein are proved correct by rigorous arguments. Being based on necessary and sufficient proofs, our approaches always provide definitive answers regarding test suite completeness and perfectness, thus never issuing inconclusive verdicts.

We leave for future works the possibility of testing our algorithms in practical situations, and comparing the results with other methods for testing test suites completeness and perfectness.

References

1. Bonifacio, A.L., Moura, A.V.: Necessity and sufficiency for checking m-completeness of test suites. Tech. Rep. IC-13-21, Institute of Computing, University of Campinas (September 2013),
   http://www.ic.unicamp.br/~reltech/2013/13-21.pdf
2. Bonifacio, A.L., Moura, A.V.: On the Completeness of Test Suites. In: Proceedings of the 29th Annual ACM Symposium on Applied Computing (SAC), Gyeongju, Korea, vol. 2, pp. 1287–1293. ACM (March 2014) ISBN: 978-1-4503-2469-4
3. Bonifacio, A.L., Moura, A.V., da Silva Simão, A.: Model partitions and compact test case suites. Int. J. Found. Comput. Sci. 23(1), 147–172 (2012)
4. Chow, T.S.: Testing software design modeled by finite-state machines. IEEE Trans Software Eng. 4(3), 178–187 (1978)

5. Dorofeeva, R., El-Fakih, K., Yevtushenko, N.: An improved conformance testing method. In: Wang, F. (ed.) FORTE 2005. LNCS, vol. 3731, pp. 204–218. Springer, Heidelberg (2005)

6. Fujiwara, S., Bochmann, G.V., Khendek, F., Amalou, M., Ghedamsi, A.: Test selection based on finite state models. IEEE Trans. Software Eng. 17(6), 591–603 (1991)

7. Gill, A.: Introduction to the theory of finite-state machines. McGraw-Hill, New York (1962)

8. Gonenc, G.: A method for the design of fault detection experiments. IEEE Trans. Comput. 19(6), 551–558 (1970)

9. Hennie, F.C.: Fault detecting experiments for sequential circuits. In: Proceedings of the Fifth Annual Symposium on Switching Circuit Theory and Logical Design, Princeton, New Jersey, USA, November 11-13, pp. 95–110. IEEE (1964)

10. Hierons, R.M.: Separating sequence overlap for automated test sequence generation. Automated Software Engg. 13(2), 283–301 (2006)

11. Hierons, R.M., Ural, H.: Reduced length checking sequences. IEEE Trans. Comput. 51(9), 1111–1117 (2002), http://dx.doi.org/10.1109/TC.2002.1032630

12. Hierons, R.M., Ural, H.: Optimizing the length of checking sequences. IEEE Trans. Comput. 55(5), 618–629 (2006), http://dx.doi.org/10.1109/TC.2006.80

13. Petrenko, A., Bochmann, G.V.: On fault coverage of tests for finite state specifications. Computer Networks and ISDN Systems 29, 81–106 (1996)

14. Petrenko, A., Yevtushenko, N.: On test derivation from partial specifications. In: Bolognesi, T., Latella, D. (eds.) FORTE. IFIP AICT, vol. 55, pp. 85–102. Springer, Heidelberg (2000)

15. Petrenko, A., Yevtushenko, N.: Testing from partial deterministic fsm specifications. IEEE Trans. Comput. 54(9), 1154–1165 (2005), http://dx.doi.org/10.1109/TC.2005.152

16. Simão, A., Petrenko, A., Yevtushenko, N.: Generating reduced tests for fsms with extra states. In: Núñez, M., Baker, P., Merayo, M.G. (eds.) TESTCOM/FATES 2009. LNCS, vol. 5826, pp. 129–145. Springer, Heidelberg (2009)

17. Simao, A., Petrenko, A., Yevtushenko, N.: On reducing test length for fsms with extra states. Softw. Test. Verif. Reliab. 22(6), 435–454 (2012), http://dx.doi.org/10.1002/stvr.452

18. Simao, A.D.S., Petrenko, P.: Checking completeness of tests for finite state machines. IEEE Trans. Computers 59(8), 1023–1032 (2010)

19. Sipser, M.: Introduction to the Theory of Computation. International Thomson Publishing (1996)

20. Ural, H., Wu, X., Zhang, F.: On minimizing the lengths of checking sequences. IEEE Trans. Comput. 46(1), 93–99 (1997), http://dx.doi.org/10.1109/12.559807

21. Yao, M.Y., Petrenko, A., von Bochmann, G.: Fault coverage analysis in respect to an fsm specification. In: INFOCOM, pp. 768–775 (1994)

Automated Error-Detection and Repair
for Compositional Software Specifications

Dalal Alrajeh and Robert Craven

Department of Computing, Imperial College London, UK
{dalal.alrajeh,robert.craven}@imperial.ac.uk

Abstract. The complexity of error diagnosis in requirements specifications, already high, is increased when requirements refer to various system components, on whose interaction the system's aims depend. Further, finding causes of error, and ways of overcoming them, cannot easily be achieved without a systematic methodology. This has led researchers to explore the combined use of verification and machine-learning to support automated software analysis and repair. However, existing approaches have been limited by using formalisms in which modularity and compositionality cannot be explicitly expressed. In this paper we overcome this limitation. We define a translation from a representative process algebra, Finite State Processes, into the action language $C+$. This enables forms of verification not supported by previous methods. We then use a logic-programming equivalent of $C+$, to which we apply inductive logic programming for learning repairs to system components while ensuring no new errors are introduced and interactions with other components are maintained. These two phases are iterated until a correct specification is reached, enabling rigorous and scalable support for automated analysis and repair of component-based specifications.

1 Introduction

Research into formal specification, verification and error diagnosis has played a significant role in improving software safety and reliability. Such methods rely on specifying the system in a formal language (e.g., temporal logic, process algebras) and using automated verification techniques such as model checking and theorem proving to check that the specified system satisfies some given property. Though such methods are useful for detecting errors in software specifications (e.g., [14]), identifying the exact causes of error and resolving them is a very difficult task that is mostly performed manually—defeating the aim of automation, and increasing the likelihood of error.

In recent years researchers in software engineering have responded to this by deploying a combination of verification and machine learning techniques to improve software specifications. For example, in [1] the authors describe a method for incrementally refining a consistent specification, expressed in first-order temporal logic, with respect to some given property using an integration of model checking and Inductive Logic Programming (ILP). In [2], the authors give a method for revising temporal specifications that may be incorrect or inconsistent using model checking and artificial neural networks. Such advances overcome some of the difficulties of generating alternative candidate repairs to detected errors, ensuring consistency of the computed solutions

D. Giannakopoulou and G. Salaün (Eds.): SEFM 2014, LNCS 8702, pp. 111–127, 2014.
© Springer International Publishing Switzerland 2014

with the available specification and property. However, a very significant drawback of such approaches is that verification and specification improvement are at system level only: they do not relate the specification to the individual system components, nor do they support compositional analysis. With this drawback come the familiar problems of modularity, scalability and realizability. (Realizability means that suggested repairs can be assigned to and achieved by individual components.) Furthermore, these approaches either require the engineer to specify an action thought to have produced the error in the output violation run; or require the engineer to simplify the diagnosis procedure by assuming that the last action in the run is the cause.

In this paper we propose a new approach for incrementally detecting errors in and repairing compositional software specifications using verification and ILP. Our framework: (i) supports error-diagnosis and repair at component level rather than system level; (ii) diagnoses multiple errors in a single iteration; (iii) can hypothesize faults at any point in a violation run, and fix them wherever they are; (iv) finds all minimal repairs with respect to a given input language; (v) guarantees deadlock-free repairs to components consistent with the original specification; and (vi) is fully automated.

Our systems specifications are given in Finite State Processes (FSPs), a well-studied process algebra [20]. FSPs enable a user to represent the behaviour at the architectural level, specifying the system in a modular manner as a composition of processes executed concurrently and interacting with each other through shared actions. FSPs contain operations common to most algebraic languages and are supported by the model checker LTSA [20]. We show how FSP descriptions can be formulated in the action language $C+$ [12] (from non-monotonic reasoning in A.I.) and its corresponding logic programming representation, $\mathcal{EC}+$ [6] which are the languages used by the verification and learning tasks respectively. $C+$ is a natural choice: similarly to FSPs, it has a semantics of LTSs and allows concise representation of domains. It also supports many forms of reasoning, including the computation of all runs of a given length that satisfy a given description, and the construction complex queries over runs, states and transition of processes. We describe a systematic translation of $C+$ into logic programs, where the resulting logic programs allows us to deploy ILP in the discovery of repairs.

The paper is structured at follows. §2 gives background, and §3 our running example. In §4 we describe verification using $C+$. §5 presents the use of $\mathcal{EC}+$ and ILP to correct FSP descriptions. Related work and a conclusion follow in §6.

2   Background

Labelled Transition Systems (LTSs)

LTSs [15] are behaviour models representing the changing states of a system, in response to actions occurring within or outside the system. Both FSPs and $C+$ use LTSs in their semantics. An LTS L is a structure (S, A, Δ, S_0), where S is a finite set of *states*, A is a finite set of *action labels* (also known as the *alphabet*), $\Delta \subseteq S \times A \times S$ is the *transition* relation, and S_0 is a set of *initial states*. An LTS is *deterministic* iff for each $s \in S$ and each action label $a \in A$, there is at most one state s' for which $(s, a, s') \in \Delta$. It is called *deadlock-free* if for each $s \in S$ reachable from an initial state in S_0, there is at least one state s' for which $(s, a, s') \in \Delta$. We use $s \xrightarrow{a} s'$ as a shorthand for $(s, a, s') \in \Delta$. A *run of length* n through an LTS (S, A, Δ, S_0) is a sequence $(s_0, a_0, s_1, \ldots, a_{n-1}, s_n)$ such that $s_0 \in S_0$ and for all i with $0 \leqslant i < n$, $(s_i, a_i, s_{i+1}) \in \Delta$. We often write such runs as expressions $(s_0 \xrightarrow{a_0} \cdots \xrightarrow{a_{n-1}} s_n)$.

Where several LTSs represent the individual components of a larger system, the individual LTSs can be composed together by synchronising the actions common to their alphabets and interleaving the remaining actions. To denote the composed behaviour of two LTSs $P = (S_P, A_P, \Delta_P, S_{P,0})$ and $Q = (S_Q, A_Q, \Delta_Q, S_{Q,0})$ we use the commutative and associative binary parallel composition operator, $\|$. The LTS $(P \parallel Q)$ is the structure $(S_P \times S_Q, A_P \cup A_Q, \Delta, S_{P,0} \times S_{Q,0})$ such that $(s_p, s_q) \xrightarrow{a} (s'_p, s'_q)$ iff either: (i) $a \in A_P \setminus A_Q$ and $s_p \xrightarrow{a} s'_p$ and $s_q = s'_q$; (ii) $a \in A_Q \setminus A_P$ and $s_q \xrightarrow{a} s'_q$ and $s_p = s'_p$; or (iii) $a \in A_P \cap A_Q$ and $s_p \xrightarrow{a} s'_p$ and $s_q \xrightarrow{a} s'_q$. (i) and (ii) represent independent execution of P and Q; (iii) gives joint execution of a shared action.

Finite State Processes (FSPs)

FSPs [20] are process algebras, based on CSP [13] and CCS [22], for describing the behaviour of components of concurrent systems. Each component is represented as a *primitive process*, comprising a number of *local processes*, which can be thought of as phases of the component's operation. The scope of a local process is the primitive process in which it is defined. A *composite process* represents the composition of a set of primitive processes. The signature of a primitive process includes a process name, names of its local processes and a set of action labels A, the *alphabet*. Primitive process operators include '$\rightarrow$' for action prefixing (showing which actions can be performed to lead to another local process) and '$|$' for choice (more than one possible action).

The language also allows for definitions of constants, integer ranges, sets of action labels. In the current paper we focus on the basic syntax for FSPs. We refer to it here as *fundamental FSPs* and define it in §4. Each 'full' FSP has an equivalent formulation in terms of fundamental FSPs—so there is no loss of expressivity [20].

A composite process represents the composition of a number of primitive processes. Similarly to LTSs, the operator $\|$ is used to denote the composed behaviour of two processes. The expression $P \parallel Q$ means that the P and Q may execute actions independently but must synchronise actions common to their alphabets. A composite process is identified by a process name preceded by the symbol "$\|$". In §4 we will describe the precise syntax and semantics of the restricted form of FSPs we work with.

$\mathcal{C}+$ and $\mathcal{E}\mathcal{C}+$

Action languages [11] are logical formalisms for representing the way systems change as a consequence of actions and events occurring in them.

The language of $\mathcal{C}+$ is built over a *multi-valued propositional signature* σ, with *fluent constants* σ^f—describing states—and the *action constants* σ^a—describing actions and events. An *atom* $c=v$ has $c \in \sigma$ and $v \in dom(c)$—the non-empty *domain* of c's values. An *interpretation* I maps constants to values; we write $I \models c=v$ iff $I(c) = v$. $I(\sigma)$ is the set of interpretations of the signature σ. A *fluent formula* is built from Boolean connectives using fluent atoms ($c=v$ where $c \in \sigma^f$) and $\perp$ and $\top$ (for logical truth); an *action formula* is made from atoms containing only action constants, with $\top$, and must contain at least one action constant. The LTSs (S, A, Δ, S_0) used in the semantics of $\mathcal{C}+$ have $S \subseteq I(\sigma^f)$ and $A = I(\sigma^a)$; S_0 is S, and $\Delta \subseteq S \times A \times S$.

Causal laws determine the states S and transition relation Δ. A *static law* has the form F **if** G, where F and G are fluent formulas: if a state satisfies G, it must also satisfy F. A *fluent dynamic law* has the form F **if** G **after** ψ, where F and G are fluent formulas, and ψ is any formula with signature $\sigma^f \cup \sigma^a$. This means: for any transition (s, a, s'), if $s \cup a \models \psi$ and $s' \models G$, then $s' \models F$. (If G is $\top$, then we abbreviate the rule as F **after** ψ.) Finally, an *action dynamic law* is an expression α **if** ψ, where α is an action formula and ψ is as above. These mean: if $s \cup a \models \psi$, then $a \models \alpha$.

An *action description* is a set of causal laws; each defines an LTS (S, A, Δ, S_0). A law **inertial** c means the value of fluent constant f persists by default; **exogenous** a means (roughly) that a can be executed, or not executed, in every state. In later sections we will use the further abbreviation of **default** α **if** β for the action dynamic law α **if** $\alpha \wedge \beta$ and **nonexecutable** α **if** β for the fluent dynamic law $\perp$ **if** $\top$ **after** $\alpha \wedge \beta$. The **default** law represents that, where β is true, then α is true by default, whilst the **nonexecutable** is understood as false is derivable from a state where $\alpha \wedge \beta$ is true.

Current implementations of $\mathcal{C}+$, such as iCCalc, [1] are based on SAT solvers. Queries specify partial information about the values of fluent and action constants in the states and transitions of a run through the transition system, and answers take the form of the complete set of runs consistent with that specification.

In [6] it is shown that a subclass of action descriptions of $\mathcal{C}+$ (those without circular dependencies in causal laws) can be represented as normal logic programs (See Appendix) whose form is closely related to that of the Event Calculus [16]. We have adapted the form of those logic programs to suit our $\mathcal{C}+$ action descriptions for FSPs. The $\mathcal{EC}+$ formulation includes a translation of the specific causal theory, as well as core, domain-independent clauses to enable reasoning and ensure the semantics is respected. Domain specific facts include those of the predicate domain/2 (giving the domain of a fluent constant) and causes/5—where a fact causes(C2,V2,Act,C1,V1) corresponds to the presence of a fluent dynamic law $C2{=}V2$ **if** $\top$ **after** $Act{=}\mathbf{t} \wedge C_1{=}V_1$.

In conjunction with information about what is initially true in a given run (facts of init/2) and what actions occur at different times (facts of happens/2), the sets of clauses of an $\mathcal{EC}+$ logic program have stable models that are in one-to-one correspondence with runs through the LTS defined by the action descriptions [6].

Inductive Logic Programming

ILP [23] is a symbolic machine-learning technique for computing a hypothesis H from a background theory B (a logic program) and examples ($E = E^- \cup E^+$) such that: (i) $B \cup H \models e^+$ for each $e^+ \in E^+$; (ii) $B \cup H \not\models e^-$ for each $e^- \in E^-$. For shorthand we write (i) and (ii) as $B \cup H \models E^+$ and $B \cup H \not\models E^-$. A hypothesis space is the set of all hypotheses $\{H_i\}$ that satisfies the conditions set above. To restrict the size of the hypothesis space, some ILP methods make use of *mode declarations* (*MD*), a form of language bias that specifies the syntactic form of the hypotheses to be learned.

---

[1] See http://www.doc.ic.ac.uk/~rac101/iccalc/

It contains both head and body declarations that describe predicates that may appear, the desired input and output behaviour and number of instantiations. We use $s(MD)$ to denote the set of all hypotheses satisfying MD.

Typically, B is assumed partial but correct. The ILP task is to generate a hypothesis H that extends B to explain the examples. ILP is applicable to problems in which B is partially incorrect and must be revised. Parts of the background suspected to be responsible are removed from B and put in the revisable theory T. The revision of a theory T involves applying a transformation to T to obtain a new theory H, denoted $r(T,H)$, by deleting rules, adding facts, adding conditions to rules or deleting conditions from rules. A repair is called *minimal* if the number of revision operations required to transform one theory into another (the sum of all deletions and additions) is minimal.

Definition 1. *An* inductive task *is a tuple* $\langle B, T, E, MD \rangle$. *$B$ is the background theory, T is a revisable theory s.t. $T \subseteq s(MD)$, $E = E^+ \cup E^-$ is the examples and MD is the mode declaration. The logic program H, where $H \subseteq s(MD)$ and $r(T, H)$, is an* inductive solution *to the task* $\langle B, T, E, MD \rangle$ *iff* $B \cup H \models E^+$ *and* $B \cup H \not\models E^-$.

3   Running Example

Our running example is based on the production cell system [7]. It comprises two conveyor belts (feed belt and deposit belt), two products (a and b), a robot arm and two tools (drill and oven). The feed belt conveys raw products for the robot arm to pick up and process; the deposit belt conveys the processed products out of the cell. We define FSPs ARM, TOOL and RAW_PRODUCT (process names are in small capitals; actions are in italic), with the sets PRODUCTTYPES = $\{a, b\}$ and TOOLSET = $\{oven, drill\}$:

ARM = IDLE,

   IDLE = ([p : PRODUCTTYPES].*getFeedbelt* $\rightarrow$ PICKED_UP[p]),

   PICKED_UP[p : PRODUCTTYPES] = (*put*[t : TOOLSET][p] $\rightarrow$ PROCESSING[t][p]

      | [p].*putDepositbelt* $\rightarrow$ IDLE | [p].*getFeedbelt* $\rightarrow$ PICKED_UP[p]),

   PROCESSING[t : TOOLSET][p : PRODUCTTYPES] = (*get*[t][p] $\rightarrow$ PICKED_UP[p]).

   TOOL(T = 'any') = (*put*[T][p : PRODUCTTYPES] $\rightarrow$ *get*[T][p] $\rightarrow$ TOOL).

   RAW_PRODUCT(P = 'any') = ([P].*available* $\rightarrow$ [P].*getFeedbelt* $\rightarrow$ TOOL_AVAILABLE

      | [P].*unavailable* $\rightarrow$ RAW_PRODUCT),

   TOOL_AVAILABLE = (*put*[t : TOOLSET][P] $\rightarrow$ *get*[t][P] $\rightarrow$ TOOL_AVAILABLE

      | [P].*putDepositbelt* $\rightarrow$ RAW_PRODUCT).

where 'any means any constant value assigned in the composed system. ARM, TOOL and RAW_PRODUCT are primitive process names. ARM has three local processes: IDLE, PICKED_UP and PROCESSING. It is initially idle. When it is idle it can pick up a product from the feed belt [p : PRODUCTTYPES].*getFeedbelt* (in which case it progresses to the PICKED_UP process). Once it has picked up a product p, it can either put the product in a tool t (*put*[t][p]) and move to the PROCESSING phase or, from the same state, place it in the deposit belt [p].*putDepositbelt* and return to the IDLE phase, or it can get another product from the feed belt and continue in the same phase. If it puts in the tool for processing then it can remove the product from the tool and return to the PICKED_UP local process and continue from there. Note that in FSP, indices may appear either before or after action labels. The composite system is defined as below.

‖TOOLS = (TOOL(*oven*) ‖ TOOL(*drill*)).

‖RAW_PRODUCTS = (RAW_PRODUCT(*a*) ‖ RAW_PRODUCT(*b*)).

‖PRODUCTIONCELL = (ARM ‖ TOOLS ‖ RAW_PRODUCTS).

Consider the property "The robot arm should not process products a and b at the same time". We are interested in checking if this situation is permissible in our composite system PRODUCTIONCELL. In the following sections we show how to detect automatically violations to such properties and repair the specification if any violations exist.

4   Compositional Verification in $\mathcal{C}+$

This section presents a new approach to verification for component-based systems represented as FSPs. It considers a fundamental FSP description as input and automatically translates it into the $\mathcal{C}+$ language. iCCalc is then used to verify that a property specified in $\mathcal{C}+$ holds in every run of the system. Our focus is on a class of properties (called safety properties [18]) which express the notion that no 'bad' state will be reached and that are expressible in Linear Temporal Logic (LTL) [21]. In what follows we give details of the FSP translation and verification using iCCalc.

Specifying FSPs in $\mathcal{C}+$

Translation from FSPs into $\mathcal{C}+$ starts from *fundamental FSPs*.

Definition 2. *Let A be a finite set of action labels, and $\mathcal{Q}$ a finite set of state labels, called* Q-labels, *of the form Q_i. Then a* fundamental FSP definition *has the form:*

$$\text{PROC} = Q_0,$$
$$Q_0 = (a_{1,1} \to Q_{1,1} \mid \cdots \mid a_{1,l_1} \to Q_{1,m_1}),$$
$$\ldots, Q_n = (a_{n,1} \to Q_{n,1} \mid \cdots \mid a_{n,l_n} \to Q_{n,m_n}).$$

where the $a_{i,j}$ are in A and the $Q_i, Q_{i,j}$ are in $\mathcal{Q}$. (It is clear that a fundamental FSP definition is also a full FSP.) We also use a representation of a fundamental FSP PROC as 4-tuple of the form $(\mathcal{Q}, A, trans, \mathcal{Q}^*)$, where $\mathcal{Q}$ and A are as above, $\mathcal{Q}^* \subseteq \mathcal{Q}$ is the set of initial local processes, and $trans \subseteq \mathcal{Q} \times A \times \mathcal{Q}$ (the transition relation) represents the effect of the actions on the FSP as above: $(Q_i, a_{j,k}, Q_{l,m}) \in trans$ iff $Q_i = (\cdots \mid a_{j,k} \to Q_{l,m} \mid \cdots)$ forms part of the fundamental FSP definition. We will refer to fundamental FSPs just as 'FSPs' where this causes no confusion. Note that Q_0 always represents the initial local state of a process. For a fundamental FSP PROC, we use $\mathcal{Q}_{\text{PROC}}, A_{\text{PROC}}, trans_{\text{PROC}}$ and $\mathcal{Q}^*_{\text{PROC}}$ to refer to elements of the tuple representation.

Any full FSP can be translated into a fundamental FSP representation behaviourally equivalent (allowing the same sequences of actions to be performed) to the original. The main features of fundamental FSPs compared to the original FSPs are: (i) definitions of sequences of action prefixes are split by creating new local processes for each action prefix, (ii) each range-indexed local process is replaced with a set of local processes, one for each value in the specified range, and (iii) each range-indexed action prefix is replaced with a choice of action prefix for each value in the range.

We work with the tuple-based representation of fundamental FSPs. The semantics is an LTS; an FSP $(Q, A, trans, Q^*)$ defines the LTS $(Q, A, \{(Q, a, Q') \mid trans(Q, a) = Q'\}, Q^*)$. Composition of the LTSs defined by fundamental FSPs is then given using the definitions in §2. (The LTS defined by a 'full' FSP is equivalent to that defined by its fundamental equivalent.) To illustrate, consider the (full) FSP definition ARM in our running example. The equivalent fundamental FSP is shown below, where we have marked the identity of states according to their Q-values.[2]

$$\text{ARM} = Q_0,$$

$$Q_0 = (b.getFeedbelt \rightarrow Q_1 \mid a.getFeedbelt \rightarrow Q_4),$$

$$Q_1 = (b.putDepositbelt \rightarrow Q_0 \mid b.getFeedbelt \rightarrow Q_1 \mid put.drill.b \rightarrow Q_2$$
$$\mid put.oven.b \rightarrow Q_3 \mid a.getFeedbelt \rightarrow Q_4),$$

$$Q_2 = (get.drill.b \rightarrow Q_1), Q_3 = (get.oven.b \rightarrow Q_1),$$

$$Q_4 = (a.putDepositbelt \rightarrow Q_0 \mid b.getFeedbelt \rightarrow Q_1 \mid a.getFeedbelt \rightarrow Q_4$$
$$\mid put.drill.a \rightarrow Q_5 \mid put.oven.a \rightarrow Q_6),$$

$$Q_5 = (get.drill.a \rightarrow Q_4), Q_6 = (get.oven.a \rightarrow Q_4).$$

When translating into $\mathcal{C}+$, we work with sets of fundamental FSPs. The fluent constants will be their names; we use the fact that signatures of $\mathcal{C}+$ are multi-valued by setting the domain of each such fluent constant to be the Q-values (the states of the local processes) for the corresponding FSP. The only action constant is ACT, with domain the union of the sets of all action labels for each fundamental FSP. The causal laws of the translation encode the particular behaviour of the FSP. Consider again the ARM process. The $\mathcal{C}+$ translation has causal laws including:

ARM=Q_1 **after** ARM=Q_0 ∧ ACT=$b.getFeedbelt$	**inertial** ARM
ARM=Q_4 **after** ARM=Q_0 ∧ ACT=$a.getFeedbelt$	**default** ACT=$a.getFeedbelt$
nonexecutable ACT=$a.getFeedbelt$ **if** ARM=Q_2	
nonexecutable ACT=$a.getFeedbelt$ **if** ARM=Q_3	

The **caused** laws encode the response to actions; the **inertial** law ensures that the local state of ARM continues in its current state unless it is caused to be otherwise; the **default** laws ensure that actions can occur by default; and the **nonexecutable** laws specify the conditions under which actions cannot occur. Further: $\sigma^f = \{\text{ARM}\}$, $dom(\text{ARM}) = \{Q_0, Q_1, Q_2, Q_3, Q_4, Q_5, Q_6\}$, $\sigma^a = \{\text{ACT}\}$, $dom(\text{ACT}) = \{put.drill.X, put.oven.X, get.drill.X, get.oven.X, X.getFeedbelt, X.putDepositbelt\}$, for $X \in \{a, b\}$.

Definition 3. *Let* F *be a set of fundamental FSPs, named* $\{\text{PROC}_1, \ldots, \text{PROC}_n\}$. *The* $\mathcal{C}+$ *translation of* F *is* $F_{\mathcal{C}+}$, *where* $\sigma^f = \{\text{PROC}_1, \ldots, \text{PROC}_n\}$ *and* $\sigma^a = \{\text{ACT}\}$, *with:*

$$dom(\text{PROC}_i) = \{Q \mid \text{PROC}_i \in F, Q \in \mathcal{Q}_{\text{PROC}_i}\} \qquad dom(\text{ACT}) = \bigcup\{A_{\text{PROC}} \mid \text{PROC} \in F\}$$

and where the laws of $F_{\mathcal{C}+}$ *are:*

---

[2] The complete FSP description is available at
http://www.doc.ic.ac.uk/~da04/sefm14/production_cell.fsp

$\{\text{PROC}{=}Q' \text{ after } \text{PROC}{=}Q \wedge \text{ACT}{=}a \mid \exists \text{PROC} \in F, (Q, a, Q') \in trans_{\text{PROC}}\}$
$\cup \{\textbf{inertial } \text{PROC} \mid \text{PROC} \in F\} \cup \{\textbf{default } \text{ACT}{=}a \mid a \in dom(\text{ACT})\}$
$\cup \{\textbf{nonexecutable } \text{ACT}{=}a \text{ if } \text{PROC}{=}Q \mid a \in A_{\text{PROC}}, \neg\exists Q'((Q, a, Q') \in trans_{\text{PROC}}\}$

As with our illustration using the ARM process, the first set of laws encodes the response to actions; and the second set ensures that local states of processes persist unless caused to change. The third set of laws ensure that synchronisation is correctly modelled: where a is in the alphabet of the processes $\text{PROC}_1, \ldots, \text{PROC}_n$, then a can occur only when each of those processes is in an appropriate local state. Our first theorem shows that any transition in an LTS defined by a fundamental FSP is matched by a transition in the LTS defined by the corresponding $\mathcal{C}+$ action description.

Theorem 1. *Let F be a set of fundamental FSPs, $F = \{\text{PROC}_1, \ldots, \text{PROC}_n\}$, such that (S, A, Δ, S_0) is the LTS defined by the composition $\|F = (\text{PROC}_1 \| \cdots \| \text{PROC}_n)$ (where no PROC_i itself contains a composition). Let $F_{\mathcal{C}+}$ be the corresponding $\mathcal{C}+$ action description, with LTS (S', A', Δ', S_0'). Then there is a mapping $\lambda : S \to S'$ such that for any $(s_1, a, s_2) \in \Delta$, $(\lambda(s_1), \{\text{ACT}{=}a\}, \lambda(s_2)) \in \Delta'$.*
Proof. (See the Appendix.)   □

This result allows us to prove that runs through the LTS defined by the FSP starting at the initial state are in 1-1 correspondence with runs through the LTS defined by the $\mathcal{C}+$ encoding, starting at its initial state.

Theorem 2. *Let F be a set of fundamental FSPs, $F = \{\text{PROC}_1, \ldots, \text{PROC}_n\}$, such that (S, A, Δ, S_0) is the LTS defined by the composition $\|F = (F_1 \| \cdots \| F_n)$. Let $F_{\mathcal{C}+}$ be the corresponding $\mathcal{C}+$ action description and (S', A', Δ', S_0') its LTS, where s_0' is $\{\text{PROC}_i{=}Q_i \mid Q_i \in s_0\}$. Then there is a run $(s_0, a_0, s_1, a_1, \ldots, a_{n-1}, s_n)$ through (S, A, Δ, S_0) iff there is a run $(s_0', a_0', s_1', a_1', \ldots, a_{n-1}', s_n')$ through (S', A', Δ', S_0'), with (i) $a_i' = \{\text{ACT}{=}a_i\}$ and (ii) $s_i' = \{\text{PROC}_k{=}Q_k \mid Q_k \in s_i\}$.*

Proof. Left to right is a trivial inductive consequence of Theorem 1. Right to left is a simple inductive proof on the length of runs (details omitted owing to space limits).   □

As a result of Theorem 2, fundamental FSPs—and therefore also *all* FSPs—have a $\mathcal{C}+$ equivalent, in the sense that runs through the transition systems defined encode the same information. Tools developed for $\mathcal{C}+$ which allow different kinds of analysis can therefore be brought to bear in reasoning about properties of FSPs, which is the aim for the rest of this section. As the translation preserves the compositionality of the original FSP specification, one may remove and add the parts of the $\mathcal{C}+$ action description corresponding to different processes without harm, to streamline verification. It may be possible to make use of theorems in [27], which show when causal laws in an action description are redundant, in order to reduce the size of the translation. This would make the representation of the action description smaller, without affecting the state space.

Detecting Errors in iCCalc

We use iCCalc for verification. It takes as input a $\mathcal{C}+$ action description and a query as a partial specification of a run. Part of that query involves a specification of the initial state, which is extracted from the FSP specification (for each primitive process).

Verification involves checking runs of the system satisfy desirable properties, expressed in iCCalc as propositional formulas of time-stamped fluent and action constants $t : C=V$, where constant C must have the value V at t (the tth state or transition in the run). In this paper, we suppose properties are given in the iCCalc language. In [6] it is shown how bounded model checking over LTL can be expressed and performed in iCCalc using these constraints. The length of runs may be adjusted and incrementally increased as needed. The minimum length of runs needed to ensure completeness of the verification process can be calculated using methods such as those in [4].

To prove a property for a system composed of several FSP processes, we check the LTS defined by the corresponding $\mathcal{C}+$ action description satisfies the negation of that property. If a run satisfying its negation is found then the original property is violated and any run produced represents a counterexample. The constraint in the third argument of the query is expressed with the constant C being either ACT, the name of a primitive process or a fluent constant, and V representing the name of some action, a local state of a process or a fluent value ($\bot$ or $\top$). For instance, consider the property mention in §3 "The robot arm should not process two different product types at the same time". This is violated if there is a run leading to a state where the robot is processing product a and b concurrently. To check if this is possible in our model, we extend our production cell description in $\mathcal{C}+$ to include the fluent constants: $\{processing.a, \quad processing.b\}$ where $processing.a$ becomes true once the action $a.getFeedbelt$ happens, and becomes false once $a.putDepositbelt$ occurs and defined as false in the initial state. A similar definition is given to $processing.b$. In $\mathcal{C}+$:

$processing.a$ **after** ACT $= a.getFeedbelt$ $\qquad$ $\neg processing.a$ **after** ACT $= a.putDepositbelt$

default $\neg processing.a$

We include predefined queries to our input files for iCCalc, using a predicate *rinit* in which the third parameter captures each process's initial local state (see Appendix). To check whether there is a run from the initial state leading to a state where the robot's arm is processing two products a and b at the same time we prompt iCCalc with the query **query** $rinit(1..m, [\mathbf{max} : processing.a, \mathbf{max} : processing.b])$ where m is an upper-bound on the length of the runs we interested in (in this example m was set to 100). In our running example, iCCalc finds all six solutions in the composed system of length four showing a case where the robot's arm gets product b from the feed belt while its processing product a and vice versa—we show three of the six here (the rest in the Appendix):

$$\mathsf{r}^1 = (s_0 \xrightarrow{a.available} s_1 \xrightarrow{b.available} s_2 \xrightarrow{a.getFeedbelt} s_3 \xrightarrow{b.getFeedbelt} s_4)$$
$$\mathsf{r}^2 = (s_0 \xrightarrow{a.available} s_1 \xrightarrow{a.getFeedbelt} s_2 \xrightarrow{b.available} s_3 \xrightarrow{b.getFeedbelt} s_4)$$
$$\mathsf{r}^3 = (s_0 \xrightarrow{b.available} s_1 \xrightarrow{a.available} s_2 \xrightarrow{a.getFeedbelt} s_3 \xrightarrow{b.getFeedbelt} s_4)$$

iCCalc produces runs representing all shortest (distinct) counterexamples to the original property from the initial state of the composed system. This is an advantage over other approaches as it allows the learning procedure (§5) to diagnose problematic runs simultaneously and hence suggest minimal repairs for all of them in a single iteration.

Because the underlying technology for the verification is propositional SAT-solving, verification is in general NP-complete w.r.t. the clausal representation iCCalc uses. In practice we have found the time iCCalc takes appears to be sensitive to the *structure* of the action descriptions; we leave the further investigation of this for future work.

5   Repairing Compositional Specifications

The detection of violation runs in the verification phase shows the composition of the processes violates the original property. However, the location of the errors and their exact causes may be unclear. Errors may occur in the composition of all or some of the processes, or be caused by a single component within the composite system. They may be caused by an over-constrained, under-specified or incorrect specification. Hence any repair must take all these considerations into account and ensure that any fix would not introduce further errors. In this section we use ILP to address these problems.

Encoding Process Descriptions

To enable the use of ILP, we first translate the $C+$ theory for a set of fundamental FSPs, from §4, into an $\mathcal{EC}+$ logic program $\mathsf{F}_{\mathcal{EC}+}$ using a variant of the $C+$ to $\mathcal{EC}+$ translation detailed in [6]. The mapping for **caused** and **nonexecutable** clauses follows that described in [6]. For each fluent constant f and action constant a the $\mathcal{EC}+$ program contains a fact fc(f) and av(a); if a value $v \in dom(c)$, there is a fact domain(c,v). Further, for every member v of the domain of a fluent constant, there is a fact fv(v). Thus, the Q-values for a process are recorded. For instance, the program obtained from encoding the extract of causal laws in §4 is:[3]

```
causes(arm, q1, b_getFeedbelt, arm, q0).
causes(arm, q4, a_getFeedbelt, arm, q0).
inertial FC :- fc(FC).
nonexecutable(a_getFeedbelt, arm, q2).
nonexecutable(a_getFeedbelt, arm, q3).
fc(arm).  av(b_getFeedbelt). av(b_getFeedbelt). fv(q0). fv(q1).
fv(q2). fv(q3). fv(q4). domain(arm, q0). domain (arm, q1).
domain(arm, q3). domain(arm, q4).
domain(act, b_getFeedbelt). domain(act, a_getFeedbelt).
```

Interpretations of $\mathsf{F}_{\mathcal{EC}+}$ are given with respect to an initial state, encoded using the predicate init/2, e.g., init(arm, q0), and runs expressed as a conjunction of happens literals. To capture multiple runs in our $\mathcal{EC}+$ description, we enrich the signature of $\mathcal{EC}+$ programs to include run constants σ^r and extend $\mathcal{EC}+$ predicates happens, caused and broken with an additional argument for runs, e.g., happens(a,t,r) means action a happens at time t in run r. The domain-independent axioms in $\mathcal{EC}+$ programs, *Axioms*, are updated accordingly. They fall into four parts, so that *Axioms* $=$ $Ax_1 \cup Ax_2 \cup Ax_3 \cup Ax_4$. The first component, Ax_1, are inspired by the event calculus, and were given in [6]; they are described in the Appendix.

We introduce the predicate alphabet(c, a), which says that action a is in the alphabet of process c. The $C+$ to $\mathcal{EC}+$ translation is extended to generate these for each action in the alphabet of every process in the $C+$ theory. To ensure the semantics of FSP descriptions are preserved when learning repairs, we further include a set of constraints in the *Axioms*. Thus, Ax_2 is:

---

[3] The full program is available at
  http://www.doc.ic.ac.uk/~da04/sefm14/production_cell.lp

```
:-   causes(C, V1, A, C, V),          :-   causes(C, V1, A,   C, V),
     causes(C, V2, A, C, V),               nonexecutable(A, C, V).
     V1 != V2.                        :-   causes(C, V, A, C, V0),
:-   causes(C, V, AV, C, V0),              not domain(C,V0).
     not domain(C,V).                 :-   nonexecutable(A, C, V),
:-   causes(C, V1, A,  C, V),              not alphabet(C, A).
     not alphabet(C, A).
```

The top-left constraint ensures determinism: a process may not be caused to be in two different local states. The middle-left states that a process cannot be caused to be in a Q state outside its domain. The bottom-left specifies that only actions in the alphabet of a process may cause it to transit to a new state. The constraints on the right say that (i) an action cannot cause a system to evolve to a new state by executing a nonexecutable action, (ii) a process cannot be caused to transit to or from a state not within its domain and (iii) a process can only restrict the occurrence of actions within its alphabet.

In addition, it is necessary to ensure any changes to the existing process description result in a component specification that is deadlock-free. To do this, we include the following in *Axioms* which state collectively that a process must at least be able to evolve to one other state from every state in its domain. Our Ax_3 contains:

```
exists_nextQstate(Process, From):-
     causes(Process, To, A, Process, From).
:-   not exists_nextQstate(Process, From).
```

Note that although the above ensures that in any model of the $\mathcal{EC}+$ program, each process is deadlock-free, it does not guarantee this for the composite system. For the latter, the program must also include definitions of composite states reachable from the initial composite state, and a constraint similar to the above but with respect to composite states. We do not include these for lack of space.

To represent runs, we augment the language with the predicate attempt(a, t, r), meaning there is an attempt to execute the action a at time t in run r. Consequently, a run is encoded in $\mathcal{EC}+$ as two sets: (i) a set of attempt facts, and (ii) a rule with happens literals in the body as defined below.

Definition 4. *Let* $r = (s_0 \xrightarrow{a_0} \cdots \xrightarrow{a_{n-1}} s_n)$ *be a run. Its $\mathcal{EC}+$ translation is* $r_{\mathcal{EC}+} = r_{Ext} \cup r_{Hap}$ *where* $r_{Ext} = \{attempt(a_0,0,r) \ldots attempt(a_{t-1},t-1,r)\}$, *and* r_{Hap} *is the clause* run:-happens($a_0,0,r$),..., happens($a_{t-1},t-1,r$) *with* run *is a predicate uniquely to run r. For simplicity, we use* $\alpha_{r_{Hap}}$ *to denote the head of clause* r_{Hap}.

Finally, we further extend the set *Axioms* with Ax_4, below. The predicate nonexecutable expresses that an action is cannot be performed at a time point within a run.

```
happens(A, T, R):-                    :-   attempt(A1, T, R),
     attempt(A, T, R),                     attempt(A2, T, R),
     not nonexcutable(A,T, R).             A1 != A2.
nonexcutable(A,T, R):-
     caused(C, V, T, R),
     nonexecutable(A, C, V).
```

The first rule means that an action happens if it has been attempted at a time in which it may occur. The second rule says that an action is not executable at a time t in a run r if it the system has evolved to a state from which it cannot occur. The constraint ensures that actions may not occur concurrently. This completes our $\mathcal{EC}+$ encoding.

Learning Repairs

Our proposed repair method locates the cause of the violation run detected during verification and revises the FSP descriptions to prevent these from occurring, whilst guaranteeing the modifications are consistent with the composite specification and do not introduce deadlock. To achieve this using ILP, the revision task $\langle B, T, E, MD \rangle$ is set by assigning specific elements of the $F_{\mathcal{EC}+}$ program to B, T and E and defining MD.

When learning repairs for process descriptions, the revision task may be explicitly guided to explore the repair of specific components or all components within a given description. The ability to specify this is particularly useful if the specification contains process descriptions that are known to be correct or cannot be modified (as is the case in legacy systems). Hence when applying the revision task to a set of FSP descriptions, their $\mathcal{EC}+$ encoding is split into two sets: those for which revisions may be explored are added to T and those which are unmodifiable are included in B. Recall that a component specification in $\mathcal{EC}+$ is represented as a collection of **caused** and **nonexecutable** clauses in which its process label appears. The background B also includes *Axioms* and the $\mathcal{EC}+$ encoding of the runs obtained from Def. 4.

As mentioned in §4, iCCalc generates the shortest runs the composed system may execute to reach an undesirable state. The purpose of the repair is to identify necessary changes to the FSP descriptions so that these sequences are no longer permissible. Therefore for each violation run r, the constant appearing in the head of its r_{Hap} rule is included in the negative examples E^-.

As we are only interested in hypotheses that influence the set of runs permissible in the LTS of a composite system, we define the mode declaration to include rules that contain a *causes* and *nonexceutable* atom in the head. (Modification to the domain and alphabet of processes is discussed in the §6.) The repair task is defined as follows.

Definition 5. *Let* $F = F^1, ..., F^{m-1}, F^m, ..., F^n$ *be a set of fundamental FSPs and* R *a set of violation runs such that each run in* R *exists in the LTS defined by* $F^1 || ... || F^n$. F^* *is said to be a repaired specification of* F *with respect to* R *if* H *is an inductive solution to the inductive task* $\langle B, T, E, MD \rangle$ *such that:*

$$B = F^1_{\mathcal{EC}+} \cup ... \cup F^{m-1}_{\mathcal{EC}+} \cup Axioms \cup \bigcup_{1 < i} \{r^i_{\mathcal{EC}+} | r^i \in R\}; \quad T = F^m_{\mathcal{EC}+} \cup ... \cup F^n_{\mathcal{EC}+};$$

$$E^- = \bigcup_{1 < i} \alpha_{r^i_{Hap}} \text{ for all } r^i \in R; \quad \text{and } F^*_{\mathcal{EC}+} = F^1_{\mathcal{EC}+}, ..., F^{m-1}_{\mathcal{EC}+} \cup H.$$

Thus far we have only discussed the use of violation runs within the proposed approach. Although not required, it is possible to integrate information about runs that satisfy the property being verified and should be preserved by the repair task. This is done by applying the translation in Def. 4 to each desirable run r_j and including the constant appearing in the head of its r^j_{Hap} in the set of positive examples E^+. It is important to note that F^* is not unique. The approach will produce all possible sets of minimal repairs from which the engineer may select which one to use.

To compute the necessary repairs, we use the non-monotonic ILP tool ASPAL [5]. The ASPAL learning algorithm maps an ILP task into Answer Set Programming (ASP) [10] and uses an ASP solver to abduce ground literals from which a hypothesis H is constructed. For our running example, we include $\text{TOOLS}_{\mathcal{EC}+}$, $\text{RAW\_PRODUCTS}_{\mathcal{EC}+}$

and $(r_{\mathcal{E}C+}^1 \cup ... \cup r_{\mathcal{E}C+}^6)$ in the background theory, $\text{ARM}_{\mathcal{E}C+}$ as the revisable theory and $(\alpha_{r_{\text{Hap}}^1} \cup ... \cup \alpha_{r_{\text{Hap}}^6})$ as the negative examples. ASPAL returns a revised theory where

```
causes(arm, q4, a_getFeedbelt, arm, q4),
causes(arm, q1, b_getFeedbelt, arm, q4)
```

are deleted, and the facts

```
nonexecutable(b_getFeedbelt, arm, q4),
nonexecutable(b_getFeedbelt, arm, q4)
```

are added. Although ASPAL is based on ASP which is NP-complete, we have noted that the repair computation time increases with the number of rules that need grounding by the ASP solver, and the number of revisions required. Heuristics for optimising the repair procedure require further study. As a result of the above, the LTS model of the $\mathcal{C}+$ equivalent of $\mathsf{F}^*_{\mathcal{E}C+}$ is no longer consistent with the violations runs $r^1, ..., r^6$ [6].

Theorem 3. *Let F be a set of fundamental FSPs and R a set of violation runs such that each run in R exists in the LTS defined by F. Let F* be the repaired specification of F with respect to R. Then each run $r \in R$ no longer exists in the LTS defined by F*.*

Proof. Induction on run length, and using the fact that there is a unique stable model.

Although the theorem above proves the repair procedure eliminates the violation runs detected, the repair process does not guarantee longer violation runs are prohibited. Therefore, the verification and learning processes are iterated to detect any additional violation runs and repair the description accordingly. Violation runs from previous iterations are accumulated in E^- to ensure they are not made permissible by later revisions. The convergence of this process is guaranteed once no further violation runs up to the completeness bound discussed in §4 are detected. Since the repair is with respect to sets of violation runs, the approach takes fewer iterations than other approaches that integrate verification and learning. Once the cycle terminates, the final description is translated back into fundamental FSPs. In our running example, checking the $\mathcal{C}+$ equivalent of $(\mathsf{F}_{\mathcal{E}C+} \cup H)$ against the same property in iCCalc shows that no further violations exist and thus the approach converges in a single iteration. Consequently, the revised theory is mapped back into FSP through an inverse application of the translation in Def. 3 (space limitations prevent our providing the full translation). The final outcome is a repaired specification in which the only process modified is *Arm*:[4]

$$\text{ARM} = Q_0,$$
$$Q_0 = (b.getFeedbelt \rightarrow Q_1 \mid a.getFeedbelt \rightarrow Q_4),$$
$$Q_1 = (b.putDepositbelt \rightarrow Q_0 \mid b.getFeedbelt \rightarrow Q_1 \mid put.drill.b \rightarrow Q_2$$
$$\mid put.oven.b \rightarrow Q_3),$$
$$Q_2 = (get.drill.b \rightarrow Q_1), Q_3 = (get.oven.b \rightarrow Q_1),$$
$$Q_4 = (a.putDepositbelt \rightarrow Q_0 \mid a.getFeedbelt \rightarrow Q_4 \mid put.drill.a \rightarrow Q_5$$
$$\mid put.oven.a \rightarrow Q_6),$$
$$Q_5 = (get.drill.a \rightarrow Q_4), Q_6 = (get.oven.a \rightarrow Q_4).$$

---

[4] Full FSP available at: http://www.doc.ic.ac.uk/ da04/ sefm14/production_cell_revised.lts

6   Conclusion and Related and Future Work

In this paper we have shown how to repair compositional specifications described in FSP, following a phase of automatic verification. We showed how an action language widely studied in A.I. ($C+$) and ILP may be used to detect violations in properties expressible in LTL, and compute minimal repairs to individual components while consistency with the rest of the specification is maintained. This also involved defining a translation from FSPs into $C+$, and thence into its logic-programming equivalent, $\mathcal{E}C+$; the correctness of our translations was proved. Although the paper focuses on revising FSP descriptions, we see the work presented here as holding exciting potential for solving a wide range of problems in component-based software engineering.

To the best of our knowledge, the translation from process algebras into logic programs has not been explored before. Several authors have proposed using logic programming to reason about software behaviour described in other formalisms [1,2,25]. [1] provides a translation for specifications expressed in LTL to event calculus logic programs. However, both that work and [2] only generate a single violation run at a time and hence require users to provide additional positive and negative example runs to ensure computed solutions are not over-generalised and to speed up the convergence of the approach. This limitation is overcome in our work by the generation of multiple violation runs in a single verification step. Further, the formalism and semantics used here allow the modelling of concurrency without the need to introduce special actions explicitly in the language (e.g., 'tick' actions in [19]), removing one threat to scalability. The work in [25] for generating Event Calculus logic programs from descriptions expressed in a tabular specification language and applying abductive logic programming to discover violations to a restricted class of invariants, namely 'single-state' invariants. That work finds a restricted class of violations, and cannot repair specifications.

[24] also use learning, to compute assumptions representing LTSs which, when composed with given components, guarantee a property's satisfaction. The learning method is L*, which finds a regular language over a given alphabet and produces a deterministic finite-state machine that accepts the language. L* requires access to an oracle that iteratively accepts and rejects a generated string, and updates a table containing state information accordingly. ILP, by contrast, uses an expressive logic-based formalism capable of capturing state information among many other constructs such as constraints over the types of computable changes; this is not possible in L*.

Our approach is somewhat related to work on controller synthesis, e.g., [7]. For instance, techniques such as [7] automatically generate controllers that, together with a given model of the environment, satisfy a given property. Although these have shown good results, such techniques find at most one solution, even if many exist. Which controller is produced is chosen at random. Although our approach has only been demonstrated to learn revisions for existing process descriptions, we believe it may be adapted to compute all minimal process descriptions for a given alphabet.

In future work, we will investigate the use of our method to check liveness properties. We will modify the approach to handle revisions to the alphabet and extend the translation to embrace non-determinism and complex features such as abstractions and priorities. We will apply the work to model distribution problems [26], compositional specification synthesis from scenarios [17] and self-adaptive software [8].

References

1. Alrajeh, D., et al.: Elaborating requirements using model checking and inductive learning. IEEE Trans. Software Eng. 39(3), 361–383 (2013)
2. Borges, R., et al.: Learning and representing temporal knowledge in recurrent networks. IEEE TNN 22(12) (2011)
3. Clark, K.: Negation as failure. In: Readings in Nonmonotonic Reasoning, pp. 311–325 (1978)
4. Clarke, E., Kroning, D., Ouaknine, J., Strichman, O.: Completeness and complexity of bounded model checking. In: Steffen, B., Levi, G. (eds.) VMCAI 2004. LNCS, vol. 2937, pp. 85–96. Springer, Heidelberg (2004)
5. Corapi, D., et al.: Inductive logic programming as abductive search. In: Proc. ICLP 2010, pp. 54–63 (2010)
6. Craven, R.: Execution mechanisms for the action language $\mathcal{C}+$. PhD thesis. Imperial College London (2007)
7. D'Ippolito, N., et al.: Synthesis of live behaviour models for fallible domains. In: Proc. ICSE 2011, pp. 211–220 (2011)
8. Filieri, A., et al.: A formal approach to adaptive software: continuous assurance of non-functional requirements. Formal Aspects of Computing 24, 163–186 (2012)
9. Gelfond, M., Lifschitz, V.: The stable model semantics for logic programming. In: Proc. ICLP 1988, pp. 1070–1080 (1988)
10. Gelfond, M., Lifschitz, V.: Classical negation in logic programs and disjunctive databases. New Generation Computing 9, 365–385 (1991)
11. Gelfond, M., Lifschitz, V.: Action languages. Electron. Trans. Artif. Intell. 2, 193–210 (1998)
12. Giunchiglia, E., et al.: Nonmonotonic causal theories. Artif. Intell. 153(1-2), 49–104 (2004)
13. Hoare, C.: Communicating Sequential Processes. Commun. ACM 21(8), 666–677 (1978)
14. Johnson, K., et al.: An incremental verification framework for component-based software systems. In: Proc. CBSE 2013, pp. 33–42 (2013)
15. Keller, R.: Formal verification of parallel programs. CACM 19(7), 371–384 (1976)
16. Kowalski, R., Sergot, M.: A logic-based calculus of events. New Generation Computing 4, 67–95 (1986)
17. Krka, I., et al.: Synthesizing partial component-level behavior models from system specifications. In: Proc. ESEC/FSE, pp. 305–314 (2009)
18. Lamport, L.: The temporal logic of actions. ACM Trans. Program. Lang. Syst. 16(3), 872–923 (1994)
19. Letier, E., et al.: Deriving event-based transition systems from goal-oriented requirements models. Autom. Softw. Eng. 15(2), 175–206 (2008)
20. Magee, J., Kramer, J.: Concurrency: state models and java programs. John Wiley and Sons (1999)
21. Manna, Z., Pnueli, A.: The temporal logic of reactive and concurrent systems. Springer-Verlag New York, Inc. (1992)
22. Milner, R.: A Calculus of Communicating Systems. Springer, New York (1982)
23. Muggleton, S., Raedt, L.D.: Inductive logic programming: theory and methods. Journal of Log. Program. 19(20), 629–679 (1994)
24. Pasareanu, C., et al.: Learning to divide and conquer: applying the l* algorithm to automate assume-guarantee reasoning. Formal Methods in System Design 32, 175–205 (2008)
25. Russo, A., Miller, R., Nuseibeh, B., Kramer, J.: An abductive approach for analysing event-based requirements specifications. In: Stuckey, P.J. (ed.) ICLP 2002. LNCS, vol. 2401, pp. 22–37. Springer, Heidelberg (2002)
26. Sibay, G.E., Uchitel, S., Braberman, V., Kramer, J.: Distribution of modal transition systems. In: Giannakopoulou, D., Méry, D. (eds.) FM 2012. LNCS, vol. 7436, pp. 403–417. Springer, Heidelberg (2012)

27. Sergot, M., Craven, R.: Some Logical Properties of Nonmonotonic Causal Theories. In: Baral, C., Greco, G., Leone, N., Terracina, G. (eds.) LPNMR 2005. LNCS (LNAI), vol. 3662, pp. 198–210. Springer, Heidelberg (2005)

Appendix

Theorem 1. Let F be a set of fundamental FSPs, $\mathsf{F} = \{\text{PROC}_1, \ldots, \text{PROC}_n\}$, such that (S, A, Δ, S_0) is the LTS defined by the composition $\|\mathsf{F} = (\text{PROC}_1 \parallel \cdots \parallel \text{PROC}_n)$ (where no PROC_i itself contains a composition). Let $\mathsf{F}_{\mathcal{C}+}$ be the corresponding $\mathcal{C}+$ action description, with LTS (S', A', Δ', S_0'). Then there is a mapping $\lambda : S \to S'$ such that for any $(s_1, a, s_2) \in \Delta$, $(\lambda(s_1), \{\text{ACT}=a\}, \lambda(s_2)) \in \Delta'$.

Proof. Members $s \in S$ have the form $(Q_1, \ldots, Q_n)$ (§2). Let λ be s.t. $\lambda(Q_1, \ldots, Q_n)$ is $\{\text{PROC}_1=Q_1, \ldots, \text{PROC}_n=Q_n\}$. $\{\text{PROC}_1=Q_1, \ldots, \text{PROC}_n=Q_n\}$ is clearly a state of the LTS defined by $\mathsf{F}_{\mathcal{C}+}$. Assume $(s_1, a, s_2) \in \Delta$, and let $s_1 = (Q_1, \ldots, Q_n)$ and $s_2 = (Q_1', \ldots, Q_n')$. We must show $(\lambda(s_1), \{\text{ACT}=a\}, \lambda(s_2))$ is in Δ'. Let F_a be those members of F whose alphabets include a, i.e., $\mathsf{F}_a = \{\text{PROC} \in \mathsf{F} \mid a \in A_{\text{PROC}}\}$. Then for all i such that $1 \leqslant i \leqslant n$, if $\text{PROC}_i \in \mathsf{F}_a$ we have that $\textit{trans}_{\text{PROC}}(Q_i, a) = Q_i'$, by definition of the transition systems defined by FSPs, and thus a law

$$\text{PROC}=Q_i' \textbf{ after } \text{PROC}_i=Q_i \wedge \text{ACT}=a$$

in $\mathsf{F}_{\mathcal{C}+}$. (Note also that if $\text{PROC}_i \notin \mathsf{F}_a$ then $\textit{trans}_i(Q_i, a)$ is undefined.) Also using Definition 3 there must be a law

$$\textbf{default } \text{ACT}=a \textbf{ if } \text{PROC}_1^*=Q_1^* \wedge \cdots \wedge \text{PROC}_m^*=Q_m^*$$

in $\mathsf{F}_{\mathcal{C}+}$, where $\text{PROC}_1^*, \ldots, \text{PROC}_m^*$ are the members of F_a and the $Q_1^*, \ldots, Q_m^*$ the corresponding values in s_1. The presence (and absence) of these causal laws, together with the **inertial** laws, means that there is a transition

$$(\{\text{PROC}_1=Q_1, \ldots, \text{PROC}_n=Q_n\}, \{\text{ACT}=a\}, \{\text{PROC}_1=Q_1', \ldots, \text{PROC}_n=Q_n'\})$$

in Δ', which is precisely $(\lambda(s_1), \{\text{ACT}=a\}, \lambda(s_2))$ given our definition of λ.   □

Logic Programs

A *normal logic program* is a set of rules of the form

$$L : -L_1, \ldots, L_m, not\ N_1, \ldots, not\ N_n \tag{1}$$

where the L, L_i and N_i are *atoms* and $0 \leqslant m$, $0 \leqslant n$. L is called the head of the rule whilst $L_1, \ldots, L_m, not\ N_1, \ldots, not\ N_n$ is referred to as the rule's body. A *literal* is an atom possibly preceded by *not*, where *not* is the negation as failure operator [3]. When a program does not contain *not* in its rules, it is called a *definite logic program*.

A (Herbrand) *model* M of a logic program P, is a set of ground atoms such that, for each ground instance C of a rule in P, M satisfies the head of C whenever it satisfies the body of C. A program is consistent if it has at least one model. A model M is *minimal* if it does not strictly include any other model. Definite programs always have a unique minimal model. Normal programs may have one, none, or several minimal models. When there is no unique minimal model, alternative semantics are often provided to single out specific models as the intended model.

Let P be a normal logic program and M be a set of atoms; then the *reduct* [9] of P with respect to M, written P^M, is

$$\{L : -L_1, \ldots, L_m \mid (1) \in P \wedge \forall i \leqslant n \, (N_i \in M)\}$$

The reduct of any normal logic program is a definite logic program, and therefore has a unique minimal model. If I is the minimal Herbrand model of P^M then M is said to be a stable model of P.

Core Axioms

We present the domain-independent axioms for our translation to $\mathcal{EC}+$ in §5. The first, event-calculus inspired component, Ax_1, are:

```
caused(C, V, 0, R)  :-           caused(C, V, T1, R) :-
   domain(C, V),                    domain(C, V),
   init(C, V).                      0 < T1,  T is T1 - 1,
                                    caused(C, V, T, R),
caused(C, V, T1, R)  :-            not broken(C, V, T, T1, R).
   domain(C, V),
   0 < T1,                        broken(C, V, T1, T2, R) :-
   T is T1 - 1,                     domain(C, V),
   happens(A, T, R),               0 =< T1,  T1 < T2,
   domain(C, V0),                  domain(C, V1),  V1 != V,
   caused(C, V0, T, R),            happens(A, T1, R),
   causes(C, V, A, C, V0).         causes(C, V1, A, C, V),
                                    caused(C, V, T1, R).
```

The top-left axiom states that anything known true initially is caused to be true. The bottom-left axiom states that if there is a fluent dynamic law (causes/5) of the right form, and its conditions on the previous state and action performed hold, then the relevant fluent atom holds. The top-right axiom states that the values of fluent constants persist inertially by default; and the bottom-right, broken/5 axiom gives the circumstances overriding that default.

iCCalc Query

```
query(rinit(N), N,
  [0:arm=q0,     0:raw_product^[a]=q0,   0:raw_product^[b]=q0,
  0:tool^[drill]=q0,    0:tool^[oven]=q0,
  -(0:being_processed^[a]),
  -(0:being_processed^[b])]).
```

Remaining Violation Runs from §4

$$r^4 = (s_0 \xrightarrow{b.available} s_1 \xrightarrow{b.getFeedbelt} s_2 \xrightarrow{a.available} s_3 \xrightarrow{a.getFeedbelt} s_4)$$

$$r^5 = (s_0 \xrightarrow{a.available} s_1 \xrightarrow{b.available} s_2 \xrightarrow{b.getFeedbelt} s_3 \xrightarrow{a.getFeedbelt} s_4)$$

$$r^6 = (s_0 \xrightarrow{b.available} s_1 \xrightarrow{a.available} s_2 \xrightarrow{b.getFeedbelt} s_3 \xrightarrow{a.getFeedbelt} s_4)$$

A General Framework
for Architecture Composability

Paul Attie[1], Eduard Baranov[2], Simon Bliudze[2],
Mohamad Jaber[1], and Joseph Sifakis[2]

[1] American University of Beirut, Lebanon
{pa07,mj54}@aub.edu.lb
[2] École Polytechnique Fédérale de Lausanne, Station 14, 1015 Lausanne, Switzerland
firstname.lastname@epfl.ch

Abstract. Architectures depict design principles: paradigms that can be understood by all, allow thinking on a higher plane and avoiding low-level mistakes. They provide means for ensuring correctness by construction by enforcing global properties characterizing the coordination between components. An architecture can be considered as an operator A that, applied to a set of components $\mathcal{B}$, builds a composite component $A(\mathcal{B})$ meeting a characteristic property Φ. Architecture composability is a basic and common problem faced by system designers. In this paper, we propose a formal and general framework for architecture composability based on an associative, commutative and idempotent architecture composition operator '$\oplus$'. The main result is that if two architectures A_1 and A_2 enforce respectively safety properties Φ_1 and Φ_2, the architecture $A_1 \oplus A_2$ enforces the property $\Phi_1 \wedge \Phi_2$, that is both properties are preserved by architecture composition. We also establish preservation of liveness properties by architecture composition. The presented results are illustrated by a running example and a case study.

1 Introduction

Architectures depict design principles: paradigms that can be understood by all, allow thinking on a higher plane and avoiding low-level mistakes. They provide means for ensuring correctness by construction by enforcing global properties characterizing the coordination between components.

Using architectures largely accounts for our ability to master complexity and develop systems cost-effectively. System developers extensively use libraries of reference architectures ensuring both functional and non-functional properties, for example fault-tolerant architectures, architectures for resource management and QoS control, time-triggered architectures and security architectures. Nonetheless, we still lack theory and methods for combining architectures in principled and disciplined fully correct-by-construction design flows.

Informally speaking, an architecture can be considered as an operator A that, applied to a set of components $\mathcal{B}$ builds a composite component $A(\mathcal{B})$ meeting a characteristic property Φ. In a design process, it is often necessary to combine more than one architectural solution on a set of components to achieve a

D. Giannakopoulou and G. Salaün (Eds.): SEFM 2014, LNCS 8702, pp. 128–143, 2014.
© Springer International Publishing Switzerland 2014

global property. System engineers use libraries of solutions to specific problems and they need methods for combining them without jeopardizing their characteristic properties. For example, a fault-tolerant architecture combines a set of features building into the environment protections against trustworthiness violations. These include 1) triple modular redundancy mechanisms ensuring continuous operation in case of single component failure; 2) hardware checks to be sure that programs use data only in their defined regions of memory, so that there is no possibility of interference; 3) default to least privilege (least sharing) to enforce file protection. Is it possible to obtain a single fault-tolerant architecture consistently combining these features? The key issue here is *architecture composability* in the integrated solution, which can be formulated as follows.

Consider two architectures A_1 and A_2, enforcing respectively properties Φ_1 and Φ_2 on a set of components $\mathcal{B}$. That is, $A_1(\mathcal{B})$ and $A_2(\mathcal{B})$ satisfy respectively the properties Φ_1 and Φ_2. Is it possible to find an architecture $A_1 \oplus A_2$ such that the composite component $(A_1 \oplus A_2)(\mathcal{B})$ meets $\Phi_1 \wedge \Phi_2$? For instance, if A_1 ensures mutual exclusion and A_2 enforces a scheduling policy is it possible to find an architecture on the same set of components that satisfies both properties?

Architecture composability is a very basic and common problem faced by system designers. Manifestations of lack of composability are also known as feature interaction in telecommunication systems [1].

The development of a formal framework dealing with architecture composability implies a rigorous definition of the concept of architecture as well as of the underlying concepts of components and their interaction. The paper proposes such a framework based on results showing how architectures can be used for achieving correctness by construction in a rigorous component-based design flow [2]. The underlying theory is inspired from BIP [3]. BIP is a component framework rooted in well-defined operational semantics. It proposes an expressive and elegant notion of interaction models for component composition. Interaction models can be studied as sets of Boolean constraints expressing interactions between components. BIP has been fully implemented in a language and supporting toolset, including compilers and code generators [4].

BIP allows the description of composite components as an expression $\gamma(\mathcal{B})$, where $\mathcal{B}$ is a set of atomic components and γ is an interaction model. Atomic components are characterized by their behaviour specified as transition systems.

An *interaction model* γ is a set of *interactions*. Each interaction is a set of actions of the composed components, executed synchronously. The meaning of γ can be specified by using operational semantics rules defining the transition relation of the composite component $\gamma(\mathcal{B})$ in terms of transition relations of the composed components $\mathcal{B}$. Intuitively, for each interaction $a \in \gamma$, $\gamma(\mathcal{B})$ can execute a transition labelled by a iff the components involved in a can execute the corresponding transitions labelled by the actions composing a, whereas other components do not move. A formal definition is given in Sect. 2 (Def. 2).

Given a set of components $\mathcal{B}$ an *architecture* is an operator A such that $A(\mathcal{B}) = \gamma(\mathcal{C}, \mathcal{B})$, where γ is an interaction model and $\mathcal{C}$ a set of coordinating components, and $A(\mathcal{B})$ satisfies a characteristic property Φ_A.

According to this definition, an architecture A is a solution to a specific coordination problem, specified by Φ_A, by using an interaction model specified by γ and $\mathcal{C}$. For instance, for distributed architectures, interactions are point-to-point by asynchronous message passing. Other architectures adopt a specific topology (e.g. ring architectures, hierarchically structured architectures). These restrictions entail reduced expressiveness of the interaction model γ that must be compensated by using the additional set of components $\mathcal{C}$ for coordination. The characteristic property Φ_A assigns a meaning to the architecture that can be informally understood without the need for explicit formalization (e.g. mutual exclusion, scheduling policy, clock synchronization).

Our Contributions. We propose a general formal framework for architecture composability based on a composition operator '$\oplus$' which is associative, commutative and idempotent. We consider that characteristic properties are the conjunction of safety properties and liveness properties. We show that if two architectures A_1 and A_2 enforce respectively safety properties Φ_1 and Φ_2, the architecture $A_1 \oplus A_2$ enforces $\Phi_1 \wedge \Phi_2$, that is both properties are preserved by architecture composition. The concept of liveness for architectures derives from the Büchi-acceptance condition. We designate a subset of states of each coordinator as "idle", meaning that it is permissible for the coordinator to remain in such a state forever. Otherwise, the controller must execute infinitely often. The main result guaranteeing liveness preservation is based on a "pairwise noninterference" check of the composed architectures that can be performed algorithmically.

The paper is structured as follows. Sect. 2 introduces the notions of components and architecture, as well as the corresponding composition operators. Sect. 3 presents the key results about the preservation of safety and liveness properties. Sect. 4 illustrates the application of our framework on an Elevator control use case. Some related work is discussed in Sect. 5, and Sect. 6 concludes.

2 The Theory of Architectures

2.1 Components and Architectures

Definition 1 (Components). *A component is a Labelled Transition System* $B = (Q, q^0, P, \rightarrow)$, *where* Q *is a set of states,* $q^0 \in Q$ *is the initial state,* P *is a set of ports and* $\rightarrow \subseteq Q \times 2^P \times Q$ *is a transition relation. Each transition is labelled by an interaction* $a \subseteq P$. *We call* P *the interface of* B. *Notations* $q \xrightarrow{a} q'$, $q \xrightarrow{a}$ *and* $q \not\xrightarrow{a}$ *are as usual;* Q_B, q_B^0, P_B *and* $\rightarrow_B$ *denote the constituents of* B.

Definition 2 (Interaction model). *Let* $\mathcal{B} = \{B_1, \dots, B_n\}$ *be a finite set of components with* $B_i = (Q_i, q_i^0, P_i, \rightarrow)$,[1] *such that all* P_i *are pairwise disjoint, i.e.* $\forall i \neq j,\ P_i \cap P_j = \emptyset$. *Let* $P = \bigcup_{i=1}^n P_i$. *An interaction model over* P *is a subset* $\gamma \subseteq 2^P$. *We call the set of ports* P *the domain of the interaction model.*

---

[1] Here and below, we skip the index on the transition relation $\rightarrow$, since it is always clear from the context.

The composition of $\mathcal{B}$ with the interaction model γ is given by the component $\gamma(\mathcal{B}) = (Q, q^0, P, \rightarrow)$, *where* $Q = \prod_{i=1}^{n} Q_i$, $q^0 = q_1^0 \ldots q_n^0$ *and* $\rightarrow$ *is the minimal transition relation inductively defined by the following rules:*

$$\frac{q_i \xrightarrow{\emptyset} q_i'}{q_1 \ldots q_i \ldots q_n \xrightarrow{\emptyset} q_1 \ldots q_i' \ldots q_n}, \qquad \frac{a \in \gamma \quad \begin{array}{l} q_i \xrightarrow{a \cap P_i} q_i' \;\; (\text{if } a \cap P_i \neq \emptyset) \\ q_i = q_i' \quad\;\; (\text{if } a \cap P_i = \emptyset) \end{array}}{q_1 \ldots q_n \xrightarrow{a} q_1' \ldots q_n'}.$$

In the sequel, when speaking of a set of components $\mathcal{B} = \{B_1, \ldots, B_n\}$, we will always assume that it satisfies all assumptions of Def. 2.

Definition 3 (Architecture). *An architecture is a tuple $A = (\mathcal{C}, P_A, \gamma)$, where $\mathcal{C}$ is a finite set of coordinating components with pairwise disjoint sets of ports, $\bigcup_{C \in \mathcal{C}} P_C \subseteq P_A$, and $\gamma \subseteq 2^{P_A}$ is an interaction model over P_A.*

Definition 4 (Application of an architecture). *Let $A = (\mathcal{C}, P_A, \gamma)$ be an architecture and let $\mathcal{B}$ be a set of components, such that $\bigcup_{B \in \mathcal{B}} P_B \cap \bigcup_{C \in \mathcal{C}} P_C = \emptyset$ and $P_A \subseteq P \stackrel{\Delta}{=} \bigcup_{B \in \mathcal{B} \cup \mathcal{C}} P_B$. The application of an architecture A to the components $\mathcal{B}$ is the component*

$$A(\mathcal{B}) \stackrel{\Delta}{=} \left(\gamma \parallel 2^{P \backslash P_A}\right)(\mathcal{C} \cup \mathcal{B}), \tag{1}$$

where, for interaction models γ' and γ'' over disjoint domains P' and P'' respectively, $\gamma' \parallel \gamma'' \stackrel{\Delta}{=} \{a' \cup a'' \mid a' \in \gamma', a'' \in \gamma''\}$ is an interaction model over $P' \cup P''$.

Architecture A enforces coordination constraints on the components in $\mathcal{B}$. The interface P_A of an architecture A contains all ports of the coordinating components $\mathcal{C}$ and some additional ports, which must belong to the components in $\mathcal{B}$. In the application $A(\mathcal{B})$, the ports belonging to P_A can only participate in the interactions defined by the interaction model γ of A. Ports which do not belong to P_A are not restricted and can participate in any interaction. In particular, they can join the interactions in γ (see (1)). If the interface of the architecture covers all ports of the system, i.e. $P = P_A$, we have $2^{P \backslash P_A} = \{\emptyset\}$ and the only interactions allowed in $A(\mathcal{B})$ are those belonging to γ. Finally, the definition of $\gamma' \parallel \gamma''$, above, requires that an interaction from each of γ' and γ'' be involved in every interaction belonging to $\gamma' \parallel \gamma''$. To enable independent progress in (1), one must have $\emptyset \in \gamma$. (Notice that $\emptyset \in 2^{P \backslash P_A}$ holds always.)

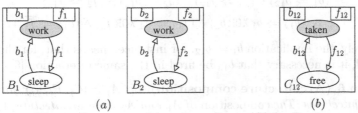

(a)   (b)

Fig. 1. Component (a) and coordinator (b) for Ex. 1.

Example 1 (Mutual exclusion). Consider the components B_1 and B_2 in Fig. 1(a). In order to ensure mutual exclusion of their work states, we apply the architecture $A_{12} = (\{C_{12}\}, P_{12}, \gamma_{12})$, where C_{12} is shown in Fig. 1(b), $P_{12} = \{b_1, b_2, b_{12}, f_1, f_2, f_{12}\}$ and $\gamma_{12} = \{\emptyset, b_1 b_{12}, b_2 b_{12}, f_1 f_{12}, f_2 f_{12}\}$.

The interface P_{12} of A_{12} covers all ports of B_1, B_2 and C_{12}. Hence, the only possible interactions are those explicitly belonging to γ_{12}. Assuming that the initial states of B_1 and B_2 are sleep, and that of C_{12} is free, neither of the two states (free, work, work) and (taken, work, work) is reachable, i.e. the mutual exclusion property $(q_1 \neq \text{work}) \vee (q_2 \neq \text{work})$ holds in $A_{12}(B_1, B_2)$

Let B_3 be a third component, similar to B_1 and B_2, with the interface $\{b_3, f_3\}$. Since $b_3, f_3 \notin P_{12}$, the interaction model of the application $A_{12}(B_1, B_2, B_3)$ is $\gamma_{12} \parallel \{\emptyset, b_3, f_3\}$. (We omit the interaction $b_3 f_3$, since b_3 and f_3 are never enabled in the same state and, therefore, cannot be fired simultaneously.) Thus, the component $A_{12}(B_1, B_2, B_3)$ is the unrestricted product of the components $A_{12}(B_1, B_2)$ and B_3. The application of A_{12} enforces mutual exclusion between the work states of B_1 and B_2, but does not affect the behaviour of B_3.

2.2 Composition of Architectures

Architectures can be intuitively understood as enforcing constraints on the global state space of the system [3, 5]. More precisely, component coordination is realised by limiting the allowed interactions, thus enforcing constraints on the transitions components can take. From this perspective, architecture composition can be understood as the conjunction of their respective constraints. This intuitive notion is formalised by the two definitions below.

Definition 5 (Characteristic predicates [6]). *Denote* $\mathbb{B} = \{\text{tt}, \text{ff}\}$ *and let* $\gamma \subseteq 2^P$ *be an interaction model over a set of ports P. Its* characteristic predicate $(\varphi_\gamma : \mathbb{B}^P \to \mathbb{B}) \in \mathbb{B}[P]$ *is defined by letting* $\varphi_\gamma \triangleq \bigvee_{a \in \gamma} \left(\bigwedge_{p \in a} p \wedge \bigwedge_{p \notin a} \overline{p} \right)$. *For any valuation* $v : P \to \mathbb{B}$, $\varphi_\gamma(v) = \text{tt}$ *if and only if* $\{p \in P \mid v(p) = \text{tt}\} \in \gamma$. *A predicate* $\varphi \in \mathbb{B}[P]$ *uniquely defines an interaction model* γ_φ, *such that* $\varphi_{\gamma_\varphi} = \varphi$.

Example 2 (Mutual exclusion (contd.)). Consider the interaction model $\gamma_{12} = \{\emptyset, b_1 b_{12}, b_2 b_{12}, f_1 f_{12}, f_2 f_{12}\}$ from Ex. 1. Since the domain of γ_{12} is $P_{12} = \{b_1, b_2, b_{12}, f_1, f_2, f_{12}\}$, its characteristic predicate is (omitting '$\wedge$'):

$$\varphi_{\gamma_{12}} = \overline{b_1}\,\overline{b_2}\,\overline{b_{12}}\,\overline{f_1}\,\overline{f_2}\,\overline{f_{12}} \vee b_1\,\overline{b_2}\,b_{12}\,\overline{f_1}\,\overline{f_2}\,\overline{f_{12}} \vee \overline{b_1}\,b_2\,b_{12}\,\overline{f_1}\,\overline{f_2}\,\overline{f_{12}}$$

$$\vee\ \overline{b_1}\,\overline{b_2}\,\overline{b_{12}}\,f_1\,\overline{f_2}\,f_{12} \vee \overline{b_1}\,\overline{b_2}\,\overline{b_{12}}\,\overline{f_1}\,f_2\,f_{12}$$

$$= (b_1 \Rightarrow b_{12}) \wedge (f_1 \Rightarrow f_{12}) \wedge (b_2 \Rightarrow b_{12}) \wedge (f_2 \Rightarrow f_{12}) \tag{2}$$

$$\wedge\ (b_{12} \Rightarrow b_1 \,\text{XOR}\, b_2) \wedge (f_{12} \Rightarrow f_1 \,\text{XOR}\, f_2) \wedge (b_{12} \Rightarrow \overline{f_{12}}).$$

Intuitively, the implication $b_1 \Rightarrow b_{12}$, for instance, means that, for the port b_1 to be fired, it is necessary that b_{12} be fired in the same interaction [6].

Definition 6 (Architecture composition). *Let* $A_j = (\mathcal{C}_j, P_j, \gamma_j)$, *for* $j = 1, 2$ *be two architectures. The* composition *of A_1 and A_2 is an architecture* $A_1 \oplus A_2 = (\mathcal{C}_1 \cup \mathcal{C}_2, P_1 \cup P_2, \gamma_\varphi)$, *where* $\varphi = \varphi_{\gamma_1} \wedge \varphi_{\gamma_2}$.

The following lemma states that the interaction model of the composed component consists precisely of the interactions a such that the projections of a onto the interfaces of both of the composed architectures (A_1, A_2, resp.) belong to the corresponding interaction models (γ_1, γ_2 resp.). In other words, these are precisely the interactions that satisfy the coordination constraints enforced by both composed architectures.

Lemma 1. *Consider two interaction models $\gamma_i \subseteq 2^{P_i}$, for $i = 1, 2$, and let $\varphi = \varphi_{\gamma_1} \wedge \varphi_{\gamma_2}$. For an interaction $a \subseteq P_1 \cup P_2$, $a \in \gamma_\varphi$ iff $a \cap P_i \in \gamma_i$, for $i = 1, 2$.*

Proposition 1. *Architecture composition '$\oplus$' is commutative, associative and idempotent; $A_{id} = (\emptyset, \emptyset, \{\emptyset\})$ is its neutral element, i.e. for any architecture A, we have $A \oplus A_{id} = A$. Furthermore, for any component B, we have $A_{id}(B) = B$.*

Notice that, for an arbitrary set of components $\mathcal{B}$ with $P = \bigcup_{B \in \mathcal{B}} P_B$, we have, by (1), $A_{id}(\mathcal{B}) = (2^P)(\mathcal{B})$ (cf. Def. 2).

Example 3 (Mutual exclusion (contd.)). Building upon Ex. 1, let B_3 be a third component, similar to B_1 and B_2, with the interface $\{b_3, f_3\}$. We define two additional architectures A_{13} and A_{23} similar to A_{12}: for $i = 1, 2$, $A_{i3} = (\{C_{i3}\}, P_{i3}, \gamma_{i3})$, where, up to the renaming of ports, C_{i3} is the same as C_{12} in Fig. 1(b), $P_{i3} = \{b_i, b_3, b_{i3}, f_i, f_3, f_{i3}\}$ and $\gamma_{i3} = \{\emptyset, b_i b_{i3}, b_3 b_{i3}, f_i f_{i3}, f_3 f_{i3}\}$.

By considering, for $\varphi_{\gamma_{13}}$ and $\varphi_{\gamma_{23}}$, expressions similar to (2), it is easy to compute $\varphi_{\gamma_{12}} \wedge \varphi_{\gamma_{13}} \wedge \varphi_{\gamma_{23}}$ as the conjunction of the following implications:

$$b_1 \Rightarrow b_{12} \wedge b_{13}, \quad f_1 \Rightarrow f_{12} \wedge f_{13}, \quad b_{12} \Rightarrow b_1 \text{ XOR } b_2, \quad f_{12} \Rightarrow f_1 \text{ XOR } f_2, \quad b_{12} \Rightarrow \overline{f_{12}},$$
$$b_2 \Rightarrow b_{12} \wedge b_{23}, \quad f_2 \Rightarrow f_{12} \wedge f_{23}, \quad b_{13} \Rightarrow b_1 \text{ XOR } b_3, \quad f_{13} \Rightarrow f_1 \text{ XOR } f_3, \quad b_{13} \Rightarrow \overline{f_{13}},$$
$$b_3 \Rightarrow b_{13} \wedge b_{23}, \quad f_3 \Rightarrow f_{13} \wedge f_{23}, \quad b_{23} \Rightarrow b_2 \text{ XOR } b_3, \quad f_{23} \Rightarrow f_2 \text{ XOR } f_3, \quad b_{23} \Rightarrow \overline{f_{23}}.$$

It is now straightforward to obtain the interaction model for $A_{12} \oplus A_{13} \oplus A_{23}$, i.e. $\{\emptyset, b_1 b_{12} b_{13}, f_1 f_{12} f_{13}, b_2 b_{12} b_{23}, f_2 f_{12} f_{23}, b_3 b_{13} b_{23}, f_3 f_{13} f_{23}\}$. Notice that this is different from the union of the interaction models of the three architectures.

Assuming that the initial states of B_1, B_2 and B_3 are sleep, whereas those of C_{12}, C_{13} and C_{23} are free, one can observe that none of the states $(\cdot, \cdot, \cdot, \text{work}, \text{work}, \cdot)$, $(\cdot, \cdot, \cdot, \text{work}, \cdot, \text{work})$ and $(\cdot, \cdot, \cdot, \cdot, \text{work}, \text{work})$ are reachable in $(A_{12} \oplus A_{13} \oplus A_{23})(B_1, B_2, B_3)$. Thus, we conclude that the composition of the three architectures, $(A_{12} \oplus A_{13} \oplus A_{23})(B_1, B_2, B_3)$, enforces mutual exclusion among the work states of all three components. In Sect. 3.1, we provide a general result stating that architecture composition preserves the enforced state properties.

2.3 Hierarchical Composition of Architectures

Proposition 2. *Let $\mathcal{B}$ be a set of components and let $A_1 = (\mathcal{C}_1, P_{A_1}, \gamma_1)$ and $A_2 = (\mathcal{C}_2, P_{A_2}, \gamma_2)$ be two architectures, such that 1) $P_{A_1} \subseteq \bigcup_{B \in \mathcal{B} \cup \mathcal{C}_1} P_B$ and 2) $P_{A_2} \subseteq \bigcup_{B \in \mathcal{B} \cup \mathcal{C}_1 \cup \mathcal{C}_2} P_B$. Then $A_2(A_1(\mathcal{B}))$ is defined and equal to $(A_1 \oplus A_2)(\mathcal{B})$.*

Condition 1 states that A_1 can be applied to the components in $\mathcal{B}$ (cf. Def. 4); condition 2 states that A_2 can be applied to $A_1(\mathcal{B})$. Note that, when $P_{A_i} \subseteq \bigcup_{B \in \mathcal{B} \cup \mathcal{C}_i} P_B$ holds for both $i \in \{1, 2\}$—for $i = 1$, this is the condition 1—and none of the architectures involves the ports of the other, i.e. $P_{A_i} \cap \bigcup_{C \in \mathcal{C}_j} P_C = \emptyset$, for $i \neq j \in \{1, 2\}$, then the two architectures are independent and their composition is commutative: $A_2(A_1(\mathcal{B})) = (A_1 \oplus A_2)(\mathcal{B}) = A_1(A_2(\mathcal{B}))$.

Proposition 3. *Let $\mathcal{B}_1, \mathcal{B}_2$ be two sets of components, such that $\bigcup_{B \in \mathcal{B}_1} P_B \cap \bigcup_{B \in \mathcal{B}_2} P_B = \emptyset$. Let $A_1 = (\mathcal{C}_1, P_{A_1}, \gamma_1)$ and $A_2 = (\mathcal{C}_2, P_{A_2}, \gamma_2)$ be two architectures, such that $P_{A_1} \subseteq \bigcup_{B \in \mathcal{B}_1 \cup \mathcal{C}_1} P_B$ and $P_{A_2} \subseteq \bigcup_{B \in \mathcal{B}_1 \cup \mathcal{B}_2 \cup \mathcal{C}_1 \cup \mathcal{C}_2} P_B$. Then $A_2(A_1(\mathcal{B}_1, \mathcal{B}_2)) = A_2(A_1(\mathcal{B}_1), \mathcal{B}_2)$.*

Intuitively, Prop. 3 states that one only has to apply the architecture A_1 to those components that have ports involved in its interface. Notice that, in order to compare the semantics of two sets of components, one has to compose them into compound components, by applying *some* architecture. Hence the need for A_2 in Prop. 3. As a special case, one can consider the "most liberal" identity architecture A_{id} (see Prop. 1). A_{id} does not impose any coordination constraints, allowing all possible interactions between the components it is applied to.

Example 4 (Mutual exclusion (contd.)). Ex. 3 can be generalised to an arbitrary number n of components. However, this solution requires $n(n-1)/2$ architectures, and so does not scale well. Instead, we apply architectures hierarchically.

Let $n = 4$ and consider two architectures A_{12}, A_{34}, with the respective coordination components C_{12}, C_{34}, that respectively enforce mutual exclusion between B_1, B_2 and B_3, B_4 as in Ex. 3. Assume furthermore, that an architecture A enforces mutual exclusion between the **taken** states of C_{12} and C_{34}. It is clear that the system $A(A_{12}(B_1, B_2), A_{34}(B_3, B_4))$ ensures mutual exclusion between all four components $(B_i)_{i=1}^4$. Furthermore, by the above propositions,

$$A(A_{12}(B_1, B_2), A_{34}(B_3, B_4)) = A(A_{12}(B_1, B_2, A_{34}(B_3, B_4))) =$$
$$A(A_{12}(A_{34}(B_1, B_2, B_3, B_4))) = (A \oplus A_{12} \oplus A_{34})(B_1, B_2, B_3, B_4).$$

3   Property Preservation

Throughout this section we use several classical notions, which we recall here.

Definition 7 (Paths, path fragments, and reachable states). *Let $B = (Q, q^0, P, \rightarrow)$ be a component. A finite or infinite sequence $q_0 \xrightarrow{a_1} q_1 \xrightarrow{a_2} \cdots \xrightarrow{a_{i-1}} q_{i-1} \xrightarrow{a_i} q_i \cdots$ is a path in B if $q_0 = q^0$, otherwise it is a path fragment. A state $q \in Q$ is reachable iff there exists a finite path in B terminating in q.*

3.1   Safety Properties

Definition 8 (Properties and invariants). *Let $B = (Q, q^0, P, \rightarrow)$ be a component. A property of B is a state predicate $\Phi : Q \rightarrow \mathbb{B}$. Φ is initial if $\Phi(q^0) = \mathtt{tt}$.*

Definition 9 (Enforcing properties). *Let $A = (\mathcal{C}, P_A, \gamma)$ be an architecture; let $\mathcal{B}$ be a set of components and Φ be an initial property of their parallel composition $A_{id}(\mathcal{B})$ (see Prop. 1). We say that A enforces Φ on $\mathcal{B}$ iff, for every state $q = (q_b, q_c)$ reachable in $A(\mathcal{B})$, with $q_b \in \prod_{B \in \mathcal{B}} Q_B$ and $q_c \in \prod_{C \in \mathcal{C}} Q_C$, we have $\Phi(q_b) = \mathrm{tt}$.*

Example 5. Consider again mutual exclusion in Ex. 1. The component $A_{12}(B_1, B_2)$ is shown in Fig. 2 (we abbreviate sleep, work, free and taken to s, w, f and t respectively). Clearly A_{12} enforces on $\{B_1, B_2\}$ the property $\Phi_{12} = (q_1 \neq \mathtt{w}) \vee (q_2 \neq \mathtt{w})$, where q_1 and q_2 are state variables of B_1 and B_2 respectively.

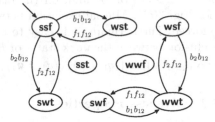

Fig. 2. Component from Ex. 5

According to the above definition, when we say that an architecture enforces some property Φ, it is implicitly assumed that Φ is initial for the coordinated components. Below, we omit mentioning this explicitly.

Theorem 1 (Preserving enforced properties). *Let $\mathcal{B}$ be a set of components; let A_1 and A_2 be two architectures enforcing on $\mathcal{B}$ the properties Φ_1 and Φ_2 respectively. The composition $A_1 \oplus A_2$ enforces on $\mathcal{B}$ the property $\Phi_1 \wedge \Phi_2$.*

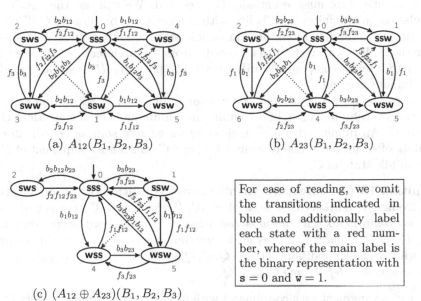

(a) $A_{12}(B_1, B_2, B_3)$

(b) $A_{23}(B_1, B_2, B_3)$

(c) $(A_{12} \oplus A_{23})(B_1, B_2, B_3)$

For ease of reading, we omit the transitions indicated in blue and additionally label each state with a red number, whereof the main label is the binary representation with $\mathtt{s} = 0$ and $\mathtt{w} = 1$.

Fig. 3. Projections of reachable states of Ex. 6 components onto $A_{id}(B_1, B_2, B_3)$

Example 6. In the context of Ex. 3, consider the application of architectures A_{12} and A_{23} to the components B_1, B_2 and B_3. The former enforces the property $\Phi_{12} = (q_1 \neq \mathtt{w}) \vee (q_2 \neq \mathtt{w})$ (the projections of reachable states of $A_{12}(B_1, B_2, B_3)$

onto the state-space of the atomic components are shown in Fig. 3(a)), whereas the latter enforces $\Phi_{23} = (q_2 \neq \mathtt{w}) \vee (q_3 \neq \mathtt{w})$ (the projections of reachable states of $A_{23}(B_1, B_2, B_3)$ onto the state-space of the atomic components are shown in Fig. 3(b)). By Th. 1, the composition $A_{12} \oplus A_{23}$ enforces $\Phi_{12} \wedge \Phi_{23} = (q_2 \neq \mathtt{w}) \vee ((q_1 \neq \mathtt{w}) \wedge (q_3 \neq \mathtt{w}))$, i.e. mutual exclusion between, on one hand, the $\mathtt{work}$ state of B_2 and, on the other hand, the $\mathtt{work}$ states of B_1 and B_3 (see Fig. 3(c)). Mutual exclusion between the $\mathtt{work}$ states of B_1 and B_3 is not enforced. Furthermore, it is easy to check that $A_1 \oplus A_2 \oplus A_3$ enforces mutual exclusion between the $\mathtt{work}$ states of B_1, B_2 and B_3 as $\Phi_{12} \wedge \Phi_{13} \wedge \Phi_{23} = ((q_1 \neq \mathtt{w}) \wedge (q_2 \neq \mathtt{w})) \vee ((q_1 \neq \mathtt{w}) \wedge (q_3 \neq \mathtt{w})) \vee ((q_1 \neq \mathtt{w}) \wedge (q_3 \neq \mathtt{w}))$.

3.2   Liveness Properties

Our treatment of liveness properties is based on the idea that each coordinator C must be "invoked sufficiently often", so that the liveness properties inherent in C are imposed on the system as a whole. So, what does sufficiently often mean? A reasonable initial idea is to require that each controller is executed infinitely often (along an infinite path). But that turns out to be too strong. For example, a mutual exclusion controller should not be invoked infinitely often if no process that it controls requests the critical resource. So, we add "idle states", so that it is permitted for a coordinator to remain forever in an idle state. A coordinator not in an idle state must eventually be executed. We will use the equivalent formulation: an (infinite) path is live with respect to a coordinator C iff either C is executed infinitely often, or is in an idle state infinitely often. A live path is one that is live with respect to all coordinators. An architecture A is live with respect to a set of components $\mathcal{B}$ iff every finite path of $A(\mathcal{B})$ can be extended to an infinite live one.

A transition $q \xrightarrow{a} q'$ executes a coordinator C iff $a \cap P_C \neq \emptyset$. An infinite path α executes C infinitely often iff α contains an infinite number of transitions that execute C. An infinite path $q_0 \xrightarrow{a_1} q_1 \cdots$ visits an idle state of coordinator C infinitely often iff, for infinitely many $i \geq 0$, $q_i \upharpoonright C$ (the state component of C in q_i) is an idle state of C.

Definition 10 (Architecture with liveness conditions). *An architecture with liveness conditions is a tuple $A = (\mathcal{C}, P_A, \gamma)$, where $\mathcal{C}$ is a set of coordinating components with liveness condition, P_A is a set of ports, such that $\bigcup_{C \in \mathcal{C}} P_C \subseteq P_A$, and $\gamma \subseteq 2^{P_A}$ is an interaction model. A coordinating component with liveness condition is $C = (Q, q^0, Q_{idle}, P_C, \rightarrow)$, where $(Q, q^0, P_C, \rightarrow)$ is a component (Def. 1) and $Q_{idle} \subseteq Q$.*

Hence, we augment each coordinator with a *liveness condition*: a subset Q_{idle} of its states Q, which are considered "idle", and in which it can remain forever without violating liveness.

Definition 11 (Live path). *Let $A = (\mathcal{C}, P_A, \gamma)$ be an architecture with liveness conditions and $\mathcal{B}$ a set of components. An infinite path α in $A(\mathcal{B})$ is live iff, for every $C \in \mathcal{C}$, α contains infinitely many occurrences of interactions containing* *some port of C, or α contains infinitely many states whose projection onto C is an idle state of C.*

That is, if $\alpha \stackrel{\Delta}{=} q_0 \xrightarrow{a_1} q_1 \xrightarrow{a_2} \cdots \xrightarrow{a_i} q_i \cdots$ then, for every $C \in \mathcal{C}$, for infinitely many i: $a_i \cap P \neq \emptyset$ or $q_i \upharpoonright C \in Q_{idle}$, where $C = (Q, q^0, Q_{idle}, P, \to)$, and $q_i \upharpoonright C$ denotes the local state of C in q_i.

The intuition behind this definition is that each liveness condition guarantees that its coordinator executes "sufficiently often", i.e. infinitely often unless it is in an idle state. When architectures are composed, we take the union of all the coordinators. Since each coordinator carries its liveness condition with it, we obtain that each coordinator is also executed sufficiently often in the composed architecture. We also obtain that architecture composition is as before, i.e. we use Def. 6, with the understanding that we compose two architectures with liveness conditions. For the rest of this section, we use "architecture" to mean "architecture with liveness conditions".

When we apply an architecture with liveness conditions to a set of components, thereby obtaining a system, we need the notion of machine closure [7]: every finite path can be extended to a live one.

Definition 12 (Live w.r.t. a set of components). *Let A be an architecture with liveness conditions and $\mathcal{B}$ be a set of components. A is live w.r.t. $\mathcal{B}$ iff every finite path in $A(\mathcal{B})$ can be extended to a live path.*

Even if $A_1, \ldots, A_m$ are each live w.r.t. $\mathcal{B}$, it is still possible for $(A_1 \oplus \cdots \oplus A_m)(\mathcal{B})$ to be not live w.r.t. $\mathcal{B}$, due to "interference" between the coordinators of the A_i. For example, consider two architectures that enforce mutually inconsistent scheduling policies, e.g. they require two conflicting interactions (those that share a component) to both be executed. Hence, we define a notion of "noninterference" which guarantees that $(A_1 \oplus \cdots \oplus A_m)(\mathcal{B})$ is live w.r.t. $\mathcal{B}$.

A system is free of *global deadlock* iff, in every reachable global state, there is at least one enabled interaction. We show in [8] how to verify that a system is free of global deadlock, using a sufficient but not necessary condition that, in many cases, can be evaluated quickly, without state-explosion. Essentially, we check, for every interaction a in the system, that the execution of a cannot possibly lead to a deadlock state. The check can often be discharged within a "small subsystem," which contains all of the components that participate in a.

We now give a criterion for liveness that can be evaluated without state-explosion w.r.t. the number of architectures. For simplicity, we assume in the sequel that each architecture A_i has exactly one coordinating component C_i.

Definition 13 (Noninterfering live architectures). *Let architectures $A_i = (\{C_i\}, P_{A_i}, \gamma_i)$, for $i = 1, 2$ be live w.r.t. a set of components $\mathcal{B}$. Then A_1 is noninterfering with respect to A_2 and components $\mathcal{B}$ iff, for every infinite path α in $(A_1 \oplus A_2)(\mathcal{B})$ which executes C_1 infinitely often: either α executes C_2 infinitely often or α visits an idle state of C_2 infinitely often.*

A set of architectures $A_i = (\{C_i\}, P_{A_i}, \gamma_i)$, for $i \in \{1, \ldots, m\}$ is *pairwise-noninterfering* w.r.t. components $\mathcal{B}$, iff for all $j, k \in \{1, \ldots, m\}, j \neq k$. A_j is noninterfering w.r.t A_k and components $\mathcal{B}$.

Theorem 2 (Pairwise noninterfering live architectures). *Let architectures $A_i = (\{C_i\}, P_{A_i}, \gamma_i)$, for $i \in \{1, \ldots, m\}$ be live and pairwise-noninterfering w.r.t. a set of components $\mathcal{B}$. Assume also that $(\bigoplus_{i=1}^{m} A_i)(\mathcal{B})$ is free of global deadlock. Then $(\bigoplus_{i=1}^{m} A_i)$ is live w.r.t. $\mathcal{B}$.*

Example 7 (Noninterference in mutual exclusion). Consider the system $(A_{12} \oplus A_{23} \oplus A_{13})(B_1, B_2, B_3)$, as in Ex. 3. Let each coordinator have a single idle state, namely the `free` state. Consider the applications of each pair of coordinators, i.e. $(A_{12} \oplus A_{23})(B_1, B_2, B_3)$, $(A_{23} \oplus A_{13})(B_1, B_2, B_3)$ and $(A_{12} \oplus A_{13})(B_1, B_2, B_3)$. For $(A_{12} \oplus A_{23})(B_1, B_2, B_3)$, we observe that along any infinite path, either C_{12} executes infinitely often, or remains forever in its idle state after some point. Hence A_{23} is noninterfering w.r.t. A_{12} and B_1, B_2, B_3. Likewise for the five other ordered pairs of coordinators. We verify that $(A_{12} \oplus A_{23} \oplus A_{13})(B_1, B_2, B_3)$ is free from global deadlock using the method of [8]. Hence by Th. 2, we conclude that $(A_{12} \oplus A_{23} \oplus A_{13})$ is live w.r.t. $\{B_1, B_2, B_3\}$.

For a finite-state system $(A_1 \oplus A_2)(\mathcal{B})$, we verify noninterference by checking for infinite paths along which C_1 (the coordinator of A_1) executes forever, while C_2 (the coordinator of A_2) does not execute and is not in an idle state. Our algorithm is: (1) generate the state-transition graph M_{12} of $(A_1 \oplus A_2)(\mathcal{B})$, by starting with the initial state and repeatedly applying all enabled interactions until there is no further change; (2) let M'_{12} result from M_{12} by removing all transitions of C_2 and all global states (and their incident transitions) whose C_2-component is an idle state of C_2; (3) find all non-trivial maximal strongly connected components of M'_{12}, if any. A strongly connected component is nontrivial if it is either a single state with a self-loop, or it contains at least two states. Existence of such a component CC of M'_{12} certifies the existence of an infinite path along which C_1 executes forever, while C_2 does not execute and is not in an idle state. Conversely, the non-existence of such a CC certifies that A_1 is noninterfering w.r.t. A_2 and $\mathcal{B}$ (Def. 13).

Let $|M_{12}|$ denote the number of nodes (states) plus the number of edges (transitions) in M_{12}. Let $|\gamma_1 \cup \gamma_2|$ denote the number of interactions in $|(A_1 \oplus A_2)(\mathcal{B})|$. Step (1) takes time $O(|M_{12}| * |\gamma_1 \cup \gamma_2|)$, since every interaction is checked in every state. Step (2) takes time $O(|M_{12}|)$, since it can be implemented using a depth-first (or breadth-first) search of M_{12}. Step (3) takes time $O(|M_{12}|)$, using [9]. Hence our algorithm has time complexity $O(|M_{12}| * |\gamma_1 \cup \gamma_2|)$.

4 Case Study: Control of an Elevator Cabin

We illustrate our results with the Elevator case study adapted from the literature [10, 11], for a building with three floors. Control of the elevator cabin is modelled as a set of coordinated atomic components shown in Fig. 4. Each floor of the building has a separate caller system, which allows floor selection inside the elevator and calling from the floor. Ports ic and fc respectively represent calls made within the elevator and calls from a floor. Ports is and fs represent cabin stops in response to these calls. Furthermore, port names, m, c, o, s, dn, up, nf,

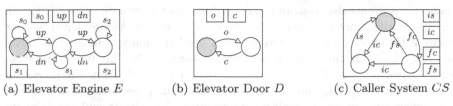

(a) Elevator Engine E (b) Elevator Door D (c) Caller System CS

Fig. 4. Elevator atomic components

fn and fr stand respectively for "move", "call", "open", "stop", "move down", "move up", "not full", "finish" and "free". Caller system components and their ports are indexed by floor numbers. $\mathcal{B} = \{E, D, CS_0, CS_1, CS_2\}$ denotes the set of atomic components.

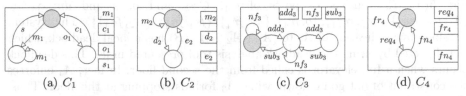

(a) C_1 (b) C_2 (c) C_3 (d) C_4

Fig. 5. Coordinating components for the elevator example

To enforce required properties, we successively apply and compose architectures. First, apply architecture $A_1 = (\{C_1\}, P_1, \gamma_1)$ to $\mathcal{B}$. C_1 is shown in Fig. 5(a). P_1 contains all ports of C_1 and all ports of $\mathcal{B}$. γ_1 comprises the empty interaction $\emptyset$ and the following interactions (for $i \in [0,2]$):

- Door control: $\{\{o, o_1\}, \{c, c_1\}\}$
- Floor selection control: $\{\{fc_i\}, \{ic_i\}\}$
- Moving control: $\{\{s_i, s, fs_i\}, \{s_i, s, is_i\}, \{up, m_1\}, \{dn, m_1\}\}$

System $A_1(\mathcal{B})$ provides basic elevator functionality, i.e., moving up and down, stopping only at the requested floors, and door control. Architecture A_1 enforces the safety property: *the elevator does not move with open doors*. Nonetheless, $A_1(\mathcal{B})$ allows the elevator to stop at a floor, and then to leave without having opened the door. To prevent this, we apply architecture $A_2 = (\{C_2\}, P_2, \gamma_2)$ where C_2 is shown in Fig. 5(b), $P_2 = \{e_2, d_2, m_2, c_1, s, m_1\}$, and $\gamma_2 = \{\emptyset, \{s, d_2\}, \{c_1, e_2\}, \{m_1, m_2\}\}$. This grants priority to the door controller after an s action. By Prop. 2, $A_2(A_1(\mathcal{B})) = (A_1 \oplus A_2)(\mathcal{B})$. $(A_2 \oplus A_1)(\mathcal{B})$ provides the same functionality as $A_1(\mathcal{B})$, and also this additional property. The property *"if the elevator is full, it must stop only at floors selected from the cabin and ignore outside calls"* [10, 11], is enforced by applying architecture $A_3 = (\{C_3\}, P_3, \gamma_3)$ with C_3 shown in Fig. 5(c), $P_3 = \{add_3, sub_3, nf_3, s, fs_i \mid i \in [0,2]\}$ and $\gamma_3 = \{\emptyset, \{add_3\}, \{sub_3\}\} \cup \{\{s, nf_3, fs_i\} \mid i \in [0,2]\}$. A elevator is full in our example if it contains two passengers. By Prop. 2, $A_3((A_1 \oplus A_2)(\mathcal{B})) = (A_1 \oplus A_2 \oplus A_3)(\mathcal{B})$. By Th. 1, $(A_1 \oplus A_2 \oplus A_3)(\mathcal{B})$ satisfies all three properties.

We specify liveness properties for $(A_1 \oplus A_2 \oplus A_3)(\mathcal{B})$ by choosing idle states for the coordinators. C_1 and C_2 have only their initial states idle, since a moving elevator must eventually stop, and an open door must eventually close. C_3 has all of its states idle, since C_3 enforces a pure safety property. We implemented our algorithm for checking noninterference, and used the implementation to verify that C_1 and C_2 are mutually noninterfering w.r.t. to $\mathcal{B}$. Our implementation showed, however, that C_3 interferes with both C_1 and C_2, since it allows an infinite sequence of add_3 and sub_3 interactions. This reflects the absence of an environment component: in reality, one assumes that clients will not hold up the elevator indefinitely by continuously moving in and out. This shows that we can detect shortcomings in component models w.r.t. liveness: they manifest as violations of noninterference.

Finally, we consider the additional property: *"requests from the second floor have priority over all other requests"* [10, 11]. This is enforced by the architecture $A_4 = (\{C_4\}, P_4, \gamma_4)$ with C_4 shown in Fig. 5(d). P_4 consists of ports of C_4, CS_2, and o, s and dn; $\gamma_4 = \{\emptyset, \{fc_2, req_4\}, \{ic_2, req_4\}, \{o, fr_4\}, \{dn, fr_4\}, \{fs_2, fn_4\}, \{is_2, fn_4\}\}$. The system obtained by application of A_4 to $(A_1 \oplus A_2 \oplus A_3)(\mathcal{B})$ has a local deadlock, which was detected by using the deadlock analysis tool presented in [8]. This deadlock occurs when a full elevator is called from the second floor. In fact, A_4 enforces the constraint of not going down, while A_3 forbids stopping at this floor. Thus, the only choice is to move upward, which is impossible. Hence the system is in a local deadlock state involving the elevator engine.

$(A_1 \oplus A_2 \oplus A_4)(\mathcal{B})$, obtained by applying A_4 to $(A_1 \oplus A_2)(\mathcal{B})$, is verified to be deadlock-free, using [8]. $\{A_1, A_2, A_4\}$ are pairwise-noninterfering w.r.t. $\mathcal{B}$, using our implementation. So by Th. 2, $(A_1 \oplus A_2 \oplus A_4)$ is live w.r.t. $\mathcal{B}$.

5   Related Work

A number of paradigms for unifying component composition have been studied in [12–14]. These achieve unification by reduction to a common low-level semantic model. Coordination mechanisms and their properties are not studied independently of behaviour. This is also true for the numerous compositional and algebraic frameworks [15–23]. Most of these frameworks are based on a single operator for concurrent composition. This entails poor expressiveness, which results in overly complex architectural designs. In contrast, BIP allows expression of general multiparty interaction and strictly respects separation of concerns. Coordination can be studied as a separate entity that admits a simple Boolean characterisation that is instrumental for expressing composability.

BIP has some similarities with CSP, which can directly express multiparty interaction by using composition operators parameterized by channel names. For example, $B|\{a\}|B'$ is the system that enforces synchronisation of a-actions of components B and B'. Nonetheless, CSP is not adequate for architecture composition as the components must be modified when additional architecture constraints are applied. Consider for example the components $B_i = a_i \to STOP$ for $i = 1, 2, 3$. To model the system described in BIP by $\{\{a_1, a_2\}, \{a_2, a_3\}\}\{B_1, B_2, B_3\}$, two channels α and β must be defined representing respectively interactions $\{a_1, a_2\}$

and $\{a_2, a_3\}$ and the components modified as follows: $B_1 = \alpha \rightarrow STOP$, $B_2 = \alpha \rightarrow STOP \square \beta \rightarrow STOP, B_3 = \beta \rightarrow STOP$. That is, in addition to renaming, B_2 must be modified to show explicitly the conflict between α and β.

Existing research on architecture composability deals mainly with resource composability for particular types of architectures, e.g. [23]. The feature interaction problem is how to rapidly develop and deploy new features without disrupting the functionality of existing features. It can be considered as an architecture composability problem to the extent that features can be modelled as architectural constraints. A survey on feature interaction research is provided in [1]. Existing results focus mainly on modelling aspects and checking feature interaction by using algorithmic verification techniques with well-known complexity limitations. Our work takes a constructive approach. It has some similarities to [24] which presents a formal framework for detecting and avoiding feature interactions by using priorities. Nonetheless, these results do not deal with property preservation through composition. Similarly, existing work on service interaction mainly focuses on modelling and verification aspects, e.g. [25, 26].

6   Conclusion

Our work makes two novel contributions towards correct-by-construction system design. First, it proposes a general concept of architecture. Architectures are operators restricting the behaviour of their arguments by enforcing a characteristic property. They can be composed and studied independently. Composition of architectures can be naturally expressed as the conjunction of the induced synchronisation constraints. This implies nice properties such as associativity, commutativity and idempotence. Nonetheless, it is not easy to understand it as an operation on interaction models. Using BIP to describe architectures proves to be instrumental for achieving this. In contrast to other formalisms, BIP is expressive enough and keeps a strict separation between behaviour and coordination aspects. *Application of architectures does not require any modification of the atomic components*. The second contribution is preservation of properties enforced by architectures. The preservation of state predicates is guaranteed by the very nature of architecture composition. This result is different from existing results stipulating the preservation of invariants of components when composed by using parallel composition operators e.g., an invariant of B_1 is also an invariant of $B_1 \| B_2$ for some parallel composition operator $\|$. Our result is about preservation of properties over the *same* state-space, which is the Cartesian product of the atomic components. That is, a property of $A_1(\mathcal{B})$ is also a property of $(A_1 \oplus A_2)(\mathcal{B})$, and so the state-space of the components $\mathcal{B}$ is unchanged.

Our work pursues similar objectives as the research on interaction of features or services, insofar as they can be modelled as architectural constraints. Nonetheless, it adopts a radically different approach. It privileges constructive techniques to avoid costly and intractable verification. It proposes a concept of composability focusing on property preservation.

142   P. Attie et al.

References

1. Calder, M., Kolberg, M., Magill, E.H., Reiff-Marganiec, S.: Feature interaction: a critical review and considered forecast. Computer Networks 41(1), 115–141 (2003)
2. Sifakis, J.: Rigorous System Design. Foundations and Trends in Electronic Design Automation 6(4), 293–362 (2012)
3. Bliudze, S., Sifakis, J.: Synthesizing glue operators from glue constraints for the construction of component-based systems. In: Apel, S., Jackson, E. (eds.) SC 2011. LNCS, vol. 6708, pp. 51–67. Springer, Heidelberg (2011)
4. Basu, A., Bensalem, S., Bozga, M., Combaz, J., Jaber, M., Nguyen, T.H., Sifakis, J.: Rigorous component-based system design using the BIP framework. IEEE Software 28(3), 41–48 (2011)
5. Wegner, P.: Coordination as constrained interaction (extended abstract). In: Ciancarini, P., Hankin, C. (eds.) COORDINATION 1996. LNCS, vol. 1061, pp. 28–33. Springer, Heidelberg (1996)
6. Bliudze, S., Sifakis, J.: Causal semantics for the algebra of connectors. Formal Methods in System Design 36(2), 167–194 (2010)
7. Abadi, M., Lamport, L.: Composing specifications. ACM Trans. Program. Lang. Syst. 15(1), 73–132 (1993)
8. Attie, P.C., Bensalem, S., Bozga, M., Jaber, M., Sifakis, J., Zaraket, F.A.: An abstract framework for deadlock prevention in BIP. In: Beyer, D., Boreale, M. (eds.) FMOODS/FORTE 2013. LNCS, vol. 7892, pp. 161–177. Springer, Heidelberg (2013)
9. Tarjan, R.: Depth-first search and linear graph algorithms. SIAM Journal on Computing 1(2), 146–160 (1972)
10. D'Souza, D., Gopinathan, M.: Conflict-tolerant features. In: Gupta, A., Malik, S. (eds.) CAV 2008. LNCS, vol. 5123, pp. 227–239. Springer, Heidelberg (2008)
11. Plath, M., Ryan, M.: Feature integration using a feature construct. Science of Computer Programming 41(1), 53–84 (2001)
12. Balarin, F., Watanabe, Y., Hsieh, H., Lavagno, L., Passerone, C., Sangiovanni-Vincentelli, A.: Metropolis: an integrated electronic system design environment. IEEE Computer 36(4), 45–52 (2003)
13. Balasubramanian, K., Gokhale, A., Karsai, G., Sztipanovits, J., Neema, S.: Developing applications using model-driven design environments. IEEE Computer 39(2), 33–40 (2006)
14. Eker, J., Janneck, J., Lee, E., Liu, J., Liu, X., Ludvig, J., Neuendorffer, S., Sachs, S., Xiong, Y.: Taming heterogeneity: The Ptolemy approach. Proceedings of the IEEE 91(1), 127–144 (2003)
15. Arbab, F.: Reo: a channel-based coordination model for component composition. Mathematical Structures in Computer Science 14(3), 329–366 (2004)
16. Fiadeiro, J.L.: Categories for Software Engineering. Springer (April 2004)
17. Ray, A., Cleaveland, R.: Architectural interaction diagrams: AIDs for system modeling. In: ICSE 2003: Proceedings of the 25th International Conference on Software Engineering, pp. 396–406. IEEE Computer Society, Washington, DC (2003)
18. Spitznagel, B., Garlan, D.: A compositional formalization of connector wrappers. In: ICSE, pp. 374–384. IEEE Computer Society (2003)
19. Bernardo, M., Ciancarini, P., Donatiello, L.: On the formalization of architectural types with process algebras. In: SIGSOFT FSE, pp. 140–148 (2000)
20. Bruni, R., Lanese, I., Montanari, U.: A basic algebra of stateless connectors. Theoretical Computer Science 366(1), 98–120 (2006)

21. Hoare, C.A.R.: Communicating Sequential Processes. Prentice Hall International Series in Computer Science. Prentice Hall (April 1985)
22. Milner, R.: Communication and Concurrency. Prentice Hall International Series in Computer Science. Prentice Hall (1989)
23. Liu, I., Reineke, J., Lee, E.A.: A PRET architecture supporting concurrent programs with composable timing properties. In: 2010 Conference Record of the Forty Fourth Asilomar Conference on Signals, Systems and Computers (ASILOMAR), pp. 2111–2115 (2010)
24. Hay, J.D., Atlee, J.M.: Composing features and resolving interactions. SIGSOFT Softw. Eng. Notes 25(6), 110–119 (2000)
25. Decker, G., Puhlmann, F., Weske, M.: Formalizing service interactions. In: Dustdar, S., Fiadeiro, J.L., Sheth, A.P. (eds.) BPM 2006. LNCS, vol. 4102, pp. 414–419. Springer, Heidelberg (2006)
26. Li, Z., Jin, Y., Han, J.: A runtime monitoring and validation framework for web service interactions. In: ASWEC, pp. 70–79 (2006)

Trace Checking of Metric Temporal Logic
with Aggregating Modalities Using MapReduce

Domenico Bianculli[1], Carlo Ghezzi[2], and Srđan Krstić[2]

[1] SnT Centre - University of Luxembourg, Luxembourg
domenico.bianculli@uni.lu
[2] DEEP-SE group - DEIB - Politecnico di Milano, Italy
{carlo.ghezzi,srdjan.krstic}@polimi.it

Abstract. Modern complex software systems produce a large amount of execution data, often stored in logs. These logs can be analyzed using trace checking techniques to check whether the system complies with its requirements specifications. Often these specifications express quantitative properties of the system, which include timing constraints as well as higher-level constraints on the occurrences of significant events, expressed using aggregate operators.

In this paper we present an algorithm that exploits the MapReduce programming model to check specifications expressed in a metric temporal logic with aggregating modalities, over large execution traces. The algorithm exploits the structure of the formula to parallelize the evaluation, with a significant gain in time. We report on the assesment of the implementation—based on the Hadoop framework—of the proposed algorithm and comment on its scalability.

1 Introduction

Modern software systems, such as service-based applications (SBAs), are built according to a modular and decentralized architecture, and executed in a distributed environment. Their development and their operation depend on many stakeholders, including the providers of various third-party services and the integrators that realize composite applications by orchestrating third-party services. Service integrators are responsible to the end-users for guaranteeing an adequate level of quality of service, both in terms of functional and non-functional requirements. This new type of software has triggered several research efforts that focus on the specification and verification of SBAs.

In previous work [8], some of the authors presented the results of a field study on property specification patterns [12] used in the context of SBAs, both in industrial and in research settings. The study identified a set of property specification patterns specific to service provisioning. Most of these patterns are characterized by the presence of aggregate operations on sequences of events occurring in a given time window, such as "the average distance between pairs of events (e.g., average response time)", "the number of events in a given time window", "the average (or maximum) number of events in a certain time interval over a certain time window". This study led to the definition of SOLOIST [9] (*SpecificatiOn Language fOr servIce compoSitions inTeractions*), a metric temporal logic with new temporal modalities that support aggregate operations

D. Giannakopoulou and G. Salaün (Eds.): SEFM 2014, LNCS 8702, pp. 144–158, 2014.
© Springer International Publishing Switzerland 2014

on events occurring in a given time window. The new temporal modalities capture, in a concise way, the new property specification patterns presented in [8].

SOLOIST has been used in the context of *offline trace checking* of service execution traces. Trace checking (also called *trace validation* [15] or *history checking* [13]) is a procedure for evaluating a formal specification over a log of recorded events produced by a system, i.e., over a temporal evolution of the system. Traces can be produced at run time by a proper monitoring/logging infrastructure, and made available at the end of the service execution to perform offline trace checking. We have proposed procedures [5,7] for offline checking of service execution traces against requirements specifications written in SOLOIST using bounded satisfiability checking techniques [16]. Each of the procedures has been tailored to specific types of traces, depending on the degree of sparseness of the trace (i.e., the ratio between the number of time instants where significant events occur and those in which they do not). The procedure described in [5] is optimized for sparse traces, while the one presented in [7] is more efficient for dense traces.

Despite these optimizations, our experimental evaluation revealed, in both procedures, an intrinsic limitation in their scalability. This limitation is determined by the size of the trace, which can quickly lead to memory saturation. This is a very common problem, because execution traces can easily get very large, depending on the running time captured by the log, the systems the log refers to (e.g., several virtual machines running on a cloud-based infrastructure), and the types of events recorded. For example, granularity can range from high-level events (e.g., sending or receiving messages) to low-level events (e.g., invoking a method on an object). Most log analyzers that process data streams [10] or perform data mining [17] only partially solve the problem of checking an event trace against requirements specifications, because of the limited expressiveness of the specification language they support. Indeed, the analysis of a trace may require checking for complex properties, which can refer to specific sequence of events, conditioned by the occurrence of other event sequence(s), possibly with additional constraints on the distance among events, on the number of occurrences of events, and on various aggregate values (e.g., average response time). SOLOIST addresses these limitations as we discussed above.

The recent advent of cloud computing has made it possible to process large amount of data on networked commodity hardware, using a distributed model of computation. One of the most prominent programming models for distributed, parallel computing is *MapReduce* [11]. The MapReduce model allows developers to process large amount of data by breaking up the analysis into independent tasks, and performing them in parallel on the various nodes of a distributed network infrastructure, while exploiting, at the same time, the locality of the data to reduce unnecessary transmission over the network. However, porting a traditionally-sequential algorithm (like trace checking) into a parallel version that takes advantage of a distributed computation model like MapReduce is a non-trivial task.

The main contribution of this paper is an algorithm that exploits the MapReduce programming model to check large execution traces against requirements specifications written in SOLOIST. The algorithm exploits the structure of a SOLOIST formula to parallelize its evaluation, with significant gain in time. We have implemented the algorithm in Java using the Apache Hadoop framework [2]. We have evaluated the approach in terms of its scalability and with respect to the state of art for trace checking of LTL properties using MapReduce [3].

The rest of the paper is structured as follows. First we provide some background information, introducing SOLOIST in Sect. 2 and then the MapReduce programming model in Sect. 3. Section 4 presents the main contribution of the paper, describing the algorithm for trace checking of SOLOIST properties using the MapReduce programming model. Section 5 discusses related work. Section 6 presents the evaluation of the approach, both in terms of scalability and in terms of a comparison with the state of the art for MapReduce-based trace checking of temporal properties. Section 7 provides some concluding remarks.

2 SOLOIST

In this section we provide a brief overview of SOLOIST; for the rationale behind the language and a detailed explanation of its semantics see [9].

The syntax of SOLOIST is defined by the following grammar: $\phi ::= p \mid \neg\phi \mid \phi \wedge \phi \mid \phi U_I \phi \mid \phi S_I \phi \mid \mathfrak{C}_{\bowtie n}^K(\phi) \mid \mathfrak{U}_{\bowtie n}^{K,h}(\phi) \mid \mathfrak{M}_{\bowtie n}^{K,h}(\phi) \mid \mathfrak{D}_{\bowtie n}^K(\phi,\phi)$, where $p \in \Pi$, with Π being a finite set of atoms. In practice, we use atoms to represent different events of the trace. I is a nonempty interval over $\mathbb{N}$; $\bowtie \in \{<,\leq,\geq,>,=\}$; n,K,h range over $\mathbb{N}$. Moreover, for the $\mathfrak{D}$ modality, we require that the subformulae pair (ϕ,ψ) evaluate to true in alternation.

The U_I and S_I modalities are, respectively, the metric "*Until*" and "*Since*" operators. Additional temporal modalities can be derived using the usual conventions; for example "*Next*" is defined as $X_I\phi \equiv \bot U_I\phi$; "*Eventually in the Future*" as $F_I\phi \equiv \top U_I\phi$ and "*Always*" as $G_I\phi \equiv \neg(F_I\neg\phi)$, where $\top$ means "true" and $\bot$ means "false". Their past counterparts can be defined using "Since" modality in a similar way. The remaining modalities are called *aggregate* modalities and are used to express the property specification patterns characterized in [8]. The $\mathfrak{C}_{\bowtie n}^K(\phi)$ modality states a bound (represented by $\bowtie n$) on the number of occurrences of an event ϕ in the previous K time instants; it is also called the "*counting*" modality. The $\mathfrak{U}_{\bowtie n}^{K,h}(\phi)$ (respectively, $\mathfrak{M}_{\bowtie n}^{K,h}(\phi)$) modality expresses a bound on the average (respectively, maximum) number of occurrences of an event ϕ, aggregated over the set of right-aligned adjacent non-overlapping subintervals within a time window K; it can express properties like "the average/maximum number of events per hour in the last ten hours". A subtle difference in the semantics of the $\mathfrak{U}$ and $\mathfrak{M}$ modalities is that $\mathfrak{M}$ considers events in the (possibly empty) tail interval, i.e., the leftmost observation subinterval whose length is less than h, while the $\mathfrak{U}$ modality ignores them. The $\mathfrak{D}_{\bowtie n}^K(\phi,\psi)$ modality expresses a bound on the average time elapsed between occurrences of pairs of specific adjacent events ϕ and ψ in the previous K time instants; it can be used to express properties like the average response time of a service.

The formal semantics of SOLOIST is defined on timed ω-words [1] over $2^\Pi \times \mathbb{N}$. A timed sequence $\tau = \tau_0\tau_1\ldots$ is an infinite sequence of values $\tau_i \in \mathbb{N}$ with $\tau_i > 0$ satisfying $\tau_i < \tau_{i+1}$, for all $i \geq 0$, i.e., the sequence increases strictly monotonically. A timed ω-word over alphabet 2^Π is a pair (σ,τ) where $\sigma = \sigma_0\sigma_1\ldots$ is an infinite word over 2^Π and τ is a timed sequence. A timed language over 2^Π is a set of timed

$(w,i) \models p$ iff $p \in \sigma_i$

$(w,i) \models \neg \phi$ iff $(w,i) \not\models \phi$

$(w,i) \models \phi \wedge \psi$ iff $(w,i) \models \phi \wedge (w,i) \models \psi$

$(w,i) \models \phi S_I \psi$ iff for some $j < i, \tau_i - \tau_j \in I, (w,j) \models \psi$ and for all $k, j < k < i, (w,k) \models \phi$

$(w,i) \models \phi U_I \psi$ iff for some $j > i, \tau_j - \tau_i \in I, (w,j) \models \psi$ and for all $k, i < k < j, (w,k) \models \phi$

$(w,i) \models \mathfrak{C}_{\bowtie n}^K(\phi)$ iff $c(\tau_i - K, \tau_i, \phi) \bowtie n$ and $\tau_i \geq K$

$(w,i) \models \mathfrak{U}_{\bowtie n}^{K,h}(\phi)$ iff $\dfrac{c(\tau_i - \lfloor \frac{K}{h} \rfloor h, \tau_i, \phi)}{\lfloor \frac{K}{h} \rfloor} \bowtie n$ and $\tau_i \geq K$

$(w,i) \models \mathfrak{M}_{\bowtie n}^{K,h}(\phi)$ iff $\max \left\{ \bigcup_{m=0}^{\lfloor \frac{K}{h} \rfloor} \{c(lb(m), rb(m), \phi)\} \right\} \bowtie n$ and $\tau_i \geq K$

$(w,i) \models \mathfrak{D}_{\bowtie n}^K(\phi, \psi)$ iff $\dfrac{\sum_{(s,t) \in d(\phi, \psi, \tau_i, K)} (\tau_t - \tau_s)}{|d(\phi, \psi, \tau_i, K)|} \bowtie n$ and $\tau_i \geq K$

where $c(\tau_a, \tau_b, \phi) = |\{s \mid \tau_a < \tau_s \leq \tau_b \text{ and } (w,s) \models \phi\}|$, $lb(m) = \max\{\tau_i - K, \tau_i - (m+1)h\}$, $rb(m) = \tau_i - mh$, and $d(\phi, \psi, \tau_i, K) = \{(s,t) \mid \tau_i - K < \tau_s \leq \tau_i \text{ and } (w,s) \models \phi, t = \min\{u \mid \tau_s < \tau_u \leq \tau_i, (w,u) \models \psi\}\}$

Fig. 1. Formal semantics of SOLOIST

words over the same alphabet. Notice that there is a distinction between the integer position i in the timed ω-word and the corresponding timestamp τ_i. Figure 1 defines the satisfiability relation $(w,i) \models \phi$ for every timed ω-word w, every position $i \geq 0$ and for every SOLOIST formula ϕ. For the sake of simplicity, hereafter we express the $\mathfrak{U}$ modality in terms of the $\mathfrak{C}$ one, based on this definition: $\mathfrak{U}_{\bowtie n}^{K,h}(\phi) \equiv \mathfrak{C}_{\bowtie n \cdot \lfloor \frac{K}{h} \rfloor}^{\lfloor \frac{K}{h} \rfloor \cdot h}(\phi)$, which can be derived from the semantics in Fig. 1.

We remark that the version of SOLOIST presented here is a restriction of the original one introduced in [9]: to simplify the presentation in the next sections, we dropped first-order quantification on finite domains and limited the argument of the $\mathfrak{D}$ modality to only one pair of events; as detailed in [9], these assumptions do not affect the expressiveness of the language.

SOLOIST can be used to express some of the most common specifications found in service-level agreements (SLAs) of SBAs. For example the property: "The average response time of operation A is always less than 5 seconds within any 900 second time window, before operation B is invoked" can be expressed as: $G(B_{start} \rightarrow \mathfrak{D}_{<5}^{900}(A_{start}, A_{end}))$, where A and B correspond to generic service invocations and each operation has a *start* and an *end* event, denoted with the corresponding subscripts.

We now introduce some basic concepts that will be used in the presentation of our distributed trace checking algorithm in Sect. 4. Let ϕ and ψ be SOLOIST formulae. We denote with $sub(\phi)$ the set of all subformulae of ϕ; notice that for *atomic* formulae $a \in \Pi$, $sub(a) = \emptyset$. The set of *atomic* subformulae (or *atoms*) of formula ϕ is defined as $sub_a(\phi) = \{a \mid a \in sub(\phi), sub(a) = \emptyset\}$. The set $sub_d(\phi) = \{\alpha \mid \alpha \in sub(\phi), \forall \beta \in sub(\phi), \alpha \not\subseteq sub(\beta)\}$ represents the set of all *direct subformulae* of ϕ; ϕ is called the *superformula* of all formulae in $sub_d(\phi)$. The notation $sup_\psi(\phi)$ denotes the set of all subformulae of ψ that have formula ϕ as *direct subformula*, i.e., $sup_\psi(\phi) = \{\alpha \mid \alpha \in sub(\psi), \phi \in sub_d(\alpha)\}$. The subformulae in $sub(\psi)$ of a formula ψ form a lattice with respect to the partial ordering induced by the inclusion in sets $sup_\psi(\cdot)$ and $sub_d(\cdot)$, with ψ and $\emptyset$ being the *top* and *bottom* elements of the lattice, respectively. We also introduce the notion of the *height* of a SOLOIST formula, which is defined recursively as:

$$h(\phi) = \begin{cases} \max\{h(\psi) \mid \psi \in \mathrm{sub}_d(\phi)\} + 1 & \text{if } \mathrm{sub}_d(\phi) \neq \emptyset \\ 0 & \text{otherwise.} \end{cases}$$

We exemplify these concepts using formula $\gamma \equiv \mathfrak{C}^{40}_{\bowtie 3}(a \wedge b)\mathsf{U}_{(30,100)}\neg c$.

Hence $\mathrm{sub}(\gamma) = \{a, b, c, a \wedge b, \neg c, \mathfrak{C}^{40}_{\bowtie 3}(a \wedge b)\}$ is the set of all subformulae of γ; $\mathrm{sub}_a(\gamma) = \{a, b, c\}$ is the set of *atoms* in γ; $\mathrm{sub}_d(\gamma) = \{\mathfrak{C}^{40}_{\bowtie 3}(a \wedge b), \neg c\}$ is the set of direct subformulae of γ; $\sup_\gamma(a) = \sup_\gamma(b) = \{a \wedge b\}$ shows that the sets of superformulae of a and b in γ coincide; and the height of γ is 3, since $h(a) = h(b) = h(c) = 0$, $h(\neg c) = h(a \wedge b) = 1$, $h(\mathfrak{C}^{40}_{\bowtie 3}(a \wedge b)) = 2$ and therefore $h(\gamma) = \max\{h(\mathfrak{C}^{40}_{\bowtie 3}(a \wedge b)), h(\neg c)\} + 1 = 3$.

3   The MapReduce Programming Model

MapReduce [11] is a programming model for processing and analyzing large data sets using a parallel, distributed infrastructure (generically called "cluster"). At the basis of the MapReduce abstraction there are two functions, *map* and *reduce*, that are inspired by (but conceptually different from) the homonymous functions that are typically found in functional programming languages. The *map* and *reduce* functions are defined by the user; their signatures are `map(k1,v1)` $\rightarrow$ `list(k2,v2)` and `reduce(k2,list(v2))` $\rightarrow$ `list(v2)`. The idea of MapReduce is to apply a *map* function to each logical entity in the input (represented by a key/value pair) in order to compute a set of intermediate key/value pairs, and then applying a *reduce* function to all the values that have the same key in order to combine the derived data appropriately.

Let us illustrate this model with an example that counts the number of occurrences of each word in a large collection of documents; the pseudocode is:

```
map(String key, String value)          reduce(String key, Iterator values):
//key: document name                    //key: a word
//value: document contents              //values: a list of counts
for each word w in value:               int result = 0
    EmitIntermediate(w,"1")             for each v in values:
                                            result += ParseInt(v)
                                        Emit(AsString(result)
```

The *map* function emits list of pairs, each composed of a word and its associated count of occurrences (which is just 1). All emitted pairs are partitioned into groups and sorted according to their key for the reduction phase; in the example, pairs are grouped and sorted according to the word they contain. The *reduce* function sums all the counts (using an iterator to go through the list of counts) emitted for each particular word (i.e., each unique key).

Besides the actual programming model, MapReduce brings in a framework that provides, in a transparent way to developers, parallelization, fault tolerance, locality optimization, and load balancing. The MapReduce framework is responsible for partitioning the input data, scheduling and executing the *Map* and *Reduce* tasks (also called *mappers* and *reducers*, respectively) on the machines available in the cluster, and for managing the communication and the data transfer among them (usually leveraging a distributed file system).

More in detail, the execution of a MapReduce operation (called *job*) proceeds as follows. First, the framework divides the input into splits of a certain size using an *InputReader*, generating key/value (k, v) pairs. It then assigns each input split to Map tasks, which are processed in parallel by the nodes in the cluster. A Map task reads the corresponding input split and passes the set of key/value pairs to the *map* function, which generates a set of *intermediate* key/value pairs (k', v'). Notice that each run of the *map* function is stateless, i.e., the transformation of a single key/value pair does not depend on any other key/value pair. The next phase is called *shuffle and sort*: it takes the intermediate data generated by each Map task, sorts them based on the intermediate data generated from other nodes, divides these data into regions to be processed by Reduce tasks, and distributes these data on the nodes where the Reduce tasks will be executed. The division of intermediate data into regions is done by a *partitioning function*, which depends on the (user-specified) number of Reduce tasks and the key of the intermediate data. Each Reduce task executes the *reduce* function, which takes an intermediate key k' and a set of values associated with that key to produce the output data. This output is appended to a final output file for this reduce partition. The output of the MapReduce job will then be available in several files, one for each Reduce task used.

4 Trace Checking with MapReduce

Our algorithm for trace checking of SOLOIST properties takes as input a non-empty execution trace T and the SOLOIST formula Φ to be checked. The trace T is finite and can be seen as a time-stamped sequence of H elements, i.e., $T = (p_1, p_2, \ldots, p_H)$. Each of these elements is a triple $p_i = (i, \tau_i, (a_1, \ldots, a_{P_i}))$, where i is the position within the trace, τ_i the integer timestamp, and $(a_1, \ldots, a_{P_i})$ is a list of atoms such that $a_{j_i} \in \Pi$, for all $j_i \in \{1, \ldots P_i\}, P_i \geq 1$ and for all $i \in \{1, 2, \ldots, H\}$.

The algorithm processes the trace iteratively, through subsequent MapReduce passes. The number of MapReduce iterations is equal to height of the SOLOIST formula Φ to be checked. The *l*-th iteration (with $1 < l \leq h(\Phi)$) of the algorithm receives a set of tuples from the $(l-1)$-th iteration; these input tuples represent all the positions where the subformulae of Φ having height $l-1$ hold. The *l*-th iteration then determines all the positions where the subformulae of Φ with height l hold.

Each iteration consists of three phases: 1) reading and splitting the input; 2) (*map*) associating each formula with its superformula; 3) (*reduce*) determining the positions where the superformulae obtained in the previous step hold, given the positions where their subformulae hold. We detail each phase in the rest of this section.

4.1 Input Reader

We assume that before the first iteration of the algorithm the input trace is available in the distributed file system of the cluster; this is a realistic assumption since in a distribute setting is possible to collect logs, as long as there is a total order among the timestamps. The input reader at the first iteration reads the trace directly, while in all subsequent iterations input readers read the output of the reducers of the previous iteration.

The input reader component of the MapReduce framework is able to process the input trace exploiting some parallelism. Indeed, the MapReduce framework exploits the

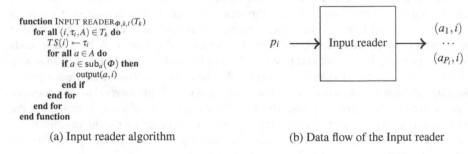

```
function INPUT READERΦ,k,l(Tk)
    for all (i, τi, A) ∈ Tk do
        TS(i) ← τi
        for all a ∈ A do
            if a ∈ suba(Φ) then
                output(a, i)
            end if
        end for
    end for
end function
```

(a) Input reader algorithm   (b) Data flow of the Input reader

Fig. 2. Input reader

location information of the different fragments of the trace to parallelize the execution of the input reader. For example, a trace split into n fragments can be processed in parallel using $\min(n, k)$ machines, given a cluster with k machines.

Figure 2b shows how the input reader transforms the trace at the first iteration: for every atomic proposition ϕ that holds at position i in the original trace, it outputs a tuple of the form (ϕ, i). The transformation does not happen in the subsequent iterations, since (as will be shown in Sect. 4.3) the output of the reduce phase has the same form (ϕ, i). The algorithm in Fig. 2a shows how input reader handles the k-th fragment T_k of the input trace T. For each time point i and for each atom p that holds in position i it creates a tuple (p, i). Moreover, for each time point i, it updates a globally-shared associative list of timestamps TS. This list is used to associate a timestamp with each time point; its contents are saved in the distributed file system, for use during the reduce phase.

4.2   Mapper

Each tuple generated by an input reader is passed to a mapper at the local node. Mappers "lift" the formula in the tuple by associating it with all its superformulae in the input formula Φ. For example, given the formula $\Phi \equiv (a \wedge b) \vee \neg a$, the tuple $(a, 5)$ is associated with formulae $a \wedge b$ and $\neg a$. The reduce phase will then exploit the information about the direct subformulae to determine all the positions in which a superformula holds.

As shown in Fig. 3, the output of a mapper are tuples of the form $((\psi, i), (\phi, i))$ where ϕ is a direct subformulae of ψ and i is the position where ϕ holds. For each received tuple of the form (ϕ, i), the algorithm shown in Fig. 3a loops through all the superformulae ψ of ϕ and emits (using the function *output*) a tuple $((\psi, i), (\phi, i))$.

Notice that the key of the intermediate tuples emitted by the mapper has two parts: this type of key is called a *composite key* and it is used to perform *secondary sorting* of the intermediate tuples. Secondary sorting performs the sorting using multiple criteria, allowing developers to sort not only by the key, but also "by value". In our case, we perform secondary sorting based on the position where the subformula holds, in order to decrease the memory used by the reducer. To enable secondary sorting, we need to override the procedure that compares keys, to take into account also the second element

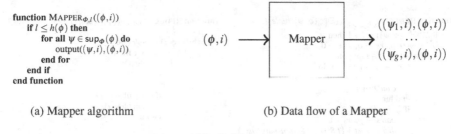

(a) Mapper algorithm   (b) Data flow of a Mapper

Fig. 3. Mapper

of the composite keys when their first elements are equal. We have also modified the key grouping procedure to consider only the first part of the composite key, so that each reducer gets all the tuples related to exactly one superformula (as encoded in the first part of the key), sorted in ascending order with respect to the position where subformulae hold (as encoded in the second part of the key).

4.3   Reducer

In the reduce phase, at each iteration l, reducers calculate all positions where subformulae with height l hold. The total number of reducers running in parallel at the l-th iteration is the minimum between the number of subformulae with height l in the input formula Φ and the number of machines in the cluster multiplied by the number of reducers available on each node. Each reducer calls an appropriate reduce function depending on the type of formula used as key in the input tuple. The initial data shared by all reducers is the input formula Φ, the index of the current MapReduce iteration l and the associative map of timestamps TS.

In the rest of this section we present the algorithms of the reduce function defined for SOLOIST connectives and modalities. For space reasons we limit the description to the algorithms for negation ($\neg$) and conjunction ($\wedge$), and for the modalities U_I, $\mathfrak{C}^K_{\bowtie n}$, $\mathfrak{M}^{K,h}_{\bowtie n}$, and $\mathfrak{D}^K_{\bowtie n}$. The other temporal modalities can be expressed in a way similar to the *Until* modality U_I. In the various algorithms we use several auxiliary functions whose pseudocode is available in the extended version of this article [6].

Negation. When the key refers to a negated superformula, the reducer emits a tuple at every position where the subformula does not hold, i.e., at every position that does not occur in the input tuples received from the mappers. The algorithm in Fig. 4e shows how output tuples are emitted. If no tuples are received then the reducer emits tuples at each position. Otherwise, it keeps track of the position i of the current tuple and the position p of the previous tuple and emits tuples at positions $[p+1, i-1]$.

Conjunction. We extend the binary $\wedge$ operator defined in Sect. 2 to any positive arity; this extension does not change the language but improves the conciseness of the formulae. With this extension, conjunction $a \wedge b \wedge c$ is represented as a single conjunction with 3 subformulae and has height equal to 1. Tuples (ϕ, i) received from the mapper may refer to any subformula ϕ of a conjunction.

In the algorithm in Fig. 4b we process all the tuples sequentially. First, we check if the height of each subformula is consistent with respect to the iteration in which they are

```
function REDUCER_{𝔇^K_{⋈n},Φ,l,TS}(𝔇^K_{⋈n}(φ,ψ),tuples[])
    if h(𝔇^K_{⋈n}(φ,ψ)) = l + 1 then
        p ← 0, pairs ← 0, dist ← 0
        for all (ξ,i) ∈ tuples do
            for j ← p + 1...i − 1 do
                updateDistInterval(j)
                emitDist(j)
            end for
            if ξ = ψ then
                pairs ← pairs + 1
                dist ← dist + (TS(i) − TS(subFmas.last))
            end if
            subFmas.addLast(i)
            updateDistInterval(i)
            emitDist(i)
            p ← i
        end for
    else
        for all (φ,i) ∈ tuples do
            output(φ,i)
        end for
    end if
end function
```

(a) 𝔇 modality

```
function REDUCER_{∧,Φ,l,TS}(ψ,tuples[])
    p ← 0, c ← 1
    while (φ,i) ∈ tuples do
        if h(ψ) = l + 1 then
            if i = p then
                c ← c + 1
            else
                if c = |sub_d(ψ)| then
                    output(ψ,i)
                end if
                c ← 1
            end if
        else
            output(φ,i)
        end if
        p ← i
    end while
end function
```

(b) Conjunction

```
function REDUCER_{U_1,Φ,l,TS}(φ_1 U_{(a,b)} φ_2,tuples[])
    if h(φ_1 U_{(a,b)} φ_2) = l + 1 then
        p ← 0
        for all (ξ,i) ∈ tuples do
            updateLTLBehavior(i)
            updateMTLBehavior(i)
            if ξ = φ_2 then
                emitUntil(i)
            end if
            p ← i
        end for
    else
        for all (φ,i) ∈ tuples do
            output(φ,i)
        end for
    end if
end function
```

(c) 𝔘 modality

```
function REDUCER_{ℭ^K_{⋈n},Φ,l,TS}(ℭ^K_{⋈n}(φ),tuples[])
    p ← 0, c ← 0
    for all (φ,i) ∈ tuples do
        c ← c + 1
        for j ← p + 1...i − 1 do
            updateCountInterval(j)
            if c ⋈ n then
                output(ℭ^K_{⋈n}(φ),j)
            end if
        end for
        updateCountInterval(i)
        if c ⋈ n then
            output(ℭ^K_{⋈n}(φ),i)
        end if
        p ← i
    end for
end function
```

(d) ℭ modality

```
function REDUCER_{¬,Φ,l,TS}(¬φ,tuples[])
    p ← 0
    for all ((φ,i)) ∈ tuples do
        for j ← p + 1...i − 1 do
            output(¬φ,j)
        end for
        p ← i
    end for
    for i ← p + 1...TS.size() do
        output(¬φ,i)
    end for
end function
```

(e) Negation

```
function REDUCER_{𝔐^{K,h}_{⋈n},Φ,l,TS}(𝔐^{K,h}_{⋈n}(φ),tuples[])
    p ← 0
    for all (ξ,i) ∈ tuples do
        for j ← p + 1...i − 1 do
            updateMaxInterval(j)
            emitMax(j)
        end for
        updateMaxInterval(i)
        emitMax(i)
        p ← i
    end for
end function
```

(f) 𝔐 modality

Fig. 4. Reduce algorithms

processed. In fact, mappers can emit some tuples before the "right" iteration in which they should be processed, since subformule of a conjunction may have different height. If the heights are not consistent, the reducer re-emits the tuples that appeared early. Since the incoming tuples are sorted by their position, it is enough to use a counter to record how many tuples there are in each position i. When the value of the counter becomes equal to the arity of the conjunction, its means that all the subformulae hold at i and the reducer can emit the tuple for the conjunction at position i. Otherwise, we reset the counter and continue.

U_I **modality.** The reduce function for the *Until* modality is shown in Fig. 4c. When we process tuples with this function, we have to check both the temporal behavior and the metric constraints (in the form of an (a, b) interval) as defined by the semantics of the modality.

Given a formula $\phi_1 U_{(a,b)} \phi_2$, we check whether it can be evaluated in the current iteration, since reducer may receive some tuples early. If this happens, reducer re-emits the tuple, as described above.

The algorithm processes each tuple (ϕ, i) sequentially. It keeps track of all the positions in the $(0, b)$ time window in the past with respect to the current tuple. For each tuple it calls two auxiliary functions, updateLTLBehavior and updateMTLBehavior. The first function checks whether ϕ_1 holds in all the positions tracked in the $(0, b)$ time window; if this not the case we stop tracing these positions. This guarantee that we only keep track of the position that exhibit the correct temporal semantics of the *Until* formula. Afterwards, function updateMTLBehavior checks the timing constraints and removes positions that are outside of the $(0, b)$ time window. Lastly, if ϕ_2 holds in the position of the current tuple, we call function emitUntil, which emits an *Until* tuple for each position that we track, which is not in the $(0, a)$ time window in the past.

$\mathfrak{C}$ **modality.** The reduce function for the $\mathfrak{C}$ modality is outlined in the algorithm in Fig. 4d. To correctly determine if $\mathfrak{C}$ modality holds, we need to keep track of all the positions in the past time window $(0, K)$. While we sequentially process the tuples, we use variable p to save the position which appeared in the previous tuple. This allows us to consider positions between each consecutive tuple in the inner "for" loop. We call function updateCountInterval, which checks if the tracked positions, together with the current one, occur within the time window $(0, K)$; positions that do not fall within the time interval are discarded. Variable c is used to count in how many tracked positions subformula ϕ holds. At the end, we compare the value of c with n according to the $\bowtie$ comparison operator; if this comparison is satisfied we emit a $\mathfrak{C}$ tuple.

$\mathfrak{M}$ **modality.** The algorithm in Fig. 4f shows when the tuples for the $\mathfrak{M}$ modality are emitted. Similarly to the $\mathfrak{C}$ modality, we need to keep track of the all positions in the $(0, K)$ time window in the past. Also, the two nested "for" loops make sure that we consider all time positions. For each position we call in sequence function updateMaxInterval and function emitMax. Function updateMaxInterval is similar to updateCountInterval, i.e., it checks whether the tracked positions, together with the current one, occur within the time window $(0, K)$. Function emitMax computes, in the tracked positions, the maximum number of occurrences of the subformula in all subintervals of length h. It compares the computed value to the bound n using the $\bowtie$ comparison operator; if this comparison is satisfied it emits the $\mathfrak{M}$ modality tuple.

$\mathfrak{D}$ **modality.** The reduce function for the $\mathfrak{D}$ modality is shown in Fig. 4a. Similarly to the case of the U_I modality, if the heights of the subformulae are not consistent with the index of the current iteration, the reducer re-emits the corresponding tuples. After that, the incoming tuples are processed in a sequential way and two nested "for" loops guarantee that we consider all time points. We need to keep track of all the positions in the $(0, K)$ time window in the past in which either ϕ or ψ occurred. Differently from the previous aggregate modalities, we have to consider only the occurrences of ϕ for which there exists a matching occurrence ψ; for each of these pairs we have to compute the distance. This processing of tuples (and the corresponding atoms and time points that they include) is done by the auxiliary function updateDistInterval. Variables *pairs* and *dist* keep track of the number of complete pairs in the current time window and their cumulative distance (computed accessing the globally-shared map *TS* of timestamps). Finally, by means of the function emitDist, if there is any pair in the time window, we compare the average distance computed as $\frac{dist}{pairs}$ with the bound n using the $\bowtie$ comparison operator. If the comparison is satisfied, we emit a $\mathfrak{D}$ modality tuple.

5   Related Work

To the best of our knowledge, the approach proposed in [3] is the only one that uses MapReduce to perform offline trace checking of temporal properties. The algorithm is conceptually similar to ours as it performs iterations of MapReduce jobs depending on the height of the formula. However, the properties of interest are expressed using LTL. This is only a subset of the properties that can be expressed by SOLOIST. Their implementation of the conjunction and disjunction operators is limited to only two subformulae which increases the height of the formula and results in having more iterations. Intermediate tuples exchanged between mappers and reducers are not sorted by the secondary key, therefore reducers have to keep track of all the positions where the subformulae hold, while our approach tracks only the data that lies in the relevant interval of a metric temporal formula.

Distributed computing infrastructures and/or programming models have also been used for other verification problems. Reference [14] proposes a distributed algorithm for performing *model checking* of LTL *safety properties* on a network of interconnected workstations. By restricting the verification to safety properties, authors can easily parallelize a bread-first search algorithm. Reference [4] proposes a parallel version of the well-known fixed-point algorithm for CTL model checking. Given a set of states where a certain formula holds and a transition relation of a Kripke structure, the algorithm computes the set of states where the superformula of a given formula holds though a series of MapReduce iterations, parallelized over the different predecessors of the states in the set. The set is computed when a fixed-point of a predicate transformer is reached as defined by the semantics of each specific CTL modality.

Table 1. Average processing time per tuple for the four properties

	Property 1		Property 2		Property 3		Property 4	
	SOLOIST	LTL	SOLOIST	LTL	SOLOIST	LTL	SOLOIST	LTL
Number of tuples	16,121	55,009	24,000	119,871	215,958	599,425	1,747,360	4,987,124
Time per event (μs)	1.172	19	1.894	21	3.707	14	7.200	30

6   Evaluation

We have implemented the proposed trace checking algorithm in Java using the Hadoop MapReduce framework [2] (version 1.2.1). We executed it on a Windows Azure cloud-based infrastructure where we allocated 10 small virtual machines with 1 CPU core and 1.75 GB of memory. We followed the standard Hadoop guidelines when configuring the cluster: the number of map tasks was set to the number of nodes in the cluster multiplied by 10, and the number of reducers was set to the number of nodes multiplied by 0.9; we used 100 mappers and 9 reducers. We have also enabled JVM reuse for any number of jobs, to minimize the time spent by framework in initializing Java virtual machines. In the rest of this section, we first show how the approach scales with respect to the trace length and how the height of the formula affects the running time and memory. Afterwards, we compare our algorithm to the one presented in [3], designed for LTL.

Scalability. To evaluate scalability of the approach, we considered 4 formulae, with different height: $\mathfrak{C}_{<10}^{50000}(a_0)$, $\mathfrak{D}_{<10}^{50000}(a_1,a_2)$, $(a_0 \wedge (a_1 \wedge a_2))\mathsf{U}_{(50,200)}((a_1 \wedge a_2)\vee a_1)$ and $\exists j \in \{0\ldots9\}\ \forall i \in \{0\ldots8\} : \mathsf{G}_{(50,500)}(a_{i,j} \to \mathsf{X}_{(50,500)}(a_{i+1,j}))$. Here the $\forall$ and $\exists$ quantifiers are used as a shorthand notation to predicate on finite domains: for example, $\forall i \in \{1,2,3\} : a_i$ is equivalent to $a_1 \wedge a_2 \wedge a_3$. We generated random traces with a number of time instants varying from 10000 to 350000. For each time instant, we randomly generated with a uniform distribution up to 100 distinct events (i.e., *atomic* propositions). Hence, we evaluated our algorithm for a maximum number of events up to 35 millions. The time span between the first and the last timestamp was 578.7 days on average, with a granularity of one second.

Figure 5 shows the total time and the memory used by the MapReduce job run to check the four formulae on the generated traces. Formulae $\mathfrak{C}_{<10}^{50000}(a_0)$ and $\mathfrak{D}_{<10}^{50000}(a_1,a_2)$ needed one iteration to be evaluated (shown in Fig. 5a and Fig. 5b). In both cases, the time taken to check the formula increases linearly with respect to the trace length; this happens because reducers need to process more tuples. As for the linear increase in memory usage, for modalities $\mathfrak{C}$ and $\mathfrak{D}$ reducers have to keep track of all the tuples in the window of length K time units and the more time points there are the more *dense* the time window becomes, with a consequent increase in memory usage. As for the checking of the other two formulae (shown in Fig. 5c and Fig. 5d), more iterations were needed because of the height of the formulae. Also in this case, the time taken by each iteration tends to increase as the length of the trace increases; the memory usage is constant since the formulae considered here do not contain aggregate modalities. Notice the increase of time and memory from Fig. 5c to Fig. 5d: this is due to the expansion of the quantifiers in formula $\exists j \in \{0\ldots9\}\ \forall i \in \{0\ldots8\} : \mathsf{G}_{(50,500)}(a_{i,j} \to \mathsf{X}_{(50,500)}(a_{i+1,j}))$.

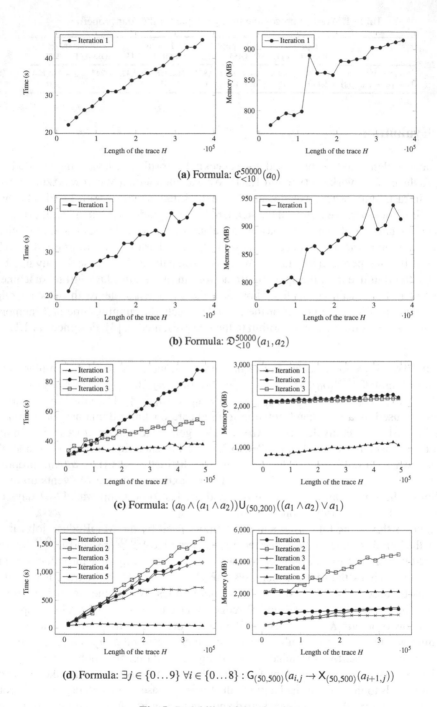

(a) Formula: $\mathfrak{C}^{50000}_{<10}(a_0)$

(b) Formula: $\mathfrak{D}^{50000}_{<10}(a_1, a_2)$

(c) Formula: $(a_0 \wedge (a_1 \wedge a_2)) \mathsf{U}_{(50,200)}((a_1 \wedge a_2) \vee a_1)$

(d) Formula: $\exists j \in \{0 \ldots 9\} \; \forall i \in \{0 \ldots 8\} : \mathsf{G}_{(50,500)}(a_{i,j} \to \mathsf{X}_{(50,500)}(a_{i+1,j}))$

Fig. 5. Scalability of the algorithm

Comparison with the LTL approach [3]. We compare our approach to the one presented in [3], which focuses on trace checking of LTL properties using MapReduce; for this comparison we considered the LTL layer included in SOLOIST by means of the *Until* modality. Although the focus of our work was on implementing the semantics of SOLOIST aggregate modalities, we also introduces some improvements in the LTL layer of SOLOIST. First, we exploited composite keys and secondary sorting as provided by the MapReduce framework to reduce the memory used by reducers. We also extended the binary $\wedge$ and $\vee$ operators to support any positive arity.

We compared the two approaches by checking the following formulae:
1) $G_{(50,500)}(\neg a_0)$; 2) $G_{(50,500)}(a_0 \rightarrow X_{(50,500)}(a_1))$; 3) $\forall i \in \{0\ldots 8\} : G_{(50,500)}(a_i \rightarrow X_{(50,500)}(a_{i+1}))$; and 4) $\exists j \in \{0\ldots 9\}\ \forall i \in \{0\ldots 8\} : G_{(50,500)}(a_{i,j} \rightarrow X_{(50,500)}(a_{i+1,j}))$.
The height of these formulae are 2, 3, 4 and 5, respectively. This admittedly gives our approach a significant advantage since in [3] the restriction for the $\wedge$ and $\vee$ operators to have an arity fixed to 2 results in a larger height for formulae 3 and 4. We randomly generated traces of variable length, ranging from 1000 to 100000 time instants, with up to 100 events per time instant. With this configuration, a trace can contain potentially up to 10 million events. We chose to have up to 100 events per time instant to match the configuration proposed in [3], where there are 10 parameters per formula that can take 10 possible values. We generated 500 traces. The time needed by our algorithm to check each of the four formulae, averaged over the different traces, was 52.83, 85.38, 167.1 and 324.53 seconds, respectively. We do not report the time taken by the approach proposed in [3] since the article does not report any statistics from the run of an actual implementation, but only metrics determined by a simulation. Table 1 shows the average number of tuples generated by the algorithm for each formulae. The number of tuples is calculated as the sum of all input tuples for mappers at each iterations in a single trace checking run. The table also shows the average time needed to process a single event in the trace. This time is computed as the total processing time divided by the number of time instants in the trace, averaged over the different trace checking runs. The SOLOIST column refers to the data obtained by running our algorithm, while the LTL column refers to data reported in [3], obtained with a simulation. Our algorithm performs better both in terms of the number of generated tuples and in terms of processing time.

7   Conclusion and Future Work

In this paper we present an algorithm based on the MapReduce programming model that checks large execution traces against specifications written in SOLOIST. The experimental results in terms of scalability and comparison with the state of the art are encouraging and show that the algorithm can be effectively applied in realistic settings.

A limitation of the algorithm is that reducers (that implement the semantics of temporal and aggregate operators) need to keep track of the positions relevant to the time window specified in the formula. In the future, we will investigate how this information may be split into smaller and more manageable parts that may be processed separately, while preserving the original semantics of the operators.

Acknowledgments. This work has been partially supported by the National Research Fund, Luxembourg (FNR/P10/03).

References

1. Alur, R., Dill, D.L.: A theory of timed automata. Theoreotical Computer Science 126(2), 183–235 (1994)
2. Apache Software Foundation: Hadoop MapReduce,
   http://hadoop.apache.org/mapreduce/
3. Barre, B., Klein, M., Soucy-Boivin, M., Ollivier, P.-A., Hallé, S.: MapReduce for parallel trace validation of LTL properties. In: Qadeer, S., Tasiran, S. (eds.) RV 2012. LNCS, vol. 7687, pp. 184–198. Springer, Heidelberg (2013)
4. Bellettini, C., Camilli, M., Capra, L., Monga, M.: Distributed CTL model checking in the cloud. Tech. Rep. 1310.6670, Cornell University (October 2013),
   http://arxiv.org/abs/1310.6670
5. Bersani, M.M., Bianculli, D., Ghezzi, C., Krstić, S., San Pietro, P.: SMT-based checking of SOLOIST over sparse traces. In: Gnesi, S., Rensink, A. (eds.) FASE 2014. LNCS, vol. 8411, pp. 276–290. Springer, Heidelberg (2014)
6. Bianculli, D., Ghezzi, C., Krstić, S.: Trace checking of metric temporal logic with aggregating modalities using MapReduce (2014) (extended version),
   http://hdl.handle.net/10993/16806
7. Bianculli, D., Ghezzi, C., Krstić, S., San Pietro, P.: From SOLOIST to CLTLB($\mathscr{D}$): Checking quantitative properties of service-based applications. Tech. Rep. 2013.26, Politecnico di Milano - Dipartimento di Elettronica, Informazione e Bioingegneria (October 2013)
8. Bianculli, D., Ghezzi, C., Pautasso, C., Senti, P.: Specification patterns from research to industry: a case study in service-based applications. In: Proc. of ICSE 2012, pp. 968–976. IEEE Computer Society (2012)
9. Bianculli, D., Ghezzi, C., San Pietro, P.: The tale of SOLOIST: a specification language for service compositions interactions. In: Păsăreanu, C.S., Salaün, G. (eds.) FACS 2012. LNCS, vol. 7684, pp. 55–72. Springer, Heidelberg (2013)
10. Cugola, G., Margara, A.: Complex event processing with T-REX. J. Syst. Softw. 85(8), 1709–1728 (2012)
11. Dean, J., Ghemawat, S.: MapReduce: Simplified data processing on large clusters. Commun. ACM 51(1), 107–113 (2008)
12. Dwyer, M.B., Avrunin, G.S., Corbett, J.C.: Property specification patterns for finite-state verification. In: Proc. of FMSP 1998, pp. 7–15. ACM (1998)
13. Felder, M., Morzenti, A.: Validating real-time systems by history-checking TRIO specifications. ACM Trans. Softw. Eng. Methodol. 3(4), 308–339 (1994)
14. Lerda, F., Sisto, R.: Distributed-memory model checking with SPIN. In: Dams, D., Gerth, R., Leue, S., Massink, M. (eds.) SPIN 1999. LNCS, vol. 1680, pp. 22–39. Springer, Heidelberg (1999)
15. Mrad, A., Ahmed, S., Hallé, S., Beaudet, É.: Babeltrace: A collection of transducers for trace validation. In: Qadeer, S., Tasiran, S. (eds.) RV 2012. LNCS, vol. 7687, pp. 126–130. Springer, Heidelberg (2013)
16. Pradella, M., Morzenti, A., San Pietro, P.: Bounded satisfiability checking of metric temporal logic specifications. ACM Trans. Softw. Eng. Methodol. 22(3), 20:1–20:54 (2013)
17. Verbeek, H.M.W., Buijs, J.C.A.M., van Dongen, B.F., van der Aalst, W.M.P.: XES, XESame, and ProM 6. In: Soffer, P., Proper, E. (eds.) CAiSE Forum 2010. LNBIP, vol. 72, pp. 60–75. Springer, Heidelberg (2011)

Increasing Consistency in Multi-site Data Stores: Megastore-CGC and Its Formal Analysis[*]

Jon Grov[1] and Peter Csaba Ölveczky[1,2]

[1] University of Oslo, Norway
[2] University of Illinois at Urbana-Champaign, USA

Abstract. Data stores for cloud infrastructures provide limited consistency guarantees, which restricts the applicability of the cloud for many applications with strong consistency requirements, such as financial and medical information systems. Megastore is a replicated data store used in Google's cloud infrastructure. Data are partitioned into entity groups, and consistency is only guaranteed if each transaction only accesses data from a single entity group. This paper extends Megastore to also provide consistency for transactions accessing data from multiple entity groups, thereby increasing the applicability of such cloud data stores. Our extension, Megastore-CGC, achieves this extra consistency without introducing significant additional message exchanges. We used the formal specification language and analysis tool Real-Time Maude throughout the development of Megastore-CGC. We introduce Megastore-CGC, its Real-Time Maude specification, and show how Real-Time Maude can estimate the performance of Megastore-CGC and model check Megastore-CGC.

1 Introduction

Database facilities are important for applications, such as payroll systems, stock exchange systems, banking, online auctions, and medical systems, where inconsistencies (such as lost or corrupted medication requests or money deposits) cannot be tolerated. Databases therefore usually provide *transactions*. A transaction is a sequence of read and write operations which are executed equivalently to an atomic execution, and where the concurrent execution of a set of transactions is equivalent to some sequential execution of the transactions.

The availability and performance of the database is crucial in many of the applications mentioned above, which would therefore benefit from running on a cloud infrastructure. However, there is currently limited support for transactions in cloud-based data stores. A main reason is that data must be *replicated* across multiple sites to achieve the availability and scalability expected from cloud services. Multi-site replication introduces many challenges, in particular regarding *performance*, since ensuring consistency requires costly message exchanges, and *fault tolerance*, since sites may go down or messages may be lost.

---

[*] This work was partially supported by AFOSR Grant FA8750-11-2-0084.

D. Giannakopoulou and G. Salaün (Eds.): SEFM 2014, LNCS 8702, pp. 159–174, 2014.
© Springer International Publishing Switzerland 2014

One of the most mature cloud-based data management systems providing some transaction support is Google's Megastore [1]. Megastore is widely used both internally at Google, backing services such as GMail and Google+, and externally through Google's Platform-as-a-Service offering Google AppEngine. Megastore is a very complex system, described informally in the overview paper [1]. To facilitate research on the Megastore approach to data management in the cloud, a precise and more detailed description is needed. We therefore define in [9] a formal model of (the) Megastore (approach) using the rewriting-logic-based Real-Time Maude formal specification language [13].

Megastore works well for many less consistency-critical applications, such as email, social media, or online newspapers, but has some limitations for more consistency-critical applications: the data must be partitioned into a set of *entity groups*, and consistency is only guaranteed if each transaction only accesses data from a single entity group. This may require a difficult (or impossible) tradeoff between scalability and consistency, as illustrated in Section 3.

In this paper, we extend Megastore to provide consistency also for transactions accessing multiple entity groups. Our extension, called Megastore-CGC ("Megastore with cross-group consistency"), achieves this additional feature without reducing Megastore's performance and fault-tolerance.

Achieving fault-tolerant transaction management is very hard [18]. We therefore formally defined Megastore-CGC in Real-Time Maude, which allowed us to use Real-Time Maude simulations and LTL model checking extensively *throughout* the development of Megastore-CGC. To the best of our knowledge, this is the first time formal methods have been used *during* the design of a cloud-based transaction protocol. We experienced that anticipating all possible behaviors of Megastore-CGC is impossible. A similar observation was made by Google's Megastore team, which implemented a pseudo-random test framework, and state that *"the tests have found many surprising problems"* [1]. Compared to such a testing framework, Real-Time Maude model checking analyzes not only a set of pseudo-random behaviors, but all possible behaviors from an initial system configuration. Furthermore, we believe that Real-Time Maude provides a more effective and low-overhead approach to testing than a real testing environment.

Several studies indicate that the test-driven development method significantly improves the quality of the resulting product [12]. In this method, a suite of tests for the planned features are written before development starts. This set of tests is then used both to give the developer quick feedback during development, and as a set of regression tests when new features are added. However, test-driven development has traditionally been considered to be unfeasible when targeting fault tolerance in complex concurrent systems due to the lack of tool support for testing large number of different scenarios. Our experience from Megastore-CGC is that with Real-Time Maude, a test-driven approach is possible also in such systems, since many complex scenarios can be quickly tested by model checking.

To summarize, the contributions of this paper are the following:

1. Section 3 defines an extension of Megastore, called Megastore-CGC, that provides consistency also for transactions accessing multiple entity groups.

2. Section 4 defines a formal model of Megastore-CGC in Real-Time Maude.
3. We use Real-Time Maude Monte Carlo simulations in Section 5 to show that the performance of Megastore-CGC is on par with that of Megastore.
4. We show in Section 6 how Real-Time Maude LTL model checking can be used to analyze the correctness of Megastore-CGC, including how such model checking can analyze the important feature *serializability* property of distributed databases: any concurrent execution of a set of transactions should produce results equivalent to a serial execution of the same transactions.

2 Preliminaries

Megastore. Megastore [1] is a replicated data store developed by Google. Data are key-value pairs called *entities*. A *transaction* is a sequence of read and write operations on entities, followed by a commit request. Entities are partitioned into *entity groups*, and each entity group is replicated at different sites. A replicated transaction log is maintained for each entity group. For transactions accessing a single entity group, Megastore ensures *atomicity* and *serializability* (consistency) by only allowing one transaction to update the log at any time.

Initially, all read operations in a transaction t are executed locally at a site s, and t's updates are buffered. Each site has a *coordinator*, which is always informed about whether the local replica is up-to-date. If the local replica is not up-to-date for an entity requested by t, a majority read is performed.

Let t read and write entities from entity group eg, and let lp be the current log position in the replicated log of eg. When t requests commit, site s prepares a log entry for eg containing t's updates, and runs the following variant of the *Paxos* consensus protocol [11] to assign this entry to log position $lp + 1$:

1. Site s sends a *proposal* containing the log entry and the next leader (normally s) to the current leader site l, which was elected during the previous commit. If l accepts the entry, s sends the proposal to the other sites. If not, e.g., due to a concurrent update of the same entity group, the transaction is aborted.
2. Site s then waits for *acknowledge* responses from all sites. If some sites fail to acknowledge, s sends an *invalidate* message to these sites.
3. When each site has acknowledged either the proposal or the invalidate message, s requests all sites to apply t's updates. Each site replicating eg then appends the chosen log entry for position $lp + 1$ to the local copy of the transaction log for eg, and subsequently updates the local data store.

In the presence of failures, s may fail to achieve consensus. In this case another site may propose itself as the leader, and starts at step (1). If multiple sites propose log entries for the same log position, Paxos ensures that only one is elected, and the others are aborted.

Real-Time Maude. Real-Time Maude [13] is a formal modeling language and high-performance simulation and model checking tool for distributed real-time systems. The modeling formalism is *expressive* and *intuitive*, allowing developers with limited formal methods experience to model complex real-time systems.

An algebraic equational specification (specifying sorts, subsorts, functions and equations defining the functions) defines the data types in a "functional programming style." Labeled rewrite rules `crl` [*l*] : *t* => *t'* if *cond* define local transitions from state *t* to state *t'*, and tick rewrite rules `crl` [*l*] : {*t*} => {*t'*} in time Δ if *cond* advance time in the *entire* state *t* by Δ time units.

A declaration   class *C* | *att*$_1$: *s*$_1$, ..., *att*$_n$: *s*$_n$ declares a class *C* with attributes *att*$_1$ to *att*$_n$ of sorts *s*$_1$ to *s*$_n$. An *object* of class *C* is represented as a term < *O* : *C* | *att*$_1$: *val*$_1$, ..., *att*$_n$: *val*$_n$ > of sort `Object`, where *O*, of sort `Oid`, is the object's *identifier*, and where *val*$_1$ to *val*$_n$ are the current values of the attributes *att*$_1$ to *att*$_n$. A *message* is a term of sort `Msg`. The state is a term of sort `Configuration`, and is a *multiset* of objects and messages. Multiset union is denoted by an associative and commutative juxtaposition operator, so that rewriting is *multiset rewriting*.

Real-Time Maude specifications are executable, and the tool provides a variety of formal analysis methods. The *timed rewriting* command (`tfrew` *t* in time <= *timeLimit* .) simulates *one* of the system behaviors by rewriting the initial state *t* up to duration *timeLimit*.

Real-Time Maude's *linear temporal logic model checker* analyzes whether *each* behavior satisfies a temporal logic formula. *State propositions* are operators of sort `Prop`, and their semantics is defined by equations of the form

eq *statePattern* |= *prop* = *b*   and   ceq *statePattern* |= *prop* = *b* if *cond*

for *b* a term of sort `Bool`, which defines *prop* to hold in all states *t* where *t* |= *prop* evaluates to `true`. A temporal logic *formula* is constructed by state propositions and temporal logic operators such as `True`, `False`, ~ (negation), /\, \/, -> (implication), [] ("always"), <> ("eventually"), and U ("until"). The model checking command (`mc` *t* |=u *formula* .)   checks whether the temporal logic formula *formula* holds in all behaviors starting from the initial state *t*.

3   Megastore-CGC

3.1   Motivation

In Megastore, the strategy for partitioning entities into entity groups depends both on application access patterns and requirements for consistency. For an application requiring consistent access to two entities *A* and *B*, *A* and *B* must belong to the same entity group. Large entity groups are therefore desired to ensure consistency for many different transactions types. However, since only one concurrent update is allowed per entity group, the system's ability to serve multiple simultaneous users depends on entity groups being relatively small. The following example illustrates that it can be hard (or impossible) to partition the entities such that the required levels of consistency and concurrency are achieved.

Example 1. Consider a hospital with thousands of employees. To enable efficient allocation of personnel to tasks (both planned and emergencies), the hospital wants to use a cloud infrastructure for a shared scheduling system used to assign each employee a status throughout the day. The system should maintain entities $\langle\langle employee,\ time\ slot\rangle,\ status\rangle$, where each employee has a set of *capabilities* (heart surgery, anesthesia, etc), and where *status* is **booked, available,** or **off-duty**. The scheduling system must satisfy the following constraints:

1. An employee can be **booked** for at most 12 hours during a 24-hour period.
2. Emergency preparedness requires having a certain number of **available** employees with a given capability in each time slot. There should, for example, always be an available heart surgeon to deal with emergencies.

Transactions booking personnel therefore need to inspect multiple entities before performing updates. For Constraint 1, other records for the same employee must be inspected. For Constraint 2, records of other employees must be inspected.

The question is how to group the records into entity groups. Grouping all entities into the same entity group would make simultaneous assignments (by different operators) impossible, which is unacceptable. Grouping all entities belonging to one employee into the same entity group allows us to enforce Constraint 1 but not Constraint 2: Let H1 and H2 be the only two **available** heart surgeons at time slot τ, and let two concurrent transactions *Book-H1* and *Book-H2* attempt to book H1 and H2, respectively, at time τ. If H1 and H2 belong to different entity groups, Megastore cannot ensure consistency across H1 and H2. Then, both *Book-H1* and *Book-H2* could see the other heart surgeon as **available**, leading to the violation of Constraint 2.

3.2 Megastore-CGC

In Megastore, the data is a set E of *entities* replicated across a set S of *sites*. E is partitioned into a set $EG = \{eg_1, \ldots, eg_n\}$ of non-empty *entity groups*. A function $R : S \to \mathcal{P}(EG)$ assigns to a site the entity groups it replicates.

In Megastore-CGC, the set of entity groups is partitioned into a set OC of *ordering classes*. A number of entity groups should belong to the same ordering class if consistent transactions across these entity groups are required. Furthermore, for each ordering class, there must be at least one site replicating all entity groups in the ordering class ($\forall oc \in OC\ \exists s \in S\ oc \subseteq R(s)$). One of the sites replicating all the entity groups in an ordering class oc is the *ordering site* of oc.

A key observation is that, in Megastore, a site replicating a set of entity groups participates in all updates on these entity groups, and should therefore be able to maintain an ordering on these updates. The idea behind Megastore-CGC is that with this ordering, one site, the ordering site, can validate transactions.

Example 2. The status of heart surgeon h at time slot τ is represented by the entity h_τ, which is part of the entity group e_h representing all time slots of h.

Let t be a transaction, initiated at site s_t, that wants to book h_τ. Since there must always be at least one heart surgeon available, t also reads the status of the other heart surgeons at time τ. These entities belong to different entity groups. t completes by changing the availability status of h_τ to **booked**, if possible.

Using Megastore, Constraint 2 could be violated if some concurrent transaction t', executing at site $s_{t'}$, attempts to book the only other available heart surgeon h' at time slot τ:

1. t reads the value of h_τ and h'_τ at s_t.
2. t' reads the value of h_τ and h'_τ at $s_{t'}$.
3. t books h_τ. This update is distributed by s_t and applied at all sites replicating h_τ, including $s_{t'}$.
4. t' books h'_τ. This update is distributed by $s_{t'}$ and applied at all replicating sites, including s_t.

This execution, which books both heart surgeons and leaves no heart surgeon for emergencies, is not serializable. Megastore-CGC can ensure also Constraint 2 if we group the entity groups for all employees with a given expertise into the same ordering class: The ordering site of the ordering class HS of all heart surgeons orders t and t', and then validates t and t' by checking whether all read operations have seen the most recent updates (according to the given order). In the above scenario, either t or t' would fail this test and be aborted.

Since Megastore-CGC makes explicit and uses the implicit ordering of updates during Megastore commits, Megastore-CGC is essentially piggybacked onto Megastore's commit protocol, which has the following advantages:

- Performance on par with Megastore, as Megastore-CGC does not introduce additional coordination messages or blocking.
- For transactions requiring the consistency level provided by Megastore, fault tolerance is identical to that of Megastore.

3.3   Megastore-CGC Without Error Handling

This section explains the behavior of Megastore-CGC without its fault-tolerance features; i.e., assuming that messages are not lost and that sites never fail.

Megastore-CGC maintains the following additional information:

- A mapping $os : OC \to S$, which assigns to each ordering class oc its *ordering site* $os(oc)$ such that $oc \subseteq R(os(oc))$ for each ordering class $oc \in OC$.
- A function $ol : OC \to Orderlist$, assigning to each ordering class its *ordering list*. Each entry in the ordering list for oc contains the updates on entity groups in oc, together with the updating transaction.

We can select any Megastore site replicating all entity groups in an ordering class oc as the ordering site for oc. The ordering list $ol(oc)$ is replicated, with each site maintaining a projection of $ol(oc)$ of updates to locally replicated entity groups.

The mapping os is stored as a special entity group eg_{os} replicated at all sites. This ensures a consistent view among all participating sites, since the ordering site of an ordering class oc may change when an ordering site fails.

When a transaction t accessing entity group(s) in ordering class oc commits, an entry for t is appended to the list $ol(oc)$ by $os(oc)$. This represents the *ordering* of t in oc, and t can then be validated: its execution is valid if and only if all read operations have seen the most recent update according to $ol(oc)$.

Let t be a transaction with ordering class oc. Megastore-CGC then extends Megastore's commit protocol (see Section 2) as follows:

- In Step 1, t is ordered once the ordering site $os(oc)$ receives t's updates. After ordering, $os(oc)$ *validates* t, using the read set of t as input (the read set is included with the log entry proposal for t, and contains the id of all entities read by t, together with the log position of the version read by t).
- If validation at $os(oc)$ is successful, the updated order is included in the apply-request of Step 3.
- If validation is not successful, the apply-step is replaced by a rollback-step, requesting all participating sites to abort t.

A more detailed description of these steps is given in Appendix A.

3.4 Failure Handling in Megastore-CGC

The transaction ordering must be consistent even when the ordering site fails and/or messages containing ordering information are lost. Our key ideas are:

- Transactions *not* requiring the additional consistency features provided by Megastore-CGC are treated as in Megastore: they are committed regardless of whether Megastore-CGC's validation features are available.
- A new ordering site is chosen if the current ordering site may be unavailable.

The commit protocol of a transaction t may be completed without t being ordered (and validated) by the ordering site. This can happen for several reasons:

1. The ordering site is down (or recovering from failure).
2. The ordering site did not receive the message containing t's updates.
3. The acknowledgment from the ordering site was lost.
4. The site executing t crashed after sending t's updates, and some other site completed the commit protocol for t (this is a feature provided by Paxos).

In this scenario, the apply message for t in Step 3 is sent without the ordering information. The next step depends on the validation requirements of t:

- If t only reads entities from one entity group, recipients of the message register t as *awaiting order* before applying t's updates.
- If t accesses multiple entity groups, t cannot be safely committed, and its updates will be replaced by an empty list of operations.

If the ordering site fails, Megastore-CGC provides a method to reinstate ordering if there is another site replicating all entity groups of the ordering class. The steps of this *ordering site failover* are:

- Let t be a transaction with ordering class oc. If the ordering site $os(oc)$ fails to order t during t's commit, s_t (the original site executing t) initiates an ordering site failover for ordering class oc.
- s_t selects the new ordering site s' from the sites replicating all entity groups in oc. If no such site (except $os(oc)$) exists, the failover procedure is canceled.
- If a new ordering site is available, s_t prepares an update to the special entity group eg_{os}, which contains the current ordering site for each ordering class.
- Once this update is accepted by a majority of sites, the new ordering site s' is elected. The mapping os is updated to $os[oc \mapsto s']$.
- Once elected, s' orders all transactions registered as *awaiting order*. This ordering is included in the *apply* message for the next transaction t'.

4   Formalizing Megastore-CGC

This section presents our formal Real-Time Maude model of Megastore-CGC, which extends and modifies our model of Megastore in [9]. The entire executable formal specification is available at http://folk.uio.no/jongr/mcgc/.

We model Megastore-CGC in an object-oriented way, where the state consists of a multiset of site objects and messages traveling between them. Each site is modeled as an object instance of the following class:

```
class Site | entityGroups : Configuration,        localTransactions : Configuration,
             coordinator : EntGroupLogPosPairSet, egOrderings : OrderClassUpdates,
             awaitingOrder : EntGroupUpdateList .
```

The attribute `entityGroups` contains one `EntityGroup` object for each entity group replicated at the site; `localTransactions` contains one `Transaction` object for each active transaction originating at the site; `coordinator` denotes the local coordinator state for each entity group; `egOrderings` contains a list of entries (t, eg, lp) for each ordering class oc, representing $ol(oc)$, where lp is the *log position* of t's update in the transaction log for entity group eg; and `awaitingOrder` is a set of entries (oc, t, eg, lp), used during failures for transactions requiring ordering later.

Each site's copy of an entity group is modeled as an object of the class

```
class EntityGroup | entitiesState : EntitySet,        transactionLog : LogEntryList,
                    replicas : EntityGroupReplicaSet, proposals : PaxosProposalSet,
                    pendingWrites : PendingWriteList .
```

`entitiesState` stores the local version of each entity. `transactionLog` denotes the local copy of the replicated transaction log. A log entry $(t\ lp\ s\ ol)$ contains the identity t of the originating transaction, the log position lp, the leader site s for the *next* log entry, and the list ol of write operations executed by t. `replicas` denotes the set of sites replicating this entity group; `proposals` denotes the local state in ongoing Paxos processes involving this entity group; and `pendingWrites` maintains a list of write operations waiting to be applied to the `entitiesState`.

A transaction request is a list of current read operations $cr(e)$ and write operations $w(e,v)$. Executing transactions are modeled as objects of the class

```
class Transaction | operations : OperationList,      status : TransStatus,
                    reads : EntitySet,               readState : ReadStateSet,
                    writes : OperationList,          paxosState : PaxosStateSet .
```

The attribute **operations** contains the remaining operations in the transaction; **reads** stores the values fetched during read operations; write operations are buffered in **writes**; **status** holds the current transaction status; and **readState** and **paxosState** store transient data during execution.

We assume that the sites are connected by a wide-area network, and we therefore do not assume FIFO delivery between the same pair of nodes.

The dynamic behavior of Megastore-CGC is defined by 72 rewrite rules.

5 Performance Estimation

This section shows how randomized Real-Time Maude simulations can estimate the following performance parameters of Megastore-CGC:

- Average time, per committed transaction, between the request arrives and the response is sent.
- Number of commits, conflict aborts, and validation aborts at each site.

We compare the performance of (our models of) Megastore-CGC and Megastore. With the right system parameters, Real-Time Maude simulations should provide realistic performance estimates. For example, it is shown in [14] that Real-Time Maude simulations of wireless sensor networks give as good performance estimates as dedicated simulation tools. Our system parameters are:

- Frequency and distribution of transaction requests.
- Number of sites.
- Number and size of entity groups and ordering classes.
- Network delay distribution between each pair of sites.
- Network and site failure rates.
- Initial values of the seeds for the random function.

We can easily change these parameters by modifying the initial state in Fig. 1. We use a scenario with three sites, four entities, two entity groups, one ordering class (containing both entity groups), and a set of transaction types reading and writing these entity groups. A local read operation requires 10 ms to complete, according to real-world measurements in [1]. After commit, we assume a delay of 100 ms for each write operation before the new value is available. Two sites, Site 1 and Site 2, are located in the same area, with the third site (RSite) at a more remote location. The probability distribution of the network delays is:

	30%	30%	30%	10%
Site 1 ↔ Site 2	10	15	20	50
Site 1 ↔ RSite	30	35	40	100
Site 2 ↔ RSite	30	35	40	100

Transaction requests are generated randomly at each site according to the following frequency distribution (where "Book $H1_A$" is a transaction that also reads the entity $H2_A$ ("heart surgeon H2 in the afternoon") before possibly booking (heart surgeon) H1 in the afternoon):

```
eq initState(N) =
{< RSite : Site |
    awaitingOrder : noAwaitingOrderSet, coordinator : ..., egOrderings : ...,
    entityGroups :
      (< H1 : EntityGroup | pendingWrites : emptyPWList, proposals : emptyProposalSet,
                            replicas : ..., entitiesState : ..., transactionLog : ... >
        < H2 : EntityGroup | ... >
        < OrderSites : EntityGroup | ... >), --- special entity group representing the map OS
      localTransactions : none, seqGen : 0 >
  < Site1 : Site | ... >
  < Site2 : Site | ... >
  < NWRK : NetworkDelays |
    connections : (conn(Site1 <-> RSite,< 1 ; 30 ; 30 > ... < 91 ; 100 ; 100 >, true) ;
                  conn(RSite <-> Site2, ... , true) ; conn(Site1 <-> Site2, ... , true)) >
  < rnd : Random | seed : N >
  < stats(Site1): SiteStatistics | avgLatency : 0, commits : 0,
                                  conflictAborts : 0, validationAborts : 0, ... >
  < stats(RSite): SiteStatistics | ... >        < stats(Site2): SiteStatistics | ... >
  < transGen(RSite): PoissonTransGen | idCounter : 1, status : waiting(10),
    workload : < 1 ; 25 ; update-H1-M > ... < 76 ; 100 ; book-H1-A > >
  < transGen(Site1): PoissonTransGen | ... >    < transGen(Site2): PoissonTransGen | ... > >}
```

Fig. 1. An initial state in our simulations (with parts of the term replaced by '...').

Site 1	Site 2	Remote site
Update $H1_M$ 50%	Update $H1_M$ 25%	Update $H1_M$ 25%
Update $H1_A$ 50%	Update $H1_A$ 25%	Update $H1_A$ 25%
	Update $H1_M$ 25%	Update $H2_A$ 25%
	Book $H2_A$ 25%	Book $H1_A$ 25%

We add "record" objects that record events during the simulation, using techniques in [14]. The initial state `initState`, shown in Figure 1, is then a multiset containing: one `Site` object for each site; one `NetworkDelays` object containing the network delay distributions; one `Random` object with the seed used to randomly select a network delay when a message is sent; one `SiteStatistics` object for each site recording statistics during simulation; and a `PoissonTransGen` object for each site, which generates transactions randomly according to the given distribution.

We simulate the system up to 1,000,000 ms using the command

```
(tfrew initState(10) in time <= 1000000 .)
```

which returns the term (with parts of the term are replaced by '...')

```
{< stats(RSite): SiteStatistics | avgLatency :  94579/631, commitCount : 631,
                                 conflictAborts : 171, validationAborts : 10, ... > ... }
```

in 145,957ms cpu time on a Pentium Intel Core i7 2,6 GHz.

We have also run these experiments on our model of Megastore, and show the result when the average (overall) transaction rate is 2.5 TPS (transactions per second). The following table shows the number of transactions successfully committed (Comm.), and aborted due to conflict (Abs.), and the average transaction latency (Avg.lat). For Megastore-CGC, we also show the number of transactions aborted due to validation failures (Val.abs), since the transactions `book-H1-A` and `book-H2-A` access multiple entity groups and could see an inconsistent read set.

	Megastore			Megastore-CGC			
	Comm.	Abs.	Avg.lat	Comm.	Abs.	Val.abs.	Avg.lat
Site 1	652	152	126	660	144	0	123
Site 2	704	100	118	674	115	15	118
RSite	640	172	151	631	171	10	150

We have also compared the performance on "Megastore-friendly" transactions where each transaction only accesses a single entity group. The performance of Megastore and Megastore-CGC is virtually the same in this experiment:

	Megastore			Megastore-CGC			
	Comm.	Abs.	Avg.lat	Comm.	Abs.	Val.abs.	Avg.lat
Site 1	684	120	122	679	125	0	120
RSite	674	138	132	677	135	0	130
Site 2	693	111	110	691	113	0	113

We also used simulations *during* the development of Megastore-CGC to esti-mate the performance of different design choices. For example, our experiments showed that aggressive failure detection may increase the number of validation aborts, since ordering may be quicker re-established in case of small transient errors (such as message losses) than if a failover is required.

6   Model Checking Verification

We use *model checking* to explore *all possible* behaviors of Megastore-CGC that can happen nondeterministically from a given initial system configuration. In addition to verifying desired properties, model checking is invaluable *during* the design process, and helped us discover many subtle bugs in (earlier versions of) Megastore-CGC that were not uncovered during extensive simulation.

We analyze the original nondeterministic model (not the randomized one used for performance estimation). For the model checking analysis to terminate, we analyze scenarios with a limited number of transactions, and restrict the message delays, transaction start times, site and communication failures, etc.

With a finite number of transactions, the system should satisfy the property that in all states from some point on:

1. All transactions have finished their execution.
2. All replicas of an entity have the same value or the coordinator of diverging site(s) is invalidated.
3. All logs for an entity group contain the same entries, unless a coordinator is invalidated.
4. The execution was serializable; i.e., it gives the same result as some execution in which the transactions are executed one after the other.

This property can be formalized as the following temporal logic formula Φ:

```
<> [] (allTransFinished /\ entityGroupsEqualOrInvalid
       /\ transLogsEqualOrInvalid /\ isSerializable)
```

allTransFinished is a state proposition that is true in a state if all transactions have finished; entityGroupsEqualOrInvalid is a state proposition that is true in all states where all replicas of each entity have the same value, unless the coordinator has been invalidated; and transLogsEqualOrInvalid is true when all transitions logs for each entity group are equal (unless a coordinator has been invalidated). The last of these propositions is defined as follows:

```
op transLogsEqualOrInvalid : -> Prop [ctor] .
ceq {REST
     < S1 : Site | coordinator : eglp(EG1, LP) ; EGLP,
                entityGroups : < EG1 : EntityGroup | transactionLog : LOG1 > ... >
     < S2 : Site | coordinator : eglp(EG1, LP) ; EGLP,
                entityGroups : < EG1 : EntityGroup | transactionLog : LOG2 > ... >}
    |= transLogsEqual = false if LOG1 =/= LOG2 .
eq {SYSTEM} |= transLogsEqualOrInvalid = true [owise] .
```

We first characterize the states where transLogsEqualOrInvalid does *not* hold, namely, the states with two sites with valid coordinators and where some entity group EG1 has different values. The last equation, with the owise ("otherwise") attribute, defines transLogsEqualOrInvalid to be true in all other states.

To analyze serializability, we use the technique in [9]. The *serialization graph* for an execution of a set of committed transactions is a directed graph where each transaction is represented by a node, and where there is an edge from a node t_1 to another node t_2 iff the transaction t_1 has executed an operation on entity e occurs *before* transaction t_2 executed an operation on the same entity, and at least one of the operations was a write operation. An execution of multiple transactions is serializable if and only if its serialization graph is acyclic [20].

In a multi-versioned replicated data store like Megastore-CGC, we need a *version order* $<<$ on the written entity values to decide the *before* relation when constructing the serialization graph. For example: a write operation $w(e, v)$ which creates a version k of entity e occurs *before* a current read $cr(e)$ iff $cr(e)$ reads a version l where $k << l$ according to the selected version order. Since every committed transaction is assigned a unique log position for each entity group it updates, we use log positions for the version order. This means that if, for example, t_i reads from log position lp and t_k commits an update at log position lp', then $t_i \rightarrow t_k$ in the serialization graph iff $lp < lp'$.

When an update transaction t_i commits, it produces a message containing:

- the log position and value of each entity it has read; and
- the set of entities written, all of them have the log position assigned to t_i.

We add a TransactionHistory object containing the current serialization graph. When a transaction commits, this object reads the above message and updates its serialization graph. The proposition isSerializable is then defined

```
op isSerializable : -> Prop [ctor] .
eq {< th : TransactionHistory | graph : GRAPH > REST}
        |= isSerializable = not hasCycle(GRAPH) .
```

We have model checked the temporal logic formula Φ with a number of different system parameters. For example, we have executed the command without site and communication failures, where the message delay is either 30 or 80, with 5 transactions, in the following setup:

Site	Transaction	Operations	Start time
Site 1	update-H1-A	read H1-A; write(H1-A, $Avail_1$)	150
RSite	update-II2-A	read II2-A; write(II2-A, $Avail_2$)	150
Site 2	update-H2-A	read H2-A; write(H2-A, $Avail_3$)	150
RSite	book-H2-A	read H1-A; read H2-A; write(H2-A, $Booked_1$)	$\{180, 210\}$
Site 2	book-H1-A	read H2-A; read H1-A; write(H1-A, $Booked_2$)	$\{180, 210\}$

We then use the following command to check whether each behavior satisfies the desired properties in Megastore-CGC:

```
(mc init1 |=u Φ .)
```

which returned `true` in 124 seconds cpu time. The number of different states reachable from the initial state is 108,279.

Performing the exact same model checking in Megastore returns the following counterexample, in which there is both an edge from `book-H1-A` to `book-H2-A` and from `book-H2-A` to `book-H1-A` in the serialization graph:

```
Result ModelCheckResult :   counterexample({initTransactions
...
< th : TransactionHistory | graph : < book-H2-A ; book-H1-A > ; < book-H1-A ; book-H2-A > ; ...>})
```

Real-Time Maude outputs a behavior invalidating Φ when model checking fails; this allowed us to easily identify the (often subtle) issues causing problems.

We have also successfully model checked Megastore-CGC in a number of other scenarios, including:

- Three transactions, two possible start times, one site failure and fixed message delay (1,874,946 reachable states, model checked in 6,311 seconds).
- Three transactions, two possible start times, fixed message delay and one message failure (265,410 reachable states, model checked in 858 seconds).

7   Related Work

Data stores such as Amazon's Dynamo [7], Google's BigTable [3], and Cassandra [10] are widely used due to their combination of high availability and scalability. However, given their lack of transaction features, several data stores with (limited) transaction support have emerged to address the need for strong consistency in many real-world applications. In addition to Megastore, ElasTraS [6], Spinnaker [16], Calvin [19], and Microsoft's Azure [2] achieve high availability and scalability by partitioning the data, and provide consistency *within* each partition. Both Megastore, Spinnaker, and Calvin use Paxos to distribute updates among sites. We are not aware of any generic method for transactional consistency *across* partitions besides Megastore-CGC. Google's Spanner [5] provides both high availability, scalability, and transactional consistency across partitions, but is less generic since it demands a complex infrastructure involving GPS hardware and atomic clocks.

We have not seen any other work on formalizing and verifying transactional data stores using formal verification tools. In [15] the authors assert the need for formal analysis of replication and concurrency control in transactional cloud data stores, and they analyze a prose-and-pseudo-code description of a Paxos-based concurrency control protocol. In contrast to our work, this description is not amenable to model checking and simulation.

A prerequisite for extending Megastore is to have detailed knowledge of it, which is a challenging task, since Megastore is an internal system at Google that is publicly described only in an informal way in [1]. In [9] we therefore develop a fairly detailed Real-Time Maude model of Megastore. The value of using Maude [4] (the "untimed" version of Real-Time Maude) for formally analyzing other cloud systems is demonstrated in [17], where the authors point out possible bottlenecks in a naïve implementation of ZooKeeper for key distribution, and in [8], where the authors analyze denial-of-service prevention mechanisms.

8 Concluding Remarks

We have used Real-Time Maude to develop an extension of Megastore, denoted Megastore-CGC, which provides consistency also for transactions that access multiple entity groups.

The main idea behind Megastore-CGC is that in Megastore, sites replicating multiple entity groups implicitly observe an ordering of updates *across* this set of partitions. We make this ordering explicit by defining *ordering sites*. An important advantage of Megastore-CGC is that ordering and validation is piggybacked onto the existing message interactions of Megastore's commit protocol, allowing Megastore-CGC to provide these features without introducing new messages or waiting. This is also reflected in our Monte Carlo simulations, which indicate that the performance of Megastore-CGC is virtually the same as that of Megastore.

The Megastore-CGC approach might be applicable to other Paxos-based transactional data stores such as Spinnaker [16] and Calvin [19]. However, one key assumption in Megastore is that each site has a *coordinator* which knows whether the local site has received all updates. Without this feature, changing the ordering site (in case of failure) becomes significantly more complex.

Designing and validating a sophisticated protocol like Megastore-CGC is very challenging. Real-Time Maude's intuitive and expressive formalism allowed a domain expert (the first author) to define both a precise, formal description and an executable prototype in a single artifact. Simulating and model checking this prototype automatically provided quick feedback about both the performance and the correctness of different design choices, even for very complex scenarios. Model checking was especially helpful, both to verify properties and to find subtle "corner case" design errors that were not found during extensive simulations.

References

1. Baker, J., et al.: Megastore: Providing scalable, highly available storage for interactive services. In: CIDR (2011), http://www.cidrdb.org

2. Campbell, D.G., Kakivaya, G., Ellis, N.: Extreme scale with full SQL language support in Microsoft SQL Azure. In: SIGMOD 2010, pp. 1021–1024. ACM (2010)
3. Chang, F., et al.: Bigtable: A distributed storage system for structured data. ACM Trans. Comput. Syst. 26(2), 4:1–4:26 (2008)
4. Clavel, M., Durán, F., Eker, S., Lincoln, P., Martí-Oliet, N., Meseguer, J., Talcott, C.: All About Maude - A High-Performance Logical Framework. LNCS, vol. 4350. Springer, Heidelberg (2007)
5. Corbett, J.C., et al.: Spanner: Google's globally-distributed database. In: OSDI 2012. USENIX (2012)
6. Das, S., Agrawal, D., Abbadi, A.E.: ElasTraS: An elastic transactional data store in the cloud. In: USENIX HotCloud. USENIX (2009)
7. DeCandia, G., et al.: Dynamo: Amazon's highly available key-value store. SIGOPS Oper. Syst. Rev. 41, 205–220 (2007)
8. Eckhardt, J., Mühlbauer, T., AlTurki, M., Meseguer, J., Wirsing, M.: Stable availability under denial of service attacks through formal patterns. In: de Lara, J., Zisman, A. (eds.) FASE 2012. LNCS, vol. 7212, pp. 78–93. Springer, Heidelberg (2012)
9. Grov, J., Ölveczky, P.C.: Formal modeling and analysis of Google's Megastore in Real-Time Maude. In: Iida, S., Meseguer, J., Ogata, K. (eds.) Futatsugi Festschrift. LNCS, vol. 8373, pp. 494–519. Springer, Heidelberg (2014)
10. Lakshman, A., Malik, P.: Cassandra: a decentralized structured storage system. SIGOPS Oper. Syst. Rev. 44, 35–40 (2010)
11. Lamport, L.: Paxos made simple. ACM Sigact News 32(4), 18–25 (2001)
12. Munir, H., Moayyed, M., Petersen, K.: Considering rigor and relevance when evaluating test driven development: A systematic review. Inform. Softw. Techn. (2014)
13. Ölveczky, P.C., Meseguer, J.: Semantics and pragmatics of Real-Time Maude. Higher-Order and Symbolic Computation 20(1-2), 161–196 (2007)
14. Ölveczky, P.C., Thorvaldsen, S.: Formal modeling, performance estimation, and model checking of wireless sensor network algorithms in Real-Time Maude. Theoretical Computer Science 410(2-3), 254–280 (2009)
15. Patterson, S., et al.: Serializability, not serial: concurrency control and availability in multi-datacenter datastores. Proc. VLDB 5(11), 1459–1470 (2012)
16. Rao, J., Shekita, E.J., Tata, S.: Using Paxos to build a scalable, consistent, and highly available datastore. Proc. VLDB 4(4), 243–254 (2011)
17. Skeirik, S., Bobba, R.B., Meseguer, J.: Formal analysis of fault-tolerant group key management using ZooKeeper. In: Proc. CCGRID. IEEE (2013)
18. Stonebraker, M., Cattell, R.: 10 rules for scalable performance in 'simple operation' datastores. Commun. ACM 54(6), 72–80 (2011)
19. Thomson, A., et al.: Calvin: Fast distributed transactions for partitioned database systems. In: Proc. SIGMOD 2012. ACM (2012), http://doi.acm.org/10.1145/2213836.2213838
20. Weikum, G., Vossen, G.: Concurrency Control and Recovery in Database Systems. Morgan Kaufman (2001)

A   Transaction Commit in Megastore-CGC

Let t be a transaction executing at site s_t, reading a set of entity groups EG and updating an entity group $eg \in EG$. All entity groups in EG belong to ordering class oc. The table below summarizes the steps of committing t in Megastore-CGC, and distinguishes the features of Megastore from the features of our CGC extension. In the table, R_{eg} denotes all sites replicating eg.

Step	Site(s)	Megastore	CGC extension
1a	s_t	Send an *acceptLeader* request to the leader s_l for the current log position.	If $s_l = os(oc)$, include t's read set and request ordering and validation from s_l.
1b	s_l	Receive *acceptLeader* request. If there are no conflicting updates within eg, send accept to s_t. Otherwise, request s_t to abort t.	If $s_l = os(oc)$ and there are no conflicting updates in eg, order and validate t by appending t's updates to $ol(oc)$ and then verifying that t has seen the most recent update for each member of EG. If validation is successful, $ol(oc)$ is included in the accept message. If validation is unsuccessful, request s_t to abort t.
1c	s_t	Receive response from s_l. If s_l requests abort, t is aborted. Otherwise, multicast an *accept* request for t to all sites replicating entity group eg, except s_t and s_l.	If $s_l \neq os(oc)$ and $s_t = os(oc)$, order and validate t. If validation is successful, s_t requests accept from the other sites. Otherwise, t is aborted. If $s_l \neq os(oc)$ and $s_t \neq os(oc)$: include t's read set in the *accept* request for $os(oc)$.
2	$R_{eg} \setminus \{os(oc),$ $s_t, s_l\}$	Receive and store the *accept* request, send acknowledgment to s_t.	
2'	$os(oc)$ if $os(oc) \neq s_t$ $\wedge\, os(oc) \neq s_l$	Receive and store the *accept* request, send acknowledgment to s_t.	Order and validate t. If validation is successful, include $ol(oc)$ in the acknowledgment message. If validation is unsuccessful, the acknowledgment is sent without including the ordering.
3	s_t	Multicast *apply* message containing t's updates.	If t was successfully ordered and validated, include $ol(oc)$ in this message. Otherwise, replace t's updates with an empty list of operations (effectively aborting t).
3'	R_{eg}	Apply t's updates to local transaction log and replicated entity store.	If the apply message contains $ol(oc)$, update the local copy of $ol(oc)$.

Some further comments on the CGC extension:

- t is ordered when the ordering site $os(oc)$ *accepts* t. If $os(oc)$ is the leader for this log position, this occurs at Step 1b. Otherwise, it occurs at Step 2'.
- After ordering, $os(oc)$ validates t, using the read set of t as input. The read set is included in the accept-request for $os(oc)$, and contains the id of all entities read by t together with the version seen (represented by the log position). The validation procedure ensures that for any pair of transactions in a read-write conflict (i.e., one is reading and the other is writing the same entity), one of the transactions is aborted unless the conflicting operations occur according to the order $ol(oc)$. Assuming transactions access entity groups within one ordering class only, this is sufficient to verify that the serialization graph [20] for any schedule is acyclic.[1]
- If validation at $os(oc)$ is successful, site s_t distributes the updated order to all sites replicating eg as part of the apply message for t. If validation is not successful, the apply-step is replaced by an empty operation list, effectively aborting t (Step 3).

---

[1] Megastore is a multi-version data store where write-write conflicts do not occur.

Evaluating the Effect of Faults
in SystemC TLM Models Using UPPAAL

Reza Hajisheykhi[1], Ali Ebnenasir[2], and Sandeep S. Kulkarni[1]

[1] Michigan State University, USA
{hajishey,sandeep}@cse.msu.edu
[2] Michigan Technological University, USA
aebnenas@mtu.edu

Abstract. Since System on Chip (SoC) systems, where integrates all components of a computer or other electronic system into a single chip, are typically used for critical scenarios, it is desirable to analyze the impact of faults on them. However, fault-impact analysis is difficult at the RTL level due to the high integrity of SoC systems and different levels of abstraction provided by modern system design languages such as SystemC. Thus, modeling faults and impact analysis at different levels of abstraction is an important task and introduces dependability-related issues from the early phases of design. In this paper, we present a method for modeling and analyzing faults in SystemC TLM programs. The proposed method includes three steps, namely timed model extraction, fault modeling and fault analysis. We use UPPAAL timed automata to formally model the SystemC TLM programs and monitor how the models behave in the presence of faults. We analyze three case studies, two with Loosely-Timed coding style, and the other with Approximately-Timed coding style.

Keywords: SystemC, Transaction Level Modeling, Fault Modeling, Fault Analysis.

1 Introduction

The continuous increase of transistor density on a single die is leading toward the production of more and more complex System on Chip (SoC) systems, with an increasing number of components. As a result, the design process for such systems has also become more complex. This has given an increasing importance to examining the behavior of SoC systems under fault and error conditions. Moreover, developing such complex systems within today's time-to-market constraints requires reasoning at an abstract level for architectural exploration and early software development. This procedure has become systematic resulting in the so-called Electronic System Level (ESL) design. For ESL design, *SystemC* [1] has become the de facto standard. It is a widely accepted language based on a C++ library that provides hardware modeling concepts (e.g., time, concurrency, events, logic value types, etc.) for the description and simulation of

D. Giannakopoulou and G. Salaün (Eds.): SEFM 2014, LNCS 8702, pp. 175–189, 2014.
© Springer International Publishing Switzerland 2014

systems at different levels of abstraction. In addition, the concept of *Transaction Level Modeling* (TLM) [2], which enables transaction-based interactions between the components of a system, improves the success of SystemC. TLM 2.0 includes two types of interfaces, *blocking* and *non-blocking*, to support different levels of timing detail. The objective of this paper is to provide an approach for analyzing the effects of different types of faults on SystemC TLM models and evaluate how the models behave in the presence of faults.

Previous work on testing/verifying SystemC focuses mainly on a) generating test cases [3,4], and b) verifying the formalized semantics of SystemC [5,6]. In the second category, which our work lies in, the designers can use techniques for software model checking of finite models created from SystemC models. Properties of interest are then checked by an exhaustive search in the finite model. To generate the finite model, some researchers have developed manual program transformations from SystemC or SystemC TLM models into equivalent state machines [7,8]. However, none of the previous work studies the behavior of the extracted finite model in the presence of faults. In [9], we propose an approach for designing fault tolerant concerns in SystemC TLM models. In our approach, we analyze the impact of specific kinds of transient faults and design a fault-tolerant SystemC TLM program with respect to those faults. However, we consider only untimed SystemC models and the blocking transport. The blocking transport interface is only able to model the start and end of a transaction, whereas the non-blocking interface allows a transaction to be broken down into multiple timing points. In [10,11,12] the authors propose fault/mutation models for SystemC TLM models. They mainly target fault localization in their methods and do not analyze the impact of faults on the SystemC TLM models. By comparison, in this paper, we propose an approach for modeling different types of faults in the extracted time-constrained finite models and analyze the impact of faults on them.

Our objective is to provide a methodology for modeling different types of faults in SystemC TLM models. To this end, the proposed approach applies model extraction, fault modeling, and model checking to analyze the effects of faults on SystemC TLM models. The proposed framework has three parts: (1) *model extraction*, (2) *fault modeling*, and (3) *impact analysis*.

– For the first part, we leverage the approaches from [13,9] to extract UPPAAL timed automata (TA) [14] from the SystemC TLM model. To obtain the desired model, we utilize two approaches: a) for blocking transport, we use the approach from [15] that generalizes the approach in [9] by incorporating timing constraints in them; b) for non-blocking transports, we refine the approach in [13] by only considering the parts of the model that are relevant for addition of fault tolerance. The motivation for choosing UPPAAL TA as the target formal language is multi-fold: UPPAAL (1) supports interactions between parallel processes including timing behaviors and dynamic sensitivity; (2) permits modeling of the program as a network of communicating processes (Similar to SystemC). Hence, it can preserve the architecture of

the SystemC TLM programs by supporting transactions in the extracted TA, and (3) enables modeling and verification of timing behaviors.
- For the second part, based on the work in [10], we incorporate different kinds of faults including message faults, permanent faults, and transient faults into the extracted TA to create a model in the presence of faults. Towards this end, we identify several rules that describe how the given faults can be modeled in the UPPAAL model.
- Finally, in the third part, we use the UPPAAL toolset to simulate and verify the TA that capture the effect of faults.

To validate our proposed method, we have conducted two case studies. The first case study utilizes blocking transport interface for communication, whereas the second case study uses non-blocking transport interface. We analyze the impact of faults on these case studies. Specifically, we consider three types of faults, namely message loss, permanent faults, and transient faults. We evaluate the time for identifying counterexamples and/or verification for these case studies and argue that the time is comparable with verification in the absence of faults.

Contributions of the Paper. We present

- an approach that supports the analysis of three types of faults, namely message loss, permanent, and transient faults in UPPAAL timed automata models extracted from SystemC TLM models;
- a fault impact analysis method that is applicable for both blocking and non-blocking transports;
- two case studies where we analyze the impact of faults on memory-mapped busses, and
- experimental evidence that the increased cost of verification due to faults is small.

Organization of the Paper. The rest of the paper is organized as follows: In Section 2, we give a brief background of SystemC TLM models. In Section 3, we identify our fault modeling approach and different types of faults considered in this paper. The modeling of these faults is formalized in the case studies in Sections 4 and 5. Finally, the concluding remarks are presented in Section 6.

2 Background: SystemC, Transaction Level Modeling, and UPPAAL Timed Automata

This section provides a brief background on SystemC and Transaction Level Modeling (Section 2.1), UPPAAL timed automata (Section 2.2), and UPPAAL model extraction (Section 2.3). The concepts presented in this section are adapted mainly from [1,2,14,13].

2.1 SystemC and Transaction Level Modeling

SystemC is an open-source C++ class library that provides executable models of hardware-software systems at different levels of abstraction. Transaction Level

Modeling (TLM) is an abstraction level above the SystemC standard to accelerate simulation by utilizing function calls instead of using individual events and
pins. In TLM, a *transaction* is an abstraction for an interaction between two
or more concurrent processes for either data transfer or synchronization. In a
TLM model, an *initiator* is a module that initiates new transactions to exchange
data or synchronize with the other module, called the *target*. Both the initiator
and target try to maintain interoperability, i.e., the ability to take TLM models from different sources and make them work together, while interacting. In
TLM 2.0, the interoperability is introduced as a layer and has a set of main
components as follows: i) *Core interface* which implements blocking transport
interface b_transport() and non-blocking transport interface nb_transport(); ii)
Generic payload which represents transaction objects; iii) *Sockets* that connect
initiator and target modules, and iv) *Base protocol* that is a set of rules for using
TLM interfaces while sending/receiving the generic payload through sockets.

2.2   UPPAAL Timed Automata

Timed Automata (TA) are state machines that enable the modeling of real-time
systems [16]. The notion of time is captured by real-valued *clock* variables. The
clock values are used to express the timing constraints and can be assigned to
locations (vertices) and *transitions* (edges) of the TA. The semantics of TA is
given by an infinite-state transition system where transitions correspond either to
a change of location (discrete transition) or to passage of time (time transition).
UPPAAL [14] is an integrated tool environment for modeling, simulation, and
verification of real-time systems modeled as networks of TA, extended with data
types. A system in UPPAAL consists of concurrent processes, each of them
modeled as a TA. Each process TA has a set of locations and transitions. To
control transitions between locations, UPPAAL uses a) *guards* that limit when
process actions can be executed, and b) *synchronization channels* that require
multiple processes to coordinate.

2.3   Model Extraction

In order to extract a formal model from a SystemC TLM model, we utilize the
rules and approaches in [9,15,13]. In [9], we propose a set of transformation rules
that extract an untimed formal model from the given SystemC TLM program.
In [15], we extend the transformation rules such that the new set also considers
the timing constraints of the given SystemC TLM program while extracting the
formal model. These rules are proposed for Loosely-Timed (LT) coding style
and blocking transport. We utilize our rules from [9,15] along with the ideas
from [13] to extract the UPPAAL models of SystemC TLM programs in the
approximately-timed coding style and non-blocking transport. The ideas from
[13] are used for transforming the SystemC scheduler and the payload event
queue (PEQ). We model the PEQ with four different TA, namely timed-ordered
list, interface, event fetch and callback invocation, and PEQ event automata.

3 Fault Modeling

In this section, first, we give a brief description of the three types of faults considered in this paper in Section 3.1. Then we discuss about general description of these faults in Section 3.2. Finally, in Section 3.3, we explain a methodology for modeling the faults in UPPAAL TA models.

3.1 Fault Categories

In our work, we distinguish between faults and bugs with the following intuition. A fault is something that we expect to happen in a program and we expect the program to provide desired behavior even if it occurs. Examples of such faults include message loss (caused due to noise), malicious components, transients, etc. By contrast, a bug is something that we expect to avoid. Examples include uninitialized variables, buffer overflow, incorrect use of blocking or nonblocking interfaces, incorrect use of timed/untimed constructs. With this distinction, intuitively, we want to ensure that the program works correctly even if faults occur. Our work focuses on the former, i.e., it assumes that the designer has decided that it is difficult/impossible to prevent the faults from occurring and, hence, it must be tolerated. We utilize this discussion in formal modeling of faults in the case studies in Sections 4 and 5. The faults considered are as follows.

- *Message faults.* Since in SystemC TLM programs transactions are performed via message passing, one of the common faults is a message fault. These faults include message corruption, loss and duplication. Modeling of message duplication is similar, and modeling of message corruption is possible using the approach for transient faults.
- *Permanent faults.* By permanent faults, we mean that the impact of the fault is long-lasting (possibly forever). In this paper, we consider *fail-stop*, *Byzantine*, and *stuck-at* faults caused in hardware. In a fail-stop fault, a component fails functionally and the other components cannot communicate with it. The Byzantine fault is one where the faulty component continues to run but produces incorrect results. The stuck-at faults cause a signal to get stuck at a fixed value (logical 0, 1, or X) and cannot switch its value.
- *Transient faults.* Transient faults are the most common types of faults that are prevalent in SoC systems [17,18]. They perturb the state of system components without causing any permanent damage. It is anticipated that most of these faults occur only once (or a small number of times). In this paper, we consider *Single Event Upsets* (SEUs). Such events may induce soft errors in storage elements (e.g., SRAM, sequential logic) due to alpha particles generated by the radioactive decay of packaging and interconnect materials.

3.2 Generic Description of Faults

The generic descriptions of the three aforementioned types of faults are discussed next.

Message Loss.   We present two methods for modeling message loss faults in the UPPAAL TA model:

- The first approach injects a new transition T into the UPPAAL TA model in parallel with a transition (L_i, L_j), where L_i and L_j are two locations in the extracted model and (L_i, L_j) represents the transition from L_i to L_j. Also the transition (L_i, L_j) corresponds to sending/receiving of a message. The transition T utilizes a channel $loss_m$ for synchronization.
- The second approach injects a transition T from location L_i to L_j. This transition does not have any synchronization channel, while the original transition (L_i, L_j) has a channel for synchronization. As a result, the faulty component assumes that the message is sent to other components and waits to receive a response.

Permanent Faults.   As discussed in Section 3.1, we consider three types of permanent faults: fail-stop, Byzantine, and stuck-at faults. These faults are modeled as follows:

- To model *fail-stop* faults, for each component c, we introduce a variable $down_c$ that denotes whether the component is working ($down_c = 0$) or failed ($down_c = 1$). This can be tailored to consider failure of all components or only to a subset of components or to a specific number of components. Furthermore, all component actions of component c are restricted to execute only if ($down_c = 0$).
- In *Byzantine faults*, one or more components behave maliciously. By default, a malicious component can arbitrarily change the variables it can write. The designer can restrict it to a subset of variables if desired. To model the malicious component, a new transition T' is injected into the component. This transition updates the value of the variable subject to Byzantine faults.
- To model the *stuck-at* faults, we disable all transitions that change the value of the variable (identified by the designer using the same mechanism discussed earlier). This is achieved by revising all actions that change the value of affected variable(s).

Transient Faults.   To model the transient fault that affects a given variable, we model it as a one-time corruption of that variable at any reachable state in the program.

3.3   Automatic Fault Injection

In this section, we describe the automatic fault injection mechanism. Faults are injected based on the following parameters which are specified by designer.

- *The fault type.* Currently, there are three types of faults as explained in Section 3.1.
- *Effect of faults on the program.* The designer needs to specify the variables affected by faults as follows:

- *Message loss.* For this type, we assume that any of the messages in the model may be lost. The designer can limit it to a subset if desired.
- *Permanent.* i) *Fail-stop*: For this type of fault, the designer needs to specify the component that is likely to fail. By default, we consider the case where any component can fail; ii) *Stuck-at*: For this type of fault, the designer needs to specify which variable(s) may be corrupted by the stuck-at component and the possible value(s); iii) *Byzantine*: Similar to the stuck-at fault, the designer needs to specify which variable(s) may be corrupted by the Byzantine component and the possible value(s). For instance, in the example of Section 4, the variable representing the action (read/write) is affected by faults. As described in Section 4, this fault can change the requested action and leads to an undesirable state. Hence, the default for this fault is that the variable can be corrupted to any value in its domain.
- *Transient.* For this type of fault, the designer needs to specify which variables are likely to be affected by a transient fault. The default for this fault is that any variable can be corrupted to any value in its domain.
- − *Number of occurrences of faults.* The designer also needs to specify the occurrences of the transient faults that may take place during the computation. The default setting value is 1.

Algorithm Description. The input of Algorithm 1 is a fault-intolerant TA model M in XML format and the parameters described above. The output is a fault-affected TA model M' in XML format.

Like the TA model, the XML file has a set of locations and transitions, which are respectively defined by the following tags: "$< location > statements < /location >$" and "$< transition > statements < /transition >$". The *statements* can be a *name*, an *invariant*, or a *type* (e.g., urgent, committed) for locations, and a *source*, a *target*, or *labels* for transitions. The source and target tags represent the position of the transition. The label tag shows whether the transition has a *synchronization* channel, an *assignment* operation, or a *guard* condition.

The Algorithm 1 utilizes three functions $Find$, $Remove$, and $Change$. The function $Find$ takes a model M and a label L and returns a transition T that has label L in model M. The function $Remove$ takes a transition T and a synchronization channel ch and removes the channel ch from T. The function $Change$ takes a transition T and a variable v and returns a transition with a changed value of v.

The algorithm scans the XML file, finds the corresponding part, and changes it as necessary for the fault. For message loss (Lines 4-8), we identify where the message loss occurs by finding a transition T that has a label $kind = synchronization$. This label represents that T is synchronizing with other modules. Utilizing T, we create T' by removing its synchronization channel, and inject it in parallel with T into the model. In the case studies, we apply this approach to generate several fault-affected models, each model considers the case where one specific message may be lost. This can be trivially generalized to generate a model that simultaneously loses multiple messages. To model the other approach

---

Algorithm 1. Automatic Fault Injection

Input: A fault-intolerant Timed Automata model M in XML format, variable v subject to faults, type of fault, and counter c.
Output: A fault-affected Timed Automata model M' in XML format.

1:   $AddMoreFaults \leftarrow true$, $cnt \leftarrow 0$
2: **while** $(AddMoreFaults = true)$ **do**
3:
4:     **Message Loss:**
5:     $T \leftarrow \text{Find}(M, kind = TransitionKind)$
6:     $T' \leftarrow T$
7:     $T' \leftarrow \text{Remove}(T', channel)$ {or $T' \leftarrow \text{Change}(T', channel)$}
8:     $AddMoreFaults \leftarrow false$
9:
10:    **Fail-stop:**
11:    $T \leftarrow \text{Find}(M, true)$
12:    **if** T has an $assignment$ statement **then**
13:      add $(down_c \leftarrow 1)$ to T's set of assignments
14:    **else**
15:      add an $assignment$ statement to T, and add $(down_c \leftarrow 1)$ to its set of assignments
16:    **end if**
17:    **if** T has a $guard$ statement **then**
18:      add $(down_c = 0)$ to T's set of guards
19:    **else**
20:      add a $guard$ statement to T, and add $(down_c = 0)$ to its set of guards
21:    **end if**
22:    $AddMoreFaults \leftarrow false$
23:
24:    **Byzantine Fault:**
25:    $T \leftarrow \text{Find}(M, kind = TransitionKind)$
26:    $T' \leftarrow T$
27:    $T' \leftarrow \text{Change}(T', v)$ {No need to change $AddMoreFaults$}
28:
29:    **Stuck-at Fault:**
30:    $T \leftarrow \text{Find}(M, kind = TransitionKind)$
31:    $T \leftarrow \text{Change}(T, v)$
32:    $AddMoreFaults \leftarrow false$
33:
34:    **Transient Fault:**
35:    $T \leftarrow \text{Find}(M, kind = TransitionKind)$
36:    **if** $(cnt \leq c)$ **then**
37:      $T \leftarrow \text{Change}(T, v)$
38:    **else**
39:      $AddMoreFaults \leftarrow false$
40:    **end if**
41:
42: **end while**

---

of modeling message loss described in Section 3.2, the synchronization channel of T' should be changed to a faulty channel (by calling function $Change$). After injecting the fault, we use a variable $AddMoreFaults$ to terminate the algorithm.

To model a fail-stop fault (Lines 10-22), we use an arbitrary transition T. If T has a label $kind=assigment$, which means T has an assignment statement, we add $down \leftarrow 1$ to its set of assignments. If it does not, we define a new label $kind=assigment$ and add $down \leftarrow 1$ to its set of assignment. This step is repeated by every transition in the component subject to fail-stop fault. Moreover, we add the guard $down=0$ to the set of T's guards. For modeling the effects of failing a specific component, the locations of a transition T ($source$ label for the starting location and $target$ label for the ending location) should be given to the algorithm.

If the fault is a Byzantine fault (Lines 24-27), we inject a new transition T' in parallel to the original transition T, which has an assignment label. The value of the variable v, which is subject to faults, is corrupted in T'. The occurrence of this fault does not terminate the algorithm, since in a Byzantine fault the faulty component continues to run but produces incorrect results, while injecting a stuck-at fault (Lines 29-32) terminates the algorithm.

For transient faults (Lines 34-40), we define a counter that controls the number of occurrence of the fault. When the counter is greater than the input c, the algorithm terminates.

4   Case Study 1: Modeling Faults in LT Coding Style

In this section, we apply our fault modeling approach in the context of our first case study. The case study is a Network on Chip (NoC) switch that uses *Loosely-Timed* (LT) coding style and the *TLM base protocol*. In this case study, we only consider permanent and message faults. Moreover, in the next section, we investigate the impact of transient faults in the Approximately-Timed (AT) coding style.

4.1   Description of Case Study 1

In this case study, we use SystemC TLM to model a Network on Chip (NoC) using memory-mapped busses. The switch has 8 processing cores: four Initiators and four Targets and a Router as an interconnect component between the Initiators and Targets. Each Initiator module generates a transaction and sends it to one of the Target modules through the Router using b_transport() interface.

We use the method in [15] (described briefly in 2.3) to extract the UPPAAL TA model from the SystemC TLM model. Next, in Figure 1, we identify the fault-free version of this model that forms the basis of models generated for different types of faults. Due to space constraints, we only present the extracted model for the Router as the Router component is the most complicated component and it suffices to demonstrate the proposed approach.

Figure 1(a) represents the Router automaton and Figure 1(b) shows the address decoding mechanism used in the Router module. The Router receives a transaction through one of the channels Init2Router and changes its state to L7. This transaction should not be received before delay1 timing point. Note that in the Router automaton, we cannot use the same channel to communicate with Initiators since their socket connections are point-to-point in the SystemC TLM model. After receiving the transaction, the Router decodes the address (Locations L12 and L13 in Figure 1(b)), obtains the TargetID, and forwards the transaction to the appropriate Target. The Router then waits to receive the response of the Target from the same channel (L10) and sends it back to the appropriate Initiator (L11).

To ensure that the extracted model captures the requirements/properties of the SystemC TLM program, we specify the properties that should hold in the absence of faults. For this purpose, we define the following specifications.

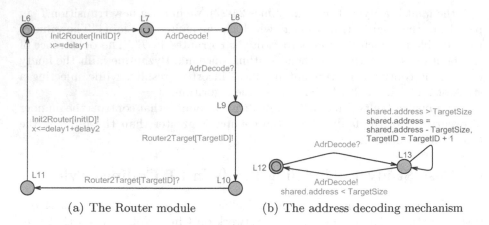

(a) The Router module   (b) The address decoding mechanism

Fig. 1. The extracted UPPAAL timed automata in LT coding style. The green text illustrates either the *guards* or *synchronization*, the blue text shows the *updates*, and the pink text represents the *names*.

```
SPEC 1: A[] not deadlock
SPEC 2: Init[id_i].CurrTrans.cmd == readCmd
        --> (Target[id_t].SentData == Router.RcvdData)
            and (Router.SentData == Init[id_i].RcvdData)
SPEC 3: Init[id_i].CurrTrans.cmd == writeCmd
        --> (Init[id_i].SentData == Router.RcvdData)
            and (Router.SentData == Target[id_t].RcvdData)
SPEC 4: Init[id_i].L1 --> (Init[id_i].L2) or (Init[id_i].L3)
SPEC 5: (Init[id_i].L2) or (Init[id_i].L3) --> Init[id_i].L1
```

The SPEC 4 and SPEC 5 show that the Initiator will eventually generate a transaction either with a write request (Location L2) or a read request (Location L3), and will eventually come back to the initial state to generate another transaction. These two requirements together imply that the Initiator module is not blocked. We can extend the set of requirements and define the same requirements as SPEC 4 and SPEC 5 for all modules in the extracted model. Using UPPAAL model checker, we have model checked the aforementioned requirements.

4.2   Modeling and Analyzing Faults in the Case Study

In this part, we extend our previous work [19] on analyzing the impact of permanent faults by a) analyzing the impact of both permanent faults and message loss, and b) injecting all the faults automatically based on approaches introduced in Section 3.2 and Algorithm 1.

Message Loss.   In this example, a message gets lost while forwarding from either the Initiator to Router, Router to Target, Target to Router, or Router to Initiator. The results are as shown in Table 1. In this, and subsequent tables, if requirement x is satisfied, we include s in the table. If it is violated, we include v. If the answer is more complicated, we include z and explain the result in the text. Moreover, SPEC 5 is for all possible Initiators. As an illustration, assume that the message gets lost while forwarding from the Router to one of the Targets. To model it, we inject the new transition T' introduced in Algorithm 1 (Lines 4-8) into the Router in Figure 1(a) from Location L9 to L10. As a result, the Router utilizes this transition and changes its state to L10 and waits to receive the response from one of the Targets. The desired Target, however, does not receive any messages from the Router and waits at its initial state, thereby violating requirements 1, 2, 3, and 5.

Table 1. Modeling and analyzing the impact of faults in the NoC switch while using LT coding style

Cause	Affected Locations	SPEC 1	2	3	4	5	Total Time (ms)
Fault-free model	–	s	s	s	s	s	13.5
Message loss	Initiator to Router	v	v	v	s	v	12.2
	Router to Target	v	v	v	s	v	12.2
	Target to Router	v	v	v	s	v	13.1
	Router to Initiator	v	v	v	s	v	13.0
Fail-stop	Initiator	v	v	v	z	v	13.1
	Router	v	v	v	s	v	13.2
	Target	v	v	v	s	v	14.1
Byzantine	Initiator	s	z	z	s	s	14.0
	Router	s	z	z	s	s	14.3
	Target	s	z	z	s	s	14.4
Stuck-at	Initiator	s	z	z	s	s	12.0
	Router	s	z	s	s	s	12.2
	Target	s	z	s	s	s	12.4

Fail-Stop. In this example, we consider three types of fail-stop: Initiator, Router, and Target failures. Regarding the second case, we utilize a variable $down_r$ to define a guard $down_r == 0$ (Lines 18 and 20 in Algorithm 1). This guard can be defined at any transitions prior to sending the transaction to the Targets. We initialize this variable to 0 that shows we have no fail-stop. During the program execution, it can be non-deterministically set to 1. For example, if the injected fault perturbs the transition from L7 to L8 in Figure 1(a), the Router cannot decode the address and will not be able to communicate with the Initiators and Targets. As a result, the Router is considered as a failed component. The modeling of the Initiator and Target failures are similar. The results for failure of different components are as shown in Table 1. Regarding the Initiator failure, the location of the fault injection affects satisfaction of SPEC 4. If the fault occurs after setting the attributes in the sending transaction, the fault does not violate SPEC 4. If the fault occurs while setting the attributes, the requirement SPEC 4 is violated. Hence, we show it as z.

Byzantine Faults. In this example, we consider the case where the variable of concern is cmd attribute, which represents the action requested (read/write). For this purpose, we inject a transition T' in parallel with the original transition T into the model (Lines 25-26 in Algorithm 1). The transition T' changes the cmd attribute such that its value is different from that in T. This change causes the Initiator to update the value of cmd non-determinately and behave maliciously.

Stuck-at Faults. Modeling of the stuck-at faults is similar to that in Byzantine faults except that once the fault occurs, the affected variables cannot change, since we do not inject a new transition T' (See Algorithm 1) for the stuck-at faults. We consider the stuck-at fault for the variable cmd to 1 in Table 1, which means the Initiator is always requesting a write action. As a result, when a write action is requested, the effects of stuck-at faults cannot be found and SPEC 3 is satisfied.

5   Case Study 2: Modeling Faults in AT Coding Style

In this section, first, we introduce our second case study that focuses on an on-chip memory-mapped communication bus between an Initiator and a Memory module. This case study utilizes *Approximately-Timed* (AT) coding style and *TLM base protocol*. Then, we model the faults described in Section 3 on this case study, and analyze the effects of each type on the extracted UPPAAL timed automata.

5.1   Description of Case Study 2 and Model Extraction

In this case study, adapted from [20], the Initiator and the Memory use non-blocking transport (nb_transport()) interface for interaction. The nb_transport() interface is intended to support the AT coding style and is particularly suited for modeling pipelined transactions. It breaks down each transaction into four phases, namely BEGIN_REQ, END_REQ, BEGIN_RESP, and END_RESP, where each phase transition is associated with a timing point. The Initiator generates a transaction and starts the communication by sending a BEGIN_REQ using the forward path nb_transport_fw to the Memory and waits to receive END_REQ or BEGIN_RESP from the backward path nb_transport_bw. After that, the Initiator can finish the transaction by sending END_RESP. The Initiator can also start another transaction by sending a new BEGIN_REQ.

We utilize the rules and approaches explained in [13,9] to extract the UP-PAAL timed automata model. Nonetheless, the UPPAAL model generated by considering all possible components is too large to perform exhaustive analysis. Hence, for evaluating the effect of given faults, we utilize simple slicing techniques by only considering components that could be affected by those faults. To ensure that the extracted model captures the requirements of the SystemC TLM model, we specify a set of requirements that should hold in the absence of faults. These requirements should be always true in the absence of faults.

```
SPEC 1: A[] not deadlock
SPEC 2: Init.SentBeginReq --> (Memory.RcvdBeginReq)
SPEC 3: (Memory.SentEndReq or Memory.SentBeginResp) --> (Init.EndResp)
SPEC 4: Init.SentBeginReq --> (Init.Initial)
SPEC 5: Init.CurrTrans.cmd == readCmd --> (Target.SentData==Init.RcvdData)
SPEC 6: Init.CurrTrans.cmd==writeCmd --> (Init.SentData==Target.RcvdData)
SPEC 7: (Init.SentBeginReq or Init.EndReq) and
        (Memory.RcvBeginReq or Memory.SentBeginResp)
        --> (Init.CurrTrans.phase == Memroy.CurrTrans.phase)
```

Among these requirements, the last requirement helps to check the execution ordering of transactions while they are executed in a pipeline. Using UPPAAL, we have model checked all the above properties for the extracted model.

5.2   Modeling and Analyzing Faults in the Case Study

In this part, we model and analyze the impact of all the aforementioned faults in Section 3.1 utilizing the approaches introduced in Section 3.2 and Algorithm 1. The experimental results (Table 2) illustrate that the time for evaluating the effect of faults is comparable ($< 125\%$) to the verification in the absence of faults.

Table 2. Modeling and analyzing the impact of faults in the memory bus system while using AT coding style

Cause	Affected Locations	SPEC							Total Time (s)
		1	2	3	4	5	6	7	
Fault-free model	–	s	s	s	s	s	s	s	5.120
Message loss	Initiator, sending BEGIN_REQ	v	v	s	v	v	v	s	4.455
	Initiator, sending END_RESP	s	s	s	s	s	s	s	4.545
	Memory, sending END_REQ	v	s	v	v	v	v	s	4.235
	Memory, sending BEGIN_RESP	s	s	v	s	v	v	s	4.235
Fail-stop	Initiator	v	v	v	v	v	v	s	4.125
	Memory	v	v	v	v	v	v	s	4.459
Byzantine	Initiator	s	s	s	s	z	z	s	5.534
	Memory	s	s	s	s	z	z	s	5.680
Stuck-at	Initiator, stuck-at 1	s	s	s	s	z	s	s	5.650
	Memory, stuck-at 1	s	s	s	s	z	s	s	5.645
	Initiator, stuck-at 0	s	s	s	s	s	z	s	5.552
	Memory, stuck-at 0	s	s	s	s	s	z	s	5.557
Transient	Initiator, cmd attribute	s	s	s	s	z	s	s	5.676
	Memory, cmd attribute	s	s	s	s	z	s	s	5.655
	Initiator, phase attribute	z	z	z	z	v	v	v	5.645
	Memory, phase attribute	s	s	s	s	z	z	v	5.675

Message Loss.   The modeling of message loss in this case study is similar to that in Section 4 with the exception that the program is using nb_transport_fw and nb_transport_bw for forwarding and receiving transactions.

Permanent Faults. In modeling fail-stop, either the Initiator or the Memory can fail. The location of injecting the variable $down_c$ explained in Section 4.2 can be different and does not change the results of Table 2. In Byzantine and stuck-at faults, we consider the case where the variable of interest is the cmd variable.

Transient Faults. We consider two instances to illustrate the transient faults: (1) where cmd attribute is corrupted, and (2) where phase argument is corrupted. As an illustration, when a transient fault affects cmd, satisfaction of SPEC 5 and SPEC 6 depends upon whether cmd is corrupted from 0 to 1 or from 1 to 0. Hence, Table 2 represents it as z and $\bar{z}$.

6 Conclusions and Future Work

In this paper, we focused on analyzing the effect of different types of faults that are of concern in the SystemC TLM program. This work is inspired by [10] that characterizes different types of faults for SystemC TLM programs. We partitioned the classes of faults in [10] into faults (that need to be tolerated) and bugs (that need to be prevented) and focused on the former.

We began with the given SystemC TLM model and used the approach in [13] to generate a fault-intolerant UPPAAL model. Subsequently, we considered three types of faults, message faults, permanent faults, and transient faults. For each type of faults, we utilized a generic approach to transform the UPPAAL model to obtain a fault-affected model. Subsequently, this model was used in UPPAAL to conclude tolerance to faults or to obtain a counterexample. We were either able to verify that the original specification is satisfied or find a counterexample demonstrating the violation of the original specification. Moreover, the time for evaluating the effect of faults was comparable ($< 125\%$) to the verification in the absence of faults. We demonstrated our approach with two case studies. These case studies covered programs that utilized LT and AT coding styles. Given the simplicity of the LT coding style, the time for verification was lower in LT coding style. However, the evaluation of the AT coding style was mitigated with appropriate program slicing that allowed us to consider only those components that are relevant to the given fault.

One future work is to combine this work with programs such as [13] that automate translation from SystemC TLM to UPPAAL timed automata.

Acknowledgements. This work has been supported by National Science Foundation awards CNS-1329807 and CNS-1318678, and CCF-1116546.

References

1. Open SystemC Initiative (OSCI): Defining and advancing SystemC standard IEEE 1666-2005, http://www.systemc.org/

2. Transaction-Level Modeling (TLM) 2.0 Reference Manual,
   http://www.systemc.org/downloads/standards/
3. Fin, A., Fummi, F., Martignano, M., Signoretto, M.: SystemC: A homogenous
   environment to test embedded systems. In: Proceedings of the Ninth International
   Symposium on Hardware/Software Codesign, CODES 2001, pp. 17–22 (2001)
4. Harris, I.G.: Fault models and test generation for hardware-software covalidation.
   IEEE Design and Test of Computers 20(4), 40–47 (2003)
5. Blanc, N., Kroening, D.: Race analysis for SystemC using model checking. ACM
   Transactions on Design Automation of Electronic Systems 15(3), 21:1–21:32 (2010)
6. Cimatti, A., Griggio, A., Micheli, A., Narasamdya, I., Roveri, M.: KRATOS: A
   software model checker for SystemC. In: Gopalakrishnan, G., Qadeer, S. (eds.)
   CAV 2011. LNCS, vol. 6806, pp. 310–316. Springer, Heidelberg (2011)
7. Habibi, A., Moinudeen, H., Tahar, S.: Generating finite state machines from SystemC. In: Gielen, G.G.E. (ed.) DATE Designers' Forum, European Design and
   Automation Association, Leuven, Belgium, pp. 76–81 (2006)
8. Niemann, B., Haubelt, C.: Formalizing TLM with Communicating Stat Machines.
   In: Proceedings of Forum on Specification and Design Languages (FDL 2006), pp.
   285–292 (2006)
9. Ebnenasir, A., Hajisheykhi, R., Kulkarni, S.S.: Facilitating the design of fault tolerance in transaction level systemc programs. Theor. Comput. Sci. 496, 50–68 (2013)
10. Le, H.M., Große, D., Drechsler, R.: Automatic TLM Fault Localization for Sys-
    temC. IEEE Trans. on CAD of Integrated Circuits and Systems 31(8), 1249–1262
    (2012)
11. Le, H.M., Große, D., Drechsler, R.: Scalable fault localization for systemc tlm
    designs. In: Macii, E. (ed.) DATE, EDA Consortium, pp. 35–38. ACM DL, San
    Jose (2013)
12. Bombieri, N., Fummi, F., Pravadelli, G.: A Mutation Model for the SystemC TLM
    2.0 Communication Interfaces. In: DATE, pp. 396–401. IEEE (2008)
13. Herber, P., Pockrandt, M., Glesner, S.: Transforming SystemC Transaction Level
    Models into UPPAAL timed automata. In: Singh, S., Jobstmann, B., Kishinevsky,
    M., Brandt, J. (eds.) MEMOCODE, pp. 161–170. IEEE (2011)
14. Behrmann, G., David, A., Larsen, K.G.: A tutorial on uppaal. In: Bernardo, M.,
    Corradini, F. (eds.) SFM-RT 2004. LNCS, vol. 3185, pp. 200–236. Springer, Hei-
    delberg (2004)
15. Hajisheykhi, R., Ebnenasir, A., Kulkarni, S.S.: Modeling and analyzing timing
    faults in transaction level systemc programs. In: Palesi, M., Mak, T.S.T., Danesh-
    talab, M. (eds.) NoCArc@MICRO, pp. 65–68. ACM (2013)
16. Alur, R., Dill, D.L.: A Theory of Timed Automata. Theor. Comput. Sci. 126(2),
    183–235 (1994)
17. Buttazzo, G.C.: Hard Real-Time Computing Systems. Springer, New York (2011)
18. Iyer, R.K., Rossetti, D.J., Hsueh, M.-C.: Measurement and modeling of computer
    reliability as affected by system activity. ACM Trans. Comput. Syst. 4(3), 214–237
    (1986)
19. Hajisheykhi, R., Ebnenasir, A., Kulkarni, S.S.: Analysis of permanent faults in
    transaction level systemc models. In: ADSN (2014)
20. Getting Started with TLM-2.0, http://www.doulos.com/knowhow/systemc/tlm2/

Formal Verification of Discrete-Time MATLAB/Simulink Models Using Boogie

Robert Reicherdt and Sabine Glesner

Technische Universität Berlin,
Ernst-Reuter-Platz 7, 10587 Berlin, Germany
{robert.reicherdt,sabine.glesner}@tu-berlin.de
http://www.pes.tu-berlin.de

Abstract. MATLAB/Simulink is a widely used industrial tool for the development of embedded systems. Many of these systems are safety critical, especially in automotive industries. At the same time, automatic formal verification techniques for Simulink, in particular on model level, are rare and often suffer from scalability issues. In this paper, we present an automatic transformation of discrete-time MATLAB/Simulink models into the intermediate verification language Boogie. This transformation enables us to use the Boogie verification framework and inductive invariant checking for the automatic formal verification of MATLAB/Simulink models. Additionally, verification objectives for common error classes are generated automatically. With our approach, we provide an automatic formal verification technique for MATLAB/Simulink and the most common error classes which scales better than existing techniques in many cases. To demonstrate the practical applicability, we have applied our approach to a number of case studies from the automotive domain.

Keywords: Formal Verification, MATLAB/Simulink, Boogie.

1 Introduction

Mathworks' MATLAB/Simulink is a widely used tool in embedded systems development, especially in automotive industries. MATLAB/Simulink enables graphical specification of embedded systems as block diagrams, the iterative refinement of these abstract models with implementation details and finally, the automatic generation of source code for various target architectures.

Even though MATLAB/Simulink is used to develop safety-critical systems, the correct functionality of systems on model level is often only verified by testing and simulation of the models, which is known to be incomplete. Since fixing of errors in late development stages is more expensive, complete formal verification methods on the model level are desirable. There are automatic approaches for the formal verification of MATLAB/Simulink models but the techniques used, like abstract interpretation and (bounded) model checking, suffer from scalability issues, i.e., the state space explosion problem.

Hence, there is a need for techniques that can be applied on model level and that are promising to scale well even for large and complex models. A

D. Giannakopoulou and G. Salaün (Eds.): SEFM 2014, LNCS 8702, pp. 190–204, 2014.
© Springer International Publishing Switzerland 2014

possible solution for this problem is the use of inductive invariant checking for the verification of MATLAB/Simulink models. With an inductive approach, we avoid unfolding the full state space of a model. Instead, we use automatic theorem proving to show that model invariants are maintained in all possible executions. This technique requires the specification of invariants which are suitable to verify the desired properties.

In our approach, we present a novel automatic transformation of MATLAB/Simulink models into the *Boogie* intermediate verification language. This enables us to use the *Microsoft Boogie Program Verifier*[15] for the verification of MATLAB/Simulink models. During the transformation, we also automatically generate invariants that enable the automatic verification of the models for some common error classes.

We require our approach to fulfill the following criteria:

Preservation of Semantics. The transformation should preserve the informal, intuitive semantics of MATLAB/Simulink or safely over-approximate the behavior of model elements if a direct transformation is not possible.

Automation. Achieve a high degree of automation for the transformation as well as for the verification.

Coverage. Support many of the frequently used blocks from the MATLAB/Simulink block library. The set of blocks should be extensible such that translation rules for further blocks can be easily added in the future.

Performance. Translation and verification should be possible in reasonable time on a standard computer system.

The rest of the paper is structured as follows: In Section 2, we briefly introduce *Simulink* and *Boogie*. Subsequently, in Section 3, we present our verification framework for MATLAB/Simulink models using the Boogie program verifier. In Section 4, the automatic translation is presented and after that in Section 5, we present our verification approach. We show our experimental results in Section 6. Finally, we present related work in Section 7 and conclude in Section 8.

2   Background

2.1   MATLAB/Simulink

MATLAB/Simulink [13,14] is an add-on to Mathworks MATLAB IDE. It enables graphical modeling and simulation of synchronous and reactive embedded systems. Simulink uses a data flow oriented block diagram notation which consists of blocks and lines. Blocks represent either some kind of functionality, like mathematical or logical functions, or are used for structuring the model such as subsystem blocks, port blocks, bus blocks etc. To represent signal flow between blocks in MATLAB/Simulink, lines are used. A line can carry multiple signals.

Every block is defined by its type and its block parameters. The block parameters consist of a set of common parameters, e. g., color, size, position, data type, etc., which can be found in every block, and a number of parameters that are specific to the block type and modify the behavior of the block.

MATLAB/Simulink enables hierarchical structuring of the model using subsystem blocks. Only subsystem blocks can contain other blocks. To model the signal flow into subsystems, the inputs of the subsystem blocks are mapped to (*Inport* and *Outport*) port blocks within the subsystem. Besides these port blocks, a `Subsystem` block can also contain special (for instance *Enable*) port blocks which are used to realize conditional execution. Another important property of `Subsystem` blocks is whether they are *atomic* or not. Non-atomic (virtual) subsystems are practically invisible to the Simulink scheduler while atomic subsystems do affect the behavior of the model.

Even though the data flow oriented notation of MATLAB/Simulink is generally concurrent, MATLAB/Simulink executes the blocks *sequentially* in a simulation. Hence, the simulation engine schedules the blocks to determine an execution order. For that MATLAB/Simulink uses so-called *execution contexts*.

An execution context is comparable to a sorted list of blocks and child execution contexts that have to be executed as an atomic operation. This means that once an execution context is entered, all blocks and nested execution contexts have to be executed before the execution is allowed to return to the parent execution context.

2.2   Boogie

Boogie[2] is a verification framework developed at Microsoft Research. It is based on *Extended Static Checking (ESC)* as presented by Detlefs et al. in [5]. The basic idea of ESC is formalizing the program for a set of properties. This is done by enhancing the code with annotations about invariants and variables as well as assertions to specify proof obligations. The annotated program is then translated into first order logic formulas, the *Verification Conditions*, and passed to an automatic theorem prover (SMT-solver). The Verifications Conditions (VC) are only satisfiable if the program is consistent with the annotations.

The Boogie framework consists of the intermediate verification language *Boogie2*[12] (formerly BoogiePL) and the Boogie program verifier tool [15], which is used to verify programs written in Boogie2. Boogie is used as intermediate framework for the verification of various programming languages. While there are interfaces to other SMT-solvers, the Boogie framework usually uses the automatic theorem solver *Z3* developed at Microsoft Research [16].

The Boogie programming language is an imperative programming language providing a number of basic types like Booleans, mathematical integers, mathematical reals and bit vector types together with some basic operations for these types. It features constants, map types, user-defined types as well as uninterpreted functions. To model control flow, Boogie offers common constructs like loops and if-else blocks as well as simple goto statements and labels.

Besides the basic operations, it is possible to use functions and operations of the theories provided by Z3 using the *bvbuiltin* directive. With that feature, it is possible to write specifications that use features of the *SMTLIB 2.0* standard and Z3-specific commands.

3 Approach

In this section, we present our approach for the verification of MATLAB/Simulink models. This approach is based on a translation of the models into the Boogie programming language. Besides the translation of the model, we also automatically generate proof obligations to verify the absence of specific error classes. So far, we consider the following error classes: overflows, underflows, division-by-zero and range violations.

3.1 Limitations and Assumptions

Even though, MATLAB/Simulink is used to model the continuous environment of embedded controllers, we only focus on discrete controller. There are blocks that include legacy code into a model. This would require a translation of respective language to Boogie and, hence, is not part of this work. There are blocks that represent calculations that are too complex or for which it is even impossible to define a sufficient mapping with the types and operations provided by Boogie.

We constrain the models by the following limitations:

1. The models should only contain blocks from the discrete library and stateless blocks, such as mathematical functions and blocks for signal routing.
2. We assume that the sample time is fixed for every block.
3. We do not support external code like C code or Matlab functions (M-code) introduced by S-Function blocks or Stateflow charts. However, these blocks may be over-approximated.
4. We over-approximate blocks like lookup tables, signal builders or blocks with arithmetic operations not expressible in the specification language.
5. We only translate vector and scalar signals and element-wise operations on matrices.
6. We assume that the model does not contain bus-capable blocks and composite data types like bus objects.

3.2 Verification Approach

The core contribution of our approach is the automatic translation of MATLAB/Simulink models that fulfill the assumptions from Section 3.1 into the Boogie2 language. Our approach is depicted in Figure 1.

With this translation, we

1. define a formal semantics for the set of supported blocks according to the informal simulation semantics and
2. automatically extract the verification objectives for the error classes of interest and
3. extract additional information from the model that helps with the verification (invariants).

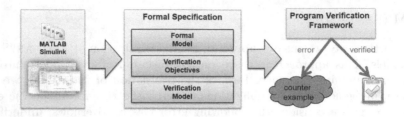

Fig. 1. The Verification Framework

Formal Model. While the notation of MATLAB/Simulink models is generally concurrent, the simulation of MATLAB/Simulink models is done sequentially, just as the code which is generated for the controllers. During a simulation, the MATLAB/Simulink environment calculates an execution order for the blocks, initializes the blocks and executes the model for a given number of time steps. Hence, in our automatic translation, we first have to calculate the order to construct a control flow graph *(CFG)*, which then can be translated into a Boogie program. Once the CFG is calculated, we translate the model according to the CFG block by block. For each supported block type, we define translation rules specifying the translation according to the block semantics, the relevant parameters and the signals connected to the inputs.

Verification Objectives. Depending on the block type, verification goals are created for each block type. For each block where overflows, underflows, division-by-zero and range violations can occur, the necessary formulas are produced according to the parameters of the concrete blocks.

Verification Model. Besides the parameters necessary for the translation of the blocks, we additionally extract information from the model that helps with the verification, e. g., saturation limits, data types, and lower and upper bounds for signals. This information is used to automatically create loop invariants in the specification. With our approach, we support two verification methods: *inductive invariant checking* and *k-induction*. The first is naturally supported by Boogie, for the second we create a special Boogie2 specification for a desired k.

Finally, the formal specification for the MATLAB/Simulink model is passed to the Boogie program verifier which either returns a counter example if the model contains an error or returns that the model is verified.

4   Transformation

In this section, we describe the transformation of MATLAB/Simulink models into the Boogie programming language. For that, we first calculate the control flow graph of a model. Then, we are able to map the control flow graph directly to the structure of a Boogie program for the model.

Example 1. Figure 2a depicts a small MATLAB/Simulink model for a simple counter. It consist of a constant with the value 1, a Sum block that outputs the

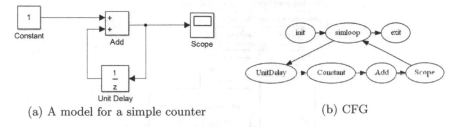

(a) A model for a simple counter   (b) CFG

Fig. 2. A Example Model and its CFG

sum of its inputs, a `Scope` block that displays its inputs and a `UnitDelay` block. A `UnitDelay` block holds the value connected to the input for one simulation cycle and outputs it in the next cycle. It also has a parameter *InitialValue* which defines the value for the first simulation step. In this model it is set to 0.

In [18], we already have presented how to calculate control and data dependences in Simulink models. This is done calculating the so-called execution contexts of a model and scheduling the blocks according to their data dependences within execution contexts. We calculate the control flow graph for a model in two steps: First, we need to calculate all execution contexts within the model using the algorithm described in [18]. With that, we also capture control flow introduced by the *Conditional Execution Behavior* parameter as well as by *execution context propagation*, which may be activated for subsystem blocks. Second, we calculate the schedule for each execution context in the model. The schedule of an execution context contains all blocks and all child execution contexts sorted according to the signal flow dependencies. The schedule is calculated using the scheduling rules defined in the MATLAB/Simulink documentation.

Example 2. The example model from Figure 2a consists of 4 blocks. All these blocks are scheduled in the root execution context of the model. The calculation of the sorted order results in the CFG depicted in Figure 2b. For simplicity, the initialization steps for the blocks are omitted and subsumed by an *init* node.

4.1   Translating the Model

Once the CFG is calculated, we translate the model to Boogie. In our translation, the MATLAB/Simulink model is mapped to a procedure in Boogie. Within the procedure, the simulation loop is realized as Boogie loop. Figure 3 depicts the structure of a translated model.

The first section contains uninterpreted functions, axioms and constants. These functions and axioms are either part of our prelude or created during the block translation. Functions defined in the prelude enable a number of commands from SMTLIB 2.0 and Z3 that are not part of the Boogie programming language and also some helper functions, e. g., casts according to the semantics of MATLAB/Simulink. Functions defined during the block translation are used to over-approximate behavior of blocks that cannot be translated to Boogie directly.

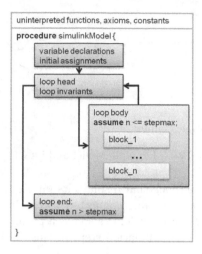

Fig. 3. General structure of a translated Model

The second section in Figure 3 is the actual Boogie procedure into which the MATLAB/Simulink model is translated. First, all variables needed for the translation of the blocks are declared. Afterward, all variables are assigned to their initial values, corresponding to the initialization step of a simulation.

The initialization is followed by the loop head which contains the loop invariants. During the translation of the blocks, invariants are added according to the block type and block parameters. To reflect the simulation semantics in our translation, we assume that the model is executed a finite, unbounded number of steps and use a symbolic constant *stepmax* as simulation bound, which is greater or equal to the number of simulation steps. Nonetheless, with inductive invariant checking and k-induction, we are able to verify the model for arbitrary many simulation steps.

The loop body contains the actual translation of the blocks according to the CFG. The translation of the blocks consist of statements for each block and the automatically created verification objectives encoded in assertions.

4.2   Translating Simulink Blocks into Boogie

For our translation, we distinguish the supported set of blocks into four classes. There are blocks which (1) have direct-feedthrough inputs, (2) do not have direct-feedthrough inputs, (3) have to be over-approximated or (4) blocks that are related to control flow.

Direct-feedthrough blocks are the most general class for translation. Every translation step done for (1) is done for (2) and (3), too.

General Blocks. When translating a block to Boogie, variables have to be created in the Boogie specification. In Simulink, a block can have multiple outputs, the so-called outports, which may either be scalar, vectors or matrices of

```
1  var add#1#0 : int;
2  /*...*/
3  loophead: // invariant
4  assert ((add#1#0 < 128) &&
       (add#1#0 >= -128));
5  /*...*/
6  add#1#0#0#0 := Constant#1#0
       + UnitDelay#1#0;
7  // verification objectives
8  assert (add#1#0 < 128);
9  assert (add#1#0 >= -128);
```

Listing 1.1. Sum block

```
1  var UnitDelay#1#0 : int;
2  var state_UnitDelay#1#0 : int;
3  state_UnitDelay#1#0 := 0;
4  /*...*/
5  loopbody:
6  UnitDelay#1#0#:=
       state_UnitDelay#1#0;
7  /*...*/
8  state_UnitDelay#1#0:=add#1#0;
```

Listing 1.2. UnitDelay block

signals. We create a variable for each possible combination of the port number and the position in a signal vector or the indices within the matrix. A variable name is constructed using an unique identifier for the block, the port number and the zero-indexed position of the signal in the vector or matrix if necessary. We represent a scalar signal as a vector of size 1.

Table 1. Mapping of data types

Matlab/Simulink	Boogie
boolean	bool
int8, uint8, int16, uint16, ..	int (mathematical integer)
single, double	real (rational numbers)

Table 1 shows the mapping of basic data types from MATLAB/Simulink to Boogie. The mapping of *double* and *single* data types is a safe over-approximation. Although the *integer* and *real* representation of Boogie are unbounded, the bounds of the data types are kept by the automatically created assertions for the over- and underflow checks. I.e., over- and underflows are always considered as a error and reported to the user.

Example 3. Consider the Sum block of Figure 2. It has two inports, one connected to the Constant block and one connected to the UnitDelay block. A Sum block adds the values of the input signals and extends the output dimensions if necessary. In our Example, both inputs are scalar signals and the variable names are prefixed by the port number and a 0 for the position in the vector. An addition like shown in Listing 1.1 fully captures the behavior of this block. Additionally to the translation of the block semantics, the verification goals for the Sum block are created. Of our error classes of interest, only over- and underflows could occur at Sum blocks. Hence, we automatically create an over- and underflow check during the translation according to the data type of the output port. Listing 1.1 shows an excerpt of the translation for the example model for the Sum block. As the output data type is an 8-bit integer, the result has to be within the interval $[-128, 127]$. Hence, we create an assertion for this interval (Line 8). Finally, in Line 4 a loop invariant is automatically created, limiting the bounds for the output signal of the Sum block to $[-128, 127]$.

Non-direct-feedthrough Blocks. The second class of blocks are those blocks that do have non-direct-feedthrough inputs. I.e., the outputs of these blocks are not directly dependent on the inputs but on the internal state. However, the inputs of these blocks are used to calculate the state for the next simulation step. In a simulation, the MATLAB/Simulink IDE first calculates the outputs for all blocks and in a second step the new states for the blocks within the model. Hence, the blocks are scheduled at the front of the respective execution context.

In our translation, we use two variables for each output of a non-direct-feedthrough block: One for the output and one for the state. Corresponding to the scheduling rules from the Simulink documentation, the outputs of these blocks are set in the beginning of the loop, and they are available to every other block they feed. The state updates are placed at the end of the loop.

Example 4. Consider the example from Figure 2a again. Listing 1.2 shows an excerpt of the translation for the UnitDelay block. The UnitDelay block in the model is a non-direct-feedthrough block. Hence, two variables are created. As mentioned in Example 1, the initial value of the block is 0. So in the initialization part in Line 3 the state variable for the UnitDelay block is set to 0. At the beginning of the loop body in Line 6 the output variable for the block is set to its state variable. Finally, at the end of the loop in Line 8, the state variable is updated with the new state: The value of the Sum block from Example 3.

Over-approximation for Blocks. In Simulink, there exist blocks that cannot be directly translated into Boogie. These blocks are, e. g., complex mathematical functions or *S-Functions*. Additionally, there are blocks where a direct translation would greatly increase the complexity of the specification and hence the verification effort, like *Lookup* tables. In our translation, we automatically over-approximate such blocks. To over-approximate blocks, we either use uninterpreted functions or the *havoc*-commands to set the outputs of blocks to an arbitrary value. In most cases we are able to define some bounds by additional assumptions or axioms for the uninterpreted functions. We prefer the use of the *havoc*-command, to reduce the number of quantifier instantiations.

Bounds can be defined for periodic functions like some trigonometric functions like *sin*, *cos* or *atan*. We also approximate the *sqrt*-function using linear functions as bounds for the intervals $(0, 1)$ and $[1, max]$ where max is the maximum positive value for the output data type. The output of a LookupTable is bounded by the minimum and maximum value in the table. For linear extrapolation the bounds are given by linear functions using the smallest slope and the smallest value and the biggest slope and the biggest value. For blocks with behavior not defined in Simulink, but in Stateflow or legacy code, like *S-Functions*, we use the limits given by the OutMin and OutMax parameter as a contract. In Stateflow charts, sometimes bounds are defined for the output data objects, which can be used for the approximation. However, in the general case the translation of *S-Functions* is dependent on user annotations.

```
1   var Sin#1#0 : real;
2   /*...*/
3   havoc Sin#1#0; //set to arbitrary value
4   assume (Sin#1#0 >= (-1.0*(10.0+4.0))) && (Sin#1#0<=(10.0+4.0)); //
        limit to approximated bounds
```

Listing 1.3. Translation for the `Sine Wave` block

Example 5. Assume there is a `Sine Wave` block which produces a sine wave dependent on the simulation time. A `Sine Wave` block has parameters for the amplitude, the frequency, the phase and its bias. For each `Sine Wave` block holds: $y = amp*sin(freq*x+phase)+bias$ When approximating the `Sine Wave` we use the fact, that $-1 \leq sin(x) \leq 1$. For every `Sine Wave` block with the amplitude a, the bias b and the simulation time t holds that $-a+b \leq a*sin(t)+b \leq a+b$. Listing 1.3 shows an excerpt of the translation for a `Sine Wave` block with an amplitude of 10.0 and a bias of 4.0.

Control Flow. In MATLAB/Simulink there also exist blocks that cause control flow. Such blocks are conditionally executed subsystems, e.g., `Enabled Subsystem` blocks, or `Switch` and `MultiPortSwitch` blocks. Control flow in MATLAB/Simulink is realized by nested execution contexts, which are only executed if a condition depending on the block type that has caused the control flow is fulfilled. When translating blocks that introduce control flow, we create a branch for every execution context a block induces. The blocks contained in each of these execution contexts are then translated into the corresponding branch.

5 Verification

In this section, we present our approach for the verification of MATLAB/Simulink models. Our approach for the verification is twofold. We are able to perform inductive invariant checking on the translated model and, with little changes to the translated model, we are also able to perform k-induction. Both come with advantages and disadvantages. However, we use the Boogie program verifier for both, inductive invariant checking and k-induction. Depending on the desired technique, we create slightly different Boogie specifications.

Inductive invariant checking is based on the idea of proving a loop by showing that a set of loop invariants holds on loop entry and on an arbitrary loop execution. The latter is shown by using arbitrary values for the variables modified by the loop (loop bound variables) which do not violate the loop invariants, performing one loop iteration and showing that the values after one loop execution still not violate the loop invariants. This is exactly the way the Boogie program verifier works. Boogie is able to perform an analysis over the loop bound variables using abstract interpretation to determine additional invariants.

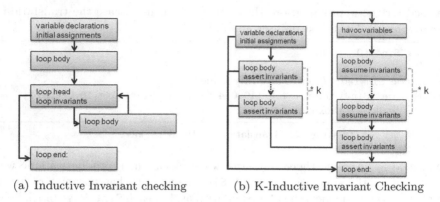

(a) Inductive Invariant checking   (b) K-Inductive Invariant Checking

Fig. 4. Inductive and k-inductive invariant checking

However, the loop invariants derived by Boogie are helpful, but not very strong. Thus, we create additional loop invariants during the translation of the the model. These invariants specify the bounds by data types and parameters of the blocks or relations of the variables with respect to control flow. A disadvantage of these stronger invariants is that they do not always match the initial state of the model. Hence we assume that a model is always executed once to reach a valid entry state for the loop. Figure 4a shows the structure of the specification for inductive invariant checking.

While inductive invariant checking scales well, especially with large state spaces, in many cases the invariants that can be automatically derived are not sufficient to verify a program or model. Instead, invariants needed to succeed with the verification have to be added manually. A related technique is k-inductive invariant checking where the induction is not only performed over one loop iteration. Instead the induction basis and the induction step are done over k loop iterations. A benefit of k-induction is that we can omit invariants related to properties that can be shown in k loop iterations

In our approach we adopt *combined-case k-induction* presented by Donaldson et al. [6] where the induction basis and the induction step is encoded into a single formula. They also extended Boogie to be able to perform k-inductive invariant checking: *K-Boogie*. However, K-Boogie is based on an old version of Boogie and Z3 which is not able to process real values. Hence we decided to encode the combined-case k-induction directly in our Boogie specification of the model. Figure 4b shows the structure of the resulting Boogie specification if k-inductive invariant checking is used. Here the loop is unrolled first k-times which forms the induction basis. After that, the loop-bound variables are set to arbitrary values (using the *havoc*-command). Now the the loop is unrolled k-times while the loop invariants are assumed. In the final $(k + 1)$ step the loop body is unrolled one more time but now all invariants and assertions for the error classes are checked.

Table 2. Experimental Results

Model	Name	Errors	Checks	Ind. Inv. Check.		k-Induction(k=2)		SLDV	
				time (s)	CE	time (s)	CE	time (s)	CE
m1	turn_indicator	0	10	3	0	4	0	5	0
m2	odometer	0	34	2	1	2	0	26	0
m3	dist_warning1	16	38	13	18	119	25	timeout	
m4	dist_warning2	0	38+4	10	11	41	0	1521	0

6   Evaluation

We have integrated our approach into our MeMo framework [18,10] to evaluate our approach. The parsing strategy in our MeMo framework is twofold. First, the model file is parsed to create a skeleton data structure for the model. Second, the model is loaded into MATLAB/Simulink. It is compiled and all the parameters that are usually inferred at the beginning of a simulation are extracted and saved to the data structure. This procedure avoids the reimplementation of the inference mechanisms of MATLAB/Simulink, whose description is informal and incomplete in the documentation. While parsing, the MeMo framework automatically integrates model references and library blocks and replaces the `Reference` blocks with the corresponding subsystems. This means that the lowest levels of hierarchy in the parsed model only consist of basic blocks.

Currently, our implementation supports 44 basic block[1] types and their common parameter configurations. It mainly comprises blocks from the following block sets: *Discrete, Lookup Tables, Math Operations, Ports & Subsystems, Signal Routing, Sources* and *Sinks*. However, more translation rules for other block types and further parameter combinations can be added in future.

We have evaluated our approach on four models supplied by industrial partners from automotive area: A turn indicator (m1), an odometer (m2) and two models of a distance control system where one, the original model (m3), is erroneous and the second is a corrected version(m4). All models are automatically translated by our tool and contain between 190 and 346 blocks after integrating all library and model references. The model m1 mainly consists of Boolean arithmetic and a few integer computations but no stateful blocks. The model m2 consists of integer computations and also contains stateful blocks. Finally, m3 and m4 consist of integer and floating point computations as well as stateful blocks, where some are only updated every ten steps.

Table 2 shows the evaluation results for the four models. We were able to automatically verify the absence of over- and underflows, division-by-zero and range violations for tree of the four case studies. The table shows the number of errors and automatically generated checks, the time needed for translation and verification and the number of counter examples (CE) returned by Boogie.

We could verify m1 using only inductive invariant checking which was not possible for m2 due to a spurious counter example. Nevertheless, we were able

---

[1] Many blocks in the Simulink block library are constructed using basic blocks.

to show the absence of those error classes for m2 automatically using k-induction with $k = 2$. We have discovered errors in the distance warning model m3 that where caused by `Integrator` blocks with missing reset which could lead to overflows at these blocks and at subsequent calculations. Two of the counter examples using inductive invariant checking were spurious counter examples that disappear when using k-induction. The nine additional CE using k-induction are violations of the loop invariants and related to the errors. The verification of these three models was done fully automatic. We have fixed the distance warning model (m4) by adding limits to the integrator and were able to verify the model using k-induction and *four* manually specified invariants.

We have verified these models using the Simulink Design Verifier (SLDV), which was not able to verify m3 within 12 hours. For m3 the SLDV reported an average run time of 1521 seconds over 5 runs. However, with our tool we have verified all models in less than two minutes and especially for m3 and m4 in significantly less time than the SLDV.

7   Related Work

There already exist some approaches for the formal verification of MATLAB/Simulink models. These approaches can be distinguished whether they use a synchronous semantics for the verification of Simulink models or not.

In [4,22], the authors present an approach for the translation of discrete-time MATLAB/Simulink models into the synchronous data flow language *Lustre*. This translation enables the use of the *SCADE Design Verifier*[11]. Furthermore, other verification backends [17,8] like model checkers, e. g., *NuSMV*, *SAL* and *Prover*, and to theorem provers, like *PVS* and *ACL* can be used for the verification of these translated models. In [19], a method is presented to show that a MATLAB/Simulink model is correctly translated by an automatic code generator using the theorem prover YICES to show output equivalence of the MATLAB/Simulink model and the generated C-code. In [20,1], a translation from MATLAB/Simulink into hybrid automata is presented. This translation enables the use of verification tools for hybrid automata like CheckMate. In [9], a verification approach based on a transformation into the input language of the *UCLID* verifier is presented and UCLID is used to verify the models. Since UCLID supports less theories than the Z3, more over-approximations have been used in that transformation. Hence, it is less precise than our approach.

However, these approaches are based on the assumption that the semantics of Simulink is synchronous. Instead, the actual semantics of Simulink is sequential and mechanisms like *Conditional Execution Behavior* and *Conditional Execution Context Propagation* are defined on the sequential simulation semantics. Hence, we provide a more precise formalization of the MATLAB/Simulink semantics.

The *Simulink Design Verifier (SLDV)*[21] by MathWorks uses abstract interpretation and model checking techniques to automatically verify the model for division-by-zero, dead code and overflows. However, these techniques are subject to scalability issues especially for models with large state spaces and in our experiments the SLDV was not able to verify all the models in a reasonable time.

An approach for the contract-based verification of MATLAB/Simulink models is presented in [3]. It is based on a manual specification of the contracts for atomic subsystems and a subsequent translation of the MATLAB/Simulink model into verification conditions for the Z3. However, the schedule for the blocks is calculated using synchronous data flow graphs instead of the actual scheduling rules of Simulink and control flow is not mentioned in this translation. Hence, this translation also is less precise than our approach.

Theoretically, our approach can be used to verify functional properties on a model, as long as the properties are directly modeled in Simulink like presented in [7], by translating the SLDV `Proof` blocks directly into Boogie assertions.

8 Conclusion and Future Work

In this paper, we have presented our approach for the formal verification of discrete-time MATLAB/Simulink model using the Boogie program verifier. The key idea of the approach is an automatic transformation of a given MATLAB/Simulink model into a specification in the Boogie programming language and a subsequent verification of the model using the Boogie program verifier. The translation is based on the simulation semantics of discrete-time MATLAB/Simulink models. Besides the translation or safe over-approximation of the set of supported blocks, the translation also creates (1) loop invariants for each block type, (2) verification goals for each block (according to the error classes of interest) and (3) a specialized Boogie specification depending on the desired verification strategy (either inductive invariant checking or k-induction).

We have evaluated our approach on four cases studies supplied by industrial partners and have been able to show the absence of over- and underflows, division-by-zero and range violations in the correct models as well as that one of the models is erroneous in less than two minutes.

In future work we want to increase the degree of automation especially for inductive invariant checking. We want to achieve this by exploiting the semantics of certain blocks to derive stronger loop invariants. We are also currently working on a formalization of the Simulink fixed point semantics in Boogie.

References

1. Agrawal, A., Simon, G., Karsai, G.: Semantic translation of Simulink/Stateflow models to hybrid automata using graph transformations. Electron. Notes Theor. Comput. Sci. 109, 43–56 (2004)
2. Barnett, M., Chang, B.-Y.E., DeLine, R., Jacobs, B., Leino, K.R.M.: Boogie: A modular reusable verifier for object-oriented programs. In: de Boer, F.S., Bonsangue, M.M., Graf, S., de Roever, W.-P. (eds.) FMCO 2005. LNCS, vol. 4111, pp. 364–387. Springer, Heidelberg (2006)
3. Boström, P.: Contract-based verification of Simulink models. In: Qin, S., Qiu, Z. (eds.) ICFEM 2011. LNCS, vol. 6991, pp. 291–306. Springer, Heidelberg (2011)

4. Caspi, P., Curic, A., Maignan, A., Sofronis, C., Tripakis, S.: Translating discrete-time Simulink to lustre. In: Alur, R., Lee, I. (eds.) EMSOFT 2003. LNCS, vol. 2855, pp. 84–99. Springer, Heidelberg (2003)
5. Detlefs, D., Leino, K.R.M., Nelson, G., Saxe, J.: Extended static checking. In: SRC Research Report 159, Compaq Systems Research Center (1998)
6. Donaldson, A.F., Haller, L., Kroening, D., Rümmer, P.: Software verification using k-induction. In: Yahav, E. (ed.) SAS 2011. LNCS, vol. 6887, pp. 351–368. Springer, Heidelberg (2011)
7. Ferrari, A., Grasso, D., Magnani, G., Fantechi, A., Tempestini, M.: The Metrô Rio ATP Case Study. In: Kowalewski, S., Roveri, M. (eds.) FMICS 2010. LNCS, vol. 6371, pp. 1–16. Springer, Heidelberg (2010)
8. Hardin, D., Hiratzka, T.D., Johnson, D.R., Wagner, L., Whalen, M.: Development of security software: A high-assurance methodology. In: Breitman, K., Cavalcanti, A. (eds.) ICFEM 2009. LNCS, vol. 5885, pp. 266–285. Springer, Heidelberg (2009)
9. Herber, P., Reicherdt, R., Bittner, P.: Bit-precise formal verification of discrete-time MATLAB/Simulink models using SMT solving. In: Proceedings of the Eleventh ACM International Conference on Embedded Software, EMSOFT 2013, Piscataway, NJ, USA, pp. 8:1–8:10. IEEE Press (2013)
10. Hu, W., Wegener, J., Stürmer, I., Reicherdt, R., Salecker, E., Glesner, S.: Memo - methods of model quality. In: Dagstuhl-Workshop MBEES: Modellbasierte Entwicklung Eingebetteter Systeme VII, pp. 127–132 (2011)
11. Joshi, A., Heimdahl, M.P.E.: Model-based safety analysis of Simulink models using SCADE design verifier. In: Winther, R., Gran, B.A., Dahll, G. (eds.) SAFECOMP 2005. LNCS, vol. 3688, pp. 122–135. Springer, Heidelberg (2005)
12. Leino, K.R.M.: This is boogie 2. Technical report (2008)
13. MathWorks. MATLAB Simulink. The MathWorks Inc.,
   http://www.mathworks.com/products/simulink/
14. MathWorks. Simulink getting started guide. The MathWorks Inc.,
   http://www.mathworks.com/help/pdf_doc/simulink/sl_gs.pdf
15. Microsoft Research. Microsoft Research Boogie, http://boogie.codeplex.com/
16. Microsoft Research. Z3 Theorem Prover, http://z3.codeplex.com
17. Miller, S.P., Whalen, M.W., Cofer, D.D.: Software model checking takes off. Commun. ACM 53(2), 58–64 (2010)
18. Reicherdt, R., Glesner, S.: Slicing MATLAB Simulink models. In: ACM/IEEE 34th International Conference on Software Engineering (ICSE 2012), pp. 551–561. IEEE (2012)
19. Ryabtsev, M., Strichman, O.: Translation validation: From Simulink to C. In: Bouajjani, A., Maler, O. (eds.) CAV 2009. LNCS, vol. 5643, pp. 696–701. Springer, Heidelberg (2009)
20. Silva, B., Krogh, B.: Formal verification of hybrid systems using CheckMate: a case study. In: American Control Conference, vol. 3, pp. 1679–1683 (2000)
21. TheMathWorks. Code verification and run-time error detection through abstract interpretation. Technical report (2008)
22. Tripakis, S., Sofronis, C., Caspi, P., Curic, A.: Translating discrete-time Simulink to lustre. ACM Transactions on Embedded Computing Systems (TECS) 4(4), 779–818 (2005)

A Formal Model for Constraint-Based Deployment Calculation and Analysis for Fault-Tolerant Systems

Klaus Becker[1], Bernhard Schätz[1], Michael Armbruster[2], and Christian Buckl[1]

[1] fortiss GmbH, An-Institut Technische Universität München,
Guerickestr. 25, 80805 München, Germany
{becker,schaetz,buckl}@fortiss.org
[2] Siemens AG, Corporate Research and Technologies,
Otto-Hahn-Ring 6, 81730 München, Germany
michael.armbruster@siemens.com

Abstract. In many embedded systems like in the automotive domain, safety-critical features are increasingly realized by software. Some of these features are often required to behave fail-operational, meaning that they must stay alive even in the presence of random hardware failures.

We propose a new fault-tolerant SW/HW architecture for electric vehicles with inherent safety capabilities that enable fail-operational features. In this paper, we introduce a constraint-based approach to calculate valid deployments of mixed-critical software components to the execution nodes. To avoid harm, faulty execution nodes have to be isolated from the remaining system. We treat the isolations of execution nodes and the required changes to the deployment to keep those software components alive that realize fail-operational features. The affected software components have to be resumed on intact execution nodes. However, the remaining system resources may become insufficient to execute the full set of software components after an isolation of an execution node. Hence, some components might have to be deactivated, meaning that features might get lost. Our approach allows to formally analyze which subset of features can still be provided after one or more isolations. We present an arithmetic system model with formal constraints of the deployment-problem that can be solved by a SMT-Solver. We evaluate our approach by showing an example problem and its solution.

Keywords: Fault-Tolerance, Fail-Operational, Mixed-Critical, Deployment, Dependability, SMT-Solver.

1 Introduction and Motivation

Many embedded systems are operated in safety-critical environments, in which unhandled faults could cause harmful system failures. This requires that those systems react on faults properly. However, handling faults by invalidating faulty data and going into a fail-safe state may cause the loss of some provided features. This is not acceptable for features that require fail-operational behavior.

D. Giannakopoulou and G. Salaün (Eds.): SEFM 2014, LNCS 8702, pp. 205–219, 2014.
© Springer International Publishing Switzerland 2014

To increase their dependability, systems must be able to resume affected features without any service interruption. If system resources get lost due to hardware failures, the remaining resources should be used efficiently to keep alive those features with the highest demand with respect to safety, reliability and availability, as defined in [1]. For instance, if an execution node becomes faulty and has to be isolated from the remaining system, another execution node has to be able to provide that features that were provided by the faulty node. However, as the remaining system-resources may become insufficient to provide the full set of features, it may be needed to explicitly deactivate some low priority features. This results in a graceful degradation of the system.

We propose a new centralized HW/SW platform for vehicles, that provides inherent safety properties and supports fail-operational features without requiring mechanical fallbacks. In this paper, we address the calculation and analysis of the deployment of software components to the execution nodes inside the proposed architecture. However, with a rising number of software and hardware components, this deployment configuration becomes more and more complex and hard to manage manually. We therefore provide an automated configuration support for deployment decisions, ranging from a semi-automated to a fully-automated approach. Our approach is based on a formal system model and a set of formal constraints describing the validity of deployments with respect to the safety-concept. Model and constraints characterize an arithmetic problem that can be solved for instance by SMT-solvers.

The main contribution is an approach to calculate and analyze different reconfigurations of the deployment to become active after execution nodes become isolated. The set of active software components – and thus also the set of provided features – is automatically reduced when the remaining system resources become insufficient to provide the initial set of components. Components are deactivated based on their priorities, which can either be assigned manually or derived automatically. Our approach allows to formally analyze at design-time if the desired system and feature properties can be fulfilled, like which set of features can still be provided after one or multiple isolations. Analyzing the deactivations of single features allows to analyze the entire system degradation.

In section 2 we present the basic concepts of the proposed platform. Section 3 shows the main contribution of this paper, which is a formal model and a constraint-based approach to calculate valid deployments and to analyze which features can be provided after isolations of nodes. Section 4 contains an automotive example, evaluating the applicability of our approach. Related work is discussed in section 5 and the conclusion and future work is given in section 6.

2   Proposed System Architecture and Safety Concept

Fault-tolerance is the ability of a system to maintain control objectives despite the occurrence of a fault, while degradation of control performance may be accepted [2]. If a system should support fail-operational features, it has to be capable to absorb loss of execution nodes. We deploy multiple instances of software components redundantly to the execution nodes. This enables the system to absorb loss of execution nodes and results in features being fail-operational, meaning that features can continue operation in the presence of a limited number of hardware failures, while ensuring the absence of harm to the users or the environment. In the following sections we briefly introduce the main ideas of the proposed platform, needed to follow the deployment concept and constraints.

2.1 System Architecture

We tackle the development of a scalable, uniform, open and thus easily expandable base platform with the aim to reduce the complexity of automotive HW/SW architectures. The basic principles of this platform have been already presented in [3] and [4].

The proposed platform is composed by a scalable set of central execution nodes (also called *Duplex Control Computers* (DCCs)) and a set of peripheral execution nodes providing the physical sensing and actuating (also called Smart-Aggregates). The DCCs assemble the *Central Platform Computer* (CPC) and are connected to each other and to the Smart-Aggregates by redundant switched Ethernet-Links. The DCCs are homogeneous for flexibility in the deployment.

The proposed system has two different power supplies, named *red* and *blue*. Each execution node is supplied by either the red or the blue power supply. Hence, if one power-supply fails, only a subset of the execution nodes get lost and the residual nodes can continue the operation. As scheduling policy, we follow the concept of logical execution times [5], meaning that the software components are executed within fixed *cycles*. Each execution node provides a certain budget of time per cycle that can be used to execute application software components. In this paper, we assume a simplified model in which all software components are scheduled with the same rate in every cycle.

2.2 Fault-Model and Safety Concept

In this paper, we focus on so called *random hardware failures*, as defined in the ISO 26262 [6] as failures that can occur unpredictably during the lifetime of a hardware (HW) element and that follows a probability distribution. If such a random hardware failure exists in an execution node, this node has to be isolated from the remaining system to avoid harm. Our proposed platform ensures the detection of random hardware failures with a sufficient failure detection coverage. Sufficient means that the probability to become out-of-control is acceptably low to meet the quantitative safety-requirements of the ISO26262 [6]. We focus on how to handle detected failures by performing adaptions to the deployment to meet the requirements w.r.t. fail-operationality. We assume a state-transition time of $0s$ from a faulty to an isolated state. Only if these assumptions hold, the deployment considerations shown later in section 3 can be applied. More information about the Fault-Model is also provided in [7].

In the safety concept of the proposed platform, application software components (ASWCs) are grouped into so called *ASWC-Clusters*. This is done to reduce the complexity of fault detection and handling mechanisms at runtime.

The ASWC-Clusters get deployed to the execution nodes. Those ASWCs are mapped to the same ASWC-Cluster that have the same *Automotive Safety Integrity Level* (ASIL) and the same requirements to behave *fail-operational*.

Each ASWC has multiple safety goals, while each safety goal has an assigned *fault-tolerance time* (*FTT*). The FTT defines the time period that a component can fail to deliver its service without harming the safety goal. The smallest of these *FTT*s is the so called *minFTT* of an ASWC. The *minFTT* of an ASWC-Cluster is the smallest *minFTT* of the ASWCs that are mapped to this cluster.

Each ASWC-Cluster has at least one actively deployed instance in the initial deployment. If the cluster is required to be fail-operational, a second instance is deployed. In this case, the first instance is called the *master* and the second instance is called the *slave*. We distinguish between hot-standby and cold-standby *slaves* (also known as hot/cold spare). A hot-standby is active (executed in schedule), while a cold-standby is passive (only in memory, not executed in schedule). In the deployment, we consider this by distinguishing between *activations* (active deployments, ASWCs are executed) and *allocations* (inactive/passive deployments). The decision whether to create a hot- or a cold standby slave depends on the *minFTT* of the ASWC-Cluster compared to the *fault-recovery time* (FRT) of the proposed platform. We assume the FRT to be a defined constant, as a maximum FRT can be shown because the platform ensures a worst-case time between fault-detection, confirmation and reconfiguration. In this paper, we neglect the time that is required to switch a cold-standby slave to become a master. With the proposed platform, a maximum switchover time can be verifed. We actually aim on a switchover-time of max. 50ms.

There exist several constraints for the deployment given by the safety concept. For instance, if an ASWC-Cluster has a master and a slave, master and slave have to be deployed onto two execution nodes with different power-supplies to avoid that both instances get lost simultaneously when a power-supply fails.

Depending on the required level of fail-operationality, meaning how many HW-failures have to be survived, additional inactive instances of a cluster are deployed. If the execution node of the master gets isolated, the slave becomes the master and if required, a passive instance becomes the new hot-standby slave. These mechanisms are presented in section 3 in a more detailed formal model.

3   Deployment Calculation and Analysis

We define the system properties and the deployment problem as shown in the following sections.

3.1   Formal System and Deployment Model

Definition 1. *A Vehicle* $\mathbb{V} = \langle F, S^A, H^A, \Phi \rangle$ *comprises a set of* Functional Features F, *an* Application Software Architecture S^A, *an* Execution Hardware Architecture H^A *and a* Configuration Φ.

Definition 2. *An Application Software Architecture $S^A = \langle S, SC \rangle$ is composed by a set $S = \{s_1, ..., s_n\}$ of Application Software Components (ASWCs) and a set $SC = \{sc_1, ..., sc_q\}$ of ASWC-Clusters with $sc_i \subseteq S$ while $\forall i, j : sc_i \cap sc_j = \emptyset$ and $\bigcup_{i=1}^{q} sc_i = S$. We describe the mapping of $s \in S$ to $sc \in SC$ with $\alpha(s) \to \{sc_i \in SC \mid sc_i \text{ contains } s\}$ and $\alpha(sc) \to \{s_i \in S \mid s_i \text{ is mapped to } sc\}$.*

Definition 3. *The set of functional features $F = \{f_1, ..., f_m\}$ contains the features of the vehicle that can be recognized by the user. A feature is realized by one or more ASWCs and the involved Sensors and Actuators, while each ASWC contributes to realize one or more features. For $s \in S$ and $f \in F$, we define this relationship as $\chi(s) \to \{f_i \in F \mid s \text{ contributes to realize } f_i\}$ and $\chi(f) \to \{s_i \in S \mid f \text{ is partly realized by } s_i\}$.*

Definition 4. *An Execution Hardware Architecture $H^A = \langle E, L \rangle$ comprises execution nodes E and communication links $L = E \times E$ between these nodes. The set of execution nodes $E = E^C \cup E^A$ is composed by a set of central execution nodes $E^C = \{e_1, ..., e_k\}$ and a set of peripheral Smart-Aggregate nodes $E^A = \{e_{k+1}, ..., e_l\}$ with attached physical Sensors and Actuators. The set E^C is also called the Central Platform Computer (CPC).*

Definition 5. *The Configuration $\Phi = \langle \delta_P(SC), \delta_A(SC), \delta(SC) \rangle$ defines how ASWC-Clusters SC are deployed to execution nodes E, either passively (δ_P) or actively (δ_A). For $sc \in SC$, we define $\delta_P(sc) \to \{e_i \in E \mid sc \text{ is in memory of } e_i, \text{ but not executed on } e_i\}$, $\delta_A(sc) \to \{e_i \in E \mid sc \text{ is in memory of } e_i \text{ and executed on } e_i\}$ and $\delta(sc) = \delta_A(sc) \cup \delta_P(sc)$.*

Our deployment approach can either be applied to ASWCs or to ASWC-Clusters. The motivation to think in clusters and not in single ASWCs is that the definition of clusters reduces the complexity with regard to the amount of combinations to be considered for deployment and master-slave switchovers. Furthermore, the ASWCs within a cluster have a kind of stronger binding to each other. Thus, we aim on a deployment of ASWCs which are bound to one cluster within the same execution node. An example for a binding quality is data-transport delay.

Fig. 1 shows a visualization of the given definitions, based on an example. Two features are realized by overall three ASWCs, while the third ASWCs s_3 contributes to both features. The three ASWCs are mapped to two different ASWC-Clusters, depending on a property *failOp* that defines the level of required fail-operationality of an ASWC. As cluster sc_1 contains ASWCs that are not required to behave fail-operational, it is deployed only once ($\delta_A(sc_1) = \{e_1\}$). The other cluster sc_2 contains an ASWC that is required to behave fail-operational ($\alpha(sc_2) = \{s_3\}$ and $failOp(s_3) = 1$). Hence, this cluster is deployed twice with one active *Master* ($\delta_A(sc_2) = \{e_2\}$) and one passive *cold-standby slave* ($\delta_P(sc_2) = \{e_1\}$). If a *hot-standby slave* would have been required, then it would hold that $\delta_A(sc_2) = \{e_1, e_2\}$, $\delta_P(sc_2) = \emptyset$.

ASWCs might contain invisible sub-components and internal communication channels. We don't model external communication channels between ASWCs in this paper for simplicity.

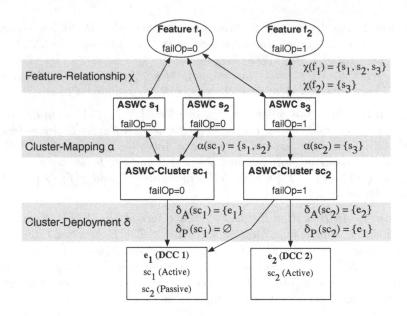

Fig. 1. Example for the definitions

3.2 Fixed Properties of the Deployment Model

Each ASWC $s_i \in S$ is defined by several properties. Property $wcet(S) \rightarrow \mathbb{N}^+$ defines the *Worst-Case Execution Time*. Property $asil(S) \rightarrow \{0..4\}$ defines the *Automotive Safety Integrity Level* (ASIL) of an ASWC [0: Quality-Management (QM), 1: ASIL-A, 2: ASIL-B, 3: ASIL-C, 4: ASIL-D]. Property $failOp(S) \rightarrow \mathbb{N}_0$ defines the fail-operational level [0: non fail-operational, n: s_i has to be provided after n isolations]. The minimum of the fault-tolerance times of an ASWC for its different safety goals is defined by $minFTT(S) \rightarrow \mathbb{N}^+$.

As defined in section 2.2, the vehicle property $frt(\mathbb{V}) \rightarrow \mathbb{N}^+$ defines the *fault-recovery time* of the vehicle $\mathbb{V}$. The frt has influence on whether the slaves are deployed as hot or as cold-standby slaves, depending on their $minFTT$.

For execution nodes $e \in E$, the following properties are defined. The property $totalTimeBudget(E) \rightarrow \mathbb{N}^+$ defines the budget of time that is provided in each cycle to execute the ASWCs. We assume here that ASWCs are executed in every cycle. The property $powerSupply(E) \rightarrow \{0,1\}$ defines the power supply of the execution node [0: Blue, 1: Red]. Finally, the property $isolated(E) \rightarrow \{0,1\}$ defines if the execution node $e_i \in E$ is isolated in the current solution instance. We do not model the amounts of required and provided volatile and non-volatile memory here for simplicity. These are handled in a similar manner as the WCET and the time-budget.

3.3   Solution Properties of the Model

In this section we describe the model-properties that represent the solution of the deployment problem.

The properties of ASWC-Clusters $sc \in SC$ depend on the mapped ASWCs. Properties $asil(SC) \rightarrow \{0..4\}$ and $failOp(SC) \rightarrow \mathbb{N}_0$ define the ASIL and the fail-operational level of a cluster. It is ensured by constraints that $\forall s_i \in \alpha(sc)$: $asil(sc) = asil(s_i)$ and $failOp(sc) = failOp(s_i)$. Property $minFTT(SC) \rightarrow \mathbb{N}^+$ is the minimum of all the $minFTT(s_i)$ for $s_i \in \alpha(sc)$. Property $sumWcets(SC)$ is defined to be equal to $\sum_{s_i \in \alpha(sc)} wcet(s_i)$. To cover deactivation scenarios that might be required after isolations of central execution nodes, each $sc \in SC$ has additionally the following properties:

- $hotStandbySlaveReq(SC) \rightarrow \{0, 1\}$:   indicates if a hot-standby *slave* is required. The valuation is derived by considering $minFTT(sc)$ and $frt(\mathbb{V})$
- $hotStandbySlavePresent(SC) \rightarrow \{0, 1\}$:   indicates if a required hot-standby *slave* can be established
- $masterPresent(SC) \rightarrow \{0, 1\}$:   indicates if the *master* can be established

The last two properties may change after isolations of execution nodes. Finally, each cluster has the properties $prioPointsMaster(SC) \rightarrow \mathbb{N}^+$ and $prioPointsHotSlave(SC) \rightarrow \mathbb{N}^+$ storing priorities of actively deployed instances of clusters. These are used to construct an order in which the cluster instances should be deactivated in case resources become insufficient. We derive the priorities depending on $asil(SC)$ and $failOp(SC)$ (cf. Listing 3). However, they could also be set in a different manner depending on the user's needs.

For execution nodes $e \in E$, $usedTimeBudget(E) \rightarrow \mathbb{N}_0$ is defined to be equal to $\sum_{sc_j \in SC \mid e \in \delta_A(sc_j)} sumWcets(sc_j)$, which is the sum of the $wcet(s)$ of those ASWCs that are active on execution node e. A constraint ensures that $\forall e \in E$: $usedTimeBudget(e) \leq totalTimeBudget(e)$.

On vehicle-level, the property $prioSumAllSCs(\mathbb{V}) \rightarrow \mathbb{N}$ is defined as the sum of the priorities of the actively deployed ASWC-Clusters in the initial deployment without any isolation. In addition, the property $prioSumActiveSCs(\mathbb{V}) \rightarrow \mathbb{N}$ is the sum of the priorities of all ASWC-Clusters $SC' \subseteq SC$ that are actively deployed in the current system situation with some isolations.

Finally, the following two properties define the solution matrices that contain the mapping of ASWCs S to ASWC-Clusters SC and the deployment of the ASWC-Clusters SC to the execution nodes E.

- $map(S, SC) \rightarrow \{0, 1\}$:   Mapping of ASWCs $s \in S$ to ASWC-Clusters $sc \in SC$. [0: $s \notin \alpha(sc)$, 1: $s \in \alpha(sc)$].
- $deploy(SC, E) \rightarrow \{0, 1, 2, 3\}$:   Deployment of ASWC-Clusters $sc \in SC$ (and it's ASWCs $s_i \in \alpha(sc)$) to execution nodes $e \in E$. [0: $e \notin \delta(sc)$, 1: $e \in \delta_P(sc)$, 2: $e \in \delta_A(sc)$ while sc is a *master* on e, 3: $e \in \delta_A(sc)$ while sc is a hot-standby *slave* on e]

Notice that the decision if an ASWC-Cluster instance becomes a master or a hot-standby slave is done dynamically at runtime by a Platform-Management component of the Runtime-Environment (RTE) of the proposed vehicle platform. This is, because there are also other reasons beside node-isolations that may lead to the deactivation of a master. Hence, the calculated master/slave deployments as shown in this paper are not used as predefined runtime-configuration, but at design-time to statically analyze the fail-operational runtime-behavior. It can be analyzed under which circumstances it is possible at runtime to keep a master respectively a slave alive in the presence of faults that lead to the isolation of execution nodes.

3.4 Basic Deployment Constraints

In this section we describe some exemplary constraints that limit the solution space of the calculated deployments to ensure the properties listed in section 2.2.

To define the constraints, we setup an arithmetic model. We use two conditional functions in the constraints. Function $Ite(I, T, E)$ has three parameters. The first parameter describes an *if-clause* I. If I is true, then the second parameter T is used in the constraint, else the third parameter E. The second function that we use is $Implies(I, T)$, which is true for $(\neg I \vee T)$. Both functions are provided by the SMT-Solver.

Listing 1 shows some basic constraints of the described deployment model.

```
1  ∀sc ∈ SC:
2  ∑_{e∈E} Ite(deploy(sc,e) ≠ 0, 1, 0) = failOp(sc) + 1
3
4  hotStandbySlaveReq(sc) = Ite(
5     And(failOp(sc) > 0, minFTT(sc) ≤ frt(V)), 1, 0)
6
7  Implies(  masterPresent(sc) = 1,
8            ∑_{e∈E} Ite(deploy(sc,e) = 2, 1, 0)  =  1)
```

Listing 1. Some basic constraints

The constraint in line 2 ensures the correct number of allocations of ASWC-Clusters. Clusters with $failOp(sc) = n$ have to be allocated $n + 1$ times. Hence, $|\delta(sc)| = n + 1$.

Lines 4-5 show the constraint that defines when a hot-standby slave is required for a ASWC-Cluster. If the cluster contains fail-operational ASWCs and has a $minFTT$ smaller or equal than the vehicle's fault-recovery time (frt), then a hot-standby slave is required for that cluster.

The constraint in lines 7-8 controls the presence of the master for each cluster. If a master is present, it is ensured that it exists exactly once. To deactivate a master, $masterPresent(sc)$ has to become 0. This allows to give feedback that sc cannot be executed in the current solution.

The hot-standby slaves are handled similarly by considering the property $hotStandbySlaveReq(SC)$. Additional constraints ensure for instance that if both the master and the hot-standby slave are present, then they have to be active on two execution nodes with different power-supplies.

3.5 Reconfigurations after Isolations

Let $E_f^C \subset E^C$ be the set of isolated execution nodes. For all $e_i \in E_f^C$, we set $isolated(e_i) = 1$. It is ensured by constraints that no ASWC-Cluster is activated anymore on one of the isolated execution nodes.

Definition 6. *A Platform-Availability-Graph (PAG) is a directed acyclic graph $G = (V, E)$. Each vertex V represents a set of alive central execution nodes $E_a^C = E^C \setminus E_f^C$. The edges E describe a transition between two vertices, meaning that some $e_i \in E^C$ move from E_a^C to E_f^C. A transition happens due to an isolation or if a power-supply disappears.*

Fig. 2(a) shows an example CPC containing four central execution nodes (DCCs) and the two power-supplies (red and blue).

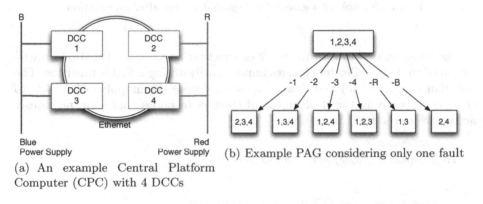

(a) An example Central Platform Computer (CPC) with 4 DCCs

(b) Example PAG considering only one fault

Fig. 2. Platform-Availability-Graph (PAG)

When considering only one fault, the PAG looks like shown in Fig. 2(b). The vertices are labeled with the Ids i of the alive nodes $e_i \in E_a^C$. The edges are labeled with the Id i of that $e_i \in E_f^C$ which has recently been isolated respectively with the power-supply (R, B) that has recently been broken down.

Fig. 3 shows how the deployment from Fig. 1 is reconfigured in case DCC 2 has to be isolated. The passive cold-standby slave of cluster sc_2 has to be activated, because the former master gets lost. Assuming that sc_1 and sc_2 cannot run simultaneously on e_1 due to resource constraints, sc_1 has to be passivated. This is allowed as sc_1 contains ASWCs that have no requirement to be active after a fault ($failOp = 0$). However, as sc_1 becomes passivated, feature f_1 cannot be provided anymore, because two of the three ASWCs that realize f_1 are passivated. Notice that all requirements concerning fail-operationality are met in this example.

We now show some formal constraints that describe the validity of follow-up deployments that become active after isolations of execution-nodes, forcing a transition in the PAG.

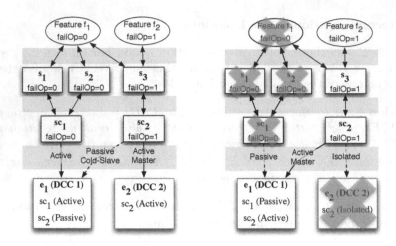

Fig. 3. Example of a gracefully degraded system after an isolation

The constraints shown in Listing 2 ensure that no present allocation or activation of an ASWC-Cluster changes unnecessarily during a PAG-transition. The notation $map_{prev}(s, sc)$ and $deploy_{prev}(sc, e)$ denote the mapping of ASWC to clusters respectively the deployment of clusters to nodes that were previously active before the PAG-transition.

```
1  ∀s ∈ S,   ∀sc ∈ SC :
2  Implies(map_prev(s, sc) = 1,   map(s, sc) = 1)
3
4  ∀sc ∈ SC,   ∀e ∈ E :
5  Implies(deploy_prev(sc, e) = 0,   deploy(sc, e) = 0)
6
7  ∀sc ∈ SC,   ∀e_m, e_s ∈ E :
8  Implies(And(deploy_prev(sc, e_m) = 2, deploy_prev(sc, e_s) = 3,
9               isolated(e_m) = 1, isolated(e_s) = 0,
10              masterPresent(sc) = 1),
11         deploy(sc, e_s) = 2)
```

Listing 2. Constraints for valid post-isolation deployments

Lines 1-2 ensure that the mapping of ASWCs to the ASWC-Clusters does not change. Lines 4-5 ensure that no reallocation of an ASWC-Cluster is performed after a PAG-Transition. Lines 7-11 ensure that if a master and a hot-standby slave were present but the execution node of the master has been isolated, then the former hot-standby slave should become the new master. The other cases, like when only a master is required, are handled in a similar manner.

In order to decide about the deactivation order for the ASWC-Clusters, each instance of a cluster gets assigned a priority. Listing 3 exemplarily shows how the cluster-priorities can be calculated and how these are summed up to the vehicle priority-points $prioSumAllSCs(\mathbb{V})$ and $prioSumActiveSCs(\mathbb{V})$.

```
 1  ∀sc ∈ SC :
 2  prioPointsMaster(sc) = asil(sc) + failOp(sc) + 2
 3
 4  prioPointsHotSlave(sc) = Ite(hotStandBySlaveReq(sc) = 1 ,
 5                               asil(sc) + failOp(sc) + 1 ,  0))
 6
 7  prioSumAllSCs(V) = ∑_{sc∈SC}(prioPointsMaster(sc)
 8                            + prioPointsHotSlave(sc))
 9
10  prioSumActiveSCs(V) = ∑_{sc∈SC} ∑_{e∈E}(
11    Ite( deploy(sc, e) = 2 ,
12         prioPointsMaster(sc),
13         Ite(deploy(sc, e) = 3,  prioPointsHotSlave(sc),  0)))
```

Listing 3. Calculation of the priority points of the single deployed instances

Finally, these priority-points can be used to decide which cluster instances have to be deactivated when the system resources become insufficient. Listing 4 depicts one simple algorithm to do this.

```
 1  priorityReduction := 0
 2  while True:
 3    s.push()
 4    s.add(prioSumAllSCs(V) − priorityReduction
 5       = prioSumActiveSCs(V))
 6    result := s.check()
 7    s.pop()
 8    if result = sat:      break
 9    priorityReduction := priorityReduction + 1
10    if prioSumActiveSCs(V) = 0: exit
```

Listing 4. Determine the set of deployable instances

Before executing this algorithm, all deployment constraints and the set of isolated execution nodes are defined. When a PAG-transition is calculated, some solution properties of the former deployment are set as fixed properties for the follow-up deployment, e.g., to avoid undesired changes in the deployment.

Line 3 pushes the already set constraints onto a stack. Line 4-5 add a new constraint defining the desired value of *prioSumActiveSCs* in the solution. Afterwards, the problem is checked and the additional constraint is removed again in line 7. If there exists a solution for the problem, line 8 evaluates to *True* and the algorithm terminates successfully with a valid follow-up deployment. If no solution exists, *prioSumActiveSCs* is decreased until a valid solution is found. Decreasing the value of *prioSumActiveSCs* allows to deactivate those cluster instances whose priorities sum up to *prioSumAllSCs*(V) − *prioSumActiveSCs*(V). This mechanism is repeated as long as the property *prioSumActiveSCs*(V) becomes zero. When this is the case, the algorithm exits unsuccessfully, meaning that no valid follow-up deployment exists (line 10). Instead of this linear search, also a more efficient binary-search or other algorithms could be applied, but this was not in focus of our work. We implemented the system model, constraints and algorithms using the Z3 SMT-Solver [8].

4   Evaluation and Example

In this section we show the applicability of our approach on a simplified example from the automotive domain. Consider the following features and ASWCs:

Feature f_i	ASWCs s_i of $\chi(f_i)$	asil(s_i)	failOp(s_i)	wcet(s_i) in ms
f_1 : Infotainment	s_1 : Infotainment	QM	0	2
f_2 : Energy-	s_2 : RemainingRangeCalc	A	0	0.7
Management	s_3 : EnergyEfficiencyAssist	A	0	0.3
f_3 : ADAS-A	s_4 : AdasSwc1	C	0	1.7
	s_5 : AdasSwc2	D	1	1
f_4 : ADAS-B	s_5 : AdasSwc2	D	1	1
f_5 : Manual-	s_6 : ManualAcceleration	D	3	1
Driving	s_7 : ManuelBraking	D	3	1
	s_8 : ManualSteering	D	3	0.5

The features f_3 and f_4 are placeholders for some Advanced Driver Assistance Systems (ADAS), like an ACC or automatic parking. Let f_4 be required to stay active after a failure, but f_3 is not required to be active after a failure. As ASWC s_5 contributes to realize both f_3 and f_4, it has $failOp(s_5) = 1$. As ASWC s_4 only realizes f_3, it is sufficient that $failOp(s_4) = 0$.

In this example, five ASWC-Clusters $\{sc_1, ..., sc_5\}$ are established. The clusters are: $\alpha(sc_1) = \{s_1\}$, $\alpha(sc_2) = \{s_2, s_3\}$, $\alpha(sc_3) = \{s_4\}$, $\alpha(sc_4) = \{s_5\}$ and $\alpha(sc_5) = \{s_6, s_7, s_8\}$. Notice that ASWC s_5 is only in one cluster, although it contributes to two features.

Considering a CPC with four execution nodes (DCCs) as shown in Fig. 2(a), a valid initial deployment for the example is shown in Fig. 4(a). Fig. 4(b) shows the follow-up deployment for the case that DCC 1 has been isolated. The colors (red/blue) of the execution nodes denote their attached power-supply.

We assume here that $minFTT(s_i) \leq frt(\mathbb{V})$ for the fail-operational ASWCs. Hence, hot-standby slaves are required. As provided execution time of the execution nodes per cycle, we assume $totalTimeBudget(e_i) = 4ms$. It can be seen in both Fig. 4(a) and Fig. 4(b) that $\forall e_i \in E : usedTimeBudget(e_i) \leq totalTimeBudget(e_i)$.

In the initial deployment, all clusters can be deployed as required. After the isolation of e_1 (= DCC 1), the master of cluster sc_4 gets lost and its slave on e_2 becomes the new master. As $failOp(sc_4) = 1$, no new slave is created as it is not required that sc_4 is still present after the next isolation. Furthermore, the slave of cluster sc_5 gets lost. As $failOp(sc_5) = 3$, an inactive instance of sc_5 must be activated to serve as new slave to prepare for the next isolation. The new slave of sc_5 can only be activated on e_3 and not on e_2, because master and slave must not depend on the same power-supply. However, to be able to execute cluster sc_5 on execution node e_3, cluster sc_3 has to be deactivated as the sum of the WCETs of sc_3 and sc_5 would exceed the time-budget of e_3. The deactivation of sc_3 forces the deactivation of feature f_3, as $\alpha(sc_3) = \{s_4\} \subseteq \chi(f_3)$.

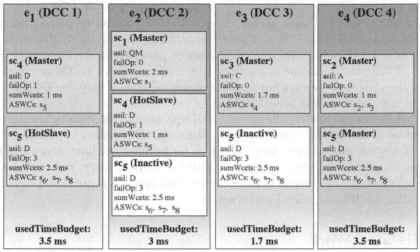

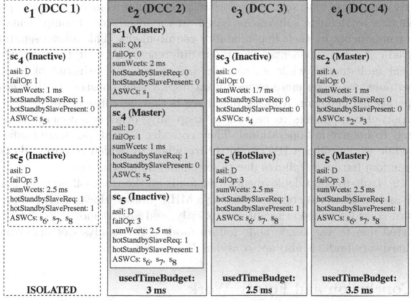

(a) Initial deployment for the example

(b) Followup deployment after DCC1 has been isolated

Fig. 4. Example about an initial and a followup deployment

The sum of priority points in the initial solution was 40. The loss of the master of sc_3 and the slave of sc_4 forces a loss of 11 priority points, because $prioPointsMaster(sc_3) = 5$ and $prioPointsHotSlave(sc_4) = 6$. Hence, when DCC1 is isolated, only 29 priority points can be provided by the system (cf. Fig. 4(b)). When this procedure is continued by isolating more DCCs in arbitrary order, the cluster sc_5 always has a master instance, even if only one DCC is left. This is important as $failOp(sc_5) = 3$.

The designer can analyze the system's fail-operational behavior by considering the set of deactivated features for each situation. This allows to analyze if all desired system and feature properties can be fulfilled, without executing the system. A valid initial deployment is calculated automatically, but can also be changed manually in order to analyze the systems graceful degradation scenarios depending on different initial deployments.

5   Related Work

In this section, we discuss related work of deployment approaches with focus on safety and fail-operationality.

In [9], the authors show an approach to analyze graceful degradation. They use a utility function to measure the set of active features. This can be seen as quite similar to our sums of priorities. To reduce complexity, they group components by defining subsystems based on the interfaces of components. We group components by their dependability requirements. This allows separation of mixed-critical components. The main differences are that they consider a fail-silent fault-model, while we consider fail-operational behavior of features. Furthermore, we focus more explicitly on deployment constraints that ensure fail-operational behavior. Another difference is that we consider the explicit deactivation of components to be able to keep alive other components that are required to behave fail-operational. They consider a fixed hardware configuration, while we consider a HW-Architecture whose provided resources decrease after random hardware failures due to execution node isolations.

In [10], fault-tolerant deployments with focus on the trade-off between performance and reliability are optimized using a MILP-Solver. However, the approach does not consider mixed criticalities explicitly, and also at most 1 replication is supported due to the single node failure model. The analysis of deployments after hardware-faults is also not considered.

6   Conclusion and Future Work

In this paper, we introduced a formal model of mixed-critical systems including the relationship of functional features and software components realizing the functional features. A set of formal arithmetic constraints describe valid deployments of the software components to a fault-tolerant HW/SW platform for vehicles. Based on the model and the constraints, an approach to calculate and analyze valid deployments of mixed-critical components was provided.

The analysis focuses on the fail-operational behavior of features in the presence of random hardware failures. It can be analyzed which features can be uphold depending on the available set of execution nodes. We implemented the model as input for an SMT-Solver, which calculates the deployment solutions. We analyzed which components and features have to become inactive after certain failures. An evaluation was shown by an automotive example.

As future work, we are going to include communication channels between components into the model. Also, we want to treat the integration of new software components into existing deployments during the use case of extensions of the vehicle by new functional features. Finally, we want to evaluate the scalability of our approach based on the layout of a concept car that we construct.

Acknowledgments. This work is partially funded by the German Federal Ministry for Economic Affairs and Energy (BMWi) under grant no. 01ME12009 through the project RACE (Robust and Reliant Automotive Computing Environment for Future eCars) (http://www.projekt-race.de/).

References

1. Avizienis, A., Laprie, J., Randell, B., Landwehr, C.: Basic concepts and taxonomy of dependable and secure computing. IEEE Trans. on Dependable and Secure Computing (1), 11–33 (2004)
2. Blanke, M., Staroswiecki, M., Wu, N.E.: Concepts and methods in fault-tolerant control. In: Proceedings of the American Control Conf., vol. 4. IEEE (2001)
3. Sommer, S., Camek, A., Becker, K., Buckl, C., Knoll, A., Zirkler, A., Fiege, L., Armbruster, M., Spiegelberg, G.: Race: A centralized platform computer based architecture for automotive applications. In: IEEE Vehicular Electronics Conference / Int. Electric Vehicle Conference (VEC-IEVC) (2013)
4. Armbruster, M., Fiege, L., Freitag, G., Schmid, T., Spiegelberg, G., Zirkler, A.: Ethernet-Based and Function-Independent Vehicle Control-Platform: Motivation, Idea and Technical Concept Fulfilling Quantitative Safety-Requirements from ISO 26262. In: Adv. Microsystems for Automotive Applications (AMAA), pp. 91–107 (2012)
5. Henzinger, T.A., Horowitz, B., Kirsch, C.M.: Giotto: A time-triggered language for embedded programming. In: Henzinger, T.A., Kirsch, C.M. (eds.) EMSOFT 2001. LNCS, vol. 2211, pp. 166–184. Springer, Heidelberg (2001)
6. International Organization for Standardization: ISO/DIS 26262-1 - Road vehicles - Functional safety, Part 1 Glossary. Technical report, ISO/TC 22 (2011)
7. Becker, K., Armbruster, M., Schätz, B., Buckl, C.: Deployment Calculation and Analysis for a Fail-Operational Automotive Platform. In: 1st Workshop on Engineering Dependable Systems of Systems (EDSoS) (2014)
8. de Moura, L., Bjørner, N.: Z3: An efficient SMT solver. In: Ramakrishnan, C.R., Rehof, J. (eds.) TACAS 2008. LNCS, vol. 4963, pp. 337–340. Springer, Heidelberg (2008)
9. Shelton, C., Koopman, P., Nace, W.: A framework for scalable analysis and design of system-wide graceful degradation in distributed embedded systems. In: Int. Workshop on Object-Oriented Real-Time Dependable Systems (WORDS), pp. 156–163. IEEE (2003)
10. Boone, B., De Turck, F., Dhoedt, B.: Automated deployment of distributed software components with fault tolerance guarantees. In: 6th Int. Conf. on Software Engineering Research, Management and Applications (SERA), pp. 21–27. IEEE (2008)

Optimising the ProB Model Checker for B Using Partial Order Reduction*

Ivaylo Dobrikov and Michael Leuschel

Institut für Informatik, Heinrich-Heine Universität Düsseldorf
Universitätsstr. 1, 40225 Düsseldorf, Germany
{dobrikov,leuschel}@cs.uni-duesseldorf.de

Abstract. Partial order reduction has been very successful at combatting the state explosion problem [4], [9] for lower-level formalisms, but has thus far made hardly any impact for model checking higher-level formalisms such as B, Z or TLA$^+$. This paper attempts to remedy this issue in the context of the increasing importance of Event-B, with its much more fine-grained events and thus increased potential for event-independence and partial order reduction. This paper provides a detailed description of a partial order reduction in ProB. The technique is evaluated on a variety of models. Additionally, the implementation of the method is discussed, which contains new constraint-based analyses.

Keywords: Model Checking, Partial Order Reduction, Static Analysis, Event-B.

1 Introduction

PROB [15] is a toolset for validating systems formalised in B, Event-B, CSP, TLA+ and Z. Initially developed for B, PROB comprises an animator, a model checker, and a refinement checker. Using the PROB model checker for consistency checking of B and Event-B models is a convenient way of searching for errors in the model. In contrast to interactive theorem provers, model checking performs tasks like invariant and deadlock freedom checking automatically.

B offers a variety of data structures and B models are often infinite state. Making such a B machine manageable for model checking requires setting bounds on the types of the variables. However, even systems with finite types can have very large state spaces. Therefore, applying various optimisation techniques is essential for practical model checking of B or Event-B specifications.

Partial order reduction reduces the state space by taking advantage of independence between actions. The reduction relies on choosing only a subset of all enabled actions in each reachable state of the state space. In the process of choosing such a subset, certain requirements have to be satisfied so that no new error states (deadlocks) are introduced and no important executions for the verification of the underlying system are pruned. There are several theories [8], [12], [20]

---

* This research is being carried out as part of the DFG funded research project GEPAVAS.

D. Giannakopoulou and G. Salaün (Eds.): SEFM 2014, LNCS 8702, pp. 220–234, 2014.
© Springer International Publishing Switzerland 2014

ensuring the soundness of such a type of reduction. Our implementation of partial order reduction uses the ample set theory which is suggested as a method for partial order reduction in [4], [8], [9].

Our optimisation uses a static analysis for determining the relations between each pair of operations or events in a B or Event-B machine, respectively. The static analysis is executed prior to the model checking and is based on both syntactic and new constraint-based analyses. These analyses are used for discovering the mutual influences of actions inside the model. In this paper we present an implementation of partial order reduction in the standard PROB model checker [15] for the formalisms B [1] and Event-B [2]. In addition, we evaluate the implementation on several case study models, and discuss the implementation and its limitations. For practical reasons, we will concentrate our review of the implementation of partial order reduction on Event-B only.

Indeed, Event-B events are much more fine-grained than typical operations in classical B (e.g. an if-then-else is decomposed into two separate events in Event-B). As such, the potential for finding independent events and partial order reduction is greater. Our intuition is that the more fine-grained nature of events in Event-B should dramatically increase the potential for partial order reduction.

In the next section, we give a brief overview of the Event-B formalism and consistency checking algorithm in PROB, as well as basic definitions and notation are introduced. In Section 3, we discuss and define formally relations between events that are relevant for this work. Section 4 presents the method and the algorithm. The evaluation and the discussion of the implementation are given in Section 5. The related work is outlined in Section 6. Finally, we discuss future improvements and features for the reduced state space search, and draw the conclusions of our work.

2   Preliminaries

Event-B. Event-B is a formal language for modelling and analysing of hardware and software systems. The formal development of a system in Event-B is a state-based approach using two types of components for the description of the system: contexts and machines.

The machines represent the dynamic part of the model and each machine is comprised primarily of variables, invariants, and events. The variables are typecast and constrained by the invariants. The variables determine the states of the machine. In turn, the states of the machine are related to each other by means of the events. Each event consists of two main parts: guards and actions. Formally, an event can be described as follows:

$$\textbf{event } e \; = \; \textbf{any } t \textbf{ where } G(x,t) \textbf{ then } S(x,t,x') \textbf{ end}$$

In the definition above, x and x' stand for the evaluation of the variables before and after the execution of the event e, respectively. The parameters t in the **any** clause are typecast and restricted in the enabling predicate $G(x,t)$ of the event. The enabling predicate of an event e will be often denoted as the guard of e.

The actions part $S(x, t, x')$ of an event is composed of a number of assignments to state variables. When the event is executed, all assignments in $S(x, t, x')$ are completed simultaneously. All non-assigned variables remain unaltered.

The event e is said to be enabled in a particular state s of the machine if $G(x, t)$ holds for the current evaluation of the variables of s. Otherwise, we say that the event e is disabled in s.

Notation and Basic Definitions. When we talk about enabled events in a particular state s, we mean all events whose enabling predicates hold in s. The set of all events that are enabled in a state s will be denoted by $enabled(s)$.

By definition, an event in Event-B may have parameters and non-deterministic assignments. Thus, in some state s an event e can have several representations, i.e. there is more than one successor state s' such that $s \xrightarrow{e} s'$. In that case, we say that e is a non-deterministic event. For simplicity, from now on we will assume that each event is *deterministic*. However, the optimisation in this work has been implemented for the general case where non-determinism is present.

An event is called a *stutter* event if it preserves the truth value of each atomic proposition of the property being checked. By property we mean an LTL formula or invariant of an Event-B machine. Formally, an event e is stuttering w.r.t. a property ϕ if for each transition $s \xrightarrow{e} s'$ it is fulfilled that for each atomic proposition p of ϕ either $s \models p$ and $s' \models p$ or $s \not\models p$ and $s' \not\models p$.

The implementation of the partial order reduction technique presented in this work is realised by the ample set theory. The reduction of the state space happens by choosing a subset of $enabled(s)$ in each state s. These subsets we will denote by $ample(s)$. In the context of partial order reduction, a state s is then said to be *fully expanded* if $ample(s) = enabled(s)$.

The Consistency Checking Algorithm. Since the main contribution of this work is the optimisation of the consistency checking algorithm for Event-B and B, we will give a quick overview of it (Algorithm 1).

The pseudo code in Algorithm 1 describes a graph traversal algorithm for exhaustive error search in a directed transition system. All unexplored nodes in the state space are stored in a standard queue data structure $Queue$ while running the consistency check for the particular Event-B machine. By popping unexplored states from the front or the end of the queue a depth-first search or a breadth-first search through $Graph$ can be simulated, respectively. A mixed depth-first/breadth-first search can be simulated by a randomised popping from the front and end of the queue. This is the standard search strategy in PROB.

Once an unexplored state has been chosen from the queue, it will be checked for errors by the function *error* (line 4). An error state, for example, can be a state that violates the invariant of the machine or that has no outgoing transitions.

If no error has been found in the current state, then it will be expanded. In this context, expansion means that all events from the current machine will be applied to the current state. Each event whose enabling predicate $G(x, t)$ holds for the current variables' evaluation will be executed and a possible new successor state will be generated. Subsequently, a new transition will be added to the state space (line 8) if not already present in $Graph$, and a new state $succ$

Algorithm 1. Consistency Checking

```
1  Queue := {root} ; Visited := {}; Graph := {};
2  while Queue is not empty do
3      state := get_state(Queue)
4      if error(state) then
5          return counter-example trace in Graph from root to state
6      else
7          for all succ,evt such that state ⟶ᵉᵛᵗ succ do        the code to
8              Graph := Graph ∪ {state ⟶ᵉᵛᵗ succ};            be optimised
9              if succ ∉ Visited then
10                 push_to_front(succ, Queue);
11                 Visited := Visited ∪ {succ}
12             end if
13         end for
14
15     end if
16 end while
17 return ok
```

---

will be adjoined to the queue (line 10) if not already visited. The algorithm runs as long as the queue is non-empty and no error state has been found.

Since the way of adding transitions to the state space will become slightly different in order to apply partial order reduction, the most relevant part of Algorithm 1 for this paper is thus the pseudo code in lines 7-13.

3   Event Relations

Finding out how the events of an Event-B machine are related to each other is a key step for applying partial order reduction. The simplest approach just analyses the syntactic structure. For this, we first need to determine the *read* and *write* sets for each event. For an event e, we denote by $read(e)$ the set of the variables that are read by e, and by $write(e)$ the set of the variables that are written by e. With $read_G(e)$ and $read_S(e)$ we will denote the sets of the variables that are read in the guard and in the actions part of the event e, respectively. To simplify the presentation we assume that each event is deterministic.

Introducing Independence. The most important event relation is independence. Formally, one can define independence between two events as follows:

Definition 1 (Independence)
Two events e_1 and e_2 are independent if for any state s with e_1, $e_2 \in enabled(s)$ it is satisfied that the executions $s \xrightarrow{e_1} s_1 \xrightarrow{e_2} s'$ and $s \xrightarrow{e_2} s_2 \xrightarrow{e_1} s''$ are feasible in the state space (enabledness), and additionally $s' = s''$ (commutativity).

Two events e_1 and e_2 are said to be *syntactically independent* if the following three conditions are satisfied:

(SI 1) The read set of e_1 is disjoint to the write set of e_2 $(read(e_1) \cap write(e_2) = \varnothing)$.

(SI 2) The write set of e_1 is disjoint to the read set of e_2 $(write(e_1) \cap read(e_2) = \varnothing)$.

(SI 3) The write sets of e_1 and e_2 are disjoint $(write(e_1) \cap write(e_2) = \varnothing)$.

Two syntactically independent events are independent by means of Definition 1 since no event can affect the guard of the other one (enabledness) and additionally the read and write sets of each of both events are disjoint to the write set of the other one (commutativity).

On the other hand, syntactical independence is obviously a quite coarse concept: two events of an Event-B machine can be independent even if some of the conditions (SI 1) - (SI 3) are violated. Take for example the following two events:

Example 1 (Event Dependency)

event $e_1 =$	**event** $e_2 =$
when	**when**
$\quad x \in \mathbb{N}$	$\quad z \geq 1 \wedge z \leq 10$
then	**then**
$\quad y := y + 1$	$\quad x := z \parallel z := z + 1$
end	**end**

Apparently, e_1 and e_2 are not syntactically independent as (SI 1) is violated $(read(e_1) \cap write(e_2) = \{x\})$. However, e_2 cannot affect the guard of e_1 because e_2 can assign to x only values between 1 and 10, and e_1 is enabled when x is a natural number. Since additionally $write(e_1) \cap read(e_2) = \varnothing$, it follows that the *enabledness* condition for independence for e_1 and e_2 is fulfilled. Further, no variable written by the one event will be read in the actions part of the other event and the write sets of e_1 and e_2 are disjoint. Thus, both events cannot interfere each other and herewith the *commutativity* condition for independence is fulfilled for e_1 and e_2. Hence, e_1 and e_2 are indeed independent events.

Since partial order reduction takes advantage of the independence between events, it is important to determine independence as accurately as possible. The higher the degree of independence in a system, the higher is the chance to reduce its state space significantly. This motivates the following, more precise approach to determine independence by using the PROB's constraint solving facilities.

Refining the Dependency Relation. We use the constraint solver to find feasible sequences of events for the analysed Event-B model. First, we define a procedure stating a Prolog predicate in PROB used for testing whether a given sequence of events is feasible. This will form the basis of our analysis.

Definition 2 (The *test_path* procedure)
*For a given Event-B machine M, let Φ and Ψ be B predicates for M, and $e_1, \ldots, e_n$ events of M. Then, we define **test_path** as follows:*

$$
test\_path(\Phi, \langle e_1, \ldots, e_n \rangle, \Psi) =
\begin{cases}
true & \text{if there is an execution } s \xrightarrow{e_1} \ldots \xrightarrow{e_n} s' \\
& \text{such that } s \models \Phi \text{ and } s' \models \Psi \\
false & \text{otherwise}
\end{cases}
$$

The predicates Φ and Ψ are used in order to constrain the search for possible test paths for M. If, for example, Φ and Ψ are both equal to the truth value $TRUE$ then $test\_path$ will return $true$ if the given sequence of events is possible from some valid state of M.

We can now refine our definition of independence. We introduce the binary relation $Dependent_M \subseteq Events_M \times Events_M$ which is intended to comprise all dependent pairs of events of a given Event-B machine M. Two events e_1 and e_2 will be denoted as dependent if $(e_1, e_2) \in Dependent_M$, otherwise they are considered to be independent. The dependency relation is defined as follows:

$$Dependent_M := \{(e, e') \mid (e, e') \in Events_M \times Events_M \wedge dependent(e, e')\},$$

where M is the observed Event-B machine, $Events_M$ is the set of events of M and $dependent$ is the procedure showed in Algorithm 2.

Algorithm 2. Determining Events' Dependency

---

1 **procedure boolean** dependent(e_1, e_2)
2   **if** $write(e_1) \cap write(e_2) \neq \varnothing$ **then**
3   **return** $true$ /* events are race dependent */
4   **else if** $(read(e_1) \cap write(e_2) = \varnothing \wedge write(e_1) \cap read(e_2) = \varnothing)$ **then**
5   **return** $false$ /* events are syntactically independent */
6   **else**
7   **return**
8       $(read_S(e_1) \cap write(e_2) = \varnothing \wedge write(e_1) \cap read_S(e_2) = \varnothing) \Rightarrow$
9       $((read_G(e_1) \cap write(e_2) \neq \varnothing \wedge test\_path(G_{e_1} \wedge G_{e_2}, \cdot \xrightarrow{e_2} \cdot, \neg G_{e_1}))$
10     $\vee (write(e_1) \cap read_G(e_2) \neq \varnothing \wedge test\_path(G_{e_2} \wedge G_{e_1}, \cdot \xrightarrow{e_1} \cdot, \neg G_{e_2}))$
11   **end if**

The procedure $dependent$ presents a refined strategy for determining the dependency between two events. The **else** branch in Algorithm 2 will be executed if at least one of the two events modifies a variable that is read by the other one. In order to test whether two events are independent, we need to check the two independence conditions *enabledness* and *commutativity*. The test for dependency is expressed by means of the predicate in lines 8-10. We are interested mainly in the case when the predicate evaluates to $false$. This is clearly fulfilled when the left side of the implication holds and the right side evaluates to $false$. In case the premise of the implication

$$(read_S(e_1) \cap write(e_2) = \varnothing \wedge write(e_1) \cap read_S(e_2) = \varnothing)$$

is satisfied, then it is assured that both events cannot affect each other (at this point we know that the write sets of e_1 and e_2 are disjoint) and thus the commutativity condition for independence is satisfied in case the events cannot disable each other. Once we know that e_1 and e_2 cannot interfere, we need to check the enabledness condition. The enabledness condition is tested by the two disjunction arguments in lines 9 and 10. If at least one of the arguments is fulfilled, we have deduced that e_1 and e_2 are indeed dependent. Otherwise, we have proven that e_1 and e_2 are independent.

Checking whether the events can disable one other is realised by means of the *test_path* procedure. If, for example, e_2 assigns a variable that is read in the guard G_{e_1} of e_1 (i.e. if $read_G(e_1) \cap write(e_2) \neq \varnothing$) then we can further check whether e_2 eventually can disable e_1. This can be additionally examined by searching for a possible transition $s \overset{e_2}{\rightarrow} s'$ such that e_1 and e_2 are enabled in s ($s \models G_{e_1} \wedge G_{e_2}$) and e_1 disabled in s' ($s' \models \neg G_{e_1}$). The call for this case is then $test\_path(G_{e_1} \wedge G_{e_2}, \cdot \overset{e_2}{\rightarrow} \cdot, \neg G_{e_1})$. If the result of the call is *true* then we have found a case in which e_2 can disable e_1 and thus inferred that e_1 and e_2 are dependent. Otherwise, we have shown that the enabling condition of e_1 cannot be affected by the execution of e_2.

The Enabling Relation. In addition to the independence of events, we are also interested in the particular way events may influence each other. Concretely, if event e_1 modifies some variables in the guard of event e_2 we are asking in which way the effect of e_1 may affect the guard of e_2. In that case, the possible direct influences of e_1 to e_2 can be *enabling* and *disabling*. The enabling relation is the residual relation needed for applying the optimisation technique in this work.

In the next section we are interested whether events can be enabled after the successively execution of a number of certain events. We will retain the enabling information between events in terms of a directed edge graph, defined as follows:

Definition 3 (Enable Graph). *An enable graph for an Event-B machine M is a directed edge graph* $EnableGraph_M = (V, E)$, *where* $V = Events_M$ *are the vertices and* $E = \{e_1 \mapsto e_2 \mid e_1, e_2 \in Events_M \wedge can\_enable(e_1, e_2)\}$ *the edges of* $EnableGraph_M$.

In Definition 3, $e_1 \mapsto e_2$ means that e_1 can enable e_2, while *can_enable* constitutes a procedure which returns *false* when $write(e_1) \cap read_G(e_2) = \varnothing$, otherwise tests if e_1 can enable e_2 by means of the *test_path* procedure. The call of *test_path* for testing whether e_1 may enable e_2 is then $test\_path(G_{e_1} \wedge \neg G_{e_2}, \cdot \overset{e_1}{\rightarrow} \cdot, G_{e_2})$.

4   Algorithm

In this section we introduce the theory of partial order reduction and the algorithm for the expansion of states by using the ample set method. The reduction of the original state space using ample sets is realised by choosing of a subset of all enabled events in each state.

The Ample Set Requirements. There are four requirements that should be satisfied by each ample set to make the reduction of the state space sound:

(A 1) Emptiness Condition
$ample(s) = \varnothing \Leftrightarrow enabled(s) = \varnothing$

(A 2) Dependency Condition
Along every finite execution in the original state space starting in s, an event dependent on $ample(s)$ cannot appear before some event $e \in ample(s)$ is executed.

(A 3) Stutter Condition

If $ample(s) \subsetneq enabled(s)$ then every $e \in ample(s)$ has to be a stutter event.

(A 4) Cycle Condition

For any cycle C in the reduced state space, if a state in C has an enabled event e, then there exists a state s in C such that $e \in ample(s)$.

The Need of Local Criteria for (A 2). We are interested in how efficiently each of the requirements can be checked. For a state s, the conditions (A 1) and (A 3) can be checked by examining the events in $ample(s)$. In contrast to conditions (A 1) and (A 3), condition (A 2) is a global property which requires for $ample(s)$ the examination of all possible executions (in the original state space) starting in s. A straightforward checking of (A 2) will demand the exploration of the original state space. Local criteria thus need to be given for (A 2) that facilitate an efficient computation of the condition.

For our implementation, we define the following two local conditions (which will replace (A 2)), where M is the observed Event-B machine, $Events_M$ the set of events in M, and s a state in the original state space:

(A 2.1) Direct Dependency Condition

Any event $e \in enabled(s) \setminus ample(s)$ is independent of $ample(s)$.

(A 2.2) Enabling Dependency Condition

Any event $e \in Events_M \setminus enabled(s)$ that depends on $ample(s)$ may not become enabled through the activities of events $e' \notin ample(s)$.

The following theorem states that (A 2.1) and (A 2.2) are sufficient local criteria for (A 2). The proof of Theorem 1 can be examined in [11].

Theorem 1 (Sufficient Local Criteria for (A 2))

Given a state s in the original state space. If $ample(s)$ is computed with respect to the local criteria (A 2.1) and (A 2.2), then $ample(s)$ satisfies (A 2) for all execution fragments in the original state space starting in state s.

Computing $ample(s)$. We can now present our algorithm for computing an ample set satisfying (A 1) through (A 3). The procedure *ComputeAmpleSet* in Algorithm 3 gets as argument a set of events. $Dependent_M$ and $EnableGraph_M$ are respectively the dependent relation and the enable graph computed for the respective Event-B machine M. The output of the *ComputeAmpleSet* is an ample set $ample(s)$ satisfying the first three conditions of the ample set constraints.

In Algorithm 3 the set T is meant to be $enabled(s)$. First, it is clear that if T is an empty set, then *ComputeAmpleSet* will return an empty set. Otherwise, if $T \neq \emptyset$, then the set returned by *ComputeAmpleSet* has at least one element (e.g. the event α chosen in one of the iterations of the **for**-loop). Thus, *ComputeAmpleSet*$(T) = \emptyset$ if and only if T is an empty set. Hence, (A 1) is satisfied by the procedure in Algorithm 3.

The first step of computing $ample(s)$, in case that T is a non-empty set, is choosing randomly an event α from T. After that, all enabled events in s that depend on α will be added to S (line 3). (S is the set which is meant to be $ample(s)$.) This step obviously does not violate the local condition (A 2.1). What remains is to check whether every execution starting from state s with one of the events in I (the set of all independent from S events) can possibly enable an event γ that is dependent on an event in S such that $\gamma \notin S$. This is realised by inspecting the enable graph of M for each $\beta \in I$ (line 6). If we find a path

$$\beta \to \gamma_1 \to \ldots \to \gamma_n \to \gamma$$

in $EnableGraph_M$ with $\gamma_1, \ldots \gamma_n, \gamma \notin S$ such that γ depends on S, then we just add β to S (line 7). Finding of such a path in $EnableGraph_M$ means that there is possibly an execution fragment starting in s that violates the local condition (A 2.2). In this case, adding β to S is necessary to ensure that S also satisfies (A 2.2). At the beginning of line 10, we then have computed in s a set of enabled events satisfying the local criteria (A 2.1) and (A 2.2). The final step is to check whether S fulfills the stutter condition (line 10). The procedure in Algorithm 3 runs until an appropriate ample set has been found or all potential ample sets fail to fulfil the conditions (A 2) and (A 3) (then we return T).

Algorithm 3. Computation of $ample(s)$

```
1  procedure set ComputeAmpleSet(T)
2      foreach α ∈ T such that α randomly chosen do
3          S := {β | β ∈ T ∧ (α, β) ∈ Dependent_M} ∪ {α};
4          I := T \ S;
5          foreach β ∈ I do
6              if there is a path β → γ₁ → ... → γₙ → γ in EnableGraph_M
                        such that γ₁, ..., γₙ, γ ∉ S ∧ γ depends on S then
7                  S := S ∪ {β}
8              end if
9          end foreach
10         if S is a stutter set then                    /* checking (A 3) */
11             return S
12         end if
13     end foreach
14     return T
```

The Ignoring Problem. Condition (A 3), which requires adding only of stutter events to the ample sets of each state (assuming that (A 1) and (A 2) are also satisfied), can sometimes cause ignoring of certain (non-stutter) events in the reduced state space. Ignoring of non-stutter events may happen when the reduction results in a cycle of stutter events only. If some events are ignored in the reduced state space of the model, then computing ample sets w.r.t. (A 1) through (A 3) may not be sufficient to preserve some of the LTL$_{-X}$ properties. The issue is also known as the *ignoring* problem [20].

To ensure that no events in the reduced state space are ignored, the cycle condition (A 4) should be guaranteed by the reduced state space. We establish (A 4) by means of the following condition:

(A 4') Strong Cycle Condition
Any cycle in the reduced state space has at least one fully expanded state.

Using the strong cycle condition (A 4') is a sufficient criterion for (A 4) (Lemma 8.23 in [4]) and easier to implement. Since at least one of the states should be fully expanded in any cycle, we expand fully each state s with an outgoing transition reaching an expanded state generated before s, as well as each state with a self loop. Note that this method of implementing the strong cycle condition (A 4') is approximative because it expands fully states unnecessarily sometimes. We have chosen this way of realising (A 4') in order to generalise our algorithm of calculating ample sets for different exploration strategies. This technique of implementing (A 4) has been also proposed in other works like in [5].

Expanding a State by Applying the Ample Events Only. To apply the ample set approach for the consistency checking algorithm, we change the way each state is expanded. Thus, the respective changes in Algorithm 1 take place in lines 7-13 of the algorithm. Basically, we can replace the code in the **else** branch of Algorithm 1 by calling the procedure *compute_ample_transitions* in Algorithm 4 with the currently processed state s as argument.

Algorithm 4. Computation of the Ample Transitions

```
1  procedure compute_ample_transitions(s)
2      T := compute all enabled events in s;
3      S := ComputeAmpleSet(T);
4      foreach evt ∈ S do
5          s' := execute_event(s,evt);
6          T := T \ {evt}
7          if (id(s) ≥ id(s')) ∧ s' ∉ Queue then        /* check (A 4) */
8              foreach e ∈ T do
9                  execute_event(s,e)
10             end foreach
11             break                    /* state s has been fully explored */
12         end if
13     end foreach
```

Algorithm 4 summarises the computation of the ample events in each state and the execution of those in the reduced state space. The presented procedure *compute_ample_transitions* gets as argument the state being expanded. The computation of the successor states and the insertion of the new determined transitions are realised by the procedure *execute_event*.

In Algorithm 4 all enabled events in the currently processed state s will be assigned to T (line 2). After that, an ample set S satisfying (A 1) through (A 3) is computed by means of the procedure *ComputeAmpleSet*. If the test of the cycle condition in line 7 fails for each loop-iteration, then only the events from S will be executed in s. Otherwise, the full expansion of s will be forced (lines 8-10), if a transition from S reaches an already expanded state s' ($s' \notin Queue$) generated before s or it is s itself ($id(s) \geq id(s')$).

5   Discussion and Evaluation

Discussion. In Section 4, we presented the background of the ample set theory and our implementation of partial order reduction (Algorithms 3 and 4). Our algorithm reduces the original state space of an Event-B machine M by using the dependency relation $Dependent_M$ and the enable graph $EnableGraph_M$. $Dependent_M$ and $EnableGraph_M$ are computed prior to the model checking by using a static analysis on the events of M. We chose to determine the dependency and enabling relations between the events in this way for performance reasons. Computing the respective relations between events on-the-fly in each state can sometimes be expensive since we use constraint based analyses in addition to syntactic analysis. In fact, timeouts are set by default in PROB for diminishing the possibility that the overhead caused by static analysis and partial order reduction outweighs the improvement achieved by the reduction of the state space. PROB can also apply partial order reduction without using its constraint solving facilities. In this case, the determination of the dependency and enabledness between events is provided by inspecting their syntactic structure only. This, however, often results in less state space reduction.

The reduction of the state space by using partial order reduction cannot only be influenced by the independence of the events of the model being verified, but also by the type of the checked property. For instance, deadlock preservation is guaranteed by any ample set satisfying conditions (A 1) and (A 2) [13], [20]. We adapted the implementation to this fact to gain more state space reduction when a model is checked for deadlock freedom only.

Another factor that can influence the effectiveness of the reduction is the number of the stutter events. For example, if we check the full invariant I, then every event that trivially fully preserves I is a stutter event. Systems specified in Event-B often have a very low number, if any, of events that trivially fulfil the invariant. This means that partial order reduction will probably only yield minor state space reduction in such cases. A possible way to detect more stutter events w.r.t. I is to use either proof information (from the Rodin provers) or PROB for checking invariant preservation for operations: any event which we can prove to preserve the invariant now becomes a stuttter event.

Evaluation. We have evaluated our implementation of partial order reduction on various models that we have received from academia and industry.[1] A part of those experiments are presented in Table 1. In particular, we wanted to study the benefit of the optimisation on models with large state spaces.

Besides having sizeable state spaces, the particular models should also have a certain number of independent concurrent events. Otherwise, the possibility of reducing the state space is very minor. If, for instance, we have a system where there is no pair of independent events or a system where any two independent events are never simultaneously enabled, then no reductions of the state space can be gained at all.

---

[1] The models and their evaluations can be obtained from the following web page http://nightly.cobra.cs.uni-duesseldorf.de/por/

Table 1. Part of the Experimental Results (times in seconds)

Model	Algorithm	States	Transitions	Analysis Time	Model Checking Time
Counters	MC	3,974	11,485	-	3.417[*]
	MC+POR	961	1,807	< 0.001	0.823[*]
	MC-NoINV	110,813	325,004	-	73.167
	MC-NoINV+POR	152	154	0.010	0.097
Fact v2	MC	112,185	381,510	-	208.150
	MC+POR	112,185	381,510	0.589	230.434
	MC-NoINV	112,185	381,510	-	197.181
	MC-NoINV+POR	27,628	62,950	0.476	50.051
BPEL v6	MC	2,248	4,960	-	7.437
	MC+POR	2,248	4,960	0.748	7.884
	MC-NoINV	2,248	4,960	-	6.944
	MC-NoINV+POR	847	1,004	0.640	2.670
Token Ring	MC	8,196	45,077	-	14.291
	MC+POR	8,176	40,565	0.011	14.671
	MC-NoINV	8,196	45,077	-	13.814
	MC-NoINV+POR	4,776	12,129	0.016	7.807
Sieve	MC	8,328	28,436	-	215.138
	MC+POR	8,142	25,237	12.437	217.754
	MC-NoINV	8,328	28,436	-	220.864
	MC-NoINV+POR	6,421	14,557	12.439	186.101
Phil v2	MC	2,350	4,528	-	9.086
	MC+POR	2,347	4,390	0.406	9.354
	MC-NoINV	2,350	4,528	-	8.870
	MC-NoINV+POR	2,346	4,336	0.378	9.167

[*] Invariant Violation

We have performed four different types of checks in order to measure the performance of our implementation of partial order reduction. By all types of tests we used the mixed depth-first/breadth-first search of ProB for the exploration of the state space. The four types of checks are abbreviated in Table 1 as follows:

MC: Model checking by using the standard consistency checking algorithm.
MC+POR: Model checking with partial order reduction.
MC-NoINV: Model checking by using the standard consistency checking algorithm without invariant violations checking.
MC-NoINV+POR: Model checking with partial order reduction without invariant violations checking.

The consistency checking algorithm and the partial order reduction algorithm are respectively Algorithm 1 and Algorithm 4. For the evaluations we used model checking for searching for deadlocks and invariant violations only.[2] Due to the fact that checking for deadlock freedom only requires the satisfaction of the

---

[2] Another options like finding a goal or searching for assertion violations have not been checked while model checking the particular model.

ample set conditions (A 1) and (A 2) for the reduced search, we additionally observed experiments with MC-NoINV+POR. For this type of checks, the results produced by MC-NoINV+POR were compared with the results of MC-NoINV.

One specification, *Counters*, in Table 1 is given that represents the best case for the reduced search in PROB. *Counters* is a toy example aiming to show the benefit of partial order reduction when each event in the model is independent from the executions of all other events. The worst case, when no reductions of the state space are gained, is represented by checking *Fact v2* and *BPEL v6* with MC+POR. *Fact v2* is an Event-B model of a simple parallel algorithm for integer factorisation. The factorisation algorithm's model was re-created from [10] for three computational slave processes searching for a factor of 53. In *Fact v2* the guard of the event *newround* was weakened. *Phil* [7] and *BPEL* [3] are case studies of the dinning philosophers problem with four philosophers and of a business process for a purchase order, respectively. Both are carried by a stepwise development via refinement; their last refinement versions *Phil v2* and *BPEL v6* are presented in Table 1. *Token Ring* is a B model of a token ring protocol and *Sieve* an Event-B model formalising a parallel version (for four processes) of the algorithm of sieve of eratosthenes for computing all prime numbers from 2 to 40.

All measurements were made on an Intel Xeon Server, 8 x 3.00 GHz Intel(R) Xeon(TM) CPU with 8 GB RAM running Ubuntu 12.04.3 LTS. The Analysis times in Table 1 are the measured runtimes for the static analysis of each machine. If the POR option is not set in an experiment, no static analysis is performed. Each experiment has been performed ten times and its respective geometric means (states, transitions and times) are reported in the results.

In general, the most considerable reductions of the state space were gained with the reduced search when only deadlock freedom checks were performed. We consider both the reductions of the number of states and transitions. In two cases (*Fact v2* and *BPEL v6*), no reductions of the state space were gained using the reduced search MC+POR. However, the model checking runtimes in those cases are not significantly different from the model checking runtimes for the standard search MC. As expected, significant reduction of the state space and thus the overall time for checking the *Counters* model were gained by both reduction searches MC+POR and MC-NoINV+POR. For the test cases MC and MC+POR of *Counters* an invariant violation was found which led to a termination of the respective search. Interesting results were obtained when applying any of the reduced searches on the *Phil v2* model. Although the model has a great magnitude of independence, the coupling between the events is so tight that no significant reductions can be gained.

6   Related Work

Several works have been devoted to optimising the PROB model checker for B and Event-B. In this section, we refer to some of the techniques have been developed and analysed for the PROB model checker.

Symmetry reduction is a technique successfully implemented in PROB for combating the state space explosion problem. Using the fact that symmetry is induced by the deferred sets in B, two sorts of exhaustive symmetry reduction algorithms in PROB have been implemented: the graph canonicalisation method [19] and the permutation flooding method [16]. The general idea of both techniques is to check only a single representative of each symmetry class of equivalent states during the consistency check of the model being verified. An approximative symmetry reduction method [17] based on computing symmetry markers for states of B machines has been also implemented in PROB. The idea of the method is that two states are considered to be symmetrically equivalent if they have the same symmetrical marker. All three methods showed good performance results when model checking B or Event-B models with a certain degree of symmetry induced by B's deferred sets.

Another notion of optimising the PROB model checker has been presented in [6]. The idea of this work is to improve the efficiency of the model checker by using the already discharged proof information from the front-end environment. The verification technique, known as proof assisted model checking, is used by default in PROB and has shown a performance improvement up to factor two on various industrial models.

Other techniques, such as using mixed breadth-first/depth-first search strategy and heuristic functions for performing directed model checking [14], have been also suggested as optimisation methods for the standard PROB model checker.

7 Conclusion and Future Work

Partial order reduction has been very successful for lower-level models such as Promela, but has had relatively little impact for higher-level modelling languages such as B, Z or TLA$^+$. Inspired by Event-B's more simpler event structures and more distributed nature, we have started a new attempt at getting partial order reduction to work for high-level formal models. We have presented an implementation of partial order reduction in PROB for Event-B (and also classical B) models. The implementation makes use of the ample set theory for reducing the state space and uses new constraint-based analyses to obtain precise relations of influence between events. Our evaluation of the reduction method has shown that considerable reductions of the state space can be gained for models with a high degree of independence and concurrency. We also observed that checking only for deadlock freedom tends to provide more significant reductions than checking simultaneously for invariant violations and deadlock freedom.

Our approach of satisfying the Cycle condition (A 4) is an approximative method for loop detection during the reduced expansion of the state space. Finding possible cycles in the reduced state space simply by checking whether the currently processed state has an outgoing transition to an already expanded state can cause less state space reductions, since the full exploration of a state can also be forced when no true cycles are discovered. For this reason, future work will concentrate on improving the reduction algorithm w.r.t. the Cycle detection condition. Further work will need to be done in elaborating the reduction algorithm presented in this work for the LTL model checker [18] in PROB.

References

1. Abrial, J.-R.: The B-Book: Assigning Programs to Meanings. Cambridge University Press, New York (1996)
2. Abrial, J.-R.: Modeling in Event-B: System and Software Engineering, 1st edn. Cambridge University Press, New York (2010)
3. Ait-Sadoune, I., Ait-Ameur, Y.: A Proof Based Approach for Modelling and Verifying Web Services Compositions. In: ICECCS 2009, pp. 1–10. IEEE Computer Society, Washington, DC (2009)
4. Baier, C., Katoen, J.-P.: Principles of Model Checking. The MIT Press (2008)
5. Barnat, J., Brim, L., Rockai, P.: Parallel Partial Order Reduction with Topological Sort Proviso. In: SEFM, pp. 222–231. IEEE Computer Society (2010)
6. Bendisposto, J., Leuschel, M.: Proof Assisted Model Checking for B. In: Breitman, K., Cavalcanti, A. (eds.) ICFEM 2009. LNCS, vol. 5885, pp. 504–520. Springer, Heidelberg (2009)
7. Boström, P., Degerlund, F., Sere, K., Waldén, M.: Derivation of Concurrent Programs by Stepwise Scheduling of Event-B Models. Formal Aspects of Computing, 1–23 (2012)
8. Clarke, E., Grumberg, O., Minea, M., Peled, D.: State Space Reduction using Partial Order Techniques. International Journal on STTT 2(3), 279–287 (1999)
9. Clarke Jr., E.M., Grumberg, O., Peled, D.A.: Model Checking. MIT Press, Cambridge (1999)
10. Degerlund, F.: Scheduling Performance of Compute-Intensive Concurrent Code Developed Using Event-B. TUCS Technical Reports 1051, pp. 1–20 (2012)
11. Dobrikov, I., Leuschel, M.: Optimising the PROB Model Checker for B using Static Analysis and Partial Order Reduction. Technical Report (2014), http://www.stups.uni-duesseldorf.de/mediawiki/images/5/5b/ Pub-DobrikovLeuschelPORtechreport.pdf
12. Godefroid, P.: Partial-Order Methods for the Verification of Concurrent Systems. LNCS, vol. 1032. Springer, Heidelberg (1996)
13. Godefroid, P., Wolper, P.: Using Partial Orders for the Efficient Verification of Deadlock Freedom and Safety Properties. In: Larsen, K.G., Skou, A. (eds.) CAV 1991. LNCS, vol. 575, pp. 332–342. Springer, Heidelberg (1992)
14. Leuschel, M., Bendisposto, J.: Directed Model Checking for B: An Evaluation and New Techniques. In: Davies, J., Silva, L., Simão, A. (eds.) SBMF 2010. LNCS, vol. 6527, pp. 1–16. Springer, Heidelberg (2011)
15. Leuschel, M., Butler, M.: ProB: An Automated Analysis Toolset for the B Method. STTT 10(2), 185–203 (2008)
16. Leuschel, M., Butler, M., Spermann, C., Turner, E.: Symmetry Reduction for B by Permutation Flooding. In: Julliand, J., Kouchnarenko, O. (eds.) B 2007. LNCS, vol. 4355, pp. 79–93. Springer, Heidelberg (2006)
17. Leuschel, M., Massart, T.: Efficient Approximate Verification of B via Symmetry Markers. In: Proceedings International Symmetry Conference, Edinburgh, UK, pp. 71–85 (January 2007)
18. Plagge, D., Leuschel, M.: Seven at one stroke: LTL model checking for High-level Specifications in B, Z, CSP, and more. STTT 12(1), 9–21 (2010)
19. Turner, E., Leuschel, M., Spermann, C., Butler, M.: Symmetry Reduced Model Checking for B. In: Proceedings TASE 2007, pp. 25–34. IEEE (2007)
20. Valmari, A.: Stubborn Sets for Reduced State Space Generation. In: Rozenberg, G. (ed.) APN 1990. LNCS, vol. 483, pp. 491–515. Springer, Heidelberg (1991)

Rapid Prototyping of a Semantically Well Founded *Circus* Model Checker

Alexandre Mota[1], Adalberto Farias[2], André Didier[1], and Jim Woodcock[3]

[1] Centre of Informatics, UFPE, Brazil
{acm,alrd}@cin.ufpe.br
[2] Department of Systems and Computing, UFCG, Brazil
adalberto@computacao.ufcg.edu.br
[3] Department of Computer Science, University of York, UK
jim.woodcock@york.ac.uk

Abstract. Nowadays academia and industry use model checkers. These tools use search-based algorithms to check the satisfaction of some property f in M. Formally, $M \models f$, where M is a transition system representation of a specification written in a language L. Such a representation may come from the semantics of L. This paper presents a rapid prototyping of a model checker development strategy for *Circus* based on its operational semantics. We capture this semantics with the Microsoft FORMULA framework and use it to analyse (deadlock, livelock, and nondeterminism of) *Circus* specifications. As FORMULA supports SMT-solving, we can handle infinite data communications and predicates. Furthermore, we create a semantically well founded *Circus* model checker as long as executing FORMULA is equivalent to reasoning with First-Order Logic (Clark completion). We illustrate the use of the model-checker with an extract of an industrial case study.

Keywords: Model Checking, *Circus*, Model-Driven Development, SMT.

1   Introduction

Model checking [1] is an automatic technique to verify whether the relation $M \models f$ holds, where M is a model (a Labelled Transition System or Kripke structure) of some formal language L and f is a temporal logic formula. *Circus* [2] has introduced another way of performing model checking, named refinement checking. The idea is similar but using the refinement relation $M_f \sqsubseteq M$, where both M and M_f are models of a same language and M_f is the most non-deterministic model known to satisfy f.

Usually a model checker is a tool that implements search procedures derived from the relation $M \models f$. Such procedures and representations of M and f are very specialized algorithms and data structures aiming at achieving the best space and time complexities. In virtue of this, it is not common to find model checkers for rich-state space languages that use elaborate data structures and that clearly follow a formal semantics. Those specialized algorithms and data structures create a gap between theory and practice. The first issue on

D. Giannakopoulou and G. Salaün (Eds.): SEFM 2014, LNCS 8702, pp. 235–249, 2014.
© Springer International Publishing Switzerland 2014

implementing model-checkers is how to guarantee that the model M conforms to the semantics (usually the Structured Operational Semantics—SOS) of the language L. The second issue is concerned with the correctness of the check $M \models f$ (or $M_f \sqsubseteq M$). For instance, FDR [3] and PAT [4] had several delivered versions due to bug fixes. And [5] analyses CSP-Z via FDR but it is not assured to be semantically well founded.

A very recent technology developed by Microsoft Research, known as FOR-MULA [6] (Formal Modelling Using Logic Programming and Analysis), seems to be appropriate for creating semantically well founded model checkers. It is based on the Constraint Programming Paradigm [7] and Satisfiability Modulo Theory (SMT) solving provided by Z3 [8]. Besides providing a high abstraction level for describing structures, FORMULA allows one to deal with some infiniteness aspects of data types as well as defining search procedures over structures.

Figure 1 shows the ideal scenario for creating semantically well founded model checkers for a formal language L. The necessary elements are a BNF grammar, an SOS, and a set of properties stated in some (temporal) logic. The first effort is describing the theoretical SOS (associated to the constructors defined by the BNF) using a Domain-Specific Language (DSL) [9] (this can be created following [10], for instance). The second task is representing this description as abstractions (how to build a model for an instance of L and how to check properties over it) in some underlying framework (besides FORMULA [6], Prolog [11] or Maude [12] are suitable for this purpose). The automatic translation from the SOS metamodel to the underlying framework can be automated by tools like Stratego/XT [13] or QVT [14]. The last task is concerned with optimisation: abstractions can be adjusted to improve space and time towards the final goals while preserving correctness [15]. Obviously that to assure correctness, the semantics of the executable framework must be formal and there must exist a refinement calculus to obtain the abstractions. But in this paper we follow the idea of Clark completion [16] of a definite clause program, which makes the assumption that the axioms in a program completely axiomatise all possible reasons for atomic formulas to be true.

In this paper we focus on the dashed square of Figure 1, considering *Circus* [2] as the formal language. We spent 2 months learning FORMULA, 8 months to create the proposed strategy for any SOS (Figure 1), and 72 hours to build the

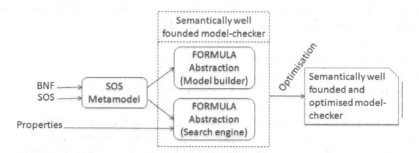

Fig. 1. A model checker product line

model checker. This fast development is result of the high-level abstraction of FORMULA. Other approaches like [17], for instance, spent a whole PhD to build a first model checker for *Circus* and the gap from theory to practice hinders the claim for a semantically well-founded tool.

The last part of Figure 1 is about optimisation. It consists in rewriting the FORMULA abstraction to obtain the fastest solution. Such a rewriting process can produce a FORMULA abstraction that is not straightforward to be compared with the original SOS, but it is assured to be semantics preserving [15]. We point out that our model checker does not have an optimal performance; it is focused on correctness by construction.

Our main contributions are: (i) a semantically well founded way to capture operational semantics using FORMULA; (ii) a model checker for *Circus* specifications that deals with infinite communications and predicates.

This paper is organised as follows. The next section gives a brief introduction to *Circus*, through an example. Section 3 presents FORMULA and how to encode *Circus* in FORMULA to create a *Circus* model checker, focusing on semantics correctness. This model checker is used in Section 4. Related work comes next in Section 5 and our conclusions and future work in Section 6.

2   Introducing *Circus* with a Small Example

Circus combines Z, CSP, and constructs of the refinement calculi [18] and Dijkstra's language of guarded commands, which is a simple imperative language with nondeterminism. All the extra constructs used are familiar: assignments, conditionals, and so on. We use label Listing$_C$ for *Circus* code listings. Listing$_C$ 1 illustrates a process that represents part of a controller of our case study. The case study is an Emergency Response System that integrates different systems to achieve an objective that is not accomplished by the systems alone. We give more details of the case study in Section 4.

```
process ERUs₀ ≘ begin

  state Control == [ allocated, total_erus : ℕ ]
  InitControl == [ Control' | allocated' = 0 ∧ total_erus' = 5 ]
  AllocateState == [ ΔControl | allocated' = allocated ]
  Allocate ≘ allocate_idle_eru → AllocateState ⨟ Choose
  ServiceState == [ ΔControl | allocated' = allocated − 1 ]
  Service ≘ service_rescue → ServiceState ⨟ Choose
  Choose ≘
      if[ Control | allocated = 0 ] → Allocate
      ∥[ Control | allocated = total_erus ] → Service
      ∥[ Control | allocated > 0 ∧ allocated < total_erus ] →
      Allocate □ Service
      fi

  • InitControl ⨟ Choose

end
```

Listing$_C$ 1. Emergency Response Units Controller (version 0)

The internal state of the process is described in schema *Control*. It contains two natural numbers: *allocated* and *total_erus*. The former records the current number of allocated Emergency Response Units (ERUs), whereas the latter is used as a constant value (in this version), defining the total number of ERUs.

The definitions that follow are action specifications. The action *InitControl* initialises the total number of ERUs to 5 and the number of allocated ERUs to 0. The action *Allocate* updates *Control* when a request is made through channel *allocate_idle_eru* (the *AllocateState* schema has a flaw and will be explained later). The action *Service* releases an ERU after a *service_rescue* event. The action *Choose* enables other actions when it is safe: (i) when all ERUs are available (guard *allocated* = 0 is valid), only the action *Allocate* can execute and (ii) when there is none available (guard *allocated* = *total_erus* is valid), only the action *Service* can execute.

The behaviour of $ERUs_0$ is described by the last sequential composition *InitControl* ; *Choose*. This means that $ERUs_0$ behaves as described by *InitControl* and then as described by *Choose*.

3 Design and Implementation

The *Circus* model checker is a FORMULA abstraction. FORMULA supports algebraic data types (ADTs) and strongly typed constraint logic programming (CLP). This allows one to create concise specifications [6], analysable by SMT-solving. The following code introduces FORMULA using a basic abstraction for digraphs. It is reproduced from the FORMULA tutorial.

```
 1  domain Digraph {                           12      conforms := !undeclVertex.
 2      primitive V   ::= (id:Integer).        13  }
 3      primitive E   ::= (src:V,dst:V).       14  model G1 of Digraph {
 4      path          ::= (beg:V,end:V).       15      V(5)
 5      path(x, y)    :- E(x,y).               16      E(V(5), V(5))
 6      path(x, z)    :- path(x,y),            17  }
 7                       path(y,z).            18  partial model G2 of Digraph {
 8      undeclVertex := E(V(x),_),             19      V(_) V(_)
 9                      fail V(x).             20      E(_, V(3))
10      undeclVertex := E(_,V(y)),             21      E(x, y) E(y, z)
11                      fail V(y).             22  }
```

A digraph is modelled as a domain containing a set of vertexes (V) and a set of edges (E). The qualifier primitive indicates that vertexes and edges cannot be generated during the analysis, but—as it is to all values in a model—their values can be instantiated (see, for example the partial model G2). The rule path links vertexes where there is a single edge or several edges. By using the definition of path, FORMULA is able to find a path between two vertexes (if it exists) by building paths between intermediate vertexes. The element undeclVertex establishes constraints upon the domain; it captures undeclared vertexes by checking if the first or the second components of edges have not been declared as vertexes (fail V(.)). Finally, the conforms constraint defines a final goal: a valid graph cannot have undeclared vertexes. We use two models to check instances of the domain Digraph. The model G1 defines a digraph with one vertex (V(5)) and a self-edge. As it has no undeclared vertexes, FORMULA detects its conformance with the Digraph domain (satisfiable). Concerning the partial model G2, there are three edges and two vertexes (some are left undetermined). These elements play the role of parameters to be instantiated by FORMULA to make G2 satisfiable. In this case, FORMULA found the instances V(3) and V(-103701) and used V(3) to validate the edge with the first vertex undetermined (E(V(3),V(3))). The value -103701 is arbitrary and was generated only because G2 has two vertexes. If we remove one vertex, only V(3) is used.

Thus a FORMULA abstraction is a set of *domains* and (partial) *models*. A domain can contain rules (a Horn clause LHS :- RHS where RHS is a set of facts) and constraints (as queries). A model is a possible representative of a domain. A model can be *satisfiable* or *unsatisfiable*. A partial model is an open model, whose unknown parts are instantiated by Z3, if a satisfiable model can be found.

Figure 2 shows FORMULA working. It takes the main goal (a special conforms clause) and the facts given in a (partial) model as starting point. From the (initial) facts and the RHS of domain rules, FORMULA tries to generate other facts iteratively (according to the LHS of domain rules) until the base stops increasing (that is, when a least fixed-point is found). Afterwards, it checks the goal. If any SMT-solving activity (instantiation, evaluation, etc.) is required, FORMULA invokes Z3 automatically [6]. Section 3.2 presents this formally.

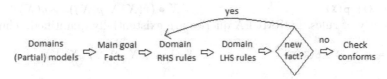

Fig. 2. Iterative analysis of FORMULA

In this sense, FORMULA works as a symbolic executor, expanding its base of facts as much as necessary. This fits well the purposes of LTS generation. To save space we provide a basic (but sufficient) description of each component used to capture the syntax, semantics, classical properties and traces refinement.

3.1 FORMULA Semantics

Executing a FORMULA abstraction means determining whether a logic program can be extended by a finite set of (primitive) facts so that a goal is satisfied [6]. This requires searching through (infinitely) many possible extensions using Z3 [8]. FORMULA is based on a concept defined as Constraint Logic Programming Satisfiability (CLP Satisfiability).

Let U be a (possibly infinite) set called a universe. Let r be an n-ary relation symbol and r^I a (finite) interpretation of r; r^I is a (finite) subset of U^n. As shorthand, we use $r(\bar{t})$ meaning r applied to elements $t_1, \ldots, t_n$ of U.

Definition 1. (CLP Satisfiability). *Given:*

- *The least Herbrand model, a function lm(.),*
- *A program Π with relation symbols $R = \{r_1, \ldots, r_n\}$,*
- *$R_p \subseteq R$ a subset of the program relations, called the primitive relations,*
- *A quantifer-free goal g over the program relations.*

Then find a finite interpretation R_p^I for primitive relations such that:

$$lm((\Pi \cup R_p^I)^*) \models \tilde{\exists} g$$

Program $\Pi \cup R_p^I$ emerges by extending Π with a fact $r(t)$ whenever $R_p^I \models r(t)$. Then R_p^I is an interpretation satisfying the problem.

The program can only be extended by primitive relations R_P. The contents of R_P^I are the facts that, when added to the program, cause the goal to be satisfied.

FORMULA rules are directly associated to First-Order Logic formulas by Clark completion [6]. Thus,

```
r(X,Y) :- p(X,Y).
```
$\equiv \quad \forall X, Y \bullet p(X, Y) \Rightarrow r(X, Y)$

```
q(X,Z) :- q(X,Y), q(Y,Z).
```
$\equiv \forall X, Z \bullet \exists Y \bullet (q(X, Y) \wedge q(Y, Z) \Rightarrow q(X, Z))$

Repetition of the right-hand side of a rule can be avoided as follows.

```
q(X) , r(X) :- p(X).
```
$\equiv \quad \forall X \bullet p(X) \Rightarrow (q(X) \wedge r(X))$

When different bodies have the same head, one can use semicolon as follows.

```
q(X) :- r(X); p(X).
```
$\equiv \quad \forall X \bullet (r(X) \vee p(X)) \Rightarrow q(X)$

Differently of rules, FORMULA queries are existentially quantified. Thus,

```
query1 := q(X,2), p(X,Y).
```
$\equiv \quad \exists X, Y \bullet q(X, 2) \wedge p(X, Y)$

```
query2 := q(X,_), fail p(X,Y).
```
$\equiv \exists X, Y, Z \bullet q(X, Z) \wedge \neg p(X, Y)$

```
1 | query3 := p(X, Y).
2 | query3 := q(Z, W).
```
$\equiv \quad \exists X, Y, Z, W \bullet p(X, Y) \vee q(Z, W)$

3.2   Embedding *Circus* in FORMULA

The representation of *Circus* syntax is straightforward as all infix operators become FORMULA constructors with a resulting disjoint union of these several elements, as illustrated in Listing_F 1 in the `CircusProcess` construct[1].

The *Circus* semantics is captured by the notions of states, events and transitions [2] (the main elements to build the LTS). In FORMULA, states and transitions are defined as relations: `State(s, A)` represents a relation where `s` is a binding and `A` is a syntactically correct *Circus* process fragment (an action), and `trans(c, ev, c')` is a ternary relation where `c` is the initial configuration, `ev` is the event that labels the transition, and `c'` is the configuration after performing `ev`. The FORMULA domain `Circus_Semantics` is (partially) described as an extension (`extends Circus_Syntax`) plus representations for states, events, transitions, expressions, etc. These elements are used to represent firing rules from *Circus* SOS (taken from [2]). In Rule (1) a local context (illustrated from a simple case of a single variable `x` of type `T` and initial value w_0) is introduced to be used in other firing rules.

---

[1] We use label Listing_F for FORMULA code listings.

```
 1   domain Circus_Syntax{
 2     ...
 3     primitive iChoice    ::= (lProc : CircusProcess , rProc : CircusProcess).
 4     primitive proc       ::= (name : String, p: Type).
 5     primitive schema     ::= (schN: String).
 6     primitive var        ::= (name: String, tName: String, p: CircusProcess).
 7     primitive assign     ::= (occur: Natural).
 8     assignDef            ::= (occur: Natural, st: Binding, st_: Binding).
 9     preSchemaOk          ::= (schN: String, st: Binding).
10     preSchemaNOk         ::= (schN: String, st: Binding).
11     schemaDef            ::= (schN: String, st: Binding, st_: Binding).
12     CircusProcess        ::= BasicProcess + Prefix + iChoice + eChoice + pGuard +
13     opChoice + seqC + hide + parll + par + proc + var + let + assign + schema.
14     ...
15   }
16   domain Circus_Semantics extends Circus_Syntax{
17     State ::= (bind: Binding, action: CircusProcess).
18     trans ::= (source: State, ev: SigmaEps, target: State).
19     ...
20   }
```

Listing$_F$ 1. *Circus* Syntax in FORMULA.

$$
\left(\begin{array}{l} \textbf{begin} \\ \quad \textbf{state} \,[\, x : T \,] \\ \quad \bullet \, A \\ \textbf{end} \end{array}\right) \xrightarrow{\epsilon} \left(\begin{array}{l} \textbf{begin} \\ \quad \textbf{state} \,[\, x : T \,] \,|\, \text{loc} \,(w_0 \in T \,|\, x := w_0) \\ \quad \bullet \, A \\ \textbf{end} \end{array}\right) \tag{1}
$$

In Rule (2) we have that a change in an abstract representation of the local context (to be used in all SOS rules for simplification purposes), represented as an antecedent, directly reflects the same change in the concrete local context (as conclusion of the rule). Without loss of generality, we ignored the condition c when embedding these SOS rules in FORMULA. Thus, in FORMULA we deal only with $(s \models A)$ instead of $(c \mid s \models A)$.

$$
\frac{(c_1 \mid s_1 \models A_1) \xrightarrow{1} (c_2 \mid s_2 \models A_2)}{\left(\begin{array}{l} \textbf{begin} \\ \quad \textbf{state} \,[\, x : T \,] \\ \quad |\, \text{loc} \,(c_1 \mid s_1) \\ \quad \bullet \, A_1 \\ \textbf{end} \end{array}\right) \xrightarrow{1} \left(\begin{array}{l} \textbf{begin} \\ \quad \textbf{state} \,[\, x : T \,] \\ \quad |\, \text{loc} \,(c_2 \mid s_2) \\ \quad \bullet \, A_2 \\ \textbf{end} \end{array}\right)} \tag{2}
$$

From now on we present some SOS rules and the corresponding FORMULA code. Explanation of syntactic and semantics elements is on demand. Rule (3) concerns the behavior of the internal choice operator. It is equivalent to CSP except for the transition that uses the *Circus* ϵ invisible event.

$$
\frac{c}{(c \mid s \models A_1 \sqcap A_2) \xrightarrow{\epsilon} (c \mid s \models A_1)} \qquad \frac{c}{(c \mid s \models A_1 \sqcap A_2) \xrightarrow{\epsilon} (c \mid s \models A_2)} \tag{3}
$$

We capture Rule (3) in FORMULA by first considering the constructor iChoice the syntactic representation for $\sqcap$. The term $(c \mid s \models A_1 \sqcap A_2)$ becomes State(s,iChoice(A1,A2)) because we ignore c as already said. Transitions are trivially represented by using the constructor trans, filled with the corresponding parameters. We point out that, differently from a Prolog representation [11], such a

FORMULA rule only fires if the term `State(s,iChoice(A1, A2))` is present in the FORMULA knowledge base. That is, in terms of behaviour, FORMULA creates two ϵ-transitions as described by Rule (3).

```
1  trans(State(s,iChoice(A1,A2)),eps,State(s, A1)),
2  trans(State(s,iChoice(A1,A2)),eps,State(s, A2)) :- State(s,iChoice(A1,A2)).
```

In Rule (4) we show another aspect of *Circus*: the state part. This rule considers an assignment (`v := e`), which is represented in FORMULA by `assign(id)` (syntax) and `assignDef(id,s,s_)` (semantics). The `id` is the (unique) identifier that links both parts of the assignment. The semantics part is responsible for interpreting the expression `e` and updating the state (binding) variable.

$$\frac{c}{(c \mid s \models v := e) \xrightarrow{\epsilon} (c \wedge (s; \, w_0 = e) \mid s; \, v := w_0 \models \text{Skip})} \tag{4}$$

In FORMULA, the variable `v` and the expression `e` are encapsulated inside a fact `assignDef(id,s,s_)`. The expression `n is State(s,assign(id))` is useful to guarantee that `State(s,assign(id))` is present in the knowledge base, as well as to capture such a reference in a variable named `n`, which is used as first parameter of `trans` in the head of the rule.

```
1  trans(n,eps,State(s_,Skip)) :- n is State(s,assign(id)),assignDef(id,s,s_).
```

As last example of embedding of *Circus* rule in FORMULA, we consider the situation of a schema when its precondition is not valid (see Rule 5). This implies the introduction of a *Chaos* action.

$$\frac{c \wedge \neg (s; \text{ pre } Op)}{(c \mid s \models Op) \xrightarrow{\epsilon} (c \mid s \models \text{Chaos})} \tag{5}$$

Similarly to assignments, schemas are handled by two parts: syntactic and semantic. The first just introduces a unique FORMULA fact `schema(schN)`, where `schN` is the name of a schema. However, differently from assignments, schemas have a precondition that can be valid or not. Ideally we should embed the schema body once and calculate the negation of its precondition as in $\neg (s; \text{ pre } Op)$. Unfortunately when one tries to do that, FORMULA reports a non stratified situation and does not compile. As a solution, we calculate $\neg (s; \text{ pre } Op)$ outside FORMULA and store the result inside the constructor `preSchemaNOk(schN,s)`. If such a constructor is present in the knowledge base then $\neg (s; \text{ pre } Op)$ holds. That is, the precondition is invalid.

```
1  trans(n,eps,State(s,Chaos)):-n is State(s,schema(schN)),preSchemaNOk(schN,s).
```

3.3   Properties Definition

The rules presented previously guide FORMULA to build the LTS for a *Circus* process as defined by the *Circus* operational semantics. To establish the properties to be checked in such an LTS we focus on three classical properties because they are supported by CSP traditional tools like FDR and PAT:

- *Deadlock*: the process reached some state from which it goes nowhere;
- *Livelock*: the process performs an infinite loop of ϵ-transitions;
- *Nondeterminism*: an event from one state lead to different states.

We define the properties in a separated domain that extends the semantic one (see Listing_F 2). A deadlock (line 13) is directly captured by the existence of a configuration C1, from which we can only find an invisible path to a configuration C2 whose action cannot be Skip and from which it is not possible to find any exit path. The rule path (lines 3–6) captures any path that exists between two configurations. A livelock is captured by an epsPath from an arbitrary configuration L to itself (line 16), where an epsPath is a sequence of ϵ-transitions between two configurations (lines 8–11). The nondeterminism property has some subtleties that deserve special attention. The rule accepts (lines 18–23) captures the initial acceptances of a process in a given configuration. Thus, accepts(P, ev) means the analysed process accepts the visible event ev in a configuration P (possibly performing ϵ-transitions before ev). It calculates all reachable states by using transitive closure. Nondeterminism (lines 24–28) is captured by checking the existence of two transitions with the same event (possibly ϵ-transitions) from the same state L (trans(L,ev1,S1) and trans(L,ev1,S2)) leading to different states (S1!=S2) in which the process can accept (accepts(S1,ev)) or reject (fail accepts(S2,ev)) the same visible event (ev!= eps). The remaining facts epsPath(S1,S3) and epsPath(S2,S4) are necessary to guarantee that S1 and S2 are reachable by the analysed process and avoiding, hence, analysing the property in the premises of the firing rules.

```
1   domain Properties extends          17  // Nondeterminism property
        Circus_Semantics {              18  accepts ::= (iS:State,
2   //Reachability anaysis              19             ev:SigmaTickeps).
3   path    ::= (fI:State, fE: State).  20  accepts(P,ev) :- trans(P,ev,_),
4   path(C1,C2) :- trans(C1,e,C2).      21                  ev != eps.
5   path(C1,C2) :- path(C1,Ci),         22  accepts(P,ev) :- trans(P,eps,R),
6                  trans(Ci,e,C2).       23                  accepts(R,ev).
7   //Invisible path                    24  Nondeterminism := trans(L,ev1,S1),
8   epsPath    ::= (iS:State,fS:State).  25    trans(L,ev1,S2), S1!=S2,
9   epsPath(P,Q) :- trans(P,eps,Q).      26    accepts(S1,ev), ev!=eps,
10  epsPath(P,Q) :- epsPath(P,S),        27    fail accepts(S2,ev),
11                  epsPath(S,Q).        28    epsPath(S1,S3), epsPath(S2, S4),
12  //Deadlock property                        S3 != S4.
13  Deadlock := epsPath(C1,C2),         29  }
14    C2.action!=Skip,fail path(C2,C3)

15  //Livelock property
16  Livelock := epsPath(L,L).
```

Listing_F 2. Properties Specification in FORMULA.

3.4   Properties: From Logics to FORMULA

A deadlock occurs in a *Circus* configuration (s_1, A_1) if the following formula holds [19].

$$\exists\, s_2, A_2 \bullet (s_1, A_1) \overset{\langle\rangle}{\Longrightarrow} (s_2, A_2) \land A_2 \neq Skip \land (\neg\exists\, l, s_3, A_3 \bullet (s_2, A_2) \overset{l}{\Longrightarrow} (s_3, A_3))$$

To obtain the equivalent FORMULA rules and queries that answer the above first-order logic formula, we need to introduce some definitions. In [19], $(s_1, A_1) \overset{t}{\Longrightarrow} (s_2, A_2)$ is defined as reachability: there exists a trace t, from which, the configuration (s_1, A_1) can reach configuration (s_2, A_2). To obtain the corresponding in FORMULA we need a more detailed definition as follows.

Definition 2. *Let s be a binding and A be a Circus action. The configuration* (s, A) *is defined in FORMULA as* `State(s, A)`.   ◇

Definition 3. *Let* (s_1, A_1) *and* (s_2, A_2) *be two Circus configurations and e be an event. The transition* $(s_1, A_1) \xrightarrow{e} (s_2, A_2)$ *is defined in FORMULA as* `trans((s1, A1), e, (s2, A2))`.   ◇

Definition 4. *Let* (s_1, A_1) *and* (s_2, A_2) *be two Circus configurations and t be a trace, such that* $t = \langle e_1, \ldots, e_k \rangle$. *The transition* $(s_1, A_1) \xRightarrow{t} (s_2, A_2)$ *is defined as* $\exists\, C_1, \ldots, C_n \bullet (s_1, A_1) \xrightarrow{e_1} C_1 \wedge \ldots \wedge C_n \xrightarrow{e_k} (s_2, A_2)$.   ◇

From the previous definitions we can prove that a FORMULA embedding is equivalent to $(s_1, A_1) \xRightarrow{t} (s_2, A_2)$.

Lemma 1. *Let* C_1 *and* C_2 *be two Circus configurations and t be a trace. If* $C_1 \xRightarrow{t} C_2$ *then* `path(C1, C2)` *holds in the FORMULA knowledge base, where*

```
1  path(C1, C2) :- trans(C1, e, C2).
2  path(C1, C2) :- path(C1, Ci), trans(Ci, e, C2).
```

                    ◇

Proof follows by induction.

   (Base case: $t = \langle e \rangle$*)*
   (a) $C_1 \xRightarrow{\langle e \rangle} C_2$ *(By hyp.)*
   (b) $C_1 \xrightarrow{e} C_2$ *(By Def. 4)*
   (c) `trans(C1, e, C2)`   *(By Def. 3)*
   (d) `path(C1, C2)`   *(By def.)*
   (Inductive case: $t = s \frown \langle e \rangle$*)*
   (a) $C_1 \xRightarrow{s \frown \langle e \rangle} C_2$ *(By hyp.)*
   (b) $\exists\, C_i \bullet C_1 \xRightarrow{s} C_i \wedge C_i \xrightarrow{e} C_2$ *(By Def. 4)*
   (c) `path(C1, s, Ci), trans(Ci,e,C2)`   *(By def. and Clark comp.)*
   (d) `path(C1, C2)`   *(By def.)* ∎

Similarly to Lemma 1, we have this new lemma.

Lemma 2. *Let* C_1 *and* C_2 *be two Circus configurations. If* $C_1 \xRightarrow{\langle\rangle} C_2$ *then* `epsPath(C1, C2)` *holds in the FORMULA knowledge base, where*

```
1   epsPath(C1, C2) :- trans(C1, eps, C2).
2   epsPath(C1, C2) :- epsPath(C1, Ci), trans(Ci, eps, C2).
```

                    ◇

And $\neg\, \exists\, l, s_3, A_3 \bullet (s_2, A_2) \xRightarrow{l} (s_3, A_3)$ in FORMULA is simply obtained by negating Lemma 1 as follows.

Corollary 1. *Let* (s_2, A_2) *be a Circus configuration, named* C_2 *for short. If* $\neg\, \exists\, l, C_3 \bullet C_2 \xRightarrow{l} C_3$ *holds then* `fail path(C2, C3)`.   ◇

Now *Circus* deadlock is simply obtained as follows.

Theorem 1. *If*
$$\exists\, s_2, A_2 \bullet (s_1, A_1) \xRightarrow{\langle\rangle} (s_2, A_2) \wedge A_2 \neq Skip \wedge (\neg \exists\, l, s_3, A_3 \bullet (s_2, A_2) \xRightarrow{l} (s_3, A_3))$$
then query `deadlock` *in FORMULA is valid, where*

```
1  deadlock := epsPath(C1, C2), C2.action != Skip, fail path(C2, C3).
```

                    ◇

4   Evaluating the Model Checker

To evaluate our *Circus* model checker, we consider the Emergency Response System (ERS) introduced in [20,21]. Figure 3 shows its outline view. The ERS model is a set of SysML [22] diagrams and the behaviour in *Circus* is obtained from Activity Diagrams with specialized stereotypes. Due to space restrictions, we show only in this article the code that corresponds to the activation, detection and recovery of faults. We add controller processes $ERUs_0$, $ERUs_1$, or $ERUs_2$ (Listings$_C$ 1 and 2). It adds details of the behaviour of the Call Centre, controlling the number of ERUs currently allocated. Version 0 has a flaw on the implementation of the schema *AllocateState*. The schema should add 1 to the previous *allocated* value. This simple mistake causes a deadlock on process $ERSystem_0$ (Listing$_C$ 2)—because channel *service_rescue* is never offered by $ERUs_0$—that is successfully detected by the model-checker. Process $ERUs_1$ fixes this problem and $ERSystem_1$ is deadlock-free. The FORMULA code and instructions to run our case study are available at http://www.dsc.ufcg.edu.br/~adalberto/circus-mc/.

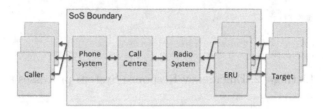

Fig. 3. Outline of the ERS

We went further and verified the fault tolerance property shown in [20] for the processes $ERSystem_1$ and $ERSystem_2$. The difference between these processes is the implementation of a recovery mechanism, modelled as process *Recovery*1. For this case, we created a deadlock assertion to check fault-tolerance. In $ERSystem_1$ the recovery is not modelled, thus it is not fault tolerant (a deadlock is found). On the other hand, $ERSystem_2$ is fault-tolerant, and the model-checker is unable to find a deadlock.

Listing$_F$ 3 illustrates a few *Circus* elements in FORMULA for our case study: the state (`Control`) and processes definitions (`CallCentreStart`, `InitiateRescueFault1Activation`, `ERSystem_0`) in Listing$_F$ 3. In this excerpt, note four constructors: (i) `State`, (ii) `schemaDef`, (iii) `ProcDef` and (iv) `genPar`. The *Control* state is defined through a `State` constructor and establishes the schema `Control`. The three `ProcDef` defines three processes (`CallCentreStart`, `InitiateRescueFault1Activation` and `ERSystem_0`). The constructor `genPar` defines the generalized parallel of the processes `InitiateRescueFault1Activation` and `ERUs_0`, through the chanset declaration with channels `allocate_idle_eru` and `service_rescue`.

process $ERUs_1 \,\hat{=}\, \mathbf{begin}$

$\ldots$

$AllocateState == [\ \Delta ERUs\ |\ allocated' = allocated + 1\ ]$

$\ldots$

end

process $InitiateRescueFault1Activation \,\hat{=}\, \mathbf{begin}$
  $CallCentreStart \,\hat{=}\, start\_rescue \rightarrow FindIdleEru$
  $FindIdleEru \,\hat{=}\, find\_idle\_erus \rightarrow (IdleEru \ \square \ (wait \rightarrow FindIdleEru))$
  $IdleEru \,\hat{=}\, allocate\_idle\_eru \rightarrow send\_rescue\_info\_to\_eru \rightarrow IR1$
  $IR1 \,\hat{=}\, (process\_message \rightarrow FAReceiveMessage) \ \square \ (fault\_1\_activation \rightarrow IR2)$
  $FAReceiveMessage = receive\_message \rightarrow ServiceRescue$
  $ServiceRescue = service\_rescue \rightarrow CallCentreStart$
  $IR2 \,\hat{=}\, IR2Out \ \square \ (error\_1\_detection \rightarrow FAStartRecovery)$
  $IR2Out \,\hat{=}\, drop\_message \rightarrow target\_not\_attended \rightarrow CallCentreStart$
  $FAStartRecovery \,\hat{=}\, start\_recovery\_1 \rightarrow end\_recovery\_1 \rightarrow ServiceRescue$
    $\bullet\ CallCentreStart$
end

process $Recovery1 \,\hat{=}\, \mathbf{begin}$
  $Recovery1Start \,\hat{=}\, start\_recovery\_1 \rightarrow log\_fault\_1 \rightarrow resend\_rescue\_info\_to\_eru \rightarrow$
  $process\_message \rightarrow receive\_message \rightarrow end\_recovery\_1 \rightarrow Recovery1Start$
    $\bullet\ Recovery1Start$
end

process $ERSystem_{i \in \{0,1\}} \,\hat{=}\, InitiateRescueFault1Activation \underset{ERUsSignals}{\parallel} ERUs_i$

process $ERSystem_2 \,\hat{=}\, ERSystem_1 \underset{RecoverySignals}{\parallel} Recovery1$

chanset $ERUsSignals == \{\!|\ allocate\_idle\_eru, service\_rescue\ |\!\}$
chanset $RecoverySignals == \{\!|\ start\_recovery\_1, end\_recovery\_1\ |\!\}$

Listing_C 2. Emergency Response System processes

```
 1  schemaDef("Control",s,s_) :- State(s,schema("Control")),
 2    s = BBinding(SingleBind("allocated",allocated),
 3          BBinding(SingleBind("total_erus"total_erus),nBind))),
 4    s_ = BBinding(SingleBind("allocated",allocated_),
 5          BBinding(SingleBind("total_erus"total_erus_),nBind))),
 6    allocated_ = 0, total_erus_ = 5.
 7  ProcDef("CallCentreStart",void,
 8    Prefix(IOComm(4,"start_rescue",""),void),proc("FindIdleEru",void))).
 9  ProcDef("InitiateRescueFault1Activation",void,proc("CallCentreStart",void)).
10  ProcDef("ERSystem_0",void,genPar(proc("InitiateRescueFault1Activation",void),
11    "{|allocate_idle_eru,service_rescue|}",proc("ERUs_0",void))).
12  ...
```

Listing_F 3. Main FORMULA elements of our case study.

5   Related Work

Palikareva *et al.* [23] propose a prototype called SymFDR, which implements
a bounded model checker for CSP based on SAT-solvers. The authors make a
comparison to show that SymFDR can deal with problems beyond FDR (such as
combinatorial complex problems). Moreover, they found that FDR outperforms

SymFDR when a counter-example does not exist. In our work we extend the class of problems analysable by SymFDR with the aid of SMT-solving. This resulted in a more expressive approach to create the LTS because we do not depend on FDR. Moreover, this makes our approach able to handle infinite state systems while SymFDR can only deal with systems that FDR can.

Leuschel [11] proposes an implementation of CSP in SICStus Prolog (a variation of Prolog) for interpretation and animation purposes. Part of the design of our model checker in FORMULA follows a similar declarative and logic representation as reported in [11]. However, as we handle infinite state systems, we indeed implement a future work of [11]. Like Leuschel's work, we do not provide a formal proof of the soundness of our approach. The reason is that, like Prolog and other languages, FORMULA does not have a publicly available formal semantics. Our hypothesis is assuming that FORMULA is sound, our one-to-one mapping used in our deep embedding is a strong evidence of semantics preservation. But to further attest this, we checked our hypothesis by performing a systematic test campaign (170 specifications) based on the classical properties mentioned here. For those examples that could also be analysed in FDR and PAT (those with a finite state space) we observed the same results.

The use of SMT-solving for model checking purposes is not new. The advances of SMT-solving bring a new level of verification. Bjørner *et al.* [24] extend the SMT-LIB to describe rules and declare recursive predicates, which can be used by symbolic model checking. Alberti *et al.* [25] propose an SMT-based specification language to improve the verification of safety properties. Our work focuses on using *Circus* as the language and a model checker with a new perspective for reasoning about infinite systems. In this sense we associate SMT-solving to increase the expressiveness of the process algebra *Circus* to provide a powerful tool for verification and reasoning of concurrent systems.

A similar approach was proposed in [12] and uses MAUDE for executing and verifying CCS (Concurrent Communicating Systems). According to that work, only behavioural aspects can be handled, whereas we deal with data aspects even if they come from an infinite domain and are involved in communications and in predicates. Moreover, that work also considers temporal logic, whereas we do not (it is not a *Circus* culture but FORMULA can handle it). We point out that MAUDE can be more powerful than FORMULA but it can be harder to guarantee convergence when applying rewriting rules. Our work is free of convergence problems because the engine of FORMULA focuses on finding the least fixed-point using SMT solving.

Still with regard to rewriting rules convergence, the $\mathbb{K}$-framework [26] may have the same issue, depending on the choice of heating and cooling rules. The framework allows one to obtain tools—like a state-space explorer—given a language syntax and a semantics in MAUDE style, using rewriting rules.

6   Conclusions and Future Work

This work proposed a new model checker for *Circus*, whose first attempt was made in [17]. It is a semantically well founded model checker that can handle infinite data (involved in communications and in predicates). The relation between FOL and FORMULA assures the semantic correctness of the model checker.

We have used our tool in more than 170 test specifications and obtained the same results (concerning correctness) against FDR and PAT. Our results indicate that our model checker can outperform FDR and PAT for data-intensive communicating systems. This is because FORMULA deals with a symbolic LTS. For non data-intensive systems, the opposite happens. Thus as future work we aim at optimising the FORMULA rules as well as using the FORMULA abstraction as a contract to create an efficient and correct implementation [15].

Our work is in the context of the COMPASS[2] project which uses the CML language. CML is based on the maturity of *Circus* and is a combination of VDM, CSP, and the refinement calculus of Morgan [18]. Our future plan includes the extension of the current model checker to deal with CML as well, which means dealing with time, probability, mobility, etc., aspects in a single language and tool support. As consequence, we aim as future work to automatize as much as possible the elements of Figure 1. This means proposing a DSL [9] for SOS rules (following [10], for example), using Stratego/XT [13] or QVT [14], giving a UTP semantics [27] to FORMULA and developing a refinement calculus.

In [28], the author shows that it is possible to analyse certain infinite state CSP processes as long as they are syntactically characterised as data independent. This is not available neither in FDR nor in PAT but it can be easily considered in FORMULA as a future work. Actually, our proposal already works with data independent systems, but we still need to generalise our solution to data independent parametrised processes.

References

1. Clarke, E., Grumberg, O., Long, D.: Model Checking and Abstraction. ACM Trans. on Programming Languages and Systems 16(5), 1512–1542 (1994)
2. Cavalcanti, A., Gaudel, M.C.: Testing for refinement in Circus. Acta Inf. 48(2), 97–147 (2011)
3. Roscoe, A.W., et al.: Model-checking CSP. A classical mind: essays in honour of CAR Hoare, pp. 353–378 (1994)
4. Liu, Y., Sun, J., Dong, J.: Developing Model Checkers Using PAT. In: Bouajjani, A., Chin, W.-N. (eds.) ATVA 2010. LNCS, vol. 6252, pp. 371–377. Springer, Heidelberg (2010)
5. Mota, A., Sampaio, A.: Model-checking CSP-Z: strategy, tool support and industrial application. Science of Computer Programming 40(1), 59–96 (2001)
6. Jackson, E.K., Levendovszky, T., Balasubramanian, D.: Reasoning about metamodeling with formal specifications and automatic proofs. In: Whittle, J., Clark, T., Kühne, T. (eds.) MODELS 2011. LNCS, vol. 6981, pp. 653–667. Springer, Heidelberg (2011)
7. Rossi, F., van Beek, P., Walsh, T. (eds.): Handbook of Constraint Programming. Elsevier (2006)

---

[2] The EU Framework 7 Integrated Project "Comprehensive Modelling for Advanced Systems of Systems" (COMPASS, Grant Agreement 287829).

8. De Moura, L., Bjørner, N.: Z3: an efficient SMT solver. In: Ramakrishnan, C.R., Rehof, J. (eds.) TACAS 2008. LNCS, vol. 4963, pp. 337–340. Springer, Heidelberg (2008)

9. Fowler, M.: Domain Specific Languages, 1st edn. Addison-Wesley Professional (2010)

10. Corradini, A., Heckel, R., Montanari, U.: Graphical Operational Semantics. In: ICALP Satellite Workshops, pp. 411–418 (2000)

11. Leuschel, M.: Design and Implementation of the High-Level Specification Language CSP(LP) in Prolog. In: Ramakrishnan, I.V. (ed.) PADL 2001. LNCS, vol. 1990, pp. 14–28. Springer, Heidelberg (2001)

12. Verdejo, A., Marti-Oliet, N.: Executing and Verifying CCS in Maude. Technical report, Dpto. Sist. Informaticos y Programacion, Univ. Complutense de (2002)

13. Visser, E.: Program transformation with Stratego/XT. In: Lengauer, C., Batory, D., Consel, C., Odersky, M. (eds.) Domain-Specific Program Generation. LNCS, vol. 3016, pp. 216–238. Springer, Heidelberg (2004)

14. Dan, L.: QVT Based Model Transformation from Sequence Diagram to CSP. In: 2010 15th IEEE International Conference on Engineering of Complex Computer Systems (ICECCS), pp. 349–354 (2010)

15. Liu, Y.A., Stoller, S.D.: From datalog rules to efficient programs with time and space guarantees. ACM Trans. Program. Lang. Syst. 31(6), 21:1–21:38 (2009)

16. Dao-Tran, M., Eiter, T., Fink, M., Krennwallner, T.: First-Order Encodings for Modular Nonmonotonic Datalog Programs. In: de Moor, O., Gottlob, G., Furche, T., Sellers, A. (eds.) Datalog 2010. LNCS, vol. 6702, pp. 59–77. Springer, Heidelberg (2011)

17. Freitas, L.: Model Checking *Circus*. PhD thesis, University of York (2005)

18. Morgan, C.: Programming from Specifications. Prentice-Hall, Inc., Upper Saddle River (1990)

19. Bryans, J., Galloway, A., Woodcock, J.: COMPASS deliverable D23.2. Technical report (2013), http://www.compass-research.eu/

20. Andrews, Z., Payne, R., Romanovsky, A., Didier, A., Mota, A.: Model-based development of fault tolerant systems of systems. In: 2013 IEEE International Systems Conference (SysCon), pp. 356–363 (2013)

21. Andrews, Z., Didier, A., Payne, R., Ingram, C., Holt, J., Perry, S., Oliveira, M., Woodcock, J., Mota, A., Romanovsky, A.: Report on timed fault tree analysis — fault modelling. Technical Report D24.2, COMPASS (September 2013)

22. Object Management Group (OMG): Systems Modelling Language (SysML) 1.3. website (June 2012)

23. Palikareva, H., Ouaknine, J., Roscoe, A.W.: SAT-solving in CSP Trace Refinement. Sci. Comput. Program. 77(10-11), 1178–1197 (2012)

24. Bjørner, N., McMillan, K., Rybalchenko, A.: Program Verification as Satisfiability Modulo Theories. In: SMT Workshop (July 2012)

25. Alberti, F., Bruttomesso, R., Ghilardi, S., Ranise, S., Sharygina, N.: Reachability Modulo Theory Library (Extended abstract). In: SMT Workshop (July 2012)

26. Rosu, G., Serbanuta, T.F.: K Overview and SIMPLE Case Study. In: Proceedings of International K Workshop (K 2011). ENTCS. Elsevier (2013) (to appear)

27. Hoare, T., He, J.: Unifying theories of programming, vol. 14. Prentice Hall, Englewood Cliffs (1998)

28. Lazić, R.: A Semantic Study of Data-independence with Applications to the Mechanical Verification of Concurrent Systems. PhD thesis, Oxford University (1999)

Learning Extended Finite State Machines*

Sofia Cassel[1], Falk Howar[2], Bengt Jonsson[1], and Bernhard Steffen[3]

[1] Dept. of Information Technology, Uppsala University, Sweden
{sofia.cassel,bengt.jonsson}@it.uu.se
[2] Carnegie Mellon University, Moffet, CA, USA
howar@cmu.edu
[3] Chair for Programming Systems, Technical University Dortmund, Germany
steffen@cs.tu-dortmund.de

Abstract. We present an active learning algorithm for inferring extended finite state machines (EFSM)s, combining data flow and control behavior. Key to our learning technique is a novel learning model based on so-called *tree queries*. The learning algorithm uses the tree queries to infer symbolic data constraints on parameters, e.g., sequence numbers, time stamps, identifiers, or even simple arithmetic. We describe sufficient conditions for the properties that the symbolic constraints provided by a tree query in general must have to be usable in our learning model. We have evaluated our algorithm in a black-box scenario, where tree queries are realized through (black-box) testing. Our case studies include connection establishment in TCP and a priority queue from the Java Class Library.

1 Introduction

Behavioral models of components and interfaces are the basis for many powerful software development and verification techniques, such as model checking, model based test generation, controller synthesis, and service composition. Ideally, such models should be part of documentation (e.g., of a component library), but in practice they are often nonexistent or outdated. To address this problem, techniques for automatically generating models of component behavior are being developed. These techniques can be based on static analysis, dynamic analysis, or a combination of both approaches. Static analysis of a component requires access to its source code; so when source code is not available, or when models must be generated on the fly, dynamic analysis is a better alternative.

In dynamic analysis, test executions are used to drive and observe component behavior. Mature techniques for generating finite-state models, describing the possible orderings of interactions between a component and its environment, have been developed to support, e.g., interface modeling [4], test generation [27], and security analysis [23]. However, faithful models should capture not only the ordering between interactions (control flow aspects), but also the constraints

---

* Supported in part by the European FP7 project CONNECT (IST 231167), and by the UPMARC centre of excellence.

D. Giannakopoulou and G. Salaün (Eds.): SEFM 2014, LNCS 8702, pp. 250–264, 2014.
© Springer International Publishing Switzerland 2014

on any data parameters passed with these interactions (data flow aspects). Data flow aspects are commonly captured by extending finite state machines with variables. Together with the data parameters passed with interactions, the variables influence the control flow by means of guards, and the control flow can cause updates of variables. Different dialects of *extended finite state machines* (EFSMs) are successfully used in tools for model-based testing [18], software model checking [19], and model-based development [11]. However, dynamic analysis techniques that generate EFSM models with guards and assignments to variables are still lacking: existing techniques either handle only a limited range of operations on data (typically only equality [16,15]), require significant manual effort [2], or rely on access to source code.

In this paper, we present a black-box technique for generating *register automata* (RAs), which are a particular form of EFSMs in which transitions are equipped with guards and assignments to variables (called *registers*). Our contribution is an active automata learning algorithm for RAs, which is parameterized on a particular *theory*, i.e., a set of operations and tests on the data domain that can be used in guards. By an appropriate choice of theory, we can infer RA models where data parameters and variables represent sequence numbers, time stamps, numbers with limited arithmetic, identifiers, etc.

Our algorithm has been evaluated in a black-box scenario, using SMT-based test generation for realizing tree queries for integers with addition ($+$), equalities ($=$), and inequalities ($<, >$). We have learned models of the connection establishment in TCP and the priority queue from the Java Class Library.

Illustrating Example. We give an example of an RA that can be generated using our technique. We begin by describing the language that it recognizes. Consider a simplistic sliding window protocol without retransmission, with a window of size two, in which the receipt of messages must be acknowledged in order. The protocol is described as a data language $\mathcal{L}_{seq}$ over messages of form $msg(d)$ and $ack(d)$, where d ranges over natural numbers. A sequence of messages $\sigma = msg(d_1) \ldots ack(d_m)$ is in the language $\mathcal{L}_{seq}$ if (i) σ has equally many msg and ack messages, (ii) the data parameter d in each $msg(d)$-message must be one more than the data parameter of the previous msg-message. (iii) the data parameter d in each $ack(d)$-message must be one more than the data parameter of the previous ack-message. (iv) whenever $msg(d)$ immediately precedes $ack(d')$, then $d - 1 \le d' \le d$. Sequences $msg(1)ack(1)msg(2)ack(2)$ and $msg(1)msg(2)ack(1)ack(2)$ are examples of data words in $\mathcal{L}_{seq}$.

Fig. 1 shows a register automaton that accepts $\mathcal{L}_{seq}$. Locations are annotated with registers. Accepting locations are denoted by double circles; l_0 is the initial location. Transitions are denoted by arrows and labeled with a message, a guard over parameters of the message and registers of the automaton, and an assignment to these registers. A sink location and its adjacent transitions are omitted in the figure. The automaton processes sequences σ by first moving from l_0 to l_1 and storing the data value of the initial msg in x_1. It then moves between locations l_1 (waiting for an ack), l_2 (waiting for two $acks$), and l_3 (accepting). $\mathcal{L}_{seq}$ is used as a running example throughout the paper.

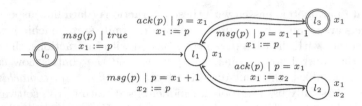

Fig. 1. A simple sliding window protocol with sequence numbers

Main Ideas. In classic active learning for finite automata (e.g., L^* [5]), each location of an inferred automaton is identified by a word that reaches it from the initial location. Two words lead to the same location if they behave the same when prepended to the same suffix (i.e., both are accepted or both rejected). Similarly, each location in the RAs we infer is identified by a data word. To determine whether two data words represent the same location, it is, however, not sufficient to check whether they behave the same when prepended to the same suffix, since we want to model relations between data parameters and not concrete data values. For example, when learning $\mathcal{L}_{seq}$, we might wrongly deduce that $msg(3)$ and $msg(1)$ represent different locations, by observing that $msg(3)ack(3) \in \mathcal{L}_{seq}$ but $msg(1)ack(3) \notin \mathcal{L}_{seq}$. To remedy this, we have generalized the L^* algorithm to the symbolic setting.

We describe our learning framework as a game between a learner and a teacher: the learner has to infer an automaton model of an unknown target language by making *queries* to a teacher who knows it. The concept of a teacher is an abstraction that helps us separate different concerns; the concrete learning framework is defined by the types of queries that the teacher can answer, and the class of languages that can be learned.

Teacher. In our framework, the Teacher answers *equivalence queries* and *tree queries*. The answer to an equivalence query tells us if a conjectured automaton is correct, i.e., it accepts the unknown language. If not, the teacher provides a counterexample, i.e., a data word that is in the language but not accepted by the conjectured automaton, or vice versa. In practice, counterexamples can be provided by, e.g., conformance testing or monitoring.

A tree query consists of a concrete prefix (e.g., a sequence of messages where data parameters are instantiated with concrete data values) and a symbolic suffix. Symbolic suffixes are obtained from concrete suffixes by replacing data values by symbolic parameters (e.g., $ack(p)$). The answer to a tree query is a *symbolic decision tree* (SDT), which describes which instantiations of the symbolic suffix are accepted and which are rejected. Fig. 2 shows examples of SDTs for $\mathcal{L}_{seq}$. We depict trees with the root location at the top and annotate locations with registers. A register in the root location with index i holds the i-th data value of the corresponding prefix. The trees describe the fragments of $\mathcal{L}_{seq}$ for suffixes of form $ack(p)$ after prefixes $msg(1)$ (Tree [a]) and $msg(1)ack(1)msg(2)$ (Tree [b]). They each have a register at the root location and two guarded initial transitions. In both trees, $ack(p)$ leads to an accepting location only when the value

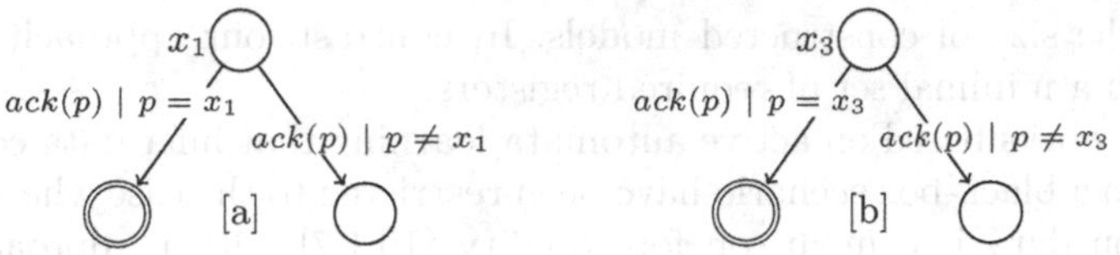

Fig. 2. Isomorphic SDTs for $ack(p)$ after [a] $msg(1)$, and [b] $msg(1)ack(1)msg(2)$

of the parameter p is equal to the value of the register in the root location (i.e., the value of the parameter from the most recent $msg(p)$).

Learner. The learner infers a register automaton that accepts the unknown target language by making tree queries and equivalence queries. At a very abstract level, our learning algorithm builds a prefix-closed set of *prefixes*, i.e., test sequences with concrete data values that reach control locations of the inferred register automaton. To determine when prefixes should lead to the same control location in the automaton, the learner compares SDTs to each other. Prefixes with equivalent SDTs (isomorphic up to renaming of registers and locations) can be unified. The transitions of SDTs will be used to create registers, guards, and assignments in the automaton. For example, the trees in Fig. 2 are equivalent — meaning that the corresponding prefixes $msg(1)$ and $msg(1)ack(1)msg(2)$ should lead to the same location.

The learner submits the hypothesis automaton to an equivalence query. If the equivalence query is successful, the algorithm terminates; otherwise, a counterexample is returned. Counterexamples guide the algorithm to make tree queries for larger fragments of the target language, e.g., for more and/or longer suffixes after a given prefix. The resulting SDTs will lead to refinements in the hypothesis: previously unified prefixes may be split, new registers may be introduced, and transitions may be refined or new ones introduced.

Related Work. The problem of generating models from implementations has been addressed in a number of different ways. Proposed approaches range from mining source code [4], static analysis [25] and predicate abstraction [3,24] to dynamic analysis [12,6,28,22]. Closest to our work are approaches that combine an automata learning algorithm with a method for inferring constraints on data. An early black-box approach to inferring EFSM-like models is [20], where models are generated from execution traces by combining passive automata learning with the Daikon tool [10].

A number of approaches combine active automata learning with different methods for inferring constraints on data parameters. All these approaches follow a pattern similar to CEGAR (counterexample guided abstraction refinement). A sequence of models is refined in a process that is usually monotonic and converges to a fixpoint. Active automata learning has been combined with symbolic execution [13,8] and an approach based on support vector machines [29] for inferring constraints on data parameters in white-box scenarios. In white-box learning scenarios (as in other static analyses) registers or state variables do not have to be inferred as they are readily available. Sometimes abstraction is used to reduce the size of constructed models. In contrast, our approach will infer models with a minimal set of required registers.

Previous works based on active automata learning that infer data constraints from tests in a black-box scenario have been restricted to the case where the only operation on data is comparison for equality [16,1,7]. Other approaches infer models without symbolic data constraints [17,23] or require manually provided abstractions on the data domain [2]. In general, black-box methods can infer complex (e.g., arithmetic) constraints only at a very high cost — if at all. Our black-box implementation is subject to these principal limitations, too.

While existing approaches extend active learning to a fix class of behavioral models, we present a general purpose automata learning algorithm that can be combined with any method for generating data constraints (meeting the requirements we discuss in this paper).

Register automata are similar to the symbolic transducers of [26]. It is an open question if some of the decidability results for symbolic transducers can be adapted to RAs to help answer for which relations and operations tree queries and equivalence queries are decidable.

Outline. In Sec. 2, we introduce register automata and data languages. In Sec. 3, we define symbolic decision trees and discuss how a tree oracle answers tree queries. We present the details of the learning algorithm in Sec. 4, and Sec. 5 presents the results of applying it in a small series of experiments. Here, we also briefly describe the implementation of a teacher for our learning framework. Conclusions are in Sec. 6.

2   Preliminaries

In this section, we introduce the central concepts of our framework: theories, data languages, and register automata.

Theories. Our framework is parameterized by a *theory*, which consists of an unbounded domain $\mathcal{D}$ of *data values*, and $\mathcal{R}$ is a set of *relations* on $\mathcal{D}$. The relations in $\mathcal{R}$ can have arbitrary arity. Known constants can be represented by unary relations. For example, the theory of natural numbers with inequality is the theory $\langle \mathbb{N}, \{<\} \rangle$ where $\mathbb{N}$ is the natural numbers and $<$ is the inequality relation on $\mathbb{N}$. In the following, we assume that some theory has been fixed.

Data Languages. We assume a set Σ of *actions*, each with an arity that determines how many parameters it takes from the domain $\mathcal{D}$. In this paper, we assume that all actions have arity 1; it is straightforward to extend our results to the case where actions have arbitrary arity. A *data symbol* is a term of form $\alpha(d)$, where α is an action and $d \in \mathcal{D}$ is a data value. A *data word* is a sequence of data symbols. For a data word $w = \alpha_1(d_1) \ldots \alpha_n(d_n)$, let $Acts(w)$ denote its sequence of actions $\alpha_1 \ldots \alpha_n$, and $Vals(w)$ its sequence of data values $d_1 \ldots d_n$. The concatenation of two data words w and w' is denoted ww'. Two data words $w = \alpha_1(d_1) \ldots \alpha_n(d_n)$ and $w' = \alpha_1(d'_1) \ldots \alpha_n(d'_n)$ are $\mathcal{R}$-*indistinguishable*, denoted $w \approx_{\mathcal{R}} w'$, if $Acts(w) = Acts(w')$ and $R(d_{i_1}, \ldots, d_{i_j}) \leftrightarrow R(d'_{i_1}, \ldots, d'_{i_j})$

whenever $R \in \mathcal{R}$ and $i_1, \ldots, i_j$ are indices between 1 and n. Intuitively, w and w' are $\mathcal{R}$-indistinguishable if they have the same sequences of actions and cannot be distinguished by the relations in $\mathcal{R}$.

A *data language* $\mathcal{L}$ is a set of data words that respects $\mathcal{R}$ in the sense that $w \approx_{\mathcal{R}} w'$ implies $w \in \mathcal{L} \leftrightarrow w' \in \mathcal{L}$. A data language can be represented as a mapping from the set of data words to $\{+, -\}$, where $+$ stands for *accept* and $-$ for *reject*.

Register Automata. Assume a set of *registers* (or variables), ranged over by $x_1, x_2, \ldots$. A *parameterized symbol* is a term of form $\alpha(p)$, where α is an action and p a formal parameter. A *guard* is a conjunction of negated and unnegated relations (from $\mathcal{R}$) over the parameter p and registers. An *assignment* is a simple parallel update of registers with values from registers or p.

Definition 1. A *register automaton* (RA) is a tuple $\mathcal{A} = (L, l_0, \mathcal{X}, \Gamma, \lambda)$, where

- L is a finite set of *locations*, with $l_0 \in L$ as the *initial location*,
- λ maps each $l \in L$ to $\{+, -\}$,
- $\mathcal{X}$ maps each location $l \in L$ to a finite set $\mathcal{X}(l)$ of registers, and
- Γ is a finite set of *transitions*, each of form $\langle l, \alpha(p), g, \pi, l' \rangle$, where
  - $l \in L$ is a source location,
  - $l' \in L$ is a target location,
  - $\alpha(p)$ is a parameterized symbol,
  - g is a guard over p and $\mathcal{X}(l)$, and
  - π (the *assignment*) is a mapping from $\mathcal{X}(l')$ to $\mathcal{X}(l) \cup \{p\}$ (meaning that the value of $\pi(x_i)$ is assigned to the register $x_i \in \mathcal{X}(l')$). □

We require register automata to be completely specified in the sense that whenever there is an α-transitions from some location $l \in L$, then the disjunction of the guards on α-transitions from l is *true*.

Let us now describe the semantics of an RA. A *state* of an RA $\mathcal{A} = (L, l_0, \mathcal{X}, \Gamma, \lambda)$ is a pair $\langle l, \nu \rangle$ where $l \in L$ and ν is a valuation over $\mathcal{X}(l)$, i.e., a mapping from $\mathcal{X}(l)$ to $\mathcal{D}$. The state is *initial* if $l = l_0$. A *step* of $\mathcal{A}$, denoted $\langle l, \nu \rangle \xrightarrow{\alpha(d)} \langle l', \nu' \rangle$, transfers $\mathcal{A}$ from $\langle l, \nu \rangle$ to $\langle l', \nu' \rangle$ on input of the data symbol $\alpha(d)$ if there is a transition $\langle l, \alpha(p), g, \pi, l' \rangle \in \Gamma$ with

1. $\nu \models g[d/p]$, i.e., d satisfies the guard g under the valuation ν, and
2. ν' is the updated valuation with $\nu'(x_i) = \nu(x_j)$ if $\pi(x_i) = x_j$, otherwise $\nu'(x_i) = d$ if $\pi(x_i) = p$.

A *run* of $\mathcal{A}$ over a data word $w = \alpha(d_1) \ldots \alpha(d_n)$ is a sequence of steps

$$\langle l_0, \nu_0 \rangle \xrightarrow{\alpha_1(d_1)} \langle l_1, \nu_1 \rangle \quad \ldots \quad \langle l_{n-1}, \nu_{n-1} \rangle \xrightarrow{\alpha_n(d_n)} \langle l_n, \nu_n \rangle$$

for some initial valuation ν_0. The run is *accepting* if $\lambda(l_n) = +$ and *rejecting* if $\lambda(l_n) = -$. The word w is *accepted (rejected) by* $\mathcal{A}$ under ν_0 if $\mathcal{A}$ has an accepting (rejecting) run over w which starts in $\langle l_0, \nu_0 \rangle$. Note that an RA defined as above does not necessarily have runs over all data words.

We define a *simple register automaton* (SRA) to be an RA with no registers in the initial location, whose runs over a given data word are either all accepting or all rejecting. We use SRAs as acceptors for data languages.

3   Tree Queries

In this section, we first define symbolic decision trees (SDTs), which are used to symbolically describe a fragment of a data language. We then state conditions for the construction of SDTs, which is done by a *tree oracle*.

Symbolic Decision Trees. A *symbolic decision tree* (SDT) is an RA $\mathcal{T} = (L, l_0, \mathcal{X}, \Gamma, \lambda)$ where L and Γ form a tree rooted at l_0. In general, an SDT has registers in the initial location; we use $\mathcal{X}(\mathcal{T})$ to denote these registers $\mathcal{X}(l_0)$. Thus, an SDT has well-defined semantics only wrt. a given valuation of $\mathcal{X}(\mathcal{T})$.

If l is a location of $\mathcal{T}$, let $\mathcal{T}[l]$ denote the subtree of $\mathcal{T}$ rooted at l. Let $\mathcal{T}$ and $\mathcal{T}'$ be two SDTs, such that $\gamma : \mathcal{X}(\mathcal{T}) \mapsto \mathcal{X}(\mathcal{T}')$ is a bijection from the initial registers of $\mathcal{T}$ to the initial registers of $\mathcal{T}$. We say that $\mathcal{T}$ and $\mathcal{T}'$ are *equivalent under* γ, denoted $\mathcal{T} \simeq_\gamma \mathcal{T}'$, if γ can be extended to a bijection from all registers of $\mathcal{T}$ to all registers of $\mathcal{T}'$, under which $\mathcal{T}$ and $\mathcal{T}'$ are isomorphic.

Let a *symbolic suffix* be a sequence of actions in Σ^*. Let u be a data word with $Vals(u) = d_1, \ldots, d_k$. Let ν_u be defined by $\nu_u(x_i) = d_i$. We require that for each data word u and each guard g over p and $Vals(u)$, the guard g has a *representative data value* in $\mathcal{D}$, denoted d_u^g, such that $\nu_u \models g[\mathsf{d}_u^g/p]$ (i.e., d_u^g satisfies p after u), and such that whenever g' is a stronger guard satisfied by d_u^g (i.e., $\nu_u \models g[\mathsf{d}_u^g/p]$) then $\mathsf{d}_u^{g'} = \mathsf{d}_u^g$.

Definition 2. For a data language $\mathcal{L}$, a data word u with $Vals(u) = d_1, \ldots, d_k$, and a set V of symbolic suffixes, a (u, V)-*tree* is an SDT $\mathcal{T}$ that has runs over all data words v with $Acts(v) \in V$, such that v is accepted by $\mathcal{T}$ under ν_u iff $uv \in \mathcal{L}$ (and rejected iff $uv \notin \mathcal{L}$) whenever $Acts(v) \in V$. Moreover, in any run of $\mathcal{T}$ over a data word v, the register x_i may contain only the value of the ith data value in uv.   □

The last requirement simplifies the matching of decision trees. It can be enforced, e.g., by requiring that whenever $\langle l, \alpha(p), g, \pi, l' \rangle$ is the jth transition on some path from l_0, then for each $x_i \in \mathcal{X}(l')$ we have either (i) $i < k+j$ and $\pi(x_i) = x_i$, or (ii) $i = k + j$ and $\pi(x_i) = p$ (recall that k is the length of u).

The *initial* α-*transitions* of an SDT are the transitions for action α from the root location l_0, guarded by *initial* α-*guards*. The SDT in Fig. 2 [a] has two initial $ack(p)$-transitions with initial $ack(p)$-guards $p = x_1$ and $p \neq x_1$.

Tree Oracles. A key concept in our approach is that of tree queries. Tree queries are made to a tree oracle, which returns an SDT. To ensure the consistency of tree queries, a tree oracle must satisfy the conditions in the following definition.

Definition 3. Let $\mathcal{L}$ be a data language. A *tree oracle* for $\mathcal{L}$ is a function $\mathcal{O}_{\mathcal{L}}$, which for a data word u and a set V of symbolic suffixes returns a (u, V)-tree $\mathcal{T}$, and satisfies the following constraints.

1. If $V \subseteq V'$, then $\mathcal{O}_{\mathcal{L}}(u, V') \simeq_\gamma \mathcal{O}_{\mathcal{L}}(u, V')$ implies $\mathcal{O}_{\mathcal{L}}(u, V) \simeq_\gamma \mathcal{O}_{\mathcal{L}}(u, V)$ for all u, u' and γ (i.e., adding more symbolic suffixes cannot make inequivalent trees equivalent).

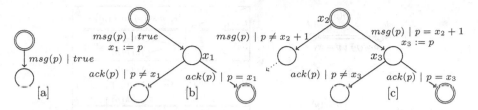

Fig. 3. [a] SDT for $msg(p)$ after prefixes ϵ and $msg(1)ack(1)$. Refined SDTs for suffix $msg(p)ack(p)$ after [b] ϵ and [c] $msg(1)ack(1)$.

2. If $V \subseteq V'$, then for each initial α-transition of $\mathcal{O}_\mathcal{L}(u, V)$ with guard g, there is some initial α transition of $\mathcal{O}_\mathcal{L}(u, V')$ with a stronger guard g' (i.e., $\nu_u \models g' \longrightarrow g$).

3. If $\langle l_0, \alpha(p), g, \pi, l \rangle$ is an initial transition of $\mathcal{O}_\mathcal{L}(u, V)$, then $\mathcal{O}_\mathcal{L}(u, V)[l] \simeq_\gamma \mathcal{O}_\mathcal{L}(u\alpha(d), \alpha^{-1}V)$, where $d = \mathsf{d}_u^g$, and γ is the identify mapping (i.e., any subtree of $\mathcal{O}_\mathcal{L}(u, V)$ must be isomorphic to the subtree after d: here $\alpha^{-1}V$ denotes the set of sequences $\alpha_1 \cdots \alpha_n$ such that $\alpha\alpha_1 \cdots \alpha_n \in V$).   □

The first two conditions in Def. 3 ensure monotonicity: First, extending V will only preserve or introduce inequivalence between trees of different prefixes. Second, by gradually extending V, we will only refine trees and not, e.g., merge transitions or forget registers. Fig. 3 [b] and [c] show SDTs that refine SDT [a]. SDT [b] refines [a] by adding an assignment $x_1 := p$ to the initial transition and by adding new transitions after the initial one. SDT [c] refines [a] by splitting the initial transition into two transitions with refined guards, and by initializing a register in the root location. The third condition ensures that it is sufficient to consider concrete prefixes with representative data values during learning.

Finally, let two data words u and u' be equivalent, denoted by $u \equiv_{\mathcal{O}_\mathcal{L}} u'$ if $\mathcal{O}_\mathcal{L}(u, V) \simeq_\gamma \mathcal{O}_\mathcal{L}(u', V)$ for some γ and any finite V. A data language $\mathcal{L}$ is *regular* if $\equiv_{\mathcal{O}_\mathcal{L}}$ has finite index. The regularity of $\mathcal{L}$ is relative to the implementation of tree queries, since $\equiv_{\mathcal{O}_\mathcal{L}}$ is defined on SDTs.

The following adaptation of the Myhill/Nerode theorem provides the basis for convergence of the automata learning algorithm presented in the next section.

Theorem 1 (Myhill-Nerode). Let $\mathcal{L}$ be a data language, and let $\mathcal{O}_\mathcal{L}$ be a tree oracle for $\mathcal{L}$. If the equivalence $\equiv_{\mathcal{O}_\mathcal{L}}$ has finite index, then there is an SRA which accepts precisely the language $\mathcal{L}$.   □

4   The SL* Algorithm

This section presents the central ideas for an active automata learning algorithm SL^* (*Symbolic L^**, reminiscent of the L^* algorithm). To construct an SRA for some unknown data language, we need to infer locations, transitions, and registers. **Locations** of an SRA can be characterized by their SDTs, which are obtained by making tree queries. Data words with equivalent SDTs will lead to the same location. The initial **transitions** of the SDTs will serve as transitions

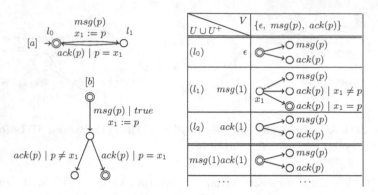

Fig. 4. Hypothesis [a] (without error location l_2) and its observation table (right). Transitions [b] for suffix $msg(p)ack(p)$ after prefix $msg(1)ack(1)$ in hypothesis.

in the SRA. The **registers** of an SDT will become registers in the location that the SDT represents. A *hypothesis* automaton is constructed and submitted for an *equivalence query*. If it matches (which will happen eventually for regular data languages), the algorithm terminates. Otherwise, the returned counterexample is processed, leading to refinement of the hypothesis.

The SL^* algorithm maintains an *observation table* $\langle U, V, Z \rangle$, where U is a prefix-closed set of data words, called *short prefixes*, V is a set of symbolic suffixes, and Z maps each element u in U to its (u, V)-tree. The algorithm also maintains a finite set U^+ of extended prefixes of the form $u\alpha(d)$ (abbreviated $u\alpha$), such that $u \in U$ and d is d_u^g, where g is an initial α-guard of $Z(u)$. Fig. 4 (right) shows an observation table for the example in Sec. 1. A set of symbolic suffixes V labels the column; rows are labeled with short prefixes from U (above the double line) and with prefixes from U^+ (below the double line). Each table cell (referred to by row label u and column label V) stores the SDT $Z(u)$.

Algorithm 1 shows a pseudocode description of SL^*. The algorithm is initialized (line 1) with U containing the empty word, the set of symbolic suffixes V being the empty sequence together with the set of all actions, and $Z(\epsilon)$ being the SDT $\mathcal{O}_{\mathcal{L}}(\epsilon, V)$. The algorithm then iterates three phases: *hypothesis construction*, *hypothesis validation*, and *counterexample processing* until no more counterexamples are found, monotonically adding locations and transitions to hypothesis automata. We detail these phases below, referring to lines in Algorithm 1.

Hypothesis Construction (lines 3-11). In this phase, the algorithm attempts to construct a hypothesis automaton by making tree queries and entering the results in an observation table. The answer to a tree query for the prefix u and the set of symbolic suffixes V is the SDT $\mathcal{O}_{\mathcal{L}}(u, V)$, stored in the table as $Z(u)$.

An observation table $\langle U, V, Z \rangle$ is

- *closed*, if for every $u \in U^+$ there is a short prefix $u' \in U$ and a γ such that $Z(u) \simeq_\gamma Z(u')$. Closedness ensures that all transitions in the automaton have a target location. If the table is not closed, then u leads to a location not covered by U, and $Z(u)$ proves it by not being equivalent to $Z(u')$ for

Algorithm 1 SL^*

Require: A set Σ of actions, a data language $\mathcal{L}$, a tree oracle $\mathcal{O}_\mathcal{L}$ for $\mathcal{L}$.
Ensure: An SRA $\mathcal{H}$ with $\mathcal{L}(\mathcal{H}) = \mathcal{L}$
1: $U \leftarrow \{\epsilon\}$, $V \leftarrow (\{\epsilon\} \cup \Sigma)$, $Z(\epsilon) \leftarrow \mathcal{O}_\mathcal{L}(\epsilon, V)$ $\qquad\qquad\qquad$ ▷ **Initialization**
2: **loop**
3: $\quad$ **repeat** $\qquad\qquad\qquad\qquad\qquad\qquad\qquad\qquad$ ▷ **Hypothesis construction**
4: $\qquad$ $U^+ \leftarrow \{u\alpha(\mathsf{d}_u^g) \; : \; u \in U, \; \alpha \in \Sigma, \text{ and } g \text{ initial } \alpha\text{-guard of } Z(u)\}$
5: $\qquad$ For each $u \in (U \cup U^+)$, $Z(u) \leftarrow \mathcal{O}_\mathcal{L}(u, V)$
6: $\qquad$ **if** $\exists u \in U^+$ s.t. $Z(u) \not\simeq_\gamma Z(u')$ for any γ and $u' \in U$ **then**
7: $\qquad\quad$ $U \leftarrow U \cup \{u\}$
8: $\qquad$ **if** $\exists u\alpha \in U^+$ and $\exists x_i \in \mathcal{X}(Z(u\alpha)) \cap Vals(u)$ s.t. $x_i \notin \mathcal{X}(Z(u))$ **then**
9: $\qquad\quad$ $V \leftarrow V \cup \{\alpha v\}$ for $v \in V$ with $x_i \in \mathcal{X}(\mathcal{O}_\mathcal{L}(u\alpha, \{v\}))$
10: $\quad$ **until** $\langle U, V, Z \rangle$ is closed **and** register-consistent
11: $\quad$ $\mathcal{H} \leftarrow Hyp(\langle U, V, Z \rangle)$
12: $\quad$ **if** $eq(\mathcal{H})$ **then Return** $\mathcal{H}$ $\qquad\qquad\qquad\qquad\qquad$ ▷ **Hypothesis validation**
13: $\quad$ **else** $\qquad\qquad\qquad\qquad\qquad\qquad\qquad\qquad$ ▷ **Counterexample processing**
14: $\qquad$ **for** $\langle u_{i-1}, \alpha_i(p), g_i, \pi_i, u_i \rangle$ in run of $\mathcal{H}$ over σ **do**
15: $\qquad\quad$ **if** g_i does not refine an initial trans. of $\mathcal{O}_\mathcal{L}(u_{i-1}, V_{i-1})$ **then** $V \leftarrow V \cup V_{i-1}$
16: $\qquad\quad$ **if** $\mathcal{O}_\mathcal{L}(u_{i-1}\alpha_i, V_i) \not\simeq_\gamma \mathcal{O}_\mathcal{L}(u_i, V_i)$ for γ used to construct $\mathcal{H}$ **then**
17: $\qquad\qquad$ $V \leftarrow V \cup V_i$
18: **end loop**

---

any short prefix u'. $\langle U, V, Z \rangle$ is closed by making u a short prefix, i.e., adding it to U.

- *register-consistent*, if $(\mathcal{X}(Z(u\alpha)) \cap Vals(u)) \subseteq \mathcal{X}(Z(u))$ for every $u\alpha \in U^+$. Register-consistency ensures that whenever a data value in u is needed to construct the SDT after $u\alpha$, then it also occurs in the tree after u. If the table is not register-consistent, then $Z(u\alpha)$ has a register that expects a value from u but $Z(u)$ does not have a register for storing this value. We make $\langle U, V, Z \rangle$ register-consistent by extending V with the appropriate abstract word αv with $v \in V$, propagating the missing register backwards to $Z(u)$.

A closed and register-consistent observation table $\langle U, V, Z \rangle$ can be used together with a set U^+ of extended prefixes to construct a hypothesis automaton $Hyp(\langle U, V, Z \rangle) = (L, l_0, \mathcal{X}, \Gamma, \lambda)$, where

- $L = U$ and $l_0 = \epsilon$,
- $\mathcal{X}$ maps each location $u \in U$ to $\mathcal{X}(Z(u))$ ($\mathcal{X}(l_0)$ is the empty set),
- $\lambda(u) = +$ if $u \in \mathcal{L}$, otherwise $\lambda(u) = -$, and
- each $u\alpha \in (U \cup U^+)$ with corresponding initial α-transition $\langle l_0, \alpha(p), g, \pi, l' \rangle$ of $Z(u)$ generates a transition $\langle u, \alpha(p), g, \pi', u' \rangle$ in Γ, where
  - u' is the (unique) prefix in U with $Z(u\alpha) \simeq_\gamma Z(u')$,
  - π' is an assignment $\mathcal{X}(Z(u')) \mapsto (\mathcal{X}(Z(u)) \cup \{p\})$. For $x_i \in \mathcal{X}(Z(u'))$, we define $\pi'(x_i) = \gamma^{-1}(x_i)$ if $\gamma^{-1}(x_i)$ stores a data value of u in $Z(u\alpha)$, and $\pi'(x_i) = p$ otherwise.

Fig. 4 shows an observation table that is closed and register-consistent. Fig. 4 [a] shows the hypothesis that can be constructed from it. In the table, rows for short prefixes (above the double line) are annotated with corresponding locations in the hypothesis. The assignment on the transition from l_0 to l_1 and the guard on the transition from l_1 to l_0 are both derived from the SDT for prefix $msg(1)$.

Hypothesis Validation (line 12). The hypothesis automaton $\mathcal{H}$ is submitted for an equivalence query. The teacher either replies 'OK', or returns a counterexample (a word that is accepted by $\mathcal{H}$ but rejected by the target system, or vice versa). If it replies 'OK', the algorithm terminates and returns $\mathcal{H}$. Otherwise, the counterexample has to be analyzed.

Counterexample Analysis (lines 13-16). A counterexample indicates either that a location is missing, (i.e., that U has to be extended), or that a transition is missing, (i.e., that SDTs need to be refined), or that we used an incorrect renaming γ between some SDTs when constructing the hypothesis. For a counterexample σ of length m we denote by σ_i its prefix of length i, and by v_i its suffix of length $m - i$. Moreover, let V_i be the singleton set $\{Acts(v_i)\}$.

In a run of $\mathcal{H}$ over σ, the i-th step $\langle u_{i-1}, \nu_{i-1} \rangle \xrightarrow{\alpha_i(d_i)} \langle u_i, \nu_i \rangle$ traverses transition $\langle u_{i-1}, \alpha_i(p), g_i, \pi_i, u_i \rangle$, i.e., prefix σ_i leads to the location corresponding to short prefix u_i from U. In order to determine at which step the run of $\mathcal{H}$ over σ diverges from the behavior of the system under learning, we analyze the sequence $u_0 = \epsilon, \ldots, u_m$ and the corresponding (u_i, V_i)-trees for $0 \leq i \leq m$ computed by $\mathcal{O}_\mathcal{L}(u_i, V_i)$, using an argument similar to the one presented in [21]: Since σ is a counterexample and V contains ϵ, there is an index j of the counterexample for which u_{j-1} together with $\mathcal{O}_\mathcal{L}(u_{j-1}, V_{j-1})$ contains a counterexample to $\mathcal{H}$, while u_j and $\mathcal{O}_\mathcal{L}(u_j, V_j)$ do not. We can then distinguish two cases.

Case 1. The guard g_j in the step of $\mathcal{H}$ from u_{j-1} to u_j does not refine an initial transition of $\mathcal{O}_\mathcal{L}(u_{j-1}, V_{j-1})$. In this case the SDT distinguishes cases that $\mathcal{H}$ does not distinguish. Adding V_{j-1} to V will result in new and refined transitions from u_{j-1} in the hypothesis. This is guaranteed by the monotonicity requirement on tree constructors in Def. 3. Consider, e.g., the counterexample $msg(1)ack(1)msg(1)ack(1)$ to the hypothesis in Fig. 4 at index 3. The hypothesis in Fig. 4 [b] has only one transition with guard *true* after $msg(1)ack(1)$. The corresponding SDT for $\mathcal{L}_{seq}$ (Fig. 3 [c]), on the other hand, has two initial transitions, and neither of them is refined by the *true*. Adding $msg(p)ack(p)$ to V will add these transitions to the hypothesis.

Case 2. The tree $\mathcal{O}_\mathcal{L}(u_j, V_j)$ is not isomorphic to the corresponding subtree after $\alpha(d_{u_{j-1}}^{g_j})$ of $\mathcal{O}_\mathcal{L}(u_{j-1}, V_{j-1})$ under the renaming of registers γ that was used in the hypothesis (only one of these trees contains a counterexample to $\mathcal{H}$). Adding V_j to V will lead to either $\mathcal{O}_\mathcal{L}(u_j, V) \not\simeq \mathcal{O}_\mathcal{L}(u_{j-1}\alpha(d_{u_{j-1}}^{g_j}), V)$ and $u_{j-1}\alpha(d_{u_{j-1}}^{g_j})$ will become a separate location, or γ will be refined. Consider again the counterexample $msg(1)ack(1)msg(1)ack(1)$ to the hypothesis in Fig. 4; this time at index 2. Here, $u_{j-1}\alpha(d_{u_{j-1}}^{g_j})$ is $msg(1)ack(1)$, and $u_j = u_2$ is ϵ. The SDTs for these two prefixes and the suffix $msg(p)ack(p)$ are shown in Fig. 3 [b]

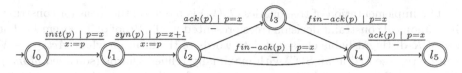

Fig. 5. Connection establishment of TCP (only non-reflexive transitions)

and Fig. 3 [c]. They are not equivalent. Adding the suffix $msg(p)ack(p)$ to V will lead to a new location for $msg(1)ack(1)$ in the next hypothesis.

Correctness and Termination. That SL^* returns a correct SRA upon termination follows by the properties of our teacher. For regular data languages, termination follows from the properties of tree queries in Sec. 3, from Theorem 1, and from the algorithm itself: SDTs will only be refined when adding symbolic suffixes, and this can happen only finitely often. Each added symbolic suffix will either lead to a new transition, a refined transition, a new register assignment or a new location. By adapting arguments from other contexts [5,16], Theorem 1 can be used to show that SL^* converges to a minimal (in terms of locations and registers) SRA for $\mathcal{L}$. Note that this minimal number of locations and transitions also depends on the particular tree oracle that is used.

Complexity. We estimate the worst case number of counterexamples and show how they lead to a correct model with n locations, t transitions, and at most r registers per location. Since each location has one access sequence, $n \leq t$, and thus we estimate the costs in t and r only. The final model is minimal relative to the implementation of tree queries: it has one location per class of $\equiv_{\mathcal{O}_{\mathcal{L}}}$. Each counterexample results in one additional suffix in the observation table, leading to a new transition or to discarding a bijection between two prefixes in U. The former can happen t times before all transitions are identified. The latter can happen at most tr times, since it corresponds to breaking a symmetry between two of at most r registers at one of $n \leq t$ locations (cf. [14]). The algorithm terminates after $O(tr)$ equivalence queries. The number of tree queries depends on the length m of the longest counterexample and on the size of the observation table. The algorithm uses a maximum of m calls per counterexample, and the size of $U \cup U^+$ in the final observation table is $t + 1$. This leads to $O(t^2r + trm)$ tree queries and yields the following theorem.

Theorem 2. *The algorithm SL^* infers a data language $\mathcal{L}$ with $O(tr)$ equivalence queries and $O(t^2r + trm)$ tree queries.* □

5 Implementation and Evaluation

We have implemented the SL^* algorithm together with a teacher for a black-box scenario and fixed set of relations on integers and rationals. We allow equalities and/or inequalities as well as simple sums of registers and pre-defined constants (e.g., $p = x_1 + x_2$ or $p = x_1 + 5$).

The implementation of tree queries $\mathcal{O}_u(V,)$ is based on the ideas for constructing canonical constraint decision trees presented in [9] (Proof of Theorem 1). The
set of $\mathcal{R}$-distinguishable classes of data words of the form uv where $Acts(v) \in V$
can be represented in an SDT with maximally refined guards (so-called *atoms*).
We use an SMT solver (Z3[1]) to generate tests for all atoms in this SDT. Finally,
atoms are merged in a bottom-up fashion based on test results.

Equivalence queries have been implemented using tree queries (similar to the
approach in [13]). We generate $\mathcal{O}_\mathcal{L}(\epsilon, w)$ for all $w \in \Sigma^k$ up to some depth k and
compare the SDTs to the hypothesis. We start with $k = 3$ and increase k until
a fixed time limit is reached (10 minutes) or until a counterexample is found.

We have inferred a simplified version of the connection establishment phase
of TCP, a bounded priority queue from the Java Class Library, and a set of five
smaller models (Alternating-bit protocol, Sequence number, Timeout, an ATM,
and a Fibonacci counter). Here, we only detail the TCP model. Fig. 5 shows the
connection establishment phase of TCP. The example uses a set of five actions:
init, *syn*, *syn−ack*, *ack*, and *fin−ack*. The transition $init(p)$ was added to get
an initial sequence number. Each synchronizing message increases this number;
all other messages use the current sequence number.

We used common optimizations for saving tests: a cache and a prefix-closure
filter. Table 1 shows the results. We report the locations, variables, and transitions for all inferred models. For each case, we state the number of constants,
relations ($\leq$ denotes the combination of equalities and inequalities), and supported terms: $p + c$ indicates sums of parameters and constants, and $p + p$ sums
of different parameters. We report the number of tree queries (TQs) and equivalence queries (EQs) made. For equivalence queries, we also state the depth k_1
at which the last counterexample was found and the greatest explored depth k_2
(up to which inferred models are guaranteed to be correct). Finally, we show
execution times.

Time consumption for learning is below one second for most of the examples;
the only "real" Java class, the priority queue, takes a little more time (4.3 seconds). The difference between k_1 and k_2 gives an idea of how likely the final
hypothesis is correct: If k_2 is bigger than k_1, then the depth was increased by
$k_2 - k_1$ without finding a new counterexample. A big difference suggests that
the learning algorithm has converged to the correct RA. For some examples
no counterexamples where found and for the Timeout example $k_2 = \infty$, i.e.,
the equivalence query terminated successfully. This was possible because all sequences of length greater than two are not in the language of this example. For
the examples with more relations ($\leq$, and $p + c$ or $p + p$) the reached depth
k_2 is smaller, regardless of the number of locations and transitions in the final
model. This is due to the exploding number of $\mathcal{R}$-distinguishable classes of data
words in such cases. One way of addressing this challenge in the future could be
introducing typed parameters and using multiple simpler disjoint domains.

---

[1] http://z3.codeplex.com

Table 1. Experimental results obtained on a 2GHz Intel Core i7 with 8GB of memory running Linux kernel 3.8.0

	Model			Language class			Queries		EQ		Times	
	Loc's	Var's	Trans's	Const's	Rel's	Op's	TQs	EQs	k_1	k_2	TQs [s]	EQs [s]
ABP	3	0	5	2	=	-	9	1	-	11	0.1	599.9
Sequence Number	3	1	4	1	=	p+c	8	1	-	10	0.1	599.9
TCP	7	1	51	1	=	p+c	187	2	6	7	0.6	599.4
PriorityQueue	8	2	33	0	≤	-	113	5	6	7	4.3	595.7
Timeout	4	1	5	1	≤	p+c	9	1	-	∞	0.2	0.1
ATM	3	1	7	3	≤	p+c	16	2	3	4	1.3	598.7
Fibonacci counter	4	2	6	0	≤	p+p	19	2	3	5	0.2	599.8

6   Conclusions

We have presented a symbolic learning algorithm which can be parameterized by methods for constructing symbolic decision trees and which infers models that capture both control and data aspects of a system. Our preliminary implementation demonstrates that the approach can infer protocols comprising sequence numbers, time stamps, and variables that are manipulated using simple arithmetic operations or compared for inequality even in a black-box scenario.

A particularly promising direction for future research will be the combination with white-box methods like symbolic execution, both for searching counterexamples as well as for supporting construction of decision trees. We also plan to investigate decidability of tree queries and equivalence queries in our learning model for different data domains.

References

1. Aarts, F., Heidarian, F., Kuppens, H., Olsen, P., Vaandrager, F.: Automata learning through counterexample guided abstraction refinement. In: Giannakopoulou, D., Méry, D. (eds.) FM 2012. LNCS, vol. 7436, pp. 10–27. Springer, Heidelberg (2012)
2. Aarts, F., Jonsson, B., Uijen, J.: Generating models of infinite-state communication protocols using regular inference with abstraction. In: Petrenko, A., Simão, A., Maldonado, J.C. (eds.) ICTSS 2010. LNCS, vol. 6435, pp. 188–204. Springer, Heidelberg (2010)
3. Alur, R., Cerný, P., Madhusudan, P., Nam, W.: Synthesis of interface specifications for java classes. In: POPL 2005, pp. 98–109 (2005)
4. Ammons, G., Bodik, R., Larus, J.: Mining specifications. In: POPL 2002, pp. 4–16 (2002)
5. Angluin, D.: Learning regular sets from queries and counterexamples. Information and Computation 75(2), 87–106 (1987)
6. Bertolino, A., Inverardi, P., Pelliccione, P., Tivoli, M.: Automatic synthesis of behavior protocols for composable web-services. In: ESEC/FSE 2009, pp. 141–150 (2009)
7. Bollig, B., Habermehl, P., Leucker, M., Monmege, B.: A fresh approach to learning register automata. In: Béal, M.-P., Carton, O. (eds.) DLT 2013. LNCS, vol. 7907, pp. 118–130. Springer, Heidelberg (2013)
8. Botinčan, M., Babić, D.: Sigma*: symbolic learning of input-output specifications. In: POPL 2013, pp. 443–456 (2013)

9. Cassel, S., Jonsson, B., Howar, F., Steffen, B.: A succinct canonical register automaton model for data domains with binary relations. In: Chakraborty, S., Mukund, M. (eds.) ATVA 2012. LNCS, vol. 7561, pp. 57–71. Springer, Heidelberg (2012)
10. Ernst, M.D., Perkins, J.H., Guo, P.J., McCamant, S., Pacheco, C., Tschantz, M.S., Xiao, C.: The Daikon system for dynamic detection of likely invariants. Sci. Comput. Programming 69(1-3), 35–45 (2007)
11. Gery, E., Harel, D., Palachi, E.: Rhapsody: A complete life-cycle model-based development system. In: Butler, M., Petre, L., Sere, K. (eds.) IFM 2002. LNCS, vol. 2335, pp. 1–10. Springer, Heidelberg (2002)
12. Ghezzi, C., Mocci, A., Monga, M.: Synthesizing Intentional Behavior Models by Graph Transformation. In: ICSE 2009 (2009)
13. Giannakopoulou, D., Rakamarić, Z., Raman, V.: Symbolic learning of component interfaces. In: Miné, A., Schmidt, D. (eds.) SAS 2012. LNCS, vol. 7460, pp. 248–264. Springer, Heidelberg (2012)
14. Howar, F.: Active learning of interface programs. PhD thesis. Technical University of Dortmund, Germany (2012)
15. Howar, F., Isberner, M., Steffen, B., Bauer, O., Jonsson, B.: Inferring semantic interfaces of data structures. In: Margaria, T., Steffen, B. (eds.) ISoLA 2012, Part I. LNCS, vol. 7609, pp. 554–571. Springer, Heidelberg (2012)
16. Howar, F., Steffen, B., Jonsson, B., Cassel, S.: Inferring canonical register automata. In: Kuncak, V., Rybalchenko, A. (eds.) VMCAI 2012. LNCS, vol. 7148, pp. 251–266. Springer, Heidelberg (2012)
17. Howar, F., Steffen, B., Merten, M.: Automata Learning with Automated Alphabet Abstraction Refinement. In: Jhala, R., Schmidt, D. (eds.) VMCAI 2011. LNCS, vol. 6538, pp. 263–277. Springer, Heidelberg (2011)
18. Huima, A.: Implementing Conformiq Qtronic. In: Petrenko, A., Veanes, M., Tretmans, J., Grieskamp, W. (eds.) TestCom/FATES 2007. LNCS, vol. 4581, pp. 1–12. Springer, Heidelberg (2007)
19. Jhala, R., Majumdar, R.: Software model checking. ACM Comput. Surv. 41(4) (2009)
20. Lorenzoli, D., Mariani, L., Pezzè, M.: Automatic generation of software behavioral models. In: ICSE 2008, pp. 501–510 (2008)
21. Rivest, R.L., Schapire, R.E.: Inference of finite automata using homing sequences. Information and Computation 103(2), 299–347 (1993)
22. Schur, M., Roth, A., Zeller, A.: Mining behavior models from enterprise web applications. In: ESEC/FSE 2013, pp. 422–432 (2013)
23. Shu, G., Lee, D.: Testing security properties of protocol implementations - a machine learning based approach. In: ICDCS 2007 (2007)
24. Singh, R., Giannakopoulou, D., Păsăreanu, C.: Learning component interfaces with may and must abstractions. In: Touili, T., Cook, B., Jackson, P. (eds.) CAV 2010. LNCS, vol. 6174, pp. 527–542. Springer, Heidelberg (2010)
25. Tkachuk, O., Dwyer, M.B.: Adapting side effects analysis for modular program model checking. In: ESEC/FSE 2003, pp. 188–197 (2003)
26. Veanes, M., Hooimeijer, P., Livshits, B., Molnar, D., Bjorner, N.: Symbolic finite state transducers: Algorithms and applications. In: POPL 2012, pp. 137–150 (2012)
27. Walkinshaw, N., Bogdanov, K., Derrick, J., Paris, J.: Increasing functional coverage by inductive testing: A case study. In: Petrenko, A., Simão, A., Maldonado, J.C. (eds.) ICTSS 2010. LNCS, vol. 6435, pp. 126–141. Springer, Heidelberg (2010)
28. Whaley, J., Martin, M.C., Lam, M.S.: Automatic extraction of object-oriented component interfaces. In: ISSTA 2002, pp. 218–228 (2002)
29. Xiao, H., Sun, J., Liu, Y., Lin, S.-W., Sun, C.: Tzuyu: Learning stateful typestates. In: ASE 2013, pp. 432–442 (2013)

Translating Event-B Machines
to Database Applications

Qi Wang[1] and Tim Wahls[2]

[1] Department of Computer Science, The University of Toronto,
Toronto, Ontario, Canada
njqi.wang@mail.utoronto.ca

[2] Department of Mathematics and Computer Science, Dickinson College,
Carlisle, Pennsylvania, USA
wahlst@dickinson.edu

Abstract. Previous work on generating implementations from Event-B models has focused on translating concrete machines that are already relatively close to code. Additionally, the generated implementations do not provide support for data persistence and for inter-operating with hand-written system components. In this work, we present the EventB-2SQL tool, which translates Event-B models to Java classes that store all model data in a relational database. Operations on sets and relations are directly translated to database queries, and Event-B carrier sets are both stored in the database and translated as generic type parameters of the generated classes. This allows developers to use objects of almost any Java class as elements of carrier sets, and to easily store these objects in the database. Additionally, using a database back-end in this manner and translating events as database transactions greatly facilitates the development of client-server and multi-threaded applications while maintaining the atomicity of events.

Keywords: Event-B, code generation, database applications, client-server applications.

1 Introduction

Previous work on generating implementations from Event-B models [6,4,5,8] is largely concerned with translating concrete machines that result from a (possibly long) refinement process. In fact, the primary purpose of refinement is to translate abstract models to models that are much closer to programming language code, typically removing higher-level Event-B features such as relations and simultaneous assignment. The implementations produced use in-memory data structures (often arrays), and so do not provide support for data persistence. While appropriate for small applications with transient data, this approach does not scale for applications that manage larger volumes of data over longer timeframes.

In this work, we present the EventB2SQL tool[1], which automatically translates Event-B models to database applications. The generated programs store

---

[1] EventB2SQL is freely available from [7]. The website includes installation and usage instructions, and the social networking example discussed in this paper.

D. Giannakopoulou and G. Salaün (Eds.): SEFM 2014, LNCS 8702, pp. 265–270, 2014.
© Springer International Publishing Switzerland 2014

Event-B sets, relations and functions in database tables, and EventB2SQL translates operations on these types to SQL queries. Hence, EventB2SQL can translate Event-B models written at a relatively high level of abstraction, with the additional advantage of automatically making all application data persistent.

2   The Translation

EventB2SQL translates an Event-B machine and any contexts that it sees to a Java class that uses JDBC to communicate with a MySQL database. The translations of all machine variables and carrier sets are stored in the database, making their values persistent across invocations of the generated program. Carrier sets are translated as tables in the database, and the Java class generated from an Event-B machine has a generic type parameter for each carrier set that the machine sees. This allows programs generated from Event-B models to manipulate Java objects, as the classes defining those objects can be used as actual type parameters when an instance of the translated class is created. Any class used as an actual type parameter must implement the `java.io.Serializable` interface so that instances can be stored in the database. The code generated by the EventB2SQL tool includes methods for iterating over carrier sets, and for adding objects to them. Additionally, the generated code includes methods for retrieving the value of each machine variable, and for retrieving the image of any domain element for functions and relations.

Each non-INITIALISATION event is translated to a Java method. Any event parameters are translated as parameters of the method. The method executes as a single database transaction, ensuring that events are atomic as required by the semantics of Event-B. If the translation of the event guard is not satisfied when the method is called, the translation of the actions is not executed and the method returns false. If the translation of the guard is satisfied, the translation of the actions is executed and the method returns true. This approach prevents any interleaving of method executions that would cause the actions of an event to be executed in a state that did not satisfy the guard of that event.[2]

To correctly translate simultaneous assignments, the EventB2SQL tool first translates the right-hand sides of all assignments in the body of an event, assigning the results to temporary variables. Because EventB2SQL represents all Event-B values as integers (as described in the following), the temporary variables are simply local variables of type `int`. After all right-hand sides have been evaluated, the values of these temporary variables are stored to the database in the locations of the corresponding machine variables. Assignments that use $:\in$ are handled similarly, with an arbitrary element of the right-hand side assigned to the temporary variable.

Space limitations preclude a full discussion of the translation of Event-B expressions and predicates into SQL queries, so we limit our presentation to three

---

[2] For backward compatibility with previous versions of EventB2SQL that did not support concurrency, the tool also generates separate methods for checking the guard and executing the actions of an event.

representative examples. Abstractly, Event-B variables that are sets (but not relations or functions) are represented as SQL tables with a single column labeled `refkey`, with each row containing one element of the set. Event-B relations and functions are represented as SQL tables with two columns labeled `id` and `value`, with each row representing a maplet (pair) in the relation.

EventB2SQL translates the Event-B predicate: $x_1 \in s_1$ as follows, assuming that `x1` is the translation of x_1 and `s1` is the translation of s_1. In general, `x1` and `s1` are nested queries and so must be renamed.

```
select count(*)
from (x1) as x1tp, (s1) as s1tp
where x1tp.id = s1tp.refkey
```

Assuming that the result of translating s_1 contains no duplicates (a property that our translation enforces), this query evaluates to 1 (`true`) if and only if $x_1 \in s_1$. Note that an expression of a primitive (integral or boolean) type evaluates to a table with a single row and a single column labeled `id`.

The composition of n Event-B relations or functions $(r_1; r_2; \ldots r_m; r_n)$ is translated to a query that joins tables representing the relations where the `value` column of each table (except the last) is equal to the `id` column of the following one, and then selecting the appropriate columns in the result:

```
select r1tp.id, rntp.value
from (r1) as r1tp, (r2) as r2tp, ..., (rm) as rmtp, (rn) as rntp
where r1tp.value = r2tp.id and ... and rmtp.value = rntp.id
```

We translate relational override $(r_1 \lessdot r_2)$ by selecting appropriate tuples from the two tables involved and unioning the results. In early versions of the tool, the generated query used `NOT IN` to select tuples in r_1 that were not overridden by tuples from r_2 in the result. However, MySQL does not execute such queries efficiently, and so the current version of the tool, uses a `LEFT JOIN` to find tuples in r_1 with `id` values that are not `id` values in r_2:

```
select r1tp.id, r1tp.value
from (r1) as r1tp left join (select id from (r2) as r2tp)
on r1tp.id = r2tp.id where r2tp.id is null
    union
select * from (r2) as r2tp
```

The database design actually used in applications generated by EventB2SQL is more complex than the abstract version presented above. The abstract version permits redundancy (the same Event-B object can be stored in multiple tables) and makes equality comparisons between complex Event-B objects such as sets and relations difficult. Hence, the EventB2SQL tool uses a highly normalized representation in which all values of the same type (set, relation, function or maplet) are stored in the same table, and any value more complex than a number or boolean is always referred to indirectly (via a unique numeric identifier). The table schemas generated by EventB2SQL are in BCNF [3], and the generated code ensures that the tables never contain duplicate entries or *null* values.

When processing an Event-B machine, the EventB2SQL tool creates a new table for each maplet and set (including relation/function) type that it encounters. The table for a maplet type has three columns labeled `refnum`, `id` and `value`, where `refnum` is an auto-generated primary key used to refer to the maplet, and `id` and `value` represent the pair of values. Whenever an Event-B operation creates a new maplet (i.e. by using $\mapsto$), the generated code first checks if the maplet already exists in the corresponding table. If so, the `refnum` of that maplet is returned. If not, a new row is inserted into the table and the `refnum` of the row is returned. While potentially expensive to execute, this approach ensures that maplets can be correctly compared by `refnum` alone, as a `refnum` always uniquely identifies a maplet.

The table created for a set type has two columns labeled `refnum` and `refkey`. All sets of this type will be stored in this table. All elements of the same set have the same value of `refnum`, and there is one row in the table for each element of each set (with the element stored in the `refkey` column). Again, whenever a new set is created, the generated code first checks the associated table to see if the set already exists. If so, the `refnum` of that set is returned. If not, a new `refnum` is generated, appropriate tuples with that `refnum` are generated and inserted into the table, and the new `refnum` is returned. Relations and functions are stored as sets of maplets, where the `refkey` value references a maplet in the appropriate maplet table. This makes the representation uniform, so that the same translation of set operations works on both sets and relations, and so that nested structures (such as sets of relations) can be stored as sets of `refnums`.

Of course, the code generated by the EventB2SQL tool is not as efficient as a hand-coded database application would likely be, although the query optimization built-in to MySQL should mitigate this to some extent. As mentioned above, earlier versions of EventB2SQL generated code that made heavy use of IN and NOT IN in SQL queries (to test membership in the result of a nested subquery). MySQL does not do an adequate job of optimizing such queries, and the performance of applications generated by early versions of EventB2SQL was not acceptable. Subsequently, we have updated the tool to generate queries that use joins in place of these forms of nested subqueries, and application performance is significantly improved.

3   Implementation and Usage Example

The EventB2SQL tool is implemented as a plugin for the Rodin platform [1]. Rodin provides tools such as editors and parsers for Event-B models, and so is an ideal environment for developing Event-B tools. When translation is initiated, the EventB2SQL tool walks the abstract syntax tree constructed by Rodin using the provided visitor pattern, generating a combination of Java code and SQL statements as previously described.

In a typical usage of EventB2SQL, a developer would:

– use Rodin to develop an Event-B model that includes the desired functionality, including refinements as needed. It is not necessary to discharge proof obligations before translation, but we recommend doing so.

- use EventB2SQL to translate the model to a Java database application (via a menu selection within Rodin)
- write client code that interacts with the translation result to produce a complete application

We have employed an Event-B model of a social networking core (adapted from the B model in [2]) as a small case study during the development of EventB2SQL. Each of the nine machines in this model (one abstract and eight refinements) sees a context that introduces carrier sets PERSON (all possible people in the network) and CONTENTS (all possible content items). Hence, the Java class generated by EventB2SQL for each of these machines has type parameters PERSON and CONTENTS, allowing client code to supply Java classes (as actual type parameters) that represent people and content items that are appropriate for the intended application.

To illustrate how to use code generated by EventB2SQL, we have written a small client application on top of the code generated from the first refinement machine[3]. This application:

- creates a connection to a MySQL database
- creates an instance of the class generated by EventB2SQL, passing the database connection as a parameter and the classes representing people and content items as type parameters
- uses this instance to:
  - call the generated `createTables` method, which creates all necessary tables in the database
  - call the INITIALISATION method (generated from the initialisation event in the model) to initialize the network state. Note that this and the previous step should only be done once.
  - call generated methods to add objects to the representations of the carrier sets. This adds the objects to the database, making them persistent.
  - call methods generated from events in the model to add people and content to the network, to share content between users and to print the current state of the network.

It is straightforward to construct a client-server application around the generated code as many copies of that code (running on different computers) can connect to a single database server. Because each event executes as a database transaction, atomicity is maintained. Similarly, applications generated by EventB2SQL are well suited for use in multi-threaded environments.

4   Future Work and Conclusion

While EventB2SQL can translate a large and useful subset of Event-B, there are some features such as set comprehensions, quantified predicates, data types defined in theories and non-deterministic assignments (formed using :|) that are

---

[3] See [7] for the full source code.

not yet supported. Other areas for future work include reducing the generated code's use of temporary tables and making further improvements in the efficiency of the generated code. We also plan to undertake larger case studies to evaluate the reliability and usefulness of applications generated with EventB2SQL, and to modify the tool as indicated by this evaluation. Finally, to produce a provably correct implementation, the soundness of the translation performed by EventB2SQL must itself be verified. We are currently investigating ways to perform such a proof.

The current version of the EventB2SQL tool improves on the state of the art in generating code from Event-B models in a number of ways: it can translate machines written at a relatively high level of abstraction, it makes the values of machine variables persistent across executions of a generated application, it allows carrier sets to contain instances of arbitrary Java classes (in a persistent way), and it simplifies the development of client-server and multi-threaded applications. Our hope is that other developers will find EventB2SQL to be useful in practice, thus promoting the use of Event-B and more generally formal methods in the software process.

References

1. Butler, M., Jones, C.B., Romanovsky, A., Troubitsyna, E. (eds.): Rigorous Development of Complex Fault-Tolerant Systems. LNCS, vol. 4157. Springer, Heidelberg (2006)
2. Catano, N., Rueda, C.: Matelas: A predicate calculus common formal definition for social networking. In: Frappier, M., Glässer, U., Khurshid, S., Laleau, R., Reeves, S. (eds.) ABZ 2010. LNCS, vol. 5977, pp. 259–272. Springer, Heidelberg (2010)
3. Codd, E.F.: Recent investigations in relational data base systems. In: IFIP Congress. pp. 1017–1021 (1974)
4. Edmunds, A., Butler, M.: Tool support for Event-B code generation. In: WS-TBFM 2010. John Wiley and Sons, Québec (2010)
5. Edmunds, A., Butler, M.: Tasking Event-B: An extension to Event-B for generating concurrent code. In: Programming Language Approaches to Concurrency and Communication-Centric Software PLACES. Springer, Saarbrucken (2011)
6. Méry, D., Singh, N.K.: Automatic code generation from Event-B models. In: Proceedings of the Second SoICT, SoICT 2011. ACM, Hanoi (2011)
7. Wang, Q., Wahls, T.: The EventB2SQL tool – Rodin plugin and usage example (2013), http://users.dickinson.edu/~wahlst/eventb2sql/eventb2sql.html
8. Wright, S.: Automatic generation of C from Event-B. In: Workshop on IM_FMT. Springer, Nantes (2009)

IKOS: A Framework for Static Analysis Based on Abstract Interpretation

Guillaume Brat, Jorge A. Navas, Nija Shi, and Arnaud Venet

NASA Ames Research Center, Moffett Field, CA 94035, USA

Abstract. The RTCA standard (DO-178C) for developing avionic software and getting certification credits includes an extension (DO-333) that describes how developers can use static analysis in certification. In this paper, we give an overview of the IKOS static analysis framework that helps developing static analyses that are both precise and scalable. IKOS harnesses the power of Abstract Interpretation and makes it accessible to a larger class of static analysis developers by separating concerns such as code parsing, model development, abstract domain management, results management, and analysis strategy. The benefits of the approach is demonstrated by a buffer overflow analysis applied to flight control systems.

1 Introduction

Our goal is to enable the use of static analysis for the certification of avionic systems. The DO-333 extension to DO-178C lists Abstract Interpretation [4] as a possibility to obtain certification credits. Unfortunately, there are few available commercial static analyzers based on Abstract Interpretation. Moreover, they often lack precision and scalability for C/C++ code, or, they are restricted to strict subsets of C. Our goal is to define a framework that can be used to develop precise, scalable static analyses based on Abstract Interpretation for flight software systems.

Abstract Interpretation [4] is a theoretical framework that provides a methodology for constructing sound static analyses. It offers mathematical guarantee that all properties computed by the analyzer hold for all possible execution paths of the program. The core idea behind this theory is the careful use of the notion of approximation: all possible values that a variable can take at a certain program point are approximated by a set that can be compactly represented (e.g., an integer interval), thus ensuring the soundness of the analysis. However, infeasible value assignments of the variable may be introduced because of the approximation. This may result into false alarms, where the analyzer detects a potential problem at a statement when the program is actually safe. These false alarms need to be as rare as possible; otherwise, it defeats the usefulness of the analysis. Nevertheless, when a statement is deemed safe, it can never cause an error, which is a key property for certification.

In this paper, we give an overview of IKOS [1] (Inference Kernel for Open Static Analyzers), an open-source framework developed at the NASA Ames Research Center that supports the development of precise and scalable static analyses. IKOS

D. Giannakopoulou and G. Salaün (Eds.): SEFM 2014, LNCS 8702, pp. 271–277, 2014.
© Springer International Publishing Switzerland 2014

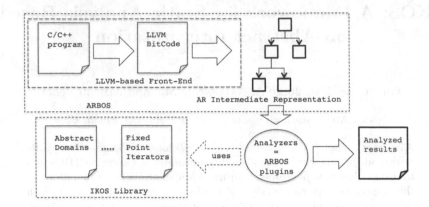

Fig. 1. The IKOS framework architecture overview

provides abstract interpretation concepts for developing specialized analyzers, which helps drive down the number of false positives without compromising scalability. Designing a specialized analyzer using standard methods is long and difficult. IKOS facilitates this process by factoring out most of the expertise required to write the analyzer. The use of IKOS in developing precise and scalable static analyses is demonstrated through the implementation of a buffer overflow analysis and its application to flight control systems. Arrays and buffers are pervasively employed in flight software (navigation, communication) and errors are often very hard to catch during standard V&V activities, like testing or code review.

2   Framework Overview

The IKOS framework, shown in Figure 1, offers capabilities to facilitate the development and integration of the traditional elements of static analyzers. IKOS relies on the ARBOS plugin framework for parsing the source code, performing semantic resolution, and creating an intermediate representation (using the AR form) more suitable for analysis (i.e., semantic equations that need to be solved using fixpoint iterations). Analyses are developed as ARBOS plugins using the Abstract Interpretation concepts available in the IKOS library (a collection of abstract domains and fixpoint iteration algorithms). Currently, results are being stored in permanent storage in the form of text files or in an SQL database (SQLite). The SQL database is convenient to extract specific information from the results. We can also visualize the results using an external tool, called IkosView, which shows the location of the checks in the source code with the traditional color coding: green for safe checks, red for unsafe checks, and orange for warnings. In the following sections, we will describe ARBOS and its AR form, then IKOS, and finally some of the analyses we have developed.

2.1   The ARBOS Plugin Framework

ARBOS is a plugin framework that allows the definition of static analyses using the AR form as intermediate representation. Currently, ARBOS includes a front-end (based on LLVM [7]), which translates C/C++ code into AR, the abstract representation of programs, and the APIs that facilitate writing static analyses as ARBOS plugins. The workflow in Figure 1 shows the various phases to obtain the AR representation of the C/C++ source code to be analyzed.

2.2   Why LLVM?

LLVM [7] is essentially a high-level, platform-independent assembly language. Although it is simpler to process than the abstract syntax tree of a C/C++ program, it heavily relies on the static single assignment form (SSA) which cannot be readily used to design an abstract interpreter. The ϕ-nodes need to be eliminated and other inadequate constructs need to be simplified using various LLVM transformation passes. An intermediate representation like CIL [9] is far more adapted to the design of static analyzers based on Abstract Interpretation than LLVM, so why choose LLVM in the first place?

The single most important issue facing the user of a static analysis tool is getting the code through the tool's parser. *All* commercial static analyzers, sound or not, use their own parsers, which may not accept C/C++ dialects or idioms that are commonplace in the embedded world, including flight systems. For example, in our experiments the code for the UAS autopilot Paparazzi listed in Table 1 was rejected by all three commercial static analyzers we had licenses for. Getting the application through those tools would have required rewriting huge chunks of code, which is unacceptable in general and for the certification of flight software in particular, where code cannot be changed at all. However, Paparazzi would compile without any problem when using the GCC compiler. As a matter of fact, all the programs we have studied would compile without any modification using GCC whereas they would require some modifications when using commercial tools. There is a special version of GCC that has been modified so as to generate LLVM bitcode, which is why we are using LLVM. CIL has its own front-end and trips when parsing nonstandard code, very much like all other C/C++ front-ends but GCC.

2.3   The Abstract Representation

The Abstract Representation (AR) generated by ARBOS can be used as an input to abstract interpreters implemented using IKOS as ARBOS plugins. Compared to the LLVM Internal Representation (IR), the AR takes a different angle on how to express the semantics of a C program. For example, the SSA form is done away with, the instruction set is more regular and the control flow is expressed in a declarative way using nondeterministic choices and assertions rather than conditional branch instructions. Due to space limitations, we cannot describe the entire AR form in this paper. Instead, we will highlight the main differences between the LLVM IR and AR using a simple example. It is worth noting that there is no loss of expressiveness when translating the LLVM IR into AR.

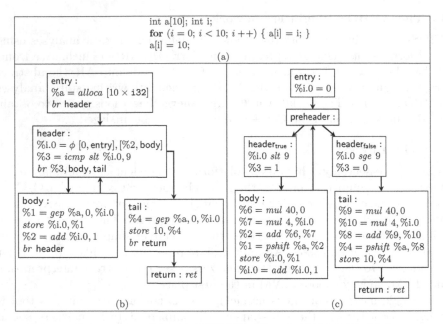

Fig. 2. Code snippet (a) with LLVM IR (b) and ARBOS AR (c) forms

Figure 2(a) shows a simple piece of code performing an array initialization with special treatment for the last element. The loop is not correctly written, which causes an out-of-bounds array access at the last statement. This example is a redacted and simplified version of a problem identified in a real flight code during V&V activities. Figures 2(b) and 2(c) show the LLVM IR and ARBOS AR forms, which have also been simplified for readability. We will now go over the details of the translation from the LLVM IR into AR.

In SSA form variables can only be assigned once, which requires the introduction of ϕ-nodes to represent the values a variable can take at a merge point in the control-flow graph. In Abstract Interpretation, a merge point corresponds to the application of a join (or widening) operation in the abstract domain. A ϕ-node represents a partial disjunction over some program variables, which can be dealt with easily when considering non-relational domains (like intervals). However, relational abstractions (like polyhedra) describe properties over *all* program variables, which makes the treatment of ϕ-nodes extremely challenging. Since IKOS is meant to be a generic abstract interpretation framework, ϕ-nodes are removed from the AR by inserting assignment instructions that simulate the effect of the ϕ-nodes on the variables concerned.

In the LLVM IR, conditional branch instructions (br) are coupled with Boolean instructions that return their result in a register (slt, sge). This implies that processing the condition in the abstract domain (e.g., by using a linear constraint solver) should be done in conjunction with assigning a discrete value to a variable (the result of the operation) and propagating the invariant across basic blocks (to take care of both branches). Since IKOS is a generic static analyzer, we need to decouple these aspects so as not to make the structure of the fixpoint iterator dependent on any particular abstract domain. This is why branch instructions are eliminated for the AR and replaced by nondeterministic choices (over blocks header$_{true}$ and header$_{false}$ in our example).

Finally, complex instructions in the LLVM IR that model pointer arithmetic (*gep*) are replaced by atomic operations on the pointer offsets expressed in bytes (e.g., the pointer shift operation *pshift*). Once all these transformations have been applied, the resulting AR form can be processed by the generic algorithms of IKOS. Instantiating these algorithms with the domain of intervals provides enough precision to statically resolve all array access checks and identify the error in the example.

2.4 The IKOS Library

IKOS is a development platform for static analyzers based on Abstract Interpretation. IKOS is actually a large library of optimized Abstract Interpretation algorithms. It is accessible through a highly generic API. IKOS is meant to offer a cost-effective way of designing specialized static analyzers. The API for abstract domains provide the usual services from the abstract interpretation theory, i.e., abstract operators, comparison operators, lattice elements such as bottom and top, and narrowing and widening operators. Currently, IKOS offers implementations for the following numerical abstract domains: constants, intervals, arithmetic congruences [3], octagons [8] and discrete symbolic domains. Other domains are under development. IKOS also provides an API for fixpoint iterators.

3   Buffer Overflow Analysis

We have used IKOS to implement an interprocedural buffer-overflow analyzer for avionic codes in C. The analysis represents less than 600 lines of C++. This analysis is interprocedural and performs a full expansion of function calls, very much like Astrée [5]. We have run our buffer overflow analysis on a set of C flight control systems ranging in size from 35 KLOC to 278 KLOC. The analysis was conducted on a MacBook Pro with a 2.8 GHz Intel Core i7 processor and 16 GB of memory. In our results presented in Table 1, we include analysis times to give an idea of the speed of the analysis. We did not try to optimize the analysis speed. We focused on the precision, which is measured as the percentage of analysis checks that are classified (as safe or unsafe) with certainty as opposed to checks that yield warnings (there may or may not be a problem).

The goal was to create an analysis that would yield less than 10% false positives on flight control codes. The results on our test suite seem to indicate that we have reached this goal since we always have a precision higher than 90%. The results also show that we have not sacrificed analysis times for precision since all analyses are done in a matter of minutes or less. We are in the process of identifying a large embedded system code base so that we can truly characterize the scalability of the analysis. Note that our measure of analysis time is really coarse since we do not attempt to separate time spent analyzing the code from

Table 1. Buffer Out-of-Range Analysis Results

Code	Size	Analysis Time	Precision
Paparazzi	35 KLOC	22s	99%
Gen2	22 KLOC	1m03s	98%
FLTz	144 KLOC	10m30s	91%
Arduplane	278 KLOC	6m30s	94%

time spent logging results to a file or a database. Our past experience with C Global Surveyor (CGS) showed that logging results takes a significant amount of time. So, we find our measured analysis times encouraging.

4   Related Work

The closest related work comes from tools relying on the abstract interpretation framework, namely C Global Surveyor, CodeHawk, Astrée, and PolySpace Verifier.

C Global Surveyor [10] (CGS) is the ancestor of IKOS, and, it has had a large influence on the design of IKOS. However IKOS is a framework to build analyzers when CGS is an analyzer. The emphasis in IKOS is to factor out the difficult concepts (abstract domains, fixed-point iterators). We also changed the front-end (GCC/LLVM instead of EDG) and the database (SQLite instead of PostGReSQL). Finally, the precision of CGS is not on par with IKOS' precision since CGS generally produces about 20% warnings when IKOS is usually in the 1% to 2% range.

CodeHawk [6] is the closest tool to IKOS. It is also a framework for developing analyses based on abstract interpretation. CodeHawk is a commercial tool and little public data is available.

Astrée [5] was customized for specific Airbus codes. The impressive results it achieves inspired us to enable the construction of specialized static analyzers. The Airbus code is essentially composed of filters, which means that Astrée focused on floating-point computation, which is not yet addressed by IKOS. IKOS is addressing a much larger class of C programs. In all honesty, we only can compare to the original version of Astrée, not the current commercial one.

PolySpace Verifier was the first of this line of static analyzers based on Abstract Interpretation. In many ways, it paved the way for the current generation of tools. Polyspace Verifier was very successful in analyzing Ada code but fell short for C and C++. In our own experience [2], scalability was a big issue and the number of warnings was also important (20% to 50% of all checks).

5   Conclusion

We have given an overview of IKOS, an open-source platform which facilitates the development of static code analyzers based on Abstract Interpretation. The front-end of IKOS relies on LLVM, but it can be easily replaced by other front-ends since the analyses run on our own intermediate representation. We demonstrated the precision and scalability of IKOS-based analyzers with an interprocedural buffer overflow analysis.

References

1. IKOS: Inference Kernel for Open Static Analyzers,
   http://ti.arc.nasa.gov/opensource/ikos/
2. Brat, G., Klemm, R.: Static Analysis of the Mars Exploration Rover Flight Software. In: Space Mission Challenge for Information Technology, pp. 321–326 (2003)
3. Bygde, S.: Abstract Interpretation and Abstract Domains with special attention to the congruence domain. Master's thesis, Mälardalen University, Sweden (2006)
4. Cousot, P., Cousot, R.: Abstract Interpretation: A Unified Lattice Model for Static Analysis of Programs by Construction or Approximation of Fixpoints. In: POPL, pp. 238–252 (1977)
5. Cousot, P., Cousot, R., Feret, J., Mauborgne, L., Miné, A., Monniaux, D., Rival, X.: The Astreé Analyzer. In: Sagiv, M. (ed.) ESOP 2005. LNCS, vol. 3444, pp. 21–30. Springer, Heidelberg (2005)
6. Kestrel Technology: CodeHawk, http://www.kestreltechnology.com
7. Lattner, C., Adve, V.: LLVM: A Compilation Framework for Lifelong Program Analysis & Transformation. In: CGO 2004 (2004)
8. Miné, A.: The Octagon Abstract Domain. Higher-Order and Symbolic Computation 19(1), 31–100 (2006)
9. Necula, G.C., McPeak, S., Rahul, S.P., Weimer, W.: CIL: Intermediate Language and Tools for Analysis and Transformation of C Programs. In: Nigel Horspool, R. (ed.) CC 2002. LNCS, vol. 2304, pp. 213–228. Springer, Heidelberg (2002)
10. Venet, A., Brat, G.P.: Precise and Efficient Static Array Bound Checking for Large Embedded C Programs. In: PLDI, pp. 231–242 (2004)

A Toolset for Support of Teaching Formal Software Development

Štefan Korečko, Ján Sorád, Zuzana Dudláková, and Branislav Sobota

Department of Computers and Informatics,
Faculty of Electrical Engineering and Informatics,
Technical University of Košice, Letná 9, 041 20 Košice, Slovakia
{stefan.korecko,zuzana.dudlakova,branislav.sobota}@tuke.sk,
jansorad@gmail.com

Abstract. Teachers of formal methods courses often experience disinterest or even disgust towards the topic from software engineering students. As one of the significant reasons of this situation we see the fact that students are not in touch with domains where their use is desired and worth the effort. In this paper we deal with a toolset we developed to improve the situation. The toolset brings to students, in a virtual form, one of the most successful domains of formal methods application - railway systems. It consists of a modified version of a railway centralized traffic control simulator called Train Director and a tool that allows signals and switches in a railway scenario, simulated by Train Director, to be controlled by a separate formally developed control program. We briefly describe the toolset and its typical use within a formal methods course and discuss its usability with respect to various formal methods.

Keywords: formal methods, teaching, software development, railway systems, virtual laboratory.

1 Introduction

Almost every university teacher who dedicated a portion of his career to introducing software engineering students to the world of formal methods (FM), especially to those heavy weighted ones that involve formal verification and refinement, faced several serious problems. And in the era we live in, the era of massification of higher education, one of the most important problems is how to motivate students to enrol into formal methods courses and to stay in them. Of course, we often get the "Why should I learn this language (method, approach, etc.)?" question in "normal" software engineering subjects as well. But there it can be easily answered by pointing out a number of (local) companies whose employees use them on regular basis. However, in FM courses we get a more serious questions, like "Why on earth should I deal with such terrifying stuff like formal semantics or, heaven forbid, mathematical proofs?". And the easy answer is not here. There are only few companies worldwide that use FM in software development and they are almost exclusively located in the most developed countries.

D. Giannakopoulou and G. Salaün (Eds.): SEFM 2014, LNCS 8702, pp. 278–283, 2014.
© Springer International Publishing Switzerland 2014

Instead of it we can, together with the authors of [3], focus on a noble goal of educating rigorous software engineers who will change the way software is produced. But will our students follow? It is our strong belief that they will if we let them play with FM in an appropriate setting. We agree with Almeida et al. [1] that FM should not be used everywhere, but primarily in cases when reliability, safety or security are a concern. We can hardly persuade students to put an extra effort to formal verification of some typical information system, a computer game or a mobile phone firmware when they already know that such software is usually released with several bugs, fixed by updates afterwards. And nothing really bad ever happens. The problem is that these are exactly the types of systems our students encounter during their university study. So, we need to introduce them to a domain where use of FM is appropriate, where they will feel the need of that extra effort. And we have to let them develop something for that domain, using FM. But what domain to choose? We should pick up one where software failures may have tragic consequences. It is also important that most of the students are familiar with the domain and can imagine these consequences affecting their lives. Moreover, there should be real-life cases from the domain where human lives are already under the control of automated systems. There are several candidates but one of the most appealing are railway systems. The fact that this domain is one of few where FM reached a mature level [2] is a nice and important bonus.

The domain has been selected, now the question is how to bring it to the students. The real railway is definitely out of our reach and to let students develop a console application on the basis of some text document form of assignment is hardly motivating. This is exactly where our toolset can help. It replaces the real railway with a virtual one, represented by a simulation game called Train Director (http://www.backerstreet.com/traindir). The modifications we made to the game allow it to be connected to a separately developed control program (module), which responds to requests from simulated trains by manipulating switches and signals. And these control modules are the very pieces of software the students develop using formal methods. The control modules are Java applications, so the toolset is usable with any FM for which a Java code generator exists. The appearance and operation of the toolset and control modules, their place in a FM course and adaptability to various FM are described in the next section. The final one deals with teaching experiences, related work and plans for future development.

2   The Toolset and Its Use

The toolset itself consists of two tools - a modified version of *Train Director*, an open source simulator of the railway centralized traffic control and *TS2JavaConn*, a Java application whose primary role is to provide communication between the simulator and control modules.

Train Director is a game that allows a user to create and simulate a railway scenario, which consists of a track layout and a train schedule. The user's task

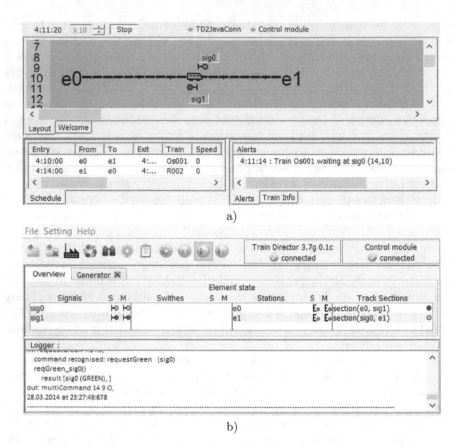

Fig. 1. The toolset during a simulation: Train Director (a) and TS2JavaConn (b)

during the simulation is to throw switches and clear signals in such a way that the trains will follow the schedule. The game has its own logic that prevents collisions and changes some signals automatically. It also provides a simple server interface for an external control. We modified the game by disabling the internal logic and implementing train collisions and naming of signals and switches. We also enhanced the server interface to be able to communicate with TS2JavaConn. The modified Train Director sends messages to TS2JavaConn every time a train stops before a red signal (*requestGreen* message), wants to enter a track layout (*reqestEnter*) or departure from a station (*reqestDepartureStation*). These messages also contain name of the corresponding signal, entry point or station, name of the train and names of following stations the train should visit according to the schedule. A *sectionLeave* message is sent when a train leaves current track section and a *sectionEnter* message when it enters a new one. For the sake of simplicity a track section always starts and ends at some signal, switch or entry point. The modified Train Director can also receive messages. These messages are commands from TS2JavaConn to, for example, start or stop a simulation or to change the state of a signal or switch. In Fig. 1 a) we can see Train Director during a simulation of simple scenario that consists of two entry points e0 and e1 and two signals sig0 and sig1. There are two track sections, e0_sig1 and sig0_e1.

TS2JavaConn (Fig. 1 b) was necessary because Train Director is a C++ application and control modules are in Java. We have chosen Java because of its popularity among students and wide support in FM tools. Having TS2JavaConn as a separate tool also allows to easily replace Train Director with another simulator. The tool provides a GUI where a user can load a control module (first button in the toolbar in Fig. 1 b), unload the module (2nd button) open a tab with a module generator (3rd button), reset the connection with the simulator (4th button) or remotely control the simulation in Train Director (round buttons). In the "Element state" part of the "Overview" tab a user can observe in which state track elements are in the simulator (S) and in the module (M). Communication between the tools can be watched in the "Logger" part. For each scenario the current version of the module generator can create a control module template in Java and in specification languages of formal methods B-Method and Perfect Developer, together with a corresponding configuration file.

The control module itself is a Java application where one "main" class contains methods that react to the messages from Train Director and variables that represent devices from the controlled scenario. How exactly these methods and variables are mapped to the messages from and devices in Train Director is defined in a mandatory text-based *configuration file*. The possibilities are wide: for data representation we can use primitive types like integer or boolean, enumerated sets or mappings. The methods can be non-parametric, where corresponding message parameters are parts of their names or parametric, where they are usual parameters. For example, in a control module for the scenario depicted in Fig. 1 a) we need two non-parametric methods (reqGreen_sig0 and reqGreen_sig1) or one parametric method (reqGreen(sig)) to handle the requestGreen messages for sig0 and sig1. The number of additional classes and libraries in control modules is not limited, so the modules can be really sophisticated and complex applications. One may ask why we bother with the non-parametric representation, but our experience shows that more complex data representation, necessary for the parametric one, usually makes an automated verification in FM tools impossible even for very simple scenarios.

The communication between the simulator and a control module can be seen in Fig. 1, which shows the tools exactly after the moment when a request for clearing the signal sig0 is received from the train Os001. As we can see in the "Logger" part, TS2JavaConn responds by calling reqGreen_sig0 method from the connected control module. The method changes the value of a variable that represents sig0 and this change is sent back to the simulator (as so-called *multiCommand* message) where it sets sig0 to green.

During a FM course the toolset is useful in both lectures and practices. In lectures the whole method taught can be illustrated by examples utilizing the toolset. Even very simple scenarios and control modules are able to demonstrate benefits (e.g. we can specify safety conditions and prove that they hold in every state of given program) and drawbacks (e.g. we cannot prove that the safety conditions we specified are the right ones) of FM. Advanced concepts can be explained as well. For example, on a refinement from a data representation that corresponds 1:1 to devices in given scenario to a more effective one or on a control module composed from reusable components for individual track types (a straight track, various junctions, etc.). On practices the toolset primarily provides a virtual laboratory environment and is usually used in the following way: First a teacher creates a new scenario, or modifies an existing one, in Train Director. When creating it he should restrict himself to simple red/green signals and two-way switches. Then he presents the scenario to students with a task to create a dependable controller for it. The students can then play with the scenario in Train Director: if it is disconnected from TS2JavaConn, switches and signals can be operated manually. After getting familiar with the scenario the students generate an empty module using TS2JavaConn and start to develop the controller itself, using given formal method and its tools. Finally, they return to the toolset and run the finished and compiled module with the scenario.

Adaptability of the toolset to various FM was one of the primary concerns during its development. It has been achieved by making the toolset as independent from actual FM tools as possible. There are only two "common points". The first one is when a new control module template is generated. Only languages of two FM are supported yet, but the module generator is based on the Apache Velocity template engine, so new ones can be added easily. The second point is when a finished module is connected to and run with the corresponding scenario. Here the only requirement is that the module has to be a Java application with an appropriate interface. And Java code generators are available for a wide variety of FM tools. For example, Perfect Developer (http://www.eschertech.com) and VDM++ Toolkit (http://www.vdmtools.jp) have built-in generators, for the Rodin tool (http://www.event-b.org) of the Event-B method they exist in a form of plug-ins (e.g. EB2J, http://eb2all.loria.fr) and for B-Method we provide our own generator, called BKPI compiler, optimized for the use with the Atelier-B tool (http://www.atelierb.eu). We had tested the toolset with all these methods and code generators and only in the case of EJ2B it was necessary to alter the generated Java code (an explicit constructor was added). In all other cases it was enough to modify configuration files of the modules.

3   Conclusions

The toolset was already used during two runs of a FM course, which teaches Petri nets and B-Method, at the home institution of the authors. Petri nets were explained with abstract models of synchronization problems while almost all examples in the B-Method part were prepared and presented using the toolset. On practices the toolset was used in the way described in section 2. Based on the students' feedback we can conclude that our belief has been confirmed. When compared to previous years the students were more engaged and even those who didn't score very well in other theoretical computer science-based subjects managed to accomplish assignments that incorporated the toolset without significant problems. Some of them reported that they enjoyed the B-Method part more that the Petri nets part despite its significantly higher difficulty. And all of them enjoyed the moment when they have finally seen their control modules running in the toolset. Of course, problems were reported, too. After the first run (in 2013) the need to write configuration files and whole control modules manually was identified as the greatest setback. To improve the situation the module generator of TS2JavaConn has been implemented. Students also reported that it takes too long to get the modules from FM side to the toolset. But this was intentional, to prevent students from using the "modify-compile-run" cycle too often.

The belief we presented is also supported by other educators. The work [4] shares our view on importance of motivation with respect to massification of higher education and points out that students will see little benefit in developing ordinary systems using FM. The authors of [2] see the importance of an appropriate experimentation platform, which is exactly what our toolset tries to establish, as high enough to make it one of their ten principles (no. 6).

The future development of the toolset will focus on an improvement of the module generator and replacement of Train Director by 3D train simulator Open Rails (www.openrails.org).

This paper dealt primarily with the actual version of the toolset and its use in a FM course. Additional information, such as the general idea behind the toolset, related work that led us to the idea, examples of control modules and the reasons why Train Director was chosen, can be found in other papers by the authors. These papers, the toolset, the BKPI compiler and a set of examples with control modules developed using various FM can be downloaded from https://kega2012.fm.kpi.fei.tuke.sk.

Acknowledgments. This work has been supported by KEGA grant project No. 050TUKE-4/2012: "Application of Virtual Reality Technologies in Teaching Formal Methods".

References

1. Almeida, J.B., Frade, M.J., Pinto, J.S., Melo de Sousa, S.: Rigorous Software Development. An Introduction to Program Verification. Springer, London (2011)
2. Cerone, A., Roggenbach, M., Schlingloff, H., Schneider, G., Shaikh, S.: Teaching Formal Methods for Software Engineering Ten Principles. In: Fun With Formal Methods, Workshop Affiliated with the 25th Int. Conf. CAV 2013 (2013)
3. Cristi, M.: Teaching formal methods in a third world country: what, why and how. In: Proceedings of the 2006 Conference on Teaching Formal Methods: Practice and Experience (2006)
4. Reed, J.N., Sinclair, J.E.: Motivating study of Formal Methods in the classroom. In: Dean, C.N., Boute, R.T. (eds.) TFM 2004. LNCS, vol. 3294, pp. 32–46. Springer, Heidelberg (2004)

Execution and Verification of UML State Machines with Erlang*

Ricardo J. Rodríguez, Lars-Åke Fredlund, Ángel Herranz, and Julio Mariño

Universidad Politécnica de Madrid, Spain
{rjrodriguez,lfredlund,aherranz,jmarino}@fi.upm.es

Abstract. Validation of a system design enables to discover specification errors before it is implemented (or tested), thus hopefully reducing the development cost and time. The Unified Modelling Language (UML) is becoming widely accepted for the early specification and analysis of requirements for safety-critical systems, although a better balance between UML's undisputed flexibility, and a precise unambiguous semantics, is needed. In this paper we introduce UMerL, a tool that is capable of executing and formally verifying UML diagrams (namely, UML state machine, class and object diagrams) by means of a translation of its behavioural information into Erlang. The use of the tool is illustrated with an example in embedded software design.

1 Introduction

A better integration with the development process is crucial for the success of UML as a language for the specification and design of safety-critical software. This requires tools capable of validating complex requirements, and linking them to operational code through an unambiguous semantics. With these goals in mind we have developed UMerL, a tool that executes and verifies UML designs consisting of UML2 *state-machine*, *class* and *object* diagrams, using the concurrent language Erlang [1]. UMerL is available (with source code) at https://bitbucket.org/fredlund1/umerl.

UMerL differs from other analysis tools [2–4] in that an executable prototype is first produced, and then the validation of the UML model is done by performing various analyses on that prototype. Using Erlang has been crucial for implementing this approach. First, Erlang's concurrency features simplified the task of coding the state machine interpreter, which has to run several state machines with little runtime overhead. Also, the availability of advanced analysis tools for Erlang like Quviq QuickCheck [5] or the McErlang model checker [6] facilitates model validation without having to introduce a new set of tools.

Outline. Sec. 2 describes UMerL. Sec. 3 relates the application of UMerL to a real industrial case in embedded software design. We focus on the execution of

* The research has received funding from the ARTEMIS JU: grant agreement 295373 (nSafeCer), from the Spanish MINECO: STRONGSOFT (TIN2012-39391-C04-02), and from the Comunidad Autónoma de Madrid: PROMETIDOS (P2009/TIC-1465).

D. Giannakopoulou and G. Salaün (Eds.): SEFM 2014, LNCS 8702, pp. 284–289, 2014.
© Springer International Publishing Switzerland 2014

state-machine diagrams in Erlang and the verification of behavioural properties by program analysis on the Erlang code. Finally, Sec. 4 concludes the paper.

2 The UMerL Tool

UMerL is an interpreter of UML state machines implemented in Erlang that executes a system modelled as a collection of UML state machines with acceptable performance. Its design also allows us to verify using model checking techniques whether a UML system meets some correctness properties. UMerL executes the UML state machines inside an object following a UML-friendly semantics: the meaning assigned to the constructs is consistent with respect to the UML (informal) semantics. An excerpt of the supported semantics and its interpretation by UMerL is described in Sec. 2.1.

System Description. In UMerL, a system description consists of a UML class diagram, a set of UML state-machine diagrams each one associated to a class and a UML object diagram. Each object has a private data store defined by the properties indicated in the class diagram. Several UML state-machine instances are running in each object, one for each UML state-machine associated to its class. To describe the system a domain specific language embedded in Erlang is used. The environment of the system can communicate with an object (and its associated state machines) by simply sending normal Erlang messages to the Erlang process associated with the object.

Verification Workflow. Figure 1 depicts the verification workflow of UMerL. A verification scenario consists of a system description and an environment model. The environment model sends messages and signals to the objects. We use Quviq QuickCheck [5] to randomly generate sequences of sensible messages. UMerL provides two functionalities: the system can be executed (with user interaction), providing early feedback regarding behaviour; or the verification scenario can be (model) checked against a set of correctness properties specified in Linear Temporal Logic (LTL) [7]. Properties are defined by the user using the McErlang tool [6], which provides a counterexample (in terms of message traces) when an LTL property is not satisfied by the system.

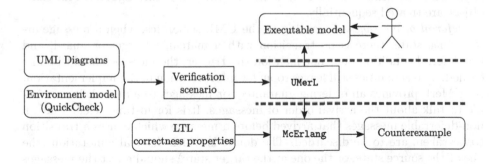

Fig. 1. Verification workflow of UMerL

Architecture. UMerL maps each object to a single Erlang process: a generic interpreter that executes transitions of the UML state machines in that object, i.e., an individual UML state machine is not mapped to an Erlang process. Every step of the generic interpreter consists in choosing, non-deterministically, one of the enabled transitions and executing it (see Section 2.1).

A message sent to an object is received by its associated process, and is broadcast to every UML state machine running in the object. Conceptually, each state machine has its own mailbox for storing incoming messages until they are processed. Mailboxes are ordered in our implementation, i.e., if a message m_1 arrives before a message m_2, then m_1 will precede m_2 in the mailbox.

2.1   Semantics

Transition execution. A transition of a UML state machine can be executed when it is enabled: the mailbox contains a message that matches the trigger and the guard (a condition expressed over the contents of the message and the object data store) evaluates to true. The execution of a transition consists of three steps: (1) processing the first eligible message in the mailbox, (2) executing the activity that updates the private data store and sends messages to other objects, and (3) entering the target state. The execution of a transition appears to occur instantaneously since the execution of transitions follows a linearizable (atomic) semantics (atomicity does not necessarily mean mutually exclusive).

Do activities. A do activity is managed by an independent Erlang process, which is terminated when the execution of a transition leads outside the state.

Entry and exit activities. The semantics of an entry is implemented by adding it to the activity of every transition entering the state; an exit is implemented by adding it to the activity of every transition leaving the state.

Processing of messages. The most interesting aspect in our implementation is the processing of messages during the execution of a transition, and the deferral of messages. A message in the mailbox is eligible when it matches the trigger of a transition, and the corresponding guard evaluates to true. Our implementation chooses the oldest eligible message providing the additional guarantee (compared to the standard semantics for UML state machines) that messages from the same object are treated sequentially.

Deferral of messages. According to the UML semantics, when a message arrives in a state, there is no transition with a matching trigger or guard, and the deferral condition does not mention the trigger, the message should be discarded. This semantics still leaves room for interpretation in the implementation. As UMerL provides an ordering guarantee for messages (see above), it is possible to talk about the arrival order of messages. It is for instance clear that all non-deferrable messages that arrived before a message which causes a transition to be taken, are to be discarded. The doubt is which deferral annotation (the one at the source state, or the one at the target state) should affect the messages that arrived later than the message which caused the transition.

An *eager* semantics would discard all the messages not deferred by the source state while a *lazy* semantics would discard all the messages not deferred by the target state. The implications are crucial. For instance, in a two step communication protocol where one machine sends two messages m_1 and m_2 in two consecutive transitions, and the other machine receives both messages, message m_2 could be discarded if the second machine does not defer it in the initial state (m_1 and m_2 could both be received when the machine is in that state).

In our experience a designer of a distributed asynchronous system regularly makes mistakes causing messages to be silently discarded. We have decided to implement several semantic options to permit a designer to experiment with different interpretations of the discarding rule: (i) enable as the default that all messages are deferrable in states which has no explicit deferral condition. The use of such an option is, we argue, preferable when modelling distributed systems using state machines as it leads to fewer errors committed and less syntactic clutter (avoiding the need to repeat defer annotations in all states); and (ii) the choice of an eager or lazy deferral semantics, the default being lazy.

3   Safety Assessment of an Embedded Software Design

As case study, we consider a system for managing door operations in a train, provided by an industrial partner in a collaborative project. The system is composed of three major parts represented by UML classes: a Train Control Management System (TCMS), a traction system, and several doors. The traction system moves the train, or stops it. The doors allow passengers to enter or exit the coaches. Finally, the TCMS is an embedded device in charge of supervising both the traction system and the doors, to ensure safe operation.

Figure 2(a) and (b) show the UML-State Machine diagrams (UML-SMs) of the Door and TCMS classes, respectively. A Door object starts closed and disabled, and can be opened once it has been enabled (which is performed by the TCMS after receiving a enableDoors message), if a passenger presses the door button (triggering the sending of buttonPressed message to a door). Once a door is again disabled, it can be closed when no obstacle is detected. The TCMS starts in state *Idle*, which represents a state where the train is stopped. A message enableDoors will be eventually sent (by the train driver) and received by the TCMS. Then, the TCMS sends to each Door an enable message, and waits for an acknowledgement message (notify). The TCMS reports that all doors have been enabled by switching an informative LED off, and waits until the message disableDoors is received. After receiving it, the TCMS sends a disable message to each Door, and it waits a safety time interval of 5 seconds, before enabling the Traction, and moving to the *MovingTrain* state. This safety time is designed to permit to verify that all doors have been correctly closed. The transition from *MovingTrain* to *StoppingTrain* is triggered by the stopTrain message, and the TCMS acts by sending the disable message to Traction. The signal trainStopped is received once the train has been completely stopped, and so TCMS moves to the *Idle* state again.

Safety Assessment. A correctness property that must be assured in the system is that *No door should be open when the train is moving*. This is a safety property,

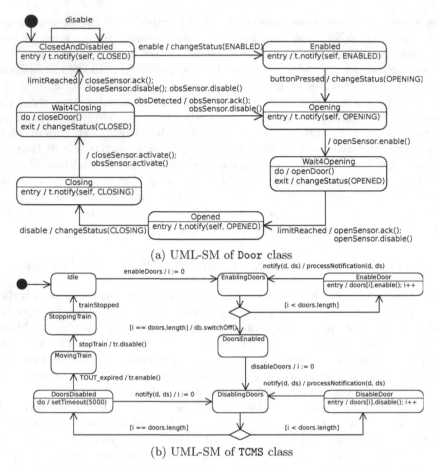

(a) UML-SM of **Door** class

(b) UML-SM of **TCMS** class

Fig. 2. UML-State Machine diagrams of (a) **Door** and (b) **TCMS** classes

i.e., stating that *something bad never happens*. Note that the state predicate "a door is open" is true when the value of attribute **status** in a **Door** object is equal to **OPENED**. The predicate "the train is moving" is true when the value of attribute **speed** (in the **Traction** class, not shown here) is greater than zero. As a verification example, given an environment model in which an **enableDoors** message is first received by TCMS, and then a **buttonPressed** message is sent to a door, the McErlang model checker can verify that the two predicates above are never true in the same system state.

The above property can also be reformulated as *all doors must be closed when the train is moving*, i.e., the status attribute of a door must be **CLOSED**. Given that the **status** attribute of a door can be either **OPEN**, **CLOSED**, **ENABLED**, **OPENING** or **CLOSING**, this is a more restrictive (and safe) formulation. If we use the same environment model, except that we assume that a **disableDoors** message also arrives at the TCMS, the McErlang tool quickly finds a counterexample to the second property. The counterexample indicates that the failure is that a door may not have had sufficient time to process earlier messages sent to it.

In brief, we have verified the above safety property for a coach with two doors in 0.35 seconds using McErlang (running under an Intel i7-2640M CPU with 8GB memory), with a resulting state space of 1,133 states, under the assumption that all messages are deferrable. The model of a coach with three (and four doors) has 7,323 (53,743 states), and its checking time is 1.74 seconds (14.88).

4   Conclusion

The experimental results obtained with our tool are quite promising. Although the tool works with only three kinds of UML diagrams and a quite restrictive syntax for state-machine diagrams (which has been crucial for defining the underlying semantics), the language is expressive enough to model embedded systems of a moderate complexity, e.g., the train doors example used here.

Several other tools exist which perform model checking on UML state machines. USMMC [2] is remarkable for being *self-contained*, it does not rely on a foreign formalism and checker, thus avoiding some inconveniences of translation-based tools like HUGO [4] or UMerL. However, UMerL does have a number of advantages too. First, an executable prototype, constructed from the UML model, provides early validation that can reveal mistakes even before attempting a detailed verification. Moreover, UMerL users can take advantage of existing analysis and testing tools for Erlang such as McErlang and QuickCheck.

To improve the usability of the tool a translation from the XMI notation is being implemented, and verification counterexamples will be presented as UML Sequence Diagrams. We also aim at specifying LTL properties at the UML level using a UML-friendly syntax, such as Object Constraint Language (OCL). Moreover, we aim at supporting hierarchical structures and pseudo-states among other UML features missing from the current prototype.

References

1. Armstrong, J., Virding, R., Wikström, C., Williams, M.: Concurrent Programming in Erlang. Prentice-Hall (1996)
2. Liu, S., Liu, Y., Sun, J., Zheng, M., Wadhwa, B., Dong, J.S.: USMMC: A Self-contained Model Checker for UML State Machines. In: Proc. of the 2013 Meeting on Foundations of Software Engineering, pp. 623–626. ACM, New York (2013)
3. Lilius, J., Paltor, I.P.: Formalising UML State Machines for Model Checking. In: France, R., Rumpe, B. (eds.) UML 1999. LNCS, vol. 1723, pp. 430–444. Springer, Heidelberg (1999)
4. Balser, M., Bäumler, S., Knapp, A., Reif, W., Thums, A.: Interactive verification of UML state machines. In: Davies, J., Schulte, W., Barnett, M. (eds.) ICFEM 2004. LNCS, vol. 3308, pp. 434–448. Springer, Heidelberg (2004)
5. Arts, T., Hughes, J., Johansson, J., Wiger, U.: Testing Telecoms Software with Quviq QuickCheck. In: ACM SIGPLAN Int. Erlang Workshop. ACM (2006)
6. Fredlund, L.Å., Svensson, H.: McErlang: a model checker for a distributed functional programming language. In: 12th ACM SIGPLAN ICFP. ACM (2007)
7. Pnueli, A.: The Temporal Logic of Programs. In: FOCS, pp. 46–57 (1977)

A Tool for Verifying Dynamic Properties in B

Fama Diagne[1,2], Amel Mammar[1], and Marc Frappier[2]

[1] Institut Telecom SudParis CNRS/SAMOVAR, France
{fama.diagne,amel.mammar}@telecom-sudparis.eu
[2] GRIL, Dep. d'informatique, Universite de Sherbrooke (Quebec), Canada
marc.frappier@usherbrooke.ca

Abstract. This paper presents a tool for verifying dynamic properties using the B formal method. For example, in a library system, typical dynamic properties would be that a member has a possibility to borrow a book or make a reservation if it is already reserved by another member. Starting from a B specification and a dynamic property, this tool generates the proof obligations that permit the user to check whether the property is verified on the B specification. The goal of such a tool is to discharge the users from tedious and error-prone activities.

1 Introduction

In this paper, we present a tool developed in JAVA for proving dynamic properties using the B formal method [1]. Verification of these properties is an important phase in the development process of many systems like information systems, access control, etc. Contrary to invariance properties, dynamic properties depend on several system states. We are interested in three types of dynamic properties: reachability, absence and precedence properties. In practice, these properties are very common and useful in several domains and applications. In a library system, for instance, a reachability property will be used to state that a member can always borrow a book. An absence property can express that if a member me_1 reserves a book bo before a member me_2, then it is impossible for me_2 to take the book bo before me_1.

2 Presentation of the Tool

Our tool implements the verification of several dynamic properties including reachability [2,3], absence [4] and precedence [5]. The verification methods implemented in the tool are based on a formal specification of the system using the B method. This formal specification consists of a set B operations acting on variables representing the state of the system. A reachability property, expressed in CTL as $\mathsf{AG}(\psi \Rightarrow EF\phi)$, specifies that from a state s satisfying ψ, the system can reach a state s' where ϕ becomes true. To prove a reachability property on a system specified by a B machine, two approaches have been developed. According to the first one, the user must provide a set of paths such that each path leads

D. Giannakopoulou and G. Salaün (Eds.): SEFM 2014, LNCS 8702, pp. 290–295, 2014.
© Springer International Publishing Switzerland 2014

from the initial state to the target one. These paths come from the use cases identified during requirements analysis to reach ψ from ϕ. Each path consists of a set of B operation calls combined with programming constructs like sequencing ";", IF and LOOP. The key idea of the approach consists in calculating the intermediate values of each variable (the post-condition of a sub-path) and proving that at each point of the path, the current values satisfy the precondition of the next action. The second approach is based on substitution refinement of the B method. This approach uses Morgan's specification statement [6] to represent a reachability property and refinement laws to prove it. An absence property of the form $\mathsf{Abs}(P_2, \mathsf{From}\ P_1\ \mathsf{Until}\ P_3)$ expresses that from a state satisfying predicate P_1, the system cannot reach a state where P_2 is true, until it has reached a state that satisfies predicate P_3. Such a property can be expressed in LTL [7] by $\Box(P_1 \Rightarrow \neg P_2 \mathsf{W} P_3)$. We have also defined a second variant of such a property of the form $\mathsf{Abs}(P_2, \mathsf{After}\ P_1 \mathsf{Until}\ P_3)$ that states that some states, represented by predicate P_2, should not be reached after the system entering a state that verifies P_1 until P_3 becomes fulfilled. In LTL, such a property is represented by: $\Box(P_1 \Rightarrow \mathsf{X}(\neg P_2 \mathsf{W} P_3))$. Finally, a precedence property of the form $\mathsf{Prec}(P_1,\ P_2)$ that expresses that if a state, presented by predicate P_2, is reached then there should exist a state, in the past, that verifies P_1. For these different properties, the tool generates a set of proof obligation that permit to verify them on a B specification modeling a given system.

The processing flow of our tool can be divided into four main steps (see Figure 1). The tool takes as input two text files that correspond to the B specification of the system and the property to verify. These files are then parsed, using the abstract syntax tree generated by the SableCC parser, to extract the information they contain. To this aim, we have extended the JAVA class *DepthFirstAdapter* generated by SableCC. This class allows one to browse the syntax tree and to perform processing on the nodes of this tree. The information extracted from the input files are stored in the JAVA objects *SpecSys* and *Spec_Prop*. These objects are used to generate the proof obligations required to verify the related dynamic property. As output, the tool produces the same B specification, provided as input, in which the generated proof obligations are added as assertions. The correctness of these assertions are then proved using AtelierB [8]. To generate the proof obligation related to a given dynamic property, several steps have to be followed. For sake of the concision, this paper gives details only for the reachability property. More details can be found in [5].

Figure 2 depicts the different steps followed by the tool to generate the proof obligations required for the verification of the reachability property according to the approach proposed in [2]. This approach introduces an algorithm that takes as input a formula that expresses the property to check and a set of guarded paths that lead to the desired state. As output, this algorithm generates a set of proof obligations that ensures that the system can reach the desired state by following these paths. A guarded path is of the form $cond \rightsquigarrow (Act_1; Act_2; ......; Act_n)$ with ";" denoting action sequencing and Act_i an action. This path can be executed only if guard $cond$ is true.

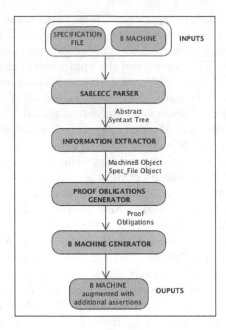

Fig. 1. Information flow of the tool

To verify a reachability property of the form $\mathbf{AG}(\psi \Rightarrow \mathbf{EF}\phi)$, the key idea of this approach is to prove that:

1. The execution of a path leads to ϕ:

$$\boxed{\psi \wedge cond \Rightarrow [(Act_1; Act_2; ......; Act_n)]\phi} \quad \mathbf{PO1}$$

where $[S]P$ denotes the weakest conditions under which the execution of substitution S terminates in a state that verifies predicate P.

2. At least one path can be executed starting from any state satisfying ψ (where m is the number of paths):

$$\boxed{\psi \Rightarrow \bigvee_{i=1,..,m} cond_i} \quad \mathbf{PO2}$$

To establish (**PO1**), one must prove that: (1) action Act_1 can run if the current state satisfies ψ and $cond$; (2) the state reached after the execution of each action Act_i satisfies the precondition of the next action Act_{i+1}, (3) ϕ is true after the execution of the last action Act_n.

According to Fig 2, this is achieved in two phases. The first phase produces the proof obligation associated with each path. It is composed of the three steps listed above. The second phase generates a proof obligation to guarantee that, from a state where ψ is true, at least one path can run (**PO2**). These phases have been implemented by defining methods that calculate the precondition and post-condition of an action. Since an action Act_i is executed with the variable values x_{i-1} obtained after the execution of the previous action Act_{i-1}, we have implemented a method to replace each variable x of action Act_i by its value x_{i-1}. This substitution method takes into account all the possible B expressions, which includes sets, relations, functions, sequences, integers, and predicates.

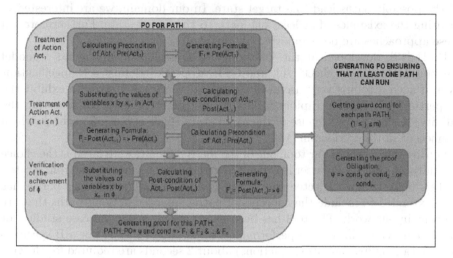

Fig. 2. Process of generating proof obligations

3   Discussion

There are three main approaches to verifying dynamic properties: testing, model checking or theorem proving. Testing is the most widely used method in practice, but it suffers from a lack of automation and limited coverage of the test space. Model checking has the advantage of being more automatic, but it quickly suffers from combinatorial explosion, thus limiting the size of the models checked as shown in [9]. Consequently, the confidence in the correctness of the system is limited to the relatively small size of the models analyzed. Theorem proving requires more human intervention and sometimes considerable expertise, but it certifies the correctness of the system, since proofs are valid for any models. However, little attention has been paid so far to proofs of temporal properties, because they are more complex to carry out than typical invariance properties.

Even if some proof-based approaches for the verification of dynamic properties have been already developed, however they are not dedicated for information systems and require consequent efforts. More detailed literature description can be found in [5]. In [10], Abrial and Mussat introduced the *leadsto* modality of UNITY for an ancestor of Event-B. UNITY's leadsto, denoted by $\psi \rightsquigarrow \phi$, is defined in LTL as $\Box(\psi \rightarrow \Diamond\psi)$. This modality is proved by showing that a set of events decrease a variant V. This work has been extended in [11] by adding

UNITY's *ensures* modality as well as minimal progress. In [12], a set of rules that permit to reason about liveness properties are presented. A variant of the reachability property is dealt with: the authors provide conditions that ensure that a program can always reach a given state whatever its behavior. For our application domain, information systems, such properties are not suitable since a user is never forced to execute an action. In other words, the behavior depends on the user's actions that cannot be controlled: it is not possible to prove that all the possible paths lead to a target state. In our domain, we are interested in ensuring the existence of at least one path to the target state. Furthermore, all these approaches are not supported by any tool.

ProB [13], developed at the University of Düsseldorf, implements a model checking technique to check LTL and CTL properties against a B specification. Even if such a tool is very useful in the initial verification steps to exhibit the properties that become rapidly falsifiable, it cannot be used for asserting the validity of a property because of the rapid state space explosion problem which is inherent in the IS domain [14].

During the design of our tool, one of the main difficulties we faced is the choice of a suitable existing B parser in order to avoid developing a new one from scratch. To this aim, we have selected the parser developed for ProB[1]. This parser has been extended to include the concepts of paths, guarded actions/paths that are relevant in our work. The tool has been experienced on several case studies for which it provides, in term of performance, interesting runtime: for a B specification containing five operations (actions) about 2 seconds are required for the generation of all the properties we have dealt with [5]. The tool can now be accessed on-line at the following url: `http://www.dmi.usherb.ca/~frappier/DynamicB`.

4   Conclusion

In this paper, we have presented a tool that automates some verification approaches for dynamic properties. From two input files representing the B specification of a system and the dynamic property to be verified, the tool automatically generates the proof obligations required to prove it. Our tool deals with reachability together with absence and precedence properties, but can be easily extended to support other types of property. Also to facilitate the use of the tool, we have implemented a graphical interface that permits the user to choose the input files. After six months of implementation, we have automated two approaches for the verification of reachability properties and two approaches for the absence properties.

We plan to extend our tool to take into account other types of property patterns that would be interesting for information systems. As an example, we can cite the response property, which permits specifying that a state is always followed by an other specific state. Such a pattern will be used to express, for instance, that a client that asks for a book is either satisfied or put in a reservation queue in order to take the book when it becomes available. Moreover, the

---

[1] `https://github.com/bendisposto/probparsers`

approach defined here can be adapted for the Event-B approach [15]. In that way, the tool can be integrated as a plugin to the Rodin platform[2].

References

1. Abrial, J.R.: The B-book: Assigning Programs to Meanings. Cambridge University Press, New York (1996)
2. Mammar, A., Frappier, M., Diagne, F.: A Proof-Based Approach to Verifying Reachability Properties. In: Chu, W.C., Wong, W.E., Palakal, M.J., Hung, C.C. (eds.) SAC, pp. 1651–1657. ACM (2011)
3. Frappier, M., Diagne, F., Mammar, A.: Proving Reachability in B using Substitution Refinement. Electron. Notes Theor. Comput. Sci. 280, 47–56 (2011)
4. Mammar, A., Frappier, M., Chane-Yack-Fa, R.: Proving the Absence Property Pattern Using the B Method. In: HASE, pp. 167–170 (2012)
5. Diagne, F.: Preuve de Propriétés Dynamiques en B. PhD thesis, Télécom Sud-Paris/Université de Sherbrooke (2013), http://www-public.it-sudparis.eu/~mammar_a/theseFamaDiagne.pdf
6. Morgan, C.C.: Programming from Specifications, 2nd edn. Prentice Hall International series in computer science. Prentice Hall (1994)
7. Pnueli, A.: The Temporal Logic of Programs. In: FOCS, pp. 46–57 (1977)
8. ClearSy: Manuel de Référence du Langage B. ClearSy, France (2007)
9. Frappier, M., Fraikin, B., Chossart, R., Chane-Yack-Fa, R., Ouenzar, M.: Comparison of Model Checking Tools for Information Systems. In: Dong, J.S., Zhu, H. (eds.) ICFEM 2010. LNCS, vol. 6447, pp. 581–596. Springer, Heidelberg (2010)
10. Abrial, J.R., Mussat, L.: Introducing dynamic constraints in b. In: Bert, D. (ed.) B 1998. LNCS, vol. 1393, pp. 83–128. Springer, Heidelberg (1998)
11. Barradas, H.R., Bert, D.: Specification and Proof of Liveness Properties under Fairness Assumptions in B Event Systems. In: Butler, M., Petre, L., Sere, K. (eds.) IFM 2002. LNCS, vol. 2335, pp. 360–379. Springer, Heidelberg (2002)
12. Hoang, T.S., Abrial, J.R.: Reasoning about Liveness Properties in Event-B. In: Qin, S., Qiu, Z. (eds.) ICFEM 2011. LNCS, vol. 6991, pp. 456–471. Springer, Heidelberg (2011)
13. Leuschel, M., Butler, M.: ProB: An Automated Analysis Toolset for the B Method. STTT 10(2), 185–203 (2008)
14. Frappier, M., Fraikin, B., Chossart, R., Chane-Yack-Fa, R., Ouenzar, M.: Comparison of Model Checking Tools for Information Systems. In: Dong, J.S., Zhu, H. (eds.) ICFEM 2010. LNCS, vol. 6447, pp. 581–596. Springer, Heidelberg (2010)
15. Abrial, J.R.: Modeling in Event-B - System and Software Engineering. Cambridge University Press (2010)

---

[2] http://www.event-b.org/install.html

WeVerca: Web Applications Verification for PHP⋆

David Hauzar and Jan Kofroň

Department of Distributed and Dependable Systems
Faculty of Mathematics and Physics
Charles University in Prague, Czech Republic

Abstract. Static analysis of web applications developed in dynamic languages is a challenging yet very important task. In this paper, we present WEVERCA, a framework that allows one to define static analyses of PHP applications. It supports dynamic type system, dynamic method calls, dynamic data structures, etc. These common features of dynamic languages cause implementation of static analyses to be either imprecise or overly complex. Our framework addresses this problem by defining end-user static analyses independently of value and heap analyses necessary just to resolve these features. As our results show, taint analysis defined using the framework found more real problems and reduced the number of false positives comparing to existing state-of-the-art analysis tools for PHP.

1 Introduction

PHP is the most common programming language used at the server side of web applications. It is notably used, e.g., by Wikipedia and Facebook. PHP as well as other dynamic languages contains dynamic features, such as dynamic type system, dynamic method calls (names of called methods are computed at run-time), and dynamic data structures (names of object fields are computed at run-time and object fields can be added at run-time). These features provide flexibility accelerating the development. However, they make applications more error-prone and less efficient. Consequently, they shift more work to tools for error detection, code refactoring, and code optimization.

For most of these tools, static program analysis is a necessary prerequisite. Unfortunately, dynamic features pose major challenges here. To precisely resolve these features, the end-user analysis (e.g., taint analysis) needs to be combined with value and heap analyses. Importantly, these analyses must interplay. To resolve dynamic accesses to data structures, the heap analysis needs to evaluate value expressions and the value analysis must track values over heap elements— array indices and object fields.

In this paper we present WEVERCA[1], an open-source static analysis framework for PHP. WEVERCA allows to define end-user static analyses independently

---

⋆ This work was partially supported by the Grant Agency of the Czech Republic project 14-11384S and by Charles University institutional funding SVV-2014-260100.
[1] http://d3s.mff.cuni.cz/projects/formal_methods/weverca/

D. Giannakopoulou and G. Salaün (Eds.): SEFM 2014, LNCS 8702, pp. 296–301, 2014.
© Springer International Publishing Switzerland 2014

of dynamic features. This is possible because: (1) WEVERCA defines an inter-play of value and heap analyses allowing to define these analyses independently of each other. (2) WEVERCA comes with default implementations of context-sensitive heap and value analyses that model associative arrays and prototype objects, track values of PHP primitive types, and model library functions, native operators, and type conversions. (3) WEVERCA defines how information from heap and value analyses are used to resolve dynamic features (i.e., to compute control-flow and resolve dynamic data accesses). As a proof of the concept, we implemented static taint analysis for detection of security problems.

2   Example

As an example, consider static taint analysis, which is commonly used for web applications. It can be used for detection of security problems, e.g., SQL injection and cross-site scripting attacks. The program point that reads user-input, session ids, cookies, or any other data that can be manipulated by a potential attacker is called *source*, while a program point that prints out data, queries a database, etc. is referred to as *sink*. Data at a given program point are *tainted* if they can pass from a source to this program point. A tainted data are *sanitized* if they are processed by a sanitization routine (e.g., `htmlspecialchars` in PHP) to remove potential malicious parts of it. Program is *vulnerable* if it contains a sink that uses data that are tainted and not sanitized.

Static taint analysis can be performed by computing the propagation of tainted data and then checking whether tainted data can reach a sink. The propagation of tainted data computed by forward data-flow analysis is shown in Tab. 1[2]. The analysis is specified by giving the lattice of data-flow facts, the initial values of variables, the transfer function, and the join operator.

Table 1. Propagation of tainted data

Lattice	L	$true$	
Top	$\top$	Bool	
Initial value	$init(v)$	$true$	if $v \in \$\_SESSION \cup ..$
		$false$	otherwise
Transfer function	$TF(LHS = RHS)$	$var = \bigvee_{r \in RHS} r$	if $var \in LHS$
		$var = var$	otherwise
	$TF(n)$	$var = var$	if n is not assignment
Join operator	$\sqcup(x,y)$	$x \vee y$	

Consider now the code in Fig. 1. At lines (1)–(9) classes for processing the output are defined. They can either log the output or show the output to the user. While the `Templ1` class uses a *sink* command to show the output, `Templ2` uses a *non-sink* command (e.g., does not send the output to the browser directly, but sanitizes it first). At lines (13)–(16) the application mode is set based on the value of `DEBUG` either to `log`—the application will log the output—or to

---

[2] For simplicity we omit the specification of sanitization.

show—the application will show the output to the user. At lines (17)–(20) the skin is set based on user input. At line (21), the array $users is initialized with the address of administrator. This value is not taken from any source and can be directly shown to the user. Note the update at line (11) is correct even if the variable $users is uninitialized. In PHP, if a non existing index is updated, it is automatically created and if the update involves next dimension, the index is initialized with an empty array. At lines (23)–(24) information about the user name and user address is assigned to the array $users. Note that this information is tainted. Finally, at lines (25)–(26) data are processed to the output.

```
1   class Templ {                              14      case true: $mode = "log"; break;
2       function log($msg) {...}               15      default: $mode = "show";
3   }                                          16  }
4   class Templ1 : Templ {                     17  switch ($_GET['skin']) {
5       function show($msg) { sink($msg); }    18      case 'skin1': $t = new Templ1(); break;
6   }                                          19      default: $t = new Templ2();
7   class Templ2 : Templ {                     20  }
8       function show($msg) { not_sink($msg); }  21  initialize($users);
9   }                                          22  $id = $_GET['userId'];
10  function initialize(&$users) {             23  $users[$id]['name'] = $_GET['name'];
11      $users['admin']['addr'] =              24  $users[$id]['addr'] = $_GET['addr'];
            get_admin_addr_from_db();          25  $t->$mode($users[$id]['name']);
12  }                                          26  $t->$mode($users['admin']['addr']);
13  switch (DEBUG) {
```

Fig. 1. Running example

The code contains two vulnerabilities. At lines (25) and (26) the method show of Templ1 can be called, its parameter $msg can be tainted and the parameter goes to the sink. Taint analysis defined using WEVERCA detects both vulnerabilities. Note that the definition of taint propagation uses just the information in Tab 1. This is possible only because WEVERCA automatically resolves control-flow and accesses to built-in data structures. That is, WEVERCA computes that the variable $t can point to objects of types Templ1 and Templ2 and that the variable $mode can contain values show and log. Based on this information, it resolves calls at lines (25) and (26). Moreover, as WEVERCA automatically reads the data from and updates the data to associative arrays and objects, at line (24), the tainted data are automatically propagated to index $users['admin']['addr'] defined at line (11). Consequently, the access of this index at line (26) reads tainted data.

3   Tool Description

The architecture of WEVERCA is shown in Fig. 2. For parsing PHP sources and providing abstract syntax tree (AST) WEVERCA uses PHALANGER[3]. The analysis is split into two phases. In the first phase, the framework computes control-flow of the analyzed program together with the shape of the heap and information about values of variables, array indices and object fields. Then it also evaluates expressions used for accessing data. The control-flow is captured in the intermediate representation (IR), while the other information is stored in the data representation.

---

[3] http://www.php-compiler.net/

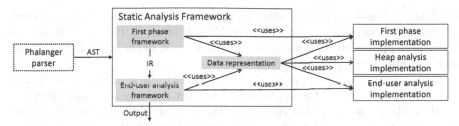

Fig. 2. The architecture of WeVerca

IR defines the order of instructions' execution and has function calls, method calls, includes, and exceptions already resolved. In the second phase, end-user analyses of the constructed IR are performed. The tool includes the following parts:

- **Data Representation** stores analysis states and allows to access them—it allows to read values from data structures, write values to data structures, and modify the shape of data structures. Next, it performs join and widening of the states and defines their partial order. Importantly, data representation defines the interplay of heap and value analyses allowing each analysis to define these operations independently. WeVerca contains implementation of heap analysis described in [1]. It supports associative arrays and objects of an arbitrary depth (in PHP, updates create indices and properties if they do not exist and initialize them with empty arrays and empty objects if needed; on contrary, read accesses do not, so updates of such structures cannot be decomposed). Accesses to these structures can be made using an arbitrary expression yielding even statically unknown values.
- **First-phase implementation** must define value analysis that tracks values of PHP primitive types and evaluates value expressions. Next, it must handle declaration of functions, classes, and constants. Finally, it must compute targets of include statements and function and method calls, and it must define context sensitivity. WeVerca contains a default implementation of the first phase providing fully context-sensitive value analysis precisely modeling native operators, native functions, and implicit conversions.
- **End-user analyses** can be specified using an arbitrary value domain. This is possible because (1) control-flow is already computed, (2) the shape of the heap is computed and dynamic data accesses are resolved—all information that data representation needs to discover accessed variables, indices, and fields are available. (3) Data representation combines heap and value analyses automatically, i.e., to perform operations with analysis states, it uses standard operations of combined analyses. The framework contains an implementation of static taint analysis as a proof-of-the-concept.

4   Results

To evaluate the precision and scalability of the framework, we used the framework to implement static taint analysis and we applied it to a NOCC webmail client[4] and a benchmark application comprising of a fragment of the myBloggie weblog system[5], with a total of over 16,000 lines of PHP code. While the benchmark application contains 13 security problems, in the case of the webmail client, the number of problems is not known.

Tab. 2 shows the summary of results together with the results of PIXY [3] and PHANTM [4], the state-of-the-art tools for security analysis and error discovery in PHP applications. The table shows that the analysis defined using WEVERCA outperforms the other tools both in error coverage and number of false positives when analyzing the benchmark application. While it took WEVERCA more than 5 minutes to analyze the webmail client and 52 alarms were reported, PIXY was even not able to analyze this application. PHANTM analyzed the application in two minutes, however, the false-positive rate of 93% makes its output almost useless.

Out of 13 problems in the benchmark application, WEVERCA discovered all of them. One of the false alarms reported by WEVERCA is caused by imprecise modeling of the built-in function `date`. WEVERCA only models this function by types and deduced that any string value can be returned by this function. However, while the first argument of the function is `"F"`, the function returns only strings corresponding to English names of months. When the value returned by this function is used to access the index of an array, WEVERCA incorrectly reports that an undefined index of the array can be accessed. Two remaining false alarms are caused by path-insensitivity of the analysis. The sanitization and sink commands are guarded by the same condition, however, there is a joint point between these conditions, which discards the effect of sanitization from the perspective of path-insensitive analysis. While the first false-alarm can be easily resolved by modeling the built-in function more precisely, the remaining false alarms would require more work. One can either implement an appropriate relational abstract domain or devise a method of path-sensitive validation of alarms.

Table 2. Comparison of tools for static analysis of PHP. W/C/F/T: **W**arnings / error **C**overage (in %) / **F**alse-positives rate (in %) / analysis **T**ime (in s). The best results are in bold.

	Lines	WeVerca W/C/F/T	Pixy W/C/F/T	Phantm W/C/F/T
myBloggie	648	16/**100**/19/2.2	16/69/44/**0.6**	43/23/93/2.5
NOCC 1.9.4	15605	52/NA/NA/332	NA	426/NA/NA/**130**

5 Related Work

The existing work on static analysis of PHP and other dynamic languages is primarily focused on specific security vulnerabilities and type analysis.

Pixy [3] performs taint analysis of PHP programs and it provides information about the flow of tainted data using dependence graphs. It involves a flow-sensitive, interprocedural, and context-sensitive data flow analysis along with

[4] http://nocc.sourceforge.net/
[5] http://mybloggie.mywebland.com/

literal and alias analysis to achieve precise results. The main limitations of Pixy include limited support for statically-unknown updates to associative arrays, ignoring classes and the `eval` command, omitting type inference, and limited support for handling file inclusion and aliasing. Alias analysis introduced in Pixy incorrectly models aliasing when associative arrays and objects are involved.

Phantm [4] is a PHP 5 static analyzer for type mismatch based on data-flow analysis; it aims at detection of type errors. To obtain precise results, Phantm is flow-sensitive, i.e., it is able to handle situations when a single variable can be of different types depending on program location. However, they omit updates of associative arrays and objects with statically-unknown values and aliasing, which can lead to both missing errors and reporting false positives.

TAJS [2] is a JavaScript static program analysis infrastructure. To gain precise results, it models prototype objects and associative arrays, dynamic accesses to these data structures, and implicit conversions. However, TAJS combines combines heap and value analysis ad-hoc, which results in intricate lattice structure and transfer functions.

6 Conclusion and Future Work

In this paper, we presented WeVerca, a framework for static analysis of PHP applications. WeVerca makes it possible to define static analyses independently of dynamic features, such as dynamic includes, dynamic method calls, and dynamic data accesses to associative arrays and objects. These features are automatically resolved using information from heap and value analyses, which are automatically combined.

Our prototype implementation of static taint analysis outperforms state-of-the-art tools for analysis of PHP applications both in error coverage and the false-positive rate. We believe that WeVerca can accelerate both the development of end-user static analysis tools and the research of static analysis of PHP and dynamic languages in general.

For future work, we plan to improve the scalability and precision of analyses provided by the framework. In particular, this includes the scalability improvements of data representation, implementation of more choices of context-sensitivity, more precise widening operators, and devising precise modeling of more library functions.

References

1. Hauzar, D., Kofroň, J., Baštecký, P.: Data-flow analysis of programs with associative arrays. In: ESSS 2014. EPTCS (2014)
2. Jensen, S.H., Møller, A., Thiemann, P.: Type analysis for JavaScript. In: Palsberg, J., Su, Z. (eds.) SAS 2009. LNCS, vol. 5673, pp. 238–255. Springer, Heidelberg (2009)
3. Jovanovic, N., Kruegel, C., Kirda, E.: Pixy: a static analysis tool for detecting Web application vulnerabilities. In: S&P 2006. IEEE (2006)
4. Kneuss, E., Suter, P., Kuncak, V.: Phantm: PHP Analyzer for Type Mismatch. In: FSE 2010. ACM (2010)

More Flexible Object Invariants
with Less Specification Overhead

Stefan Huster, Patrick Heckeler, Hanno Eichelberger, Jürgen Ruf,
Sebastian Burg, Thomas Kropf, and Wolfgang Rosenstiel

University of Tübingen, Department of Computer Science,
Sand 14, 72076 Tübingen, Germany
{huster,weissensel,heckeler,eichelberger,ruf,burg,
kropf,rosenstiel}@informatik.uni-tuebingen.de

Abstract. Object invariants are used to specify valid object states.
They play a central role for reasoning about the correctness of object-
oriented software. Current verification methodologies require additional
specifications to support the flexibility of modern object oriented programming concepts. This increases the specification effort and represents
a new source of error. The presented methodology reduces the currently
required specification overhead. It is based on an automatic control flow
analysis between code positions violating invariants and code positions
requiring their validity. This analysis helps to prevent specification errors,
possible in other approaches. Furthermore, the presented methodology
distinguishes between valid and invalid invariants within one object. This
allows a (more) flexible definition of invariants.

Keywords: Object Invariants, Dependency Analysis, Reduced Specification Overhead.

1 Introduction

Invariants specify relations on the program's data, which are expected to hold
during the program execution. Besides other contract types, e.g. pre- and post-
conditions, invariants play a central role for reasoning about the correctness of
object-oriented software [1–3]. It is generally accepted when pre- and postconditions must be valid. Preconditions must be valid at call time of a method
and postconditions at a methods completion. But there exists no unique definition regarding the scope of an invariant, which specifies when an invariant
must be valid. Different approaches exist regarding the definition of invariants
and the supported scope. To handle the flexibility of object oriented concepts,
current approaches introduce and require additional specifications. These additional specifications are used to define explicitly when an invariant or object
must be valid or which methods are allowed to invalidate an invariant. But they
also cause additional specification overhead and represent a new source of error.

This paper describes a new methodology to generate proof obligations for
invariants. Figure 1 illustrates how the presented methodology is embedded in a

D. Giannakopoulou and G. Salaün (Eds.): SEFM 2014, LNCS 8702, pp. 302–316, 2014.
© Springer International Publishing Switzerland 2014

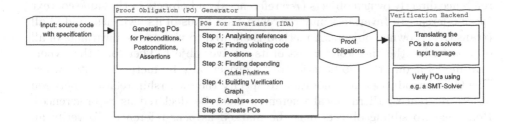

Fig. 1. Process flow diagram of our methodology

verification process. It is based on a static code analysis consisting of six steps. We begin in Step 1 to analyse all references of each invariant. In Step 2 we search code positions modifying the referenced values. These positions may invalidate the corresponding invariant. In Step 3 we search code positions depending on the validity of an invariant. In Step 4 we analyse backwards the possible call stack of each found code position and build a special call graph, called *Verification Graph*. In Step 5 we use the generated Verification Graph to analyse when invariants are invalidated and when they need to be re-established. We call this the *Scope* of an invariant. This information is used in Step 6 to generate proof obligations, ensuring the validity of an invariant whenever it is expected to hold. Therefore they are very similar to a Hoare-Triple [4]

The remainder of this paper is structured as follows: In Section 1.1 we introduce current methodologies for specifying and verifying invariants and detail their limitations. The contributions of the presented methodologies are listed in Section 1.2. A formal description of our methodology is given in Section 2. In Section 3 we show how this approach is applied to several examples. In Section 4 we conclude and introduce possible future work.

1.1 Related Work and Current Limitations

The classical Visible State Technique (VST) [5], as used in Eiffel [6] or Java Extended Static Checking [7], is the most restricted methodology verifying invariants. In this concept, invariants are allowed to reference only class fields of the same object. Each invariant must be valid in every public state. Therefore, one must show that each invariant of an object is valid before and after any public exported method has been executed. The limitations of the VST are well analysed in the literature [5, 8]. Due to its strictness the VST does not require any additional specifications. But it is also not flexible enough to support constructs like recursive methods, inheritance or invariants referring to values of multiple classes (multiclass invariants).

The ownership technique (OST) [9, 10, 5, 11] structures the set of objects in a acyclic hierarchical graph. Each object has at most one owner, which defines one context, containing all its (transitively) owned objects. Objects without any owner are part of the global context. The ownership model permits an object to reference directly owned objects (*rep* references) and objects in the same context (*peer* references). Invariants may reference class fields of its own class and of all (transitively) owned objects. A method is allowed to violate the invariants of all objects within the ancestor context of its receiver object. Therefore, the ownership model allows the modification of an object only by methods of its owner. The OST introduces a new notation to specify the ownership relations between object references. Hierarchical references must be declared as *rep*-references. References to sibling objects must be marked as *peer*-reference. To verify an invariant, one must show that each exported method preserves the invariants of its receiver object. Besides the additional required specification effort, the OST represents a very strict verification model. This model does not support the verification of recursive data structures and limits the possible cooperation between different objects. Furthermore, the ownership technique prohibits invariants of two different objects to contain a reference to one shared instance.

Barnett et al. extends the ownership technique in [12], by introducing a friendship system (FSS). This system allows the specification of invariants beyond ownership boundaries. Friendship relations control the access to privately owned fields. This allows other classes to build their invariants on it. This is realised by two new specification statements *friend* and *read*. Another extension is introduced by Barnett et al. in [14]. We refer to this approach as Explicit State Technique (EST). In that methodology, whether or not an object invariant is known to hold is expressed within the objects state in a special class field, not accessible by normal program code. Therefore, objects have to be marked explicitly as "invalid", before their class fields are updated. This is done by two special statements: *unpack* and *pack*. The first one marks an object as invalid and opens a frame in which the object state may be changed. The second statement closes the frame and enforces all invariants to hold again. This extension is used by Leino et al. in [2] to express invariants in dynamic contexts. Their approach uses an additional *dependent* and *ownerdependent* clausal to mark recursive dependencies. Furthermore, it is the first approach able to reason separately about object invariants declared in different subclasses.

The visibility technique (VIS) is introduced by Müller et al. in [5] and is based on the ownership model. A declaration within a specific class is visible in a method, if the methods module imports the module of that class. An extended approach considering visibility modifiers is presented in [15]. Invariants may reference class fields from their own class and all classes, in which that invariant is visible. Therefore, an invariant might be violated only by methods in which the invariant is visible. To prove that an invariant holds, one must show that a method preserves the invariants of all its referenced objects. As a result, the visibility technique is powerful enough to define and handle among others specifications of recursive data structures. Because the VIS is based on the ownership model it supports only very strict invariants regarding the ownership hierarchy. The VIS requires that each invariant of all objects, relevant for a method's execution, hold before the corresponding method is called. Therefore, the VIS cannot be used to verify a gradual update on a not owned object.

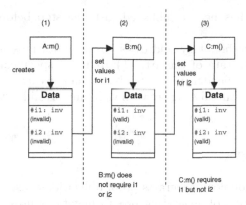

Fig. 2. Illustration of an inter-object based on partly valid objects

The Oval approach (OVL) [13] combines the ownership model and behavioural contracts. These contracts are defined by the additional specification sets *validity invariants* and *validity effects*: The first set contains objects which must be valid before and after a method is executed. The second set enumerates objects which might be violated during the execution of that method. Both sets are used to track which objects must be re-established and validated after a method was executed. This is very similar to the presented methodology which also is based on two sets, listing invariants expected to be valid and invariants which might be invalidated. However, we use a static code analysis to determine these sets automatically rather than requiring their definition manually by the programmer. Furthermore, the Oval approach allows only invariants based on its own fields or the fields of its (transitively) owned objects. As well as the pure ownership and the visibility technique, Oval cannot distinguish between valid and invalid invariants within one object. Additionally to the overhead caused by the underlying ownership model, the Oval approach requires a high specification overhead for defining the behavioural contracts. Consequently, a manual enumeration of required and effected invariants has to be performed for each method.

1.2   Contributions

Current approaches have two main limitations: (1) They require a high specification overhead to define object invariants. (2) They cannot distinguish between valid and invalid invariants within one object.

The first limitation has an additional drawback. The programmer must learn the semantic and syntax of these new specifications. Furthermore, they represent an additional source of error. This is because the programmer may define the expected scope of an invariant not correctly. This may cause the unrecognised invalidation of depending post- or preconditions, as shown in Section 3. The second limitation prevent current approaches to be used to verify method calls on partly valid objects, depending on a subset of invariants, as illustrated in Figure 2. In this example, the Data-object is invalid until the last method $C : m()$ establishes its valid state. But the operation $C : m()$ requires the validity of invariant i_1, which has been established just one step before by the method $B : m()$.

The presented methodology addresses these limitations and has following contributions to the state of the art: **(1)** Reduced specification overhead, by using an automatic dependency analysis based on existing access modifiers **(2)** More flexibility, by distinguishing between valid and invalid invariants within one object.

2   Methodology

The presented methodology generates proof obligations ensuring the validity of invariants. The process of generating proof obligations uses static code analysis to analyse when invariants are expected to hold. Altogether, the presented methodology combines six different steps, as illustrated in Figure 1. These steps are applied for each invariant.

Step 1: Analysing References. To analyse when an invariant might be violated we need to know what values are referenced by a given invariant i. The set of class fields referenced by any statement s or invariant i is specified by the set $Ref^*(s)$. It combines directly $(Ref(s))$ and transitively referenced class fields. A direct reference is any direct access to a class field f_c in class c, by calling $o.f$ on an instance o of class c. Transitively referenced fields are accessed through method calls in s, e.g. by calling a get-method. The set of methods called in s is denoted by $CalledMethods(s)$.

$$Ref^*(s) = Ref(s) \cup \{Ref(m) \,|\, m \in CalledMethods(s)\} \tag{1}$$

The set of class fields, directly modified by a given statement s, is returned by the function $Ref!(s)$.

Step 2: Finding Invariant Violations. A statement might invalidate an invariant i, if it assigns a new value to any class field f_c, referenced in i. We call such statement s *Violating Code Position* and its method $m|s \in m$ *Violating Method*. Violating code positions are searched in each method body $S_m \in M_c$ of all methods M_c of each class $c \in C$ within the set of all classes C. The set of violating code positions for one invariant i is defined by:

$$ViolatingS(i) = \forall c \in C \,\forall m \in M_c \,\forall s \in S_m \,\{s \,|\, Ref!(s) \cap Ref^*(i) \neq \emptyset\} \tag{2}$$

For reasons of simplicity, we assume that every class field f has private accessibility. Therefore, direct access to a field f_c is possible only within its declaring class c. However, this assumption causes no limitations, because we make no further assumptions regarding the definition of set- and get-methods.

Step 3: Finding Depending Code Positions. To analyse the scope of an invariant i we must know when i might be violated and when i is expected to be valid. A code position s is called *Depending Code Position* if it requires the validity of an invariant. The corresponding method $m|s \in m$ is called *Depending Method*. Depending code positions are searched in each method body $S_m \in M_c$ of each class c. A statement s accessing a field f, referred by the invariant i, depends on i in two cases: (1) If s has no (transitive) access to every $f_i \in Ref^*(i)$ (2) If there exists a different proof obligation ϱ, e.g. caused by a postcondition, containing s: $s \in S_\varrho$.

The first case is based on the idea that an invariant might be invalid, as long as its validity can be checked by the programmer. But this is only possible if all fields, referenced by an invariant are accessible. In this case we say s *can check* i. If an invariant cannot be checked, a code block may invalidate an invariant or access an invalid object. This is very similar to the task of checking manually the validity of preconditions, before calling the corresponding method. Therefore, preconditions are part of the public specification. In our concept, a programmer can use access modifiers to control the visibility of each invariant and therefore also its scope. Which code positions may access a defined class element is defined by its access modifier:

Definition 1 (Accessibility). *Each class element e_c of class c, which is either a class field f_c, a method m_c or an invariant i_c, has one access modifier $\alpha(e_c) \in AM$, while the set AM must be specified by the concrete programming language. An access modifier defines which code positions can access e_c. The predicate IsAccessible (e_c, s) returns True, if the statement s can access the class element e_c. A class element e_c of the instance o of class c might be accessed either directly by $o.f$ or transitively through a get-method. A get-method get_{f_c}, for the class field f_c, is a method of class c, returning the unmodified value of f_c. In both cases, the predicate IsAccessible(f_c, s) returns True. Furthermore, a statement can access a class element e_c transitively through references across several object instances. The predicate IsAccessible*(e_c, s) returns True, if the class element e_c can be accessed transitively by s.*

However, the syntax and semantic of each $\alpha \in AM$ depends on the selected programming language. Because we have exemplary implemented our methodology for Java, we support four different access modifiers[1]: *public, package, protected, private*. Elements e_c, declared as *public*, are accessible from any other method m_c in any other class $c \in C$. Each class $c_p \in C$ is member of one package $p \in \mathcal{P}$. Elements e_{c_p}, declared as *package*, within class c_p are accessible by all other methods m defined in class c'_p, declared in the same package p. Elements e_c, declared as *protected*, are accessible from methods defined in c and all classes extending c. Elements declared as *private* are accessible only from methods declared in the same class c.

The following predicate indicates, if a statement s can check an invariant i:

$$CanCheck(s,i) \Leftrightarrow IsAccessible^*(i,s) \wedge \forall e \in Ref^*(i) \\ \cup CalledMethods(i): IsAccessible^*(e,s) \tag{3}$$

---

[1] There exist no problem in adapting this methodology to a different semantic of access modifiers.

The second case considers dependencies between different proof obligations. For example, a postcondition might be verified only, if a corresponding invariant is valid. Therefore, a statement also depends on the validity of an invariant, if it refers to a proof obligation whose validity cannot be proven without assuming the correctness of that invariant. If a statement s requires the validity of an invariant i is given by the predicate $Requires(s, i)$.

$$Requires(s, i) \Leftrightarrow \exists \varrho = (P, S, Q) | s \in S_\varrho : \neg \Psi((P \setminus i, S, Q) \wedge \Psi(P \cup i, S, Q)) \quad (4)$$

In summary, a statement s depends on an invariant i if:

$$Depends(s, i) \Leftrightarrow \neg CanCheck(s, i) \vee Requires(s, i) \quad (5)$$

The set of depending code positions for one invariant i is defined by:

$$DependingS(i) = \forall c \in C \, \forall m \in M_c \, \forall s \in S_m \, \{s \, | Depends(s, i)\} \quad (6)$$

Step 4: Building The Verification Graph. The scope of an invariant defines when an invariant might be violated and when its validity is expected. We use a special call graph, called *Verification Graph (VG)*, to analyse the scope of each invariant.

Definition 2 (Verification Graph). *A Verification Graph $VG(i) = (V, E)$ is a tuple. Each vertex $v \in V$ has a reference m_v to a method m. Each edge $e = (v_i, v_j) \in E$ indicates a method call in m_{v_i} to the method referenced by its target m_{v_j}. Furthermore, each edge e has a reference s_e to the position of the method call in m_{v_i}. Within v_i, the edges are ordered by the position s_e in m_{v_i}. If $e_1 = (v_i, v_j) < e_2 = (v_i, v_k)$ the method m_{v_j} is called before the method m_{v_k} is called. Each method and method call is represented only once within the VG.*

The VG is built by analysing the possible call stack of each violating and depending method. We call this possible call stack *Context*.

Definition 3 (Context). *The context of any method $\hat{m}$ is defined as a set of pairs (m, s), where m refers to a method and $s \in S_m$ to a statement within the method m. Each pair corresponds to a method m, calling $\hat{m}$ with the statement $s = o.m'(\overrightarrow{p})$, and any list of parameters $\overrightarrow{p}$. If m is the source of the context, s might also be empty, denoted as $(m, \emptyset)$. The general n-order context, for $n \geq 0$, of a method m and a defined set of methods $M' \subset M$, of all methods M, is defined as:*

$$C^n(m, M') = \{(\hat{m}, s) \, | s = o.m'(\overrightarrow{p}) \in S_{\hat{m}} \wedge m' \in C^{n-1}(m) \wedge \hat{m} \notin M'\} \quad (7)$$

$$C^0(m, M') = \{(m, \emptyset) \, | m \notin M'\} \quad (8)$$

The Verification Graph $VG(i) = (V, E)$ of a given invariant i is built as follows:

$$V = V_1 = \{(m) | \exists s \in m \wedge s \in ViolatingS(i)\} \cup \quad (9)$$

$$V_2 = \{(m) | \exists s \in m \wedge s \in DependingS(i)\} \cup \quad (10)$$

$$\{(m) | m \in C(V_1, V_2) \cup C(V_2, V_1)\} \quad (11)$$

$$E = \{(v_i, v_j) | v_i, v_j \in V \wedge m_{v_i} \text{ calls } m_{v_j}\} \quad (12)$$

Data: Start vertex: v_j, Start statement: s, Searched type: $t = \{violating, depending\}$,
      Search behind s: b
Result: The closest vertex of type t wthin the context of v_j

1   if v_j *marked* then return $\emptyset$ // Skip visited vertexes ;

2   mark v_j ;   // Mark vertex as visited

3   if v_j *is* t then return v_j ;

     // Analysing all called methods in m_{v_j} before s is reached
     // by following edges $e_{j,k}$ whose position $s_{e_{j,k}}$ in m_{v_j} is smaller than s

4   foreach $e_{j,k} = (v_j, v_k) \mid s_{e_{j,k}} < s \mid$ *from* s *to* 0 do

       // Searching recursively from begin on $(m_{v_k}[0])$ in each called method

5     $\hat{v} = findNode(v_k, m_{v_k}[0], t, true)$

6   if $\hat{v} \neq \emptyset$ then return $\hat{v}$;

     // Analysing all methods called after s is reached
     // by following edges $e_{j,k}$ whose position $s_{e_{j,k}}$ in m_{v_j} is greater than s.
     // This is used if we analyse methods called before the original s was
     reached.

7   if b then

8   foreach $e_{j,k} = (v_j, v_k) \mid s_{e_{j,k}} > s \mid$ *from* s *to* n do

       // Searching recursively from begin on $(m_{v_k}[0])$ in each called
       method

9       $\hat{v} = findNode(v_k, m_{v_k}[0], t, true)$

10   if $\hat{v} \neq \emptyset$ then return $\hat{v}$;

     // Analysing all methods calling m_{v_j}

11   foreach $e_{k,j} = (v_k, v_j)$ do

       // Searching from the position calling m_{v_k} to the begin of m_{v_j}.

12     $\hat{v} = findNode(v_k, s_{e_{k,j}}, t, false)$

13   if $\hat{v} \neq \emptyset$ then return $\hat{v}$;

14 return $\emptyset$;   // No vertex found

Algorithm 1. FindNode(v_j,s,t,b) : Searching closest node

Step 5: Analysing Invariant Scopes. The scope of an invariant defines when an invariant is expected to be valid and when it is allowed to be invalid. We must guarantee, that an invariant is valid whenever a depending code position is reached. In general, the invariant must be ensured by code positions modifying any value, referenced by that invariant. In combination with depending code positions, we are searching the last violating code position called before the depending code position is reached. We call the corresponding vertexes *Ensuring Vertexes*, because they must ensure the invariants validity. These positions are found by searching the shortest paths between each depending vertex and the closest violating vertex. For one depending code position $s \in m$, we analyse two categories of methods: (1) Methods (transitively) called in m before s is reached. (2) Methods (transitively) calling m. Algorithm 1 formalises this search for a given depending code position $s \in m_{v_j}$, by calling $FindNode(v_j, s, violating, false)$. A detailed walk through, based on an example, is presented in Section 3.

Step 6: Creating Proof Obligations. Proof obligations define an expected behaviour for a defined sequence of statements.

Definition 4. *Proof Obligation. A proof obligation $\varrho = (P, S, Q)$ is a triple. It combines a set of assumptions (P), an ordered list of statements (S) and a goal (Q). Each assumption and the goal are represented as boolean predicate. To prove a proof obligation, one must show, that each possible evaluation of S, validates Q, while assuming P. The predicate $\Psi(\varrho)$ is true if ϱ can be verified.*

Here, they are used to ensure that each ensuring method respects the corresponding invariant. But it is not sufficient to analyse the violating method. This is because the invariant might be ensured within the method calling the ensuring method. For example, a set-method is marked as ensuring method. In this case, the method calling the set-method must ensure, that the set value respects the invariant. Therefore, the code block s of the corresponding proof obligation $\varrho = (P, S, Q)$ must combine statements of both methods. In general, each code block, not depending on that invariant, within the call stack of the ensuring method may ensure its validity. For one ensuring node $\check{v}$, we analyse the undirected path $p(\hat{v}, \check{v})$ to the closest depending vertex $\hat{v}$. The closest depending node is found by using $FindNode$ defined by Algorithm 1.

In summary, we create the set of proof obligation $\rho(i)$ for each invariant i:

$$D = DependingS(i) \tag{13}$$

$$E = \bigcup_{d \in D} FindNode(v(d), d, violating, false) \tag{14}$$

$$P = \bigcup_{e \in E} p = (FindNode(v(e), e, depending, false), v(e)) \tag{15}$$

$$S(p) = \bigcup_{e=(v_j, v_k) \in p} m_{v_j}[0, e] \cup m_{\check{v}} \tag{16}$$

$$\rho(i) = \bigcup_{p(\hat{v}, \check{v}) \in P} (Preconditions(\hat{v}), S(p), i) \tag{17}$$

The predicate $Preconditions(\hat{v})$ refers to the set of preconditions defined for $\hat{v}$. We use the syntax $m_{v_j}[0, e]$ to refer to the subset of statements in S_m from the begin of m (position 0) to the position referenced by the edge s_e.

2.1   Soundness

We sketch the proof of soundness, by showing that the set of generated proof obligations is sufficient to guarantee an invariants validity whenever a depending code position is reached:

Theorem 1. *If all proof obligations could be verified, every invariant i is valid, whenever one of its referenced values $v \in Ref^*(i)$ is accessed by a statement $\hat{s}$ in method $\hat{m}$, with the set of valid assumptions P and defined condition Q such that $\neg\Psi(\varrho = (P \setminus i, m, Q)) \wedge \Psi(\varrho = (P \cup i, m, Q))$.*

Proof. If $\hat{s}$ fulfils the properties defined in the theorem, we know $\hat{s} \in DependingS(i)$ (Equation 6). If i is not valid when $\hat{s}$ is evaluated, there must be one statement $\check{s}$ within method $\check{m}$ which has invalidated i and which has been evaluated before $\hat{s}$. To invalidate i, $\check{s}$ must assign an invalid value to any field referred by i: $Ref!(\check{s}) \cup Ref^*(i) \neq \emptyset$. Regarding $\check{s}$, there exist two possibilities: (1) $\check{s}$ is the last code position modifying a value referenced by i, before reaching $\hat{s}$. (2) It exists a code position $\check{\check{s}}$ which modifies a value referenced by i, which is evaluated after $\check{s}$ and before $\hat{s}$ is reached. In the first case, $FindNode(v(\hat{s}), \hat{s}, violating, false) = \tilde{v} = v(\check{s})$. In the second case, $\check{\check{s}}$ must re-establish i and $FindNode(v(\hat{s}), \hat{s}, violating, false) = \tilde{v} = v(\check{\check{s}})$. The syntax $v(s)$ refers to the vertex v whose referenced method contains s. Step 6 generates a proof obligation $\varrho = (P, S, i)$ and the statement sequence S contains as last sequence the statements of $m_{\tilde{v}}$ (Equation 16). Therefore, if ϱ can be verified, i is re-established after $m_{\tilde{v}}$ has been evaluated and before $\hat{s}$ is reached.   □

3   Case Studies

The presented methodology provides a higher flexibility in defining object invariants while requiring less specification overhead. This is shown by demonstrating the analysis process of different examples. The examples represent challenges and code examples which have been addressed by latest related work. Thereby we can compare the specification overhead of our methodology with the one required by related approaches. Furthermore, we present one example which cannot be verified using current approaches. All examples have been implemented in Java. Invariants were defined using the syntax of the Java Modelling Language, as descried in [7]. The defined access modifiers are interpreted as described in Step 3 within Section 2.

Challenge 1: Gradual Updates. Invariants may refer to multiple class elements. A gradual update of referenced values may invalidate an invariant temporary. This enables access to an invalid object. Current methodologies use additional specification elements to define when an invariant is valid. The approach presented in [14] uses *unpack* and *pack* statements. These statements mark the begin and end of an interval, in which an object is allowed to be invalid. Their usage is indicated in Listing 1. The example is based on a data type, representing a numerical interval by storing a min and max value. It provides a method $getSize()$, which guarantees a positive return value. Thereby, $getSize()$ requires the validity of the invariant $getMin() <= getMax()$.

In Listing 1.2 *pack* and *unpack* is correctly used, because $getSize$ is called, after the object invariant has been ensured by calling *pack*. In Listing 2 the *pack* statement is located after $getSize()$ and has been called on the invalid object. This is a specification error, because the programmer declares the scope of the invariant incorrectly. This causes a violated postcondition of $getSize()$. We want to demonstrate two points in this example: (1) How the presented methodology analyses the code without using additional specification elements like *pack* and

```
 1 class Interval {
 2 //@public invariant getMin() <= getMax();
 3 private int min,max;
 4 // For reasons of compactness we do not display
 5 // the constructor and the analog set/get methods for min
 6 public void setMax(int max){ this.max=max;}
 7 public int getMax(){ return this.max; }
 8 //@ensures \return >= 0;
 9 public void getSize() { return this.max-this.min; }
10 }
11 class UseInterval {
12 //@ensures \return >= 0;
13 public int main() {
14   Interval inter = new Interval(5,7);
15   //unpack inter as Interval
16   inter.setMin(8);
17   inter.setMax(9);
18   //pack inter as Interval
19   return inter.getSize();
20 }
21 }
```

Listing 1.1. Gradual update of an invariant

unpack. (2) How the automatic code analysis of the presented methodology detects the described error of Listing 1.3.

The VGs (VG_a,VG_b) for both examples are illustrated in Figure 3.

```
 1 //@ensures \return >= 0;
 2 public int main2() {
 3   Interval inter = new Interval(5,7);
 4   //unpack inter as Interval
 5   inter.setMin(8);
 6   int dist = inter.getSize();
 7   inter.setMax(9);
 8   //pack inter as Interval
 9   return dist;
10 }
```

Listing 1.2. Specification error

In the following, we use the vertex labels as reference to the different methods. In Step 1 we analyse the references of the public invariant i: $Ref^*(i) = \{min, max\}$. In Step 2 we analyse which code positions modify any referenced value. These are the methods $setMin()$ and $setMax()$: $ViolatingS = \{s_{v_3}, s_{v_4}\}$. In Step 3 we analyse which code positions depend on i. The method $getSize()$ is the only depending code position: $DependingS = \{s_{v_5}\}$. This is because the

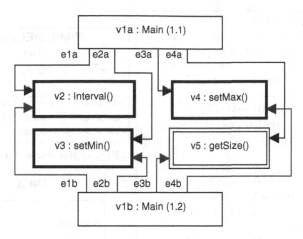

Fig. 3. The VGs for the Listings (a) 1.1 and (b) 1.2

postcondition $\varrho_{v_5} = (i, (max - min), (max - min) >= 0)$ cannot be verified without assuming i. In Step 4, we build the VG, illustrated in Figure 3. In Step 5, we search the ensuring methods of each depending code position. In example (a) the analysis follows first edge $e4a$ and next edge $e3a$. The first edge is followed by lines 11-13 of Algorithm 1 and the second edge by lines 3-6, within the first recursive call. Thereby we reach vertex $v4$ and we find the closest violating method. In example (b) the analysis follows first edge $e3b$ and next edge $e2b$. Here, vertex $v3$ is the closest violating method. In Step 6, we create the proof obligations ensuring i. Therefore, we search for each ensuring vertex the closest depending vertex. In these examples, there is no depending vertex within the context of both ensuring vertexes. Therefore, the context covers the full program until each ensuring vertex is reached. The proof obligations are: $\varrho_A = (\emptyset, m_{v_2} \cup m[14] \cup m_{v_3} \cup m_{v_4}, i)$, $\varrho_B = (\emptyset, m_{v_2} \cup m[14] \cup m_{v_3}, i)$. Using Z3 as verification back-end, we can prove the validity of ϱ_A and ϱ_B.

Challenge 2: Recursive Data-Structures. Figure 4 contains an example for a recursive data structure width following private invariant: $inv1 = ((val >= 0) \wedge (prev.val < 0)) \vee ((val < 0) \wedge (prev.val >= 0))$. Recursive data structures have been addressed by Leino et al. in [2]. They require the additional specification statements *peer*, *dependent* and *owner dependent*. The presented methodology does not require any additional specification elements. Our analysis recognises that the public *setPrev*-method (m_1) and the constructor (m_2) are the only two methods modifying the value *val*. Because the invariant is private, both public methods must ensure the invariant. The two proof obligations are $\varrho_1 = (\emptyset, m_1, i)$ and $\varrho_2 = (\emptyset, m_2, i)$.

Challenge 3: Dependencies on an Invariant Subset. Current methodologies do not distinguish between valid and invalid invariants within one object. Methods cannot require the validity of an invariant subset only. Current methodologies cannot be used to verify the example in Figure 5 or in Listing 1.3.

```
 1 class Starter {
 2 // Post: Return Value > 0;
 3 static main(int a) {
 4   if (a < 2)
 5   { throw new Exception(); }
 6   Data d = new Data();
 7   d.setA(a); d.setB(0);
 8   return DataProcessorA.
       process(d);
 9 } }
10 class DataProcessorA {
11 static int process(Data d) {
12   assert(d.getA()>2);
13   int b = 2 * sqrt(d.getA());
14   d.setB(b);
15   return DataProccessorB.
       process(d);
16 } }
17 class DataProcessorB {
18 // Post: Return Value > 0;
19 static int process(Data d)
20 { return d.getC()/d.getB();}
21 }
```

Listing 1.3. Partly valid objects

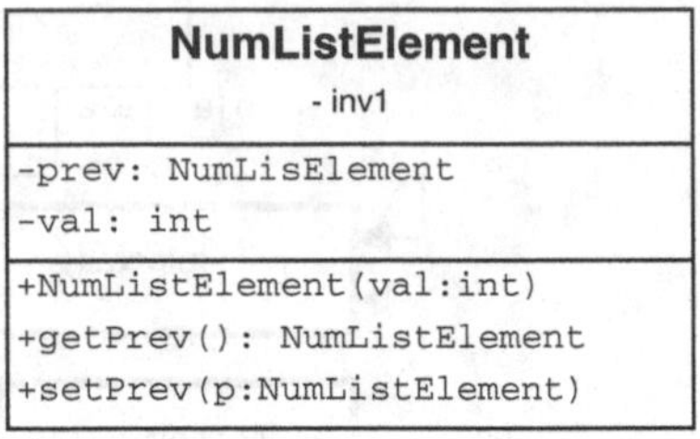

NumListElement
- inv1
-prev: NumLisElement
-val: int
+NumListElement(val:int)
+getPrev(): NumListElement
+setPrev(p:NumListElement)

Fig. 4. Recursive data structure

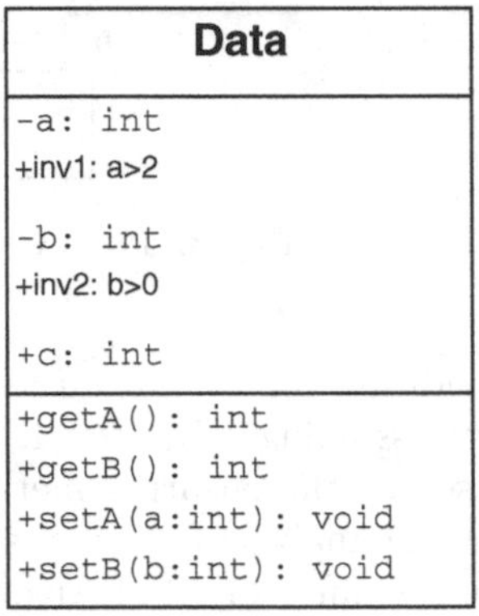

Data
-a: int
+inv1: a>2
-b: int
+inv2: b>0
+c: int
+getA(): int
+getB(): int
+setA(a:int): void
+setB(b:int): void

Fig. 5. Data model of Listing 3

This Listing uses the data structure shown in Figure 5, which contains two invariants $(i_1 = inv1)$ and $(i_2 = inv2)$. The $Data$-object is passed as an argument to the $DataProcesorA : process$-method and later further to the $DataProcessorB : process$-method. The $DataProcessorA : process$-method uses the square root of the a-field-value to calculate a new b-field-value. Because of the defined assertion, it relies on the invariant i_1. But at call time of $DataProcessorA : process$, the invariant i_2 is invalid. The invariant i_2 is required not until $DataProcessorB : process$ is called. This method uses the b-field-value as divisor in Line 19 of Listing 1.3. This implies the obligation $b! = 0$, which cannot be assured without assuming i_2. In summary, both methods $DataProcessorA : process$ and $DataProcessorB : process$ rely on a different subset of invariants defined within the $Data$-object. We use this example to demonstrate how the presented methodology distinguishes between valid and invalid invariants within one object. This example causes two Verification Graphs $VG(i_1)$ and $VG(i_2)$, one for each invariant. They are both illustrated in Figure 6. Again, we start by analysing the references of each invariant: $Ref^*(i_1) = \{a\}$, $Ref(i_2) = \{b\}$. These values may be modified by following code position: $Violating(i_1) = \{s_{v_4}\}$, $Violating(i_2) = \{s_{v_3}\}$. The depending code positions are $DependingS(i_1) = \{m_{v_5}[12]\}$ and $DependingS(i_2) = \{m_{v_6}[20]\}$. We use the syntax [•] to identify the corresponding code position by their

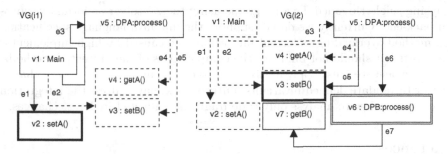

Fig. 6. The VG for the example of Goal 6

line number in Listing 1.3. The ensuring method for $m_{v_5}[12]$ is m_{v_2}, following the edges $e3, e2, e1$. For m_{v_6} the ensuring method is m_{v_3}, following the edges $e6$ and $e5$. There is no depending code position within the context of m_{v_2} and m_{v_3}. Therefore, we add the all statements to S, until $setA()$ respectively $setB()$. The corresponding proof obligations are: $\varrho_{i_1} = (\emptyset, main[4-6] \cup m_{v_2}, i_1)$, $\varrho_{i_2} = (\emptyset, main[4-6] \cup m_{v_2} \cup m_{v_3} \cup m_{v_2}[12-13] \cup m_{v_3}, i_2)$. Both proof obligations can be verified, using the Z3 as verification back-end.

Results. The analysis of Challenge 1, 2, and 3 shows that the presented methodology does not require specification overhead like current state of the art methods. Furthermore, the automatic analysis prevents errors caused by the wrong usage of additional specification elements, as shown in Challenge 1. The presented methodology recognised the violated postcondition in Listing 1.3, caused by the access to an invalid object. The determination between valid and invalid invariants within one object enables the verification of Challenge 3, which is not possible with current state of the art approaches.

4   Conclusion and Future Work

We have introduced a new methodology to specify and verify object invariants. This methodology uses access modifiers to control the scope of an object invariant. An automatic control flow analysis is used to analyse when invariants may be invalidated and when they must be re-established. This reduces the specification overhead and helps to prevent errors through the usage of specification statements, as we have shown in Challenge 1 in Section 3. The presented methodology distinguishes between invalid and valid invariants within one object. Thereby, it supports more flexible scopes of invariants, as we have shown in Challenge 3. The computational overhead does highly depend on the analysed program structure. In general, public invariants cause a larger number of paths that need to be considered to validate an invariant, because more code positions may invalidate an public invariant. The same applies to invariants with a large number of references. Therefore, the higher flexibility may cause a higher number of proof obligations. The reduced specification overhead causes a higher computational overhead. We have implemented the presented methodology within a tool analysing single threaded Java programs using the Z3 solver as formal verification back-end. Currently we do not support the full Java language specification (e.g. method overloading). Current limitations are caused by high implementation efforts but should not influence the completeness of the presented methods. At the moment we must apply all six steps to each source file after every change in order to validate defined invariants. Future work may address the integration of a change review to analyse only code fragments, affected by latest changes.

References

1. Summers, A.J., Drossopoulou, S., Müller, P.: The need for flexible object invariants. In: International Workshop on Aliasing, Confinement and Ownership in Object-Oriented Programming, pp. 1–9. ACM (2009)
2. Leino, K.R.M., Müller, P.: Object invariants in dynamic contexts. In: Odersky, M. (ed.) ECOOP 2004. LNCS, vol. 3086, pp. 491–515. Springer, Heidelberg (2004)
3. Barnett, M., Fähndrich, M., Müller, P., Leino, K.R.M., Schulte, W., Venter, H.: Specification and verification: The spec# experience (2009)
4. Hoare, C.A.R.: An axiomatic basis for computer programming. Communications of the ACM 12(10), 576–580 (1969)
5. Müller, P., Poetzsch-Heffter, A., Leavens, G.T.: Modular invariants for layered object structures. Sci. Comput. Program. 62(3), 253–286 (2006)
6. Meyer, B.: Eiffel: The Language. Prentice-Hall, Inc., Upper Saddle River (1992)
7. Leavens, G.T., Baker, A.L., Ruby, C.: Jml: a java modeling language. In: Formal Underpinnings of Java Workshop, at OOPSLA 1998 (1998)
8. Huizing, K., Kuiper, R.: Verification of object oriented programs using class invariants. In: Maibaum, T. (ed.) FASE 2000. LNCS, vol. 1783, pp. 208–221. Springer, Heidelberg (2000)
9. Dietl, W., Müller, P.: Object ownership in program verification. In: Clarke, D., Noble, J., Wrigstad, T. (eds.) Aliasing in Object-Oriented Programming. LNCS, vol. 7850, pp. 289–318. Springer, Heidelberg (2013)
10. Müller, P.: Modular Specification and Verification of Object-Oriented Programs. LNCS, vol. 2262. Springer, Heidelberg (2002)
11. Müller, P.: Reasoning about object structures using ownership. In: Meyer, B., Woodcock, J. (eds.) Verified Software. LNCS, vol. 4171, pp. 93–104. Springer, Heidelberg (2008)
12. Barnett, M., Naumann, D.A.: Friends need a bit more: Maintaining invariants over shared state. In: Kozen, D. (ed.) MPC 2004. LNCS, vol. 3125, pp. 54–84. Springer, Heidelberg (2004)
13. Lu, Y., Potter, J., Xue, J.: Validity invariants and effects. In: Ernst, E. (ed.) ECOOP 2007. LNCS, vol. 4609, pp. 202–226. Springer, Heidelberg (2007)
14. Barnett, M., DeLine, R., Fähndrich, M., Leino, K.R.M., Schulte, W.: Verification of object-oriented programs with invariants. Journal of Object Technology 3, 2004 (2004)
15. Leavens, G.T., Muller, P.: Information hiding and visibility in interface specifications. In: Proceedings of the 29th International Conference on Software Engineering, ICSE 2007, pp. 385–395. IEEE Computer Society, Washington, DC (2007)

Verified Functional Iterators
Using the FoCaLiZe Environment

Catherine Dubois and Renaud Rioboo

CEDRIC-ENSIIE, 1 square de la résistance, 91025 Évry, France
{Catherine.Dubois,Renaud.Rioboo}@ensiie.fr

Abstract. Collections and iterators are widely used in the Object community since they are standards of the Java language. We present a certified functional implementation of collections and iterators addressing the Specification And Verification of Component Based Systems 2006 challenge. More precisely we describe a FoCaLiZe implementation providing these functionalities. Our approach uses inheritance and parameterization to describe functional iterators. Our code can be run in Ocaml and is certified using Coq. We provide general specifications for collections, iterators and removable iterators together with complete implementation for collections using lists as representation and iterators over those.

1 Introduction

Iterators on data structures like lists, sets, vectors, trees, etc. are available in many programming languages, usually as resources of their standard library. In functional languages, iterating facilities are mainly provided as higher order functions (e.g. `fold_left` or `fold_right` for iteration on lists in SML or Ocaml). In object oriented languages like Java, Eiffel or C#, they are provided as objects with methods allowing the enumeration of the data structure elements (e.g. `hasNext` and `next` in the Java `Iterable` interface). Usually the iterable data structure contains a method (e.g. `iterator` in Java collections), each invocation of which creates an iterator. Following the ITERATOR design pattern [7], iterators give a clean way for element-by-element access to a collection without exposing its underlying representation. Following this view, purely functional iterators can also be implemented, such as in [6] or in the Ocaml Reins Data Structure Library[1]. Thus we can consider the type of an iterator as an abstract data-type equipped with 3 functions `start`, `hasnext` and `step`: `start` is applied to a collection and computes an iterator; `hasnext` takes an iterator as an argument and returns a boolean indicating whether the enumeration is finished or not; and `step i`, when `i` is an iterator, returns an element not yet visited and the new iterator. Thus the underlying collection is provided as an argument to `start` and is not used anymore after that.

---

[1] See `http://ocaml-reins.sourceforge.net/api/Reins.Iterator.S.html` for the interface of the Iterator module.

D. Giannakopoulou and G. Salaün (Eds.): SEFM 2014, LNCS 8702, pp. 317–331, 2014.
© Springer International Publishing Switzerland 2014

In this paper, we propose a verified implementation of such functional iterators. Here verified means that this implementation has been proved correct with respect to the specification. Specification, implementation and proof are done using the FoCaLiZe[2] environment (which is a successor of FoCaL) [5]. As far as we know, it is the first verified implementation of functional iterators in the flavor of those proposed e.g. by Filliâtre in [6]. In this study we are mainly looking for a way to specify the behavior of an iterator without exposing its internal representation or the representation of the collection it traverses and to evaluate how convenient it is for specifying and proving generic algorithms using such iterators.

This work can also be seen as a contribution to the 2006 SAVCBS (Specification And Verification of Component Based Systems) challenge asking for a specification of the Iterator interface as provided in Java or its equivalent in another language[3]. Different solutions [1] have been proposed, most of them focusing on the verification of non-interference between calls that directly modify the collection and interleaved uses of one or more iterators.

The FoCaLiZe language in which our development is done, is functional. However it borrows some features to the Object world, such as inheritance, redefinition that ease reuse of specifications, code and proofs. Furthermore parameterization facilitates the definition of generic iterators and derived functions.

The rest of this paper is structured as follows. Section 2 presents FoCaLiZe very quickly. Then we introduce in Section 3 the main ingredients to use iterators. Iterators allow the enumeration of values contained in another data structure, often collections. Thus we stick to this view and propose a FoCaLiZe specification of collections and an implementation for sequences as collections in Section 4. Then we present in Section 5 a FoCaLiZe implementation of iterators for collections which are sequences. Some existing approaches are presented and discussed in Section 6. Section 7 concludes and presents some future work.

2   A Quick Presentation of FoCaLiZe

The FoCaLiZe environment provides a set of tools to describe and implement functions and logical statements together with their proof. A FoCaLiZe source program is analyzed and translated into Ocaml sources for execution and Coq sources for certification. The FoCaLiZe language has an object oriented flavor allowing inheritance, late binding and redefinition.

FoCaLiZe concrete programming units are *collections* which contain entities in a model akin to classes and objects or types and values. In the following, to avoid confusion with collections as data containers, a FoCaLiZe collection is called an Fcollection. Fcollections have *methods* which can be called using the "!" notation as in Code 1. They are derived from *species* which describe and implement methods. In an Fcollection the concrete *representation* of entities is abstracted and a programmer refers to it using the keyword Self in FoCaLiZe sources.

---

[2] http://focalize.inria.fr
[3] http://www.eecs.ucf.edu/~leavens/SAVCBS/2006/challenge.shtml

Species may inherit from other species and may have parameters which may either be Fcollections or entities providing parametric polymorphism. As shown in Code 4 parameters are declared in sequence and may have dependencies: this excerpt describes a species parameterized by 2 Fcollections named resp. Elt and L. The first one is expected to derive from the Setoid species, it means that it provides at least all the methods appearing in the interface of Setoid, i.e the list of methods appearing in Setoid or inherited, with their type where the type of entities is made abstract. The second parameter L is expected to provide methods in the interface of Utils(Elt) where Utils is a parameterized species which is applied to the effective Fcollection Elt. We can notice the dependency between the first and the second argument.

A species defines a set of entities together with functions and properties applying to them. At the beginning of a development, the representation of these entities is usually abstract, it is precised later in the development. However the type of these entities is referred as Self in any species. Species may contain specifications, functions and proofs, all of theses being called *methods*. More precisely species may specify a method (signature, property keywords as in code 4) or implement it (let, proof of, theorem keywords as in code 1 or 2). A let defined function must match its signature and similarly a proof introduced by proof of should prove the statement given by the property keyword. Statements belong to first order typed logic.

Within FoCaLiZe, proofs are written using the FoCaLiZe proof language and are sent to the Zenon prover which produces Coq proofs. The FoCaLiZe proof language is a declarative language in which the programmer states a property and gives hints (by) to achieve its proof which is performed by Zenon. She typically introduces a context with variables (assume) and hypothesis (hypothesis) and then states a result (prove). Elements of the proof are then listed (by) and these can be either an hypothesis (hypothesis), an already proved statement (step), an existing statement (property) or a definition (definition of, or type). When a proof has steps it is ended by conclude or qed by clauses. Code 9 shows the skeleton of a FoCaLiZe proof tree. The automatic prover Zenon is a first order automatic theorem prover which supports algebraic data types and induction developed by D. Doligez (see for instance [2]).

For more details on FoCaLiZe please refer to the reference manual. More explanations about FoCaLiZe syntax will be given in next sections when necessary.

3   Using Iterators

In this section we present a sample use of our iterators implementation. Our demonstration package IterTools proposes a function copy (see Code 1) that copies elements from a collection c of type Col, using an iterator it of type It. We use a tail recursive function copy_aux that uses an iterator (it) and a collection (a). Since FoCaLiZe is a functional language the state change of an object is implemented using an extra result and the next operation returns a pair made of an iterator together with the visited element. The species presented here is parameterized by four Fcollections Elt, L, Col and It specifying operations for elements of the collections, lists of such elements, collections of such elements and iterators on the previous collections. These Fcollections derive from species which will explained in the following sections. The overall hierarchy of species is shown in Figure 1 (without parameters for sake of clarity).

We can notice that the copy function provided by the species IterTools uses the same implementation for both the source and the target collections. It can be generalized to allow different implementations. In that case, two Fcollections Col1 (implementation of the source collection) and Col2 (implementation of the target collection), both having the interface Collection(Elt, L), will be provided as parameters of the species. Furthermore the It parameter would have as interface Iterator(Elt, L, Col1).

Code 1

```
species IterTools (Elt is Setoid,
                   L is Utils(Elt),
                   Col is Collection(Elt, L),
                   It is Iterator(Elt, L, Col)) =

let rec copy_aux (it, a) =
if It!has_next(it) then
    let res = It!next (it) in
    copy_aux (snd(res), Col!add(fst(res), a))
else a;

let copy (c) = copy_aux (It!start (c), Col!empty);
```

At this step, we have identified some necessary operations of collections and iterators. Collections have to provide 2 operations, empty and add, these are the methods Col!empty and Col!add provided by the Fcollection parameter Col. For iterators, we need 3 operations, start, has_next and next provided by the Fcollection parameter It.

Correctness of copy relies on the theorem copy_spec whose statement is given in Code 2, establishing that the original collection and its copy have the same elements. The statement uses the contains method provided by collections. Inside the proof, we use an invariant property, copy_invariant (also in Code 2) which refers to the abstract model of an iterator stated by the logical predicate model. For an iterator i, a collection c and a list of elements l the model(i, c, l) statement should describe logically the elements of c belonging to the list l which are not yet visited by the iterator i. This informal specification and further constraints on the model predicate will be formalized in Section 5. The invariant property copy_invariant relates two collections between recursive calls in the copy_aux function. An element x is either an element of the collection c not yet visited by an iterator or contained in an auxiliary collection a.

Code 2 *excerpt of species IterTools*

```
theorem copy_spec :
```

```
all e: Elt, all c : Col,
   Col!contains (e, c) <-> Col!contains (e, copy(c))
proof = (* 50 lines *);

theorem copy_invariant:
  all it: It, all a: Col, all c: Col, all l: list(Elt),
    It!model(it, c, l) ->
    (all x: Elt, Col!contains(x, a) -> Col!contains(x, c)) ->
      (all x: Elt, Col!contains(x, copy_aux(it, a)) <->
        ((L!mem(l, x) || Col!contains(x, a))))
proof = (* 150 lines *);
```

The above theorems allow us to state that if the copy_aux function terminates it performs the right action. In order to show termination we must prove that the recursive call in copy_aux decreases for some well founded order it_order defined below (see Code 3).

Code 3 *excerpt of species IterTools*
```
let it_order(it1, it2) =
  (0 <= It!measure_it(it2))  &&
  (It!measure_it(it1) < It!measure_it(it2));

theorem well_wrapper_it: well_wrapper(it_order)
proof =(* 30 lines of Coq *);

theorem rec_call_decreases: all it: It, all res: Elt * It,
It!has_next(it) -> (It!next(it) = res) -> it_order(snd(res), it)
  proof = (* 150 lines *);
```

The well_wrapper statement is part of FoCaLiZe standard library and states that the ordering it receives as argument is well founded. Since it is not a first order statement we cannot prove it using the Zenon prover and have to do the proof in Coq. Proofs are here omitted but performed by unfolding the different definitions and making use of the (Zwf_well_founded 0) Coq property that establishes that the usual order on positive integers is well founded. In order to prove that the recursive call decreases (theorem rec_call_decreases) we rely on a property stating that when iterating we decrease some measure of an iterator. We thus have identified two other operations it_measure_it and mea_decreases which we specify in Code 10.

We can see that though the 6 lines of effective code in Code 1 use a simple accumulator they must be completed by 10 lines of specification statements in Code 2 which are not obvious to guess. Furthermore their proofs are quite tedious and the overall species is globally 350 lines of mixed FoCaLiZe and Coq code.

4   Collections

Though the word collection is a keyword of the FoCaLiZe language we use it in the normal UML/Java sense and we present the functionalities we implemented.

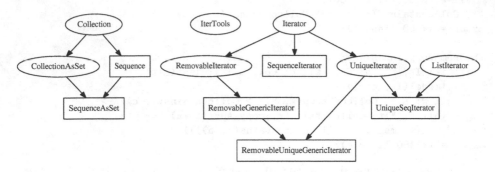

Ellipses correspond to specification species. Rectangles correspond to implementation species (complete species)

Fig. 1. The Overall Hierarchy

4.1   Specification Hierarchy

Basic collections contain a finite number of values and we have methods to add and remove values in a collection, check if a value is in a collection and transform a collection into a list of values as in Code 4. We can also compute the size of a collection, check if a collection is empty etc.

Code 4

```
species Collection (Elt is Setoid, L is Utils(Elt))  =
  signature contains: Elt -> Self -> bool;

  signature add: Elt -> Self -> Self;
  property add_contains: all c: Self, all e x: Elt,
    contains(x, add(e, c)) <-> ( (x = e) || contains(x, c));

  signature remove: Elt -> Self -> Self;
  property remove_contains:
    all c: Self, all e : Elt, all x : Elt, not (x = e)) ->
      (contains (x, (remove (e, c))) <-> contains (x, c));

  signature tolist : Self -> list(Elt);
  property tolist_contains :
    all c: Self, all e : Elt, contains (e, c)
        <-> L!mem (tolist(c), e);
```

We then distinguish between collections which are sets. Thus we define, using inheritance, a new species (`CollectionAsSet`) describing these collections as sets. A new property, `unique_contains`, is added, it explains that such collections have no redundant element (Code 5)

Code 5

```
species CollectionAsSet (Elt is Setoid, L is Utils(Elt))  =
  inherit Collection(Elt, L) ;

  property unique_contains : all c : Self, all e : Elt,
    not(contains (e, remove (e, c))) ;
end;;
```

4.2   Implementations

In the previous subsection, a specification of basic collections is presented. We could go further into specifications by providing specifications for sequences, maps and then provide one or more implementations for each category. Here we simply provide an implementation of sequences using a simple implementation based on lists (seen as the elements of an inductive type providing 2 constructors: cons and empty). In FoCaLiZe a species is complete when all its signatures have an implementation and all its statements have received a proof. Thus the species given in Code 6 contains the definition of every function and the proof of every property specified in `Collection`. It also exports the functions **head** and **tail** with their specifications which have their obvious meaning.

In this case all functions have a simple termination proof (**structural** keyword as in Code 7) since their code performs simple pattern matching on lists and recursive calls on the tail of their initial parameter. All properties can be proved by induction over lists which is supported by the Zenon prover as shown in the proof of **unique_contains** (Code 9). Statements <2>1 and <2>1 are the base and inductive steps, statement <2>3 is the property we prove inductively and the <2>f step enables to abstract the list representation.

Code 6

```
species Sequence (Elt is Setoid, L is Utils(Elt)) =
inherit Collection(Elt, L);

representation = list(Elt);

let contains (e: Elt, l: Self) = L!mem (l, e);
```

We also provide a `SequenceAsSet` complete species where we use the invariant that lists have no doubles as in Code 7.

Code 7

```
species SequenceAsSet(Elt is Setoid, L is Utils(Elt)) =
inherit Sequence(Elt, L), CollectionAsSet(Elt, L);

let torep (l : Self ) : list(Elt) = l;

let rec nodouble (l) =
    match l with
```

```
   | [] -> true
   | h :: q -> nodouble (q) && not(L!mem (q, h))
termination proof = structural l;
```

For correctness of the invariant we follow [17] and need to prove that all functions returning an element of Self preserve the invariant property as shown in Code 8. These proofs use induction on lists and the overall code is 170 lines of FoCaLiZe code.

Code 8 *excerpt of species SequenceAsSet*
```
theorem remove_preserves_inv : all l : Self, all e : Elt,
  nodouble (torep(l)) -> nodouble (torep(remove (e, l)))
proof =
<1>1 prove all l: list(Elt), all e: Elt,
     nodouble(l) -> nodouble(remove(e, l))
     (* 40 lines proof *)
<1>2 qed by step <1>1 definition of torep;
```

We can now prove uniqueness of an element in a sequence implemented as a list in Code 9 which statement is in Code 5

Code 9 *excerpt of species SequenceAsSet*
```
proof of unique_contains =
<1>1 assume c : Self,
     assume e : Elt,
     prove  not( L!mem (remove(e, c), e))
     <2>1 prove not(L!mem (remove(e, []), e)) (* 2lines *)
     <2>2 prove all l : list(Elt),  not(L!mem (remove(e, l), e))
          -> all x : Elt,  not(L!mem (remove(e, x::l), e))
          (* 30 lines *)
     <2>3 prove all l : list(Elt), not(L!mem (remove(e, l), e))
          by step <2>1, <2>2
     <2>f qed by step <2>3
<1>f qed by step <1>1
          property tolist_contains
          definition of tolist;
```

5   Iterators

Once collections have been specified, we can use them to specify iterators. We were inspired functional iterators of [6] for the interface and by JML specifications of [8] for the logical description.

5.1   Specification Hierarchy

In this paper we mainly describe finite linear iterations but many other may be considered. In order to provide a library which can easily be reused we heavily use inheritance and parameterization. We begin with basic iterator functionalities as in Code 10. An Fcollection implementing collections Col is a parameter of the specification species of iterators Iterator.

Code 10

```
species Iterator (Elt is Setoid,
                  L is Utils(Elt),
                  Col is Collection(Elt, L)) =

signature start : Col -> Self;

signature has_next : Self -> bool;

signature step_it : Self -> Elt * Self;
property step_it_empty :
  all c : Col, Col!is_empty (c) -> not(has_next (start (c)));
property step_it_nonempty :
  all c : Col, not(Col!is_empty (c)) -> has_next (start (c));

signature measure_it : Self -> int;
property mea_positive : all a : Self, 0 <=  measure_it (a) ;
property mea_decreases :
  all i1: Self, all res: Elt * Self, has_next(i1) ->
    step_it(i1) = res -> measure_it (snd(res)) < measure_it (i1);
```

The mea_decreases property expresses that when stepping an iterator we decrease a measure and thus enables us to prove the termination of the iteration.

As outlined in Section 3 and following [3] and [8], we rely on the user of our hierarchy for writing a model logical statement relating an iterator, a collection and a list of values. An implementation of the model signature should be a statement describing the list of elements of collection which have not been visited by the iterator.

Code 11 *excerpt of species Iterator*

```
signature model : Self -> Col -> list(Elt) ->  prop;

(** elements of l are in c *)
property model_includes: all it: Self, all c: Col, all l : list(Elt),
   model(it, c, l) -> all e: Elt, L!mem(l, e) -> Col!contains(e, c);

(** should start with full collection *)
property model_start : all c : Col, model (start (c), c, Col!tolist(c)) ;

(** when has_next is true l should not be empty *)
property model_has_next_true :
   all it : Self, all l : list(Elt), all c : Col,
   model (it, c, l) -> has_next(it) -> not(l = []);

(** when has_next is false there should remain no element to treat *)
property model_has_next_false :
   all it : Self, all l : list(Elt), all c : Col,
   model (it, c, l) -> not (has_next(it)) -> l = [];
```

```
[* we should return an element among those to be treated *)
property model_step :
   all it it2 : Self, all e : Elt, all l : list(Elt), all c : Col,
     model (it, c, l) -> has_next(it) -> step_it (it) = (e, it2)  ->
       L!mem (l, e);


property model_step_exists: all it it2: Self, all c: Col, all e: Elt,
   all l: list(Elt), has_next(it) ->
     model(it, c, l) -> step_it(it) = (e, it2) ->
       (* there exists a list which is a model  for it2 *)
       (ex l2: list(Elt), model(it2, c, l2));
```

The properties in Code 11 explicit the informal specifications given in section 3 of the model statement which is thus a key component of our implementation. The last statement expresses that when stepping an iterator we still have some model.

We now can specify iterators that visit only once an element of a set using inheritance as in Code 12.

Code 12
```
species UniqueIterator (Elt is Setoid,
                        L is Utils(Elt),
                        Col is CollectionAsSet(Elt, L)) =
inherit Iterator(Elt, L, Col) ;

property model_step_unique :
all it it2: Self, all e: Elt, all l l2: list(Elt), all c : Col,
  model (it, c, l) -> has_next(it) -> step_it (it) = (e, it2)  ->
    model(it2, c, l2) -> not(L!mem(l2, e));
end
```

The Java informal specifications introduce the notion of iterators from which the last iterated element can be removed from the collection it belongs to. This is achieved using the optional remove functionality, on the contrary we rely on FoCaLiZe inheritance to specify the remove functionality. In Code 13 we define a species of removable iterators that inherits from basic iterators and adds new specifications.

Code 13
```
species RemovableIterator(Elt is Setoid,
                          L is Utils(Elt),
                          Col is Collection(Elt, L)) =
  inherit Iterator(Elt, L, Col) ;

  signature remove: Self -> Self ;
  property remove_spec :
    all it it2: Self, all e: Elt, all l l2: list(Elt), all c : Col,
      model (it, c, l) -> has_next(it) ->
        step_it (it) = (e, it2)  -> model(it2, c, l2) ->
```

```
          model(remove(it2), Col!remove(e, c), 12);

    signature get_collection: Self -> Col ;
end
```

The statement remove_spec explains the behavior of the remove function, we also provide a `get_collection` operation to retrieve the new collection that results from the application of remove on an iterator.

5.2   Implementations

In this subsection, we describe our implementation of iterators which use sequences as representation and also a generic implementation of removable iterators.

First, in the species `SequenceIterator` (see Code 14), we represent an iterator by a sequence containing the elements left to be treated by the iterator. We use operations from `Sequence` (head, tail as in Section 4) to traverse the values.

Code 14

```
species SequenceIterator (Elt is Setoid, L is Utils(Elt),
                    LCol is Sequence(Elt, L)) =
inherit Iterator(Elt, L, LCol);

representation = LCol ;

let tolist (l : Self) = LCol!tolist (l);

logical let model (it: Self, c, l) =
  (all x : Elt, L!mem (l, x)
   <->
   L!mem (tolist(it), x));

let start (c : LCol) : Self = c;

let has_next (it : Self) = not(LCol!is_empty (it));

let step_it (it) =
  if has_next (it) then (LCol!head (it), LCol!tail (it))
  else focalize_error ("no more elements") ;

let measure_it (c) = LCol!size (c);
```

We have defined the `model` statement which expresses that the list of elements to visit should be the list view of the iterator. Here this view is the list view of the underlying sequence as defined by the `tolist` function.

The overall `SequenceIterator` species is 150 lines of FoCaLiZe code where proofs mostly involve unfolding definitions. For iterators that visit an element only once we implemented the `UniqueSeqIterator` species by simple inheritance and we proved the `model_step_unique` property in 40 lines of FoCaLiZe.

We use a species `RemovableGenericIterator` to implement the remove feature. It takes an iterator as argument as in Code 15. To implement removable iterators we encapsulate a general iterator with the necessary information to keep track of the last element returned and of the collection of remaining values after deletion. In Code 15 we use the `PFailed` value to reflect that no element can be removed from the collection. As in Java we enforce that only the last visited element can be removed.

Code 15

```
type partial('a) =
  | PFailed
  | PUnfailed('a);;

species RemovableGenericIterator(Elt is Setoid, L is Utils(Elt),
                                 Col is Collection(Elt, L),
                                 It is Iterator(Elt, L, Col)) =

inherit RemovableIterator(Elt, L, Col);

(* basic iterator, last element returned, current collection *)
representation = It * (partial(Elt) * Col) ;

logical let model(it, c, l) =
  It!model(fst(it), c, l);

let get_collection(it: Self) = snd (snd (it) );

let remove(it: Self): Self =
  let i = fst(it) and re = snd(it) in
  let e = fst(re) and col = snd(re) in
  match e with
    | PFailed -> it
    | PUnfailed(x) -> (i, (PFailed , Col!remove(x, col)));

let start(c) = (It!start(c), (PFailed, c));

let step_it(it) =
  if has_next(it)
  then
    let c = It!step_it(fst(it)) in
      (fst(c), (snd(c), (PUnfailed(fst(c)), snd(snd(it)))))
  else focalize_error("no more elements");
```

This species implements all of the basic iterators specifications (for instance has_next or model_start of `Iterator`) together with features of `remove`. Basic iterator methods are implemented by de-structuring the iterator's representation and using the corresponding methods of the embedded basic iterator.

We also provide a `RemovableUniqueGenericIterator` species which inherits removable iterators and proves that an element is only visited once. The overall code for the two species implementing remove facilities is 300 lines of FoCaLiZe code.

6 Related Work

Collections and iterators have been studied from a verification point of view by different researchers, mainly in the context of Java or C#. Existing approaches differ a lot and some of them are mentioned below.

Besides static verification methods, run-time verification has been used, it allows for example the verification of safe enumeration, by monitoring and predictive analysis such as in [16].

Formal specification and deductive methods and tools have tackle the problem of safe iterators or safe use of iterators. A very early specification of Alphard like iterators using traces has been given by Lamb in [12]. Iterators have also been studied in the context of the refinement calculus [10]. In this work, iterators are translated into catamorphisms.

Some approaches (see e.g. [11] and [15]) and use higher order separation logic to verify some properties on iterators. It is strongly linked to an imperative implementations with shared mutable heap structures and thus not in the scope of our approach.

Model oriented specification to describe how iterators behave is a largely adopted approach (see e.g. [18], [8], [4], [9], [14]). Contracts are associated to collections and iterators in the form of pre and post-conditions and invariants. In Java and JML context, this kind of specification may use model fields [3] such as in [8] where the abstract model of a collection is a bag. From specification and code, verification conditions are generated and then proved, automatically or not, by a theorem prover. Our approach is close to this model based style, however we don't fix a choice for the model. We only specified it as a logical statement and its definition is left to the implementor of the iterators. This avoids explicit bag abstraction and we believe, allows more flexibility to describe iterators.

Such uses of specification contracts, model fields in particular, usually allow modular verification. Our approach facilitates also this modular verification since we are able to verify functions dealing with iterators according to their interface and thus using only the specifications of iterators (`model_start`, `model_next` etc.).

The standard Coq library provides a modular specification for finite maps and sets very similar to those found in the Ocaml library implemented using lists and efficient trees. Iterators are not featured, however a `fold` function is proposed. Also Filliâtre (see [6]) generalizes a `fold` function into efficient persistent iterators for Ocaml.

The Isabelle Collections Framework (ICF) [13] provides a unified framework for using verified collection data structures in Isabelle/HOL formalizations. They come with iterators which are implemented as generalized fold combinators. The ICF supports maps, sets and sequences together with generic algorithms using the Isabelle abstraction facilities. Iterators are created using a continuation function, a state transformer function and an initial state. Support for reasoning is achieved using an invariant and specifications are provided for maps, sets and sequences. Our implementation only provides some support for sequences but we have designed a general framework in which maps and sets can be implemented. The ICF heavily relies on higher order functions whereas FoCaLiZe emphasizes on first order statements which are often easier to understand by programmers. We thus remain in the same spirit than the Java Collection Framework but we use persistent data and allow certification.

7   Conclusion

In this paper we have presented a formal specification of collections and iterators together with a verified implementation of iterators for sequential lists, using the FoCaLiZe environment. The overall FoCaLiZe formal development with specifications, code and proofs, contains around 1600 lines[4]. We have used as much as possible FoCaLiZe inheritance and parameterization in order to get a flexible, adaptable and reusable formal development.

As perspectives we plan to specify and implement iterators for other kind of collections such as trees or maps. Then, in our development it is possible to state that when there is no more element to visit, every element in the collection has been visited. It would also be interesting to exploit the fact that a sequence is an ordered aggregate of elements and thus specify and define iterators that enumerate the elements of such a collection respecting their order.

Furthermore since we have defined iterators as a species they are normal FoCaLiZe values and we are able to manipulate them as in Code 15. This should allow the combination of different iterators and thus provide generic species implementing combinators of iterators.

References

1. Proceedings of the 2006 Conference on Specification and Verification of Component-based Systems. ACM, New York (2006)
2. Bonichon, R., Delahaye, D., Doligez, D.: Zenon: An extensible automated theorem prover producing checkable proofs. In: Dershowitz, N., Voronkov, A. (eds.) LPAR 2007. LNCS (LNAI), vol. 4790, pp. 151–165. Springer, Heidelberg (2007)
3. Breunesse, C.-B., Poll, E.: Verifying jml specifications with model fields. In: Formal Techniques for Java-like Programs. Proceedings of the ECOOP 2003 Workshop (2003)
4. Cok, D.R.: Specifying java iterators with jml and esc/java2. In: Proceedings of the 2006 Conference on Specification and Verification of Component-based Systems, SAVCBS 2006, pp. 71–74. ACM (2006)

---

[4] Available at the unlisted url http://www.ensiie.fr/~rioboo/iterators.fcl

5. Dubois, C., Hardin, T., Vigui Donzeau-Gouge, V.: Building certified components within focal. In: Loidl, H.-W. (ed.) Revised Selected Papers from the Fifth Symposium on Trends in Functional Programming, TFP 2004, München, Germany. Trends in Functional Programming, vol. 5, pp. 33–48. Intellect (2006)
6. Filliâtre, J.-C.: Backtracking iterators. In: Proceedings of the ACM Workshop on ML 2006, Portland, Oregon, USA, pp. 55–62. ACM (2006)
7. Gamma, E., Helm, R., Johnson, R., Vlissides, J.M.: Design patterns: elements of reusable object-oriented software. Addison-Wesley, Reading (1994)
8. Huisman, M.: Verification of java's abstractcollection class: A case study. In: Boiten, E.A., Möller, B. (eds.) MPC 2002. LNCS, vol. 2386, pp. 175–194. Springer, Heidelberg (2002)
9. Jacobs, B., Meijer, E., Piessens, F., Schulte, W.: Iterators revisited: Proof rules and implementation. In: Workshop on Formal Techniques For Java-like Programs, FTFJP (2005)
10. King, S., Morgan, C.: An iterator construct for the refinement calculus. In: Fourth Irish Workshop on Formal Methods (2000)
11. Krishnaswami, N.R.: Reasoning about iterators with separation logic. In: Proceedings of the 2006 Conference on Specification and Verification of Component-based Systems, SAVCBS 2006, pp. 83–86. ACM (2006)
12. Lamb, D.A.: Specification of iterators. IEEE Trans. Software Eng. 16(12), 1352–1360 (1990)
13. Lammich, P., Lochbihler, A.: The isabelle collections framework. In: Kaufmann, M., Paulson, L.C. (eds.) ITP 2010. LNCS, vol. 6172, pp. 339–354. Springer, Heidelberg (2010)
14. Leino, K.R.M., Monahan, R.: Dafny meets the verification benchmarks challenge. In: Leavens, G.T., O'Hearn, P., Rajamani, S.K. (eds.) VSTTE 2010. LNCS, vol. 6217, pp. 112–126. Springer, Heidelberg (2010)
15. Malecha, G., Morrisett, G.: Mechanized verification with sharing. In: Cavalcanti, A., Deharbe, D., Gaudel, M.-C., Woodcock, J. (eds.) ICTAC 2010. LNCS, vol. 6255, pp. 245–259. Springer, Heidelberg (2010)
16. Meredith, P., Roşu, G.: Runtime verification with the RV system. In: Barringer, H., et al. (eds.) RV 2010. LNCS, vol. 6418, pp. 136–152. Springer, Heidelberg (2010)
17. Rioboo, R.: Invariants for the FoCaL language. Annals of Mathematics and Artificial Intelligence 56(3-4), 273–296 (2009)
18. Weide, B.W.: Savcbs 2006 challenge: Specification of iterators. In: Proceedings of the 2006 Conference on Specification and Verification of Component-based Systems, SAVCBS 2006, pp. 75–77. ACM (2006)

Tool Support for Teaching Hoare Logic*

Tadeusz Sznuk and Aleksy Schubert

Institute of Informatics, University of Warsaw
ul. Banacha 2, 02–097 Warsaw, Poland
{tsznuk,alx}@mimuw.edu.pl

Abstract. Currently, software verification is perceived as an overly difficult and hard to understand task. This image can be changed through effective instruction of prospect programmers during their studies. Teaching Hoare logic is a process that can be made more appealing to students if appropriate tools are employed. Having an environment tailored to the style and content of a particular lecture is especially beneficial. We argue that current state of related technology is such that it is possible to implement a tool that can be adapted to a particular style of classes with manageable effort. We illustrate our point by showing a tool called HAHA (Hoare Advanced Homework Assistant) and presenting a statistical analysis of its effectiveness in teaching Hoare logic.

1 Introduction

Refined dependable software development methods, especially ones based on Hoare logic, are difficult and as a result are perceived as tedious and impractical. One way to achieve this it to replace the instruction with pen and paper on introductory courses of Hoare logic with one supported by a tool. The methodical approach of Hoare logic is much harder to execute than convincing oneself about correctness of the very same program in a less formal way, which contributes to the perception that it is tedious and boring. What is worse, the chances of making a mistake can be argued to be similar for both approaches. The fact that the whole logical inference is performed on paper, without any aid from the computer (save, perhaps, in the matter of typesetting) further enforces the view that Hoare logic is impractical. One way to avoid this is to present these methods to future programmers during their curriculum in an attractive, modern way.

The most direct approach here is to use automated formal verification software to facilitate checking the correctness of Hoare programs. Although systems such as ESC/Java [7,25], Frama-C [5,8], Verifast [19], Microsoft VCC [9], KeY [3], to mention only few, have not yet made their way into the everyday toolbox of an average developer [20], they have proven to be usable in the verification process of software projects.

The design of these systems is focused on large scale software development, rather than education, and these two goals are, at least in some aspects, conflicting. One of the reasons is that rich feature set of languages such as C or Java

---

* This work was partly supported by Polish government grant N N206 493138.

D. Giannakopoulou and G. Salaün (Eds.): SEFM 2014, LNCS 8702, pp. 332–346, 2014.
© Springer International Publishing Switzerland 2014

(e.g. the complexity of heap handling in Verifast [19] is an additional burden in getting the basic ideas through), as well as the need to handle the organisation of creation and evolution of real code (e.g. in the form of full fledged support for Design by Contract software development [27]), invariably result in complexity of the underlying formal logic, which limits its use in an introductory course.

There are tools such as KeY-Hoare [6] or Why3 [14], which are designed with the goal in mind to serve as educational aids, but were started from general purpose verification tools. Unfortunately, variants of Hoare logic which are implemented by them are seldom compatible with these from existing teaching materials of courses in particular faculties. This means pedagogical experience of tutors is, at least to some descent, lost when such a tool is adopted for instruction. It should also be noted that the high automation they offer can distract students and allow them to solve exercises by trial and error with little regard to the design of the logic. This calls for a tool in which only basic techniques are implemented, but which can easily be adapted to different courses.

One more crucial point here is that the usefulness of the tools for teaching is usually presented through qualitative descriptions. Hardly anyone tries to use statistical methods of quantitative psychology [30] to estimate the impact that introduction of a tool has on the educational process. We address the discussed shortcomings of previous approaches and propose a Hoare logic teaching assistant, HAHA, designed specifically to teach the logic. Moreover, we present a quantitative study of the impact adoption of such tool has on teaching results.

The paper is structured as follows. Section 2 gives an overview of the requirements for the tool and its current features. The experiment concerning the results of teaching students with our tool is presented in Section 3. This is followed by a presentation of related work in Section 4. We conclude in Section 5

2   Presentation of HAHA[1]

Requirements for the Tool. The basis of our study are the tutoring activities in our faculty. We gathered requirements on a tool to support teaching in the following two scenarios. The first of them involves giving instruction on Hoare logic in a standard undergraduate course on semantics and verification of programs. The second one involves teaching advanced topics in software verification.

As a secondary non-functional requirement on the development we took the constraint that the internal design of the tool must be such that the tool is relatively easy adaptable to other teaching environments.

Teaching Hoare logics. We would like the teaching process to be similar to the original one. This means we require the syntax of the programs to be close to original Hoare logic with possible extensions, but in the manner easily digestible by students who are acquainted with programming languages such as Pascal or Java. In addition, we would like the process of verification to give the impression that it is done as part of program development, in particular we would not like to

---

[1] The tool is available from http://haha.mimuw.edu.pl

change the environment to the one of interactive prover to assist in discharging verification conditions. Instead we would like the students to give assertions between instructions that are subsequently verified by an automatic theorem prover. In case the prover cannot discharge the supplied conditions we would like to make it possible to give it additional help rather by means of additional axioms than through an interactive proof. The latter solution would only be possible if significantly more time was available to instruct students how to do interactive proofs. It is an unavoidable feature of this part of software verification that it requires deep technical fluency in the proving technology [28,16].

Traditionally assignments in our courses suggest students to fill in all assertions in program code. Contrary to the common tendency to make only loop invariants obligatory, we decided that we want to force students to fill in all intermediate assertions. This might seem surprising, since the need to write many formulae increases the amount of work necessary to create a verified program. However, we believe that, in the case of a teaching aid, our approach is more beneficial. First, this suggests students to match the assertions with relevant Hoare logic rules and in this way it reinforces the process of teaching the logic. Second, it gives the students a tangible experience of how much information must be maintained at each step of the program to make it execute correctly — the process of making the verification work is also a tangible experience of how it is easy to overlook transformation of some tiny detail in this information packet.

Alternatives to Development. Before we started development of our own tool we reviewed the literature on existing tools (see Section 4). We decided to have a closer look at Why3 [4,14] and KeY-Hoare [6]. We verified small programs with both tools to have an impression of how they match our requirements. We have no room to make a detailed comparison with them, but we give an overview of encountered problems with their adaptation to our scenario.

Why3 is a very mature tool. It gives the possibility to work with C or Java code and brings Emacs interface with syntax colouring for the native Why language, WhyML. Still, the tool does not have the possibility to enforce filling in assertions between all instructions. One more obstacle, which makes it less suitable for our purposes is the syntax of WhyML. It is not similar to the languages the students are used to work with so it would present some kind of difficulty for them. We could start instruction with Java or C code, but in the end we would have to expose students to the native syntax. Therefore, we gave this option up.

Key-Hoare is another mature tool that is an adaptation of the very attractive KeY platform to the needs of a Hoare logic course. Still, the logic behind the tool is not pure Hoare logic, but Hoare logic with updates. Therefore, the first obstacle in adoption of the tool was the need to extend the lecture material about Hoare logic to include the updates. Another difficulty with Key-Hoare is that it exposes a student to the KeY prover where a considerable number of logic rules can be applied at each step of verification. A student must be instructed which of them should be used and which of them avoided in typical cases. We believed that we did not have enough time during classes to explain it. At last, the prover environment gave a good impression on which logic rules are available at each point, but it also did not give the impression of a typical software development environment and this was one of our requirements.

After taking these observations, we decided to develop our own, based upon Eclipse, environment called Hoare Advanced Homework Assistant, or HAHA. We describe it in more detail below.

2.1   Overview of HAHA

The user interface of HAHA is presented in Fig. 1. The main pane of the window is filled with the source code of the program one works with. It features an editor for simple while programs and has all features that are expected of a modern IDE, such as syntax highlighting, automated completion proposals and error markers. Once a program is entered, it is processed by a verification conditions generator, which implements the rules of Hoare logic. The resulting formulae are then passed to an automated prover. If the solver is unable to ascertain the correctness of the program, error markers are generated to point the user to the assertions which could not be proven. A very useful feature is the ability to find

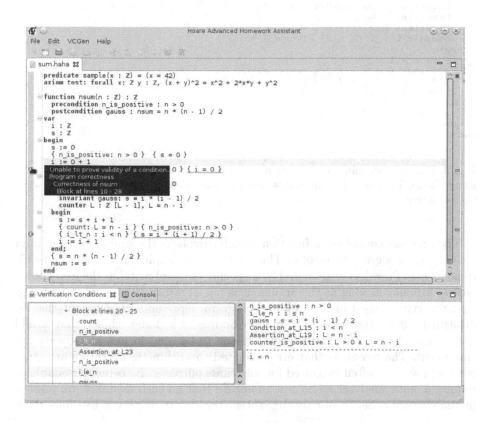

Fig. 1. The user interface of HAHA

counterexamples for incorrect assertions. These are included in error descriptions displayed by the editor.

The input language of HAHA is that of while programs over integers and arrays. We designed it so that its mechanisms and data types match those supported by state of the art satisfiability solvers, e.g. Z3 [10] or CVC4 [2]. As the language is fairly standard, we do not give its grammar. Instead, we discuss pivotal features of the HAHA syntax through an example presented in Fig. 2.

```
predicate sample(x : Z) = (x = 42)
axiom test: forall x: Z y : Z, (x + y)^2 = x^2 + 2*x*y + y^2

function nsum(n : Z) : Z
  precondition n_is_positive : n > 0
  postcondition gauss : nsum = n * (n − 1) / 2
var
  i : Z
  s : Z
begin
  s := 0
  { n_is_positive: n > 0 }  { s = 0 }
  i := 0
  { n_is_positive: n > 0 } { s = 0 } { i = 0 }
  while i < n do
    invariant n_is_positive: n > 0
    invariant i_le_n : i <= n
    invariant gauss: s = i * (i − 1) / 2
    counter L : Z [L − 1], L = n − i
  begin
    s := s + i
    { count: L = n − i } { n_is_positive: n > 0 }
    { i_lt_n : i < n } { s = i * (i + 1) / 2 }
    i := i + 1
  end;
  { s = n * (n − 1) / 2 }
  nsum := s
end
```

Fig. 2. Example program. The function computes the sum of numbers from 1 to $n - 1$ using a loop. The postcondition states that the final result is equal to the result of the Gauss' formula.

The program consists of a function, which calculates the sum of integers from 1 to $n - 1$, for a given value of n. The specification simply states that the result (which, as in Pascal, is represented by a special variable) matches the well known Gauss' formula, as long as the argument is not negative. Here it must be noted that the type Z, used in the example program, represents unbounded (that is, arbitrarily large) integers. This is one example of a design choice that would not necessarily be valid for a verifier meant to be used in actual software development. The reason is that errors related to arithmetic overflows are quite common, and are often exploited for malicious purposes. It seems reasonable to require a static analyser to be able to ensure that no such mistakes are present in the checked code. In our setting, these considerations play a less important role, so we were able to choose a simpler model of arithmetic. On the other hand, it might be actually desirable to be able to illustrate difficulties associated with the necessity of avoiding or handling overflows. For this reason we have created a variant of our tool to allow the use of `Int` variables, modelled as 32-bit vectors, in which way we exercised, in our view successfully, the non-functional requirement concerning adaptability of HAHA.

Structure of the language appears to be fairly self explanatory. Let us note that, following the example of Eiffel, loop invariants can be named. This is also extended to other types of assertions. The names are useful for documentation purposes, and make error messages as well as solver logs much easier to read. It is possible to give multiple invariants for a single loop. Similarly, a sequence of assertions is interpreted as a conjunction. This is notably different from the approach taken in some textbooks and course material, in which an implication is supposed to hold between two consecutive assertions not separated by any statement. We believe the former interpretation to be clearer, but, to illustrate the ease with which HAHA can be modified to fit the requirements of a particular course, we have implemented the latter in a variant of our tool. Finally, let us remark that an explicit application of the weakening rule can be unambiguously represented with the help of the `skip` statement.

In the example program, each pair of consecutive statements is separated by assertions. For each instruction the correctness of the two surrounding assertions is checked by the application of the Hoare logic rule for the instruction combined with implicit application of the weakening rule. As long as loop invariants are provided, these midconditions can be inferred automatically through Dijkstra's weakest precondition calculation [11]. However, no such inference is performed in HAHA as a result of the requirement stated in Section 2.

HAHA supports proofs of both partial and total correctness. We follow here the traditional pattern used in our classes. To facilitate the latter, we allow a specifically designated invariant to be parameterised by an auxiliary integer variable. The conditions generated for such an invariant, which we call a *counter*, ensure that the loop condition holds precisely when the invariant formula is true for an argument of 0. It must also be proved that, if the invariant holds before the loop for an argument of $L \in \mathbb{N}$, it will hold for a number $L' \in \mathbb{N}$ strictly smaller than L after the loop body is executed. Concrete syntax used by HAHA for the purpose of termination proving can be seen in the example program, although proving termination of this particular loop is not a very challenging task. The expression in square brackets represents the aforementioned value of L'.

This solution is different from frequently used constructs of *loop variant* as in Why3 or *decreases* statement as in JML. However, these solutions focus, as mentioned before, on ease of intent specification while we focus on giving the students the impression of what information a programmer should control to write correct programs. Our solution forces students not only to provide the formula that decreases with each loop iteration, but also to explicate the way *how* the formula is decreased. Students can provide such formula only when they have good command of all the control flow paths of the program. Other courses may opt for the mentioned above design with loop variants. A smooth introduction of such a construct requires binary Hoare calculus, which is a desirable extension of the basic formalism. To extend the portfolio of existing options, we are working on adding support for the binary assertions.

Before we conclude this brief examination of the capabilities of HAHA, let us focus on the very first lines of the example program. They contain definitions of an axiom and a predicate. They are only an illustration, and are not actually used in the remaining code. When creating specifications for more complex procedures, however, it is often desirable to use predicates to simplify notation. Our experience shows that this is especially useful in code operating on arrays, as it tends to employ rather complex assertions. Axioms, in turn, are helpful when the automated solver cannot prove a true formula.

3   Description of the Experiment

In general terms the goal of our study was to check if the students that had been taught with HAHA performed worse or better in their evaluation. A natural setup here is to try to reject the null hypothesis (H_0) that *scores of students taught with the tool are greater or equal to the scores of students taught traditionally.* Here is a description of our experiment to do this.

Experiment environment.   The base environment of the experiment was the course of *Semantics and program verification (Semantyka i weryfikacja programów* in Polish).[2] The students are traditionally instructed on two kinds of classes, namely, on lectures and on blackboard exercises. The lectures give the theoretical background for the material while during blackboard exercises students are exposed to problems such as defining formal semantics for a given intuitive description of a language or verification of a small program using Hoare logic. The problems are solved in cooperation between students and tutors. The lectures are given to all students who enrolled on the course while the blackboard exercises are given to smaller exercise groups of 15–20 students each.

The course is traditionally divided into three approximately equal in weight topics: operational semantics, denotational semantics, and program verification. Each of them ends with a homework graded by tutors. The basis for the ultimate score of a student is the final exam. The students are given there three problems concerning the three topics of the course. The course has been run several times and is instructed with an established routine. The lectures are given with help of slides that undergo only minor changes each year. The blackboard exercises are given using standard sets of problems to be dealt with.

Experiment setup.   The experiment was run twice. The first run was conducted in 2012/13 semester and the second one in 2013/14. Each of the runs gave a student two exam attempts. In case a student attempted an exam twice, only the second attempt was taken into account in our calculations. The whole body

---

[2] A description of the course curriculum can be found in page
   http://informatorects.uw.edu.pl/en/courses/view?prz_kod=1000-215bSWP

of students was divided in two populations: G_0, where the instruction was done traditionally, and G_1, where the instruction was done with help of HAHA. Students decided to enroll to particular blackboard classes groups, some of which instructed subjects with HAHA and some traditionally [29]. However, students were not aware of this variation of instruction at the time of their choice.

The groups G_0, G_1 were subsequently subdivided into control subpopulations $G_{0,i,j}$ where $i \in \{1,2\}$ corresponds to the number of exam attempts and $j \in \{12,13\}$ corresponds to the year of experiment. Similarly, for test subpopulations we have $G_{1,i,j}$. Out of the students who enrolled the course in 2012/13 we excluded from the computations students who did not return any homework nor attempted exams.[3] We assume they effectively did not take part in the experiment so they could not be counted. To ensure independence of the tests we excluded in the run of 2013/14 in addition those students who attempted the experiment in 2012/13 run. The sizes of the populations are gathered in Fig. 3.[4] We should mention here that the sizes of the populations $G_{1,2,12}$ and $G_{1,2,13}$ are very small

Group	Size
$G_{0,1,12}$	47
$G_{0,2,12}$	17
$G_{0,1,13}$	41
$G_{0,2,13}$	14
G_0	119
$G_{1,1,12}$	31
$G_{1,2,12}$	5
$G_{1,1,13}$	24
$G_{1,2,13}$	8
G_1	68

Fig. 3. Group sizes

so any statistical results for them are the matter of coincidence. We present the analysis for them only for completeness.

HAHA tool was introduced to the standard setup of the course for the third part of the instruction, when Hoare logic was presented. All students were warned at the first lecture that some of them would be trained with help of a new tool to avoid astonishment on their side. We also believe that the Eclipse environment is perceived neither as a hot novelty nor as an antique tool, which is confirmed by the Evans Data Corp. survey [13].

The tool was presented only during the blackboard exercises. It was not mentioned during the lecture except for the initial short message. Each run the students of the course from G_0 were divided into three classes groups instructed by two teachers T_1, T_2. Accordingly, the students of G_1 in each semester consisted of two classes groups instructed by two teachers T_2 and T_3. One of the teachers T_2 instructed both classes groups in G_0 and in G_1. The teacher T_3 is a co-author of the tool and the current paper.

The instruction consisted in exposing the students to the same set of problems as in the previous years. However, the examples were shown in the HAHA editor displayed through a projector on a screen visible for the whole group. Students chosen by a tutor had an opportunity to determine the Hoare formulae written in HAHA. After the series of instructional classes finished, a homework was given as in the previous years. The students instructed with help of HAHA were encouraged, but not forced, to return their homework done in HAHA. The homework assignment was prepared by the teacher T_1 who did it in the previous years, however to ensure it can be prepared smoothly with HAHA it

---

[3] When these students are included the p-values support our claim even stronger.

[4] The supplementary material with raw data and R source code is available from http://haha.mimuw.edu.pl/experiment2013/data.zip

was modified slightly by T_3. In the end 12 students returned their homework in HAHA format in 2012/13 run and 14 in 2013/14. Each run only one of these returned homeworks was graded not with the maximal number of points.

The results of instructions were checked during the final exams. In each of the total four attempts the students in G_0 and G_1 were given the same assignments. One of them consisted in filling in missing assertions of Hoare logic in a given program, which was a typical kind of assignment on exams in this subject for several years. Both groups had to do it on a supplied piece of paper that contained the program and free space to fill in with formulae.[5] The assignment was again prepared by T_1 (who was not involved neither in development of HAHA nor in teaching with HAHA). After the exam the assignments were collected and graded in points ranging from 0 to 10. The grading was done by the teacher T_1, the one who prepared the assignment and who did not do instruction with HAHA.

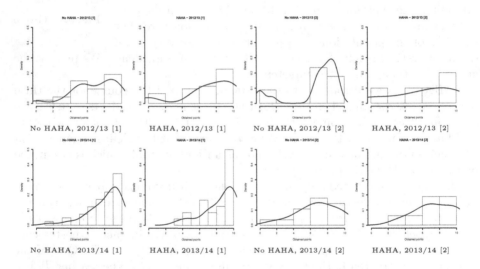

Fig. 4. Scores of students trained traditionally (No HAHA) and with HAHA (HAHA) for the exams in 2012/13 and 2013/14 in the first ([1]) and second ([2]) attempts

Experiment results and discussion.   The main result of the experiment is the comparison between the performance of students in G_0 and in G_1. The histograms of the scores obtained by the groups are presented in Fig. 4. (In all pictures, an idealised distribution of the scores is drawn, as given by the R tool.) We can immediately see that the distributions are not normal.

---

[5] The texts of the assignments are included in the supplementary documentation of the experiment.

We can now turn to the analysis of the statistics for the students' scores. The results for all the groups are presented in Fig. 5, which shows the mean (E) value of each group, median (M) and the standard deviation (σ). The picture here is relatively clear. There is only one exception to the rule that the mean of the group that was taught without HAHA (the upper part of the table) is lower than the one for the corresponding group that was taught traditionally. Still, this exception takes place in situation where the test group was very small so this may be an accidental situation. The same situation holds for medians. This suggests that the control population G_0 has systematically lower scores in this experiment than the treatment one, G_1.

Group	E	M	σ
$G_{0,1,12}$	6.908511	7.50	2.468042
$G_{0,2,12}$	6.676471	8.00	3.066661
$G_{0,1,13}$	7.963415	8.50	1.953811
$G_{0,2,13}$	6.714286	7.00	2.439375
$G_{1,1,12}$	7.109677	8.00	3.192111
$G_{1,2,12}$	6.100000	7.00	4.006245
$G_{1,1,13}$	8.375000	9.25	1.906796
$G_{1,2,13}$	7.437500	7.25	2.321291

Fig. 5. Means (E), medians (M) and standard deviations (σ) of student's scores

We would like to strengthen this argument by showing that these differences are not pure coincidence. We give here a substantial statistical evidence that the scores in G_1 are not worse than scores in G_0, which means that the students taught with help of HAHA perform not worse than students taught in the traditional way. We use for this the confidence level of $p \leq 0.05$. For our verification, we use the nonparametric Mann-Whitney test (also called Willcoxon test), as the use of standard parametric tests assumes the distributions are normal. We can indeed apply the test since its prerequisites are met:

Groups	z-score	p
$G_{0,1,13}$-$G_{1,1,13}$	1.17971100	0.1190576
$G_{0,2,13}$-$G_{1,2,13}$	-0.07922324	0.5315725
$G_{0,1,14}$-$G_{1,1,14}$	1.27021700	0.1020037
$G_{0,2,14}$-$G_{1,2,14}$	0.72321340	0.2347744

Fig. 6. Comparison of students' results

Hypotheses The null hypotheses H_0 for the current study is that the median of scores in the groups within G_0 (represented by a random variable Y_1) are greater or equal to the median of scores in the groups within G_1 (represented by Y_2), i.e. $H_0 : Y_1 - Y_2 \geq 0$. The alternative hypothesis H_A is that the median in G_0 are less than the one in G_1.

Uniformity of populations We also can assume that in case the distribution of results from G_0 and G_1 is the same, the probability of an observation from G_0 exceeding one from G_1 is equal to the probability of an observation from G_1 exceeding one from G_0. We discuss this assumption later, but in summary the background of both groups is the same and their members were chosen randomly from the point of view of the experiment.

Independence We can assume that the observations in G_0 and G_1 are independent since they concern answers to the same problem given in disjoint groups in the conditions of an exam during which communication between students was prohibited.

Comparable responses The scores are numeric so they can be easily compared one with another so a single ranking of the subjects can be formed.

The z-scores and p-values for the test[6] are presented in Fig. 6. We can see that the statistics confirms our observation that the median in all cases except from the second one is greater in the group who was taught with HAHA. Since the p-values are bigger than 0.05 the results are not statistically significant. However, we can combine them using a meta-analysis technique called Stouffer-Lipták method [26]. If we combine all the four p-values from the table in Fig. 6 using weights, as suggested by Lipták, that are square roots of the populations sizes $(8.831761, 4.690416, 8.062258, 4.690416$, respectively) then we obtain the combined $p = 0.04166557$. In case we take the two tests that compare populations of bigger sizes then the combined $p = 0.0420251$. In each of the cases we can reject H_0 and conclude that we obtained statistically significant result that the median of students who were taught with HAHA is higher than the one for students who were taught traditionally.

There are a few more issues that should be discussed here.

Bias of more talented students. First of all the process of group assignment is mostly random, but can be influenced by students [29]. One possible bias that could affect our results is that the students in G_1 could have been more talented than average.

This can be rejected by an additional check. The assignments 1 and 2, which consist in defining of an operational and denotational semantics for toy languages, have similar mathematical nature as the one with Hoare logic. In case G_1 consisted of more talented students, also the scores for the other assignments during the exam should be consistently higher for them.

The statistics for the other assignments are presented in Fig. 7. The mean of the scores in G_0 for the assignment 1 was consistently higher than the one in the subgroups of G_1. In one case the median for the assignment was smaller for G_0 than for G_1. This was in case of the small group that attempted the exam

Group	E	M
Assignment 1		
$G_{0,1,12}$	8.510638	9.00
$G_{1,1,12}$	7.516129	8.00
$G_{0,2,12}$	5.617647	6.50
$G_{1,2,12}$	5.600000	7.00
$G_{0,1,13}$	7.463415	7.00
$G_{1,1,13}$	6.958333	7.00
$G_{0,2,13}$	7.428571	8.00
$G_{1,2,13}$	6.125000	5.00
Assignment 2		
$G_{0,1,12}$	4.814894	5.00
$G_{1,1,12}$	4.848387	5.40
$G_{0,2,12}$	2.205882	1.00
$G_{1,2,12}$	1.800000	1.00
$G_{0,1,13}$	5.219512	6.00
$G_{1,1,13}$	4.791667	4.50
$G_{0,2,13}$	2.964286	3.25
$G_{1,2,13}$	1.625000	0.50

Fig. 7. Scores in other assignments

for the second time. In case of assignment 2 the situation is more complicated since both mean and median scores are higher for G_0 than for G_1 in all cases except for the first big group of 2012/13 exam. In that case the difference of the medians measured by the Mann-Whitney test results in $Z = -0.2125$ and $p = 0.4158$. This means that the difference was hardly meaningful [12]. As a result, we do not see any significant bias here that could testify that students in G_1 were more talented.

Problem of instruction by T_3. For the validity of the study it is important to judge more thoroughly the impact of the instruction of the co-author of the tool, referred here as T_3. The basic ground to think that the results are correct is that

---

[6] The results were obtained with help of the R package **coin** [17,18] with its heuristics to handle ties in input data.

the person who graded the studied assignments was not involved in development of HAHA nor in teaching with the tool. Moreover, the results of the 2012/13 exam (see Fig. 8, $T_{3,i,j}$ is the subgroup of $G_{1,i,j}$ taught by T_3) show that the scores of the group taught by the teacher were even smaller than ones in G_0 so they made the results of G_1 even smaller.

Discussion of instruction by T_2. Since one of the tutors instructed both with help of HAHA and without HAHA, it is interesting to compare the results obtained by the corresponding exercise groups $T_{2,0,i,j} \subseteq G_{0,i,j}$ and $T_{2,1,i,j} \subseteq G_{1,i,j}$. The sizes of these groups were $|T_{2,0,1,12}| = 17$, $|T_{2,1,1,12}| = 19$, $|T_{2,0,2,12}| = 5$, $|T_{2,1,2,12}| = 1$, $|T_{2,0,1,13}| = 16$, $|T_{2,1,1,13}| = 11$, $|T_{2,0,2,13}| = 0$, $|T_{2,1,2,13}| = 6$. The comparison of the

Group	E	M
$T_{3,1,12}$	5.041667	6.00
$T_{3,2,12}$	5.875000	6.75
$T_{3,1,13}$	8.625000	9.50
$T_{3,2,13}$	8.250000	8.25

Fig. 8. Results of groups trained by T_3

medians using the Mann-Whitney test is presented in Fig. 9. We can see that there was no data for $T_{2,0,2,13}$-$T_{2,1,2,13}$ case. This was caused by the size of $T_{2,0,2,13}$ equal to zero. As we see, the scores are statistically significant for the bigger groups. This reinforces the claim that instruction with HAHA gives rise to better results.

Independence and uniformity of populations. Important assumption in the experiment is that the results of G_0 and G_1 groups are independent one from the other. The main reason to think so is that the populations in those groups were separate and the exams that gave the sample results took place at different times. Moreover, the solutions to

Group	z-score	p
$T_{2,0,1,12}$-$T_{2,1,1,12}$	1.7494	0.04011
$T_{2,0,2,12}$-$T_{2,1,2,12}$	-1.2060	0.88610
$T_{2,0,1,13}$-$T_{2,1,1,13}$	2.0081	0.02232
$T_{2,0,2,13}$-$T_{2,1,2,13}$		*no data*

Fig. 9. Comparison between groups trained by T_2

assignments during the exam were individual, i.e. all kinds of cooperation were explicitly forbidden under standard sanctions.

The experiment lasted several weeks so in principle the students from the tested group could interfere significantly with those in the control group. Actually, students from the groups taught traditionally could even attend classes taught with HAHA. In one case, a student from a group of students instructed traditionally actually returned his homework written in HAHA. Incidentally, this was a student known to attend classes with HAHA. This student was included into the population taught with HAHA. Still, the students were strongly encouraged to attend groups they were enlisted in so such cases were marginal.

In 2012/13 we checked additionally how much information on the tool spread to the groups taught traditionally. We did it with help of an anonymous survey during the exam. This survey showed that in all students except 17 indicated no familiarity with HAHA. Therefore, the number of people who admitted familiarity was strictly less than the number of people in the part of G_1 corresponding to the semester. Moreover, the number of people who answered that used HAHA was exactly equal to the number of people who returned homework written in HAHA. Therefore, we can conclude that the number of people who used HAHA in G_0 was marginal.

4   Related Work

The limited space does not make it possible to give an overview of all program verification tools. We focus here on those with reported applications in teaching.

KeY-Hoare [6] is a tool that serves purposes very similar to HAHA. It uses a variant of Hoare logic with explicit state updates which allows one to reason about correctness of a program by means of symbolic forward execution. In contrast, the assignment rule in more traditional Hoare logics requires backwards reasoning, which can be argued to be less natural and harder to learn. Implementation of the system is based on a modification of the KeY [3] tool.

Why3 [4,14] is a platform for deductive program verification based on the WhyML language. It allows computed verification conditions to be processed using a variety of provers, including SMT solvers and Coq. WhyML serves as an intermediate language in verifiers for C [5,8], Ada [22] and Java. It has also been used in a few courses on formal verification and certified program construction.

Another tool used in education that must be mentioned here is Dafny [24]. It can be used to verify functional correctness and termination of sequential, imperative programs with some advanced constructs, such as classes and frame conditions. Input programs are translated to language of the Boogie verifier, which uses Z3 to automatically discharge proof obligations.

Some courses on formal semantics and verification use the Coq proof assistant as a teaching aid [28,16]. Reported results of this approach are quite promising, but the inherent complexity of a general purpose proof assistant appears to be a major obstacle [28]. One method that has been proposed to alleviate this issue is to use Coq as a basis of multiple lectures on subjects ranging from basic propositional logic to Hoare logic [16]. In this way the overhead necessary to learn to effectively use Coq or a similar tool becomes less prominent.

The complexity of general purpose provers is often a troublesome issue in education. One can attempt to resolve this problem by creating tools tailored to specific applications, which sacrifice generality for ease of use. One example of such a system is SASyLF [1], which is a proof assistant used for teaching language theory. Another program worth mentioning here is CalcCheck [21]. It is used to check validity of calculational proofs in the style of a popular textbook [15]. This approach is very similar to what we advocate for teaching Hoare logic, as it employs a tool created to fit the style of existing educational material.

5   Conclusions and Further Work

We have implemented a tool to support instruction of Hoare logic to students. This tool resides in a mainstream software development environment Eclipse, which can give the impression to students that the technique matches contemporary trends in software development tools. It turns out that students instructed with this tool improved their scores in statistically significant way.

As the design of HAHA assumes it can be adapted to other curricula, we invite everybody to consider its adaptation to their teaching needs. The tool is released with a flexible open-source licence (EPL) that makes this available.

This tool can also be used to teach advanced formal verification methods. In fact, the experience of implementation of an existing verification method can give the students the real working understanding of similar methods. HAHA can serve as a platform to assign such a development task.

There are still many ways this endeavour could be extended. The presentation of counterexamples can be enhanced in various ways. Additional different verification condition generation procedures could open the tool for different settings, for instance as an aid in instruction of first-year students where forcing them to write machine checkable loop invariants can improve their command of programming. It would also be convenient to enable execution of edited programs and their debugging as in GNATprove [23].

Acknowledgement. We would like to thank Prof. Andrzej Tarlecki for encouragement in development of HAHA and for letting us make our study in the course of his lecture. This study would be impossible without tutoring of Bartek Klin who kindly agreed to instruct students with HAHA. We also thank Ewa Madalińska-Bugaj for preparation of assignment problems and grading them.

References

1. Aldrich, J., Simmons, R.J., Shin, K.: SASyLF: an educational proof assistant for language theory. In: Proceedings of the 2008 International Workshop on Functional and Declarative Programming in Education, pp. 31–40. ACM (2008)
2. Barrett, C., Conway, C.L., Deters, M., Hadarean, L., Jovanović, D., King, T., Reynolds, A., Tinelli, C.: CVC4. In: Gopalakrishnan, G., Qadeer, S. (eds.) CAV 2011. LNCS, vol. 6806, pp. 171–177. Springer, Heidelberg (2011)
3. Beckert, B., Hähnle, R., Schmitt, P.H. (eds.): Verification of Object-Oriented Software. LNCS (LNAI), vol. 4334. Springer, Heidelberg (2007)
4. Bobot, F., Filliâtre, J.-C., Marché, C., Paskevich, A.: Why3: Shepherd your herd of provers. In: Boogie 2011: First International Workshop on Intermediate Verification Languages, pp. 53–64 (2011)
5. Boldo, S., Marché, C.: Formal verification of numerical programs: From C annotated programs to mechanical proofs. Mathematics in Computer Science 5(4), 377–393 (2011)
6. Bubel, R., Hähnle, R.: A Hoare-style calculus with explicit state updates. In: Instenes, Z. (ed.) Proc. of Formal Methods in Computer Science Education (FORMED). ENTCS, pp. 49–60. Elsevier (2008)
7. Cok, D.R., Kiniry, J.R.: ESC/Java2: Uniting ESC/Java and JML: Progress and issues in building and using ESC/Java2, including a case study involving the use of the tool to verify portions of an Internet voting tally system. In: Barthe, G., Burdy, L., Huisman, M., Lanet, J.-L., Muntean, T. (eds.) CASSIS 2004. LNCS, vol. 3362, pp. 108–128. Springer, Heidelberg (2005)
8. Cuoq, P., Kirchner, F., Kosmatov, N., Prevosto, V., Signoles, J., Yakobowski, B.: Frama-C - A software analysis perspective. In: Eleftherakis, G., Hinchey, M., Holcombe, M. (eds.) SEFM 2012. LNCS, vol. 7504, pp. 233–247. Springer, Heidelberg (2012)
9. Dahlweid, M., Moskal, M., Santen, T., Tobies, S., Schulte, W.: VCC: Contract-based modular verification of concurrent C. In: ICSE Companion, pp. 429–430. IEEE (2009)

10. de Moura, L., Bjørner, N.: Z3: An efficient SMT solver. In: Ramakrishnan, C.R., Rehof, J. (eds.) TACAS 2008. LNCS, vol. 4963, pp. 337–340. Springer, Heidelberg (2008)
11. Dijkstra, E.W.: A Discipline of Programming. Series in Automatic Computation. Prentice-Hall, Englewood Cliffs (1976)
12. Elston, R.C.: On Fisher's method of combining p-values. Biometrical Journal 33(3), 339–345 (1991)
13. Evans Data Corp. Users' Choice: 2011 Software Development Platforms. Evans Data Corp. (2011)
14. Filliâtre, J.-C., Paskevich, A.: Why3 — where programs meet provers. In: Felleisen, M., Gardner, P. (eds.) ESOP 2013. LNCS, vol. 7792, pp. 125–128. Springer, Heidelberg (2013)
15. Gries, D., Schneider, F.B.: A logical approach to discrete math. Springer, New York (1993)
16. Henz, M., Hobor, A.: Teaching experience: Logic and formal methods with Coq. In: Jouannaud, J.-P., Shao, Z. (eds.) CPP 2011. LNCS, vol. 7086, pp. 199–215. Springer, Heidelberg (2011)
17. Hothorn, T., Hornik, K., van de Wiel, M.A., Zeileis, A.: Implementing a class of permutation tests: The coin package. Journal of Statistical Software 28(8) (2008)
18. Hothorn, T., Hornik, K., van de Wiel, M.A., Zeileis, A.: Package 'coin': Conditional Inference Procedures in a Permutation Test Framework. In: CRAN (2013)
19. Jacobs, B., Smans, J., Philippaerts, P., Vogels, F., Penninckx, W., Piessens, F.: Verifast: A powerful, sound, predictable, fast verifier for C and Java. In: Bobaru, M., Havelund, K., Holzmann, G.J., Joshi, R. (eds.) NFM 2011. LNCS, vol. 6617, pp. 41–55. Springer, Heidelberg (2011)
20. Johnson, B., Yoonki, S., Murphy-Hill, E., Bowdidge, R.: Why don't software developers use static analysis tools to find bugs? In: Proc. of ICSE 2013, pp. 672–681. IEEE (2013)
21. Kahl, W.: The teaching tool CalcCheck a proof-checker for Gries and Schneider's "logical approach to discrete math". In: Jouannaud, J.-P., Shao, Z. (eds.) CPP 2011. LNCS, vol. 7086, pp. 216–230. Springer, Heidelberg (2011)
22. Kanig, J.: Leading-edge ada verification technologies: combining testing and verification with GNATTest and GNATProve – the Hi-Lite project. In: Proceedings of the 2012 ACM Conference on High Integrity Language Technology, pp. 5–6. ACM (2012)
23. Kanig, J., Schonberg, E., Dross, C.: Hi-lite: the convergence of compiler technology and program verification. In: Proceedings of the 2012 ACM Conference on High Integrity Language Technology, pp. 27–34. ACM, New York (2012)
24. Leino, K.R.M.: Dafny: An automatic program verifier for functional correctness. In: Clarke, E.M., Voronkov, A. (eds.) LPAR-16 2010. LNCS (LNAI), vol. 6355, pp. 348–370. Springer, Heidelberg (2010)
25. Leino, K.R.M., Nelson, G., Saxe, J.B.: ESC/Java user's manual. Technical note, Compaq Systems Research Center (October 2000)
26. Lipták, T.: On the combination of independent tests. Magyar Tud Akad Mat Kutato Int Közl 3, 171–196 (1958)
27. Meyer, B.: Applying "Design by Contract". IEEE Computer 25(10), 40–51 (1992)
28. Pierce, B.C.: Lambda, the ultimate TA: using a proof assistant to teach programming language foundations. In: Proc. of ICFP, pp. 121–122 (2009)
29. Stępień, A., Kośla, K., Krysiak-Klejnberg, M., Kudelska, A.: USOSweb enrolling direct enrollment in groups. Technical report, University of Warsaw (2008)
30. Trierweiler, S.J., Stricker, G.: The Scientific Practice of Professional Psychology. Springer (1998)

A Two-Phase Static Analysis
for Reliable Adaptation[*]

Pierpaolo Degano, Gian-Luigi Ferrari, and Letterio Galletta

Dipartimento di Informatica, Università di Pisa, Pisa, Italy
{degano,giangi,galletta}@di.unipi.it

Abstract. Adaptive systems are designed to modify their behaviour in response to changes of their operational environment. We adopt a language-based approach to the development of such systems, with particular attention to preventing them from failures in adaptation. The kernel of our proposal is a simple core language, equipped with a type and effect system that computes a sound approximation of program behaviour. The effect is exploited at loading time to verify that programs correctly adapt themselves to all possible running environments.

1 Introduction

Adaptive software is designed and programmed to dynamically adjust its behaviour in order to respond to specific features or to changes of its execution environment, and never fail. The development of adaptive systems requires a variety of new design and programming abilities, and it often involves cross-environment actions using different collections of hardware and software resources. This issue has been investigated from different perspectives (control theory, artificial intelligence, programming languages) and several proposals have been put forward; for a survey, see [22,14]. A main question is about which features are needed to make a program aware of its running environment, and able to efficiently adapt.

Typically, an adaptive system is made up of a massive number of interacting components. Each component must keep consistent its overall structure and its own private resources, after the adaptation steps. Recent work extend standard model-checking techniques to guarantee that both functional and non-functional requirements are preserved. E.g., the logic LTL has been suitably extended for specifying and verifying *transitional properties* which hold during adaptation [25]; also, a quantitative model-checking is proposed in [10] to support verification of parametric models at runtime. Verification can be made more effective if systems are programmed with an ad hoc language, with high-level constructs for expressing adaptation patterns. Indeed, the provided linguistic abstractions impose a good practice to programmers, with a positive fallout on correctness and modularity, mainly because low level details are masked.

We follow this line of research and we propose the core of a programming language, called ML_{CoDa}, specifically designed for adaptation. Also, we endow

---

[*] Work partially supported by the MIUR-PRIN project *Security Horizons*.

D. Giannakopoulou and G. Salaün (Eds.): SEFM 2014, LNCS 8702, pp. 347–362, 2014.
© Springer International Publishing Switzerland 2014

it with a static analysis guaranteeing programs to be always able to adapt in every working environment, which is crucial for proving transitional properties.

Our static analysis is carried out in two phases: a type and effect system (at compile time) and a control flow analysis (at loading time). While type-checking we also compute an abstraction over-approximating the capabilities that must be offered at runtime by the various environments that will host the program. When entering in a new context, before running the program this abstraction is exploited to check that no failure will arise because the actual hosting environment lacks a required capability.

Below, we introduce the main features of the language and of our static analysis. Then Section 2 briefly presents the dynamic semantics of ML_{CoDa}. Sections 3 and 4 introduce our type and effect system, and our loading time analysis. Section 5 discusses related work and future work. All the proofs of our results and some additional technical details are in [11].

The language design. The notion of *context* is fundamental for adaptive software. It includes any kind of computationally accessible information coming both from outside (e.g., sensor values, available devices, code libraries etc. offered by the environment), and from inside the application boundaries (e.g., its private resources, user profiles, etc.). There have been different proposals to include the notion of context inside programming languages. Context-Oriented Programming (COP) [9] is one among the most successful approaches. It extends standard programming languages with suitable constructs to express context-dependent behaviour in a modular fashion; there basic ones are *behavioural variations* and *layers*. A behavioural variation is a chunk of code that can be activated depending on information picked up from the context, so to dynamically modify the execution. A layer is an elementary property of the context, that can be activated/deactivated at runtime. A set of active layers specify the context. Usually, behavioural variations are bound to layers: activating/deactivating a layer corresponds to activating/deactivating the corresponding behavioural variation.

The kernel of our proposal is ML_{CoDa}, a core of ML with COP features. Its main novelty is to be a two-component language: a declarative constituent for programming the context and a functional one for computing (see [11] for more details and for an applicative scenario). We emphasise that the nature of the context requires customised abstractions for its description, that are different from those used for programming applications. This observation, together with separation of concerns, motivated us to define the language with a bipartite structure, one for the context and one for applications.

Our context is a Datalog knowledge base [20,16]. Adaptive programs can therefore query the context by simply verifying whether a given property holds in it, in spite of the complex deductions that this may require.

As for programming adaptation, we propose two mechanisms. The first one is *context-dependent binding* that allows program variables to assume different values depending on the properties of the context; so our programs are widely open. The second mechanism extends *behavioural variations*. Usually, these are not first class objects in COP languages, rather they are expressed as partial definitions of procedures or classes or methods or modules, see e.g. [9]. Instead, in ML_{CoDa} behavioural variations are first class, so they can be referred to by identifiers, and passed as arguments to, and returned by functions. Since a behavioural variation is a value, it can be supplied by the context and composed with existing ones. This facilitates programming dynamic adaptation patterns, as well as reusable and modular code.

Despite the bipartite nature of ML_{CoDa} we avoid the impedance mismatch [17], i.e. the problem of representing data in the context differently from the application, because the two components of the language share the same type system (see Section 3).

We assume that the virtual machine of the language provides its users with a collection of system variables, values, functions and predicates through a predefined API. Consequently, the programmer can exploit data, functions and pieces of the context supplied by the virtual machine. Obviously, the actual values returned by the API are only available at runtime.

We devise an execution model where the compiler produces a triple (C, e, H), where C is the application context, e is the program object code and H is an approximation of e, used to verify properties about the program. Given such a triple, at loading-time the virtual machine performs a *linking* and a *verification* phase. The linking phase resolves system variables and links the application context to the system one, so obtaining the initial context that, of course, is checked for consistency. In the spirit of Proof-Carrying code [19] and of the Java Bytecode Verifier [21], the verification phase exploits the approximation H to check that the program e will adapt to *all* the changes in the operating contexts that may occur at runtime. In this simple model, if both phases succeed program evaluation begins, otherwise it is aborted.

2   The Dynamic Semantics of ML_{CoDa}

We briefly define the syntax and the operational semantics of ML_{CoDa}, concentrating on the new constructs, the others being standard.

Syntax. ML_{CoDa} consists of two sub-languages: a Datalog with negation to describe the context and a core ML extended with COP features.

The Datalog part is standard: a program is a set of facts and clauses. We assume that each program is safe [6]; to deal with negation, we adopt *Stratified Datalog* under the Closed World Assumption.

The functional part inherits most of the ML constructs. In addition to the usual ones, our values include Datalog facts F and behavioural variations. Also, we introduce the set $\tilde{x} \in DynVar$ of *parameters*, i.e., variables assuming values depending on the properties of the running context, while $x, f \in Var$ are standard identifiers, disjoint from parameters. Our COP constructs include behavioural variations $(x)\{Va\}$, each consisting of a variation Va, i.e. a list $G_1.e_1, \ldots, G_n.e_n$ of expressions e_i guarded by Datalog goals G_i (x possibly free in e_i). At runtime, the first goal G_i satisfied by the context determines the

(TELL2)

$$\rho \vdash C, tell(F) \rightarrow C \cup \{F\}, ()$$

(RETRACT2)

$$\rho \vdash C, retract(F) \rightarrow C \backslash \{F\}, ()$$

(DLET1)

$$\frac{\rho[(G.e_1, \rho(\tilde{x}))/\tilde{x}] \vdash C, e_2 \rightarrow C', e_2'}{\rho \vdash C, dlet\, \tilde{x} = e_1\, when\, G\, in\, e_2 \rightarrow C', dlet\, \tilde{x} = e_1\, when\, G\, in\, e_2'}$$

(DLET2)

$$\rho \vdash C, dlet\, \tilde{x} = e_1\, when\, G\, in\, v \rightarrow C, v$$

(PAR)

$$\frac{\rho(\tilde{x}) = Va \qquad dsp(C, Va) = (e, \theta)}{\rho \vdash C, \tilde{x} \rightarrow C, e\,\theta}$$

(APPEND3)

$$\rho \vdash C, (x)\{Va_1\} \cup (y)\{Va_2\} \rightarrow C, (z)\{Va_1\{z/x\}, Va_2\{z/y\}\} \qquad z\ \text{fresh}$$

(VAAPP3)

$$\frac{dsp(C, Va) = (e, \{\overrightarrow{c}/\overrightarrow{y}\})}{\rho \vdash C, \#((x)\{Va\}, v) \rightarrow C, e\{v/x, \overrightarrow{c}/\overrightarrow{y}\}}$$

Fig. 1. The reduction rules for new constructs of ML_{CoDa}

expression e_i to be selected (*dispatching*). The *dlet* construct implements the context-dependent binding of a parameter $\tilde{x}$ to a variation Va. The *tell/retract* constructs update the context by asserting/retracting facts. The append operator $e_1 \cup e_2$ concatenates behavioural variations, so allowing for dynamic compositions. The application of a behavioural variation $\#(e_1, e_2)$ applies e_1 to its argument e_2. To do so, the dispatching mechanism is triggered to query the context and to select from e_1 the expression to run, if any. The syntax follows:

$$Va ::= G.e \mid G.e, Va$$
$$v ::= c \mid \lambda_f x.e \mid (x)\{Va\} \mid F$$
$$e ::= v \mid x \mid \tilde{x} \mid e_1 e_2 \mid let\, x = e_1\, in\, e_2 \mid if\, e_1\, then\, e_2\, else\, e_3 \mid$$
$$dlet\, \tilde{x} = e_1\, when\, G\, in\, e_2 \mid tell(e_1) \mid retract(e_1) \mid e_1 \cup e_2 \mid \#(e_1, e_2)$$

Semantics. For the Datalog evaluation we adopt the top-down standard semantics for stratified programs [6]. Given a context $C \in Context$ and a goal G, $C \vDash G\, with\, \theta$ means that the goal G, under the substitution θ replacing constants for variables, is satisfied in the context C.

The small-step operational semantics of ML_{CoDa} is defined for expressions with no free variable, but possibly with free parameters, allowing for openness. For that, we have an environment $\rho: DynVar \rightarrow Va$, mapping parameters to variations. A transition $\rho \vdash C, e \rightarrow C', e'$ says that in the environment ρ, the expression e is evaluated in the context C and reduces to e' changing C to C'. We assume that the initial configuration is $\rho_0 \vdash C, e_p$ where ρ_0 contains the bindings for all system parameters, and C results from linking the system and the application contexts.

Fig. 1 shows the inductive definitions of the reduction rules for our new constructs; the other ones are standard, and such are the congruence rules that reduce subexpressions, e.g. $\rho \vdash C, tell(e) \rightarrow C', tell(e')$ if $\rho \vdash C, e \rightarrow C', e'$. See [11] for full definitions. We briefly comment below on the rules displayed.

The rule for $tell(e)/retract(e)$ evaluates the expression e until it reduces to a fact F, which is a value of ML_{CoDa}. Then, the evaluation yields the unit value $()$ and a new context C', obtained from C by adding/removing F. The following example shows the reduction of a *tell* construct, where we apply the function $f = \lambda x.\,if\,e_1\,then\,F_2\,else\,F_3$ to unit, assuming that e_1 reduces to false without changing the context:

$$\rho \vdash C, \texttt{tell}(\texttt{f}\,()) \rightarrow^* C, \texttt{tell}(\mathsf{F_3}) \rightarrow C \cup \{\mathsf{F_3}\}, ()$$

The rules (DLET1) and (DLET2) for the construct *dlet*, and the rule (PAR) for parameters implement our context-dependent binding. To simplify the technical development we assume here that e_1 contains no parameters. The rule (DLET1) extends the environment ρ by appending $G.e_1$ in front of the existent binding for $\tilde{x}$. Then, e_2 is evaluated under the updated environment. Notice that the *dlet* does *not* evaluate e_1 but only records it in the environment. The rule (DLET2) is standard: the whole *dlet* yields the value which eventually e_2 reduces to.

The (PAR) rule looks for the variation Va bound to $\tilde{x}$ in ρ. Then the dispatching mechanism selects the expression to which $\tilde{x}$ reduces. It is defined as the partial function dsp:

$$dsp(C, (G.e, Va)) = \begin{cases} (e, \theta) & \text{if } C \vDash G \, with \, \theta \\ dsp(C, Va) & \text{otherwise} \end{cases}$$

A variation is inspected from left to right to find the first goal G satisfied by C, under a substitution θ. If this search succeeds, the dispatching returns the corresponding expression e and θ. Then $\tilde{x}$ reduces to $e\,\theta$, i.e. to e whose variables are bound by θ. Instead, if the dispatching fails because no goal holds, the computation gets stuck since the program cannot adapt to the current context. Our static analysis is designed to prevent this kind of runtime errors.

As an example of context-dependent binding consider the expression $\texttt{tell}(\tilde{x})$, in an environment ρ that binds the parameter $\tilde{x}$ to $e' = \mathsf{G_1.F_5}, \mathsf{G_2.f}\,()$ ($\texttt{f}$ is defined above) and in a context C that satisfies the goal G_2 but not G_1:

$$\rho \vdash C, \texttt{tell}(\tilde{x}) \rightarrow C, \texttt{tell}(\texttt{f}\,()) \rightarrow^* C, \texttt{tell}(\mathsf{F_3}) \rightarrow C \cup \{\mathsf{F_3}\}, ()$$

In the first step, we retrieve the binding for $\tilde{x}$ (recall it is e'), where $dsp(C, e') = dsp(C, \mathsf{G_1.F_5}, \mathsf{G_2.f}\,()) = (\texttt{f}\,(), \theta)$, for a suitable substitution θ.

The rules for $e_1 \cup e_2$ sequentially evaluate e_1 and e_2 until they reduce to behavioural variations. Then, they are concatenated (bound variables are renamed to avoid name captures, see rule (APPEND3)). As an example of concatenation, let T be the goal always true, and consider the function $d = \lambda x.\lambda y.\, x \cup (w)\{\mathsf{T}.y\}$.

$$\overline{C, \epsilon \cdot H \to C, H} \qquad \overline{C, tell\, F \to C \cup \{F\}, \epsilon} \qquad \overline{C, retract\, F \to C \backslash \{F\}, \epsilon}$$

$$\frac{C, H_1 \to C', H_1'}{C, H_1 + H_2 \to C', H_1'} \qquad \frac{C, H_2 \to C', H_2'}{C, H_1 + H_2 \to C', H_2'} \qquad \frac{C, H_1 \to C', H_1'}{C, H_1 \cdot H_2 \to C', H_1' \cdot H_2}$$

$$\overline{C, \mu h.H \to C, H[\mu h.H/h]} \qquad \frac{C \vDash G}{C, ask\, G.H \otimes \Delta \to C, H} \qquad \frac{C \nvDash G}{C, ask\, G.H \otimes \Delta \to C, \Delta}$$

Fig. 2. Semantics of History Expressions

It takes as arguments a behavioural variation x and a value y, and extends x by adding a default case which is always selected when no other case apply. (Note in passing that this way of "extending" programs may require an intricate definition with standard COP features [9].) In the following computation we apply d to $p = (x)\{G_1.c_1, G_2.x\}$ and to c_2 (c_1, c_2 constants):

$$\rho \vdash C, d\, p\, c_2 \;\to\; C, (x)\{G_1.c_1, G_2.x\} \cup (w)\{T.c_2\} \;\to\; C, (z)\{G_1.c_1, G_2.z, T.c_2\}$$

The behavioural variation application $\#(e_1, e_2)$ evaluates the subexpressions until e_1 reduces to $(x)\{V a\}$ and e_2 to a value v. Then the rule (VaApp3) invokes the dispatching mechanism to select the relevant expression e from which the computation proceeds after v replaced x. Also in this case the computation gets stuck if the dispatching mechanism fails. As an example, consider the above behavioural variation p and apply it to the constant c in a context C that satisfies the goal G_2 but not G_1. Since $dsp(C, p) = dsp(C, (x)\{G_1.c_1, G_2.x\}) = (x, \theta)$ for some substitution θ, we get

$$\rho \vdash C, \#((x)\{G_1.c_1, G_2.x\}, c) \;\to\; C, c$$

3   Type and Effect System

We now associate $\mathrm{ML_{CoDa}}$ expressions with a type and an abstraction H, called *history expression*. During the verification phase the virtual machine uses H to ensure that the dispatching mechanism will always succeed at runtime. First, we define History Expressions and then the rules of our type and effect system.

History Expressions. A history expression is a term of a simple process algebra that soundly abstracts program behaviour [4]. Here, it approximates the sequence of actions that a program may perform over the context at runtime, i.e., asserting/retracting facts and asking if a goal holds. The syntax follows

$$H ::= \epsilon \mid h \mid \mu h.H \mid tell\, F \mid retract\, F \mid H_1 + H_2 \mid H_1 \cdot H_2 \mid \Delta$$
$$\Delta ::= ask\, G.H \otimes \Delta \mid fail$$

The empty history expression ϵ abstracts programs which do not interact with the context; $\mu h.H$ represents possibly recursive functions, where h is the recursion variable; the "atomic" history expressions $tell\,F$ and $retract\,F$ are for the analogous expressions of $\mathrm{ML_{CoDa}}$; the non-deterministic sum $H_1 + H_2$ stands for the conditional expression $if\text{-}then\text{-}else$; the concatenation $H_1 \cdot H_2$ is for sequences of actions, that arise, e.g., while evaluating applications; Δ is an *abstract variation*, that mimics our dispatching mechanism and is defined as a list of history expressions H_i, each guarded by an $ask\,G_i$.

Given a context C, the behaviour of a history expression H is formalized by the transition system inductively defined in Fig. 2. Transitions $C, H \rightarrow C', H'$ formalize that H reduces to H' in C yielding C'. Most rules are standard in process algebras, so we only comment on those dealing with the context.

An action $tell\,F$ reduces to ϵ and yields a context C' where the fact F has just been added; similarly for $retract\,F$. The rules for abstract variation scan it and look for the first goal G satisfied in the current context; if this search succeeds, Δ reduces to the history expression H guarded by G; otherwise the search continues on the rest of Δ. If no satisfiable goal exists, the stuck configuration $fail$ is reached, representing that the dispatching mechanism fails.

Typing rules. Here we only give a logical presentation of our type and effect system, and we omit its two-step inference algorithm. We assume that our Datalog is typed, i.e. each predicate has a fixed arity and a type. Many papers exist on this topic, and we can follow, e.g., a light version of [18]. From here onwards, we simply assume that there exists a Datalog typing function γ that given a goal G returns a list of pairs $(x, \text{type-of-}x)$, for all the variables x of G.

The rules of our type and effect systems have the usual type environment Γ binding the variables of an expression:

$$\Gamma ::= \emptyset \mid \Gamma, x : \tau$$

where $\emptyset$ denotes the empty environment and $\Gamma, x : \tau$ denotes an environment having a binding for the variable x (x does not occur in Γ).

In addition, we introduce the parameter environment K that maps a parameter $\tilde{x}$ to a pair consisting of a type and an abstract variation Δ. The information in Δ is used to resolve the binding for $\tilde{x}$ at runtime. Formally:

$$K ::= \emptyset \mid K, (\tilde{x}, \tau, \Delta)$$

where $\emptyset$ is the empty environment and $K, (\tilde{x}, \tau, \Delta)$ has a binding for the parameter $\tilde{x}$ ($\tilde{x}$ not in K).

Our typing judgements have the form $\Gamma; K \vdash e : \tau \triangleright H$, expressing that in the environments Γ and K the expression e has type τ and effect H.

The syntax of types is

$$\tau ::- \tau_c \mid \tau_1 \xrightarrow{K|H} \tau_2 \mid \tau_1 \xRightarrow{K|\Delta} \tau_2 \mid fact_\phi \qquad \phi \in \wp(Fact)$$

We have basic types $\tau_c \in \{int, bool, unit, \ldots\}$, functional types, behavioural variation types, and facts. Some types are annotated for analysis reason. In the type

(SREFL)
$$\frac{}{\tau \leq \tau}$$

(SFACT)
$$\frac{\phi \subseteq \phi'}{fact_{\phi} \leq fact_{\phi'}}$$

(SFUN)
$$\frac{\tau_1' \leq \tau_1 \qquad \tau_2 \leq \tau_2' \qquad K \sqsubseteq K' \qquad H \sqsubseteq H'}{\tau_1 \xrightarrow{K|H} \tau_2 \leq \tau_1' \xrightarrow{K'|H'} \tau_2'}$$

(SVA)
$$\frac{\tau_1' \leq \tau_1 \qquad \tau_2 \leq \tau_2' \qquad K \sqsubseteq K' \qquad \Delta \sqsubseteq \Delta'}{\tau_1 \xRightarrow{K|\Delta} \tau_2 \leq \tau_1' \xRightarrow{K'|\Delta'} \tau_2'}$$

(TSUB)
$$\frac{\Gamma; K \vdash e \,:\, \tau' \triangleright H' \qquad \tau' \leq \tau \quad H' \sqsubseteq H}{\Gamma; K \vdash e \,:\, \tau \triangleright H}$$

(TFACT)
$$\frac{}{\Gamma; K \vdash F \,:\, fact_{\{F\}} \triangleright \epsilon}$$

(TTELL)
$$\frac{\Gamma; K \vdash e \,:\, fact_{\phi} \triangleright H}{\Gamma; K \vdash tell(e) \,:\, unit \triangleright H \cdot \left(\sum_{F \in \phi} tell\, F \right)}$$

(TRETRACT)
$$\frac{\Gamma; K \vdash e \,:\, fact_{\phi} \triangleright H}{\Gamma; K \vdash retract(e) \,:\, unit \triangleright H \cdot \left(\sum_{F \in \phi} retract\, F \right)}$$

(TPAR)
$$\frac{K(\tilde{x}) = (\tau, \Delta)}{\Gamma; K \vdash \tilde{x} \,:\, \tau \triangleright \Delta}$$

(TVARIATION)
$$\frac{\begin{array}{c}\forall i \in \{1, \ldots, n\} \qquad \gamma(G_i) = \overrightarrow{y_i} \,:\, \overrightarrow{\tau_i} \qquad \Gamma, x : \tau_1, \overrightarrow{y_i} \,:\, \overrightarrow{\tau_i}; K' \vdash e_i \,:\, \tau_2 \triangleright H_i \\ \Delta = ask\, G_1.H_1 \otimes \cdots \otimes ask\, G_n.H_n \otimes fail\end{array}}{\Gamma; K \vdash (x)\{G_1.e_1, \ldots, G_n.e_n\} \,:\, \tau_1 \xRightarrow{K'|\Delta} \tau_2 \triangleright \epsilon}$$

(TVAPP)
$$\frac{\Gamma; K \vdash e_1 \,:\, \tau_1 \xRightarrow{K'|\Delta} \tau_2 \triangleright H_1 \qquad \Gamma; K \vdash e_2 \,:\, \tau_1 \triangleright H_2 \qquad K' \sqsubseteq K}{\Gamma; K \vdash \#(e_1, e_2) \,:\, \tau_2 \triangleright H_1 \cdot H_2 \cdot \Delta}$$

(TAPPEND)
$$\frac{\Gamma; K \vdash e_1 \,:\, \tau_1 \xRightarrow{K'|\Delta_1} \tau_2 \triangleright H_1 \qquad \Gamma; K \vdash e_2 \,:\, \tau_1 \xRightarrow{K'|\Delta_2} \tau_2 \triangleright H_2}{\Gamma; K \vdash e_1 \cup e_2 \,:\, \tau_1 \xRightarrow{K'|\Delta_1 \otimes \Delta_2} \tau_2 \triangleright H_1 \cdot H_2}$$

(TDLET)
$$\frac{\Gamma, \overrightarrow{y} \,:\, \overrightarrow{\tau}; K \vdash e_1 \,:\, \tau_1 \triangleright H_1 \qquad \Gamma; K, (\tilde{x}, \tau_1, \Delta') \vdash e_2 \,:\, \tau_2 \triangleright H_2}{\Gamma; K \vdash dlet\, \tilde{x} = e_1\, when\, G\, in\, e_2 \,:\, \tau_2 \triangleright H_2}$$

where $\gamma(G) = \overrightarrow{y} : \overrightarrow{\tau}$
if $K(\tilde{x}) = (\tau_1, \Delta)$ then $\Delta' = G.H_1 \otimes \Delta$
else (if $\tilde{x} \notin K$ then $\Delta' = G.H_1 \otimes fail$)

Fig. 3. Typing rules for new constructs

$fact_\phi$, the set ϕ soundly contains the facts that an expression can be reduced to at runtime (see the rules of the semantics (TELL2) and (RETRACT2)). In the type $\tau_1 \xrightarrow{K|H} \tau_2$ associated with a function f, the environment K is a precondition needed to apply f. Here, K stores the types and the abstract variations of parameters occurring inside the body of f. The history expression H is the latent effect of f, i.e. the sequence of actions which may be performed over the context while evaluating the function. Analogously, in the type $\tau_1 \xrightarrow{K|\Delta} \tau_2$ associated with the behavioural variation $bv = (x)\{Va\}$, K is a precondition for applying bv, and Δ is an abstract variation representing the information that the dispatching mechanism uses at runtime to apply bv.

We now introduce the orderings $\sqsubseteq_H, \sqsubseteq_\Delta, \sqsubseteq_K$ on H, Δ and K, respectively (often omitting the indexes when unambiguous). We define $H_1 \sqsubseteq H_2$ iff $\exists H_3$ such that $H_2 = H_1 + H_3$; $\Delta_1 \sqsubseteq \Delta_2$ iff $\exists \Delta_3$ such that $\Delta_2 = \Delta_1 \otimes \Delta_3$ (note that Δ_2 has a single trailing term $fail$); $K_1 \sqsubseteq K_2$ iff ($(\tilde{x}, \tau_1, \Delta_1) \in K_1$ implies $(\tilde{x}, \tau_2, \Delta_2) \in K_2 \wedge \tau_1 \leq \tau_2 \wedge \Delta_1 \sqsubseteq \Delta_2$), where $\tau_1 \leq \tau_2$ is defined in Fig. 3.

Fig. 3 shows the typing rules for the new constructs, omitting the standard ML ones. A few comments are in order.

The rules for subtyping and subeffecting are at top of Fig. 3. As expected they say that subtyping relation is reflexive (rule (SREFL)); a type $fact_\phi$ is a subtype of a type $fact_{\phi'}$ if $\phi \subseteq \phi'$ (rule (SFACT)); functional types are contravariant in the types of arguments and covariant in the result type and in the annotations (rule (SFUN)); analogously for behavioural variations types (rule (SVA)). The rule (TSUB) allows us to freely enlarge types and effects by applying the rules above.

The rule (TFACT) says that a fact F has type $fact$ annotated with the singleton $\{F\}$ and empty effect. The rule (TTELL)/(TRETRACT) asserts that the expression $tell(e)/retract(e)$ has type $unit$, provided that the type of e is $fact_\phi$. The overall effect is obtained by concatenating the effect of e with the nondeterministic summation of $tell\,F/retract\,F$ where F is any of the facts in the type of e. For example, consider the function $\mathtt{f} = \lambda\mathtt{x}.\,\mathtt{if}\,\mathtt{e_1}\,\mathtt{then}\,\mathtt{F_2}\,\mathtt{else}\,\mathtt{F_3}$ that returns either fact $\mathtt{F_2}$ or $\mathtt{F_3}$. Let H be the latent effect of f, then $f() : fact_{\{F_2, F_3\}} \triangleright H$, and the overall type of $\mathtt{tell}(f())$ will be $unit$ and its effect $H \cdot (tell\,F_2 + tell\,F_3)$.

Rule (TPAR) looks for the type and the effect of the parameter $\tilde{x}$ in the environment K. The rule (TDLET) requires that e_1 has type τ_1 in the environment Γ extended with the types for the variables $\overrightarrow{y}$ of the goal G. Also, e_2 has to type-check in an environment K extended with the information for parameter $\tilde{x}$. The type and the effect for the overall $dlet$ expression are the same of e_2.

In the rule (TVARIATION) we guess an environment K' and the type τ_1 for the bound variable x. We determine the type for each subexpression e_i under K' and the environment Γ extended by the type of x and of the variables $\overrightarrow{y_i}$ occurring in the goal G_i (recall that the Datalog typing function γ returns a list $(z, \text{type-of-}z)$ for all variable z of G_i). Note that all subexpressions e_i have the same type τ_2. We also require that the abstract variation Δ results from concatenating $usk\,G_i$ with the effect computed for e_i. The type of the behavioural variation is annotated by K' and Δ. Consider, e.g. the behavioural variation $bv_1 = (x)\{G_1.e_1, G_2.e_2\}$. Assume that the two cases of this behavioural variation have type τ and effects H_1 and H_2, respectively, under $\Gamma, x : int$ (goals have no variables) and the guessed environment K'. Hence, the type of bv_1 will be $int \xrightarrow{K'|\Delta} \tau$ with $\Delta = ask\, G_1.H_1 \otimes ask\, G_2.H_2 \otimes fail$ and the effect empty.

The rule (TVApp) type-checks behavioural variation applications and reveals the role of preconditions. As expected, e_1 is a behavioural variation with parameter of type τ_1 and e_2 has type τ_1. We get a type if the environment K', that acts as a precondition, is included in K according to $\sqsubseteq$. The type of the behavioural variation application is τ_2, i.e. the type of the result of e_1. Its effect is obtained by concatenating the ones of e_1 and e_2 with the history expression Δ, occurring in the annotation of the type of e_1. Consider, e.g. bv_1 above, its type and its empty effect. Assume to type-check $e = \#(bv_1, 10)$ in the environments Γ and K. If $K' \sqsubseteq K$, the type of e is τ and its effect is $\epsilon \cdot \Delta = ask\, G_1.H_1 \otimes ask\, G_2.H_2 \otimes fail$.

The rule (TAppend) asserts that two expressions e_1, e_2 with the same type τ, except for the abstract variations Δ_1, Δ_2 in their annotations, and effects H_1 and H_2, are combined into $e_1 \cup e_2$ with type τ, and concatenated annotations and effects. More precisely, the resulting annotation has the same precondition of e_1 and e_2 and abstract variation $\Delta_1 \otimes \Delta_2$, and effect $H_1 \cdot H_2$. E.g., consider again the above bv_1 and its type $int \xrightarrow{K'|\Delta} \tau$; let $bv_2 = (w)\{G_3.c_2\}$, and let its type be $int \xrightarrow{K'|\Delta'} \tau$ and its effect be H_2. Then the type of $bv_1 \cup bv_2$ is $int \xrightarrow{K'|\Delta \otimes \Delta'} \tau$ and the effect is $\epsilon \cdot H_2 = H_2$.

Our type and effect system is sound with respect to the operational semantics. To concisely state our results, the following definitions are helpful.

Definition 1 (Typing dynamic environment). *Given the type and parameter environments Γ and K, we say that the dynamic environment ρ has type K under Γ (in symbols $\Gamma \vdash \rho : K$) iff $dom(\rho) \subseteq dom(K)$ and $\forall \tilde{x} \in dom(\rho)$. $\rho(x) = G_1.e_1, \ldots, G_n.e_n$ $K(\tilde{x}) = (\tau, \Delta)$ and $\forall i \in \{1, \ldots, n\}$. $\gamma(G_i) = \overrightarrow{y_i} : \overrightarrow{\tau_i}$ $\Gamma, \overrightarrow{y_i} : \overrightarrow{\tau_i}; K \vdash e_i : \tau' \triangleright H_i$ and $\tau' \leq \tau$ and $\bigotimes_{i \in \{1, \ldots, n\}} G_i.H_i \sqsubseteq \Delta$.*

Definition 2. *Given H_1, H_2 then $H_1 \preccurlyeq H_2$ iff one of the following case holds*

(a) $H_1 \sqsubseteq H_2$;   (b) $H_2 = H_3 \cdot H_1$ for some H_3;
(c) $H_2 = \bigotimes_{i \in \{1, \ldots, n\}} ask\, G_i.H_i \otimes fail \,\wedge\, H_1 = H_i, \exists i \in [1..n].$

Intuitively, the above definition formalises the fact that the history expression H_1 could be obtained from H_2 by evaluation.

The soundness of our type and effect system easily derives from the following standard results (the proofs are in [11]).

Theorem 1 (Preservation). *Let e_s be a closed expression; and let ρ be a dynamic environment such that $dom(\rho)$ includes the set of parameters of e_s and such that $\Gamma \vdash \rho : K$. If $\Gamma; K \vdash e_s : \tau \triangleright H_s$ and $\rho \vdash C, e_s \rightarrow C', e'_s$ then $\Gamma; K \vdash e'_s : \tau \triangleright H'_s$ and $\exists \overline{H}$ such that $\overline{H} \cdot H'_s \preccurlyeq H_s$ and $C, \overline{H} \cdot H'_s \rightarrow^* C', H'_s$.*

The Progress Theorem assumes that the effect H is *viable*, namely it does not reach *fail* (i.e. it is not the case that $C, H_s \rightarrow^+ C', fail$), because the dispatching mechanism succeeds at runtime. The control-flow analysis sketched in Section 4 guarantees viability. In the statement of the theorem we write $\rho \vdash C, e \nrightarrow$ to intend that there exists no transition outgoing from C, e, i.e. that e is *stuck*.

Theorem 2 (Progress). *Let e_s be a closed expression such that $\Gamma; K \vdash e_s : \tau \triangleright H_s$; and let ρ be a dynamic environment such that $dom(\rho)$ includes the set of parameters of e_s, and such that $\Gamma \vdash \rho : K$. If $\rho \vdash C, e_s \nrightarrow$ and H is viable for C, then e_s is a value.*

The following proposition ensures that the history expression of e over-approximates the actions that may be performed over the context during the evaluation.

Proposition 1 (Over-approximation). *Let e_s be a closed expression. If $\Gamma; K \vdash e_s : \tau \triangleright H_s \wedge \rho \vdash C, e_s \rightarrow^\star C', e'$, for some ρ such that $\Gamma \vdash \rho : K$, then $\Gamma; K \vdash e' : \tau \triangleright H'$ and there exists a sequence of transitions $C, H_s \rightarrow^\star C', H'$.*

The following theorem ensures the correctness of our approach.

Theorem 3 (Correctness). *Let e_s be a closed expression such that $\Gamma; K \vdash e_s : \tau \triangleright H_s$; let ρ be a dynamic environment such that $dom(\rho)$ includes the set of parameters of e_s, and that $\Gamma \vdash \rho : K$; and let C be a context such that H_s is viable i.e. $C, H_s \nrightarrow^+ C'$, fail. Then either the computation terminates yielding a value ($\rho \vdash C, e_s \rightarrow^\star C'', v$) or it diverges, but it never gets stuck.*

4   A Sketch of the Loading-time Analysis

In this section we illustrate how our loading-time analysis works. As said at the end of Section 1, in the execution model of ML_{CoDa} the compiler produces the triple (C_p, e_p, H_p) made of the application context, the object code and the effect over-approximating the behaviour of the application. Using it, the virtual machine of ML_{CoDa} performs a linking and verification phases at loading time. During the linking phase, system variables are resolved and the initial context C is constructed, combining C_p and the system context. Still, the application is "open" with respect to its parameters. This calls for the verification phase: we verify whether applications adapt to all evolutions of C that may occur at runtime, i.e., that all dispatching invocations will always succeed. Only programs which pass this verification phase will be run. To do that efficiently and to pave the way for checking further properties, we build a graph $\mathcal{G}$ describing the possible evolutions of the initial context, exploiting the history expression H_p.

To support the analysis, we assume to give a distinct label $l \in Lab$ to each subterm of the history expression in hand. A result of the analysis is a pair of functions $\Sigma_\circ, \Sigma_\bullet : Lab \rightarrow \wp(Context \cup \{*\})$ where $*$ is a distinguished context representing a dispatching failure. For each label l, $\Sigma_\circ(l)$ over-approximates the set of contexts that may arise before evaluating H^l (call it *pre-set*); instead $\Sigma_\bullet(l)$ over-approximates the set of contexts that may result from the evaluation of H^l (call it *post-set*). We define the specification of our analysis in the Flow Logic style, through the validity relation

$$\models \subseteq \mathcal{AE} \times \mathbb{H}$$

where $\mathcal{AE} = (Lab \rightarrow \wp(Context \cup \{*\}))^2$ is the domain of the results of the analysis and $\mathbb{H}$ the set of history expressions. We write $(\Sigma_\circ, \Sigma_\bullet) \vDash H^l$, when the pair $\mathcal{E} = (\Sigma_\circ, \Sigma_\bullet)$ is an *acceptable analysis estimate* for the history expression H^l. We only show the most significant inductive rules defining the validity relation:

$$(\text{ATELL}) \quad \frac{\forall C \in \Sigma_\circ(l) \qquad C \cup \{F\} \in \Sigma_\bullet(l)}{(\Sigma_\circ, \Sigma_\bullet) \vDash tell\, F^l}$$

$$(\text{AASK2}) \quad \frac{* \in \Sigma_\bullet(l)}{(\Sigma_\circ, \Sigma_\bullet) \vDash fail^l}$$

$$(\text{AASK1}) \quad \frac{\begin{array}{c} \forall C \in \Sigma_\circ(l) \\ (C \vDash G \implies (\Sigma_\circ, \Sigma_\bullet) \vDash H^{l_1} \qquad \Sigma_\circ(l) \subseteq \Sigma_\circ(l_1) \qquad \Sigma_\bullet(l_1) \subseteq \Sigma_\bullet(l)) \\ (C \nvDash G \implies (\Sigma_\circ, \Sigma_\bullet) \vDash \Delta^{l_2} \qquad \Sigma_\circ(l) \subseteq \Sigma_\circ(l_2) \qquad \Sigma_\bullet(l_2) \subseteq \Sigma_\bullet(l)) \end{array}}{(\Sigma_\circ, \Sigma_\bullet) \vDash (askG.H^{l_1} \otimes \Delta^{l_2})^l}$$

$$(\text{ASEQ1}) \quad \frac{\begin{array}{c} (\Sigma_\circ, \Sigma_\bullet) \vDash H_1^{l_1} \\ (\Sigma_\circ, \Sigma_\bullet) \vDash H_2^{l_2} \qquad \Sigma_\circ(l) \subseteq \Sigma_\circ(l_1) \qquad \Sigma_\bullet(l_1) \subseteq \Sigma_\circ(l_2) \qquad \Sigma_\bullet(l_2) \subseteq \Sigma_\bullet(l) \end{array}}{(\Sigma_\circ, \Sigma_\bullet) \vDash (H_1^{l_1} \cdot H_2^{l_2})^l}$$

$$(\text{AREC}) \quad \frac{(\Sigma_\circ, \Sigma_\bullet) \vDash H^{l_1}}{\Sigma_\circ(l) \subseteq \Sigma_\circ(l_1) \qquad \Sigma_\bullet(l_1) \subseteq \Sigma_\bullet(l)} \over (\Sigma_\circ, \Sigma_\bullet) \vDash (\mu h.H^{l_1})^l}$$

$$(\text{AVAR}) \quad \frac{\mathbb{K}(h) = (\mu h.H^{l_1})^{l'}}{\Sigma_\circ(l) \subseteq \Sigma_\circ(l') \qquad \Sigma_\bullet(l') \subseteq \Sigma_\bullet(l)} \over (\Sigma_\circ, \Sigma_\bullet) \vDash h^l}$$

The rule (ATELL) prescribes that the estimate $\mathcal{E}$ is acceptable if for all context C in the pre-set, the context $C \cup \{F\}/C\backslash\{F\}$ is in the post-set; similarly for *retract*. The rules (AASK1/2) handle the abstract dispatching mechanism. The first states that $\mathcal{E}$ is acceptable for $H = (askG.H_1^{l_1} \otimes \Delta^{l_2})^l$, provided that, for all C in the pre-set of H, if the goal G succeeds in C then the pre-set of H_1 includes that of H and the post-set of H includes that of H_1. Otherwise, the pre-set of Δ^{l_2} must include the one of H and the post-set of Δ^{l_2} is included in that of H. The rule (AASK2) requires $*$ to be in the post-set of $fail$. The rules (ASEQ1/2) handle the sequential composition of history expressions. The first states that $\mathcal{E}$ is acceptable for $H = (H_1^{l_1} \cdot H_2^{l_2})^l$ if it is valid for both H_1 and H_2. Moreover, the pre-set of H_1 must include that of H and the pre-set of H_2 includes the post-set of H_1; finally, the post-set of H includes that of H_2. The rule (ASEQ2) is omitted here an takes care of the sequentialization when H_1 is empty. By the rule (AREC) $\mathcal{E}$ is acceptable for $H = (\mu h.H_1^{l_1})^l$ if it is acceptable for $H_1^{l_1}$ and the pre-set of H_1 includes that of H and the post-set of H includes that of H_1. The rule (AVAR) says that the estimate $\mathcal{E}$ is acceptable for a variable h^l if the pre-set of the history expression introducing h, namely $\mathbb{K}(h)$, is included in that of h^l, and the post-set of h^l includes that of $\mathbb{K}(h)$. We also omit the rule (ASUM) that handles the non-deterministic choice in the obvious way.

By exploiting the result of the analysis, we introduce the notion of *viability*. Intuitively, we say that a history expression is *viable* for a given initial context if the failure context occurs only in the post-set corresponding to $fail$ subterms.

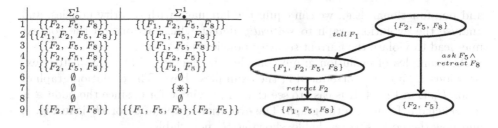

	$\Sigma_\circ^1$	$\Sigma_\bullet^1$
1	$\{\{F_2, F_5, F_8\}\}$	$\{\{F_1, F_2, F_5, F_8\}\}$
2	$\{\{F_1, F_2, F_5, F_8\}\}$	$\{\{F_1, F_5, F_8\}\}$
3	$\{\{F_2, F_5, F_8\}\}$	$\{\{F_1, F_5, F_8\}\}$
4	$\{\{F_2, F_5, F_8\}\}$	$\{\{F_2, F_5\}\}$
5	$\{\{F_2, F_5, F_8\}\}$	$\{\{F_2, F_5\}\}$
6	$\emptyset$	$\emptyset$
7	$\emptyset$	$\{*\}$
8	$\emptyset$	$\emptyset$
9	$\{\{F_2, F_5, F_8\}\}$	$\{\{F_1, F_5, F_8\},\{F_2, F_5\}\}$

Fig. 4. The analysis result (on right) and the evolution graph (on left) for the context $C = \{F_2, F_5, F_8\}$ and the history expression $H_a = ((tell\ F_1^1 \cdot retract\ F_2^2)^3 + (ask\ F_5.retract\ F_8^5 \otimes ask\ F_3.retract\ F_4^6 \otimes fail^7)^4)^8$.

Below we illustrate how viability is checked using a couple of examples. Consider the history expression

$$H_a = ((tell\ F_1^1 \cdot retract\ F_2^2)^3 + (ask\ F_5.retract\ F_8^5 \otimes (ask\ F_3.retract\ F_4^6 \otimes fail^7)^8)^4)^9$$

and the initial context $C = \{F_2, F_5, F_8\}$, consisting of facts only. For each label l occurring in H_a, Fig. 4 shows the corresponding values of $\Sigma_\circ^1(l)$ and $\Sigma_\bullet^1(l)$, respectively. The column describing $\Sigma_\bullet$ contains $*$ only for $l = 7$ which is the label of $fail$, so H_a is viable for C.

Now consider the following history expression that fails to pass the verification phase, when put in the same initial context C used above:

$$H_a' = ((tell\ F_1^1 \cdot retract\ F_2^2)^3 + (ask\ F_3.retract\ F_4^5 \otimes fail^6)^4)^7$$

Indeed H_a' is not viable because the goal F_3 does not hold in C, and this is reflected by the occurrences of $*$ in $\Sigma_\bullet^2(4)$ and $\Sigma_\bullet^2(7)$ as shown in Fig. 5.

By using the pre- and the post-sets we build the evolution graph $\mathcal{G}$ describing how the initial context C evolves at runtime. The abstract machine use $\mathcal{G}$ to study how the application interacts with and affects the context. Reachability of specific contexts is easily checked on this graph. It can help verifying, besides viability, various other properties of the application behaviour, both functional

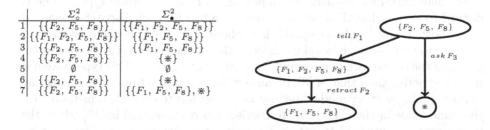

	$\Sigma_\circ^2$	$\Sigma_\bullet^2$
1	$\{\{F_2, F_5, F_8\}\}$	$\{\{F_1, F_2, F_5, F_8\}\}$
2	$\{\{F_1, F_2, F_5, F_8\}\}$	$\{\{F_1, F_5, F_8\}\}$
3	$\{\{F_2, F_5, F_8\}\}$	$\{\{F_1, F_5, F_8\}\}$
4	$\{\{F_2, F_5, F_8\}\}$	$\{*\}$
5	$\emptyset$	$\emptyset$
6	$\{\{F_2, F_5, F_8\}\}$	$\{*\}$
7	$\{\{F_2, F_5, F_8\}\}$	$\{\{F_1, F_5, F_8\},*\}$

Fig. 5. The analysis result (on left) and the evolution graph (on right) for the context $C = \{F_2, F_5, F_8\}$ and the history expression $H_a' = ((tell\ F_1^1 \cdot retract\ F_2^2)^3 + (ask\ F_3.retract\ F_4^5 \otimes fail^6)^4)^7$

and non-functional. E.g., we can equip the language with security policies, and analyse the evolution graph to *statically* detect which actions on the context may lead to violate the current security policies [11].

As examples of evolution graph consider the context C and the history expressions H_p and H'_p introduced in the examples above. The evolution graph of C for H_p is in Fig. 4. It is easy to see that H_p is viable for C since the node $*$ is not reachable from C in the graph. The evolution graph of C for H'_p is in Fig. 5, and now the node $*$ is reachable, showing H'_p not viable.

5   Conclusion

We presented ML_{CoDa}, a two-component language for programming adaptive applications and its two phases static analysis. In the first, a type and effect system type-checks programs and computes a sound abstraction of their behaviour. In the second phase, a loading time analysis uses the abstraction to verify that the program will adapt to all contexts occurring at runtime, i.e., that the dispatching mechanism will always succeed.

We successfully experimented the control-flow analysis on a proof-of-concept implementation in F#. We are currently implementing our constructs for adaptation and security within F#, so to tune our linguistic proposal and to assess our static analyses. We also plan to investigate whether our static machinery can be beneficial to architectural description languages for self adaptation, e.g. [7,24].

Related Work. Below, we consider only adaptive programming languages, and neglect other approaches, e.g. the great deal of work on mixing functional and logic languages [1,5] and the agent-based one.

Starting from the initial proposal by Costanza [9], *ContextL*, some experimental programming languages adopting this paradigm have been implemented (see [3,23] for an overview). Here, we concentrate on proposals concerning static verification of COP languages, and we relate them with our approach.

The Java-like language *ContextFJ* [8] offers layers, scoped layer activation and deactivation. However, it does not consider constructs for expressing inheritance and adopts a class-in-layer [13] strategy to express behavioural variations. Since layers may introduce methods not appearing in classes, a static type system is defined to ensure that there always exists a binding for each dispatched method call. Another Java-like language [12] has inheritance, and uses the class-in-layer strategy to express behavioural variations. Also in this case, a static type system prevents the occurrence of erroneous invocations at runtime. This type system is more restrictive than that of [8], because it forbids layers from introducing any new methods. So every method defined in a layer has to override a method with the same name in the class. This restriction has been relaxed in [15] where the type system is extended to handle dynamic layers composition. *Featherweight EventCJ* [2] is a further Java dialect that activate layers in reaction to events triggered by the environment (*layer transitions*). Model checking is then used to verify that layer transitions satisfy some expected safety properties.

All the approaches above differ from our proposal in a main aspect, namely the *context*, that for those is a stack of layers carrying no data. Furthermore, their notion of context only captures what we called the application context: all the properties holding in the running context are determined by only considering the code of the application. Our approach instead introduces the notion of *open* context, the properties of which not only depend on the application code, but *also* on the actual shape of the system context, where the application is about to run. This difference is reflected in the two phases of our static analysis, and justifies the need for a loading time analysis.

References

1. Antoy, S., Hanus, M.: Functional logic programming. Communications of the ACM 53(4), 74–85 (2010)
2. Aotani, T., Kamina, T., Masuhara, H.: Featherweight eventcj: a core calculus for a context-oriented language with event-based per-instance layer transition. In: Proceedings of the 3rd International Workshop on Context-Oriented Programming, COP 2011. ACM, New York (2011)
3. Appeltauer, M., Hirschfeld, R., Haupt, M., Lincke, J., Perscheid, M.: A comparison of context-oriented programming languages. In: International Workshop on Context-Oriented Programming, COP 2009, pp. 6:1–6:6. ACM, NY (2009)
4. Bartoletti, M., Degano, P., Ferrari, G.L., Zunino, R.: Local policies for resource usage analysis. ACM Trans. Program. Lang. Syst. 31(6) (2009)
5. Bellia, M., Degano, P., Levi, G.: The call by name semantics of a clause language with functions. In: Clark, K.L., Tärnlund, S.A. (eds.) Logic Programming, APIC Studies in Data Processing, vol. 16, pp. 281–295. Academic Press, London (1982)
6. Ceri, S., Gottlob, G., Tanca, L.: What you always wanted to know about datalog (and never dared to ask). IEEE Trans. on Knowl. and Data Eng. 1(1) (March 1989)
7. Cheng, S.W., Garlan, D.: Stitch: A language for architecture-based self-adaptation. Journal of Systems and Software 85(12), 2860–2875 (2012)
8. Clarke, D., Sergey, I.: A semantics for context-oriented programming with layers. In: International Workshop on Context-Oriented Programming, COP 2009, pp. 10:1–10:6. ACM, New York (2009)
9. Costanza, P.: Language constructs for context-oriented programming. In: Proceedings of the Dynamic Languages Symposium, pp. 1–10. ACM Press (2005)
10. Filieri, A., Ghezzi, C., Tamburrelli, G.: A formal approach to adaptive software: continuous assurance of non-functional requirements. Formal Aspects of Computing 24(2), 163–186 (2012)
11. Galletta, L.: Adaptivity: linguistic mechanisms and static analysis techniques. Ph.D. thesis, Comp. Sci. Dept., University of Pisa (2014), http://www.di.unipi.it/~galletta/phdThesis.pdf
12. Hirschfeld, R., Igarashi, A., Masuhara, H.: ContextFJ: a minimal core calculus for context-oriented programming. In: Proceedings of the 10th International Workshop on Foundations of Aspect-Oriented Languages, pp. 19–23. ACM (2011)
13. Hirschfeld, R., Costanza, P., Nierstrasz, O.: Context-oriented programming. Journal of Object Technology 7(3), 125–151 (2008)
14. Huebscher, M.C., McCann, J.A.: A survey of autonomic computing degrees, models, and applications. ACM Comput. Surv. 40(3), 7:1–7:28 (2008)

15. Igarashi, A., Hirschfeld, R., Masuhara, H.: A type system for dynamic layer composition. In: FOOL 2012, p. 13 (2012)
16. Loke, S.W.: Representing and reasoning with situations for context-aware pervasive computing: a logic programming perspective. Knowl. Eng. Rev. 19(3), 213–233
17. Meijer, E., Schulte, W., Bierman, G.: Programming with circles, triangles and rectangles. In: XML Conference and Exposition (2003)
18. Mycroft, A., O'Keefe, R.A.: A polymorphic type system for prolog. Artificial Intelligence 23(3), 295–307 (1984)
19. Necula, G.C., Lee, P.: Safe, untrusted agents using proof-carrying code. In: Vigna, G. (ed.) Mobile Agents and Security. LNCS, vol. 1419, pp. 61–91. Springer, Heidelberg (1998)
20. Orsi, G., Tanca, L.: Context modelling and context-aware querying. In: de Moor, O., Gottlob, G., Furche, T., Sellers, A. (eds.) Datalog 2010. LNCS, vol. 6702, pp. 225–244. Springer, Heidelberg (2011)
21. Rose, E.: Lightweight bytecode verification. J. Autom. Reason. 31(3-4), 303–334
22. Salehie, M., Tahvildari, L.: Self-adaptive software: Landscape and research challenges. ACM Trans. Auton. Adapt. Syst. 4(2), 14:1–14:42 (2009)
23. Salvaneschi, G., Ghezzi, C., Pradella, M.: Context-oriented programming: A software engineering perspective. Journal of Systems and Software 85(8), 1801–1817
24. Sanchez, A., Barbosa, L.S., Riesco, D.: Bigraphical modelling of architectural patterns. In: Arbab, F., Ölveczky, P.C. (eds.) FACS 2011. LNCS, vol. 7253, pp. 313–330. Springer, Heidelberg (2012)
25. Zhang, J., Goldsby, H.J., Cheng, B.H.: Modular verification of dynamically adaptive systems. In: Proceedings of the 8th ACM International Conference on Aspect-oriented Software Development, AOSD 2009, pp. 161–172. ACM, NY (2009)

Formal Modelling and Verification
of Cooperative Ant Behaviour in Event-B

Linas Laibinis[1], Elena Troubitsyna[1], Zeineb Graja[2,3],
Frédéric Migeon[3], and Ahmed Hadj Kacem[2]

[1] Åbo Akademi University, Turku, Finland
{Linas.Laibinis,Elena.Troubitsyna}@abo.fi
[2] Research Laboratory on Development and Control of Distributed Applications
(ReDCAD), Faculty of Economics and Management, University of Sfax, Tunisia
zeineb.graja@redcad.org, ahmed.hadjkacem@fsegs.rnu.tn
[3] Institute for Research in computer Science in Toulouse (IRIT),
Paul Sabatier University, Toulouse, France
{zeineb.graja,frederic.migeon}@irit.fr

Abstract. Multi-agent technology is a promising approach to development of complex decentralised systems that dynamically adapt to changing environmental conditions. The main challenge while designing such multi-agent systems is to ensure that reachability of the system-level goals emerges through collaboration of autonomous agents despite changing operating conditions. In this paper, we present a case study in formal modelling and verification of a colony of foraging ants. We formalise the behaviour of cooperative ants in Event-B and verify by proofs that the desired system-level properties become achievable via agent collaboration. The applied refinement-based approach weaves proof-based verification into the formal development. It allows us to rigorously define constraints on the environment and the ant behaviour at different abstraction levels and systematically explore the relationships between system-level goals, environment and autonomous ants. We believe that the proposed approach helps to structure complex system requirements, facilitates formal analysis of various system interdependencies, and supports formalisation of intricate mechanisms of agent collaboration.

Keywords: Self-organizing MAS, cooperative ants, formal verification, refinement, Event-B.

1 Introduction

Self-organising multi-agent systems (MAS) are decentralised systems composed of a number of autonomous actors – agents – that cooperate with each other to achieve system-level goals [6]. Each autonomic agent follows a number of rules that govern its own behaviour as well as agent interactions. The absence of a centralised controlling mechanism and a loosely-coupled system architecture enhance system adaptability. However, they also make the design of self-adaptive MAS a challenging task, since the designers should demonstrate that the desired system-level behaviour emerges from the behaviour of individual agents.

D. Giannakopoulou and G. Salaün (Eds.): SEFM 2014, LNCS 8702, pp. 363–377, 2014.
© Springer International Publishing Switzerland 2014

In this paper, we propose an approach to formal development of a self-organising MAS by refinement in Event-B. Event-B [1] is a formal approach for designing distributed systems correct-by-construction. The main development technique of Event-B – refinement – allows the designers to transform an abstract specification into a detailed model through a chain of correctness-preserving transformations. Each refinement step is verified by proofs guaranteeing that a refined model preserves the externally observable behaviour. Refinement also allows us to formally define relations between formal models representing the system behaviour at different levels of abstraction. Hence it constitutes a suitable mechanism for establishing relationships between the system-level goals, the behaviour of autonomic agents, and their interactions.

In this paper, we undertake a formal development of a colony of foraging agents. We adopt the systems approach [11] that promotes an integrated modelling of the system with its environment. In our modelling, we further extend the systems approach by integrating the third component – the observer. The observer detects that the system level goal has been reached and the system can successfully terminate.

We start from an abstract specification in which all three layers – the system environment (the grid with distributed food), the ant colony, and the observer are modelled in a formal abstract way. In the chain of model refinements, we introduce a detailed representation of the ant behaviour and link their actions with the changes in the environment while, at the same time, elaborating on the logical conditions of system-level goal reachability. Our models incorporate the perceive-decide-act pattern for modelling the ant behaviour as well as the ant decision rules, including the heuristics for moving and harvesting food [2]. We discuss the benefits of formal modelling, the introduced modelling assumptions, and point out the modelling aspects that require integration with other modelling techniques such as stochastic analysis and simulation.

The paper is structured as follows. In Section 2 we briefly describe the basics of self-organising MAS, while Section 3 presents our formal modelling framework – Event-B. In Section 4 we describe our case study – the colony of foraging ants – and outline the formal development strategy. Section 5 presents our formal development in detail. In Section 6 we discusses the results achieved by our approach. Finally, in Section 7 we conclude and overview the related work.

2   Self-organising Cooperative MAS

Multi-Agent Systems (MAS) exhibiting a self-organised behaviour is a promising approach to design complex decentralised software systems. The main challenge when designing self-organising MAS is to ensure that the desired system-level behaviour emerges from the interactions of individual agents. Since self-organising systems do not have a centralised controlling mechanism, each individual agent should adapt its behaviour according to its individual perception of the operating environment and the rules governing its behaviour. The mechanism of self-adaptation should be described by the means of local information. Therefore, the functionality of the overall system should emerge from the interactions between the agents [4]. While designing a MAS, we assume that each agent has a life cycle, called the perceive-decide-act cycle, which consists of sensing its local environment, then deciding according to its own environment perceptions which actions to perform, and, finally, executing them.

This paper focuses on studying cooperative MAS. The main idea that stems from the adaptive MAS theory is to ensure that each agent acts in cooperation with its neighbours and in accordance with the state of its operational environment [8,6]. This behavioural pattern has resulted in the following three meta-rules [3] of the cooperative MAS design:

- The agent should be able to understand every received signal from its environment and its neighbours;
- The representations that the agent has about its environment should allow it to make decisions;
- The decisions that an agent make should enable it to perform an action which is useful for the other agents and the environment.

Natural self-organising systems, such as, e.g., ant colonies, provide us with the valuable behavioural patterns that can facilitate design of decentralised cooperative interaction mechanisms [6]. The individual capabilities of ants to drop pheromone, smell nest, food or other agents lead to discovery of the cooperative mechanisms to perceive the environment, make decisions and act.

Traditionally, the behaviour of self-organising systems is studied via simulation and model-checking. Simulation allows the designers to experiment with various system parameters and create certain heuristics facilitating the system design [2]. Model checking provides support in the discovery of deadlocks and property violations [7]. However, to cope with the complexity of self-organising MAS, the designer also need techniques that support not only verification, but also the development process itself. Moreover, such techniques should support disciplined development and facilitate reasoning about various aspects of the system behaviour at different levels of abstraction.

We believe that the Event-B framework provides a suitable basis for formal model-driven development of cooperative MAS. In the next section we give a brief overview of the Event-B framework, while in Section 5 we will demonstrate our approach to development of cooperative MAS in Event-B.

3   Formal Development in Event-B

The Event B formalism [1] is a state-based formal approach that promotes the correct-by-construction development paradigm and formal verification by theorem proving. Event B is particularly suitable for modelling distributed and reactive systems and had been actively used within several EU projects for modelling complex software-intensive systems from various domains.

In Event-B, a system specification (model) consists of two parts – machine and context, as shown in Fig. 1. The dynamic part of the model — a machine – is defined using the notion of an *abstract state machine* [1]. A machine encapsulates the model state, represented as a collection of model variables, and defines operations on this state, i.e., contains the the dynamic part (behaviour) of the modelled system. Another part of the model, called *context*, contains the static

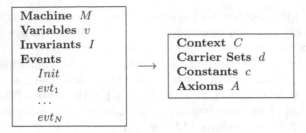

Fig. 1. Event-B machine and context

part of the system. In particular, a context can include user-defined carrier sets, constants and their properties, which are given as a list of model axioms.

The machine is uniquely identified by its name M. The state variables, v, are declared in the **Variables** clause and initialised in the $Init$ event. The variables are strongly typed by the constraining predicates I given in the **Invariants** clause. The invariant clause might also contain other predicates defining properties that should be preserved during system execution.

The dynamic behaviour of the system is defined by the set of atomic events specified in the **Events** clause. Generally, an event can be defined as follows:

$$\textbf{ANY } vl \textbf{ WHERE } g \textbf{ THEN } S \textbf{ END},$$

where vl is a list of new local variables (parameters), the guard g is a state predicate, and the action S is a statement (assignment). In case when vl is empty, the event syntax becomes **WHEN** g **THEN** S **END**.

The occurrence of events represents the observable behaviour of the system. The guard defines the conditions for the action to be executed, i.e., when the event is *enabled*. If several events are enabled at the same time, any of them can be chosen for execution. If none of the events is enabled, the system deadlocks.

The action of an event is a parallel composition of assignments. The assignments can be either deterministic or non-deterministic. A deterministic assignment, $x :=$ $E(x, y)$, has the standard syntax and meaning. A nondeterministic assignment is denoted either as $x :\in Set$, where Set is a set of values, or $x :| P(x, y, x')$, where P is a predicate relating initial values of x, y to some final value of x'. As a result, x can get any value belonging to Set or according to P.

Event-B employs a top-down refinement-based approach to system development. Development starts from an abstract system specification that models the most essential functional requirements. While capturing more detailed requirements, each refinement step typically introduces new events and variables into the abstract specification. Moreover, Event-B formal development supports data refinement, allowing us to replace some abstract variables with their concrete counterparts. In that case, the invariant of the refined machine formally defines the relationship between the abstract and concrete variables.

The consistency of Event-B models, i.e., verification of model well-formedness, invariant preservation as well as correctness of refinement steps, is demonstrated by discharging the relevant proof obligations. The Rodin platform [13] provides an automated support for modelling and verification. In particular, it automatically generates the required proof obligations and attempts to discharge them.

4 The Foraging Ants Case Study

Case Study Description. A colony of foraging ants is a nature-inspired cooperative MAS. The global objective of the colony is to bring the food, scattered in the environment, to the nest. Each ant has the ability to perceive, primarily by smell, different characteristics (e.g., closeness of food, nest or other ants) of its environment. The ant perception depends on its position in the environment. We assume that the stronger is the smell, the closer is the food. Each ant can autonomically perform such actions as moving, harvesting and carrying-up food, unloading food at the nest, as well as dropping pheromone. Pheromone is a chemical substance that ants put for marking paths to the discovered food. The autonomic behaviour of an ant can be summarised by the following rules:

1. Each ant starts by exploring the environment and moving randomly;
2. If it smells food, it moves to the direction where the smell is strongest;
3. If it smells pheromone, it moves to the direction where the smell is strongest;
4. When reaching the food at a certain location, an ant harvests as much food as it can carry and returns to the nest;
5. While an ant returns to the nest carrying food, it drops pheromone along the way to attract other ants to the food source.

We assume that the environment is composed of a set of connected locations. One specific location is reserved for the nest of the colony. A location might contain a certain limited amount of food. Moreover, a location can be marked by some quantity of (gradually evaporating) pheromone.

The aim of the formal development is to specify the following requirements.

- (R1) The main goal of the colony is to bring all the food to the nest;
- (R2) Before performing an action, an ant should make a decision based on its current perceptions of the environment;
- (R3) A combination of the ant perceptions should allow it to make an unambiguous decision;
- (R4) The decision an ant makes should lead to its specific action;
- (R5) An ant should avoid conflicts with other ants on the same food source;
- (R6) An ant should avoid conflicts with other ants on the same area.

The requirements (R5) and (R6) essentially mean that, given a choice, an ant should avoid the areas already exploited by other ants. This ensures a more efficient food foraging by exploring more territory for yet undiscovered food.

The Formal Refinement Strategy. Traditionally, modelling of self-organising MAS is structured according to three views:

- modelling the environment,
- modelling autonomic agents and their interactions,
- modelling the system-level properties (observer-view).

One of the advantages of Event-B is that it supports the systems [11] approach, i.e., allows us to model the system behaviour together with its environment. In this paper, we further extend the systems approach by defining our model as an integration of the environment, agent and observer views. It allows us to formally derive the interconnections between these layers through the development process. Moreover, such an integrated modelling approach allows us to discover the constraints that the environment should satisfy, precisely define how the agent behaviour affects the environment, and link the system-level goals with both agent and environment dynamics.

Next we present the strategy that we will follow in our formal development of the case study. The main idea behind the proposed strategy is to derive a detailed model demonstrating that the local ant behaviour leads to achieving the defined system-level goal (the requirement R1). The reachability is proved as a result of formalisation of all three views: environment, agent and observer as well as their inter-relationships. The overall refinement strategy is as follows.

1. **Initial model.** The initial abstract model introduces the location grid (including the nest) with the distributed food and models the effect of ants activity – all the food is gradually transferred to the nest. Reaching this goal is eventually observed by the observer.
2. **First refinement.** The specification obtained at this level introduces into the model a representation of the ants and their behaviour, following the perceive- decide-act cycle. Moreover, we elaborate of the act stage.
3. **Second refinement.** At this level, we focus on the decision stage. We introduce different types of possible ant decisions as well as the dynamic food load the ants are carrying. This refinement allows us also to establish a link between the act and decide stages.
4. **Third refinement.** At this level, we complete refinement of the perceive-decide-act cycle by introducing different ant perceptions and the decision rules based on these perceptions.
5. **Fourth refinement.** At the final refinement step, we elaborate on the link between the cooperative ant behaviour and system-level properties. We introduce the conditions guaranteeing that an ant in a particular functioning mode (exploration, going after perceived food, returning to the nest, etc.) always gets closer to its current target.

In our refinement strategy, each subsequent refinement step elaborates on the previously-introduced models, verifying at the same time the consistency between the models. Moreover, different refinement steps focus on modelling and verifying different requirements (R1)–(R6). For instance, the second refinement step ensures the requirement (R4), while the third refinement step focuses on formalising the requirements (R3), (R5), and (R6).

5   Formal Development of the Foraging Ants Case Study

Next we present our formal development of the colony of foraging ants. Due to the space limit, we will present excerpts from our formal models and only discuss the main modelling solutions as well as verified properties.

The Initial Model. In our formal development, we aim at establishing an explicit link between the system-level goals and the ant behaviour. In our case, we have to demonstrate that the ants will harvest all the food distributed in the environment. In the initial specification, we abstractly model the process of harvesting food and reaching the goal – reaching the state in which all the food initially distributed over the environment is transferred to the colony nest.

In the context component of our abstract model, we introduce constants and properties required to represent the grid (the environment) on which the ants are moving to harvest the food. We model the grid as a finite adirectional graph over a set of interconnected locations. The locations are modelled as the abstract set *Locations*, with *Nest* – a fixed location in the grid – representing the nest of the colony to which the ants should bring the food.

$$
\begin{array}{l}
\textsf{axm1}:\ Nest \in Locations \wedge Locations\backslash\{Nest\} \neq \varnothing \\
\textsf{axm2}:\ Grid \in Locations \leftrightarrow Locations \wedge Grid = Grid\sim
\end{array}
$$

Here $\leftrightarrow$ designates a total relation, i.e., each location has at least one adjacent location, connected by *Grid*. *Grid* is also symmetric (the axiom axm2). To make a decision about where to move next, each ant should analyse its close vicinity – a set of nearby locations. To represent this set, we explicitly introduce the function *Next*, defined as a relational image of *Grid* for the given location *loc*.

$$
\begin{array}{l}
\textsf{axm3}:\ Next \in Locations \rightarrow \mathbb{P}(Locations) \\
\textsf{axm4}:\ \forall loc.\, loc \in Locations \Rightarrow Next(loc) = Grid[\{loc\}]
\end{array}
$$

Finally, in the context component we also introduce the initial food distribution in the grid, defined as a constant function over the grid locations:

$$
\begin{array}{l}
\textsf{axm5}:\ QuantityFoodMax \in \mathbb{N}1 \\
\textsf{axm6}:\ InitFoodDistr \in Locations \rightarrow 0..QuantityFoodMax \\
\textsf{axm7}:\ InitFoodDistr(Nest) = 0 \wedge (\exists loc.\, loc \in Locations\backslash\{Nest\} \wedge InitFoodDistr(loc) > 0)
\end{array}
$$

Here *QuantityFoodMax* is the constant restricting the maximal amount of food for any single location. In other axioms, we require that the initial food amount in the nest is equal to 0, and there is at least one location outside the nest that contains some non-zero amount of food. Without these constraints, the system-level goal would be automatically satisfied, i.e., the system would terminate right after initialisation.

In our abstract model, the main complexity lies in the context that defines the system environment. The dynamic part of the model – the machine – is rather simple. After the system initialisation, the event Change becomes enabled. It models non-deterministic changes in food distribution on the grid. Eventually the event Observer becomes enabled, indicating that all the food is now transferred to *Nest*. We also introduce two variables *GoalReached* and *QuantityFood*:

$$
\begin{array}{l}
\textsf{inv1}:\ GoalReached \in bool \\
\textsf{inv2}:\ QuantityFood \in Locations \rightarrow 0..QuantityFoodMax
\end{array}
$$

The current state of food distribution in the grid is modelled by the variable *QuantityFood*. It is defined as a function (array) over the grid locations, associating each location with the food amount currently stored in it. The variable is initialised by *InitFoodDistr*, introduced in the context. The boolean variable *GoalReached* indicates whether the system reached its main goal.

The system goal is reached when there is no food left in the grid, i.e.,

$$\forall loc.\, loc \in Locations \backslash \{Nest\} \;\Rightarrow\; QuantityFood(loc) = 0$$

Once this happens, the variable $GoalReached$ is assigned $TRUE$ (by Observer). This in turn disables the event Change, effectively terminating the system.

The event Change abstractly models possible changes in the grid food distribution. Essentially, it non-deterministically specifies the general tendency for the food to be transferred from non-nest locations to $Nest$. This behaviour is enforced by permitting non-deterministic decrease (or at least non-increase) of the food amount outside $Nest$ or, similarly, its non-deterministic increase in $Nest$.

> EVENT Change
>   ANY $loc, newQF$ WHERE
> $grd1 : loc \in Locations \wedge newQF \in \mathbb{N}$
> $grd2 : loc = Nest \Rightarrow newQF \geq QuantityFood(loc)$
> $grd3 : loc \neq Nest \Rightarrow newQF \leq QuantityFood(loc)$
> $grd4 : GoalReached = FALSE$
>   THEN
> $act1 : QuantityFood(loc) := newQF$
>   END

Even though modelling of ants is abstracted away in the initial model, it is implicitly assumed that all the changes in the grid food distribution happen because of some ant activities. In the subsequent refinements, this relationship will be made explicit, constraining the nondeterminism of our abstract model.

The First Refinement. In our first refinement step, we introduce abstract representation of ants and their behaviour stages. In particular, we adopt the widely used pattern $Perceive \rightarrow Decide \rightarrow Act$ to model the cyclic ant behaviour. Moreover, we distinguish two groups of ants – the ants that are currently engaged in the food foraging and the ants that are resting in the nest.

In the context of the refined model, we introduce the abstract set $Ants$ to model the colony of ants. Moreover, we define the enumerated set $StepCycle = \{perceive, decide, act\}$ that defines the constants to indicate specific cyclic stages of the ant behaviour. In the dynamic part of the refined model, we introduce three new variables to model ants and their behaviour.

> $inv8 : WorkingAnts \subseteq Ants$
> $inv9 : AgentStage \in WorkingAnts \rightarrow StepCycle$
> $inv10 : currentLoc \in Ants \rightarrow Locations$

The variable $WorkingAnts$ stores the set of the ants currently involved in food foraging. The variable $AgentStage$ indicates the current behaviour stage for each working ant. Finally, the variable $currentLoc$ associates each ant (whether working or resting) with its current location on the grid.

The abstract event Change is now refined (and renamed into Act) to model possible actions of a particular ant. The event is parameterised with a local variable ant, which is required to be a working ant in the stage act (the guard $grd5$). Note that the local variable (parameter) loc of the abstract event Change, which signified an arbitrary possible grid location, is now constrained to be equal to $currentLoc(ant)$, i.e., the current location of ant.

The ant action may also result in the ant moving to an adjacent location. The new action $act2$ specifies this: the ant may move to a new location (one of possible locations specified by $Next(currentLoc(ant))$) or stay where it is now.

```
EVENT Act
REFINES Change
  ANY newQF, ant WHERE
    grd1 : newQF ∈ ℕ
    grd2 : currentLoc(ant) = Nest  ⇒  newQF ≥ QuantityFood(currentLoc(ant))
    grd3 : currentLoc(ant) ≠ Nest  ⇒  newQF ≤ QuantityFood(currentLoc(ant))
    grd4 : GoalReached = FALSE
    grd5 : ant ∈ WorkingAnts ∧ AgentStage(ant) = act
  THEN
    act1 : QuantityFood(currentLoc(ant)) := newQF
    act2 : currentLoc(ant) :∈ Next(currentLoc(ant)) ∪ {currentLoc(ant)}
  END
```

The new events Perceive, Decide, and NewCycle are introduced to model the cyclic ant behaviour. The events Perceive and Decide abstractly model the perceive and decide stages of the ant behaviour. These events will be elaborated (refined) in the subsequent refinement steps. The event NewCycle is enabled when all the working ants completed their act stage (i.e., executed Act). It starts a new cycle by moving all the working ants into the perceive stage.

As a part of verifying model correctness, Event-B allows us to formally prove convergence of the newly introduced events (system transitions) in the refined models. The convergence is proved by providing a natural number expression (variant) and then formally demonstrating that this expression is decreased by any execution of new events. We have proved convergence of the new events Perceive and Decide (thus guaranteeing that the act stage will be reached for all the working ants), using the following variant expression:

$$card(\{a \cdot a \in WorkingAnts \wedge AgentStage(a) = perceive\}) +$$
$$card(\{a \cdot a \in WorkingAnts \wedge AgentStage(a) \in \{perceive, decide\}),$$

where *card* is the set cardinality operator.

The Second Refinement. The first refinement step has allowed us to establish the connection between the dynamical changes in the system environment (the food distribution in the grid) and the actors (ants) that cause these changes. In the second refinement, we elaborate on the ant decision stage. We also introduce the notions of ant load (i.e., the amount of food an ant is carrying) and grid pheromone distribution (i.e., quantities of ant pheromone in grid locations).

To model the outcome of the decision stage, in the model context we introduce the enumerated set *Decision* = {*move*, *harvest*, *dropPheromoneAndMove*, *dropPheromone*, *dropFood*, *doNothing*}, with the constants for respective ant decisions. The ant decisions are constrained by the corresponding environment and its own conditions, such as the presence of food and currently carried load. To reason about this, we add the constant *MaxLoad* (for the maximal amount a single ant can carry) as well as the functions *TotalLoad* and *TotalFood*, returning the total amount of food for a set of ants or a set of locations.

```
axm2 :  MaxLoad ∈ ℕ1
axm3 :  TotalLoad ∈ (Ants → ℕ) → (ℙ(Ants) → ℕ)
axm4 :  TotalFood ∈ (Locations → ℕ) → (ℙ(Locations) → ℕ)
```

In the dynamic part of the model, we introduce three new variables:

```
inv2 .  load ⊂ WorkingAnts → Decision
inv3 :  AgentDecision ∈ WorkingAnts → Decision
inv4 :  DensityPheromone ∈ Locations → ℕ
```

The first variable, *load*, models the current load each ant is carrying. The second one, *AgentDecision*, stores the latest decision made by every working ant. Finally, the variable *DensityPheromone* reflects the current amount of dropped pheromone in specific grid locations. Having the corresponding type and variable for ant decisions allows us to refine the abstract event Decide as follows:

```
EVENT Decide
REFINES Decide
  ANY ant WHERE
    grd1 : ant ∈ WorkingAnts ∧ AgentStage(ant) = decide
    grd2 : GoalReached = FALSE
  THEN
    act1 : AgentDecision(ant) :∈ Decision
    act2 : AgentStage(ant) := act
  END
```

The event is still abstract since the environment perceptions of an ant, which are the basis for making ant decisions, will be introduced later. As a result, here the ant decision is made nondeterministically from the set *Decision*. Nevertheless, we can now rely on the information about the last decision of each ant (stored in *AgentDecision*) to elaborate on the act stage. In the previous model, this stage is represented by a single event Act. Now we refine the event Act to introduce the instances of Act corresponding to each possible ant decision. For example, below we show the event that models dropping food by an ant after reaching the nest. This event is proved to be a valid refinement of Act.

```
EVENT Act_Drop_Food
REFINES Act
  ANY ant WHERE
    grd1 : ant ∈ WorkingAnts ∧ AgentStage(ant) = act
    grd2 : AgentDecision(ant) = dropFood
    grd3 : currentLoc(ant) = Nest ∧ GoalReached = FALSE
  THEN
    act1 : QuantityFood(Nest) := QuantityFood(Nest) + load(ant)
    act2 : load(ant) := 0
  END
```

In a similar way, such events as, for example, Act_Move, Act_HarvestFood, and Act_DropPheromone, are introduced and proved to be specific refinements of the abstract event Act. The first event changes the ant's current location (not affecting the food and pheromone distributions), while the second and third ones update respectively the grid pheromone and food distributions.

In the abstract model, the food distribution in the event Change is updated with a high degree of nondeterminism. After two refinements, the introduced system details and constraints allow us to eliminate this nondeterminism completely. In fact, we can prove (as an invariant property) that no food is lost:

```
inv5 : TotalFood(QuantityFood)(Locations) + TotalLoad(load)(Ants) =
       TotalFood(InitFoodDistribution)(Locations)
```

Here we use the context functions *TotalFood* and *TotalLoad* to state that all the food from the initial food distribution is now either in the grid locations or is carried up by the ants. We can also explicitly relate the reaching of the main goal with the food absence outside the nest.

```
inv6 : GoalReached = TRUE ⟹ TotalFood(QuantityFood)(Ants\{Nest}) = 0
inv7 : GoalReached = TRUE ⟹
       QuantityFood(Nest) = TotalFood(InitFoodDistribution)(Locations)
```

Finally, we can now prove that all the events affecting the food distribution are convergent, using the following variant expression:

$$TotalFood(QuantityFood)(Locations \setminus \{Nest\})$$

The Third Refinement. The second refinement step has allowed us to build a link between the ant decisions and its subsequent actions. While further elaborating on the ants behaviour, we have also refined the definition of the system level goal and the conditions that lead to it. Next, we focus on introducing different ant perceptions and formulate the decision rules allowing an ant to decide on its next action based on a combination of its current perception values.

We assume that each ant has the ability to perceive from a distance the food, dropped pheromone, nest and other ants. The exact strength of each perception depends on the ant's current location and the direction (i.e., the next location) it is facing. In other words, knowing the current food, pheromone or ant distribution on the grid, as well as the ant's location and direction, we can argue that the value of a specific perception can be unambiguously determined. This reasoning allows us to introduce the ant perceptions as abstract functions in the context. Specifically, the food perception can be defined as follows:

---

axm5 : $MaxFoodSmell \in \mathbb{N}1$
axm6 : $FoodPerception \in (Locations \to \mathbb{N}) \to (Locations \times Locations \nrightarrow 0..MaxFoodSmell)$

The first parameter of *FoodPerception* is the current food distribution on the grid. The second parameter is a pair of locations, the first element of which is the current location and the second one is a possible next location (a position in the vicinity). The resulting value is the perception strength. We also assume that there is a upper limit for it (e.g., the maximal food smell).

In a similar way, we introduce *PheromonePerception* and *AntPerception*. The final perception, *NestPerception*, can be defined slightly simpler: since the nest location is stationary, the first parameter can be omitted.

---

axm11 : $MaxNestSmell \in \mathbb{N}1$
axm12 : $NestPerception \in (Locations \times Locations \nrightarrow 0..MaxNestSmell)$

When foraging, an ant should evaluate different alternatives in its vicinity based on a combination of all its perceptions: food, pheromone, other ants, and nest. In other words, four perception values should be merged into a single value, which is then can be compared with the corresponding values for each possible direction. In the concrete system implementations, the perception values are often partitioned into the distinct intervals with the corresponding attached weights. In our formal development, we abstract away from the concrete heuristics allowing for producing a single perception value[1]. Instead, we define a generic abstract function, *Favour*,

---

axm14 : $Favour \in \mathbb{N} \times \mathbb{N} \times \mathbb{N} \times \mathbb{N} \to \mathbb{N}$

---

which can be instantiated in many different ways.

For the given food, pheromone, and ants distributions fd, pd, ad, and a pair of locations ($loc \mapsto next$), the overall perception value can be calculated as follows:

---

[1] How such heuristics can be obtained, see, for instance, [2].

Favour (*FoodPerception fd* (*loc* ↦ *next*), *PheromonePerception pd* (*loc* ↦ *next*),

   AntsPerception ad (*loc* ↦ *next*), *NestPerception* (*loc* ↦ *next*))

In the dynamic part of the model, we introduce two new variables:

> inv4 : *nextLocation* ∈ *WorkingAnts* → *Location*
> inv5 : *DensityAnts* ∈ *Locations* → ℕ

The first variable, *nextLocation*, stores the next location an ants decides to move to based on its environment perceptions. The variable *DensityAnts* contains the dynamic information about the quantity of ants in grid locations.

Based on the perception functions introduced in the model context, we can now elaborate on the ant decide stage. Specifically, the abstract event Decide is now split into its several versions (Decide_MoveExplore, Decide_MoveReturn, Decide_HarvestFood, ...) that cover different ant decisions. The introduced perception functions are most useful for the events where an ant should decide the next location to proceed to. For instance, the event Decide_MoveExplore presented below should rely on all the ant perceptions.

```
EVENT Decide_MoveExplore
REFINES Decide
  ANY ant, nextDir, maxFav WHERE
    grd1 : ant ∈ WorkingAnts ∧ AgentStage(ant) = decide
    grd2 : GoalReached = FALSE ∧ nextDir ∈ Next(currentLoc(ant))
    grd3 : maxFav = FAVOUR(ant ↦ nextDir)
    grd4 : maxFav = max({dir · dir ∈ Next(currentLoc(ant)) | FAVOUR(ant ↦ dir)}
  THEN
    act1 : AgentDecision(ant) := move
    act2 : AgentStage(ant) := act
    act2 : NextLocation(ant) := nextDir
  END
```

where *FAVOUR*(*ant* ↦ *nextDir*) stands for

Favour(*FoodPerception* (*QuantityFood*) (*currentLoc*(*ant*) ↦ *nextDir*),

   PheromonePerception (*DensityPheromone*) (*currentLoc*(*ant*) ↦ *nextDir*),

   AntsPerception (*DensityAnts*) (*currentLoc*(*ant*) ↦ *nextDir*),

   NestPerception (*currentLoc*(*ant*) ↦ *nextDir*))

The event allows an ant to choose the most favourable direction to move next. It is the location *nextDir* belonging to *Next*(*currentLoc*(*ant*)) and giving the maximal *FAVOUR*(...) value based on the current ant perceptions.

The Fourth Refinement. One of the main purposes of the presented formal development is to formally establish the reachability of the main system goal: "All the distributed food will be eventually transferred to the nest". In the second refinement, we already proved that all the events affecting the food distribution are convergent and the amount of food outside the nest is constantly decreasing.

However, this result does not concern the events modelling the ants moving in search of the food or drawn by the left pheromone, ants returning to the nest, etc. We have to ensure that the ants do not stay forever in such modes of operation. We can achieve this by deriving the necessary conditions (constraints) on the ant perception functions that essentially control ant movements.

When ants are returning to the nest (or going after the food/pheromone smell), they have a specific target to reach, after which they switch to a different activity (operational mode). The property we have to ensure is that, if an ant moves to the next location according to the used perception functions, it always gets closer to the target of its current operational mode. We ensure this by adding additional expected constraints (axioms) for the abstract perception functions in the model context. Then we are going to use these constraints in the model machine component to prove termination of the ants in particular operation modes. For instance, we constrain the definition of *NestPerception* as follows:

$$\text{axm17}: \ \forall loc, next, prc. \ loc \in Locations \land next \in Next(loc) \ \land$$
$$prc = NestPerception(loc \mapsto next) \ \land$$
$$prc = max(\{dir \cdot dir \in Next(loc) \mid NestPerception(loc \mapsto dir)\}) \ \Rightarrow$$
$$next = Nest \ \lor \ (\exists loc'. \ loc' \in Next(next) \land NestPerception(loc' \mapsto dir) > prc)$$

This axiom states that, if an ant proceeds to the direction with the maximal nest perception value, it either immediately reaches the nest or there exists the next location after that with an even higher perception value. Since we have introduced the constant for the maximal nest smell, the nest perception value cannot go up indefinitely. In similar fashion, we add the corresponding constraints to the other perception as well as the *Favour* function.

In the model machine component, we explicitly introduce ant operation modes by partitioning the working ants into separate classes. For instance, the variable AntsApproachingNest is introduced for the ants returning to the nest.

$$\text{inv7}: \ AntsApproachingNest \subseteq WorkingAnts$$

The corresponding model events are refined to update this variable if necessary.

Moreover, we formulate the variant in order to formally demonstrate termination of the ants in this operation mode:

$$\Sigma \ (ant \cdot \ ant \in AntsApproachingNest \mid (maxNestSmell - max($$
$$\{ \ dir \cdot dir \in Next(currentLoc(ant)) \mid NestPerception(currentLoc(ant) \mapsto dir)\})))$$

The decreasing of this variant (for the corresponding events) is proved by relying on the axiom axm17 presented above. In a similar way, we formulate the necessary conditions and prove termination for the other ant operation modes.

6   Discussion

The presented formal development of the foraging ants case study has been carried out within the Rodin platform [13] – the integrated tool support for Event-B. The Rodin platform has significantly facilitated both modelling and verification of our models. In particular, it has generated over 480 proof obligations, most of which were automatically discharged. Majority of those proof obligations came from the last two refinement steps, indicating the rising level of complexity.

By formulating many important notions as abstract sets and functions (with only essential properties postulated) in the model context, we have not only achieved better understanding of the environment-system interdependencies but also arrived at a parametric system model. Indeed, the obtained generic definitions can be instantiated with different system-specific parameters and hence the proposed models can be reused to model a family of cooperative MAS. For instance, generic definitions of the ant decision rules (perception and *Favour* functions) allow us to instantiate them in many ways, assigning different weights for various perceptions or their combinations.

In the last refinement step we derived the constraints for ensuring termination of ants staying in particular operation modes. These constraints can be seen as the conditions to be checked for concrete instances of the perception functions.

Our derived models also demonstrate the interplay between the global and local reasoning. Even though the ant perception functions (which are the basis for local ant decisions) are defined globally, they merely represent our global assumptions that each ant has particular capabilities to perceive its vicinity.

We formalised the problem of system-level goal reachability as a termination problem. We had to constrain the environment by requiring that no new food sources appear on the grid, otherwise the system would become non-convergent. The proved termination for ants in particular modes can be seen as piece-wise invariant, since it can be violated at the points of ants switching the operating modes. The termination proof is based on the standard Event-B technique using variants. To obtain a general termination result, one can consider *almost certain termination* approach [9] based on the probabilistic reasoning. However, such an approach would complicate the refinement process because of intricate properties of models containing both probabilistic and demonic non-determinism.

To evaluate quantitative characteristics of the modelled system (e.g., how effective are cooperation strategies of concrete instances of the decision rules), the designers should bridge Event-B with other approaches. We are planning to investigate how runtime simulation or model checking can be used for this aim.

7   Related Work and Conclusions

Self-organising systems have attracted significant research attention over the last decade. Majority of the approaches rely on simulation and model checking to explore the impact of different parameters on the system behaviour. In [7], *Gardelli* uses stochastic Pi-Calculus for modelling self-organising MAS for intrusion detection capabilities. The *SPIM* tool is used to assess the impact of, e.g., the number of agents and frequency of inspections, on the system behaviour. In [5], a hybrid approach for modelling and verifying self-organising systems has been proposed. This approach uses stochastic simulations to model the system described as a Markov chain and probabilistic model checking (using the *PRISM* tool) for verification. Konur et al. [10] also use *PRISM* and probabilistic model checking to verify the behaviour of a robot swarm. The authors verify the system properties expressed in the *PCTL* logic for several scenarios.

In this paper, we have experimented with a technique that not only allows the designers to verify certain system-level properties of self-organising MAS, but also provides a support throughout the development process. In our work, we start from a high-level system model and *derive* the specification that details the individual agent mechanisms leading to reaching the desired goal.

The derivational approach has been also adopted in our previous work [12]. There we have studied the mechanisms of goal decomposition by refinement and ensuring data integrity in cooperative MAS. In contrast, in this paper we propose how to create a parameterised generic model of the system environment and establish the link between actions of autonomic agents and the environment state. Moreover, we demonstrate how to formally represent agent perception and decision rules as generic system parameters.

In this paper, we presented a case study in formal development of a nature-inspired self-organising MAS. We demonstrated how to derive a detailed specification of a colony of foraging ants by refinement. Formal derivation has provided us with a structured and disciplined framework for the development of a complex system with intricate agent interactions. We believe that the proposed approach is promising for modelling the logical aspects of self-organising systems.

Self-organising MAS are complex multi-facet phenomena and hence require a range of approaches for their modelling and analysis. The proposed approach should be integrated with stochastic analysis techniques, in order to identify the most optimal system parameters that would allow the system to achieve its objectives not only in terms of logical correctness but also performance, reliability and required resources. Integration with such techniques constitutes one of the directions of our future research.

References

1. Abrial, J.-R.: Modelling in Event-B. Cambridge University Press (2010)
2. Bonjean, N., Mefteh, W., Gleizes, M.-P., Maurel, C., Migeon, F.: ADELFE 2.0. In: Handbook on Agent-Oriented Design Processes. Springer
3. Camps, V.: Vers une théorie de l'auto-organisation dans les systèmes multi-agents basée sur la coopération: application à la recherche d'information dans un système d'information répartie. PhD thesis, Paul Sabatier university (1998)
4. Capera, D., Georgé, J.-P., Gleizes, M.P., Glize, P.: The AMAS theory for complex problem solving based on self-organizing cooperative agents. In: WETICE, pp. 383–388 (2003)
5. Casadei, M., Viroli, M.: Using probabilistic model checking and simulation for designing self-organizing systems. In: Proceedings of the 2009 ACM Symposium on Applied Computing, pp. 2103–2104. ACM, New York (2009)
6. Di Marzo Serugendo, G., Gleizes, M.-P., Karageorgos, A. (eds.): Self-organising Software - From Natural to Artificial Adaptation. Natural Computing Series. Springer (October 2011), http://www.springerlink.com
7. Gardelli, L., Viroli, M., Omicini, A.: Exploring the Dynamics of Self-Organising Systems with Stochastic π-Calculus: Detecting Abnormal Behaviour in MAS. In: Trappl, R. (ed.) Proceedings of 18th European Meeting on Cybernetics and Systems Research (EMCSR 2006), Vienna, Austria, vol. 2, pp. 539–544 (2006)
8. Gleizes, M.-P., Camps, V., Georgé, J.-P., Capera, D.: Engineering systems which generate emergent functionalities. In: Weyns, D., Brueckner, S.A., Demazeau, Y. (eds.) EEMMAS 2007. LNCS (LNAI), vol. 5049, pp. 58–75. Springer, Heidelberg (2008)
9. Hallerstede, S., Hoang, T.S.: Qualitative Probabilistic Modelling in Event-B. In: Davies, J., Gibbons, J. (eds.) IFM 2007. LNCS, vol. 4591, pp. 293–312. Springer, Heidelberg (2007)
10. Konur, S., Clare, D., Fisher, M.: Analysing robot swarm behaviour via probabilistic model checking. Robot. Auton. Syst. 60(2), 199–213 (2012)
11. Laibinis, L., Troubitsyna, E.: Refinement of Fault Tolerant Control Systems in B. In: Heisel, M., Liggesmeyer, P., Wittmann, S. (eds.) SAFECOMP 2004. LNCS, vol. 3219, pp. 254–268. Springer, Heidelberg (2004)
12. Pereverzeva, I., Troubitsyna, E., Laibinis, L.: Formal Development of Critical Multi-agent Systems: A Refinement Approach. In: EDCC, pp. 156–161 (2012)
13. Rodin platform. Automated tool environment for Event-B, http://rodin-b-sharp.sourceforge.net/

A Formal Privacy Policy Framework
for Social Networks*

Raúl Pardo[1] and Gerardo Schneider[2]

[1] Dept. of Computer Science and Engineering, Chalmers, Sweden
[2] Dept. of Computer Science and Engineering, University of Gothenburg, Sweden
pardo@chalmers.se, gerardo@cse.gu.se

Abstract. Social networks (SN) provide a great opportunity to help people interact with each other in different ways depending on the kind of relationship that links them. One of the aims of SN is to be flexible in the way one shares information, being as permissive as possible in how people communicate and disseminate information. While preserving the spirit of SN, users would like to be sure that their privacy is not compromised. One way to do so is by providing users with means to define their own privacy policies and give guarantees that they will be respected. In this paper we present a privacy policy framework for SN, consisting of a formal model of SN, a knowledge-based logic, and a formal privacy policy language. The framework may be tailored by providing suitable instantiations of the different relationships, the events, the propositions representing what is to be known, and the additional facts or rules a particular social network should satisfy. Besides, models of Facebook and Twitter are instantiated in our formalism, and we provide instantiations of a number of richer privacy policies.

1 Introduction

A *social network* is a structure made up of a set of *agents* (individuals or organisations), which are connected via different kinds of relationships. People and organisations use social networks (SN) to interact on a peer-to-peer manner and also to broadcast information related to themselves or others with selected subgroups of other agents. Users expect that social network services (SNS) provide flexibility and easy-to-use interfaces for achieving the intended objectives in a fast and reliable manner. This flexibility, however, comes with the potential problem of compromising organisations' and individuals' privacy.

Privacy in SN may be compromised in different ways: from direct observation of what is posted (seen by non-allowed agents), by inferring properties of data (*metadata privacy leakages*), indirectly from the topology of the SN (e.g., knowing who our friends are), to more elaborate intentional attackers such as *sniffers* or *harvesters* [6]. In this paper we are mainly concerned with the first

---

* Supported by the Swedish funding agency SSF under the grant *Data Driven Secure Business Intelligence*.

D. Giannakopoulou and G. Salaün (Eds.): SEFM 2014, LNCS 8702, pp. 378–392, 2014.
© Springer International Publishing Switzerland 2014

3 kinds of privacy issues. In order to tackle them, we look into the problem of defining a formal language for writing rich privacy policies in the context of social networks. We aim at defining a privacy policy language able to express at least the following (kinds of) policies: i) All privacy policies currently supported by existing SN like Facebook; ii) Privacy policies describing properties on attributes, i.e. not only coarse-grained properties as the fact that someone has post something, but about the content of the post itself; iii) Conditional privacy policies, which depend on the amount of current knowledge or permissions in the SN; iv) Privacy policies based on knowledge in a group of agents and distributed knowledge among several agents.

In order to achieve the above we propose a solution based on the definition of a rather general privacy policy framework that may be specialised for concrete SN instances. More concretely, our contributions are:

1. We propose a formal *privacy policy framework* consisting of: i) a generic model for social networks, formalised as a combination of hyper-graphs and Kripke structures; ii) the syntax and semantics of a knowledge-based logic to reason about the social network and privacy policies; iii) a formal language to describe privacy policies (based on the logic mentioned above), together with a conformance relation to be able to state whether a certain social network satisfies a given policy. (Section 2.)
2. We specify how the above privacy policy framework may be instantiated in order to be used in practice. (Section 3.)
3. Our definition of *instantiated privacy policy framework* allows us to model not only existing SN with their corresponding privacy policies, but also richer ones. We show the expressiveness of our approach by presenting instantiations of Twitter, Facebook, and richer privacy policies. (Section 4.)

2   Privacy Policy Framework

In this section we define $\mathcal{PPF}$, a formal *privacy policy framework* for social networks. The framework is not only able to deal with explicit disclosure of information, but it also is equipped with internal machinery for detecting implicit knowledge.

Definition 1. *The tuple* $\langle \mathcal{SN}, \mathcal{KBL_{SN}}, \models, \mathcal{PPL_{SN}}, \models_C \rangle$ *is a privacy policy framework (denoted by $\mathcal{PPF}$), where*

- $\mathcal{SN}$ *is a social network model;*
- $\mathcal{KBL_{SN}}$ *is a knowledge-based logic;*
- $\models$ *is a satisfaction relation defined for $\mathcal{KBL_{SN}}$;*
- $\mathcal{PPL_{SN}}$ *is a privacy policy language;*
- $\models_C$ *is a conformance relation defined for $\mathcal{PPL_{SN}}$.*   □

In what follows we define in more detail each of the components of $\mathcal{PPF}$.

2.1   The Social Network Model $\mathcal{SN}$

$\mathcal{SN}$ is a generic model for social networks representing the topology of the social network, modelling the different *connections* between agents, their knowledge, and the actions they are allowed to perform.

Preliminaries. Before providing the definition of $\mathcal{SN}$ let us define Ag to be a finite and nonempty set of *agents*, $\mathcal{C}$ a finite and nonempty set of *connections*, representing the relations between agents (e.g. friendship, colleague, blocked, restricted), and Σ a finite and nonempty set of *actions*, representing what is allowed to be performed by the agents (e.g. posting, looking up an agent). Also, let Π be a finite set of privacy policies defined by

$$\Pi = \{ [\![\psi_j]\!]_i \mid i \in Ag, \ j \in \{1, 2, \ldots, n_i\} \text{ and } \psi_j \in \mathcal{PPL}_{\mathcal{SN}} \}$$

containing all the privacy policies for each agent i (there are n_i privacy policies for each agent i, if $n_i = 0$ then there is no privacy policy associated with agent i).

Definition 2. *Given a nonempty set of propositions $\mathbb{P}$, we define a social network model $\mathcal{SN}$ to be a hypergraph of the form $\langle W, \{R_i\}_{i \in \mathcal{C}}, \{A_i\}_{i \in \Sigma}, \nu, KB, \pi \rangle$, where*

- *W is a nonempty set of possible worlds. Every world represents one of the agents defined in the set Ag.*
- *$\{R_i\}_{i \in \mathcal{C}}$ is a family of binary relations $R_i \subseteq W \times W$, indexed by connections. Given agents $x, y \in W$, we write xR_iy iff $(x, y) \in R_i$.*
- *$\{A_i\}_{i \in \Sigma}$ is a family of binary relations $A_i \subseteq W \times W$, indexed by actions. Given agents $x, y \in W$, we write xA_iy iff $(x, y) \in A_i$.*
- *ν is a valuation function returning the set of propositions which are true in a given world (i.e. $\nu : W \to 2^{\mathbb{P}}$).*
- *KB is a function giving the set of accumulated non-trivial knowledge for each agent, stored in what we call the knowledge base of the agent.* [1]
- *π is a function returning the set of privacy policies defined for a given agent (i.e. $\pi : W \to 2^{\Pi}$).* □

We define a bijective function between agents and worlds $AW : Ag \to W$; hereafter we will interchangeably refer to elements of W as *worlds* or *agents*. We will sometimes use the indexes to denote the corresponding connections. So, given $\mathcal{C}$ to be the set $\{Friendship, Colleague\}$, then instead of writing $R_{Friendship}$ and $R_{Colleague}$ we will write $Friendship$ and $Colleague$ respectively. In addition we define $SN|_c$ to be the *projection over the connection* $c \in \mathcal{C}$ for a given social network model SN, as the graph $SN|_c = \langle W, R_c \rangle$, where W is the set of worlds of SN and R_c is the binary relation defined in SN for the connection c. Finally, given a set of agents $G \subseteq Ag$ and a projection $SN|_c$, we define the following predicate $clique(SN|_c, G)$ iff $\forall i, j \in G. \ iR_cj \wedge jR_ci$.

---

[1] We will formally define this function in subsection 2.2, since its definition requires a formal specification of $\mathcal{KBL}_{\mathcal{SN}}$ subformulae.

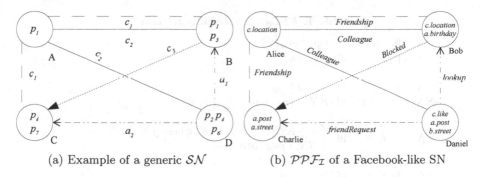

(a) Example of a generic $\mathcal{SN}$ (b) $\mathcal{PPF_I}$ of a Facebook-like SN

Fig. 1. Examples of social network models

Example 1. We illustrate how a small fragment of a generic social network could be modelled according to definition 2. The $\mathcal{SN}$ consists of: i) 4 agents, $Ag = \{A, B, C, D\}$; ii) a set of 3 connections, $\mathcal{C} = \{c_1, c_2, c_3\}$; iii) the set $\Sigma = \{a_1, a_2\}$, representing the actions allowed among users.

A graphical representation of the defined social network is given in Fig. 1a. The dashed line and the plain line represent the c_1 and c_2 relations, respectively. They are not directed because we assume these relations are symmetric. On the other hand, the c_3 relation (represented by a dotted line) relates only B and C, and it is directed.

The allowed actions are represented by the dashed and dotted directed arrows. Actions represent interaction between 2 agents. In the example, action a_1 has D as source and B as target. Associated to each world there is a set of propositions over $\{p_1, p_2, \ldots, p_7\} \subseteq \mathbb{P}$ explicitly representing basic knowledge of the agent. For instance, in Fig. 1a it is shown that agent C knows p_4 and p_7.   □

2.2   The Knowledge-Based Logic for Social Networks $\mathcal{KBL_{SN}}$

We define here a logic for representing and reasoning about knowledge. We give semantics to the logic $\mathcal{KBL_{SN}}$ over a knowledge-based representation built on top of the social network model $\mathcal{SN}$.

Definition 3. *Given $i, j \in Ag$, $a \in \Sigma$, $p \in \mathbb{P}$, and $G \subseteq Ag$, the knowledge-based logic $\mathcal{KBL_{SN}}$ is inductively defined as:*

$$\gamma ::= \neg\gamma \mid \gamma \wedge \gamma \mid \psi \mid \phi$$
$$\psi ::= P_i^j a \mid GP_G^j a \mid SP_G^j a$$
$$\phi ::= p \mid \phi \wedge \phi \mid \neg\phi \mid K_i\phi \mid E_G\phi \mid S_G\phi \mid D_G\phi.$$

The intuitive meaning of the modalities is as follows.
- $K_i\phi$ (Basic knowledge): Agent i knows ϕ.
- $E_G\phi$ (Everyone knows): Every agent in the group G knows ϕ.
- $S_G\phi$ (Someone knows): At least one agent in the group G knows ϕ.
- $D_G\phi$ (Distributed knowledge): ϕ is distributed knowledge in the group of agents G (i.e. the combination of individual knowledge of the agents in G).

Table 1. $\mathcal{KBL}_{\mathcal{SN}}$ satisfiability relation

$$SN, u \models \neg p \quad \text{iff} \quad \neg p \in \nu(u)$$
$$SN, u \models p \quad \text{iff} \quad p \in \nu(u)$$

$$SN, u \models \neg\phi \quad \text{iff} \quad SN, u \not\models \phi$$
$$SN, u \models \phi \wedge \psi \quad \text{iff} \quad SN, u \models \phi \text{ and } SN, u \models \psi$$

$$SN, u \models K_i\delta \quad \text{iff} \quad \begin{cases} \delta \in KB(i) \text{ if } \delta = K_j\delta', \text{ where } j \in Ag \\ SN, i \models \delta \text{ otherwise} \end{cases}$$

$$SN, u \models P_i^j a \quad \text{iff} \quad (i, j) \in A_a$$
$$SN, u \models GP_G^j a \quad \text{iff} \quad (n, j) \in A_a \text{ for all } n \in G$$
$$SN, u \models SP_G^j a \quad \text{iff} \quad \text{there exists } n \in G \text{ such that } (n, j) \in A_a$$

$$SN, u \models S_G\delta \quad \text{iff} \quad \text{there exists } i \in G \text{ such that } SN, i \models K_i\delta$$
$$SN, u \models E_G\delta \quad \text{iff} \quad SN, i \models K_i\delta \text{ for all } i \in G$$

$$SN, u \models D_G\delta \quad \text{iff} \quad \begin{cases} SN, u \models S_G\delta' \text{ and } SN, u \models S_G\delta'' \text{ if } \delta = \delta' \wedge \delta'' \\ SN, u \models S_G\delta \qquad\qquad\qquad\qquad \text{otherwise} \end{cases}$$

– $P_i^j a$ (Permission): Agent i is allowed to perform action a to agent j.
– $GP_G^j a$ (Global Permission): All agents specified in G are allowed to perform action a to agent j.
– $SP_G^j a$ (Someone is Permitted): At least one agent specified in G is allowed to perform action a to agent j.

We will denote with $\mathcal{F}_{\mathcal{KBL}}$ the set of all well-formed formulae of $\mathcal{KBL}_{\mathcal{SN}}$ as defined by the grammar given in above definition. Similarly, $\mathcal{F}_{\mathcal{KBL}}^K$ will denote those defined by the syntactic category ϕ and $\mathcal{F}_{\mathcal{KBL}}^P$ will denote the subformulae of the logic defined by the syntactic category ψ. The function giving the knowledge base of an agent, informally described in section 2.1, has the following type $KB : Ag \to 2^{\mathcal{F}_{\mathcal{KBL}}^K}$. We define in what follows the satisfaction relation for $\mathcal{KBL}_{\mathcal{SN}}$ formulae.

Definition 4. *Given a $SN = \langle W, \{R_i\}_{i \in \mathcal{C}}, \{A_i\}_{i \in \Sigma}, \nu, KB, \pi \rangle$, the agents $i, j, u \in Ag$, a finite set of agents $G \subseteq Ag$, an action $a \in \Sigma$, $\delta \in \mathcal{F}_{\mathcal{KBL}}^K$, and $\phi, \psi \in \mathcal{F}_{\mathcal{KBL}}$, the satisfiability relation $\models$ is defined as shown in Table 1.* $\square$

Note that we explicitly add the negation of a proposition. It represents knowing the negation of a fact (e.g $K_i\neg p$) which is different than not knowing it (i.e. $\neg K_i p$). Moreover, it is important to point out that $\mathcal{KBL}_{\mathcal{SN}}$ is not minimal as the last 5 modalities can be defined in terms of more basic cases as follows: $S_G\delta \triangleq \bigvee_{i \in G} K_i\delta$, $E_G\delta \triangleq \bigwedge_{i \in G} K_i\delta$, $GP_G^j a \triangleq \bigwedge_{i \in G} P_i^j a$, $SP_G^j a \triangleq \bigvee_{i \in G} P_i^j a$ and $D_G\delta$ is already defined in terms of S_G as shown in its semantical definition. Note that as the set G is finite, so are the disjunction and the conjunction for S_G, E_G, GP_G^j and SP_G^j.

Example 2. $\mathcal{KBL_{SN}}$ enables the possibility of reasoning about epistemic and deontic properties. As stated in $\mathcal{SN}$ showed in Example 1, D is allowed to execute a_1, which will affect B. In $\mathcal{KBL_{SN}}$ we can formally check the previous statement by checking satisfiability of the following judgement: $SN, B \models P_D^B\ a_1$.

We can also build more complex expressions in which we actually leverage the reasoning power of $\mathcal{KBL_{SN}}$. For instance, we can check whether the following holds for agent A:

$$SN, A \models \neg K_B\ p_1 \wedge \neg K_C K_A\ p_1 \implies \neg SP_{\{B,C\}}^A\ a_1,$$

which means that if agent B does not know p_1 and agent C does not know that agent A knows p_1 then it is not permitted for any of the agents B and C to execute the action a_1 to the agent A.   □

Apart from checking properties in the model, $\mathcal{KBL_{SN}}$ also permits to reason about certain properties that hold in general. Given a social network SN, $i, j \in Ag$, and formulae $\phi, \psi \in \mathcal{F}_{\mathcal{KBL}}^K$, we can state and prove the following lemma on the influence of the individuals knowledge and their combination as distributed knowledge.

Lemma 1. $SN, i \models K_i\phi \wedge K_j\psi \implies D_{\{i,j\}}\phi \wedge \psi.$ □

2.3   The Privacy Policy Language for Social Networks $\mathcal{PPL_{SN}}$

$\mathcal{KBL_{SN}}$ is an expressive language for specifying and reasoning about epistemic and deontic properties of agents in SN models. However, the language is not completely suitable for writing privacy policies, and thus a different language is needed for this purpose. Privacy policies in social networks can be seen as explicit statements in which agents specify what cannot be known about them or what is not permitted to be executed. The syntax of the privacy policy language $\mathcal{PPL_{SN}}$ is based on that of $\mathcal{KBL_{SN}}$, but adapted to express privacy policies.

Definition 5. *Given the agents $i, j \in Ag$ and a nonempty set of agents $G \subseteq Ag$, the syntax of the* privacy policy language $\mathcal{PPL_{SN}}$ *is inductively defined as follows:*

$$\delta ::= \delta \wedge \delta \mid [\![\phi \implies \neg\psi]\!]_i \mid [\![\neg\psi]\!]_i$$
$$\phi ::= \psi \mid \neg\psi \mid \phi \wedge \phi$$
$$\psi ::= E_G\gamma \mid S_G\gamma \mid D_G\gamma \mid K_i\gamma \mid GP_G^j a \mid SP_G^j a \mid P_i^j a \mid \psi \wedge \psi.$$
$$\gamma ::= p \mid \gamma \wedge \gamma$$

$\mathcal{PPL_{SN}}$ may be seen as formed by a subset of formulae definable in $\mathcal{KBL_{SN}}$ wrapped with the $[\![\ ]\!]_i$ operator, specifying which agent has defined the privacy policy. As before, we define $\mathcal{F}_{\mathcal{PPL}}$ to be the set of $\mathcal{PPL_{SN}}$ well-formed formulae defined as given by the grammar in the above definition. A basic privacy policy for an agent i, given by δ in definition 5, is either a direct restriction ($[\![\neg\psi]\!]_i$) or a

Table 2. $\mathcal{PPL}_{\mathcal{SN}}$ conformance relation

$$
\begin{array}{ll}
SN \models_C \tau_1 \wedge \tau_2 & \text{iff } SN \models_C \tau_1 \wedge SN \models_C \tau_2 \\
SN \models_C [\![\neg\psi]\!]_i & \text{iff } SN, i \models \neg\psi \\
SN \models_C [\![\phi \implies \neg\psi]\!]_i & \text{iff } SN, i \models \phi \text{ then } SN \models_C [\![\neg\psi]\!]_i
\end{array}
$$

conditional restriction ($[\![\phi \implies \neg\psi]\!]_i$). $\mathcal{F}^C_{\mathcal{PPL}}$ will denote sbuformulae belonging to the syntactic category ϕ (conditions) and $\mathcal{F}^R_{\mathcal{PPL}}$ subformulae of the syntactic category ψ (restrictions). Instead of defining a satisfaction relation for $\mathcal{PPL}_{\mathcal{SN}}$, we define the following *conformance* relation to determine when a $\mathcal{SN}$ respects a given privacy policy.

Definition 6. *Given a* $SN = \langle W, \{R_i\}_{i \in \mathcal{C}}, \{A_i\}_{i \in \Sigma}, \nu, KB, \pi \rangle$, *an agent* $i \in Ag$, $\phi \in \mathcal{F}^C_{\mathcal{PPL}}$, $\psi \in \mathcal{F}^R_{\mathcal{PPL}}$ *and* $\tau_1, \tau_2 \in \mathcal{F}_{\mathcal{PPL}}$; *the* conformance *relation* $\models_C$ *is defined as shown in Table 2.* □

Example 3. The following are the privacy policies for agent A (cf. Example 1): $\pi(A) = \{[\![\neg S_{\{B,C,D\}} \ p_1]\!]_A, [\![K_B \ p_1 \implies \neg P^A_B \ a_1]\!]_A\}$. The intuitive meaning of the first policy is that nobody can know p_1 (apart from A who is the only agent left in the $\mathcal{SN}$). The second one means that if agent B knows p_1 then she is not permitted to execute the action a_1 to A. □

3 $\mathcal{PPF}$ Instantiation

In the previous section we have presented a generic framework for defining privacy policies in social networks. In order to be usable, the framework needs to be instantiated, as specified in the following definition.

Definition 7. *We say that a* $\mathcal{PPF}$ *is an* instantiated privacy policy framework *iff an instantiation for the following is provided:*

- *The set of agents* Ag;
- *The set of propositions* $\mathbb{P}$ *($p \in \mathbb{P}$ may be given a structure);*
- *The set of connections* $\mathcal{C}$;
- *The set of auxiliary functions over the above connections;*
- *The set of actions* Σ;
- *A set of properties written in* $\mathcal{KBL}_{\mathcal{SN}}$ *(these properties may be seen as assumptions on the social network);*
- *A set of constraints over the policies defined in the language* $\mathcal{PPL}_{\mathcal{SN}}$.   □

We write $\mathcal{PPF}_{Name}$ for the instantiation of a $\mathcal{PPF}$ on a specific social network *Name*. In what follows we show an example of instantiation.

Example 4. We present here $\mathcal{PPF}_{\text{FBook-like}}$, an instantiation of the privacy policy framework given in Example 1 for a Facebook-like social network. (Fig. 1b shows the $\mathcal{SN}$ for the instantiated $\mathcal{PPF}$.)
Agents We redefine the set of agents to be $Ag = \{Alice, Bob, Charlie, Daniel\}$.

Propositions We define a structure for the propositions, by requiring them to be of the form *owner.attribute* (e.g. *Alice.street*).

Connections. In this particular instantiation we consider only the following connections: $\mathcal{C} = \{Friendship, Colleague, Blocked\}$.

Auxiliary functions. The following auxiliary functions (from Ag to 2^{Ag}) will help to retrieve the corresponding sets associated to the above defined connections: $friends(i) = \{u \mid iR_{Friendship}u$ and $uR_{Friendship}i\}$; $colleagues(i) = \{u \mid iR_{Colleague}u$ and $uR_{Colleague}i\}$; $blocked(i) = \{u \mid iR_{Blocked}u\}$; These functions are notably useful when writing formulae (both in $\mathcal{KBL}_{SN}$ and $\mathcal{PPL}_{SN}$), since it allows to refer to groups of agents defined by their relationships.

Actions. The set of actions is instantiated as $\Sigma = \{sendRequest, lookup\}$.

Assumptions on the $\mathcal{SN}$. Different social networks are characterised by different properties. We use $\mathcal{KBL}_{SN}$ for defining these properties (or assumptions). In a Facebook-like social network some attributes are a composition of others. We introduce here the notion of *record*, that is a complex attribute composed by others. We assume that the attribute *location* of an agent is composed by the following attributes: *street*, *country*, and *city*. Given agents $u, i, j, h \in Ag$ and the group $G = \{i, j, h\}$ we assume the following property holds:

$$SN, i \models S_G\, u.country \wedge S_G\, u.city \wedge S_G\, u.street \implies D_G\, u.location \quad (1)$$

moreover if $i = j = h$ we can derive the following property:

$$SN, i \models K_i(u.country \wedge u.city \wedge u.street) \implies K_i\, u.location \quad (2)$$

In addition we can also model facts that we assume to be true in the social network. For example, we could assume that if some information is distributed knowledge among users who are friends, then this information becomes known to all of them individually. Formally we say that given a set of agents $G \subseteq Ag$, an agent $u \in Ag$ and a formula $\phi \in \mathcal{F}_{KBL}^K$, for all $i \in G$ the following holds:

$$\text{if } SN, u \models D_G\phi \text{ and } clique(SN|_{Friendship}, G) \text{ then } SN, i \models K_i\phi. \quad (3)$$

Constraints over privacy policies. A common constraint in social networks is that agents can only write policies about their own data. In $\mathcal{PPL}_{SN}$ it is possible to write $[\![\neg K_j\, u.attribute]\!]_i$ where $i, j, u \in Ag$ and $i \neq j \neq u$. This policy, defined by agent i, forbids agent j to know *attribute* from agent u. Agent i is thus constraining the accessibility of certain information about an agent other than herself. To solve this we could add the following constraint: Given an agent $i \in Ag$ and her privacy policies, $\bigwedge_{j \in 1,...,n} \tau_j \in \pi(i)$, where $\tau_j = [\![\phi]\!]_i$, if $\phi = \neg\phi'$ or $\phi = \phi'' \implies \neg\phi'$ then it is not permitted that $u.attribute \in \phi'$ for any $u \in Ag$. $u \neq i$, meaning that agents can only define policies about their own data. Likewise, users should not be able to write permission restrictions over other users. In order to address this issue we extend the previous restriction with the following: given an agent $j \in Ag$, an action $a \in \Sigma$ and the set $G \subseteq Ag$, it is not the case for $i \neq j$ that $P_u^j a$, $SP_G^j a$ or $GP_G^j a \in \phi'$. □

For a given instantiation we could prove more properties besides the ones given as assumptions. The following lemma exemplifies the kind of properties we can prove about instantiated privacy policy frameworks in general and for $\mathcal{PPF}_{\text{FBook-like}}$ in particular.

Lemma 2. *Given* $u \in Ag$, *if* $SN, u \models D_G$ ($u.country \wedge u.city \wedge u.street$), *and assuming the group of agents* $G \subseteq Ag$ *are all friends to each other (i.e.* $clique(SN|_{Friendship}, G)$), *then* $SN \not\models_C [\![\neg S_{\{Ag \setminus \{u\}\}} u.location]\!]_u$. □

4   Case Studies

$\mathcal{PPF}$ may be instantiated for various social networks. We show here how to instantiate Twitter and Facebook. Though our formalisation is expressive enough to fully instantiate the social networks under consideration, due to lack of space we will only show minimal instantiations which allow us to represent all the existing privacy policies in the mentioned social networks.

Before going into the details of our instantiation, we describe some preliminaries. In the rest of the section we will use i, j, u to denote agents ($i, j, u \in Ag$), and G to denote a finite subset of agents ($G \subseteq Ag$), where Ag is the set of agents registered in the instantiated social network. Given an attribute att of an agent u (denoted by $u.att$), we will sometimes need to distinguish between different occurrences of such an attribute. In that case we will write $u.att_\eta$ ($\eta \in \{1, \ldots, n_u\}$, with n_u being the maximum number of occurrences of the attribute; by convention, if there are no occurrence of $u.att$, we have that $n_u = 0$). For example, if we assume that agent u's location changes and we want to refer to these different locations we will write $u.location_\eta$.

4.1   Twitter Privacy Policies

Twitter is a microblogging social network. Users share information according to the connections established by the *follower* relationship, which permits (depending on the privacy policies) a user to access the tweets posted (or tweeted) from the followed user. Users interact by posting (or tweeting) 140 characters long messages called *tweets*. Let us define the instantiation $\mathcal{PPF}_{\text{Twitter}}$ as follows.

Propositions. The proposition in $\mathcal{PPF}_{\text{Twitter}}$ are defined by the set $\mathbb{P} = \{owner.email, owner.location_i, owner.tweet_j, owner.retweet_{tweetRef}\}$ where $owner \in Ag$, and attributes are the following: *email*, is the user's email; $location_\eta$ represents a location of a given user ; $tweet_\eta$ the tweets a given user has tweeted; and $retweet_{tweetRef}$ representing the fact or retweeting (or sharing a tweet already tweeted by another user) where $tweetRef$ is the reference to the original tweet.

Connections. The set of connections only includes the follower relationship, $\mathcal{C} = \{Follower\}$.

Auxiliary functions. We define the function

- $followers(i) = \{u \mid u \in Ag \wedge iR_{Follower}u\}$

which returns all the agents u who i is following.

Actions. Actions are defined as $\Sigma = \{tweet, lookup, sendAd\}$, where $tweet$ represents tweeting (posting a tweet), $lookup$ represents the possibility of reaching a user's profile and $sendAd$ sending an advertisement to a user.

Twitter does not have a large amount of privacy policies since the aim is to make information accessible to as many people as possible. Yet there are important considerations concerning privacy. These policies are specified in $\mathcal{PPF}_{\text{Twitter}}$ as follows.

- Protect my Tweets: Two cases: i) Only those in u's group of followers can see her tweets: $[\![\neg S_{\{Ag\backslash followers(u)\backslash\{u\}\}}\, u.tweet_\eta]\!]_u$; ii) Only u's followers may see her retweets: $[\![\neg S_{\{Ag\backslash followers(u)\backslash\{u\}\}}\, u.retweet_{tweetRef}]\!]_u$.
- Add my location to my tweets: Twitter provides the option of adding the agents' location to their tweets. The following policy specifies that nobody can see the user's locations: $[\![\neg S_{\{Ag\backslash\{u\}\}}\, u.location_\eta]\!]_u$.
- Let others find me by my email address: $[\![\neg K_i\, u.email \implies \neg P_i^u\, lookup]\!]_u$, meaning that if an agent i does not know u's email, then she is not allowed to find u by looking her up.
- Tailor ads based on information shared by ad partners: Assuming G to be the group of ads partners, the policy is defined as $[\![\neg SP_G^u\, sendAd]\!]_u$, meaning that none of the advertisement companies taking part in the system is able to send advertisements to user u.

4.2   Facebook Privacy Policies

Facebook is a social network system in which people share information by means of posts. Each user owns a *timeline* which contains all her posts and information about the main events which can be handled by the social network (e.g. birthday, new relationships, attendance to events). The main connection between users is *friendship*, though it is possible to create special relations.

We show here the instantiation $\mathcal{PPF}_{\text{Facebook}}$. Since we are modelling just the parts of Facebook relevant for defining privacy policies, we borrow the set $\mathcal{C}$ from the instantiation presented in Example 4. We also borrow the set of auxiliary functions and we add $friends^2(i) = \bigcup_{j \in friends(i)} friends(j)$; it allows us to write formulae about friends of friends. We extend the set Σ with the action $postTimeline$ (representing posting on a user's timeline), and the actions $inviteEvent, inviteGroup$ and tag, which represent sending an invitation to join an event or a group and being tagged on a picture. As for the structure of the propositions, we define the set $\mathbb{P} = \{owner.post_\eta^j, owner.like_\eta, owner.location, owner.phone, owner.email\}$ where $owner \in Ag$, $owner.post_\eta^j$ represents the posts $owner$ posted on the j's timeline (e.g. $Alice.post_1^{Bob}$ is the first post of Alice in Bob's timeline), $owner.like_\eta$ are the posts $owner$ has liked and *owner.location*, *owner.phone* and *owner.email* are, respectively, the actual location, phone and the email attributes of *owner*. Similarly to $\mathcal{PPF}_{\text{Twitter}}$, we do not specify properties for the $\mathcal{SN}$ nor restrictions over policies.

Privacy Settings and Tools. In what follows we go through all privacy policies a user can define in the section "Privacy and Tools" of Facebook, and we provide their formalisation in $\mathcal{PPF}_{\text{Facebook}}$. The policies are defined depending on the set of users which they affect.

Who can see my stuff? In the first section Facebook enables users to set a default audience for their posts. In $\mathcal{PPF}_{\text{Facebook}}$ we can formally specify these restrictions as follows: [Public] no policy since everyone is able to access the posts; [Friends] $[\![\neg S_{\{Ag\backslash friends(u)\backslash\{u\}\}} u.post_n^j]\!]_u$; [Only me] $[\![\neg S_{\{Ag\backslash\{u\}\}} u.post_n^j]\!]_u$; [Custom] $[\![\neg S_{\{G\}} u.post_n^j]\!]_u$. The intuition behind these policies is specifying the group of agents who are not allowed to know the information about u's posts.

Who can contact me? In a second section users are provided with the possibility of deciding who can send them friend requests: [Everyone] No need of privacy policy; [Friends of Friends] $[\![\neg SP_{\{Ag\backslash friends^2(u)\}}^u sendRequest]\!]_u$; note that we specify who cannot send the friend request, which in this case are the agents who are not in the group of friends of friends.

Who can look me up? Finally, a user can be looked up by its email address or phone number. Given $a \in \{phone, email\}$, specified as [Everyone] No privacy policy is needed since; [Friends of Friends] $[\![(\neg K_i\ u.a \implies \neg P_i^u\ lookup)]\!]_u \wedge [\![(\neg SP_{\{Ag\backslash friends^2(u)\backslash\{u\}\}}^u lookup)]\!]_u$, where $i \in friends^2(u)$; [Friends] $[\![\neg K_i\ u.a \implies \neg P_i^u\ lookup]\!]_u \wedge [\![\neg SP_{\{Ag\backslash friends(u)\backslash\{u\}\}}^u lookup]\!]_u$, where $i \in friends(u)$.

Timeline and Tagging. Besides the previous policies, Facebook allows to define a set of policies related with who can post on our wall and how to manage our tags. We show now their formalisation in $\mathcal{PPF}_{\text{Facebook}}$.

Who can post on my timeline. Facebook offers the possibility of controlling the people allowed to write in a user's wall: [Only me] $[\![\neg SP_{\{Ag\backslash\{u\}\}}^u postTimeline]\!]_u$; [Friends] $[\![\neg SP_{\{Ag\backslash friends(u)\backslash\{u\}\}}^u postTimeline]\!]_u$.

Who can see things on my timeline? In Facebook it is possible to establish a bounded audience for the posts located in a user's wall. We formally define the privacy policies as: [Everyone] No privacy policy needed; [Friends of friends (implicitly includes friends)] $[\![\neg S_{\{Ag\backslash friends(u)\backslash friends^2(u)\backslash\{u\}\}} i.post_n^u]\!]_u$; [Friends] $[\![\neg S_{\{Ag\backslash friends(u)\backslash\{u\}\}} i.post_n^u]\!]_u$; [Only me] $[\![\neg S_{\{Ag\backslash\{u\}\}} i.post_n^u]\!]_u$; [Custom] $[\![\neg S_{\{Ag\backslash G\backslash\{u\}\}} i.post_n^u]\!]_u$.

Manage Blocking. Facebook offers the possibility of restricting or blocking the access to our information to a predefined set of users. It also allows to block users from doing more concrete actions as sending apps invitations, events invitations or apps. This is done by defining blocked and restricted users. Since these policies are similar, we define only the policies related with blocked users. Facebook defines blocking as *"Once you block someone, that person can no longer see things you post on your timeline, tag you, invite you to events or groups, start a conversation with you, or add you as a friend"* we formally define the previous statement in $\mathcal{PPF}_{Facebook}$ with the following set of privacy policies. A blocked user cannot: i) see things you post on your time line: $[\![\neg S_{Blocked(u)} \; u.post_{\eta}^u]\!]_u$; ii) tag you: $[\![\neg SP_{Blocked(u)}^u \; tag]\!]_u$; iii) invite to events or to join groups: $[\![\neg SP_{Blocked(u)}^u \; inviteEvent]\!]_u \wedge [\![\neg SP_{Blocked(u)}^u \; inviteGroup]\!]_u$; iv) send a friend request: $[\![\neg SP_{Blocked(u)}^u \; sendRequest]\!]_u$.

4.3 More Complex Policies

We have shown how to specify all the privacy policies of Twitter and Facebook. We show here how to express other policies, which the aforementioned SN do not offer.

A More Expressive Language One of the advantages of $\mathcal{PPF}$ is its flexibility when defining the structure of the propositions. It allows us to talk about any information related to the users, which is present in the system. For instance, as it has been seen in the Facebook privacy policies, the user cannot control any information about what she likes. The normal behaviour is to assign the same audience of the post she liked (clicking the "like" button on the post). In order to express policies about it, we can leverage the structure of the propositions of $\mathcal{PPF}_{Facebook}$ by using the attribute $like_{\eta}$. The privacy policy $[\![\neg S_{\{Ag \setminus friends(u)\}} \; u.like_{\eta}]\!]_u$ means that only u's friends can know what u liked.

Similar to retweet, in Facebook one can *share* a given post. Similarly to liking, sharing is available to the same audience as the post, but sharing entails the consequence of expanding the audience of the post. Specifically, all people included in the audience of posts of the user who is sharing will be added to the original audience of the re-shared post. In $\mathcal{PPF}_{Facebook}$ we could prevent this by explicitly restricting the audience of our posts as we did in *Who can see my stuff?* or by writing (assuming Σ to be extended with the action *share*) $[\![\neg SP_{friends(u)}^u share]\!]_u$, where explicitly is stated who could share my posts but without limiting their audience.

We have seen in Lemma 2 how distributed knowledge could be used to make some inference on the knowledge of certain agents. Its use for defining privacy policies would allow social network users to control information which could be inferred by a group of agents. For instance, an agent $u \in Ag$ could define the policy $[\![K_i \; u.location \implies \neg D_{\{friends(u) \setminus \{i\}\}} \; u.location]\!]_u$ for a given agent $i \in friends(u)$, meaning that if one of u's friends already know u's location then the distributed knowledge between the rest of u's friends is not allowed. This example also exposes the usefulness of conditional privacy policies.

Interaction among Several Social Networks SN usually focusses on one particular kind of leisure. For instance, Twitter and Facebook both focus on sharing information among followers and friends, while others have a completely different focus, e.g. Spotify (music), Instagram (photos), and Youtube (videos). We have so far shown how to formalise single SN. We discuss it what follows some examples of privacy policies involving more than one social network.

For example, in Twitter it is possible to connect the account to a Facebook account. If a user enables it, she can choose to post her tweets and retweets on her Facebook timeline. The idea is that permissions should be set allowing or disallowing Twitter to post on a user's Facebook timeline. Due to the expressivity of $\mathcal{PPF}$ we can create an instantiation being the composition of Facebook and Twitter. For instance, if we combine $\mathcal{PPF}_{\text{Twitter}}$ and $\mathcal{PPF}_{\text{Facebook}}$, assuming a common set of agents Ag, and the union of the connections, auxiliary functions, actions, assumptions and restrictions over policies of both SN, we can write the following privacy policy: $[\![\neg S_{\{Ag\backslash(friends(u)\cap Followers(u))\backslash\{u\}\}} \ u.location]\!]_u$. That is, only agents who are followers of u in Twitter, and friends in Facebook are allowed to know u's location. More complex properties of this kind could be formalised in $\mathcal{PPF}$.

5 Related Work

The approach we have followed in this paper has been to formally define privacy policies based on a variant of of *epistemic logic* [4], where it is possible to express the knowledge of *multi-agent systems* (MAS). One way to give semantics to the logic is to use *possible worlds semantics* (also known as *Kripke models*), where it is not explicitly represented what the agents know, but rather the *uncertainty* in their knowledge. This has the advantage of allowing to represent complex formulae about who knows what (including nesting of knowledge and other operators generalising the notion). Another way to give semantics to epistemic logic is to use *interpreted systems* which represents agent's knowledge as a set of runs (computational paths). Both ways of giving semantics come with advantages and disadvantages: Kripke models come with a heritage of fundamental techniques allowing to prove properties about the specification, while interpreted systems are quite intuitive to model MAS [8]. The common key in both approaches is modelling the uncertainty of the agent by using an equivalence relation. If one thinks about all the worlds that a given agent could consider possible in a social network system, it is easy to see that modelling them would lead to creating an enormous state space. Instead of modelling uncertainty we explicitly store what the agents know. This allows a more concise representation of the individuals' knowledge. Unlike previous work on epistemic logic, in our formalism worlds represent agents.

Moreover we explicitly model a restricted version of permission, i.e. our model explicitly shows which actions are allowed to be executed by the agents. Aucher *et al.* [1] show a different way of combining epistemic and deontic aspects in logic. They preserve the equivalence relation for epistemic properties and use an extra equivalence relation for representing permission. The logic is quite expressive but it suffers from the aforementioned state explosion problem. Furthermore the framework is defined as a mono agent system not being suitable for SN. We took their idea of combining epistemic and deontic operators in one language, but we restricted the semantic model according to the needs of SN.

In [10] Seligman *et al.* present a language based on epistemic logic, with the traditional Kripke semantics for the logic extended with a friendship relationship. By doing that they are able to reason about knowledge and friendship. Moreover they model a set of events using general dynamic dynamic logic (GDDL) by defining an *update* operation over the mentioned Kripke model. This enables the possibility of update the model as the events in the social network occur. Using GDDL they implement the concept of public and private announcement, which appear regularly in the communications among the agents. Although this approach is quite expressive, its focus is not on privacy or security issues, but in reasoning about the general knowledge of the agents. As mentioned before it comes with the price of having a immense state space and it complicates a practical implementation and the definition of an efficient (computationally speaking) model checking algorithm. Ruan and Thielscher [9] present a very similar formalism, but only public announcement is defined. Their focus is not on privacy either, but in the analysis of the "revolt or stay at home" effect, i.e. how the knowledge is spread among the agents.

There are other approaches for privacy not based on epistemic logic. One of the most interesting is Relationship-based access control (REBAC) [5]. The main difference with epistemic logic is that in REBAC the reasoning is focused on the resources own by the agents of the system. This approach is highly suitable for a practical implementation of a policy checking algorithm. On the other hand their approach would not detect certain kind of implicit knowledge flow. For instance, certain information about a user can be known after a friend of her is posting some information about both. The formalism is equipped with a formal language based on hybrid logic [2].

Datta *et al.* present in [3] the logic PrivacyLFP for defining privacy policies based on a restricted version of first-order logic (the restriction concerns that quantification over infinite values is avoided by considering only relevant instances of variables). The logic is quite expressive as it can represent things others than the kind of policies we are aiming at in this paper (their application domain being medical data). Though promising as a formalism for SN, the authors write that the logic might need to be adapted in order to be used for online social networks. To the best of our knowledge this has not been done.

6   Final Discussion

We have presented in this paper a framework for writing privacy policies for social networks. Our approach allows for the instantiation of the framework to formalise existing social networks, and other more complex privacy policies. One particularity of our approach is that worlds represent agents, closely following the structure of real social networks.

This paper is a first step towards a full formalisation of privacy policies for social networks. Our current and future work includes: **Adding real-time:** So far we cannot express policies with deadlines. This might be interesting in case policies are transient (e.g., "nobody is permitted to know my location during the first two weeks of May"). **Modeling dynamic networks:** The model we have of social networks is static, as well as the conformance relation between policies and the network. In practice the social network evolves, new friends come into place, others are blocked, etc. We aim at extending our formal model to capture such temporal aspect. **Adding roles and ontologies:** Agents in the SN could play different roles, e.g. individuals, companies, advertisement, etc. Providing $\mathcal{PPF}$ with the ability of detecting these roles would enhance its expressivity. **Developing an enforcing mechanism:** We have not mentioned how the policies might be enforced at runtime. We will explore how to extract a runtime monitor from the policy. Finally, we would like to explore the application of privacy-by-design [7] to a formalisation of social networks.

Acknowledgment. Thanks to Bart van Delft, Pablo Buiras, and the anonymous reviewers for their useful comments on a preliminary version of this paper.

References

1. Aucher, G., Boella, G., Torre, L.: A dynamic logic for privacy compliance. Artificial Intelligence and Law 19(2-3), 187–231 (2011)
2. Bruns, G., Fong, P.W., Siahaan, I., Huth, M.: Relationship-based access control: its expression and enforcement through hybrid logic. In: CODASPY 2012, pp. 117–124. ACM (2012)
3. Datta, A., Blocki, J., Christin, N., DeYoung, H., Garg, D., Jia, L., Kaynar, D.K., Sinha, A.: Understanding and protecting privacy: Formal semantics and principled audit mechanisms. In: Jajodia, S., Mazumdar, C. (eds.) ICISS 2011. LNCS, vol. 7093, pp. 1–27. Springer, Heidelberg (2011)
4. Fagin, R., Halpern, J.Y., Moses, Y., Vardi, M.Y.: Reasoning about knowledge, vol. 4. MIT Press, Cambridge (1995)
5. Fong, P.W.: Relationship-based access control: Protection model and policy language. In: CODASPY 2011, pp. 191–202. ACM (2011)
6. Greschbach, B., Kreitz, G., Buchegger, S.: The devil is in the metadata - new privacy challenges in decentralised online social networks. In: PerCom Workshops, pp. 333–339. IEEE (2012)
7. Le Métayer, D.: Privacy by design: A formal framework for the analysis of architectural choices. In: CODASPY 2013, pp. 95–104. ACM (2013)
8. Lomuscio, A., Ryan, M.: On the relation between interpreted systems and kripke models. In: Wobcke, W., Pagnucco, M., Zhang, C. (eds.) Agents and Multi-Agent Systems Formalisms, Methodologies, and Applications. LNCS (LNAI), vol. 1441, pp. 46–59. Springer, Heidelberg (1998)
9. Ruan, J., Thielscher, M.: A logic for knowledge flow in social networks. In: Wang, D., Reynolds, M. (eds.) AI 2011. LNCS (LNAI), vol. 7106, pp. 511–520. Springer, Heidelberg (2011)
10. Seligman, J., Liu, F., Girard, P.: Facebook and the epistemic logic of friendship. In: TARK 2013 (2013)

Author Index